PEARSON

ALWAYS LEARNING

Gary Goshgarian • Kathleen Krueger

Dialogues
An Argument Rhetoric and Reader

Custom Edition for University of Nevada Las Vegas

Taken from:
Dialogues: An Argument Rhetoric and Reader, Eighth Edition
by Gary Goshgarian, Kathleen Krueger

Cover Art: Courtesy of Pearson Learning Solutions.

Taken/Excerpts taken from:

Dialogues: An Argument Rhetoric and Reader, Eighth Edition
by Gary Goshgarian, Kathleen Krueger
Copyright © 2015, 2011, 2009 by Pearson Education, Inc.
New York, NY 10013

Pearson Education, Inc., 330 Hudson Street, New York, New York 10013
A Pearson Education Company
www.pearsoned.com

Printed in the United States of America

1   16

000200010272036399

EJ

ISBN 10: 1-323-44693-1
ISBN 13: 978-1-323-44693-5

Contents

I Tweet, Therefore I Am: Life in the Hall of Mirrors   539
Andrew Lam

So many of us have been raised on video games, cell phones and iPods, and who spent the large bulk of their lives in chatrooms, Skypes and posting on YouTube that we become news reporters and newsmakers without much of an effort. And many of us have learned to split our attention, with one eye on the electronic mirror, and the other on reality.

The Flight from Conversation   543
Sherry Turkle

"We've become accustomed to a new way of being "alone together." Technology-enabled, we are able to be with one another, and also elsewhere, connected to wherever we want to be. We want to customize our lives. We want to move in and out of where we are because the thing we value most is control over where we focus our attention. We have gotten used to the idea of being in a tribe of one, loyal to our own party."

My Facebook, My Self   547
Jessica Helfand

"There's something deeply engaging in the ebbs and flows of personal stories in which actual truth is gloriously trumped by an individual's own flawed, if heartfelt rendition of life as he or she deems fit"

READING THE VISUAL: Strictly Private   551

Facebook, the Mean Girls and Me   552
Taffy Brodesser-Akner

"Am I pathetic? Maybe. But what I also am, finally, is a popular seventh-grader. I think of my younger self, eating her lunch alone, wondering when this agony will be over. I wish I could tell her I haven't forgotten about her. I wish I could tell her I've made it OK."

You Gotta Have (150) Friends   555
Robin Dunbar

"Put simply, our minds are not designed to allow us to have more than a very limited number of people in our social world. The emotional and psychological investments that a close relationship requires are considerable, and the emotional capital we have available is limited."

Streams of Content: Limited Attention   558
danah boyd

"Those who are most enamored with services like Twitter talk passionately about feeling as though they are living and breathing with the world around them, peripherally aware and in-tune, adding content to the stream and grabbing it when appropriate. This state is delicate, plagued by information overload and weighed down by frustrating tools."

Chapter 17   Family Values   566

Family: Idea, Institution, and Controversy   566
Betty G. Farrell

Q: What did Eve say to Adam on being expelled from the Garden of Eden?

A: "I think we're in a time of transition."

Preface

Dialogues: *An Argument Rhetoric and Reader* focuses on promoting meaningful discussion, that is, the effective exchange of opinions and ideas. In this book, we move away from traditional models of confrontation and dispute and, instead, promote ways to create dialogue by examining different points of view with an open mind. This exploration of multiple perspectives on an issue helps students reach informed positions and develop their own compelling cases. While dialogue and consensus are encouraged, we realize that not all arguments can be resolved to everyone's satisfaction. However, understanding the principles of persuasive writing and the techniques of argument provides students with the tools to engage productively in negotiation. And although students may not always reach a consensus of opinion, they will be able to discuss diverse issues in a thoughtful and productive way.

New to This Edition

The eighth edition reflects the efforts of the previous edition to teach students how to create effective arguments. At the same time, we continue to encourage discussion and understanding rather than confrontation and dispute. For this edition we have incorporated the insights and suggestions of many instructors who used the last edition. Some changes to this edition include:

The Rhetoric

Each of the rhetoric chapters has been revised and updated, and they include new study and discussion questions and expanded apparatus. Furthermore, we have added new sample readings (student and professional) with analyses and replaced others in these chapters. Likewise, we have refreshed some examples and discussion in the visuals chapter. Finally, the examples of documentation using electronic sources have been updated and expanded in the "Documentation Guide: MLA and APA Styles," which concludes with two annotated and fully documented sample student essays, each incorporating visual devices.

The Reader

Part Two contains over sixty essays and visuals, many which are new to this edition, and several new chapters on topics likely to matter to students including "Moral Quandries in Medicine," "New Issues in Higher Education," and "Riding the Ecomonic Roller Coaster. We extensively revised the remaining chapters, including "Gender Matters," "Race and Ethnicity," and "Our Lives Online." We kept readings that reviewers said worked very well in class, and added new ones based on their suggestions and feedback.

In addition to magazines and journals, today's students increasingly find their information online. Online social networks such as Facebook and Twitter have created online communities through which students connect and share information. Blogs, which operate as online diaries, present viewpoints and invite others to discuss ideas and experiences. This edition includes a few readings pulled from blogs, reflecting the new ways we create and share points of view. We also added more selections from scholarly resources to challenge more advanced students who are ready to tackle demanding readings.

Writing assignments that follow each section encourage students to address issues further, prompting them to formulate critical responses to the different points of view expressed in the section.

Organization of the Book

As the title indicates, this book is divided into two parts. The rhetoric section consists of nine chapters explaining the strategies of reading and writing arguments. The reader section consists of eight thematic units containing over sixty essays that present a challenging collection of thought-provoking contemporary arguments.

Part One: The Rhetoric

Part One of the book is designed to stimulate critical thinking, reading, and writing, and to introduce students to research skills. It explores how issues are argued while emphasizing the actual process of persuasive writing, from brainstorming exercises to shaping the final product. Each of the nine chapters in Part One focuses on a particular facet or principle of persuasive writing, including a new visuals chapter that addresses how visuals can act as arguments in and of themselves, or as auxiliary support for written arguments.

Chapter 1 offers an overview of argumentation, clarifies key terminology, and introduces the processes of debate, dialogue, and deliberation. Chapter 2 focuses on critical reading, presenting a series of activities designed to help students evaluate arguments and recognize their primary components. An extensive section on testing arguments for logical fallacies ends the chapter. Chapter 3 discusses how to begin writing arguments. It helps students find worthwhile and interesting topics to write about by demonstrating techniques for brainstorming, limiting topics, and formulating claims. Chapter 4 examines the presence of audience, encouraging students to think about the different kinds of readers they may have to address. This chapter suggests ways to evaluate readers' concerns and strategies to reach different audiences.

Chapter 5 focuses on the organization of the argument essay by analyzing two basic types of arguments—position and proposal. Outlining is reviewed as a tool to ensure effective organization. Chapter 6 considers the importance of evidence. We demonstrate that the effectiveness of a writer's argument largely depends on how well the writer uses evidence—facts, testimony, statistics, and observations—to support his or her ideas. Chapter 7 introduces the socially constructed Toulmin model of logic as a way of testing the premises of the writer's argument.

Chapter 8 explores the principles of visual argument in art, advertisements, editorial cartoons, photographs, and ancillary graphics such as charts and tables. Focusing on developing visual literacy skills, the chapter shows students how to apply the tools of critical analysis to the many visual arguments they encounter every day. Finally, Chapter 9 discusses research strategies, including locating and evaluating print and electronic sources, note-taking, and drafting and revising argument essays. The Documentation Guide provides documentation formats and annotated sample student papers for both MLA and APA styles.

Part Two: The Readings

With over sixty contemporary essays and visuals, the readings offer a wide range of challenging and stimulating issues that we think will be of interest both to students and instructors. The topics are selected to encourage discussion, and attempt to represent the diversity of opinion connected to the controversial issues we face today.

The goal of Part Two is to examine broad themes that offer diverse points of view, including consumerism, gender, technology, race, religion, the economy, human rights and personal rights. Each chapter presents a variety of readings that provide multiple viewpoints surrounding an issue. Charts, graphs, cartoons and photographs are interspersed through the chapter to demonstrate the importance of visual information in framing and supporting arguments.

Study Apparatus

The study apparatus of the book is designed to help students thoughtfully consider the issues, their own opinions on these issues, and how they might engage in meaningful dialogue. Questions encourage critical thinking about each article's content and style. Each chapter in Part Two features an introduction to the chapter theme and its subsections. A brief headnote to each reading provides students with context and pertinent information regarding the reading. "Before You Read" and "As You Read" questions help frame the reading. Following each reading are "Questions for Analysis and Discussion" that stimulate thinking on the content, argument, and writing strategies of the author. Some questions ask students to consider how other authors in the section would respond to a particular essay's argument or evidence, encouraging critical thinking across the theme or chapter. "Writing Assignments" follow the end of each subsection of readings, helping students to synthesize the information they have read and their own opinions.

Resources for Instructors and Students

Now Available for Composition

MyWritingLab is an online homework, tutorial, and assessment program that provides engaging experiences to today's instructors and students. By incorporating rubrics into the writing assignments, faculty can create meaningful assignments, grade them based on their desired criteria, and analyze class performance through advanced reporting. For students who enter the course under-prepared, *MyWritingLab* offers a diagnostic test and personalized remediation so that students see improved results and instructors spend less time in class reviewing the basics. Rich multimedia resources are built in to engage students and support faculty throughout the course. Visit *www.mywritinglab.com* for more information.

Interactive Pearson eText

An e-book version of *Dialogues*, Eighth Edition, is also available in MyWritingLab. This dynamic, onlineversion of the text is integrated into MyWritingLab to create an enriched, interactive learning experience for writing students.

CourseSmart

Students can subscribe to *Dialogues*, Eighth Edition, as a CourseSmart eText (at CourseSmart.com). The site includes all of the book's content in a format that enables students to search the text, bookmark passages, save their own notes, and print reading assignments that incorporate lecture notes.

Instructor's Manual

The Instructor's Manual has been updated to assist and guide instructors as they teach each chapter. In addition to summarizing how instructors might teach each chapter, the manual provides answers to all the questions in the textbook. Questions from each reading that are particularly appropriate for class discussion are indicated in boldface, with suggestions on how instructors might use specific questions to stimulate class dialogue.

Acknowledgments

Many people behind the scenes deserve much acknowledgment and gratitude. It would be impossible to thank all of them, but there are some for whose help we are particularly grateful. First, we would like to thank all the instructors and students who used the first seven editions of *Dialogues*. Their continued support has made this latest edition possible. Also, we would like to thank those instructors who spent hours answering lengthy questionnaires on the effectiveness of the essays and who supplied many helpful comments and suggestions in the preparation of this new edition: Tracy L. Ferrell, University of Colorado, Boulder; Ashley Green, MacMurray College; Brian Hays, Westmoreland County Community College; Donna Hewlett, Bellevue University; Rhea Mendoza, Hartnell College; Donna Metcalf, Benedictine University at Springfield; Carol Narigon, Wright State University; Guy Shebat, Youngstown State University; and Charla R. Strosser, Southern Utah University.

A very special thanks goes to Kathryn Goodfellow, for her extraordinary contribution in locating articles and writing the study apparatus for Part Two, as well as for her considerable work creating the Instructor's Manual.

Finally, our thanks to the people at Pearson, especially our editor Katharine Glynn and her ever-efficient assistant editor, Rebecca Gilpin. We are very appreciative of their fine help.

Gary Goshgarian
Kathleen Krueger

PART ONE

Strategies for Reading and Writing Arguments

Understanding Persuasion: Thinking Like a Negotiator

LEARNING OJBECTIVES

After studying this chapter, you should be able to:

1. Explain what is an arguable topic and what is not. (p. 4)
2. Describe how to set up a debate to explore the strengths and weaknesses of an argument. (p. 7)
3. Explain how to identify a writer's claim. (p. 8)
4. Formulate the claim to an argument of your own. (p. 9)
5. Explain how to anticipate objections of your opposition. (p. 10)
6. Describe how to create a constructive dialogue with your opposition. (p. 13)

Think of all the times in the course of a week when someone tries to convince you of something. You listen to the radio on the way to school or work and are relentlessly bombarded by advertisements urging you to buy vitamins, watch a particular television show, or eat at the new Mexican restaurant in town. You open a newspaper and read about the latest proposals to lower the drinking age, raise the age for retirement, and provide tax relief for the poor. The phone rings and the caller asks you to donate money to a local charity or tries to convince you to vote for candidate X. There is a knock on your bedroom door and your sister wants to borrow your iPad and the keys to your car. Whether the issue is as small as borrowing your iPad or as important as taxes, everywhere you turn you find yourself called on to make a decision and to exercise a choice.

If you think about all these instances, you'll discover that each decision you finally do make is heavily influenced by the ability of others to persuade you. People who have mastered the art of argument are able to influence the thoughts and actions of others. Your ability to understand how argument works and to use it effectively will help you become aware of the ways in which you are influenced by others, as well as become more persuasive yourself. Anyone can learn to argue effectively by learning the techniques needed to create successful arguments.

This book is designed to help you achieve two goals: (1) to think critically about the power of other people's arguments and (2) to become persuasive in your own arguments.

Argument

Broadly speaking, *persuasion* means influencing someone to do something. It can take many forms: fast-paced glittering ads, high-flying promises from salespeople, and emotional appeals from charity groups—even physical threats. What will concern us in this book is *argument*—the form of persuasion that relies on reasoning and logical thought to convince people. While glitter, promises, emotional appeals, and even veiled threats may work, the real power of argument comes from the arguer's ability to convince others through language.

Because this is a book about writing, we will concentrate on the aspects of persuasion that most apply in writing, as opposed to those that work best in other forms (advertisements or oral appeals, for instance). Although written arguments can be passionate, emotional, or even hurtful, a good argument demonstrates a firm foundation of clear thinking, logical development, and solid supporting evidence to persuade a reader that the view expressed is worth hearing. The ultimate goal might be to convince readers to change their thinking on an issue, but that does not always happen. A more realistic goal might be to have your listeners seriously consider your point of view and to win their respect through the logic and skill of your argument.

Most of what you write in college and beyond will attempt to persuade someone that what you have to say is worthy of consideration, whether it's a paper stating your views on immigration laws, an analysis of "madness" in *King Lear,* a letter to the editor of your school newspaper regarding women's varsity basketball, or a lab report on the solubility of salt. The same demands of persuasion and argument will carry into your professional life. Such writing might take the form of business reports, memos to colleagues, progress reports on students, medical evaluations, results of a technical study, proposals, and maybe even a sales speech. In searching for a job or career, you might have to sell yourself in letters of inquiry.

The success or failure of those attempts will depend strongly on how well you argue your case. Therefore, it's important that as a college student you learn the skills of writing persuasive arguments. Even if you never write another argument, you will read, hear, and make them the rest of your life.

What Makes an Argument?

Arguments, in a sense, underlie nearly all forms of writing. Whenever you express ideas, you are usually attempting to persuade somebody to agree with you. However, not every matter can be formally argued. Nor are some things worth the effort. So, before we go on to discuss the different strategies, we should make clear which subjects do and do not lend themselves to argument.

Facts Are Not Arguable

Because facts are readily verifiable, they can't be argued. Of course, people might dispute a fact. For instance, you might disagree with a friend's claim that Thomas Jefferson was the second president of the United States. But to settle your dispute, all you have to do is consult an encyclopedia. What makes a fact a fact and, thus, inarguable, is that it has only one answer. It occurs in time and space and cannot be disputed. A fact either *is* or *is not* something. Thomas Jefferson was the third president of the United States, not the second. John Adams was the second. Those are facts. So are the following statements:

- The distance between Boston and New York City is 214 miles.
- Martin Luther King Jr.'s birthday is now celebrated in all 50 states.
- I got a 91 on my math test.
- The Washington Monument is 555 feet high.
- The Japanese smoke more cigarettes per capita than any other people on earth.
- My dog Fred died a year ago.
- Canada borders the United States to the north.

All that is required to prove or disprove any of these statements is to check with some authority for the right answer. Sometimes facts are not easily verifiable. Consider for instance, "Yesterday, 1,212,031 babies were born in the world" or "More people have black hair than any other color." These statements may be true, but it would be a daunting, if not impossible, challenge to prove them. And what would be the point?

Opinions Based on Personal Taste or Preference Are Not Arguable

Differing opinions are the basis of all argument. However, you must be careful to distinguish between opinions based on personal taste and opinions based on judgments. Someone who asks your "opinion" about which color shoes to buy is simply seeking your color preference—black versus brown, say. If someone asks your "opinion" of a certain movie, the matter could be more complicated.

Beyond whether or not you liked it, what might be sought is your aesthetic evaluation of the film: a judgment about the quality of acting, directing, cinematography, set design—all measured by critical standards you've developed over years of movie-going. Should you be asked your "opinion" of voluntary euthanasia, your response would probably focus on moral and ethical questions: Is the quality of life more important than the duration of life? What, if any, circumstances justify the taking of a life? Who should make so weighty a decision—the patient, the patient's family, the attending physician, a health team?

The word *opinion* is commonly used to mean different things. As just illustrated, depending on the context, opinion can refer to personal preference, a reaction to or an analysis of something, or an evaluation, belief, or judgment, all of which are different. In this text, we categorize all these different possibilities as either opinions of taste or opinions of judgment.

Opinions of taste come down to personal preferences, based on subjective and, ultimately, unverifiable judgments. Each of the following statements is an opinion of taste:

- George looks good in blue.
- Pizza is my favorite food.
- Brian May of the group Queen is the greatest living rock guitarist.
- Video games are a waste of time.

Each of these statements is inarguable. Let's consider the first: "George looks good in blue." Is it a fact? Not really, since there is no objective way to measure its validity. You might like George in blue, whereas someone else might prefer him in red. Is the statement then debatable? No. Even if someone retorts, "George does *not* look good in blue," what would be the basis of argument but personal preference? And where would the counter-argument go? Nowhere.

Even if a particular preference were backed by strong feelings, it would not be worth debating, nor might you sway someone to your opinion. For instance, let's say you make the statement that you never eat hamburger. You offer the following as reasons:

1. You're turned off by the sight of ground-up red meat.
2. When the meat is cooked, its smell disgusts you.
3. Hamburgers remind you of the terrible argument that broke out at a family barbecue some years ago.
4. You once got very sick after eating meat loaf.
5. You think beef cattle are the dirtiest of farm animals.

Even with all these "reasons" to support your point of view, you have not constructed an argument that goes beyond your own personal preference. In fact, the "reasons" you cite are themselves grounded in personal preferences. They amount to explanations rather than an argument. The same is true of the statements about pizza, musicians, and video games.

Opinions Based on Judgments Are Arguable

An *opinion of judgment* is one that weighs the pros and cons of an issue and determines their relative worth. That "something" might be a book, a song, or a public issue, such as capital punishment. Such an opinion represents a position on an issue that is measured against standards other than those of personal taste—standards that are rooted in values and beliefs of our culture: what's true and false, right and wrong, good and bad, better and worse. Consequently, such an opinion is arguable.

In other words, personal opinions or personal preferences can be transformed into bona fide arguments. Let's return to the example of hamburger. Suppose you want to turn your own dislike for ground meat into a paper persuading others to give up eating beef. You can take several approaches to make a convincing argument. For one, you can take a health slant, arguing that vegetarians have lower mortality rates than people whose diets are high in animal fat and cholesterol or that the ingestion of all the hormones in beef increases the risk of cancer. You might even take an environmental approach, pointing out that the more beef we eat, the more we encourage the conversion of woodlands and rain forests into grazing land, thus destroying countless animals and their habitats. You can even take an ethical stand, arguing from an animal-rights point of view that intensive farming practices create inhumane treatment of animals—that is, crowding, force-feeding, and force-breeding. You might also argue that the killing of animals is morally wrong.

The point is that personal opinions can be starting points for viable arguments. But those opinions must be developed according to recognized standards of values and beliefs.

The Uses of Argument

Many arguments center on issues that are controversial. Controversial issues, by definition, create disagreement and debate because people hold opposing positions about them. And, most of the time, there are more than two sides. Depending on the issue, there may be multiple opinions and perspectives. Because these views are often strongly held, we tend to view argument only in the form of a *debate,* an encounter between two or more adversaries who battle with each other over who is right. The media does much to contribute to the way we picture argument, particularly in the area of politics.

Every four years or so, the image returns to our television screens. Two candidates, dark-suited and conservatively dressed, hands tightly gripping their respective podiums, face off for all of America to watch. Each argues passionately for his or her solution to war, the economy, environmental crises, poverty, educational failings, high taxes, and countless other problems. Each tries desperately to undermine the arguments of the opponent in an effort to capture the votes of those watching. It's a winner-take-all debate, and it's often the image we see in our minds when we think of argument.

Argument *is* a form of persuasion that seeks to convince others to do what the arguer wants. Argument allows us to present our views and the reasons behind those views clearly and strongly. Yet argument can serve more productive purposes than the earlier mentioned illustration. Although argument can be a debate between two or more opponents who will never see eye to eye, in the world outside presidential debates and television sound bites, argument can also begin a *dialogue* between opposing sides. It can enable them to listen to each other's concerns and to respond in a thoughtful way. Rather than attempt to demolish their opponents arguments, these negotiators can often arrive at positions that are more valuable because they try to reconcile conflicting viewpoints by understanding and dealing directly with their opponents concerns. Through the practice of *debate, dialogue,* and *deliberation,* real change can happen. In this chapter, we explore these three essential elements of argument and explain how they will enable you to be more effective when you write to persuade others.

Debate

Think for a moment of all the associations the word *debate* suggests to you: winning, losing, taking sides, opposition, and competition. Debate is how we traditionally think of argument. It is a situation in which individuals or groups present their views as forcefully and persuasively as possible, often referring to their opponents' arguments only to attack or deride them. Practiced with just this goal in mind, debate can serve the purpose of presenting your position clearly in contrast to your opposition's, but it does little to resolve controversial issues. Focusing too much on the adversarial qualities of debate can prevent you from listening and considering other viewpoints. You can become so preoccupied with defeating opposing arguments that you fail to recognize the legitimacy of other opinions. This may lead you to ignore them as you fashion your own argument.

Consider the last time you debated an issue with someone. Perhaps it was an informal occasion in which you attempted to convince that person of your point of view. It may have been about an instructor or the best place to spend spring break or what movie to see. Your aim was to persuade the other person to "see it your way," and, if it was a typical debate, you were successful only if the other individual acquiesced. Debates are traditionally won or lost, and losers often feel frustrated and disappointed. Even more important, reasonable concerns on the losing side are often overlooked or not addressed. Debate does not provide a mechanism for compromise. It is not intended to provide a path toward common ground or a resolution in which all parties achieve a degree of success and positive change is made. Although some issues are so highly contentious that true consensus can never be achieved, an effective argument must acknowledge and respond to opposition in a thoughtful and productive manner.

But debate is an important way to develop your arguments because it allows you to explore their strengths and weaknesses. It can be a starting point for argument rather than a conclusion. Debate contains some of the essential elements of argument: Someone with a strong opinion tries to demonstrate the effectiveness of that view, hoping to persuade others to change positions or to take a particular course of action. When we debate, we have two objectives: to state our views clearly and persuasively and to distinguish our views from those of our opponents. Debate can help us develop our arguments because it encourages us to *formulate a claim, create reasons to support it,* and *anticipate opposition.*

Formulating Claims

The claim is the heart of your argument. Whether you hope to protest a decision, change your readers' minds, or motivate your audience to take action, somewhere in your argument must be the assertion you hope to prove. In an argument essay, this assertion or claim functions as the *thesis* of the paper, and it is vital to the argument. The claim states precisely what you believe. It is the *position* or opinion you want your readers to accept or the action you want them to take. Thus, it's very important to state your claim as clearly as possible. It will form the basis for the rest of your argument.

Claims often take the form of a single declarative statement. For example, a claim in an argument essay about homelessness might look like this:

> If we look further into the causes of homelessness, we will discover that in many cases it is not the homeless individual who is at fault but rather conditions that exist in our society that victimize certain individuals.

A claim for an essay about teen pregnancy might be stated even more simply:

> People who blame the rise in teenage pregnancies on the sexual references in popular music ignore several crucial realities.

Sometimes writers signal their claims by certain words: *therefore, consequently, the real question is, the point is, it follows that, my suggestion is.* Here's an example:

> Therefore, I believe that scientists can find other effective ways to test new medicines and surgical techniques other than relying on helpless laboratory animals.

Because some arguments make recommendations for solving problems, your claim might be framed as a conditional statement that indicates both the problem and a consequence. This can be accomplished with split phrases such as *either . . . or, neither . . . nor, if . . . then.* For example,

> If we continue to support a system of welfare that discourages its recipients from finding employment, the result will be a permanent class of unemployed citizens who lack the skills and incentives to participate in their own economic benefit.

Claims must have support to convince a reader, so they are often followed by "because" statements—that is, statements that justify a claim by explaining why something is true or recommended or beneficial:

> Outlawing assisted suicide is wrong because it deprives individuals of their basic human right to die with dignity.

Formulating your claim when you debate is a first step for three basic reasons:

1. It establishes the subject of your argument.
2. It solidifies your own stand or position about the issue.
3. It sets up a strategy on which your argument can be structured.

There are no hard-and-fast rules for the location of your claim. It can appear anywhere in your essay: as your opening sentence, in the middle, or as your conclusion. However, many writers state their claim early in the essay to let their readers know their position and to use it as a basis for all the supporting reasons that follow. In later chapters, we will look at strategies for arriving at a claim and ways to organize your reasons to support it effectively.

Creating Reasons

We have all seen a building under construction. Before the roof can be laid or the walls painted or the flooring installed, the support beams must be carefully placed and stabilized. Reasons are the support beams of an argument essay. Whether your claim will be considered correct, insightful, or reasonable will depend on the strength and persuasiveness of your reasons.

Reasons answer some basic questions about your claim:

1. Why do you believe your claim to be true?
2. On what information or assumptions do you base your claim?
3. What evidence can you supply to support your claim?
4. Do any authorities or experts concur with your claim?

You can derive reasons from personal experience, readings, and research. Your choices will depend on your claim and the information and evidence you need to make your reasons convincing. Let's use one of the examples from our discussion about claims to demonstrate what we mean:

> **Your Claim:** Outlawing assisted suicide is wrong because it deprives individuals of the basic human right to die with dignity.
>
> **Question 1:** Why do you believe your claim to be true?
>
> **Response:** When individuals are terminally ill, they suffer many indignities. They lose control of their bodily functions and must be dependent on others for care. A prolonged illness with no hope of recovery causes the individual and family members to suffer needlessly. When death is imminent, individuals should be given the right to decide when and how to end their lives.
>
> **Question 2:** On what information or assumptions do you base your claim?
>
> **Response:** I believe that no individual wants to suffer more than necessary. No one wants to lose his or her independence and rely on others. Everyone wants to be remembered as a whole human being, not as a dying invalid.

Question 3: What evidence can you supply to support your claim?

Response: This is based on personal examples and on readings about how terminal illness is dealt with in hospitals and clinics.

Question 4: Do any authorities or experts concur with your claim?

Response: Yes, many authorities in the field of medicine agree with my claim. I can use their statements and research to support it.

By examining the responses to the questions, you can see how reasons can be created to support your claim. The answer to the first question suggests several reasons why you might be opposed to outlawing assisted suicide: the indignities suffered by the terminally ill, unnecessary suffering, the right to control one's own fate. The second question explores your assumptions about what the terminally ill might experience and provides additional reasons to support your claim. The third and fourth questions suggest ways to support your claim through personal examples, references to ideas and examples found in readings related to your topic, and the support of experts in the field.

Credibility is an essential element in creating reasons. To be a successful debater, you must be believable; you must convince your audience that you are knowledgeable about your subject and that the facts, statistics, anecdotes, and whatever else you use to support your reasons are accurate and up-to-date. This means constructing your reasons through research and careful analysis of all the information available. For example, if you argue in an essay that there are better ways to run the U.S. Post Office, you will need to understand and explain how the current system operates. You can use the facts and statistics that you uncover in your research to analyze existing problems and to support your ideas for change. Being thoroughly informed helps you present and use your knowledge persuasively. Acquainting yourself with the necessary information will make you appear believable and competent. In later chapters, we will discuss how to formulate reasons to support your claim and how to evaluate evidence and use it effectively.

Another way to achieve credibility is to avoid logical fallacies, which will undermine the logic or persuasiveness of your argument. *Logical fallacies,* a term derived from the Latin *fallere,* meaning "to deceive," are unintentional errors in logic or deliberate attempts to mislead the reader by exaggerating evidence or using methods of argument that appeal to prejudice or bias. In Chapter 2, we will review the most common forms of logical fallacies so you can recognize them in the arguments of others and avoid them in your own writing.

Anticipating Opposition

Because debate anticipates opposition, you need to be certain that your reasons can withstand the challenges that are sure to come. Your goal as a successful debater is not only to present your reasons clearly and persuasively but to be prepared for the responses of people holding other views. For instance, in an essay on discrimination in women's collegiate sports, you may state that the operating budget of the women's varsity basketball team at your school is a fraction of that for the men's team. As evidence, you might point to the comparative lack of advertising, lower attendance at games, and lesser coverage than for the men's team. Unless you anticipate other perspectives on your issue, your argument could fall apart should someone suggest that women's basketball teams have lower budgets simply because they have smaller paying audiences. Not anticipating such a rebuttal would weaken your position. Had you been prepared, you could have acknowledged that opposing point and then responded to it by reasoning that the low budget is the cause of the problem, not the result of it. Putting more money into advertising and coverage could boost attendance and, thus, revenue.

In short, it is not enough simply to present your own reasons, no matter how effectively you support them. Unless you are familiar with opposing reasons, you leave yourself open to being undermined. To make your case as effective as possible, you must acknowledge and respond to the strongest reasons that challenge your own. To present only the weakest points of those who disagree with you or to do so in a poor light would likely backfire on your own credibility.

The following are strategies we recommend to help you become more aware of views that are different from your own and ways you might respond to them.

"Yes, but. . ." Exchanges

One way to be aware of the reasons on the other side is to research your topic carefully. After you've done some reading, a useful method to explore the way others might respond to your ideas is to engage in a "Yes, but . . ." exchange. Imagine you are face-to-face with someone holding a different position, and as you run down the list of your own reasons, his or her response is "Yes, but . . . [something]." What might that "something" be? Your task is first to acknowledge the validity of the other individual's viewpoint, and then to respond to that idea with reasons of your own. Consider, for instance, how a debate about affirmative action programs might proceed. You begin:

> Affirmative action programs discriminate against white males by denying them employment for which they are qualified.

From what you've heard and read, your opponent might respond this way:

> Yes, there are probably instances in which white males have lost employment opportunities because of affirmative action programs, but without these programs, minority candidates would never be considered for some job openings regardless of their qualifications.

Another reason might be:

> Race and gender should not be considerations when hiring an applicant for a job.

From your readings, you may uncover this opposing reason:

> Yes, in an ideal society, race and gender would never be factors for employers, but since we don't live in such a society, affirmative action programs ensure that race and gender don't become negative considerations when an individual applies for a job.

Imagining your debate in a "Yes, but . . ." exchange will help you work through a number of possibilities to strengthen your reasons in the light of opposition and to become more aware of other viewpoints.

Pro/Con Checklists

Another method to help you become more aware of opposing viewpoints is to create a pro/con checklist. Making such a checklist is useful for several reasons. First, it helps you

Sample Pro/Con Checklist

CLAIM: Human cloning should be outlawed because it is unnecessary and unethical.

PRO	CON
Human cloning is unnecessary because we have better ways to treat infertility.	Current fertility treatments are very expensive and are often unsuccessful.
Because we have too many unwanted children in the world already, we should not create more.	People have a right to have their own children.
Cloning is an unnatural process.	It is no more unnatural than many of the ways we currently treat infertility.
Human cloning will devalue the uniqueness of each individual.	A clone will still be a unique and separate human being.

solidify your own stand on the issue. It puts you in the position of having to formulate points on which to construct an argument. Second, by anticipating counterpoints, you can better test the validity and strength of your points. By listing potential resistance, you can determine the weak spots in your argument. Third, tabulating your own points will help you decide how to organize your reasons—which points to put at the beginning of your paper and which to put in the conclusion. Depending on the issue, you may decide for the sake of impact to begin with the strongest point and end with the weakest. This is the strategy of most advertisers—hitting the potential customer right off with the biggest sales pitch. Or you may decide to use a climactic effect by beginning with the weakest point and building to the strongest and most dramatic. Last, by ordering your key points, you can create a potential framework for constructing your argument. The box above shows an example of a pro/con checklist.

Moving from Debate to Dialogue

Debate is an important step in constructing an argument. It propels us to find a strong position and to argue that position as effectively as possible. But if we define *argument* as only debate, we limit the potential power of argument in our society. One common misconception is that all arguments are won or lost. This may be true in formalized debates, but in real life, few arguments are decided so clearly; and when they are, the conflicting issues at the heart of the debate can persist and continue to create dissent among individuals and groups. The prolonged tensions and sometimes violent confrontations that surround the issue of abortion may be the outcome of a debate that supposedly was resolved by a Supreme Court decision, *Roe* v. *Wade,* but remains a continuing problem because the debate did not engender a dialogue in which conflicting sides listened to each other and reconsidered their views from a more informed perspective. Argument must do more than provide an opportunity to present one's views against those of an opponent. We need to use it as a vehicle to explore other views as well and to help us shape a process in which change can happen and endure.

Dialogue

Take another moment to consider words that come to mind when you think of *dialogue:* discussion, listening, interaction, and understanding. By definition, a dialogue includes more than one voice, and those voices are responsive to each other. When we have a dialogue with someone, we don't simply present our own views. We may disagree, but we take turns so that no one voice monopolizes the conversation. The object of a dialogue is not to win or lose; the object is to communicate our ideas and to listen to what the other person has to say in response.

For example, you may find a policy in a particular class regarding makeup tests unfair. Since your instructor seems to be a reasonable person, you visit her office to discuss your objections. Your dialogue might proceed like this:

You: Professor, your syllabus states that if a student misses a test, there are no makeups. I think that this is unfair because if a student is genuinely ill or has an important conflict, the student will be penalized.

Professor: I can understand your concern, but I have that policy because some students use makeups to gain extra time to study. And, by asking other students about the questions on the test, they gain an advantage over students who take the test when it's scheduled. I don't think that's fair.

You: I hadn't thought of that. That's a good reason, but I'm still worried that even if I have a legitimate excuse for missing a test, my grade in the course will suffer. What can I do if that happens?

Professor: Let me think about your problem. Perhaps there's a way that I can be fair to you and still not jeopardize the integrity of my exams.

You: What if a student provides a physician's note in case of illness or a few days' advance notice in case of a conflict? Would you be able to provide an alternative testing day if that should happen?

Professor: That might be a good way to deal with the problem, as long as the makeup could be scheduled soon after. I'm going to give this more thought before I decide. I appreciate your suggestions. Stop by tomorrow and we can come to an agreement.

This hypothetical dialogue works because each participant listens and responds to the ideas of the other. Each has an important stake in the issue, but both focus on finding constructive ways to deal with it rather than trying to prove that the other is wrong. As a result, a compromise can be reached, and each person will have made a contribution to the solution.

When we move from debate to dialogue, we move from an arbitrary stance to one that allows for change and modification. Dialogue requires that both sides of the debate do more than simply present and react to each other's views in an adversarial fashion; it demands that each side respond to the other's points by attempting to understand them and the concerns they express. Often it is difficult for those participating in a debate to take this important step. In such cases, it will be your task, as a student of argument, to create the dialogue between opposing sides that will enable you to recognize common concerns and, if possible, to achieve a middle ground.

Creating a dialogue between two arguments involves identifying the writers' claims and key reasons. This is a skill we discuss in Chapter 2, when we look at strategies for reading and analyzing argument essays.

Deliberation

Deliberate is a verb that we don't use very much and we probably don't practice enough. It means to consider our reasons for and against something carefully and fully before making up our minds. We often speak of a jury deliberating about its verdict. Jury members must methodically weigh all the evidence and testimony that have been presented and then reach a judgment. Deliberation is not a quick process. It takes time to become informed, to explore all the alternatives, and to feel comfortable with a decision.

Deliberation plays an important part in the process of developing arguments. *Debate* focuses our attention on opposition and the points on which we disagree. *Dialogue* creates an opportunity to listen to and explore the arguments that conflict with our own. Deliberation, the careful consideration of all that we have learned through debate and dialogue, enables us to reach our own informed position on the conflict. Because we have participated in both debate and dialogue, we have a more complete understanding of the opposing arguments, as well as the common ground they may share. We are able to take the concerns of all sides into account.

Deliberation does not always resolve an issue in a way that is pleasing to all sides. Some issues remain contentious and irreconcilable, so that the parties are unable to move beyond debate. And, just as a jury sometimes reaches a verdict that is not what either the defense or the prosecution desires, deliberation does not ensure that all concerns or arguments will be considered equally valid. However, deliberation does ensure that you have given the arguments of all sides careful attention. And, unlike a jury, you have much broader parameters to determine your position. You do not have to decide *for* or *against* one side or the other. Your deliberations may result in an entirely new way of viewing a particular issue or solving a problem.

Consider, for example, a debate about whether a new football stadium should be built in a city experiencing economic problems, such as high unemployment and a failing public school system. One side of the debate may argue that a new stadium would result in additional jobs and revenue for the city from the influx of people who would come to watch the games. Another side may argue that the millions of dollars intended to subsidize a new stadium would be better spent creating job-training programs and promoting remedial education for schoolchildren. Your deliberation would involve several steps:

1. Becoming informed about the issue by reading and researching the information available
2. Creating a dialogue by listening to the arguments of all sides in the debate and trying to understand the reasons behind their claims

3. Weighing all the arguments and information carefully
4. Determining your own position on the issue

Your position might agree with one side or the other, or it might propose an entirely different response to the situation—say, a smaller stadium with the extra funds available to the schools, or a delay in the construction of a stadium until the unemployment problem is solved, or an additional tax to fund both, and so on. It would then be your task to convince all sides of the value of your position.

Deliberation enables you to use argument productively. It allows you to consider all sides of a problem or issue and to use your own critical analysis to find a way to respond.

As you learn more about writing your own arguments, you'll find that debate, dialogue, and deliberation can help you identify different perspectives, search for shared concerns, and develop your own position on an issue.

Review: Basic Terminology

Argument Essay

An essay that attempts to convince or persuade others through reason, logic, and evidence to do what the writer wants or believe as the writer wishes.

Claim

The statement in your essay that expresses your position or stand on a particular issue. The claim states precisely what you believe. It is the viewpoint you want your readers to accept or the action you want them to take.

Reasons

The explanation or justification behind your claim. To be effective, reasons must be supported by evidence and examples.

Debate

The act of presenting your claim and reasons, and challenging and being challenged by someone who holds a different viewpoint. Debate often focuses on differences between opponents rather than on shared concerns and values.

Dialogue

The act of listening and responding to those who hold viewpoints that are different from your own on a particular issue. The object of a dialogue is to find common ground by trying to understand other viewpoints while sharing your own. It is intended to reduce conflict rather than promote it.

Deliberation

The careful and informed consideration of all sides of an issue before reaching a conclusion or position on it. Deliberation can result in the resolution of a contentious issue.

Taking a "War of Words" Too Literally

Deborah Tannen

The following essay provides important insights into the ways in which we often approach argument in our society. This article by Deborah Tannen is adapted from her book, *The Argument Culture: Moving from Debate to Dialogue,* which explores how U.S. culture promotes a warlike, adversarial approach to problem-solving. Tannen is a professor of linguistics at Georgetown University. She is the author of the best-sellers *You Just Don't Understand: Women and Men in Conversation* and *Talking from 9 to 5: Women and Men at Work.* As you read Tannen's article, think about whether you have had experiences similar to those Tannen describes, when disagreements could have been settled more successfully through dialogue and thoughtful deliberation rather than through conflict.

1   I was waiting to go on a television talk show a few years ago for a discussion about how men and women communicate, when a man walked in wearing a shirt and tie and a floor-length skirt, the top of which was brushed by his waist-length red hair. He politely introduced himself and told me that he'd read and liked my book *You Just Don't Understand,* which had just been published. Then he added, "When I get out there, I'm going to attack you. But don't take it personally. That's why they invite me on, so that's what I'm going to do."

2   We went on the set and the show began. I had hardly managed to finish a sentence or two before the man threw his arms out in gestures of anger, and began shrieking—briefly hurling accusations at me, and then railing at length against women. The strangest thing about his hysterical outburst was how the studio audience reacted: They turned vicious—not attacking me (I hadn't said anything substantive yet) or him (who wants to tangle with someone who screams at you?) but the other guests: women who had come to talk about problems they had communicating with their spouses.

3   My antagonist was nothing more than a dependable provocateur, brought on to ensure a lively show. The incident has stayed with me not because it was typical of the talk shows I have appeared on—it wasn't, I'm happy to say—but because it exemplifies the ritual nature of much of the opposition that pervades our public dialogue.

4   Everywhere we turn, there is evidence that, in public discourse, we prize contentiousness and aggression more than cooperation and conciliation. Headlines blare about the Star Wars, the Mommy Wars, the Baby Wars, the Mammography Wars; everything is posed in terms of battles and duels, winners and losers, conflicts and disputes. Biographies have metamorphosed into demonographies whose authors don't just portray their subjects warts and all, but set out to dig up as much dirt as possible, as if the story of a person's life is contained in the warts, only the warts, and nothing but the warts.

5   It's all part of what I call the argument culture, which rests on the assumption that opposition is the best way to get anything done: The best way to discuss an idea is to set up a debate. The best way to cover news is to find people who express the most extreme views and present them as "both sides." The best way to begin an essay is to attack someone. The best way to show you're really thoughtful is to criticize. The best way to settle disputes is to litigate them.

6   It is the automatic nature of this response that I am calling into question. This is not to say that passionate opposition and strong verbal attacks are never appropriate. In the words of Yugoslavian-born poet Charles Simic, "There are moments in life when true invective is called for, when it becomes an absolute necessity, out of a deep sense of justice, to denounce, mock, vituperate, lash out, in the strongest possible language." What I'm questioning is the ubiquity, the knee-jerk nature of approaching almost any issue, problem or public person in an adversarial way.

7   Smashing heads does not open minds. In this as in so many things, results are also causes, looping back and entrapping us. The pervasiveness of warlike formats and language grows out of, but also gives rise to, an ethic of aggression: We come to value aggressive tactics for their own sake—for the sake of argument. Compromise becomes a dirty word, and we often feel guilty if we are conciliatory rather than confrontational—even if we achieve the result we're seeking.

8   Here's one example. A woman called another talk show on which I was a guest. She told the following story: "I was in a place where a man was smoking, and there was a no-smoking sign. Instead of saying 'You aren't allowed to smoke in here. Put that out!' I said, 'I'm awfully sorry, but I have asthma, so your smoking makes it hard for me to breathe. Would you mind terribly not smoking?' When I said this, the man was extremely polite and solicitous, and he put his cigarette out, and I said, 'Oh, thank you, thank you!' as if he'd done a wonderful thing for me. Why did I do that?"

9   I think the woman expected me—the communications expert—to say she needs assertiveness training to confront smokers in a more aggressive manner. Instead, I told her that her approach was just fine. If she had tried to alter his behavior by reminding him of the rules, he might well have rebelled: "Who made you the enforcer? Mind your own business!" She had given the smoker a face-saving way of doing what she wanted, one that allowed him to feel chivalrous rather than chastised. This was kinder to him, but it was also kinder to herself, since it was more likely to lead to the result she desired.

10   Another caller disagreed with me, saying the first caller's style was "self-abasing." I persisted: There was nothing necessarily destructive about the way the woman handled the smoker. The mistake the second caller was making—a mistake many of us make—was to confuse ritual self-effacement with the literal kind. All human relations require us to find ways to get what we want from others without seeming to dominate them.

11   The opinions expressed by the two callers encapsulate the ethic of aggression that has us by our throats, particularly in public arenas such as politics and law. Issues are routinely approached by having two sides stake out opposing positions and do battle. This sometimes drives people to take positions that are more adversarial than they feel—and can get in the way of reaching a possible resolution. . . .

12   The same spirit drives the public discourse of politics and the press, which are increasingly being given over to ritual attacks . . . I once asked a reporter about the common journalistic practice of challenging interviewees by repeating criticism to them. She told me it was the hardest part of her job. "It makes me uncomfortable," she said. "I tell myself I'm someone else and force myself to do it." But, she said she had no trouble being combative if she felt someone was guilty of behavior she considered wrong. And that is the crucial difference between ritual fighting and literal fighting: opposition of the heart.

13   It is easy to find examples throughout history of journalistic attacks that make today's rhetoric seem tame. But in the past such vituperation was motivated by true political passion, in contrast with today's automatic, ritualized attacks—which seem to grow out of a belief that conflict is high-minded and good, a required and superior form of discourse.

14   The roots of our love for ritualized opposition lie in the educational system that we all pass through.

15   Here's a typical scene: The teacher sits at the head of the classroom, pleased with herself and her class. The students are engaged in a heated debate. The very noise level reassures the teacher that the students are participating. Learning is going on. The class is a success.

16   But look again, cautions Patricia Rosof, a high school history teacher who admits to having experienced just such a wave of satisfaction. On closer inspection, you notice that only a few students are participating in the debate; the majority of the class is sitting silently. And the students who are arguing are not addressing subtleties, nuances or complexities of the points they are making or disputing. They don't have that luxury because they want to win the argument—so they must go for the most dramatic statements they can muster. They will not concede an opponent's point—even if they see its validity—because that would weaken their position.

17   This aggressive intellectual style is cultivated and rewarded in our colleges and universities. The standard way to write an academic paper is to position your work in opposition to someone else's. This creates a need to prove others wrong, which is quite different from reading something with an open mind and discovering that you disagree with it. Graduate students learn that they must disprove others' arguments in order to be original, make a contribution and demonstrate intellectual ability. The temptation is great to oversimplify at best, and at worst to distort or even misrepresent other positions, the better to refute them.

18   I caught a glimpse of this when I put the question to someone who I felt had misrepresented my own work: "Why do you need to make others wrong for you to be right?" Her response: "It's an argument!" Aha, I thought, that explains it. If you're having an argument, you use every tactic you can think of—including distorting what your opponent just said—in order to win.

19   Staging everything in terms of polarized opposition limits the information we get rather than broadening it.

20   For one thing, when a certain kind of interaction is the norm, those who feel comfortable with that type of interaction are drawn to participate, and those who do not feel comfortable with it recoil and go elsewhere. If public discourse included a broad range of types, we would be making room for individuals with different temperaments. But when opposition and fights overwhelmingly predominate, only those who enjoy verbal sparring are likely to take part. Those who cannot comfortably take part in oppositional discourse or choose not to—are likely to opt out.

21   But perhaps the most dangerous harvest of the ethic of aggression and ritual fighting is—as with the audience response to the screaming man on the television talk show—an atmosphere of animosity that spreads like a fever. In extreme forms, it rears its head in road rage and workplace shooting sprees. In more common forms, it leads to what is being decried everywhere as a lack of civility. It erodes our sense of human connection to those in public life—and to the strangers who cross our paths and people our private lives.

1. Do you agree with Tannen's assertion that public discussions about controversial issues have been turned into "battles and duels" by the media? Why or why not? Look through current newspapers or magazines for evidence of this trend. Do other forms of media, such as television and radio, also encourage the same?

2. How has the "argument culture" affected our ability to resolve issues? Think of current controversies that have been negatively affected by the tendency of some to defend their own "turf" rather than listen and respond constructively to others with differing views?

3. Tannen cites a woman who called in to a talk show and questioned whether her conciliatory approach to a potential conflict was the best course of action (paragraphs 8 and 9). In your journal, discuss your own experiences confronting someone whose behavior you found unacceptable. What approaches proved successful for you? Do you agree with Tannen that the woman was wise to avoid conflict?

4. In your own experience, have you found that schools and teachers promote and reward students who engage in heated debate with other students, as Tannen contends in paragraphs 18 to 20? Do you think this strategy discourages students who are uncomfortable with this confrontational behavior? Have you found that a "winner-take-all" approach to argument is a productive way to solve disagreements? What problems can arise from this approach? Any benefits?

SAMPLE ARGUMENTS FOR ANALYSIS

Read the following two essays to find the basic components in writing arguments and to practice debate, dialogue, and deliberation. After you have read each essay carefully, respond to these questions about them:

1. Identify each writer's claim and restate it in your own words. What do you think is the writer's purpose in writing the essay?

2. What reasons does each writer use to support his claim? Make a list of the reasons you find in each essay. Are the reasons convincing?

3. Find examples of the ways each writer supports those reasons. How convincing is the evidence he presents? Is it pertinent? Reliable? Sufficient? Is it slanted or biased?

4. Does the writer acknowledge views about the subject that are different from his own? Where does he do this? What is the writer's attitude toward those who hold different views? Does he try to understand those views or does he respond only negatively toward them?

5. Using debate, dialogue, and deliberation, complete the following activities individually or in small groups:

   a. To become acquainted with opposing reasons, write a "yes, but . . ." exchange or a pro/con checklist.

b. Using your checklist or exchange, create a dialogue between two or more opposing sides on the issue that attempts to find points of disagreement as well as common ground or shared concerns among them. Look for opportunities for each side to listen and respond constructively to the other.

c. Deliberate. Review the reasons and examples from a number of perspectives. What reasons on either side do you find the most compelling? What concerns have particular merit? How can you balance the interests of all sides of the issue? Formulate a claim that takes into account what you have learned from listening and considering several perspectives and provide reasons to support it.

The Case Against Tipping

Michael Lewis

Many people have strong views about tipping. Some consider it an optional act of kindness to express appreciation for good service, an additional expense over what they have already paid. For others it is an essential part of their day's wages, and thus their income. The following essay by Michael Lewis explores this dichotomy. Lewis is a contributing editor at *Vanity Fair* and the author of several best-selling books including *Liar's Poker* (1990), *Moneyball: The Art of Winning an Unfair Game* (2004), and most recently, *Home Game: An Accidental Guide to Fatherhood* (2009).

As you read this article, which originally appeared in the *New York Times Magazine* in 1997 and was updated by the author for this edition, think about your own attitudes toward the practice of tipping. What motivates a tip? If you have ever been on the receiving end, did you find that relying on others' generosity for your income left you vulnerable to their whims?

1　No lawful behavior in the marketplace is as disturbing to me as the growing appeals for gratuities. Every gentle consumer of cappuccinos will know what I'm getting at: Just as you hand your money over to the man behind the counter, you notice a plastic beggar's cup beside the cash register. "We Appreciate Your Tips," it reads in blue ink scrawled across the side with calculated indifference. The young man or woman behind the counter has performed no especially noteworthy service. He or she has merely handed you a $2 muffin and perhaps a ruinous cup of coffee and then rung them up on the register. Yet the plastic cup waits impatiently for an expression of your gratitude. A dollar bill or two juts suggestively over the rim—no doubt placed there by the person behind the counter. Who would tip someone a dollar or more for pouring them a cup of coffee? But you can never be sure. The greenbacks might have been placed there by people who are more generous than yourself. People whose hearts are not made of flint.

2　If you are like most people (or at any rate like me), you are of two minds about this plastic cup. On the one hand, you do grasp the notion that people who serve you are more likely to do it well and promptly if they believe they will be rewarded for it. The prospect of a tip is, in theory at least, an important incentive for the person working behind the

•

counter of the coffee bar. Surely, you don't want to be one of those people who benefit from the certain hop to the worker's step that the prospect of a tip has arguably induced without paying your fair share of the cost. You do not wish to be thought of as not doing your share, you cheapskate.

3   And these feelings of guilt are only compounded by the niggling suspicion that the men who run the corporation that runs the coffee shops might be figuring on a certain level of tipping per hour when they decide how generous a wage they should extend to the folks toiling at the counters. That is, if you fail to tip the person getting you that coffee, you may be directing and even substantially affecting that person's level of income, especially in today's down economy.

4   That said, we are talking here about someone who has spent all of 40 seconds retrieving for you a hot drink and a muffin. When you agreed to buy the drink and the muffin you did not take into account the plastic-cup shakedown. In short, you can't help but feel you are being had.

5   There in a nutshell is the first problem with tipping: the more discretion you have in the matter the more unpleasant it is. Tipping is an aristocratic conceit—"There you go, my good man, buy your starving family a loaf"—best left to an aristocratic age. The practicing democrat would rather be told what he owes right up front. Offensively rich people may delight in peeling off hundred-dollar bills and tossing them out to groveling servants. But no sane, well-adjusted human being cares to sit around and evaluate the performance of some beleaguered coffee vendor.

6   This admirable reticence means that, in our democratic age at least, gratuities are inexorably transformed into something else. On most occasions where they might be conferred—at restaurants, hotels and the like—tips are as good as obligatory. "Tipping is customary," reads the sign in the back of a New York City taxi, and if anything, that is an understatement. Once, a long time ago, I tried to penalize a cabdriver for bad service and he rolled alongside me for two crowded city blocks, shouting obscenities through his car window. A friend of mine who undertipped had the message drummed home more perfectly: a few seconds after she stepped out of the cab, the cab knocked her over. She suffered a fracture in her right leg. But it could have been worse. She could have been killed for . . . undertipping! (The driver claimed it was an accident. Sure it was.)

7   There, in a nutshell, is the second problem with tipping: the less discretion you have in the matter, the more useless it is as an economic incentive. Our natural and admirable reluctance to enter into the spirit of the thing causes the thing to lose whatever value it had in the first place. It is no accident that the rudest and most inept service people in America—New York City cabdrivers—are also those most likely to receive their full 15 percent. A tip that isn't a sure thing is socially awkward. But a tip that is a sure thing is no longer a tip really. It's more like a tax.

8   Once you understand the impossibility of tipping in our culture, the plastic cup on the coffee-bar counter can be seen for what it is: a custom in the making. How long can it be before the side of the coffee cup reads "Tipping Is Customary"? I called Starbucks to talk this over, and a pleasant spokeswoman told me that this chain of coffee bars, at least, has no such designs on American mores. The official Starbucks line on their Plexiglas container is that it wasn't their idea but that of their customers. "People were leaving loose change on the counter to show their gratitude," she said. "And so in 1990 it was decided to

put a tasteful and discreet cup on the counter. It's a way for our customers to say thanks to our partners." (Partners are what Starbucks calls its employees.)

9   Perhaps. But you can be sure that our society will not long tolerate the uncertainty of the cup. People will demand to know what is expected of them, one way or the other. Either the dollar in the cup will become a routine that all civilized coffee buyers will endure. Or the tasteful and discreet cup will disappear altogether, in deference to the straightforward price hike.

10   A small matter, you might say. But if the person at the coffee-bar counter feels entitled to a tip for grabbing you a coffee and muffin, who won't eventually? I feel we are creeping slowly toward a kind of baksheesh economy in which everyone expects to be showered with coins simply for doing what they've already been paid to do. Let's band together and ignore the cup. And who knows? Someday, we may live in a world where a New York City cabdriver simply thanks you for paying what it says on the meter.

QUESTIONS FOR DISCUSSION AND WRITING

1. Do you think Lewis has had much experience in a job that relies on tips? What evidence can you find to demonstrate this?

2. Do you agree with Lewis? In your journal, respond to Lewis's ideas by exploring your own views on tipping. What experiences have you had that support your own view?

A Generation of Slackers? Not So Much
Catherine Rampell

Catherine Rampell is an economics journalist for *The New York Times,* where she served as the founding editor of the Economix blog. She is the recipient of the Weidenbaum Center Award for Evidence-Based Journalism and is a Gerald Loeb Award finalist. This article appeared on May 28, 2011, in *The New York Times.*

1   You'd think there would be a little sympathy. This month, college graduates are jumping into the job market, only to land on their parents' couches: the unemployment rate for 16- to 24-year-olds is a whopping 17.6 percent.

2   The reaction from many older Americans? This generation had it coming. Generation Y—or Millennials, the Facebook Generation or whatever you want to call today's cohort of young people—has been accused of being the laziest generation ever. They feel entitled and are coddled, disrespectful, narcissistic and impatient, say authors of books like *The Dumbest Generation* and *Generation Me.* And three in four Americans believe that today's youth are less virtuous and industrious than their elders, a 2009 survey by the Pew Research Center found.

3   In a sign of humility or docility, young people agree. In that 2009 Pew survey, two-thirds of millennials said older adults were superior to the younger generation when it

came to moral values and work ethic. After all, if there's a young person today who's walked 10 miles barefoot through the snow to school, it was probably on an iPhone app.

4   So is this the Laziest Generation? There are signs that its members benefit from lower standards. Technology has certainly made life easier. But there may also be a generation gap; the way young adults work is simply different. It's worth remembering that to some extent, these accusations of laziness and narcissism in "kids these days" are nothing new—they've been levied against Generation X, Baby Boomers and many generations before them. Even Aristotle and Plato were said to have expressed similar feelings about the slacker youth of their times.

5   But this generation has had it easy in some ways. They can access just about any resource, product or service anywhere from a mere tap on a touch screen. And as many critics have noted, it's also easier to get A's. The typical grade-point average in college rose to about 3.11 by the middle of the last decade, from 2.52 in the 1950s, according to a recent study by Stuart Rojstaczer, professor emeritus at Duke, and Christopher Healy of Furman University.

6   College students also spend fewer hours studying each week than did their counterparts in 1961, according to a new working paper by Philip S. Babcock of the University of California, Santa Barbara, and Mindy Marks of the University of California, Riverside. That doesn't mean all this leftover time is spent on PlayStation 3's.

7   There is ample evidence that young people today are hard-working and productive. The share of college students working full time generally grew from 1985 onward—until the Great Recession knocked many millennials out of the labor force, according to the Labor Department. And while many college students today—like those of yesterday—get financial help from their parents, 44 percent of students today say that work or personal savings helped finance their higher educations, according to a survey of recent graduates by Rutgers University.

8   "I don't think this is a generation of slackers," said Carl Van Horn, a labor economist at Rutgers. "This image of the kid who goes off and skis in Colorado, I don't think that's the correct image. Today's young people are very focused on trying to work hard and to get ahead."

9   Defying the narcissism stereotype, community service among young people has exploded. Between 1989 and 2006, the share of teenagers who were volunteering doubled, to 26.4 percent from 13.4 percent, according to a report by the Corporation for National and Community Service. And the share of incoming college freshmen who say they plan to volunteer is at a record high of 32.1 percent, too, U.C.L.A.'s annual incoming freshman survey found.

10   Perhaps most important, many of the behaviors that older generations interpret as laziness may actually enhance young people's productivity, say researchers who study Generation Y. Members of Gen Y, for example, are significantly more likely than Gen Xers and boomers to say they are more productive working in teams than on their own, according to Don Tapscott, author of "Grown Up Digital: How the Net Generation is Changing Your World," a book based on interviews with 11,000 millennials.

11   To older workers, wanting help looks like laziness; to younger workers, the gains that come from teamwork have been learned from the collaborative nature of their childhood activities, which included social networks, crowd-sourcing and even video games

like World of Warcraft that "emphasize cooperative rather than individual competition," Mr. Tapscott says.

12   Employers also complain about millennials checking Facebook and Twitter on the job, or working with their ear buds in. Older workers have a strong sense of separate spheres for work and play: the cubicle is for work, and home is for fun. But to millennials, the boundaries between work and play are fuzzier, said Michael D. Hais, co-author of "Millennial Makeover: MySpace, YouTube, and the Future of American Politics."

13   Think of the corporate cultures at prototypical Gen Y employers like Facebook and Google, he says, where foosball, volleyball courts and subsidized massages are office fixtures. The prevailing millennial attitude is that taking breaks for fun at work makes people more, not less, productive. Likewise, they accept that their work will bleed into evenings and weekends.

14   Some experts also believe that today's young people are better at quickly switching from one task to another, given their exposure to so many stimuli during their childhood and adolescence, said John Della Volpe, the director of polling at Harvard's Institute of Politics. (The jury is still out on that one.)

15   Of course, these explanations may be unconvincing to older bosses, co-workers and teachers on the other side of this culture clash. But at least they can take comfort in one fact: someday, millennials will have their own new generation of know-it-all ne'er-do-wells to deal with.

QUESTIONS FOR DISCUSSION AND WRITING

1. Do you consider yourself a member of Generation Y? Or would you describe yourself as a Millennial or one of the Facebook Generation? Why did you pick that particular term? What character traits would you assign to the group you identify with? List six traits with which you associate. Do you find a match with any of the traits discussed in this article?

2. What does the author think of the tendency of the older generation to define or criticize the younger generation? How does she explain this tendency?

3. List three criticisms of Generation Y that Rampell refers to in the piece. Cite a piece of evidence in the piece that she uses to refute or question the criticism. What is the source of that evidence? Is it an analysis by an economist? An analyst of the digital world? A survey conducted by universities? Other?

4. Which critique of Generation Y did you find most untrue or objectionable? Which did you find to be true?

5. Respond specifically to claims that:
   a. Today's youth are less virtuous and industrious than their elders.
   b. Youth today are lazy.
   c. Youth today work best collaboratively.

6. Cite one book, university study, or survey mentioned in this essay that piqued your curiosity, made you want to read further. What book, study

or survey would that be, and what attracts you to it? Do you think the author's references to other books added to the quality of her argument?

7. Was "A Generation of Slackers? Not So Much" a good title for this piece? Why or why not?

EXERCISES

1. Try to determine from the following list which subjects are arguable and which are not.
   a. Letter grades in all college courses should be replaced by pass/fail grades.
   b. Sororities and fraternities are responsible for binge drinking among college students.
   c. Lobster is my favorite seafood.
   d. Professor Greene is one of the best professors on campus.
   e. Children are better off if they are raised in a traditional nuclear family.
   f. Advertisements now often appear in commercial films using a strategy called product placement.
   g. Minorities make up only 10 percent of upper management positions in corporate America.
   h. The earth's population will be 7.2 billion by the year 2014.
   i. Juveniles who commit serious crimes should be sent to adult prisons.
   j. Last night's sunset over the mountains was spectacular.
   k. Advertisers often mislead the public about the benefits of their products.
   l. AIDS testing for health care workers should be mandatory.
   m. Bilingual education programs fail to help non-English-speaking children become part of mainstream society.
   n. Scenes of Nativity often displayed at Christmas time should not be allowed on public property.
   o. The tsunami that struck Asia in December of 2004 is the worst natural disaster in recorded history.
   p. Couples should have to get a license before having children.
   q. Given all the billions of galaxies and billions of stars in each galaxy, there must be life elsewhere.
   r. Secondhand smoke causes cancer.

2. In your argument notebook, create a pro/con checklist for the following topics. Make two columns: pro on one side, con on the other. If possible, team up with other students to brainstorm opposing points on each issue. Try to come up with five or six solid points and counterpoints.
   a. I think women are better listeners than men.
   b. If a juvenile is charged with a serious crime and his/her parents are found to be negligent, the parents should be charged with the crime as well.
   c. "Hard" sciences such as math are more difficult than "soft" sciences such as sociology.

    d. There should be a mandatory nationwide ban of cigarette smoking in all places of work including office buildings, restaurants, bars, and clubs.

    e. The university should reduce tuition for those students who maintained an A average during the previous year.

    f. ROTC should be made available to all students in U.S. colleges and universities.

    g. A majority of American people support prayer in school.

    h. Mandatory national ID cards would reduce the threat of terrorism in this country.

3. Use one of these topics to construct a dialogue in which the object is not to oppose the other side but to respond constructively to its concerns. As a first step, analyze the reasons provided by both sides and make a list of their concerns, noting whether any are shared. Then create a dialogue that might take place between the two.

4. Write about a recent experience in which you tried to convince someone of something. What reasons did you use to make your claim convincing? Which were most successful? What were the opposing reasons? How did you respond?

Reading Arguments: Thinking Like a Critic

LEARNING OBJECTIVES

After studying this chapter, you should be able to:

1. Describe why it is important to read critically. (p. 28)
2. Name and apply the six basic steps in reading critically. (p. 28)
3. Define many or all of the 17 major logical fallacies. (p. 47)

We read for a variety of purposes. Sometimes it's to find information about when a particular event will take place or to check on the progress of a political candidate or to learn how to assemble a piece of furniture. Other times, we read to be entertained by a favorite newspaper columnist, or to discover the secrets behind making a pot of really good chili. But if you've ever picked up a book or read a blog, a newspaper editorial, or a piece of advertising and found yourself questioning the ideas and claims of the authors, then you've engaged in a special kind of reading called *critical reading*. When you look beyond the surface of words and thoughts to think about the ideas and their meaning and significance, you are reading critically.

Critical reading is active reading. It involves asking questions and not necessarily accepting the writer's statements at face value. Critical readers ask questions of authors such as these:

- What do you mean by that phrase?
- Can you support that statement?
- How do you define that term?
- Why is this observation important?
- How did you arrive at that conclusion?
- Do other experts agree with you?
- Is this evidence up-to-date?

By asking such questions, you are weighing the writer's claims, asking for definitions, evaluating information, looking for proof, questioning assumptions, and making judgments. In short, you are actively engaged in thinking like a critic.

Why Read Critically?

When you read critically, you think critically. Instead of passively accepting what's written on a page, you separate yourself from the text and decide what is convincing to you and what is not. Critical reading is a process of discovery. You discover where an author stands on an issue, and you discover the strengths and weaknesses of an author's argument. The result is that you have a better understanding of the issue. By asking questions of the author and by analyzing where the author stands with respect to others' views on the issue, you become more knowledgeable about the issue and more able to develop your own informed viewpoint on the subject.

Critical reading not only sharpens your focus on an issue, it also heightens your ability to construct and evaluate your own arguments. That will lead you to become a better writer because critical reading is the first step to critical writing. Good writers look at the written word the way a carpenter looks at a house—they study the fine details and how those details connect to create the whole. It's the same with critical reading. The better you become at analyzing and reacting to another's written work, the better you are at analyzing and reacting to your own, by asking: Is it logical? Are my points clearly stated? Do my examples really support my ideas? Have I explained this term clearly? Is my conclusion persuasive? In other words, critical reading will help you use that same critical eye with your own writing, making you both a better reader and a better writer.

Additionally, as you sharpen your skills as a reader and a writer, you will also develop your critical skills as an interpreter of arguments embodied not in words but in visual images. As you will see in Chapter 8, argumentation is not limited to verbal presentation. Photographs, political cartoons, and advertisements, among others, express potent and persuasive arguments in visual imagery.

Even though you may already employ many of the strategies of critical reading, we'd like to offer some suggestions and techniques to make you an even better critical reader.

Preview the Reading

Even before you begin reading, you can look for clues that may reveal valuable information about the subject of the article, the writer's attitude about the subject, the audience the writer is addressing, and the purpose of the article. As a prereading strategy, try to answer the following questions:

1. *Who is the writer?* Information about the writer is sometimes provided in a short biographical note on the first or last page of the reading. The writer's age, education, current profession, and professional background can tell you about his or her experience and perspective on the subject. For instance, a physician who is writing about assisted suicide may have a very different attitude toward that subject than an individual who has a degree in divinity. A writer who has held a high-ranking position in a government agency or a political appointment will bring that experience to bear in a discussion of a political issue. A writer's background and professional training can provide knowledge and credibility; you may be more inclined to believe an expert in a field than someone with little or no experience. However, direct experience can also limit the writer's perspective. A review of this information before you read can help you better evaluate the writer as an authority.

2. *Where was the article originally published?* Often the publication in which the article originally appeared will indicate the writer's audience and purpose. Some publications, such as scholarly journals, are intended to be read by other professionals in a particular field. Writers for such a journal assume that readers are familiar with the terminology of that profession and possess a certain level of education and experience. For example, an author writing about cancer research in a scholarly medical journal such as the *Journal of the American Medical Association (JAMA)* would assume a high degree of medical expertise on the part of the readers. An author writing about the same cancer research in *Newsweek* would provide a greatly simplified version with little medical terminology. Popular magazines you see at newsstands are designed to communicate to a larger, more general audience. Writers make an effort to explain difficult concepts in terms an inexperienced reader can understand. Knowing where the article was originally published will prepare you for the demands of the reading. It may also prepare you for the writer's point of view. Publications are usually designed for a specific audience. *The Wall Street Journal,* for example, has a readership largely comprising people interested in the economy, business, or investments. The articles in it reflect the concerns and interests of the business community. In contrast, an article appearing in *High Times,* a publication that endorses the use and legalization of marijuana, has a very different set of readers. By familiarizing yourself with the publication in which the article originally appeared, you can learn much about the writer's likely political and professional opinions, knowledge you can use to judge the credibility of his or her argument.

3. *When was the article originally published?* The date of publication can also provide background about what was happening when the article was published. It will indicate factors that might have influenced the writer and whether the evidence used in the reading is current or historical. For instance, an article written about the economy during a recession would be strongly influenced by factors of high unemployment and business failures. The writer's argument might not be as convincing during a period of growth and stability. Some readings are timeless in their consideration of basic truths about people and life; others can be challenged about whether their arguments still apply to current circumstances.

4. *What does the title reveal about the subject and the author's attitude toward it?* The title of an article often indicates both the subject of the article and the writer's attitude toward it. After you have identified the subject, look carefully at the words the writer has used to describe it. Are their connotations negative or positive? What other words do you associate with them? Does the title make reference to another written work or to a well-known slogan or familiar saying? Sometimes writers use their titles to suggest a parallel between their subject and a similar situation in recent times or a particular event in history. An article about the possibility of an annihilating nuclear attack in 2020 might be titled "Hiroshima in the Twenty-First Century." These choices are deliberate ways to inform readers about a writer's views and ideas on a subject. By considering the language in the title, you will be more aware of the writer's intent.

Let's try a preview of the first reading in this chapter. By carefully reading the introductory paragraph, you can learn the following information:

Preview Question 1: Who is the writer? As the introduction tells us, Henry Wechsler is the director of the College Alcohol Studies Program at the Harvard School of

Public Health. His professional title suggests that he is knowledgeable about alcohol use, particularly at the college level, because he directs a program that studies this area. You are about to read an essay, then, written by an expert in the field of alcohol research.

Preview Question 2: Where was the article originally published? By reading further in the paragraph, you find that the article was originally published in the *Boston Globe*. This is a widely circulated newspaper located in a major American city. The writer would expect the article to be read by a large cross-section of people with diverse economic and educational backgrounds. Because Boston is the city where Harvard and many other colleges are located, readers might have a special interest in issues that affect the college community.

Preview Question 3: When was the article originally published? The introduction tells you that the article first appeared on October 2, 1997. Although this was written some 17 years ago, the topic is still relevant to current concerns.

Preview Question 4: What does the title reveal about the subject and the author's attitude toward it? The title of the article, "Binge Drinking Must Be Stopped," suggests an emphatic and nonnegotiable attitude on the part of the author.

As you can see, your preview of the article has provided much valuable information that will help prepare you to begin the critical reading process.

Skim the Reading

Just as an athlete would never participate in a competitive event without first stretching his or her muscles and thoroughly warming up, you will find that successful critical reading is a process that benefits from a series of activities aimed at increasing your understanding of the writer's ideas. The first time through, you may wish to skim the reading to get a general idea of its subject and intent. Further readings should be slower and more thoughtful so that each reason presented can be analyzed and evaluated and each idea judged and considered. Now that you have previewed the material about the author, the original publication and date, and the title, you are ready to skim the reading to find its basic features.

When you skim a reading, you are trying to discover the topic and the claim. Start by reading the first one or two paragraphs and the last paragraph. If the reading is a relatively short newspaper article, such as the following sample essay, this may be enough to give you a general idea of the writer's topic and point of view. If the reading is longer and more complex, you will also need to examine the first sentence or two of each paragraph to get a better sense of the writer's ideas.

SAMPLE ARGUMENT FOR ANALYSIS

For practice, let's skim the first reading in this chapter. To organize your impressions from skimming the reading, it's a good idea to write down some of them in your journal.

Binge Drinking Must Be Stopped

Henry Wechsler

"Binge" drinking is a problem that plagues many colleges and universities across America. Fueled by an "alcohol culture," students will drink to excess at apartment parties or fraternity houses just off campus. But the disturbing fact is that thousands of them die each year as a result of alcohol abuse. And, as argued in the following essay, too many college administrators are apparently turning a blind eye to the problem. Dr. Henry Wechsler is a social psychologist with a long-term commitment to research on alcohol and drug abuse among young people. A lecturer in the Department of Society, Human Development and Health, at the Harvard School of Public Health, he is the principal investigator of the college alcohol study. Since its inception in 1992, the study has surveyed over 50,000 students at 120 colleges in 40 states, producing dozens of publications that have focused national attention on college binge drinking and its harmful effects. Dr. Wechsler is the author of 18 books and monographs including most recently *Dying to Drink* (2003). This essay was originally published in the *Boston Globe* in 1997 and has been updated by the author for this edition of *Dialogues*.

1   A recent study conducted for the National Institute on Alcohol Abuse and Alcoholism estimated that over 1800 college students 18–24 years of age died from alcohol related injuries in the past year. We should be saddened and outraged by these tragic deaths of young men and women just starting to fulfill their life's promise.

2   These deaths are an extreme and unfortunate consequence of a style of drinking that is deeply entrenched and widespread in American colleges. Binge drinking is a reality of college life in America and perhaps the central focus of fraternity house life.

3   Since the Harvard School of Public Health study on college binge drinking was released in 1994, colleges have been deluged with reports on alcohol abuse. Even before our results became public, it was inconceivable that college administrators were unaware of the existence of alcohol problems at their institutions.

4   A quick ride in a security van on a Thursday, Friday, or Saturday night could provide all the information needed. A conversation with the chief of security could easily reveal where the binge drinking takes place and which students, fraternities, and alcohol outlets are violating college rules or local ordinances.

5   An incoming freshman learns during the first week of school where the alcohol and parties are and often has a binge drinking experience even before purchasing a textbook. If students can find it so easily, so can college administrators. It is not that complicated: Drunken parties are usually at certain fraternity houses and housing complexes just off campus. The beer that fuels these parties is bought in the liquor stores offering cut rate prices for large purchases. Heavy drinking also takes place in the many bars encircling most campuses where large quantities of alcohol are sold cheaply.

6   If we know so much about the problem, why is it that we have not been able to do much about it? First, because colleges, like problem drinkers, do not recognize that they have a problem. And those that do think that they have solved it through half-measures. It

has been there for so long that they have adapted to it. They are lulled into complacency as long as the problem does not seem to increase or a tragedy does not occur.

7   Second, the solutions that are offered are usually only partial: a lecture, an awareness day, a new regulation in the dorms. The root of the problem is seldom touched. The focus is on the students, and not on the suppliers and marketers of the alcohol. The supply of large quantities of cheap alcohol is viewed as outside the purview of college officials. "It's off campus" is a euphemism for "that's not my job." The bar or liquor store may be off campus, but it is controlled by licensing boards that city officials and colleges can substantially influence. The fraternity house may be off campus and not owned by the college, but it is affiliated with and depends on the college for its existence. Many colleges and universities simply wink at the activities of the fraternities and claim no responsibility.

8   Third, when new policies are established, they are often assumed to be in effect without proper verification. It is easy to say there is no drinking allowed in a dormitory or a fraternity, but enforcement is necessary to put the policy into effect. Legally, no alcohol can be sold to people under age 21, but 86 percent of college students drink.

9   We can no longer be shocked at what is happening on many college campuses and in many fraternities. This is no longer a time merely to form a committee to study the situation. It is time to act.

10   Action needs to be taken on many fronts: the college president's office, the fraternity and sorority system, the athletics department, community licensing boards, and foremost, those students who are sick of the drinking they see around them.

11   Parents who pay for college tuitions should demand a safe environment for their children. Binge drinking need not remain an integral part of college life. University presidents must make it their responsibility to produce change.

After skimming "Binge Drinking Must Be Stopped," you might record the following (we indicate in parentheses the paragraphs in which we found our ideas):

> Wechsler starts off with a reference to a study that reports on the large number of college student deaths as the result of alcohol-related injuries. He says we should be saddened and outraged by this. Then he suggests that binge drinking has become very common on college campuses, particularly in fraternities (paragraphs 1 and 2). Wechsler believes parents should insist that colleges provide a safe environment for their children by finding solutions for binge drinking. University presidents must take responsibility for solving this problem (paragraph 11).

By skimming the article, you now have some sense of what the reading will be about and the writer's position. Before beginning a closer reading of the text, you will want to take one additional step to prepare yourself to be an active and responsive reader: Consider your experience with the topic.

Consider Your Own Experience

Your next step in the reading process is to consider your own experience. Critical reading brings your own perspective, experience, education, and personal values to your reading. Sometimes you begin with very little knowledge about the subject of your reading. It may be a topic that you haven't given much thought or one that is unfamiliar and new. Other times you may start with some of your own ideas and opinions about the subject. By taking the time to consider what you know and how your own experiences and values relate to the author's ideas, you can add a dimension to your reading that enables you to question, analyze, and understand the writer's ideas more effectively. You will be a more active critical reader because you can respond to the writer's ideas with ideas of your own.

Before beginning a close reading, take the time to reflect on these questions:

- What do I know about this subject?
- What have I heard or read about it recently?
- What attitudes or opinions do I have about the subject?

Exploring what you already know or think about a subject can have several benefits: You can use your knowledge to better understand the situation or issue described in the reading; you can compare your own experience with that of the writer; you can formulate questions to keep in mind as you read; and you can become more aware of your own opinions about the subject. For instance, you may be reading an article about the benefits of the proposed plan for improving your state's welfare system. If you have some knowledge about this proposal from reading news stories or hearing discussions about it, you will begin your reading with some understanding of the issue. If you have had actual experience with the welfare system or know of others' experiences, you can provide examples of your own to challenge or support those of the writer. If you have taken the time to consider questions you have about the proposed plan, you will be actively seeking answers as you read. And, by exploring your own views on the subject before you read, you will find that the ideas in the article will enrich, inform, and possibly change your opinion.

After previewing and skimming the reading, John, a freshman composition student, wrote the following reflection on the topic of binge drinking in his journal:

> It would be hard to be a student at college and not notice the heavy drinking that goes on every weekend. Some people just can't have fun unless they drink too much. It's a fact of college life—for some people. And if you live in a small college community, sometimes that's all there is to do on Saturday night. I've seen some kids really ruin their lives with too much partying. They forget why they came to college in the first place—or maybe that is why they came. But not everybody drinks to excess. Most of us just like to get a little buzz and socialize and have fun. Most of us will go just so far and stop, but there's always a few who can't seem to stop until they pass out or puke their guts out on the sidewalk. Yeah, we've all been told the dangers of drinking too much, but some people aren't mature enough to see that they're hurting themselves. Binge drinking happens every weekend around here. It's not a pretty sight, but I'm not sure how the college president or anybody else could stop it. College students have always partied to relieve tension and to socialize. It's been going on for years. Why is college drinking suddenly such a big issue? And, if the drinking takes place outside of campus, how can the college stop it? If students want to get alcohol, even if they're underage, they'll find a way. Why should the college tell us whether we can drink or not?

John clearly has considerable experience with the topic and some strong opinions of his own. By considering them before he begins a close reading of the article, he is ready to explore and challenge the ideas he encounters in the reading.

Annotate the Reading

Annotating the text is the next stage of critical reading to help you become a thoughtful and careful reader. *Annotating* is responding to the ideas in the reading right on the pages of your text. (If you don't own the publication the essay appears in, make a photocopy.) There are many different ways to annotate a reading, but many readers use the following methods:

- Highlight or underline passages that you consider significant.
- Write questions in the margins that respond to the writer's ideas or that you wish to follow up with further investigation.
- Circle words or phrases that need to be defined or made clearer.
- Add comments or brief examples of your own that support or challenge the writer's.
- Draw lines between related ideas.
- Note the writer's use of transitions and qualifiers that subtly shade meaning.
- Point out with arrows or asterisks particularly persuasive examples.
- Mark difficult-to-understand sections of the text that need a closer look.

Annotation is a way to create an active dialogue between you and the writer by responding in writing to individual points in the reading. Your annotations become a personal record of your thoughts, questions, objections, comments, and agreements with the writer. Annotation can help you read like a critic because it makes you slow down and pay attention to each idea as you read. As an additional benefit, your written comments in the margin will serve as a reminder of your response to the ideas in the essay when you read it again. Figure 2.1 is an example of some of the ways you might annotate "Binge Drinking Must Be Stopped."

Binge Drinking Must Be Stopped

1   A recent study conducted for the National Institute on Alcohol Abuse and Alcoholism estimated that over 1800 college students 18–24 years of age died from alcohol related injuries in the past year. We should be saddened and outraged by these tragic deaths of young men and women just starting to fulfill their life's promise.

Does everyone at college drink?

2   These deaths are an extreme and unfortunate consequence of a style of drinking that is deeply entrenched and widespread in American colleges. Binge drinking is a reality of college life in America and perhaps the central focus of fraternity house life.

claim

3   Since the Harvard School of Public Health study on college binge drinking was released in 1994, colleges have been deluged with reports on alcohol abuse. Even before our results became public, it was inconceivable that college administrators were unaware of the existence of alcohol problems at their institutions.

find more info on this
flooded

4   A quick ride in a security van on a Thursday, Friday, or Saturday night could provide all the information needed. A conversation with the chief of security could easily reveal where the binge drinking takes place and which students, fraternities, and alcohol outlets are violating college rules or local ordinances.

Is this the job of a college administrator?

5   An incoming freshman learns during the first week of school where the alcohol and parties are and often has a binge drinking experience even before purchasing a textbook. If students can find it so easily, so can college administrators. It is not that complicated: Drunken parties are usually at certain fraternity houses and housing complexes just off campus. The beer that fuels these parties is bought in the liquor stores offering cut rate prices for large purchases. Heavy drinking also takes place in the many bars encircling most campuses where large quantities of alcohol are sold cheaply.

qualifier
How does he know this?

6   If we know so much about the problem, why is it that we have not been able to do much about it? First, because colleges, like problem drinkers, do not recognize that they have a problem. And those that do think that they have solved it through half-measures. It has been there for so long that they have adapted to it. They are lulled into complacency as long as the problem does not seem to increase or a tragedy does not occur.

who is "we"?

Is this contradicted by the next ¶?

7   Second, the solutions that are offered are usually only partial: a lecture, an awareness day, a new regulation in the dorms. The root of the problem is seldom touched. The focus is on the students, and not on the suppliers and marketers of the alcohol. The supply of large quantities of cheap alcohol is viewed as outside the purview of college officials. "It's off campus" is a euphemism for "that's not my job." The bar or liquor store may be off campus, but it is controlled by licensing boards that city officials and colleges can substantially influence. The fraternity house may be off campus and not owned by the college, but it is affiliated with and depends on the college for its existence. Many colleges and universities simply wink at the activities of the fraternities and claim no responsibility.

Don't colleges try to do something about binge drinking?

Agreed. These don't change behaviour much

less offensive substitute word

What does he mean?

8   Third, when new policies are established, they are often assumed to be in effect without proper verification. It is easy to say there is no drinking allowed in a dormitory or a fraternity, but enforcement is necessary to put the policy into effect. Legally, no alcohol can be sold to people under age 21, but 86 percent of college students drink.

Impressive statistic

9   We can no longer be shocked at what is happening on many college campuses and in many fraternities. This is no longer a time merely to form a committee to study the situation. It is time to act.

Who is "we"? Has it changed?

10   Action needs to be taken on many fronts: the college president's office, the fraternity and sorority system, the athletics
department, community licensing boards, and foremost, those
students who are sick of the drinking they see around them.

*His solution. What
should they do?*

11   Parents who pay for college tuitions should demand a safe
environment for their children. Binge drinking need not remain
an integral part of college life. University presidents must make
it their responsibility to produce change.

*Who is responsible?
Don't the drinkers
have some
responsibility?*

essential

*Are college students
"children"?*

Figure 2.1

Summarize the Reading

Before you can begin to analyze and evaluate what you read, it's important to understand
clearly what the writer is saying. *Summarizing* is a type of writing used to capture the
essential meaning of a reading by focusing only on the writer's main points. When you
summarize, you "tell back," in a straightforward way, the writer's main ideas. Although
summaries can vary in length depending on the length of the original reading, all summaries share these qualities:

◼ **A summary is considerably shorter than the original.**   Because a summary is
concerned only with the writer's main ideas, supporting details and examples are
usually omitted. The length of a summary will vary depending on your purpose and
the length and content of the original.

◼ **A summary is written in your own words.**   Although it may be necessary to
use certain of the writer's words for which there are no substitutes, a summary is
written in your own words. If you find it necessary to include a short phrase from the
original, then quotation marks must be used to set it off. (In Chapter 9, we discuss
ways to use summary in a researched argument paper and the need to document the
ideas in your summary with a citation.)

◼ **A summary is objective.**   When you summarize, your job is to "tell back" the writer's
main ideas with no comments or personal opinions of your own. Of course, once you
have completed your summary, you are free to respond to it in any way you wish.

◼ **A summary is accurate.**   It's a good idea to reread several times before you attempt
to summarize a reading because it's important that you truly understand what the
writer means. Sometimes it takes many tries to capture that exact meaning.

◼ **A summary is thorough.**   Even though a summary is, as we've explained, much
shorter than the original, a good summary contains each of the writer's main points.

Summarizing is an important step in critical reading because you need to understand
a writer's ideas thoroughly before you can explain them, in writing, to others. Don't be
discouraged when you first try to summarize a reading. Over time and with practice you
will feel more comfortable writing summaries.

A good method to begin summarizing a reading is to write a one-sentence summary of the ideas in each paragraph. (Brief paragraphs that elaborate the same point can be summarized together.) By considering each paragraph separately, you will be sure to cover all the main ideas in the reading and be able to see at a glance how the ideas in the essay are connected to each other and how the writer has chosen to sequence them.

Let's go back to the essay "Binge Drinking Must Be Stopped" and try a one-sentence summary of each paragraph (we combine short paragraphs that are about the same idea):

Paragraph 1: According to a recent study, some 1,800 college students 18–24 years of age died from alcohol-related injuries this past year—a tragic reality.

Paragraph 2: Colleges should be aware of the problem of excessive drinking among their students because studies have been released about it.

Paragraph 3: By speaking with law enforcement professionals in their own communities, colleges could become aware of where alcohol laws are being broken.

Paragraph 4: Freshmen learn where to find alcohol when they first arrive on campus: fraternities, student housing, and bars close to campus.

Paragraph 5: Colleges aren't doing anything about the problem because they have accepted it and don't want to admit it exists.

Paragraph 6: Because the cause of the problem is the availability of alcohol off campus, colleges don't think it is their responsibility to act even though they could exercise a strong influence over the places that sell alcohol to students.

Paragraph 7: Colleges don't check to see whether their own alcohol policies are being enforced.

Paragraphs 8 and 9: Rather than just talk about this problem, we need to do something about it at many different levels within the college and the community.

Paragraph 10: College presidents need to take responsibility for reducing the practice of excessive drinking at their colleges to provide a safe place for students.

Your one-sentence summary of each paragraph should reveal the essential parts of the essay: the claim and the main reasons the writer uses to support the claim. Once you have identified these important elements, you are ready to begin your summary. It might look something like this (note that we've added the name of the writer and the title of the article):

In his essay "Binge Drinking Must Be Stopped," Henry Wechsler expresses his concern about the common practice of excessive drinking on college campuses. He suggests that colleges are failing in their responsibility to deal with this problem adequately. Although colleges should be informed about the problem, they won't acknowledge its seriousness. Because it doesn't happen on their campuses, they don't feel that it is their responsibility. Wechsler thinks that colleges could exercise their influence off campus in ways that would help to solve the problem. And, even when colleges do have alcohol policies to restrict drinking, they don't check to see if their policies are being enforced. The problem of binge drinking needs to be dealt with now at many different levels within the college and the community. Wechsler thinks that college presidents need to take responsibility for dealing with binge drinking so that it is no longer an important part of college life.

In looking over this summary, you'll notice that we begin with a general sentence that presents the writer's topic and claim. Then, after reviewing our one-sentence paragraph summaries, we have chosen the writer's main reasons to include in the rest of our paragraph. We have tried to eliminate any ideas that are repeated in more than one paragraph, so we can focus on only the major points.

Summarizing a reading means taking all the separate ideas the writer presents, deciding which ones are important, and weaving them together to create a whole. Our next step in the critical reading process is to consider the ways in which the writer has presented those ideas.

Analyze and Evaluate the Reading

To *analyze* something means to break it down into its separate parts, examine those parts closely, and evaluate their significance and how they work together as a whole. You already began this process when you summarized the main idea in each paragraph of your reading. But analysis goes beyond identifying the ideas in the essay. When we analyze, we consider how each part of the essay functions. We are discovering and evaluating the assumptions and intentions of the writer, which lie below the surface of the writing and which we consider separately from the meaning of the essay itself. Analysis helps us consider how successfully and effectively the writer has argued.

Although there is no set formula for analyzing an argument, we can offer some specific questions you should explore when reading an essay that is meant to persuade you:

- What are the writer's assumptions? What does the writer take for granted about the readers' values, beliefs, or knowledge? What does the writer assume about the subject of the essay or the facts involved?
- What kind of audience is the writer addressing?
- What are the writer's purpose and intention?
- How well does the writer accomplish those purposes?
- What kinds of evidence has the writer used—personal experience or scientific data or outside authorities?
- How convincing is the evidence presented? Is it relevant? Is it reliable? Is it specific enough? Is it sufficient? Is it slanted or dated?
- Does the writer's logic seem reasonable?
- Did the writer address opposing views?
- Is the writer persuasive?

For the sake of illustration, let's apply these questions to our reading:

- *What are the writer's assumptions?*

    The writer assumes that the estimated number of alcohol-related student deaths indicates a widespread problem of binge drinking on college campuses. He thinks that colleges have a responsibility to control the behavior of their students. He assumes that college students will continue to binge drink without any such controls.

■ *What kind of audience is the writer addressing?*

He seems to be addressing college administrators, parents of college students, and readers who have a special interest in college life.

■ *What are the writer's purpose and intention?*

He wants to make his readers aware that a problem exists and that colleges are not effectively dealing with it.

■ *How well does the writer accomplish this purpose?*

He makes a strong argument that colleges refuse to acknowledge that there's a problem.

■ *What kinds of evidence has the writer used?*

He refers to a recent study for the National Institute on Alcohol Abuse and Alcoholism as well as others by the Harvard School of Public Health, and he uses examples of student hangouts that he has heard about but not experienced personally. He seems familiar with college programs on alcohol awareness. He implies that he consulted with the campus security chief for some of his information.

■ *How convincing is the evidence?*

Wechsler mentions a scientific study in paragraph 1 with figures and then again in paragraph 3; but he does not offer much in the way of details concerning the second study. Although Wechsler could provide more solid evidence that the problem is widespread, his examples of places where students can find alcohol seem convincing.

■ *Does the writer's logic seem reasonable?*

Wechsler effectively links the evidence he presents to his claim that excessive drinking on college campuses is being ignored by college administrators.

■ *Did the writer address opposing views?*

No. We never hear how college administrators respond to this criticism. We also don't know if college students agree with the description of their behavior.

■ *Is the writer persuasive?*

The writer is persuasive if we assume that the problem is widespread and that colleges can have a major impact on students' behavior when they are not on campus.

Argue with the Reading

Asking questions and challenging assumptions are important ways to read critically. Although you may not feel qualified to pass judgment on a writer's views, especially if the writer is a professional or an expert on a particular subject, you should keep in mind that as a part of the writer's audience, you have every right to determine whether an argument is sound, logical, and convincing. Your questions about and objections to the writer's ideas will help you evaluate the effectiveness of his or her argument and form your own judgment about the issue.

You may wish to record some of these thoughts in your annotations in the margins of the text. However, a good strategy for beginning writers is to respond at greater length in a journal. You might start by jotting down any points in the essay that contradict your own experience or personal views. Note anything you are skeptical about. Write down any questions you have about the claims, reasons, or evidence. If some point or conclusion seems forced or unfounded, record it and briefly explain why. The more skeptical and questioning you are, the more closely you are reading the text and analyzing its ideas. In particular, be on the lookout for logical fallacies, those instances in which the writer— whether unintentionally or purposefully—distorts or exaggerates evidence or relies on faulty logic to make a point. We discuss these fallacies extensively later in this chapter.

Likewise, make note of the features of the text that impress you—powerful points, interesting wording, original insights, clever or amusing phrases or allusions, well-chosen references, or the general structure of the essay. If you have heard or read different views on the issue, you might wish to record them as well.

As an example, let's consider some questions, challenges, and features that might have impressed you in our sample essay:

- Wechsler claims that binge drinking is a common practice at colleges across America. Is that true? Does binge drinking take place at all colleges or only on certain campuses? Do all students engage in this practice, or is it more common among certain age groups, gender, fraternity members as opposed to nonmembers, residential students? Do college students drink more than noncollege students in the same age group?
- The statistic about the number of student deaths (paragraph 1) and percentage of college students who drink (paragraph 8) is convincing.
- Colleges exist to educate students. Are they responsible for monitoring students' behavior when they are not attending classes or socializing off campus? Is it realistic to expect colleges to do this?
- Are colleges really denying that the problem exists? Don't they have counseling services to help students with drinking problems? What else can they do?
- Wechsler's points about the influence that colleges have in their communities (paragraph 7) are persuasive.
- Mentioning the concerns of students who don't drink and the parents of college students is a clever strategy Wechsler uses to expand his audience and pressure colleges to act.

Create a Debate and Dialogue Between Two or More Readings

Few of us would expect to be experts on tennis or golf after watching one match or tournament. We know that it takes time and effort to really begin to understand even the fundamentals of a sport. Reading a single article on a particular subject is the first step in becoming educated about the issues at stake, but a single essay provides us with only one perspective on that subject. As we continue to read about the subject, each new article will offer a new perspective and new evidence to support that view. The more we read, the more complex and thorough our knowledge about the subject becomes. Creating a dialogue between two or more readings is the next step in the process of critical reading.

When you annotate a reading in the earlier stages of critical reading, you begin a dialogue between yourself and the writer. When you create a dialogue between two or more readings, you go one step further: You look at the ideas you find in them to see how they compare and contrast with each other, how they are interrelated, and how the information from one reading informs you as you read the next. By creating a dialogue between the ideas you encounter in several readings, you will be able to consider multiple viewpoints about the same subject.

SAMPLE ARGUMENT FOR ANALYSIS

Begin reading this second selection on binge drinking by following the steps we've outlined in this chapter:

1. Preview the information about the author, where the article first appeared, the date of publication, and the title.
2. Skim the reading to discover the writer's topic and claim.
3. Consider your own experience, values, and knowledge about the subject.
4. Annotate the reading.
5. Summarize the essay.
6. Analyze and evaluate the effectiveness of the reading.
7. Argue with the reading.

Stop Babysitting College Students
Froma Harrop

> Froma Harrop presents another viewpoint on the subject of binge drinking and college students in the following essay, which appeared in the *Tampa Tribune.* Harrop, an editorial writer and columnist for the *Providence Journal,* argues that college students should be the ones held responsible for their behavior, not businesses and educational institutions.

1   Anyone suspicious that the American university experience has become a four-year extension of childhood need look no farther than the colleges' latest response to the binge-drinking "problem." Now, in a grown-up world, college administrators would tell students who down four or five stiff drinks in a row that they are jerks.

2   If they commit violent acts as a result, the police get called. If they drive after drinking, they go to the slammer. If they die from alcohol poisoning, they have nothing but their own stupidity to blame.

3   But if they can drink responsibly, then let them have a good time.

4   Forget about hearing any such counsel, for that would turn students into self-directing adults. Better to blame the problem on all-purpose "cultural attitudes" and "societal pressures" abetted by the villainous alcohol industry.

5   Thus, demands grow for better policing of off-campus liquor outlets. That is, turn local businesses into babysitters. There are calls to ban sponsorship of college events by

companies selling alcohol or the marketing of such beverages on campus. That is, protect their charges from evil influences and trample on free speech. (What should colleges do with the frequent references in Western literature to the glories of drink? Rabelais, for example, said, "There are more old drunkards than old physicians.")

6   One former college official has suggested that universities stop serving champagne at parents' weekend brunches or at fundraising events. Remove the bad example for the sake of the children. (Somehow it is hard to believe that a college with any sense of self-preservation would insist that its big-check writers remain cold sober.)

7   The truth is, most Americans can drink without a problem. Careful use of alcohol relaxes and warms the drinker with a sense of well-being. Winston Churchill and Franklin Roosevelt saved Western civilization without ever missing a cocktail hour. Students have long enjoyed their own drinking traditions. Brahms' Academic Overture, the stately piece heard over and over again at college commencements, took its melody from a student drinking song.

8   Where is there a campus drinking crisis, anyway? Six college students have supposedly died this year from excessive drinking. These cases are lamentable, but many more college students died from sports-related injuries or car accidents.

9   An even more interesting question is: How many noncollege people in their late teens or early 20s have died from alcohol poisoning? Take note that no one is memorizing this particular statistic—even though the majority of high school students do not go on to college. That number is not etched on our national worry list for the following strange reason: Our society considers the 19-year-old who has a job an adult, while universities see the 19-year-old pre-law student as a child. Working people who cause trouble because they drink are punished. College students are given others to blame.

10   College administrators should know that, from a purely practical point of view, playing hide-the-bottle does no good when dealing with an alcoholic. Indeed, anyone who has hung around Alcoholics Anonymous or Al-Anon can immediately identify such behavior as "enabling." Rather than allow the problem drinker to sink into the mire of his addiction until he can no longer stand it and takes steps to straighten out, the enabler tries to save him. Rest assured that students interested in getting smashed for the night will find the booze.

11   Let us end here with yet another proposition: that binge drinking is more about binge than drinking. It would seem that someone who gulps five glasses of Jim Beam in five minutes is not looking for a pleasant high. Binge drinking is a stunt that has more in common with diving off bridges or swallowing goldfish than the quest for inebriation.

12   What any increase in binge drinking probably indicates is that the students really don't know how to drink. Binging may just be the latest evidence of decline in our nation's table arts. Instead of savoring wine and spirits in the course of a civilized meal, young people are administering them. The colleges' response is to put condoms on bottles.

Construct a Debate

Now that you have a good understanding of Froma Harrop's views on college students' binge drinking, you are ready to consider the ideas in both the essays you read. Our first step will be to consider the differences between these two writers by constructing a debate.

From your summaries of the readings, select the main ideas that seem directly opposed to each other. To highlight those differences, create two columns, one for each writer. Here are a few of the ideas Wechsler and Harrop debate in their essays:

Wechsler	*Harrop*
Binge drinking is a major problem on college campuses: A student has died.	Binge drinking is not a major problem on campuses: Few students have died.
Colleges have a responsibility to take action about this problem.	Students are responsible for their own drinking.
Colleges should prevent off-campus suppliers of alcohol from selling it to college students.	Colleges should not "police" off-campus suppliers of alcohol.
Colleges should provide a safe environment for students.	College students are adults and should take care of themselves.
Binge drinking continues because colleges aren't treating it as an important problem.	Binge drinking happens because some college students haven't learned to drink responsibly.

These are just a sampling of the many ideas that might be debated by these writers. You should be able to come up with several more.

By considering differences, you can see at a glance the ways in which these writers oppose each other. Your next step is to find the ideas they have in common. This may take more searching, but it's an important step in creating a dialogue between them. To get you started, we'll list a few of the ideas we found. See if you can come up with a few more:

1. Both writers acknowledge that drinking takes place on college campuses.
2. Both writers indicate that binge drinking can be a problem and that students have died as a result.
3. Both writers agree that colleges are aware that binge drinking takes place off campus.

Now that you have found both differences and common ideas, you are ready to create a dialogue. When you create a dialogue between two readings, you find ways for the writers to speak to each other that recognize their differences and points of agreement.

Your dialogue will reveal how the ideas in both readings interrelate. Let's try to create a dialogue using some of the ideas we found:

Wechsler: Binge drinking is a serious problem on college campuses. It's an activity that has become commonplace.

Harrop: I agree that college students engage in binge drinking, but six deaths this year don't necessarily indicate that this is a crisis.

Wechsler: Just because more students haven't died doesn't mean that it isn't a dangerous activity and should be ignored. Colleges need to take steps to ensure that more students aren't harmed by this common practice.

Harrop: It's unfortunate that students have died, but why should we think it is the college's responsibility to police student drinking? College students are adults and should suffer the consequences of their behavior. It's their choice whether to drink and how much.

Wechsler: Colleges are responsible for their students. They need to find ways to prevent students from getting alcohol. They are responsible to the parents who pay the tuition and to the other students who have to tolerate excessive drinking among their peers.

Harrop: Practically speaking, colleges can't prevent students from drinking. Students who want to drink will find a way because they are adults with drinking problems, not children in need of supervision.

Complete this dialogue by finding additional ways in which the writers' ideas speak to each other.

As you can see, the dialogue helps us explore the readings in far greater depth than if we had read both essays in isolation. Each writer's ideas help us to evaluate the ideas of the other. By interrelating them in a dialogue, we can better appreciate how the perspective of each writer changes the way similar facts and information are interpreted. For instance, Henry Wechsler is outraged by the estimated 1,800 alcohol-related student deaths. In contrast, Froma Harrop does not find the deaths of six college students from excessive drinking an alarming statistic when she compares it with the number of college students who have died from other accidental causes. It is up to us as readers to decide which writer's interpretation is more persuasive.

SAMPLE ARGUMENTS FOR ANALYSIS

To practice creating your own dialogue between readings, read the following two letters to the editor, which appeared in two newspapers before and after Henry Wechsler's article. Read them critically, going through the steps we outlined in this chapter, and add them to the dialogue already created between Wechsler and Harrop. We think you'll find that your understanding of the issue will increase and that you'll feel more confident about forming your own position on the question of college binge drinking.

Letter from *The Washington Post*

To the Editor:

1   When we saw the headline "Party Hardly" and the revolting picture of four bare-chested, probably underage fraternity brothers guzzling cheap beer, we thought, "Finally! Your paper is tackling an issue that affects every college student." Much to our chagrin, however, the article wasted two pages of newsprint glorifying drunkenness and poor study habits.

2   Perhaps you need to be aware of some ugly facts before your next article on college drinking: One out of every four student deaths is related to alcohol use (research shows that as many as 360,000 of the nation's 12 million undergraduates will die as a result of

alcohol abuse); alcohol is a factor in 66 percent of student suicides and 60 percent of all sexually transmitted diseases; studies show that between 33 percent and 59 percent of drinking college students drive while intoxicated at least once a year (with as many as 30 percent driving impaired three to 10 times per year); and alcohol consumption was a factor in at least half of the cases of a study of college women who had been raped by an acquaintance.

3   Alcohol affects not only those who drink it: Those students who do not drink are affected by their classmates or roommates who do. Students at schools with high levels of binge drinking are three times more likely to be pushed, hit or sexually assaulted than are students at schools with less drinking. Students who live with people who drink heavily often are kept awake by obnoxious behavior or the sound of their roommates vomiting in the trash can.

4   The shame does not lie solely with your paper, however. *The Princeton Review,* which ranks "party schools" based on how much students use alcohol and drugs, how few hours students study every day and the popularity of fraternities and sororities, should focus on what most feel is the real purpose of a college education: to learn—not to learn how to party.

Kathryn Stewart
Corina Sole

Letter from *The Times-Picayune*

To the Editor:

1   The entire nation is justifiably concerned about recent tragic deaths caused by alcohol abuse on our college campuses. College students everywhere know where to procure alcohol and where to consume it without being "hassled."

2   Public dialogue asks if institutions are doing enough to control the situation. Unfortunately, it must be stated that colleges and universities are doing all they can.

3   A typical university fosters an alcohol awareness program, provides the services of a substance abuse coordinator, disciplines students for infractions, and provides an atmosphere in which young people can grow responsibly.

4   There is more that must be done. Parents at one time held their sons and daughters accountable for the company they kept. A student who deliberately associates with a group known for its excesses, or who joins an organization suspended or expelled by the institution, is choosing bad company. Peer pressure does the rest.

5   The courts restrict the ability of colleges to discipline students for off-campus behavior unless the activity in question has a fairly direct relationship with institutional mission.

6   They require due process, including confrontation by witnesses, for any disciplinary action. Peer pressures in the college-age group are so strong that testimony of witnesses is frequently difficult to obtain.

7   Until we return to a system in which colleges can function, at least in part, in loco parentis (in place of the parent), other agencies of society will have to step in.

8   To be fully effective, a college would need the ability to impose severe sanctions, including dismissal, on the base of reasonable proof of misbehavior or association with bad elements. Advocates of unrestrained constitutional rights will have difficulty with this, but the student enters a contractual relationship with a college to pursue an education.

9   The educators, not the legal system, should do the educating. Colleges exist to form good citizens, conscious of their own rights and the rights of others. Colleges and universities should be evaluated on the basis of the results of their educational work.

James C. Carter, S.J.
Chancellor,
Loyola University,
New Orleans

Deliberate About the Readings

As we explained in Chapter 1, deliberation is a way to arrive at your own position on a particular issue. You can't begin deliberation until you have really listened to and reflected on the complexities each issue involves. Once you have engaged in all the steps in the process of critical reading, you are ready to deliberate.

In your deliberation, first consider each of the writer's claims and main points. Then, thinking like a critic, find a way to respond that defines your own position on the issue. Using the four readings in this chapter, a deliberation in your journal about college binge drinking might look like this:

> All the writers see binge drinking as a problem, although they differ about where they place the blame and how they plan to solve the problem. Wechsler thinks that binge drinking among college students occurs because colleges are indifferent to it and refuse to recognize its seriousness. He urges colleges to use their influence and power to prevent students from obtaining alcohol. He doesn't seem to think that the students who engage in binge drinking have a lot of control over their behavior. Carter, Sole, and Stewart all agree with Wechsler about the seriousness of the problem; however, they disagree about where to place the blame. Carter thinks that colleges are doing all they can and should be given more legal power to discipline students who binge drink. Sole and Stewart suggest that the media is to blame by endorsing values that encourage students to drink and party rather than concentrate on their studies. Only Harrop places the blame squarely on the shoulders of the binge drinkers themselves. She feels strongly that students need to be treated as adults with drinking problems and suffer the consequences of their actions.

> After reading these writings, I am convinced that binge drinking is a problem worthy of our attention. The statistics that Wechsler, Stewart, and Sole cite are convincing and impressive. I also know from my own experience that many students drink excessively, and I think that six deaths are too many for us to ignore. I also think that binge drinking is a problem that affects the entire college community, not just the drinkers, as Stewart and Sole point out. However, I tend to agree with Harrop that students must be held responsible for their own actions. I disagree with Carter that schools should act like parents. College is about becoming an adult in all areas of our lives, not just academics.

Any solution to the problem of binge drinking needs to include the students who abuse alcohol. Unless those students also see their drinking habits as a problem, nothing the college or legal system can impose will affect their behavior. Perhaps a combination of actions, including broader and stronger efforts to educate students about alcohol abuse, greater enforcement and harsher penalties for underage drinking by the legal system, and efforts by colleges to restrict alcohol availability in the community and on the campus, would make a significant dent in this problem.

Now try writing your own deliberation, in which you consider the points you find most important in each reading, to arrive at your own position on the issue of binge drinking.

Look for Logical Fallacies

When you read the arguments of others, you need to pay attention to the writer's strategies, assertions, and logic to decide if the argument is reasonable. Like the cross-examining attorney in a court case, you must examine the logical connections between the claim, the reasons, and the evidence to reveal the strengths and weaknesses of the writer's argument.

Sometimes writers make errors in logic. Such errors are called **logical fallacies**, a term derived from the Latin *fallere,* meaning "to deceive." Used unintentionally, these fallacies deceive writers into feeling that their arguments are more persuasive than they are. Even though an argument may be well developed and contain convincing evidence, a fallacy creates a flaw in the logic of an argument, thereby weakening its structure and persuasiveness.

Preview: Logical Fallacies

- Ad hominem argument
- Ad misericordiam argument
- Ad populum argument
- Bandwagon appeal
- Begging the question
- Circular reasoning
- Dicto simpliciter
- False analogy
- False dilemma
- Faulty use of authority
- Hasty generalization
- Non sequitur
- Post hoc, ergo propter hoc
- Red herring
- Slippery slope
- Stacking the deck
- Straw man

Not all logical fallacies are unintentional. Sometimes a fallacy is deliberately employed—for example, when the writer's goal has more to do with persuading than with arriving at the truth. Every day we are confronted with fallacies in media commercials and advertisements. Likewise, every election year, the airwaves are full of candidates' bloated claims and pronouncements rife with logical fallacies of all kinds.

Recognizing logical fallacies when they occur in a reading is an important step in assessing the effectiveness of the writer's argument. This final section of our chapter will acquaint you with some of the most common logical fallacies.

Ad Hominem Argument

From the Latin "to the man," the **ad hominem** argument is a personal attack on an opponent rather than on the opponent's views. Certainly the integrity of an opponent may be important to readers. Nonetheless, writers are usually more persuasive and credible when they focus on issues rather than character flaws. If, for instance, you are reading a paper against the use of animals in medical research and the writer refers to the opposition as "cold-hearted scientists only interested in fame and fortune," you might question whether the writer objects to the scientists' views or to their personal prosperity. Name-calling and character assassination should make you suspicious of the writer's real motives or balanced judgment. Personal criticisms, even if true, can be overemphasized and, therefore, undercut the writer's credibility.

However, there may be cases in which an ad hominem argument is a legitimate rhetorical tool. When the special interests or associations of an individual or group appear to have a direct impact on their position on an issue, it is fair to raise questions about their lack of objectivity on that basis. For example, the organizer of a petition to build a state-supported recycling center may seem reasonably suspect if it is revealed that he owns the land on which the proposed recycling center would be built. Although the property owner may be motivated by sincere environmental concerns, the direct relationship between his position and his personal life makes this fair game for a challenge.

Examples of Ad Hominem Arguments

- How could Tom accuse her of being careless? He's such a slob.
- Of course he doesn't see anything wrong with violent movies. The guy's a warmonger.
- We cannot expect Ms. Lucas to know what it means to feel oppressed; she is the president of a large bank.

Ad Misericordiam Argument

Its name also derived from Latin, the **ad misericordiam** argument is the appeal "to pity." This appeal to our emotions need not be fallacious or faulty. A writer, having argued several solid points logically, may make an emotional appeal for extra support. Your local Humane Society, for instance, might ask you to donate money so it can expand its facilities for abandoned animals. To convince you, the society might point out how, over the last few years, the number of strays and unwanted pets has tripled. And because of budget constraints, the society has been forced to appeal to the public. It may claim that a donation of $25 would house and feed a stray animal for a month. Any amount you give, the society might explain, will ultimately aid the construction of a new pet "dormitory" wing. To bolster the appeal, the Humane Society literature might then describe how the adorable puppy and kitten in the enclosed photo will have to be put to death unless the overcrowding of the society's facilities is relieved by donations such as yours.

When an argument is based solely on the exploitation of the reader's pity, however, the issue gets lost. There's an old joke about a man who murdered his parents and appealed to the court for leniency because he was an orphan. It's funny because it ludicrously illustrates how pity has nothing to do with murder. Let's take a more realistic example. If you were a lawyer whose client was charged with bank embezzlement, you would not get very far, basing your defense solely on the fact that the defendant was abused as a child. Yes, you may touch the hearts of the jurors, even move them to pity. Yet that would not exonerate your client. The abuse the defendant suffered as a child, as woeful as it is, has nothing to do with his or her crime as an adult. Any intelligent prosecutor would point out the attempt to manipulate the court with a sob story while distracting it from more important factors such as justice.

Examples of Ad Misericordiam Arguments

■ It makes no difference if he was guilty of Nazi war crimes. The man is 88 years old and in frail health, so he should not be made to stand trial.

■ Paula is 16 years old and lives on welfare with her mother; she suffers serious depression and functions like a child half her age. She should not be sent to adult court, where she will be tried for robbery, so she can spend her formative years behind bars.

Ad Populum Argument

From the Latin "to the people," an **ad populum** argument is just that—an argument aimed at appealing to the supposed prejudices and emotions of the masses. Writers attempt to manipulate readers by using emotional and provocative language to add appeal to their claims. The problem with the ad populum argument, however, is that such language sometimes functions as a smoke screen hiding the lack of ideas in the argument. You'll find examples of this fallacy on the editorial pages of your local newspaper—for example, the letter from parents raising a furor because they don't want their child or the children of their friends and neighbors taught by teachers with foreignaccents; or the columnist who makes the ad populum case against capital punishment by inflating the number of innocent people wrongfully executed by the state; or the writer who argues that if gays and lesbians are allowed to serve in the military, our national defense will be jeopardized by "sex maniacs."

Examples of Ad Populum Arguments

■ High school students don't learn anything these days. Today's teachers are academically underprepared.

■ If you want to see the crime rate drop, tell Hollywood to stop making movies that glorify violence.

■ Doctors oppose health reform because it will reduce their large incomes.

Bandwagon Appeal

This familiar strategy makes the claim that everybody is doing this and thinking that. If we don't want to be left out, we had better get on the **bandwagon** and do and think the same things. The basic appeal in this argument is that of belonging to the group, behaving like the majority. It plays on our fears of being different, of being excluded. Of course, the appeal is fallacious inasmuch as we are asked to "get with it" without weighing the evidence of what is being promoted: "Smart shoppers shop at Sears"; "America reads Danielle Steel."

Examples of Bandwagon Appeals

■ Everybody's going to the System of a Down concert.

■ Nobody will go along with that proposal.

■ The majority of the American people want a constitutional amendment outlawing flag burning.

Begging the Question

Similar to circular reasoning, **begging the question** passes off as true an assumption that needs to be proven. For instance, to say that the defendant is innocent because he passed a polygraph test begs the question: Does passing a polygraph test mean somebody is innocent? Sometimes the begged question is itself loaded in a bigger question: "Are you ever going to act like you are equal and pay for one of our dates?" The begged question here is whether paying the costs of a date is a measure of sexual equality.

Examples of Begging the Question

■ That foolish law should be repealed.

■ She is compassionate because she's a woman.

■ If you haven't written short stories, you shouldn't be criticizing them.

Circular Reasoning

Circular reasoning is another common fallacy into which many writers fall. In it, the conclusion of a deductive argument is hidden in the premise of that argument. Thus, the argument goes around in a circle. For instance: "Steroids are dangerous because they ruin your health." This translates: Steroids are dangerous because they are dangerous. Sometimes the circularity gets camouflaged in a tangle of words: "The high cost of living in today's America is a direct consequence of the exorbitant prices manufacturers and retailers are placing on their products and services." Cut away the excess, and this translates: The high cost of living is due to the high cost of living. Repetition of key terms or ideas is not evidence. Nor does it prove anything. Instead of simply restating your premise, find solid evidence to support it.

Examples of Circular Reasoning

 People who are happy with their work are cheerful because they enjoy what they're doing.

■ Smoking is bad for you because it ruins your health.

■ Bank robbers should be punished because they broke the law.

Dicto Simpliciter

The fallacy known as **dicto simpliciter** comes from the Latin *dicto simpliciter ad dictum secundum quid,* which roughly translates as "from a general truth to a specific case regardless of the qualifications of the latter." In its briefer form, it means "spoken simply" and refers to a sweeping generalization that doesn't always apply. A dicto simpliciter argument makes the logical fallacy of exploiting an overly simplistic or unqualified "rule of thumb" while disregarding exceptions to that rule. For example, it's generally understood that birds fly. We know that at the local zoo, Kiki, the kiwi, is a bird and is housed in the aviary. But to conclude that because she's a bird Kiki can therefore fly is fallacious reasoning. And the reason is that the kiwi bird is an exception—one of the few types of birds that are flightless.

Examples of Dicto Simpliciter Arguments

 If torture can save the lives of those who would be killed by terrorists, then the government should employ torture as a preemptive measure of protection.

■ Exercise is good for people. Now that Bob is out of the hospital, he should get back to the treadmill.

■ Guns kill. So we cannot allow the average citizen to possess a weapon.

Here's another more familiar matter where dicto simpliciter arguments might be heard. It is generally accepted that men are physically stronger than women. However, it would be a fallacious claim that women shouldn't be allowed in military combat since they aren't strong enough to carry weapons. This statement is a logical fallacy since it does not account for the exceptions to the rule—women who are stronger than the average. In other words, this argument exploits a stereotype.

False Analogy

An analogy compares two things that are alike in one or more ways. In any form of writing, analogies are very useful, as they expand meaning and demonstrate imagination. In arguments, they can be wonderful tools for persuasion. Unfortunately, they can also lead the writer astray and make his or her argument vulnerable to attack.

The problem with **false analogies** arises when the two things compared do not match up feature for feature, and ideas being compared do not logically connect or are pressed beyond legitimacy. The result is a false analogy. For instance, a candidate for a high-powered job may ask to be employed because of his extraordinary heroics during the Iraq War. He may even claim that being a CEO is like fighting a battle: He needs to be brave, tough in mind and body, and willing to take and deal out punishment. Although the argument might sound appealing, running a company involves more than combat skills. Certainly it is important for a corporate executive to be strong and tough-minded. However, an office full of five-star generals might not be expert at dealing with economic recession or product liability. The fallacy is an imperfect analogy: Business and soldiering overlap minimally.

A sound analogy will clarify a difficult or unfamiliar concept by comparing it with something easily understood or familiar.

Examples of False Analogy

- The ship of state is about to wreck on the rocks of recession; we need a new pilot.
- This whole gun control issue is polarizing the nation the way slavery did people living above and below the Mason-Dixon Line. Do we want another Civil War?
- Letting emerging nations have nuclear weapons is like giving loaded guns to children.

False Dilemma

A **false dilemma** involves the simplification of complex issues into an either/or choice. For example, "Either we legalize abortion or we send young women to back-alley butchers," "Love America or leave it," "Either we keep gun ownership legal or only criminals will have guns." Such sloganizing ultimatums, although full of dramatic impact, unfortunately appeal to people's ignorance and prejudices.

Examples of False Dilemma

- English should be the official language of the United States, and anybody who doesn't like it can leave.
- Movies today are full of either violence or sex.
- Either we put warning labels on records and compact discs, or we'll see more and more teenage girls having babies.

Faulty Use of Authority

The **faulty use of authority** occurs when someone who is an expert in one area is used as an authority for another unrelated area. For instance, the opinions of a four-star general about the use of force against an uncooperative foreign tyrant carry great weight in a discussion of U.S. foreign policy options. However, the opinions of that same individual about the Supreme Court's ruling on the question of assisted suicide are less compelling. His military expertise does not guarantee that his views on euthanasia are particularly valuable.

Advertisers frequently resort to the faulty use of authority to promote their products. Celebrities are asked to endorse products they may have no special knowledge about or any interest in, aside from the sizable check they will receive for their services. Another example occurs when well-known popular figures rely on their achievements in one area to lend credibility to their views in another. For instance, the late Benjamin Spock, famous for his work on child development, became a spokesperson for the nuclear disarmament movement. Because of his reputation, people were willing to listen more closely to his views than to others who were less well known, yet his expertise in child-rearing gave him no more authority in the area of nuclear disarmament than any other well-educated person. While Dr. Spock may, indeed, have been knowledgeable about nuclear arms, his expertise in that area would have to be demonstrated before he could be used as an effective authority on the subject.

Examples of Faulty Use of Authority

- You should buy these vitamins because Lady Gaga recommended them on television last night.
- The American Bar Association states that secondhand smoke is a serious cancer threat to nonsmokers.
- Americans shouldn't find hunting objectionable because one of our most popular presidents, Theodore Roosevelt, was an avid hunter.

Hasty Generalization

As the name indicates, **hasty generalization** occurs when a writer arrives at a conclusion based on too little evidence. It's one of the most frequently found fallacies. If the local newspaper's restaurant critic is served underdone chicken at Buster's Diner during her first and only visit, she would be making a hasty generalization to conclude that Buster's serves terrible food. Although this may be true, one visit is not enough to draw that conclusion. If, however, after three visits she is still dissatisfied with the food, she is entitled to warn her readers about eating at Buster's.

Hasty generalizations can also occur when the writer relies on evidence that is not factual or substantiated. A generalization can only be as sound as its supporting evidence. Writers should provide multiple and credible examples to support their points. Be wary of sweeping, uncritical statements and words such as *always, all, none, never, only,* and *most.* Note whether the writer qualifies the claim with words that are limiting, such as *many, some, often,* and *seldom.*

Examples of Hasty Generalizations

- That shopping mall is unsafe because there was a robbery there two weeks ago.
- I'm failing organic chemistry because the teaching assistant doesn't speak English well.
- This book was written by a Stanford professor, so it must be good.

Non Sequitur

From the Latin for "does not follow," a **non sequitur** fallacy draws a conclusion that does not follow logically from the premise. For instance, suppose you heard a classmate make the following claim: "Ms. Marshall is such a good teacher; it's hard to believe she wears such ugly clothes." The statement would be fallacious because the ability to teach has nothing to do with taste in clothing. Some of the worst teachers might be the best dressers. Although you might want to believe a good teacher would be a good dresser, there is no reason to think so. Writers must establish a clear connection between the premise and the conclusion. And unless one is made through well-reasoned explanations, readers will not accept the cause-and-effect relationship.

Political campaigns are notorious for non sequiturs: "Candidate Jones will be a great senator because she's been married for twenty years." Or, "Don't vote for candidate Jones because she is rich and lives in an expensive neighborhood." Whether the voters decide to vote for candidate Jones should not depend on the length of her marriage or the neighborhood in which she lives—neither qualifies her for or disqualifies her from public office. The non sequiturs attempt to suggest a relationship between her ability to be a successful senator and unrelated facts about her life.

Examples of Non Sequitur

- Mr. Thompson has such bad breath that it's a wonder he sings so well.
- She's so pretty; she must not be smart.
- I supported his candidacy for president because his campaign was so efficiently run.

Post Hoc, Ergo Propter Hoc

The Latin **post hoc, ergo propter hoc** is translated as "after this, therefore because of this." A post hoc, ergo propter hoc argument is one that establishes a questionable cause-and-effect relationship between events. In other words, because event Y follows event X, event X causes event Y. For instance, you would be making a post hoc argument if you claimed, "Every time my brother Bill accompanies me to Jacobs Field, the Cleveland Indians lose." The reasoning here is fallacious because we all know that although the Indians lose whenever Bill joins you at Jacobs Field, his presence does not cause the team to lose. Experience tells us that there simply is no link between the two events. The only explanation is coincidence.

Our conversations are littered with these dubious claims: "Every time I plan a pool party, it rains"; "Whenever I drive to Chicago, I get a flat tire"; "Every movie that Harry recommends turns out to be a dud." What they underscore is our pessimism or dismay, rather than any belief in the truth of such statements.

It's not surprising that post hoc reasoning is often found in arguments made by people prone to superstition—people looking for big, simple explanations. You would be committing such a fallacy if, for instance, you claimed that you got a C on your math test because a black cat crossed your path that morning or because you broke a mirror the night before. Post hoc fallacies are also practiced by those bent on proving conspiracies. Following the assassination of President Kennedy in 1963, there was considerable effort by some to link the deaths of many people involved in the investigation to a government cover-up, even though the evidence was scanty. Today, we hear Democrats protest that America goes to war every time Republicans are in office and Republicans protest that America gets poorer when Democrats are in office.

Examples of Post Hoc, Ergo Propter Hoc Arguments

- Just two weeks after they raised the speed limit, three people were killed on that road.
- I saw Ralph in the courthouse; he must have been arrested.
- It's no wonder the crime rate has shot up. The state legislature voted to lower the drinking age.

You might also have heard people argue that since the women's liberation movement, the number of latchkey children has risen sharply. The claim essentially says that the women's movement is directly responsible for the rise in working mothers over the last 30 years. Although it is true that the women's movement has made it more acceptable for mothers to return to the workforce, the prime reason is particular to the individual. For some, it is simple economics; for others, personal fulfillment; for others still, a combination of the two. The feminist movement is one among many factors linked with women in the workforce and the consequent rise in latchkey children.

Red Herring

A **red herring**, as the name suggests, is evidence that is fallaciously used to distract the audience from the true issues of an argument. The term is derived from the practice of using the scent of a red herring to throw hunting dogs off the trail of their real prey. In modern life, this fallacy is more often used to confuse the audience by providing irrelevant information or evidence. For instance, when the head coach of a major league team was accused of using team funds on personal expenses, he defended himself by pointing to the team's winning record under his leadership. While the team had undeniably performed well during this period, his response was irrelevant to the charges made against him. He had hoped to distract his accusers from the real issue, which involved his lack of honesty and abuse of power. A red herring may distract the audience momentarily, but once it is discovered, it indicates that the individual has little or no effective reasons or evidence to support his or her position.

Examples of Red Herrings

■ Even though that hockey player was convicted of vehicular homicide, he shouldn't go to jail because he is such a great athlete.
■ Susan didn't hire John for the job because his wife is always late for meetings.
■ The teacher gave me an F in the course because she doesn't like me.

Slippery Slope

The **slippery slope** presumes one event will inevitably lead to a chain of other events that end in a catastrophe—as one slip on a mountaintop will cause a climber to tumble down and bring with him or her all those in tow. This domino-effect reasoning is fallacious because it depends more on presumption than hard evidence: "Censorship of obscene material will spell the end to freedom of the press"; "A ban on ethnic slurs will mean no more freedom of speech"; "If assault rifles are outlawed, handguns will be next." America's involvement in Vietnam was the result of a slippery slope argument: "If Vietnam falls to the Communists, all of Southeast Asia, and eventually India and its neighbors, will fall under the sway of communism." Even though Vietnam did fall, the result has not been the widespread rise of communism in the region; on the contrary, communism has fallen on hard times.

Examples of Slippery Slope Arguments

■ Legalized abortion is a step toward creating an antilife society.
■ A ban on ethnic slurs will mean no more freedom of speech.
■ If we let them build those condos, the lake will end up polluted, the wildlife will die off, and the landscape will be scarred forever.

Stacking the Deck

When writers give only the evidence that supports their premise, while disregarding or withholding contrary evidence, they are **stacking the deck**. (Science students may know this as "data beautification," the habit of recording only those results that match what an experiment is expected to predict.) A meat-packing manufacturer may advertise that its all-beef hot dogs "now contain 10 percent less fat." Although that may sound like good news, what we are not being told is that the hot dogs still contain 30 percent fat.

This stacking-the-deck fallacy is common not only in advertising but also in debates of controversial matters. The faculty of a college, for instance, may petition for the firing of its president for failing to grant needed raises while an expensive new football stadium is being built. The complaint would not be fair, however, if the faculty ignored mentioning that the stadium funds were specifically earmarked for athletic improvement by a billionaire benefactor. Also, if the complaint left unrecognized the many accomplishments of the president, such as the successful capital campaign, the plans for a new library, and the influx of notable scholars, it would be an example of stacking the deck.

As you progress through the chapters in this book, you will find that thinking like a critic is the key to understanding and responding to arguments. It will make you a stronger reader and a more effective writer. In Chapter 3, we explore ways that you can think like a writer to find and develop topics for your own argument essays.

Examples of Stacking the Deck

■ Parents should realize that private schools simply encourage elitism in young people.
■ We cannot take four more years of her in office, given the way she voted against the death penalty.
■ Dickens's *Bleak House* is six hundred pages of boring prose.

Straw Man

A **straw man** literally refers to a straw-stuffed dummy in the shape of a man and dressed in clothes: a scarecrow, for instance, or an effigy for burning or target practice. Metaphorically, the term refers to something less than a real person, or a weak or ineffective substitute. As a rhetorical term, the *straw man* (or straw person) refers to a strategy of refuting another person's actual position by substituting an exaggerated or distorted version of that position. What makes it a fallacy is that the user declares the opponent's conclusion to be wrong because of flaws in another, lesser argument: The straw man user presents a fictitious or misrepresented version of the opponent's argument, and refutes that. In short, it's a setup of the opponent, a deliberate misstatement or overstatement of his or her position. And it is easier to refute somebody whose real ideas have been pushed to the extreme—reduced to a dismissible straw man.

It's no surprise that the straw man argument is a familiar strategy in politics, as candidates will attack opponents on positions often much weaker than their best arguments. Consider, for example, this statement: "Senator Jane Smith claims that we should not fund the superbomber program. Do we really want her to leave our country defenseless?" In reality, Smith may be opposed to the superbomber program for technical, economic, or even strategic reasons, or she may be in favor of an alternative defense system. However, like a red herring, the opponent tries to refute Senator Smith's position by attacking a position that Smith doesn't hold—that she wants to leave the country defenseless. In short, the arguer arrives at a conclusion that easily dismisses the "straw man" he has set up while disregarding Smith's real arguments.

Examples of Straw Man Arguments

- Home schooling is dangerous because it keeps kids isolated from society.
- Discrimination in hiring is *not* unfair. An employer has to discriminate between competent and incompetent, good and bad workers. Otherwise, we'd be hiring people least qualified for the job.
- People who are opposed to urbanization just want to go back to living in caves.

EXERCISES

1. In your journal, list examples of logical fallacies you find in essays, news articles, editorials, advertising, junk mail, and other persuasive materials that you confront on a daily basis. Based on the information you and other group members collect, draw some hypotheses about which fallacies are most prevalent today and why. If your instructor asks you to do so, convert those hypotheses into an outline of an argument essay for your campus newspaper.

2. Explain the faulty logic of the following statements. Of what fallacy (or fallacies) is each an example?
   a. When did you stop hiring other people to take your exams for you?
   b. He's too smart to play football; besides, he broke his leg ten years ago.
   c. If we don't stop the publication of this X-rated material now, it won't be long before our children will be reading it at school.
   d. Karen must be depressed; she wore dark clothes all weekend.

e. How can you accuse me of being late? You're such a slowpoke.

f. Rap music isn't music because it's just noise and words.

g. He's at least 6 feet 6 inches tall, so he must be a terrific basketball player.

h. WGBB is the most popular radio station on campus because it has more listeners than any other station.

i. Indians living on reservations get the necessities of life at government expense, so they have no worries.

j. Take Tummy Tops laxatives instead of Mellow Malt, because Tummy Tops contains calcium while Mellow Malt has aluminum and magnesium.

k. Lite Cheese Popcorn contains 34 percent fewer calories!

l. Any decent person will agree that Nazism has no place in modern society.

3

Finding Arguments:
Thinking Like a Writer

LEARNING OBJECTIVES

After studying this chapter, you should be able to:

1. Describe where to look to identify topics worthy of an argument paper. (p. 62)
2. Explain how to use various sources to find one worth writing about. (p. 65)
3. Describe how to generate ideas to explore in your topic. (p. 68)
4. Explain how to formulate a working claim. (p. 71)

When confronted with an issue we feel strongly about, most of us have no trouble offering an energetically delivered opinion. Yet when we are asked to *write* an argument, we feel paralyzed. To express our ideas in written form forces us to commit ourselves to some position or to endorse a particular action. We have to take a risk and make a public statement about what we think and feel and believe. Our written words can be scrutinized. That makes us vulnerable, and nobody likes to feel exposed.

It is helpful to think of writing an argument as one way to explore our ideas about a subject or an issue. As such, writing can be a means of growth and discovery. Investigating new ideas can be intimidating, but it's also exciting. This chapter will demonstrate how writers begin the process of researching ideas to write about in argument essays. As novelist E. M. Forster explained, "How will I know what I think until I've seen what I've said?"

Exploration, of course, takes time. We are not recommending a writing process that begins an hour before a paper is due; rather, we are recommending what successful writers do: Take time to think your writing through. This means starting assignments early, working through all the stages, and allowing time to revise and polish your work before you submit it. Learning to write well is the same as learning to perform any other skilled activity. You have to practice your strokes or your scales to be a good tennis player or pianist; likewise, you have to practice your craft to be a good writer. As you gain more experience, some of the stages of the writing process will go more quickly for you on most projects. Even when you become a polished logician, however, you may find yourself writing about a topic that requires you to work out the assumptions in your argument slowly and painstakingly. That's okay. All writers do that.

The Writing Process

Many rhetorical theorists have tried to describe the writing process, but that's a little like describing snowflakes: Each one is different. Each person has a different way of writing, especially depending on the job. Think about it. You can dash off a note to your roommate in a second; if you're writing a job application letter, you'll probably take a great deal more time. If you have only 20 minutes to answer an essay question on a history exam, you'll get it done somehow; but give you an entire semester to write a term paper on the same subject, and you will probably spend several weeks (if not months) doing the job. The scope and length of the assignment dictate a different writing process.

What most people studying the writing process agree on is that almost everyone goes through four distinct stages when writing: prewriting, drafting, rewriting, and editing.

Prewriting

When something prompts you to write (your instructor gives you an assignment, your boss tells you to write a report, a letter requires an answer, or you feel strongly about a controversy and want to write a letter to the editor), you spend time either mentally or physically preparing to respond. You may make notes, go to the library, interview someone, or just stare out the window. This is the *prewriting* stage in which you're letting the ideas you'll use begin to incubate, to take form. In this chapter, we provide strategies you can use to make this early stage of writing work for you.

Drafting

In the second stage, you begin, however haltingly, to put words to paper. Some people make an outline; others write a bare-bones rough draft in an attempt to get some ideas down on paper. Many people like to start by sketching out their conclusions so that they can see where their writing must take them. Others prefer the linear, start-with-the-introduction system that moves them through the task. The first goal in the drafting stage is to get the framework of the writing in place so you can start adding material to fill it out. At some point in the process, you also take your potential readers into account in order to get some idea of their expectations and receptivity.

Rewriting

Once you have a rough draft framed, you're ready to do the hard work of writing: *rewriting*. At this stage, you may move parts of your paper around or make a new outline or add or cut material to fill in gaps or eliminate imbalances. You will have your readers much more clearly in mind because your goal is to persuade them; what you know about their background, experiences, and values will help you decide on a final shape for your paper, even if it means throwing away a lot of what went into the rough draft. (A bad paper that's finished is still a bad paper; that's why you need to allow time for flexibility. Writers who are pressed for time sometimes have to polish something that's not good and hope their readers will not notice, a technique that does not usually work.) All writing is rewriting. So at this stage, most good writers turn to other writers for feedback—a sense of what prospective readers will think of their writing. In a classroom, this is done by exchanging drafts with classmates or having conferences with your instructor.

Editing

To maximize your chance of persuading readers, your writing needs to be as readable as possible. That's why, after you've rewritten it, you need to work on your sentence structure so that words "flow" smoothly. Or you may need to change words here and there to heighten their impact. If others have read your paper and offered feedback, you may wish to act on some of their suggestions for improvement. You always need to edit and proofread what you've written so that careless errors don't distract your readers from getting the message you're trying to convey.

In a nutshell, that's the writing process. Now let's look at how you might exploit the features of that process when you start writing arguments.

Finding Topics to Argue

Every writer knows the experience of being blocked—of having a topic but not knowing what to say about it or of having only one point to make about an issue. Even worse is having an assignment but no topic. To help generate ideas, writers need to tap both internal and external resources.

In Your Immediate Vicinity

The world around you is full of arguments; you just need to take a moment to see them. Look at the front page and editorial pages of your campus newspaper, for instance. What's going on? Look at billboards and bulletin boards. What are people having meetings about? What changes are coming up? Listen to the conversations of people on the bus or waiting in line at the bookstore or in the library. What's up? What have you been reading for a class that gets you thinking? You might want to know how a theory for the origin of the universe was derived, or what the results of a recent study of employment success for former welfare recipients were based on, or even why two experts in the field of early childhood learning draw different conclusions from the same evidence. The reading you do for your own enjoyment may also provide some interesting ideas. A science fiction novel may make you wonder about the plausibility of alien life. Reading a murder mystery may make you think about the value of forensic anthropology. Look through the magazines in your room or at the ads on television or at the junk mail that fills your mailbox. Even casually reading magazines and newspapers on a daily or weekly basis will turn up issues and controversies. What claims are people making? What are people asking you to do or think or wear or look like or support? These are sources of potential arguments; all you have to do is become aware of them. As Thoreau put it, "Only that day dawns to which we are awake."

In Your Larger Worlds

Don't limit yourself to campus. Often there are debates and discussions going on in your workplace, in your place of worship, on your block, in your town. You belong to a number of communities; each has its issues of interest, and in those issues you can find plenty to write about. And those environments aren't the only places you'll find sources for arguments; the world turns on proposals, positions, and controversies. It's almost impossible to turn on the radio or television today without seeing someone presenting an opinion. Your computer (or the one available on your campus) can connect you to a global community engaged in debate and dialogue on every issue imaginable. On the Internet, you can participate in a number of discussions about controversial issues through listservs, Usenet newsgroups, blogs, and chat rooms. Make a list of the issues that interest you. What are the headlines in the newspaper? What's Congress voting on? What are the hot spots around the globe (or in the larger universe)? Don't stick to the familiar; there is much experimental territory just waiting to be explored.

Keeping a Journal

You've probably noticed that we encourage recording ideas and observations in a journal, a technique used by many professional writers. The journal doesn't have to be fancy; the cheap supermarket variety works just as well as the $2,000 laptop. (If you're comfortable at a keyboard, a USB flash drive makes a great notebook and fits in your shirt pocket, too—although you might want to keep a backup copy.)

Writers use journals as portable file cabinets of ideas. In a journal, we record anything in language that interests us, not just materials for current projects. We may copy a word or phrase or sentence we hear that we like, or photocopy and staple in a piece by a writer we admire, or even add things that infuriate or amuse us. A journal becomes a supermarket of ideas and strategies, but there's something very positive about the simple act of copying words. Somehow, physically writing or typing them makes them yours; you learn something about technique in doing the physical work of copying. (That's why we don't recommend making too many photocopies; you don't mentally store the information in the same way you do when you copy a passage yourself.)

For the novice argument writer, a journal is invaluable. You can use yours to include notes on possible topics; examples of good introductions and conclusions; catchy words, phrases, and titles; examples of logical fallacies—just about anything a writer might need. A journal is also particularly helpful for creating *dialogues,* the voices and opinions of others who may hold views that are different from your own on particular issues. By keeping a record or notes on what people have to say in newspapers, magazine articles, television talk shows, and casual conversation about various controversial issues, you'll have a ready resource to consult when you begin to deliberate about your position on a particular issue.

When you begin keeping the journal, set yourself a formal goal: for example, adding 100 words a day or writing five days out of the week. Then *stick to it*. Journals don't fill themselves. It takes discipline to keep a journal, and discipline is a characteristic of good writers. If you don't do the groundwork, your creativity won't break through. Throughout this text, we've scattered suggestions and exercises for using journals; if you want to master the power of argument fully, we encourage you to *do* the exercises. Don't just read them. Write!

Developing Argumentative Topics

Topics alone aren't arguments, and many inexperienced writers have trouble making the jump from subject to argument. For example, you may be interested in heavy metal music. That's a subject—a big one. What can you argue about it? You could ask yourself, "What are the facts about heavy metal? When did it start? How can it be defined? What differentiates it from the mainstream rock played on most commercial radio stations? How has it evolved over the last 45 years? Why are some groups played, it seems, once an hour, and others almost totally ignored?" You can ask functional questions, such as "Who were the most influential figures in heavy metal music? Is heavy metal as relevant as it had been?" You might ask aesthetic questions about the importance of melody or lyrics or harmony, or ethical questions such as whether the music industry should put parental advisory labels on albums. You could even consider moral questions such as whether heavy metal music videos encourage sexism or violence. In recognizing the multiple possibilities of issues, you may find you have more to say on a topic than you think.

Getting Started

Sometimes getting started can be the most difficult step in the writing process. Where do I begin? What should I include? What ideas will work best? How shall I organize it all? You may have a hundred ideas in your head about the topic or—even worse—none at all. When this happens, there are a number of tried-and-true techniques that professional writers use to redirect those anxious questions and concerns into productive writing. While you may not need to use all the strategies each time you begin to write, you'll find that trying out each one of them will help you discover what works best for you.

Brainstorming

Brainstorming can help you get your ideas on paper in an informal and unstructured way. When you brainstorm, you write down as many ideas as you can about your subject, usually in short phrases, questions, or single words. Don't worry about placing them in any special order or even about making complete sense. The one rule to observe while you're brainstorming is not to judge the ideas that pop into your head and spill out onto your paper. When you give yourself permission to write down anything that seems related to your subject, you'll be surprised at the number of ideas that will occur to you. By not rejecting anything, you'll find that one idea will naturally lead to another. Even an idea that you may throw out later can lead you to an idea that may be a real gem. And the more ideas you record in your brainstorm, the more choices you will have to consider later as you sift through this record of your thoughts and decide what is and is not useful.

After reading the essays in Chapter 2 of this book, John, our first-year composition student, decided to write his first paper on college binge drinking. The topic was in the news because a student at another college in his state had died as the result of excessive drinking at a fraternity party. John began his prewriting preparation by brainstorming about the subject. Here's what he came up with:

binge drinking	want to forget all about the week
drinking until you feel sick	makes us feel grown up
getting together with friends for a good time	nothing better to do on Saturday night
partying after a tough week at school	why does the college care?
so many bars, so little time	people can really hurt themselves
half the people underage	prevention—how?
whose responsibility is it?	part of the college experience
am I responsible for my friends?	ignore it—will it go away?
could I get arrested?	trying to act cool
nobody checks anyway	what starts as fun can lead to death
feeling terrible the next morning	definition of an adult
smelling like a beer can	do other cultures experience this?
role of the college administration	why drink to excess?
rite of passage	
impact of peer pressure	

As you can see, John had many different ideas about binge drinking, and the more he brainstormed, the more he discovered what they were. After looking over his brainstorm, John chose a few of the ideas that especially interested him to explore further.

John was lucky to have a subject before he began brainstorming. But what happens if you don't have a particular topic in mind or your instructor doesn't assign one? You may find it difficult to come up with a topic, and you're not alone. Students often comment that the hardest part of writing is deciding what to write about.

Finding Ideas Worth Writing About

Let's suppose you're not assigned a specific paper topic and are left on your own to come up with an issue worth arguing about. That can be daunting, of course. When asked where he gets the ideas for his stories, best-selling author Stephen King's joke response was "Utica"—as if there were an idea shop in that New York town. Other writers respond with the tongue-in-cheek claim that there's a post office box in, say, Madison, Wisconsin, where you can write for ideas, but to qualify you need to be published. The point is that ideas for fiction as well as nonfiction are all around us. You just have to know where to look.

Again, one of the most useful prewriting strategies for coming up with an idea is brainstorming—just as you might do if you had a topic to expand upon. Take out a piece of paper and jot down whatever comes to mind in response to these questions:

- What issues in print or television news interest you?
- What issues make you angry?
- What problems in your dorm/on campus/in your town/in your country concern you?
- What political issue concerns you most?
- What aspects about the environment worry you?
- If you were a professor/dean/college president/mayor/governor/senator/president, what would be the first thing you'd do?
- What policies/practices/regulations/laws would you like to see changed?
- What do you talk about or argue over with friends or classmates?
- What ideas from books or articles have challenged your thinking?
- What books/movies/music/fashions/art do you like, and why?
- What television shows do you like/hate, and why?
- What personalities in politics/show business/the media/academia do you have strong feelings about?

Here's a quick brainstorming list one student developed:

Issues That Interest Me

1. The war on terrorism
2. Excessive salaries for athletes
3. People who protest movie violence but oppose bans on assault rifles
4. The benefits of stem cell research
5. Reality TV
6. Social messages in rap music
7. Environment-unfriendly vehicles
8. Immigration policies
9. Bullying in cyberspace
10. Movies

Another strategy is to brainstorm these items with a group of classmates. Begin by choosing a subject in the day's news, then play free association with it. Say the subject is *sports* and you begin saying the word. The next student then says the first word that comes to mind; then the next student responds with a new word, et cetera, et cetera. For instance: sports; baseball; San Francisco Giants; World Series; the latest player trades. And maybe eventually you and the group will generate ideas worth debating—the need for better coaching, salary caps, the use of steroids, team loyalty or the lack thereof, the designated hitter rule.

Once you have brainstormed a list, organize the issues according to categories—for example, sports, politics, social issues, environment, the media, television, education, and so on. Then transfer the list to your journal. Now, whenever an assignment comes up, you'll have a database of ideas worth writing about.

Next try to focus these ideas by deciding the following:

- Which subjects do I know something about?
- Have I had personal experiences with any particular subject?
- How do I feel about the subject? (Angry? Glad? Sad? Neutral?)
- What is my stand on the subject? Should I defend it? Argue against it? Do I feel strongly enough to make suggestions for changes?
- Would this be a subject I'd want to do more research on?
- Who would be my audience—friends? instructor? parents? And how much does he, she, or they know about the topic?

In subsequent chapters, we'll discuss how to frame an argument on a topic, the ways of approaching your audience, the kinds of evidence to present, and so forth. But at this point, we're simply interested in helping you come up with a checklist of arguable subjects worth writing about. Whatever you come up with in your checklist, each topic should have three basic things:

1. It should be interesting.
2. It should appeal to readers.
3. It should have a specific slant.

Clustering

Some writers find that visualizing their ideas on a page helps them explore their subject in new ways. Clustering[1] is a technique you can use to do that. It involves choosing a key word, a phrase, or even a short sentence, and placing it in the center of a blank page with a circle around it. Next you try to think of ideas, words, or other short phrases that you can associate or relate to your key word or phrase. As you do, write them in the blank area surrounding the center and circle them and draw lines, linking them to your center circled word or phrase. As you accumulate more and more clusters, the words and phrases within them will generate ideas on their own; these can be linked to the words that inspired them. When you have exhausted your cluster, you will have a complex network of ideas that should provide many ways to begin to explore your subject. By choosing any one idea or a combination of these words or ideas as a starting point, you can move to freewriting to find ways of developing these ideas further.

Figure 3.1 shows how John used clustering to find new ways of thinking about binge drinking, the topic he had chosen for his paper. When John examined his cluster, he found a map of the many ideas he might explore further:

- Should colleges play the role of in loco parentis and regulate student drinking or is drinking a matter of personal responsibility?
- What role does peer pressure play in binge drinking?

---

[1]Clustering is a technique explored by Gabriele L. Rico in her book, *Writing the Natural Way: Using Right Brain Techniques to Release Your Expressive Powers* (Los Angeles: J. P. Tarcher, 1983).

Figure 3.1 Sample Cluster

■ Are print ads and television commercials for beer partly responsible for binge drinking among young people?
■ Is the extent of binge drinking on college campuses exaggerated or overstated?
■ If a student violates campus drinking rules, what should the consequences be?

John's cluster revealed the complexity of the issue and became a starting point for him to investigate the subject in greater depth.

Freewriting

The next step is freewriting, which goes one step beyond brainstorming and which helps get a focus on the subject while developing things to say about it. Instead of simply listing phrases, questions, and words related to your subject, freewriting involves writing freely, and without stopping, whatever thoughts and ideas you have about your subject, without worrying about sentence structure, spelling, or grammar. As in brainstorming, when you freewrite, it's important not to censor your ideas. Your aim is to discover what you know about your subject, and the best way you can do that is by giving your mind permission to go wherever it pleases. Freewriting isn't intended to be a finished part of your paper; instead, it's a way to generate the ideas and focus that you can use later as you begin to draft the paper itself.

Freewriting can begin with anything: your topic, a particularly interesting idea you've read about, or an experience that you can connect with your subject. If you have used brainstorming or clustering before freewriting, these activities can provide you with a key word or phrase to get you started. For instance, John found a good idea from his brainstorm to begin his freewriting:

> Getting together with friends for a good time. That's what everyone looks forward to every weekend. Put away the books, get out of the dorm, and party. Four, five, sometimes more drinks. Feeling no pain. Binge drinking just seems to happen. It isn't something you plan to do. When you're having a good time, you don't think about how terrible you're going to feel the next day or about all the stupid things you're doing. It's easy to get alcohol in town. Nobody ever checks for proof, and if they do you just go to another place down the street. It's so easy to get a phony ID anyway. And the crowds are so large, no one looks carefully. If college students want to drink, who's to say they can't? We're old enough to vote, die for our country, sign a contract. Why not drinking? And how are you ever going to learn to drink if you don't do it? College students drink for lots of reasons. Why? Well, it gets them in a party mood. It's fun. It makes us feel like adults. It's so cool. Everyone does it. There's nothing wrong with drinking, but is it a problem if you drink too much? Every weekend. They let it get out of control. Drunk driving, alcohol poisoning, stupid accidents. Binge drinking is drinking gone overboard. You can get in a car accident and end up killing or maiming yourself, another person. Even a friend. Then how would I feel? That's all I can think of right now.

John used his freewriting to think on paper. While he didn't come up with any conclusions about how he felt about binge drinking, he did produce a number of ideas that he explored later, when he worked on the first draft of his paper:

- College students binge drink for many reasons.
- Binge drinking can be a problem.
- Drinking is related to feeling adult.
- Binge drinking is not a planned behavior, but it can get to be a habit.

One of the best reasons for using freewriting before you begin the first draft of your paper is to avoid the most intimidating sight a writer can see: a blank page. Unfortunately, sometimes that blank page is the result of a blank mind and undue concern about how your writing and ideas will appear to others. When you freewrite, you write for yourself alone. It is a way to make your ideas flow. Freewriting generates ideas that will help you begin to think about your subject before worrying about polishing your writing for an audience.

Asking Questions

Once you have a subject in mind, a good strategy for generating ideas is to make a list of questions you have about the subject. Your questions can cover areas in which you need more information, as well as questions you might like to answer as you think and write about your topic. For instance, John tried this strategy for his topic of college binge drinking and came up with the following questions:

Why do college students binge drink?

How many college students actually binge drink?

Is binge drinking a result of peer pressure?

Do students binge drink to show they are adults?

Do most college students find binge drinking acceptable?

Is binge drinking strictly a college student activity or do other age and economic groups do this as well?

Do college students stop binge drinking once they leave college?

Who should be responsible for binge drinking? The drinkers? The college? The law?

Why do college administrations feel that they must respond to the problem of drinking if it is off campus?

Do colleges have a legal responsibility to protect their students?

Are the alcohol prevention programs on campus effective?

How often does binge drinking result in fatal accidents?

It's easy to see how one question can lead to another. By choosing one question or several related ones, John had real direction for exploring his topic and focusing his paper as he began his research and his first draft.

Engaging in Dialogue with Others

Talking to other people is a great source of ideas. None of the techniques we've discussed so far have to be solitary activities. By sharing your ideas and listening to the responses of others, you will find a wealth of new ideas and perspectives. In fact, you'll be engaging in the kind of *dialogue* we discussed in Chapter 1. You can do this in a number of ways: participate either in small peer groups in your class or in larger class discussions; speak individually with your instructor; seek out members of your community, on campus or outside your school; share ideas with others electronically through Internet chat rooms, e-mail, or listservs; or talk with family and friends. As Larry King and other talk show hosts prove every day, people love to talk. So, take advantage of it—and take notes.

Refining Topics

Once you have found—through the strategies we've discussed—subjects that strike you as interesting, you have to begin narrowing down your topic to a manageable size. The next step, then, is to look over your list and reduce it to those topics that are legitimately arguable. (See Chapter 1 for a refresher.)

Reducing Your Options

Your first step is to determine whether your subject is manageable. You don't want a subject that is too broad or unwieldy or that requires prohibitive amounts of research. For example, you would not want to argue that "welfare needs to be reformed." You could write a book about that if you had time to do all the research. To write a short paper, you have to narrow your subject. "The only people who should be eligible for welfare support should be disabled people and mothers of preschool children" is a manageable reduction of your first idea, and one that you can handle in an average-length paper (see Figure 3.2). The more narrow your topic, the more you restrict your research and tighten the focus of your argument.

Figure 3.2 "Reducing Your Options" Diagram

Avoiding Overspecialized Topics

However, don't pick a topic that requires extensive specialized knowledge, such as how to reduce the trade deficit or the problems inherent in thermonuclear fusion. The issue you choose should be one you know a little something about and, to keep you interested, about which you have strong convictions. Also, it should be an issue you are willing to spend a reasonable amount of time exploring on your own online, in interviews, or perhaps in the library. Aside from writing a convincing argument, a parallel goal of any project you research is to become better informed and more appreciative of the complexity of the issue. Therefore, select a topic on which you wish to be well informed and that you are willing to investigate and reflect on.

Formulating a Working Claim

Once you have decided on your topic and used some of the strategies we've discussed, you are ready to create a working claim. As we explained in Chapter 1, the claim is the heart of your essay. It functions as a thesis statement. It states what you believe or what action you'd like your readers to take. In Chapter 1, we provided examples of the different ways you can state your claim. However, at this early stage of your writing, it would be difficult to create a claim that would be perfect for the paper you have yet to research and write. It's too early in the game to commit yourself. After all, your research may yield some surprising results, and you want to be open to all sides of the issue. At best, you can create a working claim—that is, a statement of your opinion or position on your topic that you can use temporarily to help you focus and organize your paper and limit your research.

After John, our first-year composition student, considered his subject of binge drinking by brainstorming, clustering, freewriting, asking questions about the topic, and engaging in dialogue with others, he realized what an enormous and complex topic it was and that he needed to narrow it. He began by asking questions about binge drinking. How prevalent is binge drinking? Who should be responsible for the regulation of student drinking? Are students themselves solely responsible? Should a college or university act in loco parentis? What are the consequences of ignoring the problem of binge drinking? What is the role of peer pressure in binge drinking? How can binge drinking be discouraged or controlled? What role does advertising play? Can binge drinking be fatal?

As John thought about the answers to these questions, he began to narrow the focus of his broad topic to one that he could explore in a paper of reasonable length. He decided that he would focus only on the issue of how to control or eliminate binge drinking on college campuses.

John's next step was to formulate a *working claim* for his paper on binge drinking. When he sat down to create his working claim, he examined and reflected on his topic and decided on the following *working claim*:

> Binge drinking is a serious problem on college campuses, and if we continue to ignore it or treat it as normal and acceptable student behavior, no one will ever find an effective way to eliminate it.

By creating a working claim early in his writing process, John benefited in a number of ways. He took a clear position about his topic and expressed his point of view. While he had the opportunity to change his viewpoint as he thought further about his topic, his working claim served as a baseline. John's working claim also helped him organize the reasons he needed to support his position.

Let's take a look at John's working claim to see how it is organized. His claim can be divided into three parts:

1. Binge drinking is a problem on college campuses.
2. It is ignored or simply accepted as normal student behavior.
3. No one has yet found an effective way to solve this problem.

All these statements are arguable because, as we discussed in Chapter 1, they are based on judgment and interpretation, not on indisputable facts or personal opinion. As he developed his paper, John needed to decide on reasons to effectively convince his readers that these three parts of his working claim are true.

In addition, John's working claim helped him decide what he needed to investigate further. As John researched and became more knowledgeable about his topic, he revised his working claim to better reflect what he had learned. But at this stage of his paper, his working claim provided him with several specific areas that he needed to investigate in order to argue persuasively about them:

1. Is binge drinking really a problem on college campuses? How significant is it?
2. How is binge drinking ignored and by whom?
3. Is binge drinking regarded as normal student behavior and by whom?
4. What has been done to eliminate binge drinking?
5. What are some ways this problem can be dealt with?

In Chapter 9, we look at a number of ways available to John to research his topic. By using the questions suggested by his working claim as a guide, John had plenty of avenues to explore.

Thinking like a writer will help you make the jump from simply having an opinion on a subject to finding ways to express that opinion in an argument essay. In Chapter 4, we look at the way in which audience influences and affects the choices we make about what to include in an argument essay and how to present our arguments.

SAMPLE STUDENT ARGUMENT FOR ANALYSIS

Stephanie Bower, a student majoring in English literature, was interested in the subject of television news reporting. She realized what a complicated and multifaceted topic it is and that she needed to focus on a particular aspect of broadcast news. She began refining

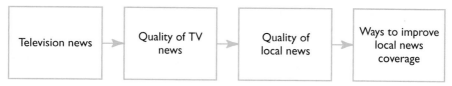

Figure 3.3 Stephanie's "Reducing Options" Diagram

her topic by asking questions about TV news reporting. What does the viewing audience expect of television news? What is the responsibility of news broadcast? Are the when, where, why, what, and how enough? What are the qualities of a newscast that satisfy my expectations for good news coverage? Which news programming do I find inadequate? What differences exist between national and local news coverage? What is the state of reporting on my local news channels? What are the strengths and weaknesses of those channels? What role does advertising play in a broadcast? How can local television news be improved? What are critics of the television news industry saying about the caliber of local news? What would I discover if I were to examine the quality of local news on a minute-by-minute basis? What recommendations could be made to improve the news?

As Stephanie thought about the answers, she realized that although each question poses an interesting issue to explore, she had to narrow the topic to one that she could cover in a paper of reasonable length. She thought back to some recent local news stories that had interested her, discovering to her dismay how complicated social issues had been pressed into just a few seconds. Worse, she was stunned to discover that extended coverage was given to a story about an abandoned dog. Reflecting on this, Stephanie realized she had material for a specific topic: local news—what was wrong with it and how it might be improved. The box diagram in Figure 3.3 reflects her thought process as she narrowed down her topic.

Her working claim, then, both limited the range of her topic and very clearly expressed her point of view about it:

> Local television news is known for its bare-bones coverage and journalistic mediocrity. Now, competing with the convenience of Internet news sources and the far more in-depth coverage available in newspapers, local television news must reconsider its responsibilities and its approach.

Bower 1

Stephanie Bower
Professor Van Zandt
English 111
March 18, 2013

What's the Rush?
Speed Yields Mediocrity in Local Television News

1   Down to the second, time is a factor in television. National television
news has outlets for lengthy reports and analysis in hour-long news magazines

like *Dateline* and panel discussions like *Meet the Press*, but local news is rendered almost exclusively in a "short story" format. Most local TV news stories are just twenty or thirty seconds long. These stories state the basic facts, but they simply do not have time to do more. Dane Claussen notes that "the entire transcript of a half-hour local television news broadcast will fit onto less than one page of a newspaper" ("Cognitive Dissonance"). Floyd McKay, a journalism professor and former broadcaster, says local TV news gives little attention to "content that doesn't glitter or titillate and no attention at all to subjects requiring more than a couple of minutes of air time. There are very few local equivalents of the PBS News Hour and documentaries on local topics are rarely produced" ("How We Clicked . . . "). Though television newscasts operate in minutes and seconds, the brevity of local news stories is not just a natural feature of the medium. Rather, these stories are often the result of local news stations that lack resources and reporters, or that lack effort and enterprise. Because of these limitations and shortcomings, local television news has developed a reputation for journalistic mediocrity. With quality online news sources available at your convenience, local television news faces more competition than ever. Local newscasts must reconsider their responsibilities and their approach.

2   Television is still the most popular source of local news, according to a 2011 Federal Communications Commission special report (Waldman, 76). Steven Waldman says that "neither the ongoing migration of viewers to cable TV nor the growth of the Internet has changed the basic fact that most Americans turn to their local TV news team for local news" (77). People want news that is specifically relevant to their communities. Local stations have the potential to reach large regional audiences looking for coverage of the issues affecting their towns and cities. Yet local news is known for its focus on sensational crime coverage and "soft" news, which focuses on human interest stories, sports, and entertainment. Education, health care, local government, and local business and economic matters receive scant coverage in a typical thirty minute local newscast. Waldman cites a 2009 study conducted in Los Angeles which found that "stories about local civic issues impacting L.A. residents' lives, like transportation, community health, the environment, education, taxes, activism, and fundraisers took up one minute and 16 seconds of the monitored half-hour broadcasts" (84).

3   Online news sources and increased cable news viewership have caused some decline in local news viewership, making the business that much more competitive (Belt and Just). News directors may feel pressure "to produce the cheapest type of news that they think will draw and hold viewers—namely, low effort stories featuring crime, lifestyle, and entertainment" (Belt and Just). Yet these kinds of stories offer little real informational value to viewers. Not all news stories demand a great deal of time and depth, but many stories require more than the twenty or thirty seconds they are allotted during a local newscast. A news story that runs for

Bower 3

thirty seconds can tell viewers the who, what, when, where, and how of a story, but it cannot delve into an analysis of a situation or its contextual significance.

4   Why don't more stations air high quality, in-depth local news coverage? The answer seems to come down to money matters. In the world of corporate-owned and advertiser-dependent media, it becomes unclear whether local journalism outlets are impartial civic informers or cogs in the machinery of big business. During sweeps weeks, local stations engage in a high-stakes war to see who wins the important time slots. Stations suddenly run "Special Reports" and exclusive interviews that are rarely seen at other times, mainly because they are expensive and time-consuming to produce. Many local market stations cannot spend money on the equipment, resources, and manpower required to do in-depth reporting. Investigative journalism is one of the first areas to be cut back due to budget limitations, and truly in-depth investigative reporting is replaced with "increasingly frivolous exposes" (Waldman, 86–87).

5   Because there are not enough reporters working to fill the time with hard news, stations become dependent on news wires and video feeds. It is cheaper to get video from the satellite feeds than to send a photographer and reporter out in the field, and it is faster to rephrase a story taken from the news wires than to research and report on an original story. Stories taken from the news wires and satellite video feeds account for many of the "quick-hit" fifteen or twenty second pieces aired during local newscasts. These stories may contain legitimate news, but they are typically not stories covering local news topics.

6   Health-related stories are popular with viewers and are frequently included in local news lineups. Yet the quick-hit format of the stories is particularly troublesome in this arena. Elizabeth Jensen writes that local newscasts frequently feature health information, but their reports are "brief, often lack necessary perspective . . . and occasionally contain 'egregious errors' with potentially serious consequences." Jensen cites a large study which showed that the median length of health stories in local newscasts was just thirty-three seconds, and of these only 27% included an interview with someone in the health profession. She writes that local news tends to cover the "sexy" stories—high profile diseases of the moment, such as West Nile virus, avian flu, or swine flu—far more often than the things that are more likely to affect people's health, like diabetes or heart disease. These are certainly topical news stories; however, the amount of coverage these stories receive coupled with a lack of time and depth may create unnecessary alarm.

7   On February 13, 2013, I examined the story line-ups for the local 6 p.m. newscast on WHDH-TV, Boston's NBC affiliate station. Excluding commercials, the full air time available for this newscast was twenty-one minutes. Of this, two minutes and twenty seconds were spent on graphics and teases for upcoming stories. Four minutes and fifteen seconds were given to weather, and four minutes and fifteen

seconds were given to sports. Local news accounted for ten minutes and fifty seconds of the coverage. Of the local news stories, the longest was about a highway car fire (three minutes). One minute and forty-five seconds were allotted to stories about a local murder case and a convenience store robbery. Two minutes of the newscast were devoted to a "soft" story about the police rescue of a chicken that was stuck in a snow bank. Even the time given to the longest piece of local news coverage was significantly shorter than the time given to sports or weather. Other local news stories ranged from fifteen to forty seconds in length. These stories could do little more than highlight key facts and perhaps include a sound bite or two. Stations are forced to select stories that can be told quickly and that require little background or context, and even if a story does need context, there isn't time to provide it.

8   Local news occasionally devotes time to entertainment stories—particularly if the story benefits the affiliate station and its network. For example, during the 5:30 p.m. newscast on February 13, 2013, WHDH allotted two minutes and ten seconds to a story about the NBC show *Chicago Fire,* which was currently airing new episodes, including interviews with two of the show's stars. This kind of promotional entertainment coverage benefits the network, but it draws even more time away from quality local news coverage.

9   Todd Belt and Marion Just conducted a five-year, in-depth study of fifty local markets to determine the relationship between what a local news station covers and its level of commercial success. Are viewers as turned off by stories on public affairs and issues as news directors fear? Do they need fast-paced, attention-grabbing stories, as the industry seems to believe? Their study suggests that this is not the case. Belt and Just found that "audiences preferred news stories that reflected journalistic enterprise—station initiated investigations or on the spot reporting instead of merely reporting the news from other sources." Stations that included this kind of reportage fared better financially overall. They write, "Journalistic enterprise is one of the factors that leads to larger audiences and, therefore, greater advertising. . . . Stations that practice low effort journalism risk getting trapped in a downward spiral of declining ratings" (Belt and Just). The findings suggest that news producers are incorrect in their stubborn belief that audiences prefer soft news and that investigative journalism is not worth the cost or effort.

10   If more time is given to news, it naturally must be taken from coverage of something else. So what has to go? Stations could take some time back from the promotional graphics that devour precious seconds with useless visuals, or they could have less repetition of stories in back-to-back newscasts. Another option is to take time from the twenty-second "quick hit" wire stories, particularly those that cover national news. Of course these stories are news and they are of interest to viewers, but if viewers want the national news tidbits, then isn't national network news the place to find them?

Bower 5

11   Another possible solution is to take the time back from the "Coming up next!" news teases designed to lure viewers to stay through the commercial break. Local news stations often run one-and-a-half to two minutes of tease video per half-hour newscast. This time, in addition to the time spent on promotional station graphics, branding slogans and music, could be spent expanding on news stories. Teases may work, and it is valuable for busy viewers to know what is coming up in case a story may be of particular interest to them. But stations should not underestimate their audiences by assuming they need to be continually wooed into watching a half hour of news. The story is what the viewers really want. Teases have no journalistic value and take time away from reporters and their pieces.

12   Today's news consumer has countless options for where, when, and how to get the news. There are many quality news sources online, and news apps and Twitter feeds can quickly provide the what and when of a story. Local television news has to offer something unique—coverage that is community-based, high-quality, in-depth, and relevant. Yet most news organizations do not yet have a model for earning the kind of profits online that they earn through television advertising, and TV is still the flagship enterprise for local news, and the top resource for local news consumers.

13   Local news affiliates may not have the financial resources or tremendous market sizes of their parent networks, but they still provide the important service of informing communities about their local schools, citizens, governments, and breaking news. Surely, it must be frustrating for professional television journalists to abandon insightful analysis and instead package the facts into a minute and thirty seconds of lead, soundbite, and tag. Research indicates that viewers want in-depth local news stories that are relevant to their lives and their communities. The question is whether local news stations will risk altering standard formats to give reporters the freedom and resources to tell these stories.

Works Cited

Belt, Todd L., and Marion R. Just. "The Local News Story: Is Quality a Choice?" *Political Communication,* April 2008, Vol. 25, pages 194–215.

Claussen, Dane S. "Cognitive Dissonance, Media Illiteracy, and Public Opinion on the News." *American Behavioral Scientist.* Vol. 48, Oct 2004, p. 212.

Jensen, Elizabeth. "Study Laments Anemic Reporting." *Television Week.* Vol. 25, March 13, 2006.

McKay, Floyd. "How We Clicked Quality Journalism off Our TV Screens." Crosscut .com. May 25, 2012.

Waldman, Steven and the Working Group on Information Needs of Communities. "The Information Needs of Communities: The Changing Media Landscape in a Broadband Age." Federal Communications Commission Report. July 2011.

1. Where does Stephanie Bower state her claim? Do you agree with Stephanie's working claim here? Did you have a strong opinion about local TV news before you read Stephanie's piece? Did reading her paper change your mind, or reinforce your thinking?

2. Did Stephanie sufficiently narrow her topic? Is her evidence convincing? Considering that some of her evidence is from leading critics of the world of journalism, did she make their information accessible to you and relevant to her claim?

3. Examine two instances in which Stephanie cites quotations from experts in the field to develop her argument. Comment on the way she incorporated the quotations into the text. Was it done successfully or awkwardly?

4. What two factors, according to Stephanie, account for mediocrity in local news? Do you agree? Disagree?

5. What are some of the brandings such as "I-Team" or "Storm Center" or "in-depth coverage" your local stations use? How do these brandings affect you? Do they earn your respect, your curiosity, or even your disdain? Explain your reaction.

6. What suggestions does Stephanie offer to improve the quality of local TV news? Which suggestions do you think could be realistically implemented? Which are obstacles too great to control in your opinion?

7. In your journal, select a local TV newscast, one that is broadcast nightly at the same time. Watch it every day if you can, or at least three times. Like Stephanie, break down the content of the newscast recording the length of time in minutes and seconds of the story, the topic of the story, and the depth of the story. Evaluate the content.

8. How do you respond to Stephanie's question, "Is journalism an impartial civic informer or a big business?" To shape your answer, use some of the evidence Stephanie presented in her paper and find some of your own.

EXERCISES

1. Get together with a small group of students in your class and brainstorm possible topics for an argument essay concerning a controversial issue on your campus or in your community. Try to think of at least ten topics that are current and that most people in your group find interesting and arguable.

2. Make a visit to the periodicals section of your college library and look through current issues of periodicals and newspapers on the shelves to find out what issues and subjects are being debated in America and around the world. Find one or more topics that interest you and make copies of those articles for further reading and response in your journal.

3. Take some time to explore the Internet by doing a key word search using a Web search engine. In your journal, describe the results of your search. How many different sites

devoted to your topic did you locate? What did you find surprising about the comments and opinions expressed by the participants?

4. Engage in a dialogue with other students, family members, friends, or people in the community who might have some interest and opinions on a potential topic. In your journal, record and respond to their diverse views.

5. Choose a topic that you might wish to investigate for an argument essay and use some of the strategies suggested in this chapter to get started: brainstorm, cluster, freewrite, and question.

6. Formulate a list of questions about your potential topic.

7. After you have followed some of the strategies for exploring your topic, formulate a working claim. In your journal, identify which parts of your claim will need to be supported by reasons in your essay. Which parts of your claim will need to be investigated further?

4

Addressing Audiences: Thinking Like a Reader

LEARNING OJBECTIVES

After studying this chapter, you should be able to:

1. Identify the different types of audience. (p. 82)
2. Explain how to adapt your argument to your target audience. (p. 84)
3. Identify the five components of the classical argument. (p. 90)
4. Explain how to distinguish denotative and connotative meanings of words. (p. 104)
5. Describe the need for language to be concrete. (p. 106)
6. Identify the major figures of speech. (p. 107)
7. Describe the importance of avoiding clichés and unnecessary euphemisms. (p. 110)
8. Know when to define technical terms. (p. 111)

As we've discussed in previous chapters, the purpose of writing an argument is to prompt your listeners to consider your point of view and, thus, win your listeners' respect through the logic and skill of your thinking. When used productively, argument is a way to resolve conflict and achieve common ground among adversaries. Thus, one of the primary ways to measure the success of your argument is to gauge how effectively it reaches and appeals to your audience. Knowing something about your audience will enable you to use your knowledge to make your arguments most effective.

Creating an argument would be a simple task if you could be guaranteed an audience of readers just like yourself. If everyone shared your cultural, educational, religious, and practical experiences, persuading them to accept your point of view would require very little effort. Clearly, however, this is not the case. A quick look around your classroom will reveal the many differences that make argument a challenging activity. Is everyone the same age? Race? Gender? Ethnicity? Do you all listen to the same music? Dress alike? Live in the same neighborhood? Vote for the same candidates? Attend the same place of worship? Unless you attend a very unusual school, the answer to most of these questions will be a resounding "no." People are different; what interests you may bore the person behind you, whereas what puts you to sleep may inspire someone else to passionate activism. And what you see on the surface isn't the whole story about your classmates, either. That rough-looking guy who works as a mechanic may write poetry in his spare time; that conservatively dressed woman may spend her weekends touring the countryside on a motorcycle. It's too easy to make assumptions about people's values and beliefs just by looking at them. If you want to persuade these people, you're going to have to assess them very carefully.

Knowing your audience will help you determine almost every aspect of the presentation of your case:

- The kind of language you use
- The writing style (casual or formal, humorous or serious, technical or philosophical)
- The particular slant you take (appealing to the reader's reason, emotions, ethics, or a combination of these)
- What emphasis to give to the argument
- The type of evidence you offer
- The kinds of authorities you cite

Also, this knowledge will let you better anticipate any objections to your position. In short, knowing your audience lets you adjust the shape of your argument the way you would select a different playlist on your iPod depending on your guests or audience.

If, for instance, you're writing for your economics professor, you would use technical vocabulary you would not use with your English professor. Likewise, in a newspaper article condemning alcohol abusers, you would have to keep in mind that some of your readers or their family members might be recovering alcoholics; they may take exception to your opinions. A travel piece for an upscale international magazine would need to have a completely different slant and voice than an article for the travel section of a small local newspaper.

Knowing your audience might make the difference between a convincing argument and a failing argument. Suppose, for instance, you decide to write an editorial for the student newspaper opposing a recently announced tuition hike. Chances are you would have a sympathetic audience in the student body because you share age, educational status, and interests. Most students do not like the idea of a higher tuition bill. That commonality might justify the blunt language and emotional slant of your appeal. It might even allow a few sarcastic comments directed at the administration. That same argument addressed to your school's board of trustees, however, would probably not win a round of applause. With them it would be wiser to adopt a more formal tone in painting a sympathetic picture of your financial strain; it's always smart to demonstrate an understanding of the opposition's needs, maybe even a compromise solution. In this case, your appeal to the trustees would be more credible if you acknowledged the university's plight while recommending alternative money-saving measures such as a new fundraising program.

Or suppose you write an article with a religious thrust arguing against capital punishment. You argue that even in the case of confessed murderers, state execution is an immoral practice running counter to Christian doctrine; for supporting evidence you offer direct quotations from the New Testament. Were you to submit your article to a religious publication, your reliance on the authority of the scriptures would probably appeal to the editors. However, were you to submit that same article to the "My Turn" column for *Newsweek,* chances are it would be turned down, no matter how well-written. The editors aren't necessarily an ungodly lot, but *Newsweek,* like most other large-circulation e-zines, is published for an audience made up of people of every religious persuasion, as well as agnostics and atheists. *Newsweek* editors are not in the business of publishing material that excludes a large segment of its audience. Knowing your readers works in two ways: It helps you decide what materials to put into your argument, and it helps you decide where to publish your argument, whether it be on an electronic bulletin board, in a local paper, or on the op-ed page of *The Wall Street Journal.*

The Target Audience

The essays in this book come from a variety of publications, many of them magazines addressed to the "general" American readership. Others, however, come from publications directed to men or women, the political right or left, or from publications for people of particular ethnic, racial, and cultural identities. They are written for *target audiences.* When writers have a "target" audience in mind, particularly readers who share the same interests, opinions, and prejudices, they can take shortcuts with little risk of alienating anybody, because writers and readers have so many things in common. Consider the following excerpts concerning the use of animal testing in scientific research:

> Contrary to prevailing misperception, in vitro tests need not replace existing in vivo test procedures in order to be useful. They can contribute to chemical-safety evaluation right now. In vitro tests, for example, can be incorporated into the earliest stages of the risk-assessment process; they can be used to identify chemicals having the lowest probability of toxicity so that animals need be exposed only to less noxious chemicals.

It is clear from the technical terminology (e.g., *in vitro, in vivo, toxicity*), professional jargon (*test procedures, chemical-safety evaluation, risk-assessment process*), and the formal, detached tone that the piece was intended for a scientifically educated readership. Not surprisingly, the article, "Alternatives to Animals in Toxicity Testing," was authored by two research scientists, Alan M. Goldberg and John M. Frazier, and published in *Scientific American.* Contrast it with another approach to the topic:

> Almost 30 years ago, Queen had been a child herself, not quite two years old, living in Thailand under the care of her mother and another female elephant, the two who had tended to her needs every day since her birth. They taught her how to use her trunk, in work and play, and had given her a sense of family loyalty. But then Queen was captured, and her life was changed irrevocably by men with whips and guns. One man herded Queen by whipping and shouting at her while another shot her mother, who struggled after her baby until more bullets pulled her down forever.

What distinguishes this excerpt is the emotional appeal. This is not the kind of article you would find in *Scientific American* or most other scientific journals. Nor would you expect to see this kind of emotional appeal in a newsmagazine such as *Newsweek* or *TIME*, or a general interest publication such as the Sunday magazine of many newspapers. The excerpt comes from an animal rights newsletter published by PETA, People for the Ethical Treatment of Animals. Given that particular audience, the writer safely assumes immediate audience sympathy with the plight of elephants. There is no need for the author to qualify or apologize for such sentimentalizing statements as "Queen had been a child herself" and "They taught her how to use her trunk, in work and play, and had given her a sense of family loyalty." In fact, given the context, the author is probably more interested in reminding readers of a shared cause rather than winning converts to the cause of animal rights.

Sometimes targeting a sympathetic audience is intended to move people to action—to get people to attend a rally or to contribute money to a cause or to vote for a particular political candidate. During the recent presidential campaign, fundraising letters went out asking for donations to one particular candidate who pledged to fight the high cost of health care. In one of several blogs supporting that candidate, the pharmaceutical industry was portrayed as a "greedy goliath" that was no different than "illegal drug cartels, extorting money from hapless consumers." As used in this blog, the strategy in appealing to a target audience is to streamline the issue into an "us-versus-them" conflict—in this case, the consumer as innocent victim and the manufacturers as bad guys. The blogger went on to argue that drug manufacturers inflate their prices astronomically, citing as evidence how company CEOs enjoy incomes in the tens of millions of dollars. "The pharmaceutical industry exists for the sole purpose of preying upon Americans who are sick, unhealthy, in discomfort and injured," said the blogger. "Their goal is to insure [*sic*] that only your symptoms are treated." Crackling with charged language, the blog invited voters to join the effort to change a system that exploited the taxpaying consumer and bloated company profits.

While pharmaceutical companies may indeed inflate the cost of their products, the campaign blog was a one-way argument, addressed to people already sympathetic to the cause. But the blog lacked perspectives from the other side. Nothing was said about the billions of dollars spent by pharmaceutical companies to develop and bring to market a new drug, or the fact that only a small percentage of drugs that reach the market ever turns a profit. Nor was there mention of the fact that the FDA is funded by the pharmaceutical companies and not taxpayer dollars, or the fact that the time frame for turning a profit is a limited number of years, after which patents expire, allowing the generic makers to market the same product at reduced costs. In short, the function of the campaign letters and blogs was not to plumb the depths of the issue and offer a balanced argument. On the contrary, most of the target audience was already sold on the cause. The basic intention was to convert conviction into money and votes. And the means was charged, motivational rhetoric.

The General Audience

Unless you're convinced that your readers are in total agreement with you or share your philosophical or professional interests, you may have some trouble picturing just whom you are persuading. It's tempting to say you're writing for a "general" audience; but, as we said at the beginning of this chapter, general audiences may include very different people with different backgrounds, expectations, and standards. Writing for such audiences, then, may put additional pressure on you.

In reality, of course, most of your college writing will be for your professors. This can be a little confusing because you may find yourself trying to determine just what audience your professor represents. You may even wonder why professors expect you to explain material with which they are familiar. You may feel that defining technical terms to your psychology instructor who covered them in class the week before, or summarizing a poem that you know your English professor can probably recite, is a waste of time. But they have a good reason: They assume the role of an uninformed audience to let you show how much *you* know.

Of course, if you are arguing controversial issues you may find yourself in the awkward position of trying to second-guess your instructor's stand on an issue. You may even be tempted to tone down your presentation so as not to risk offense and, thus, an undesirable grade. However, most instructors try not to let their biases affect their evaluation of a student's work. Their main concern is how well a student argues a position.

For some assignments, your instructor may specify an audience for you: members of the city council, the readers of the campus newspaper, Rush Limbaugh's radio listeners, and so on. But if no audience is specified, one of your earliest decisions about writing should be in choosing an audience. If you pick "readers of the *National Review*," for instance, you'll know you're writing for mostly male, conservative, middle-aged, middle-class whites; the expectations of these readers are very different than for readers of *Jet* or *Vibe*. If you are constrained to (or want the challenge of) writing for the so-called general audience, construct a mental picture of who those people are so you'll be able to shape your argument accordingly. Here are some of the characteristics we think you might include in your definition.

The "general" audience includes those people who read *TIME* magazine and your local newspaper. That means people whose average age is about 35, whose educational level is high school plus two years of college, who make up the vast middle class of America, who politically stand in the middle of the road, and whose racial and ethnic origins span the world. You can assume that they read the daily newspaper and/or online news sites, watch the television news, and are generally informed about what is going on in the country. You can assume a good comprehension of language nuances and a sense of humor. They are people who recognize who Shakespeare was, though they may not be able to quote passages or name ten of his plays. Nor will they necessarily be experts in the latest theory of black holes or be able to explain how photosynthesis work. However, you can expect them to be open to technical explanations and willing to listen to arguments on birth control, gun control, weight control, and the immigration laws. More importantly, you can look upon your audience as people willing to hear what you have to say.

Guidelines for Knowing Your Audience

Before sitting down to write, think about your audience. Ask yourself the following questions: Will I be addressing other college students, or people from another generation? Will my audience be of a particular political persuasion, or strongly identified with a specific cultural background? How might the age of my readers and their educational background influence the way they think about a given issue? On what criteria will they make their decisions about this issue? A good example of profiling your audience was evident in the 2012 presidential election. On the one hand, the Republicans gambled that "corporate expertise" was the chief criteria for voters. The Democrats, on the other hand, focused on a need for "economic and social change." As the election results showed, the Democrats had assessed their audience more accurately than did the Republicans.

As the earlier example illustrates, an effective argument essay takes into account the values, beliefs, interests, and experiences of its audience. If you simply choose to argue what you feel is important without regard to your audience, the only person you persuade may be yourself! An effective argument tries to establish common ground with the audience. While this may be difficult at times, recognizing what you have in common with your audience will enable you to argue most persuasively.

Before you can do this, however, you will need to create a profile of your audience. You may find the audience checklist below helpful in assessing an audience. If you like visual prompts, write the answers to these questions on a card or a slip of paper that you can hang over your desk or display in a window on your computer screen while you're working on your argument. Looking at these questions and answers occasionally will remind you to direct your arguments on your particular audience.

Using Debate and Dialogue

Debate and dialogue, two of the methods of developing arguments discussed in Chapter 1, can also be used to sharpen your awareness of audience. For an example of how this can happen, let's revisit John, our first-year composition student who had decided to write his

Audience Checklist

1. Who are the readers I will be addressing?
   - ▪ What will be their age group?
   - ▪ Are they male, female, or both?
   - ▪ What will be their educational background?
   - ▪ What is their socioeconomic status?
   - ▪ What are their political, religious, occupational, or other affiliations?
   - ▪ What values, assumptions, and prejudices do they have about life?
2. Where do my readers stand on the issue?
   - ▪ Do they know anything about it?
   - ▪ If so, how might they have learned about it?
   - ▪ How do they interpret the issue?
   - ▪ How does the issue affect them personally?
   - ▪ Are they hostile to my stand on the issue?
3. How do I want my readers to view the issue?
   - ▪ If they are hostile to my view, how can I persuade them to listen to me?
   - ▪ If they are neutral, how can I persuade them to consider my viewpoint?
   - ▪ If they are sympathetic to my views, what new light can I shed on the issue? How can I reinspire them to take action?
4. What do I have in common with my readers?
   - ▪ What beliefs and values do we share?
   - ▪ What concerns about the issue do we have in common?
   - ▪ What common life experiences have we had?
   - ▪ How can I make my readers aware of our connection?

argument essay on the topic of binge drinking. After reading critically in his subject area (Chapter 2) and formulating a working claim (Chapter 3), John turned his attention to the question of audience. He found that using debate and dialogue helped him answer some of the questions in the audience checklist and provided essential information about how his audience might respond to his ideas.

John decided that his audience would be a general one composed of people of all ages. He anticipated that most people in his audience would not endorse excessive drinking, but with such a diverse group of people he was unsure exactly what reasons would fuel their opposition and how strongly they would agree or disagree with his reasons. John found that using two strategies, first, a "Yes, but . . ." exchange and, second, an imaginary dialogue between different perspectives, helped to answer questions 2 and 3 on the audience checklist: Where do my readers stand on the issue? and how do I want my readers to view the issue? He used the answers to these questions to develop ways to engage his readers in the essay.

Working with classmates in small peer groups, John found that a "Yes, but . . ." exchange revealed specific points that his audience might use to oppose his reasons. For instance, John began with the following statement:

College administrators have a responsibility to deter binge drinking by their students.

He received several responses from his peer group:

Yes, college administrators have a responsibility to their students, but that responsibility should be limited to academic matters.

Yes, binge drinking by students should be a concern to college administrators, but college administrators shouldn't interfere with the private lives or habits of their students.

Yes, college administrators should try to deter binge drinking by students, but they will be ineffective unless they receive support from the community and parents.

Although each of John's classmates agreed that college administrators had a valid interest in student binge drinking, there was considerable disagreement over how far that interest should extend and how effective any action taken by administrators would be. The "Yes, but . . ." exchange gave John greater insight into the ways others might respond to his ideas. As he developed his argument, he was able to acknowledge and address such concerns by his potential audience.

In a similar fashion, John used dialogue to gain insight into question 4 on the audience checklist: What do I have in common with my readers? In particular, John wanted to discover any concerns and values he and his readers might share about binge drinking. To create a dialogue, John interviewed several of his classmates, his teachers, members of his family, and a few individuals from the community; he also read articles by health professionals concerned with alcohol abuse and young adults. His goal was to listen to a wide spectrum of views on the subject and to keep an open mind. He used his journal to record comments and his own impressions. What emerged from this dialogue were several areas of shared concerns: Most agreed that binge drinking was an unhealthy practice that should be discouraged, and while there were many different suggestions about the measures that should be taken to eliminate it, all agreed that the students who engaged in binge drinking must ultimately accept responsibility for ending it. No solution would work, all agreed, unless the drinkers themselves were willing to stop. John found this information helpful because he knew that his audience would be more willing to listen to his argument if he could identify these shared values and concerns.

By engaging in both debate and dialogue, John gained knowledge that enabled him to appeal to his audience more effectively.

Adapting to Your Readers' Attitudes

Writing for a general audience is a challenge because in that faceless mass are three kinds of readers you'll be addressing:

1. People who agree with you
2. People who are neutral—those who are unconvinced or uninformed on the issue
3. People who don't share your views, and who might be hostile to them

Each of these different subgroups will have different expectations of you and give you different obligations to meet if you are to present a convincing argument. Even readers sympathetic to your cause might not be familiar with specialized vocabulary, the latest developments around the issue, or some of the more subtle arguments from the opposition. Those hostile to your cause might be so committed to their own viewpoints that they might not take the time to discover that you share common concerns. And those neutral to the cause might simply need to be filled in on the issue and its background. If you're going to persuade your readers, you'll have to tailor your approach to suit their attitudes.

When addressing an audience, whether general or one of a particular persuasion, you must try to put yourself in its place. You must try to imagine the different needs and expectations these readers bring to your writing, always asking yourself what new information you can pass on and what new ways of viewing you can find for addressing the issue you're arguing. Depending on whether you anticipate a neutral, friendly, or unfriendly group of readers, let's look at some of the strategies you might use.

Addressing a Neutral Audience

Some writers think a neutral audience is the easiest to write for, but many others find this the most challenging group of readers. After all, they're *neutral;* you don't know which way they're leaning, or what may make them commit to your position. Your best role is the conveyor of knowledge: The information you bring, and the ways in which you present it, are the means by which you hope to persuade a neutral audience. Here are some of the ways to convey that information.

Fill in the Background

There are some issues about which few people are neutral: abortion, capital punishment, drug legalization, same-sex marriage, gun control. However, there are other issues about which some readers have not given a thought. For instance, if you're part of a farming community, your concern about preserving good farmland might make you feel concerned about unchecked industrial development in your area. To make a convincing case for readers from, say, Chicago or New York City, you first would have to explain the shortage of prime agricultural land. On the other hand, were you a writer from a large town, you might need to explain to readers from rural Vermont or Iowa why you think they should be concerned over mandatory recycling in large cities. In both cases, your task would be to provide your readers with the information they need to evaluate the issue by relating some of the history and background behind the controversy. All the while, you need to encourage them to weigh the evidence with an open mind.

Present a Balanced Picture

Part of educating a neutral audience about your position involves presenting a balanced picture of the issue by presenting multiple perspectives about the issue, not just one. Even though you are trying to help your readers understand why your position has value, you will be more persuasive if you treat *all* views fairly, including opposing views. You should clearly and accurately lay out the key arguments of all sides; then demonstrate why your position is superior. Your readers need to feel that you have looked at the total picture and reached your position after carefully weighing all views, a process you hope your readers will engage in as well. Let your readers make their decisions based on their own analysis of the information you have provided. Don't be guilty of stacking the deck, a logical fallacy we discussed in Chapter 2. Not representing the other sides at all, or representing them unfairly and inaccurately, can leave you open to criticisms of distortion, and it may make your readers feel that you're misleading them.

Personalize the Issues

One sure way of gaining readers' attention is to speak their language—that is, address their personal needs, hopes, and fears. (It's what skillful politicians do all the time on the campaign trail.) If you want to engage your readers' attention, demonstrate how the problem will affect them personally. On the matter of farmland, explain why if nothing is done to prevent its loss, the prices of corn and beans will triple over the next three years. On the recycling issue, explain how unrestricted trash dumping will mean that city dwellers will try to dump more trash in rural areas. However, although personalizing the issue is an effective way to make your readers aware of the importance of your issue, you should avoid creating an ad misericordiam argument. To be fully credible, you should be certain that the reasons and evidence you present to your readers are anchored in fact rather than emotion.

Show Respect

When you're an informed person talking about an issue to people with less knowledge than you, there's a dangerous tendency to speak down to them. Think how you feel when someone "talks down" to you. Do you like it? How persuasive do you think you can be if your readers think you're talking down to them? Don't condescend or patronize them. Try not to simplify a complex issue so much that it is reduced to a false dilemma: "If we don't increase school taxes immediately, our children will no longer receive a quality education." Don't assume that your audience is so ill informed that it cannot envision a middle ground between the two alternatives. On the contrary, treat your readers as people who want to know what you know about the issue and who want you to demonstrate to them clearly and accurately why you think they should agree with you. Invite them into the discussion, encouraging them with sound reasons and strong evidence to consider the merits of your side. Although your audience may not be as informed as you, they are willing to listen and deserve respect.

Addressing a Friendly Audience

Writing an argument for the already converted is much easier than writing for a neutral audience or one that is hostile. In a sense, half the battle is won because no minds have to be changed. You need not brace yourself for opposing views or refutations. Your role is simply to provide readers with new information and to renew enthusiasm for and commitment to your shared position. Nonetheless, we do have some suggestions for keeping your argument fair and balanced.

Avoid Appealing to Prejudices

One of the risks of addressing a sympathetic audience is appealing to prejudices rather than reasons and facts. Although it might be tempting to mock those who don't agree with you or to demean their views, don't. Stooping to that level only diminishes your own authority and undermines your credibility. Two of the logical fallacies we discussed in Chapter 2 address this problem. The first, an ad hominem argument, is a personal attack on those who disagree with your position. Unfortunately, this approach will reflect negatively on *you*. Use reason and hard evidence instead of insults and ridicule to underscore the weakness of other arguments while you make your readers aware of your mutual concerns. The second fallacy is an ad populum argument and involves using the presumed prejudices of your audience members to manipulate their responses to your argument. Once again, this approach will make you appear unreasonable and biased and may backfire if your audience does not share your prejudices. Instead, encourage your readers to respect different viewpoints, recognizing the merits of their arguments even though you ultimately disagree. It's simply a more reasonable approach, one that allows you and your readers to share informed agreement, and it will win the respect of friends and foes alike.

Offer New Information About the Issue

Even when your readers agree with you, they may need to have their memories refreshed regarding the history of the issue. In addition, you should provide readers with important new information on the issue. Such new developments might involve recent judicial decisions, newly enacted legislation, or new scientific data that could serve to strengthen your position and their agreement or require a reconsideration of your views. Unless you are absolutely up-to-date about the progress of your issue, you will appear to be either ill informed or deliberately withholding information, seriously undermining your credibility with your audience, even a friendly one. Your willingness to share and educate your audience will enhance the persuasiveness of your views.

Addressing an Unfriendly Audience

As difficult as it may be to accept, some readers will be totally at odds with your views, even hostile to them. Writing for such a readership, of course, is especially challenging—far more than for neutral readers. So how do you present your argument to people you have little chance of winning over?

THE CLASSICAL ARGUMENT

The so-called classical argument is a rhetorical structuring device dating back to the Greek philosopher, Aristotle. It is characterized by five specific components that move logically and smoothly from one to the other, making for an effective argument. This formal strategy is still used today in framing written arguments, particularly position arguments, such as those included in the reading chapters of this book. The five components of the classical argument are as follows: introduction, background, confirmation, refutation, and conclusion. Now let's look at these parts individually.

Introduction

Here the writer attempts to capture the attention of the audience by introducing the topic and convincing the reader that it is important. The introduction also prepares the reader for the argument that follows, by revealing the writer's style and tone. Oftentimes writers will end the introduction with the argument's thesis statement.

Background

What follow in the background are the material and the information informing the reader of the historical and social context of the issue being argued. Here the writer gives his or her stand, defines terms, and supplies background circumstances and other information that suggest why the problem needs to be addressed.

Support

This is where the writer lays out the specific reasons and evidence (facts, statistics, examples, expert testimony, personal experiences, etc.) that substantiate the thesis of the argument. Rhetoricians who teach the classical model of arguments usually suggest that the support consists of three separate reasons with evidence for each, moving from the most logical to that with the most impact—but all linked in from one to the next and all confirming the core claim of the argument. Here the writer may appeal to reason, emotions, and/or one's ethical and moral sense in effort to persuade readers—or what Aristotle called *logos, pathos,* and *ethos.*

For instance, say you are arguing that colleges should place less emphasis on SAT scores than on other forms of assessment for admission. Your opening reason might be that entrance exams do not show a student's true potential and accomplishments. Even the brightest students from impoverished communities may have been denied learning opportunities due to limited finances, weak school systems, or lack of time to devote to studies. Thus, they aren't able to show their true potential on the SAT. Next you could offer that standardized tests are not the sum of a student and do not necessarily reflect an individual's academic merits and achievements. Colleges should put more emphasis on students' grades, their social and community activities, letters of recommendation, and interviews. Then for impact, you might add a personal reason: that you know people who did not score well on the SAT but who did extraordinarily well in college, achieving high honors. In fact, you yourself scored 150 points above your sister, and she graduated magna cum laude, while you graduated with no such distinction from the same school. Had the SAT score been the only criterion, she would not have been accepted to your alma mater.

Concession and Refutation

This is usually the main body of the argument and the longest section. Here the writer takes account of the opposition's key points and any anticipated objections, and then rebuts those points. It is important that these follow each other. That is, not to acknowledge the other side of the argument is to leave yourself open to attack. No audience expects an argument to have but one side. Therefore, a competent argument must address key points of the opposition as well as objections that readers might raise.

This strategy demonstrates that the writer is well aware of the multiple sides to the argument. As in sports, the best offense is a good defense. Once opposing points are acknowledged, the writer then exposes the flaws in the opposition's argument, refuting concessions just made. Here a good arguer may point out errors in logic or judgment as well as negative effects of the opposition's stand. And to strengthen the refutation, the writer should offer evidence and support. For example, returning to the SAT argument mentioned earlier, you might concede that colleges should use some forms of evaluation since they have to assess the academic abilities of students applying to their institutions. But then you might go on to argue that students may do poorly on these tests for reasons other than intelligence. And such one-shot tests do not have the assessment power of full high school performance portfolios and teachers' letters of evaluation.

Conclusion

The most effective conclusion in a well-done argument is not simply a restatement of the thesis from the introduction. Yes, here the writer wraps thing up, creates closure, and sums up the argument that connects to the thesis. However, this is the finale, and a good arguer will want to end matters with impact, a final emotional or ethical appeal or rallying cry aimed at winning over the audience. And this might mean reminding the audience of the background circumstances that make the writer's solution so important. Or the writer could underscore beliefs and values shared with the audience in order to sway it into accepting his or her argument.

Classical Argument

Introduction	Captures attention of the audience
	Introduces the topic and why it's important to the reader
	Prepares readers for the argument to follow
	Reveals style and tone
	Makes thesis statement:
	1. Why is this an issue
	2. Why is this important to readers
Background	Historical and social context of the issue
	Summary of why the problem needs to be addressed
	Writer's stand on the issue
Support	Statement of writer's position with specific points of the argument:
	1. Most logical reason with evidence
	2. Additional reason with evidence
	3. Reason with the most impact
Concession	Summary of opposition views
	Takes account of opposition's key points and anticipated objections.
	Concedes to some strengths in opposition
Refutation	Exposes weaknesses in the opposition's views
	Points out errors in logic or judgment
	Points out how negative outcome of opposition stand outstrips benefits
Conclusion	Sums up argument connecting to thesis
	Makes final appeal to shared beliefs and values of audience to encourage the audience to accept your argument

Figure 4.1 Diagram of Classical Argument

The Rogerian Approach: Seek Common Ground and Show Empathy

One sure fire strategy in writing for an unfriendly audience is the so-called Rogerian approach—a strategy that evolved in the 1970s out of the writings of Carl Rogers. Considered one of the most influential American psychologists of the past century, Rogers made contributions to the fields of psychotherapy, counseling, education, and conflict resolution. In his humanistic approach to these fields, he stressed the importance of the individual and the need for empathy.

In the Rogerian approach to argumentation, your goal is to find ways to connect with your audience through empathy and common experiences rather than going on the attack or trying to persuade the other side that you are right and they are wrong. Your strategy is to validate your own point of view by making concessions to the other side, saying that you understand and respect the opinion of the opposition.

What distinguishes the Rogerian argument from the classical is the stronger emphasis on the emotional and ethical appeals rather than strictly logical ones. In other words, the Rogerian approach—to unfriendly audiences in particular—is to build an emotional or psychological bridge, a common ground through empathy. While the Rogerian approach doesn't actually concede to or even agree with the opposition, it does cite some of the opposition points as valid. In other words, the Rogerian argument shows respect for contrary views, even recognizing the logic of their argument. At the same time, the arguer states his or her own stance on the issue, thus preventing unnecessary conflict and a deadlock. And, if handled properly, instead of an "I win/you lose" outcome, both sides emerge as winners in the end.

For example, let's say that you are trying to persuade a group of senior citizens in your community to support a tax increase to fund local schools. After analyzing your audience, you conclude that many seniors are living on limited incomes and are more concerned about the financial burden of additional taxes than the school system— something that is no longer a priority in their lives. This factor alone might make them an unfriendly audience, one not easily receptive to your position. Thus a good strategy to begin your argument might be to let them know that you are well acquainted with the difficulties of living on limited means. You might even refer to relatives or friends who are in a similarly difficult financial position. By letting the members of your audience know that you empathize with and understand their hardships, they will be more willing to listen to you. And in this way you can establish an emotional and psychological bond.

Next, you could remind your audience of the beliefs and values you have in common. While it is unlikely that senior citizens still have children attending school, they nonetheless may value education and understand its importance. You let them know that you share this value, one that underlies your support for additional public school funding. This, then, is your common ground. And your thesis is that a tax increase would ensure that today's kids receive the same quality of education that existed when the seniors themselves had young children. A tax increase today might benefit their grandchildren.

In so recognizing the concerns of your readers as legitimate and worthy of attention, you demonstrate that you are aware of and respect their views. But this means learning what their concerns are. In our example, it would be wise first to read up on specific reasons why seniors would choose not to support a tax increase for public school programs. Perhaps there's an imbalance in how the tax revenues would be applied. Perhaps some senior programs need to be funded also. Perhaps the proposed tax hike is too high. By doing some research and addressing those concerns, you will make your audience aware that you understand its opposition. In the end, this may make your readers more receptive to your argument.

In summary, the Rogerian argument begins by establishing a common ground with an audience—beliefs, opinions, and common values. Showing respect, the writer demonstrates a good understanding of the audience's views. Then in the core of the argument, the writer objectively states his or her own position. Without sounding dismissive or superior, the writer explains how his or her position is valid while explaining how that position differs form the audience's stand. Finally, the writer states the thesis, making some concessions while inviting the audience to also give a little. In the end, the author demonstrates how adopting his or her perspective to some degree benefits both sides.

Convey a Positive Attitude

Whether or not they know it, an unfriendly audience will benefit from seeing the issue from another side. In a Rogerian approach, try to view yourself as someone shedding a different light on the problem. View the opposition as people who are potentially interested in learning something new. Without being defensive, arrogant, or apologetic, make your claim, enumerate your reasons, and lay out the evidence for your readers to evaluate on their own. Regard them as intelligent people capable of drawing their own conclusions. You may not win converts, but you might at least lead some to recognize the merits of your opinions. You might even convince a few people to reconsider their views.

Remember the Golden Rule

Even though it may not agree with you, treat the opposition with respect. Look upon the opposition as reasonable people who just happen to disagree with you. Demonstrate your understanding of their side of the issue. Show that you have made the effort to research the opposition. Give credit where credit is due. If some of their counterpoints make sense, say so. In short, treat those from the other side and their views as you would want to be treated. You may just win a few converts.

SAMPLE ARGUMENTS FOR ANALYSIS

How a writer appeals to his or her audience can have a positive or a negative effect on the way the writer's message is received. The following three articles—two by professionals and one by a student—are all concerned with the deleterious effects of cigarette smoking. Each writer is concerned with the efficacy and/or legitimacy of various regulations on smoking and the resulting treatment of smokers. Under its powers to regulate tobacco, the Food and Drug Administration in 2009 banned candy and fruit-flavored cigarettes, but not mentholated cigarettes. In "Let's Ban All Flavors of Cigarettes," Derrick Z. Jackson questions why menthol, which makes up 30 percent of the $87 billion U.S. cigarette market, was not included in the ban. The next piece, "The Bogus 'Science' of Secondhand Smoke," attacks claims by anti-smoking lobbies that even the smallest quantities of secondhand smoke can set the cancer process in motion. No apologist for the smoking industry, scientist Gio Batta Gori challenges the so-called scientific evidence used to support this claim. And our student piece by Danise Cavallaro questions the decision-making apparatus of her relatives and contemporaries who smoke despite statistics and numbers that show what a deadly decision they are making. For the first essay, by Derrick Z. Jackson, we have used annotations to illustrate some of the strategies he uses to appeal to his audience and the assumptions he makes about them. As a class exercise, read each of these essays and then consider the following questions:

1. Locate the claim or thesis statement and summarize the main ideas in each essay.
2. What kind of audience is each writer addressing? Neutral? Friendly? Hostile? What evidence can you find to support this?

Review: Addressing Audiences

A Neutral Audience

■ Fill in the background.
■ Present a balanced picture.
■ Personalize the issues.
■ Show respect for your readers.

A Friendly Audience

■ Avoid appealing to prejudices.
■ Offer new information about the issue.

An Unfriendly Audience

■ Seek common ground.
■ Show empathy.
■ Convey a positive attitude.
■ Remember the golden rule.

To Improve Your Credibility with Your Audience, Avoid These Fallacies

Ad hominem argument	Leveling a personal attack against an opponent. Reliance on ad hominem arguments undercuts your credibility and may make you appear mean-spirited and desperate. Focus instead on the substance of an opponent's claim.
Ad misericordiam argument	Attempting to exploit the audience's emotions rather than appealing to logic and reason. Avoid using arguments that rely only on wrenching the reader's heart strings rather than logic and real evidence.
Ad populum argument	Appealing to the audience's presumed prejudices rather than proven facts. Even if you know the prejudices of your audience, such an appeal at best only persuades those already convinced. Rely on the force of logic and supporting evidence rather than bias and stereotyping.
Stacking the deck	Presenting only evidence that supports your points and withholding contrary evidence. Instead, acknowledge that conflicting evidence exists and respond to it.
False dilemma	Presenting an issue as an either-or choice and ignoring the possibility of a middle ground. Treat your audience as intelligent equals who are aware that at least several thoughtful alternatives are likely to exist.

3. Which writers attempt to present a balanced picture to the audience? Provide examples.
4. Do the writers convey a positive attitude toward the audience? Do any of the writers antagonize the audience? How is this done?
5. Have these writers committed any of the logical fallacies we've discussed? Where do these errors occur, and how would you correct them?
6. How well does each writer establish common ground with the audience?
7. What is the purpose of each essay? How effectively does each writer accomplish this purpose?

Let's Ban All Flavors of Cigarettes

Derrick Jackson

> Derrick Z. Jackson is a journalist and regular columnist and associate editor for the *Boston Globe*. A graduate of the University of Wisconsin-Milwaukee and post-graduate journalism fellow at Harvard University, he is the recipient of various honorary degrees. He also teaches journalism courses at Simmons College in Boston. This article appeared in his column on September 30, 2009.

Let's Ban All Flavors of Cigarettes

1 It was a good first step by the Food and Drug Administration to ban candy- and fruit-flavored cigarettes this month under its new powers to regulate tobacco. The next and much bigger step is ending Menthol Madness.

2 As cancer-stick observers know, Big Tobacco really did not mind closing the candy store on cigarettes flavored like Hershey's or Life Savers. They were not even one percent of the market. Menthol is by far the most prominent cigarette flavoring of all. But it was exempted from an immediate ban in the smoking-prevention act signed by President Obama in June.

charged language
Assumes reader appreciates allusion to Big Brother

3 The reason is simple: Menthol cigarettes are nearly 30 percent of the $87 billion U.S. cigarette market. Menthol masks the harshness of smoking with its cooling effect and minty taste. The tobacco lobby and political allies bemoaned the impact of a menthol ban on jobs and government coffers. In 2007, tobacco sales generated $26 billion in state and federal tax revenues.

Assumes reader shares cynicism about tobacco industry's motives

4 When Obama signed the prevention act, he proclaimed that the tobacco industry's "millions upon millions in lobbying and advertising" on its "lies" to deny the deadly effects of smoking have "finally failed."

Though liberal author? not afraid to criticize Obama

5 That is a lie as long as the menthol exemption exists. The exemption means that government coffers remain more important than the coffins for the annual 443,000 lives lost to tobacco. The concern over tax revenues still overrides the $193 billion in annual health-related economic costs from smoking—a figure provided by the Centers for Disease Control.

Assumes politically savvy reader

6 The FDA can still ban menthol. Public health-minded politicians negotiated an explicit provision in the prevention act that commits the FDA to study menthol within one year. Any serious study should clearly result in a ban.

7 Medical journal studies over the last four years have found that smokers of menthol cigarettes are significantly more likely to have difficulty quitting smoking and that tobacco companies have deliberately manipulated menthol levels (as they did with nicotine) to lure younger smokers with "milder" taste. While menthol cigarettes are nearly 30 percent of the overall U.S. market, 44 percent of smokers ages 12 to 17 reported smoking menthol brands.

Assumes reader is comfortable with medical journals and medical data

8 The menthol exemption also leaves dangling in political midair explosive charges of racism. Menthol cigarettes are vastly disproportionately popular among African-Americans, with 80 percent of black smokers preferring menthol. According to the government, 30 percent of all cancer deaths are tied to cigarette smoking and African-Americans are 21 percent more likely to have lung cancer than white Americans. Smoking is tied to heart disease and strokes, and African-American men are twice as likely as white men to have strokes.

Uses facts and reason not emotion

9 This was enough for seven former US health secretaries to protest the exemption. One of them, Joseph Califano, told the *New York Times* that the exemption was "clearly putting black children in the back of the bus." This week, the American Legacy Foundation, established in the tobacco settlement with the states, urged the FDA to ban menthol along with the other flavors. "Literally many hundreds of tobacco industry documents conclusively establish that the tobacco industry has for decades systematically developed and marketed menthol products," the foundation said, ". . . to lure youth and younger tobacco users by masking the harsh flavor."

Assumes literate reader who recognizes these references

10 But with at least a year to go before possible banning, Big Tobacco is systematically hooking as many new smokers as possible. Martin Orlowsky, the CEO of Lorillard, which makes the top-selling menthol Newport, said this month, "We will continue to leverage the very strong brand equity position Newport has, particularly in key markets where the opportunity—that is, menthol opportunity—is greatest."

strong language

sketches opposition plans

11   As to where those "key markets" are, Reynolds American CEO Susan Ivey said in 2006, "If you look at the demographics of menthol, it is very urban. It has always had a strong African-American component. It's always had actually a strong Caucasian component. What has changed a lot in the last five years is a lot of additional Hispanic in that demographic. . . . we would see that menthol would have additional opportunity."

12   The FDA cannot close that window of opportunity too   *strong call to action*
soon.

The Bogus "Science" of Secondhand Smoke
Gio Batta Gori

Gio Batta Gori, an epidemiologist and toxicologist, is a spokesman and consultant for the tobacco industry. He is a former deputy director of the National Cancer Institute's Division of Cancer Cause and Prevention and the recipient of the U.S. Public Health Service Superior Service Award in 1976 for his efforts to define less hazardous cigarettes. This article appeared on washingtonpost.com, January 30, 2007.

1   Smoking cigarettes is a clear health risk, as most everyone knows. But lately, people have begun to worry about the health risks of secondhand smoke. Some policymakers and activists are even claiming that the government should crack down on secondhand smoke exposure, given what "the science" indicates about such exposure.

2   Last July, introducing his office's latest report on secondhand smoke, then-U.S. Surgeon General Richard Carmona asserted that "there is no risk-free level of secondhand smoke exposure," that "breathing secondhand smoke for even a short time can damage cells and set the cancer process in motion," and that children exposed to secondhand smoke will "eventually . . . develop cardiovascular disease and cancers over time."

3   Such claims are certainly alarming. But do the studies Carmona references support his claims, and are their findings as sound as he suggests?

4   Lung cancer and cardiovascular diseases develop at advancing ages. Estimating the risk of those diseases posed by secondhand smoke requires knowing the sum of momentary secondhand smoke doses that nonsmokers have internalized over their lifetimes. Such lifetime summations of instant doses are obviously impossible, because concentrations of secondhand smoke in the air, individual rates of inhalation, and metabolic transformations vary from moment to moment, year after year, location to location.

5   In an effort to circumvent this capital obstacle, all secondhand smoke studies have estimated risk using a misleading marker of "lifetime exposure." Yet, instant exposures also vary uncontrollably over time, so lifetime summations of exposure could not be, and were not, measured.

6   Typically, the studies asked 60–70 year-old self-declared nonsmokers to recall how many cigarettes, cigars, or pipes might have been smoked in their presence during their

lifetimes, how thick the smoke might have been in the rooms, whether the windows were open, and similar vagaries. Obtained mostly during brief phone interviews, answers were then recorded as precise measures of lifetime individual exposures.

7   In reality, it is impossible to summarize accurately from momentary and vague recalls, and with an absurd expectation of precision, the total exposure to secondhand smoke over more than a half-century of a person's lifetime. No measure of cumulative lifetime secondhand smoke exposure was ever possible, so the epidemiologic studies estimated risk based not only on an improper marker of exposure, but also on exposure data that are illusory.

8   Adding confusion, people with lung cancer or cardiovascular disease are prone to amplify their recall of secondhand smoke exposure. Others will fib about being nonsmokers and will contaminate the results. More than two dozen causes of lung cancer are reported in the professional literature, and over 200 for cardiovascular diseases; their likely intrusions have never been credibly measured and controlled in secondhand smoke studies. Thus, the claimed risks are doubly deceptive because of interferences that could not be calculated and corrected.

9   In addition, results are not consistently reproducible. The majority of studies do not report a statistically significant change in risk from secondhand smoke exposure, some studies show an increase in risk, and, astoundingly, some show a reduction of risk.

10   Some prominent anti-smokers have been quietly forthcoming on what "the science" does and does not show. Asked to quantify secondhand smoke risks at a 2006 hearing at the UK House of Lords, Oxford epidemiologist Sir Richard Peto, a leader of the secondhand smoke crusade, replied, "I am sorry not to be more helpful; you want numbers and I could give you numbers . . . , but what does one make of them? . . . These hazards cannot be directly measured."

11   It has been fashionable to ignore the weakness of "the science" on secondhand smoke, perhaps in the belief that claiming "the science is settled" will lead to policies and public attitudes that will reduce the prevalence of smoking. But such a Faustian bargain is an ominous precedent in public health and political ethics. Consider how minimally such policies as smoking bans in bars and restaurants really reduce the prevalence of smoking, and yet how odious and socially unfair such prohibitions are.

12   By any sensible account, the anachronism of tobacco use should eventually vanish in an advancing civilization. Why must we promote this process under the tyranny of deception?

13   Presumably, we are grown-up people, with a civilized sense of fair play, and dedicated to disciplined and rational discourse. We are fortunate enough to live in a free country that is respectful of individual choices and rights, including the right to honest public policies. Still, while much is voiced about the merits of forceful advocacy, not enough is said about the fundamental requisite of advancing public health with sustainable evidence, rather than by dangerous, wanton conjectures.

14   A frank discussion is needed to restore straight thinking in the legitimate uses of "the science" of epidemiology—uses that go well beyond secondhand smoke issues. Today, health rights command high priority on many agendas, as they should. It is not admissible to presume that people expect those rights to be served less than truthfully.

Smoking: Offended by the Numbers
Danise Cavallaro

Danise Cavallaro is a former English major, and it's clear from her word choice, tone, and the slant she takes that she is addressing her peers. As she mentions in her essay, many college students smoke, even if only at parties. In this essay, updated for this edition of *Dialogues*, Cavallaro wonders why anyone would ever want to smoke at all.

Cavallaro 1

Danise Cavallaro
Professor Mitrani
English 102
13 October 2013

Smoking: Offended by the Numbers

1 I majored in English because I hate mathematics and numbers. I hate these numbers too, but at least they are non-mathematically interesting: 11; 445; 1,200; 50,000.

- Eleven is the number of chemical compounds found in cigarettes that have been proven to cause cancer.
- Four hundred forty-five is the number of people per day who are diagnosed with smoking-related lung cancer.
- One thousand two hundred is the number of people who die every day from tobacco.
- Fifty thousand is the number of people who die every year from secondhand smoke-related diseases ("Facts").

2 I thought that I would defy the rules of journalism and write out those numbers in longhand because they seem awfully small on the page when I looked at them numerically. I thought if they looked bigger on the page, they might hold a little more meaning. They're even larger when they're not written in longhand. Yankee Stadium, filled, holds just over 52,000 people. That's roughly all the people who die from secondhand smoke per year, plus about five-and-a-half days' worth of the daily death toll from firsthand smoke. That's not even counting the nearly 5 million people worldwide who die each year from a smoking-related disease—which would be 96 sold-out Yankee Stadiums. Now go back to thinking about just one Yankee Stadium. If you were at a baseball game, who would you be there with? Your parents or your family? Your boyfriend or girlfriend, your best friends, your roommate from college? Don't forget about yourself. Now imagine each of them hooked up on an oxygen tank, struggling to do something as simple as breathe, unable to pull enough air

Cavallaro 2

into their lungs to cheer a run or a tag-out at home. They're living, still very much medically alive, but think of their quality of life: struggling to breathe, severely limited activity, and feigned happiness at most things.

3 In my now 28 years of being alive, I have never once felt the urge to light a cigarette. However, I have a lot of friends and family who have. I'm still struggling to understand what makes cigarettes appealing. Kissing my ex fresh after he squashed his cigarette underneath his heel tasted similar to what I'd imagine licking an ashtray would be like. My best friend lives in Manhattan, complains to no end about how expensive things are, but has no problem forking over $9–$11 for a pack of cigarettes. Her parents give her a hard time about it every time she's home; and she usually retorts with, "At least my cigarettes are safer than the unfiltered ones you rolled in the Army!" This argument in no way rationalizes her decisions, which contribute to raising the risks of her contracting lung cancer and emphysema. My uncle watched my grandfather slowly lose a two-year battle with lung cancer caused by working with asbestos and smoking unfiltered cigarettes for more than 40 years, but he would take smoke breaks while visiting him in the hospital. He still smokes today. It makes me sick.

4 With all this firsthand knowledge, such as the statistics I cited above, along with the deluge of widely available facts and help (Are we not living in the Information Age?) and as smart as these select people are, how could anyone not be motivated to quit by the numbers alone? The anti-smoking ad campaigns are not strong enough (though the chemical additives put into tobacco are very powerful), and, for whatever silly economic reason, cigarettes are marketed as cool. People still buy them even though they're a waste of money, and smoke them even though they carry a high mortality rate, all in the name of being able to exercise their rights as autonomous Americans.

5 I wonder if smokers still think in that hard-headed "never going to happen to me" American way when they're gasping for breath as they walk up the stairs. It's no secret that nicotine is an extremely addictive drug, and one of the hardest to give up. As with many things, if quitting were easy more people would do it. Mount Everest would be as popular as Disneyland if it were merely a hill.

6 To help lower those numbers in America, I propose a national anti-smoking campaign similar to "Scared Straight," a program for would-be juvenile offenders that worked well by showing exactly what the troubled youths would become if they kept to the path they were on. The popular anti-tobacco website, "thetruth.com," famous for its silently-shocking TV commercials depicting nonviolent boycotts of tobacco companies, is a good start. Certainly, more can be done. It starts with the youth of today.

7 Bring in a cancer-ravaged lung to a high school health class. Consider the postmortem donation as a gift to science—the science of staying alive. Black and

Cavallaro 3

white X-rays of lungs filled with shadowy malignant growths don't shock and revolt nearly as much as once-live flesh does, or ever will. While nicotine-yellowed teeth are becoming increasingly easier to whiten with do-it-yourself kits, it's impossible to peek at the inside of your own lungs to see the damage that's been done. Please plaster huge pictures of cancer- or emphysema-ravaged lungs across billboards along I-95. The media must realize that not being politically correct and therefore not afraid to shock or offend, may actually save lives. Grossing out the populace could be a highly effective tool—statistics and numbers printed on paper hardly look menacing, but disintegrating lung tissue is guaranteed to shock.

8   Within the past few years, the media have broadcast more edgy anti-smoking campaigns. Television commercials depict people regrettably living with tobacco-related tracheotomies, amputations, and late-stage cancers. The folks they show are openly remorseful, are suffering and are acutely aware of the chosen circumstances that brought them to their current situation. Unfortunately, the commercials show victims who are middle-aged or older. Nine in ten tobacco users start before they reach their 18th birthday, so this portrayed demographic may not resonate with youth (kidshealth.org).

9   One of the many problems with adolescent smoking is that the more deadly side effects are not felt until many years after high school, when smoking is less of a faux-cool habit and more of a way of life. Asthma, while not to be scoffed at, is a condition that is treatable and seldom lethal. Lung cancer, the most common cause of cancer death among men and women, is not optimistically treatable and is highly lethal. However, lung cancer is also the most preventable. Therefore, I propose banning the depiction of smoking in movies and television geared towards young adults. Adolescents, an extremely malleable age group, are obviously influenced by the media and seek to imitate the clothing, hairstyles, music, and lifestyles portrayed by the media. Remove the idea that smoking is an acceptable way of life, and it will reduce the numbers of people for whom smoking will become a way of life. America needs to be more honest with this easily influenced age group.

10   I also propose making cigarettes more expensive, as teenagers are famous for being broke. The harder it is for youth (or anyone) to afford this deadly habit, the less likely that it could actually become a habit. Given that the current recession has caused a lot of Americans to rethink their necessities, perhaps a $12 or $15 pack of cigarettes would help adjust priorities.

11   The problem with all this is, again, the numbers. America was founded on tobacco fields, funded by the trade of dried tobacco leaf between England and the Native Americans. Even a giant cornerstone of our economy rests on cigarettes. The biggest tobacco companies in the world have branched out and now own major corporations that supply nearly everything consumable. In his book *Ashes to Ashes: America's Hundred-Year Cigarette War*, the Public Health and the

Cavallaro 4

Unabashed Triumph of Philip Morris, Richard Kluger details how Philip Morris not only dominated the cigarette industry but has managed through its acquisitions of other companies—from beer to frozen vegetables—in the 1980s to insulate itself from an attack on its tobacco engine. To take down Philip Morris would be to upset an economic juggernaut to which many other companies on the NASDAQ are inexorably linked. It would be catastrophic to this country's economy. The "economic downturn" beginning in 2008 was hailed as the closest this country has been to a full-out Depression since the 1930s, and removing just Philip Morris from our economy would no doubt send America to shambles. Let's look at another huge facet of our economy—health care. Wouldn't it be nice to save over $150 billion each year in health care costs directly attributable to smoking? What could be done with all those newfound numbers?

12   It may be quite impossible to financially overturn the tobacco companies while it appears that addicted individuals might keep their cigarette plants a-humming forever. For example, my aforementioned best friend has a pack-per-week habit, which increases during midterms, finals, and immediately following bad dates. One pack of cigarettes a week, at $10 a pack, amounts to $520 per year. That's a lot of money for a law school student with no job—most of a month's rent, half a year's worth of cell phone bills, and a lot of delicious dinners at a good restaurant. I know many people who smoke a pack a day, which amounts to over $3,000 a year, even if they buy cheaper brands. The numbers add up, and it can be a hard choice where to apply your numbers.

13   Be selfish, America. Keep your numbers to yourself.

Cavallaro 5

Works Cited

"Facts." American Legacy Foundation, 2012. Web. 22 Oct. 2012.

Izenberg, Neil, MD. "Smoking Stinks!" *Kindshealth.org*. N.d. Web. 1 Oct. 2009.

Kluger, Richard. *Ashes to Ashes: America's Hundred-Year Cigarette War, the Public Health and the Unabashed Triumph of Philip Morris*. New York: Knopf, 1996. Print.

Choosing Your Words

Whether addressing friends, foes, or the undecided, you must take care that your readers fully understand your case. In part, this is accomplished by choosing your words carefully and by accurately defining any technical, unfamiliar, foreign, or abstract terms. Here are a few specific tips to follow to inform your readers without turning them off.

Distinguishing Denotation and Connotation

Many words, even the most common, carry special suggestions or associations, **connotations,** that differ from the precise dictionary definitions, **denotations.** For example, if you looked up the word *house* in the dictionary, one of the synonyms you'd find is *shelter.* Yet if you told people you live in a shelter, they would think that you live in a facility for the homeless or some kind of animal sanctuary. That is because *shelter* implies a covering or structure that protects those within from the elements or from danger. In other words, the term is not neutral, as is the word *house.* Likewise, dictionary synonyms for *horse* include *steed* and *nag,* but the former implies an elegant and high-spirited riding animal, while the latter suggests one that is old and worn out.

The denotations of words may be the same, but their connotations will almost always differ. And the reason is that dictionary denotations are essentially neutral and emotion-free, while connotations are most often associated with attitudes or charged feelings that can influence readers' responses. Therefore, it is important to be aware of the shades of differences when choosing your words. Consider the different meanings the connotations of the bracketed choices lend these statements:

> By the time I got home I was _____ [sleepy, exhausted, weary, beat, dead].
>
> My boyfriend drives around in a red _____ [car, vehicle, buggy, clunker, jalopy].
>
> I could hear him _____ [shout, yell, bellow, scream, shriek].

Connotations can also be personal and, thus, powerful tools for shaping readers' responses to what you say. Consider the word *pig.* The dictionary definition, or denotation, would read something like this: "A domestic farm animal with a long, broad snout and a thick, fat body covered with coarse bristles." However, the connotation of *pig* is far more provocative, for it suggests someone who looks or acts like a pig; someone who is greedy or filthy; someone who is sexually immoral. (Most dictionaries list the connotations of words, although some connotations might only be found in a dictionary of slang; for example, *The New Dictionary of American Slang,* edited by Robert L. Chapman, or *Slang!* by Paul Dickson.)

There is nothing wrong with using a word because of its connotations, but you must be aware that connotations will have an emotional impact on readers. You don't want to say something unplanned. You don't want to offend readers by using words loaded with unintentional associations. For instance, you wouldn't suggest to advertisers that they "should be more creative when hawking their products" unless you intended to insult them. Although the term *hawking* refers to selling, it is unflattering and misleading because it connotes somebody moving up and down the streets peddling goods by shouting. Linguistically, the word comes from the same root as the word *huckster,* which refers to an aggressive merchant known for haggling and questionable practices.

Connotatively loaded language can be used to create favorable as well as unfavorable reactions. If you are arguing against the use of animals in medical research, you will get a stronger response if you decry the sacrifice of "puppies and kittens" rather than the cooler, scientific, and less charged "laboratory animals."

You can understand why politicians, newspaper columnists, and anyone advocating a cause use connotative language. The loaded word is like a bullet for a writer making a strong argument. Consider the connotative impact of the italicized terms in the following excerpts taken from essays in this text:

> "When you agreed to buy the drink and the muffin you did not take into account the plastic-cup *shakedown*. (Michael Lewis, "The Case Against Tipping," Chapter 1)

> The *menthol exemption* also leaves dangling in political *midair explosive charges* of racism. (Derrick Jackson, "Let's Ban All Flavors of Cigarettes," page 96)

> "The English language has been *hacked and torn apart* in the effort to promote equality, but the result is a disconnection from reality." (Shannon O'Neill, "Literature Hacked and Torn Apart: Censorship in Public Schools," Chapter 9)

Each of the italicized words was selected not for its denotations but its negative connotations. In the first example, Michael Lewis could have simply said "take into account the plastic cup" or said "take into account the plastic tipping cup." Instead he added the word "shakedown" which implies a criminal act of intimidation or extortion on the part of the coffee establishment. Similarly, Derrick Jackson suggests that claims against "menthol exemption" may be "midair explosive charges" of racial discrimination, evoking powerful images of bombs (a punning use of "charges") going off in protest against the government's allowing the cigarettes industry to continue marketing potentially deadly menthol products to African Americans.

Being Specific

To help readers better understand your argument, you need to use words that are precise enough to convey your exact meaning. If you simply say, "The weather last weekend was *terrible*," your readers are left to come up with their own interpretations of what the weather was like. Was it hot and muggy? Cold and rainy? Overcast and very windy? Some of each? Chances are your readers won't come up with the same weather conditions you had in mind. However, if you said, "Last weekend it rained day and night and never got above 40 degrees," readers will have a more precise idea of the weekend's weather. And you will have accomplished your purpose of saying just what you meant.

The terms *general* and *specific* are opposites just as *abstract* and *concrete* are opposites. General words do not name individual things but classes or groups of things: animals, trees, women. Specific words refer to individuals in a group: your pet canary, the oak tree outside your bedroom window, the point guard. Of course, *general* and *specific* are themselves relative terms. Depending on the context or your frame of reference, a word that is specific in one context may be general in another. For instance, there is no need to warn a vegetarian that a restaurant serves veal Oscar and beef Wellington when simply *meat* will do. In other words, there are degrees of specificity appropriate to the situation. The following list illustrates just such a sliding scale, moving downward from the more general to the more specific.

General	animal	person	book	clothing	food	machine
	feline	female	novel	footwear	seafood	vehicle
	cat	singer	American	shoes	fish	fighter jet
Specific	Daisy, my pet	Beyonce	*The Great Gatsby*	her Nikes	tuna	F-17

General words are useful in ordinary conversation when the people you're addressing understand your meaning and usually don't ask for clarification. The same is true in writing when you are addressing an audience familiar with your subject. In such instances, you can get away with occasional broad statements. For example, if you are running for class president, your campaign speeches would not require a great number of specifics as much as general statements of promise and principles:

> If elected, I intend to do what I can to ensure a comfortable classroom environment for each student at this college.

But when your audience is unfamiliar with your subject or when the context requires concrete details, generalities and abstract terms fall flat, leaving people wondering just exactly what you are trying to communicate. Let's say, for instance, you write a note to your dean explaining why you'd like to change the room where your English class meets. You wouldn't get very far on this appeal:

> Room 107 Richards is too small and uncomfortable for our class.

However, if you offer some specifics evoking a sense of the room's unpleasantness, you'd make a more persuasive case for changing the room:

> Room 107 Richards has 20 fixed seats for 27 students, leaving those who come in late to sit on window sills or the floor. Worse still is the air quality. The radiators are fixed on high and the windows don't open. By the end of the hour, it must be 90 degrees in there, leaving everybody sweaty and wilted including Prof. Hazzard.

What distinguishes this paragraph is the use of concrete details: "20 fixed seats for 27 students," latecomers forced to "sit on window sills or on the floor," radiators "fixed on high," "the windows don't open," "90 degrees," and everybody was left "sweaty and wilted including Prof. Hazzard." But more than simply conjuring up a vivid impression of the room's shortcomings, these specifics add substance to your argument for a room change.

Concrete language is specific language—words that have definite meaning. Concrete language names persons, places, and things: *Barack Obama, Mary Shelley, New Zealand, Venice Boulevard, book, toothpaste*. Concrete terms conjure up vivid pictures in the minds of readers because they refer to particular things or qualities that can be perceived by the five senses—that is, they can be seen, smelled, tasted, felt, and heard. Abstract words, in contrast, refer to qualities that do not have a definitive concrete meaning. They denote intangible qualities that cannot be perceived directly by the senses but are inferred from the senses—*powerful, foolish, talented, responsible, worthy*. Abstract words also denote concepts and ideas—*patriotism, beauty, victory, sorrow*. Although abstract terms can be useful depending on the context, writing that relies heavily on abstractions will fail to communicate clear meaning. Notice in the pairs below how concrete and specific details convert vague statements into vivid ones:

Abstract   He was very nicely dressed.

Concrete   He wore a dark gray Armani suit, white pinstriped shirt, and red paisley tie.

Abstract   Jim felt uncomfortable at Jean's celebration party.

Concrete   Jim's envy of Jean's promotion made him feel guilty.

Abstract   That was an incredible accident.

Concrete   A trailer truck jackknifed in the fog, causing seven cars to plow into each other, killing two, injuring eight, and leaving debris for a quarter mile along Route 17.

Abstract language is also relative. It depends on circumstances and the experience of the person using them. A *cold* December morning to someone living in Florida might mean temperatures in the 40s or 50s. To residents of North Dakota, *cold* would designate air at subzero temperatures. It all depends on one's point of view. A *fair trial* might mean one thing to the prosecutor of a case, yet something completely different to the defense attorney. Likewise, what might be *offensive* language to your grandmother would probably not faze an average college student.

When employing abstract language, you need to be aware that readers may not share your point of view. Consequently, you should be careful to clarify your terms or simply select concrete alternatives. Following is an excerpt from a student paper as it appeared in the first draft. As you can see, it is lacking in details and specifics and has a rather dull impact.

> **Vague:** Last year my mother nearly died from medicine when she went to the hospital. The bad reaction sent her into a coma for weeks, requiring life-support systems around the clock. Thankfully, she came out of the coma and was released, but somebody should have at least asked what, if any, allergies she had.

Although the paragraph reads smoothly, it communicates very little of the dramatic crisis being described. Without specific details and concrete words, the reader misses both the trauma and the seriousness of the hospital staff's neglect, thus dulling the argument for stronger safeguards. What follows is the same paragraph revised with the intent of making it more concrete.

> **Revised:** Last year my mother nearly died from a codeine-based painkiller when she was rushed to the emergency room at Emerson Hospital. The severe allergic reaction sent her into a coma for six weeks, requiring daily blood transfusions, thrice weekly kidney dialysis, continuous intravenous medicines, a tracheotomy, and round-the-clock intensive care. Thankfully, she came out of the coma and was released, but the ER staff was negligent in not determining from her or her medical records that she was allergic to codeine.

Using Figurative Language

Words have their literal meaning, but they also can mean something beyond dictionary definitions, as we have seen. The sentence "Mrs. Jones is an angel" does not mean that

Mrs. Jones is literally a supernatural winged creature, but a very kind and pleasant woman. What makes the literally impossible meaningful here is figurative language.

Figurative language (or a **figure of speech**) is comparative language. It is language that represents something in terms of something else—in figures, symbols, or likeness (Mrs. Jones and an angel). It functions to make the ordinary appear extraordinary and the unfamiliar appear familiar. It also adds richness and complexity to abstractions. Here, for instance, is a rather bland literal statement: "Yesterday it was 96 degrees and very humid." Here's that same sentence rendered in figurative language: "Yesterday the air was like warm glue." What this version does is equate yesterday's humid air to glue on a feature shared by each—stickiness. And the result is more interesting than the original statement.

The comparison of humid air to glue is linked by the words *like*. This example represents one of the most common figures of speech, the simile. Derived from the Latin *similis,* the term means similar. A simile makes an explicit comparison between dissimilar things (humid air and glue). It says that *A* is like *B* in one or more respects. The connectives used in similes are most often the words *like, as,* and *than:*

- A school of minnows shot by me like pelting rain.
- His arms are as big as hams.
- They're meaner than junkyard dogs.

When the connectives *like, as,* or *than* are omitted, then we have another common figure of speech, the **metaphor.** The term is from the Greek *meta* (over) + *pherin* (to carry or ferry) meaning to carry over meaning from one thing to another. Instead of saying that A is like B, a metaphor equates them—A *is* B. For example, Mrs. Jones and an angel are said to be one and the same, although we all know that literally the two are separate entities.

- This calculus problem is a real pain in the neck.
- The crime in this city is a cancer out of control.
- The space shuttle was a flaming arrow in the sky.

Sometimes writers will carelessly combine metaphors that don't go with each other. Known as **mixed metaphors,** these often produce ludicrous results. For example:

- The heat of his expression froze them in their tracks.
- The experience left a bad taste in her eyes.
- The arm of the law has two strikes against it.

When a metaphor has lost its figurative value, it is called a **dead metaphor:** the *mouth* of a river, the *eye* of a needle, the *face* of a clock. Originally these expressions functioned as figures of speech, but their usage has become so common in our language that many have become **clichés** ("golden opportunity," "dirt cheap," "a clinging vine"). More will be said about clichés later, but our best advice is to avoid them. Because they have lost their freshness, they're unimaginative and they dull your writing.

Another common figure of speech is **personification,** in which human or animal characteristics or qualities are attributed to inanimate things or ideas. We hear it all the time: Trees *bow* in the wind; fear *grips* the heart; high pressure areas *sit* on the Northeast.

Such language is effective in making abstract concepts concrete and vivid and possibly more interesting:

■ Graft and corruption walk hand in hand in this town.
■ The state's new tax law threatens to gobble up our savings.
■ Nature will give a sigh of relief the day they close down that factory.

As with other figures of speech, personification must be used appropriately and with restraint. If it's overdone, it ends up calling undue attention to itself while leaving readers baffled:

Drugs have slouched their way into our schoolyards and playgrounds, laughing up their sleeves at the law and whispering vicious lies to innocent children.

For the sake of sounding literary, drugs here are personified as pushers slouching, laughing, and whispering. But such an exaggeration runs the risk of being rejected by readers as pretentious. If this happens, the vital message may well be lost. One must also be careful not to take shortcuts. Like dead metaphors, many once-imaginative personifications have become clichés: "justice is blind," "virtue triumphed," "walking death." While such may be handy catch phrases, they are trite and would probably be dismissed by critical readers as lazy writing.

Another figure of speech worth mentioning is the **euphemism,** which is a polite way of saying something blunt or offensive. Instead of toilets, restaurants have *restrooms.* Instead of a salesperson, furniture stores send us *mattress technicians.* Instead of false teeth, people in advertisements wear *dentures.* The problem with euphemisms is that they conceal the true meaning of something. The result can be a kind of double-talk—language inflated for the sake of deceiving the listener. Business and government are notorious for such practices. When workers are laid off, corporations talk about *restructuring* or *downsizing.* A few years ago, the federal government announced *a revenue enhancement* when it really meant that taxes were going up; likewise, the Environmental Protection Agency referred to acid rain as *poorly buffered precipitation*; and when the CIA ordered a *nondiscernible microbinoculator,* it got a poison dart. Not only are such concoctions pretentious, they are dishonest. Fancy-sounding language camouflages hard truths.

Fancy-sounding language also has no place in good writing. When euphemisms are overdone, the result is a lot of verbiage and little meaning. Consider the following example before the euphemisms and pretentious language are reduced:

Overdone: In the event that gaming industry establishments be rendered legal, law enforcement official spokespersons have identified a potential crisis situation as the result of influence exerted by the regional career-offender cartel.

Readers may have to review this a few times before they understand what's being said. Even if they don't give up, a reader's job is not to rewrite your words. Writing with clarity and brevity shows respect for your audience. Here is the same paragraph with its pretentious wordiness and euphemisms edited down:

Revised: Should casino gambling be legalized, police fear organized crime may take over.

Of course, not all euphemisms are double-talk concoctions. Some may be necessary to avoid sounding insensitive or causing pain. To show respect in a sympathy card to bereaved survivors, it might be more appropriate to use the expression *passed away* instead of the blunt *died*. Recently, terms such as *handicapped* or *cripple* have given way to less derogatory replacements such as *a person with disabilities*. Likewise, we hear *a person with AIDS* instead of *AIDS victim*, which reduces the person to a disease or a label.

As with metaphors and personification, some euphemisms have passed into the language and become artifacts, making their usage potentially stale. People over age 65 are no longer "old" or "elderly," they're *senior citizens;* slums are *substandard housing;* the poor are *socially disadvantaged*. Although such euphemisms grew out of noble intentions, they tend to abstract reality. A Jules Feiffer cartoon from a few years ago captured the problem well. It showed a man talking to himself:

> I used to think I was poor. Then they told me I wasn't poor, I was needy. They told me it was self-defeating to think of myself as needy, I was deprived. Then they told me underprivileged was overused. I was disadvantaged. I still don't have a dime. But I have a great vocabulary.

Although euphemisms were created to take the bite off reality, they can also take the bite out of your writing if not used appropriately. As Feiffer implies, sometimes it's better to say it like it is; depending on the context, "poor" simply might have more bite than some sanitized cliché. Similarly, some old people resent being called "seniors" not just because the term is an overused label, but because it abstracts the condition of old age. Our advice regarding euphemisms is to know when they are appropriate and to use them sparingly. Good writing simply means knowing when the right expression will get the response you want.

Avoiding Clichés

A cliché (or trite expression) is a phrase that is old and overused to the point of being unoriginal and stale. At one time, clichés were fresh and potent; overuse has left them flat. In speech, we may resort to clichés for quick meaning. However, clichés can dull your writing and make you seem lazy for choosing a phrase on tap rather than trying to think of more original and colorful wording. Consider these familiar examples:

apple of his eye
bigger than both of us
climbing the walls
dead as a doornail
head over heels
last but not least
mind over matter
ripe old age
short but sweet
white as a ghost

The problem with clichés is that they fail to communicate anything unique. To say you were "climbing the walls," for example, is an expression that could fit a wide variety of contradictory meanings. Out of context, it could mean that you were in a state of high anxiety, anger, frustration, excitement, fear, happiness, or unhappiness. Even in context, the expression is dull. Furthermore, because such clichés are ready-made and instantly handy, they blot out the exact detail you intended to convey to your reader.

Clichés are the refuge of writers who don't make the effort to come up with fresh and original expressions. To avoid them, we recommend being alert for any phrases you have heard many times before and coming up with fresh substitutes. Consider the following brief paragraph, which is full of clichés marked in italics, and its revision:

> **Trite:** *In this day and age,* a university ought to be concerned with ensuring that its women students take courses that will strengthen their understanding of their own past achievements and future *hopes and dreams.* At the same time, any school *worth its salt* should be *ready and able* to provide *hands-on experience,* activities, and courses that reflect a commitment to diversity and inclusiveness. Education must *seize the opportunity* of leading us *onward and upward* so that we don't slide back to the male-only curriculum emphasis of the *days of old.*

> **Revised:** A university today ought to be concerned with ensuring that its women students take courses that will strengthen their understanding of their own past achievements and future possibilities. At the same time, any decent school should provide experience, activities, and courses that reflect a commitment to diversity and inclusiveness. Education must lead us forward so that we don't revert to the male-only curriculum emphasis of the past.

Defining Technical Terms

Special or technical vocabulary that is not clear from the context can function as an instant roadblock to freely flowing communication between you and your readers—sympathetic to your views or not. You cannot expect a novice in political science to know the meaning of *hegemony* or a nonmedical person to know exactly what you mean by *nephrological necrosis.* To avoid alienating nonexpert readers, you'll have to define such uncommon terms.

You can do so without being obtrusive or disrupting the flow of your writing with "time-outs" here and there to define terms. Notice how smoothly definition has been slipped into the following passage:

> "In fact, the phenomenon is known as recidivism—that is, a convict re-offends after having been released from confinement." (Arthur Allen, "Prayer in Prison: Religion as Rehabilitation")

Clarifying Familiar Terms

Even some familiar terms can lead to misunderstanding because they are used in so many different ways with so many different meanings: *liberal, Native American, lifestyle, decent, active.* It all depends on who is using the word. For instance, to an environmentalist the expression *big business* might connote profit-hungry and sinister industrial conglomerates that pollute the elements; to a conservative, however, the phrase might mean the commercial and industrial establishment that drives our economy. Likewise, *liberal* does not mean the same thing to a Democrat as it does to a Republican. Even if you're writing for a sympathetic audience, be as precise as you can about familiar terms. Remember the advice of novelist George Eliot: "We have all got to remain calm, and call things by the same names other people call them by."

Stipulating Definitions

For a word that doesn't have a fixed or standard meaning, writers often offer a *stipulative* definition that explains what they mean by the term. For instance, *Merriam-Webster's Dictionary* offers two standard definitions of *consumerism*: (1) the "promotion of the consumer's interests"; and (2) "the theory that an increasing consumption of goods is economically desirable; *also* : a preoccupation with and an inclination toward the buying of consumer goods."* But in the essay, "Spent: America After Consumerism" (Chapter 10), author Amitai Etzioni offers this stipulative definition: "Consumerism: the obsession with acquisition." The term *obsession* takes the standard definition a few steps further into darker, disturbing connotations that beyond basic "consumption" or preoccupation with goods. Drawing from Abraham Maslow's "hierarchy of human needs," Etzioni says that once fundamental creature comforts ("safety, shelter, food, clothing, health care, education") have been sated, people get satisfaction "from affection, self-esteem, and, finally, self-actualization." However, Etzioni decries the current trend to satisfy these higher needs by the acquisition of more and more goods, including pricey brand names that many people can barely afford. This is when "consumerism becomes a social disease." It is this stipulative meaning that drives his discussion in the essay.

Writers also offer stipulative definitions for terms that are used for the first time. This is done to communicate a new concept. Oftentimes the invented term is unusual but catchy. In the same Etzioni essay, the author invents the term *megalogues*—a term coined from the prefix *mega-* meaning "very large"(literally *million*) and suffix *-logues* to mean "discourse"—as in *monologue* or *dialogue*. Etzioni stipulates the term to mean a dominant social discussion involving "millions of members of a society exchanging views with one another at workplaces, during family gatherings, in the media, and at public events." He further stipulates that "megalogues" are "often contentious and passionate, and . . . tend to lead to changes in a society's culture and its members' behavior." Past examples are women's rights and minority; more recent examples are the rights for gays to marry and the legitimacy of the 2003 invasion of Iraq.

Sometimes authors will take common words and invent a new term that stipulates a hybrid definition. One such example is *child-man* in the essay "Child-Man in the Promised Land" (Chapter 11). Here social critic Kay S. Hymowitz argues that adolescence in males today has been extended. Forty years ago, most men got married and started families by the time they were in their mid-20s. Today, however, the average age of marriage and family is dramatically older. And the reason is that today's single young men are in no hurry to grow up. These are what Hymowitz calls the "child-men"—males who prefer hanging out in "semi-hormonal adolescence and . . . self-reliance." This new hybrid group of single young males (or SYM) consists of single twentysomething college-educated males who prefer "to hang out in a playground of drinking, hooking up, playing Halo 3, and, in many cases, underachieving." She goes on to say they share interests in "stupid fun," anti-social behavior, and "gross-out humor." They're drawn to high-tech gadgets and video games; they prefer "battling cyborgs, exploding toilets, and the NFL" to serious dramas; and they're very much at home on the Internet. While the media and marketplace encourage this restless "Peter Pan" syndrome, Hymowitz is concerned that today's "child-men" not only avoid marriage but "any deep attachments."

---

*Definition of Consumerism. By permission. From Merriam-Webster's Collegiate ® Dictionary, 11th Edition. © 2013 by Merriam-Webster, Inc. (www.Merriam-Webster.com).

In fact, she says, they fear commitment. "[T]hey can't stand to think of themselves as permanently attached to one woman."

Stipulating your terms is like making a contract with your reader: You set down in black and white the important terms and their limits. The result is that you eliminate any misunderstanding and reduce your own vulnerability. And that can make the difference between a weak and a potent argument.

Avoiding Overdefinition

Where do you stop explaining and begin assuming your reader knows what you mean? What terms are "technical" or "specialized" or "important" enough to warrant definition? You certainly don't want to define terms unnecessarily or to oversimplify. In so doing, you run the risk of dulling the thrust of your claims while insulting the intelligence of your readers. Just how to strike a balance is a matter of good judgment about the needs and capabilities of your audience.

A good rule of thumb is to assume that your readers are almost as knowledgeable as you. This way, you minimize the risk of patronizing them. Another rule of thumb is the synonym test. If you can think of a word or short phrase that is an exact synonym for some specialized or important term in your argument, you probably don't need to define it. However, if you need a long phrase or sentence to paraphrase the term, you may want to work in a definition; it could be needed. And don't introduce your definitions with clauses like "As I'm sure you know" or "You don't need to be told that." If the audience didn't need to know it, you wouldn't be telling them, and if they do know what the terms mean, you may insult their intelligence with such condescending introductions.

Using Sarcasm and Humor Sparingly

Although we caution you against using sarcasm or humor too often, there are times when they can be very effective techniques of persuasion. Writers will often bring out their barbs for the sake of drawing blood from the opposition and snickers from the sympathetic. But artful sarcasm must be done with care. Too strong, and you run the risk of trivializing the issue or alienating your audience with a bad joke. Too vague or esoteric, and nobody will catch the joke. It's probably safest to use these touches when you are writing for a sympathetic audience; they're most likely to appreciate your wit. There is no rule of thumb here. Like any writer, you'll have to decide when to use these techniques and how to work them in artfully.

Review: To Choose Your Words Carefully . . .

- Consider both denotative and connotative meanings.
- Be as specific and concrete as your context requires.
- Use figurative language to add richness and complexity.
- Check figurative language for precision and clarity.
- Be alert for clichés and unnecessary euphemisms.
- Define technical terms that are not clear from the context.
- Define familiar terms and terms with multiple meanings.

EXERCISES

1. Let's say you were assigned to write a position paper defending the construction of a nuclear power plant in your state. What special appeals would you make were you to address your paper to the governor? To residents living next to the site where the proposed plant is to be built? To prospective construction workers and general contractors? To local environmentalists?

2. Choose one of the following claims, then list in sentence form three reasons supporting the argument. When you've finished, list in sentence form three reasons in opposition to the claim:

   ▨ Snowboarders are a menace to skiers.
   ▨ To save lives, a 55-mile-per-hour speed limit should be enforced nationwide.
   ▨ Condoms should be advertised on television.
   ▨ Students with drug convictions should be denied federally subsidized student aid.

3. Let's assume you have made up your mind on gun control. Write a brief letter to the editor of your local newspaper stating your views on the issue. In your letter, fairly and accurately represent arguments of the opposition while pointing out any logical weaknesses, flaws, impracticalities, and other problems you see. What different emphasis would your letter have were it to appear in a gun owner's newsletter? In a pro–gun control newsletter?

4. Write a letter to your parents explaining why you need an extra hundred dollars of spending money this month.

5. Each of the following sentences will take on a different meaning depending on the connotations of the words in brackets. Explain how each choice colors the writer's attitude and the reader's reaction to the statement.

   ▨ Sally's style of dress is really [weird, exotic, unusual].
   ▨ If a factory is [polluting, stinking up, fouling] the air over your house, you have a right to sue.
   ▨ Anyone who thinks that such words have no effect is [unaware, ignorant, unconscious] of political history.
   ▨ The anti-immigration passion being stirred up in this country has become [popular, trendy, common].
   ▨ It was clear from the way she [stomped, marched, stepped] out of the room how she felt about the decision.

6. Identify the figures of speech used in the following sentences from essays in this book. In each example, note the two things being compared and explain why you think the comparisons are appropriate or not:

   ▨ "But such a Faustian bargain is an ominous precedent in public health and political ethics." (Gio Batta Gori, "The Bogus 'Science' of Secondary Smoke")
   ▨ "Biographies have metamorphosed into demonographies whose authors don't just portray their subjects' warts and all, but set out to dig up as much dirt as possible, as if the story of a person's life is contained in the warts, only the warts, and nothing but the warts." (Deborah Tannen, "Taking a 'War of Words' Too Literally")

■ "Many colleges and universities simply wink at the activities of the fraternities and claim no responsibility." (Henry Wechsler, "Binge Drinking Must Be Stopped")

■ "And so in 1990 it was decided to put a tasteful and discreet cup on the counter. It's a way for our customers to say thanks to our partners." (Michael Lewis, "The Case Against Tipping")

■ "Just as planes and ships disappear mysteriously into the Bermuda Triangle, so do the selves of girls go down in droves." (Mary Pipher, "Saplings in the Storm")

■ "Natural selection cannot push the buttons of behavior directly; it affects our behavior by endowing us with emotions that coax us toward adaptive choices." (Steven Pinker, "Why They Kill Their Newborns")

■ "As cancer-stick observers know Big Tobacco did not mind closing the candy store on cigarettes flavored like Hershey's or Life Savers." (Derrick Jackson, "Ban All Flavors of Cigarettes")

■ "If unchecked, we could find ourselves in a time when it's acceptable for books, like 'witches,' to be burned." (Shannon O'Neill, "Literature Hacked and Torn Apart: Censorship in Public Schools")

7. Rewrite the following paragraph to eliminate the clichés and trite expressions.

It is not that we don't care about what goes on up in space; it's that the vast majority of red-blooded Americans are hard put to see what these untold billions of dollars can do. While great strides have been made in space research, we ask ourselves: Is life any safer? Are material goods all the more abundant? Are we living to a ripe old age because of these vast expenditures? Beyond the shadow of a doubt, the answer is a resounding no. Those in Congress with a vested interest need to be brought back to reality, for the nation's pressing problems of crime, homelessness, and unemployment are right here on Mother Earth. Nothing is sacred including the budget for NASA, which should follow the footsteps of other programs and be slashed across the board. Yes, that will be a rude awakening to some who will have to bite the bullet, but there are just so many tax dollars to go around. And in the total scheme of things, wasting it on exploring the depths of outer space is not the way it should be.

5

Shaping Arguments: Thinking Like an Architect

LEARNING OBJECTIVES

After studying this chapter, you should be able to:

1. Identify and explain the basic three-part structure of an argument paper. (p. 117)
2. Show how to construct a formal outline of an argument essay. (p. 127)
3. Identify and describe the features of the two basic types of arguments. (p. 128)
4. Describe how and when narrative arguments make effective cases for controversial issues. (p. 151)

Just as there is no best way to build a house, there is no best way to structure an argument. Some essays take an *inductive* approach. Such an essay begins with a specific circumstance and then presents reasons and evidence in support of or in opposition to that circumstance. For example, someone may point out that it is perfectly legal to own and walk a pit bull on a leash. However, given the breed's record for viciousness, ownership should not be allowed. Other arguments adopt a *deductive* approach, which begin with an idea or philosophical principle, move to a specific circumstance, then conclude with why that circumstance is right and should be maintained or wrong and should be changed. For example, it is assumed that domesticated animals should not present a threat to the safety of people in the community. Therefore, someone may argue that pit bulls, a potentially dangerous breed, should not be allowed as domesticated pets.

Some essays express their conclusions in the opening paragraphs. Others build up to them in the last paragraph. Still others make use of narrative in part or as a whole—that is, a story or series of episodes or anecdotes structured on a timeline. The effect is to dramatize the criteria of the author's argument rather than to argue them explicitly from point to point. As an architect designing a blueprint will tell you, the structure of a building depends on the site, the construction crew, and the prospective owners. Arguments are the same. Depending on your topic, your goals, and your readers, you'll write very different kinds of arguments.

Although no two arguments look alike, every argument has three basic structural parts: a beginning, a middle, and an end. This isn't a simplistic definition. As in architecture, each part of a structure is there for a purpose; leave out one of the parts, and the whole collapses. So let's look at those parts and the jobs they do.

Components of an Argument

What follows is an organizational pattern for argument papers—a pattern to which, with some variations, most of the essays in this book conform. We offer it to help you plan your own argument papers. Although this model provides the structure, framework, and components of most arguments, it is not a formula written in stone. You should not feel bound to follow it every time you construct an argument. In fact, you might find it more effective to move blocks of writing around or to omit material. For instance, on issues unfamiliar to your readers, it might make sense to begin with background information so the context of your discussion will be understood. With familiar issues, it might be more persuasive to open with responses to opposing views. On especially controversial topics, you might wish to reserve your responses for the main body of the paper. Or, for dramatic effect, you might decide to save your responses until the very end, thereby emphasizing your consideration of other perspectives. As a writer, you're free to modify this model any way you like; or you may want to try different models in different drafts of your paper to see which arrangement works best in each case. As with building houses, your choices in building arguments are numerous.

The Beginning

The beginning of your argument accomplishes, in a small space, three important goals:

■ It introduces you, the writer. Here your audience meets you—senses your tone, your attitude toward your subject, and the general style of the piece.
■ It appeals to your readers' reason, emotions, and/or sense of ethics. This can be done in a simple value statement, an anecdote, or some high-impact statistics intended to raise your readers' interest and concern.
■ It identifies the topic and indicates your stand.

Depending on the issue and the audience, the beginning of an argument can be several paragraphs in length. In most arguments, the beginning will end with a clear statement of the claim you are making—your thesis.

Although "Once upon a time . . ." is probably the most remembered introduction, it's not always the most effective; more ingenuity on your part is needed to "hook" your readers. For example, in *The Village Voice,* columnist Nat Hentoff began a column calling for eliminating duplication in the U.S. military by saying that he had telephoned the Pentagon press office for a comment on the subject. "Oh," said the officer with whom he spoke, "You want the *other* press office." As Hentoff remarked, he could have ended the column at that point; instead, he went on to develop his idea, confident that this introductory example would make his readers sympathetic to his point.

Composing good beginnings requires hard work. That's why many writers keep a journal in which they copy the strategies of writers they admire; that's how we happened to have a copy of Hentoff's introduction. As beginning arguers, you may want to develop your own repertoire of start-up strategies by copying strategies you admire into your own argument journal.

The Middle

The middle portion of your argument is where you do the argumentative work: presenting your information, responding to other views, making your case. If you think of it in terms of building construction, here's where you pour a foundation and lay the framework; put in all the walls, floors, and systems; and have the building inspector examine your work. There are a number of substages.

Provide Background Information

Before you can begin presenting your reasons, you want to be sure that your audience has the information necessary to understand the issue. Background information should answer any of the following questions depending on your topic:

- How significant is the issue? How many people are affected by it? Who are the people most affected?
- What facts, statistics, or information do your readers need to know to follow your reasons?
- What terminology or key words need to be defined so your readers will understand your meaning?
- What factors have caused the problem or situation to develop?
- What will be the consequences if the situation is not corrected?

If handled correctly, this part of your essay can be the most persuasive and convincing because it lets your readers know why you are concerned and the reasons behind that concern. Moreover, it gives your readers the opportunity to share your concern. For example, in "Let's Ban All Flavors of Cigarettes," Derrick Z. Jackson begins his essay with the claim that the Food and Drug Administration's recent ban of fruit-flavored cigarettes is a good but negligible start toward prevention compared to a ban that would include mentholated cigarettes. He wonders cynically if the government is more interested in state and federal tax revenue. His statistics are grimly persuasive: fruit-flavored cigarettes represent less than 1 percent of the market compared to menthol, which makes up 30 percent of the $87 billion market, generating over $25 billion in tax revenue.

Respond to Other Points of View

As we discussed in Chapter 4, it is important to let your audience know that you have seriously deliberated other points of view before reaching your own position. By doing this, you appear informed and open-minded. In this part of your essay, you should briefly review a number of viewpoints that are different from your own. If you've engaged in debate and dialogue, as we suggested in Chapter 1, you should be aware of opposing views and common concerns. Now is your opportunity to identify them and respond. You might even acknowledge the sincerity of those holding contrary views and cite the merits of their positions. Such acknowledgments help establish your authority as a writer. They will also help you define your own position more specifically for your readers by contrasting it with others.

Present Reasons in Support of Your Claim

The reasons supporting your claim comprise the heart of your essay and, therefore, its largest portion. Here you explain those reasons and present supporting evidence—facts, statistics, data, testimony of authorities, examples—to convince your readers to agree with your position or take a particular course of action. Depending on the issue, this part of your essay usually takes several paragraphs, with each reason clearly delineated for your readers.

Anticipate Possible Objections to Your Reasons

Even with a friendly audience, readers will have questions and concerns about your reasons. If you ignore these objections and leave them unanswered, you will weaken the effectiveness of your argument. Therefore, it is always wise to anticipate possible objections so you can respond to them in a constructive fashion that will strengthen and clarify your ideas. The kind of objections you anticipate, of course, will depend on your familiarity with your audience—their interests, values, beliefs, experiences, and so on. If you have carefully analyzed your audience, as suggested in Chapter 4, you will be more aware of the objections likely to surface in response to your reasons. Raising objections and responding to them will once again demonstrate your awareness of alternative viewpoints. It will also give you an opportunity to strengthen your reasons and increase your credibility.

The End

The end is usually a short paragraph or two in which you conclude your argument. Essentially, your ending summarizes your argument by reaffirming your stand on the issue. It might also make an appeal to your readers to take action. Some writers include an anecdote, a passionate summation, or even a quiet but resonant sentence. Lincoln's

Review: The Structure of an Argument

The Beginning . . .
- Introduces you as a writer
- States the problem
- Establishes your position and appeal
- Presents your claim (thesis)

The Middle . . .
- Provides background information
- Responds to other points of view
- Presents arguments supporting the claim
- Anticipates possible objections

The End . . .
- Summarizes your position and implications
- Invites readers to share your conclusion and/or take action

"Gettysburg Address," for example, ends with the quiet "government of the people, by the people, and for the people . . . ," which is one of the most memorable phrases in American political history. Looking over the essays in this book, you will find that no two end quite alike. As a writer, you have many choices; experimentation is usually the best way to decide what will work for you. Many writers copy effective conclusions into their journals so they can refresh their memories when writing their own arguments.

SAMPLE ARGUMENT FOR ANALYSIS

To illustrate this three-part argument structure, we have included two sample argument essays for you to read. The first is "Skeletons in the Attic" by Clara Spotted Elk, a consultant for Native American interests. Although it is quite brief, the essay, published in the *New York Times,* contains all the essential components of an argument essay. It is followed by an analysis of its key structural features.

Skeletons in the Attic
Clara Spotted Elk

1   Millions of American Indians lived in this country when Columbus first landed on our shores. After the western expansion, only about 250,000 Indians survived. What happened to the remains of those people who were decimated by the advance of the white man? Many are gathering dust in American museums.

2   In 1985, I and some Northern Cheyenne chiefs visited the attic of the Smithsonian's Natural History Museum in Washington to review the inventory of their Cheyenne collection. After a chance inquiry, a curator pulled out a drawer in one of the scores of cabinets that line the attic. There were the jumbled bones of an Indian. "A Kiowa," he said.

3   Subsequently, we found that 18,500 Indian remains—some consisting of a handful of bones, but mostly full skeletons—are unceremoniously stored in the Smithsonian's nooks and crannies. Other museums, individuals and federal agencies such as the National Park Service also collect the bones of Indian warriors, women, and children. Some are on display as roadside tourist attractions. It is estimated that another 600,000 Indian remains are secreted away in locations across the country.

4   The museum community and forensic scientists vigorously defend these grisly collections. With few exceptions, they refuse to return remains to the tribes that wish to rebury them, even when grave robbing has been documented. They want to maintain adequate numbers of "specimens" for analysis and say they are dedicated to "the permanent curation of Indian skeletal remains."

5   Indian people are tired of being "specimens." The Northern Cheyenne word for ourselves is "tsistsistas"—human beings. Like people the world over, one of our greatest responsibilities is the proper care of the dead.

6   We are outraged that our religious views are not accepted by the scientific community and that the graves of our ancestors are desecrated. Many tribes are willing to

accommodate some degree of study for a limited period of time—provided that it would help Indian people or mankind in general. But how many "specimens" are needed? We will not accept grave robbing and the continued hoarding of our ancestors' remains.

7   Would this nefarious collecting be tolerated if it were discovered that it affected other ethnic groups? (Incidentally, the Smithsonian also collects skeletons of blacks.) What would happen if the Smithsonian had 18,500 Holocaust victims in the attic? There would be a tremendous outcry in this country. Why is there no outcry about the Indian collection?

8   Indians are not exotic creatures for study. We are human beings who practice living religions. Our religion should be placed not only on a par with science when it comes to determining the disposition of our ancestors but on a par with every other religion practiced in this country.

9   To that end, Sen. Daniel K. Inouye will soon reintroduce the "Bones Bill" to aid Indians in retrieving the remains of their ancestors from museums. As in the past, the "Bones Bill" will most likely be staunchly resisted by the collectors of Indian skeletons—armed with slick lobbyists, lots of money and cloaked in the mystique of science.

10   Scientists have attempted to defuse this issue by characterizing their opponents as radical Indians, out of touch with the culture and with little appreciation of science. Armed only with a moral obligation to our ancestors, the Indians who support the bill have few resources and little money.

11   But, in my view, the issue should concern all Americans—for it raises very disturbing questions. American Indians want only to reclaim and rebury their dead. Is this too much to ask?

Analyzing the Structure

Now let's examine this essay according to the organizational features discussed so far.

The Beginning

Paragraph 1 clearly introduces the nature of the problem: The remains of the Indians "decimated by the advance of the white man" have wrongfully ended up "gathering dust in American museums." It isn't until paragraph 6 that Spotted Elk spells out her position: "We are outraged that our religious views are not accepted by the scientific community and that the graves of our ancestors are desecrated." (Because this essay was written for newspaper publication, the paragraphs are shorter than they might be in a formal essay; you may not want to delay your thesis until the sixth paragraph in a longer essay.) Notice, too, that in the introduction the author's persona begins to assert itself in the brief and pointed summation of the American Indians' fate. When Spotted Elk mentions the staggering decline in the population of her ancestors, we sense a note of controlled but righteous anger in her voice. Citation of the gruesome facts of history also appeals to the reader's ethical sense by prompting reflection on the Indians' demise.

The Middle

■ **Background Information**   Paragraphs 2 and 3 establish the context of the author's complaint. Paragraph 2 is personal testimony to the problem—how she and other Native Americans viewed unceremonious "jumbled bones" in the museum drawer and were stunned by the representative insensitivity of their host curator, who treated the human remains as if they were a fossil. Paragraph 3 projects the problem to progressively larger contexts and magnitudes—from the single Kiowa in a drawer to the 18,500 in the Smithsonian at large; from that institution's collection to the estimated 600,000 remains in other museums, federal agencies and institutions, and "roadside tourist attractions." The broader scope of the problem is underscored here.

■ **Response to Other Points of View**   In paragraph 4, Spotted Elk tersely sums up the opposing position of the "museum community and forensic scientists": "they refuse to return remains to the tribes." She also states their reasoning: "They want to maintain adequate numbers of 'specimens' for analysis and say they are dedicated to the 'permanent curation of Indian skeletal remains.'"

■ **Reasons in Support of the Claim**   Paragraphs 5 through 9 constitute the heart of Spotted Elk's argument. Here she most forcefully argues her objections and offers her reasons with supporting details: Indians resent being treated as specimens and want to bury their dead as do other religious people (paragraphs 5 and 6). She follows with a concession that many Indians would accommodate some degree of anthropological study for a period of time, but do not approve of the huge permanent collections that now fill museums.

In paragraph 7, the author continues to support her claim that American Indians have been discriminated against with regard to the disposition of ancestral remains. She writes that there would be a public outcry if the remains of other ethnic groups such as Holocaust victims were hoarded. Her proposal for change appears in paragraph 8: "Our religion should be placed not only on a par with science when it comes to determining the disposition of our ancestors but on a par with every other religion practiced in this country." This is the logical consequence of the problem she has addressed to this point. That proposal logically leads into paragraph 9, where she mentions efforts by Senator Daniel Inouye to see the "Bones Bill" passed into law. Throughout, Spotted Elk uses emotional words and phrases—*grisly, unceremoniously, slick lobbyists, cloaked in mystique*—to reinforce her points.

■ **Anticipation of Possible Objections**   In paragraph 10, the author addresses objections of the opposition, in this case those "[s]cientists [who] have attempted to defuse this issue by characterizing their opponents as radical Indians, out of touch with the culture and with little appreciation of science." She refutes all three charges (of being "radical," as well as out of touch with Indian culture and science) with the phrase "[a]rmed only with a moral obligation to our ancestors"—a phrase that reaffirms her strong connection with her culture. On the contrary, it is science that is out of touch with the "living religion" of Native Americans.

The End

The final paragraph brings closure to the argument. Briefly the author reaffirms her argument that Native Americans "want only to reclaim and rebury their dead." The question that makes up the final line of the essay is more than rhetorical, for it reminds us of the point introduced back in paragraph 5—that American Indians are no different than any other religious people with regard to the disposition of their ancestors. A powerful question brings the essay's conclusion into sharp focus.

As we stated in the beginning of this chapter, there is no best structure for an argument essay. As you develop your own essay, you may find it more effective to move certain structural features to locations that serve your purposes better. For instance, you may find that background information is more persuasive when you include it as support for a particular reason rather than provide it prior to your reasons. Possible objections might be raised along with each reason instead of saved for later. Ron Karpati's essay, "I Am the Enemy," provides a good example of a different approach to structuring an argument essay. Read the essay to see if you can pick out the structural elements he included and how he organized them. Following the essay, we've provided a brief analysis of its organization.

SAMPLE ARGUMENT FOR ANALYSIS

I Am the Enemy
Ron Karpati

> Ron Karpati, a pediatrician and medical researcher of childhood illnesses, defends the use of animals in medical research. This article first appeared in *Newsweek*'s "My Turn" column.

1 I am the enemy! One of those vilified, inhumane physician-scientists involved in animal research. How strange, for I have never thought of myself as an evil person. I became a pediatrician because of my love for children and my desire to keep them healthy. During medical school and residency, however, I saw many children die of leukemia, prematurity and traumatic injury—circumstances against which medicine has made tremendous progress, but still has far to go. More important, I also saw children, alive and healthy, thanks to advances in medical science such as infant respirators, potent antibiotics, new surgical techniques and the entire field of organ transplantation. My desire to tip the scales in favor of the healthy, happy children drew me to medical research.

2 My accusers claim that I inflict torture on animals for the sole purpose of career advancement. My experiments supposedly have no relevance to medicine and are easily replaced by computer simulation. Meanwhile, an apathetic public barely watches, convinced that the issue has no significance, and publicity-conscious politicians increasingly give way to the demands of the activists.

3 We in medical research have also been unconscionably apathetic. We have allowed the most extreme animal-rights protesters to seize the initiative and frame the issue as one of "animal fraud." We have been complacent in our belief that a knowledgeable public would sense the importance of animal research to the public health. Perhaps we have been mistaken in not responding to the emotional tone of the argument created by those sad posters of animals by waving equally sad posters of children dying of leukemia or cystic fibrosis.

4   Much is made of the pain inflicted on these animals in the name of medical science. The animal-rights activists contend that this is evidence of our malevolent and sadistic nature. A more reasonable argument, however, can be advanced in our defense. Life is often cruel, both to animals and human beings. Teenagers get thrown from the back of a pickup truck and suffer severe head injuries. Toddlers, barely able to walk, find themselves at the bottom of a swimming pool while a parent checks the mail. Physicians hoping to alleviate the pain and suffering these tragedies cause have but three choices: create an animal model of the injury or disease and use that model to understand the process and test new therapies; experiment on human beings—some experiments will succeed, most will fail—or finally, leave medical knowledge static, hoping that accidental discoveries will lead us to the advances.

5   Some animal-rights activists would suggest a fourth choice, claiming that computer models can simulate animal experiments, thus making the actual experiments unnecessary. Computers can simulate, reasonably well, the effects of well-understood principles on complex systems, as in the application of the laws of physics to airplane and automobile design. However, when the principles themselves are in question, as is the case with the complex biological systems under study, computer modeling alone is of little value.

6   One of the terrifying effects of the effort to restrict the use of animals in medical research is that the impact will not be felt for years and decades: drugs that might have been discovered will not be; surgical techniques that might have been developed will not be, and fundamental biological processes that might have been understood will remain mysteries. There is the danger that politically expedient solutions will be found to placate a vocal minority, while the consequences of these decisions will not be apparent until long after the decisions are made and the decision making forgotten.

7   Fortunately, most of us enjoy good health, and the trauma of watching one's child die has become a rare experience. Yet our good fortune should not make us unappreciative of the health we enjoy or the advances that make it possible. Vaccines, antibiotics, insulin and drugs to treat heart disease, hypertension and stroke are all based on animal research. Most complex surgical procedures, such as coronary-artery bypass and organ transplantation, are initially developed in animals. Presently undergoing animal studies are techniques to insert genes in humans in order to replace the defective ones found to be the cause of so much disease. These studies will effectively end if animal research is severely restricted.

8   In America today, death has become an event isolated from our daily existence—out of the sight and thoughts of most of us. As a doctor who has watched many children die, and their parents grieve, I am particularly angered by people capable of so much compassion for a dog or a cat, but with seemingly so little for a dying human being. These people seem so insulated from the reality of human life and death and what it means.

9   Make no mistake, however: I am not advocating the needlessly cruel treatment of animals. To the extent that the animal-rights movement has made us more aware of the needs of these animals, and made us search harder for suitable alternatives, they have made a significant contribution. But if the more radical members of this movement are successful in limiting further research, their efforts will bring about a tragedy that will cost many lives. The real question is whether an apathetic majority can be aroused to protect its future against a vocal, but misdirected, minority.

Analyzing the Structure

The Beginning

In paragraph 1, Karpati introduces himself as a scientist and a pediatrician with a personal and professional interest in his topic. While his first sentence proclaims, "I am the enemy," Karpati almost immediately lets his readers know that he is only an enemy to those who oppose his work; he describes himself as a caring doctor who wishes to help children stay healthy. His second sentence informs the reader that his topic will be the use of animals as research subjects; in the next sentences, he strongly implies that advances in medicine are the results of research using animals. His claim, stated in paragraph 3, is that such research is important to public health. By using the example of ill or injured children who might benefit from this work, Karpati makes a strong emotional appeal to his readers.

The Middle

Background Information

This information appears in several places in the essay. Paragraph 1 includes a list of advances in medicine that have come about, the reader assumes, through animal research. Later, in paragraph 7, Karpati lists specific drugs and surgical procedures that have resulted from using animals as research subjects. However, Karpati seems more interested in informing readers how he, a scientist who uses animals to conduct his research, is characterized negatively by animal-rights supporters.

Response to Other Points of View

Because Karpati's essay is largely a defense of his position, he focuses heavily on the views of those who oppose him. In paragraph 2, he briefly summarizes the accusations of animal-rights supporters. In paragraph 3, he suggests that these objections are voiced by extremists. He also says that he is aware of the reasons why others wish to eliminate animal research. In paragraph 4, he acknowledges that "pain [is] inflicted on these animals in the name of medical science." He agrees with the opposition that "life is often cruel"; yet his examples imply that human suffering is more compelling to physicians than is the suffering of animals. In paragraph 9, he refers back to this point and lauds the animal-rights movement in making researchers more sensitive to the issue of animal suffering.

Reasons in Support of the Claim

In paragraphs 4 through 8, Karpati presents his reasons to support his claim that medical research using animals should be continued for the benefit of human health. In paragraphs 4 and 5, he explains that the alternatives to animal research—experimenting on human subjects, relying on accidental discoveries, or using computer simulation—are not satisfactory. In paragraph 6, he warns that the impact of restricting animal research will have a far-reaching and negative impact on medical science. Paragraph 7 cites how animal research has contributed to the healthy lives that most of his readers take for granted. Finally, in paragraph 8, he reasserts the importance of human life over the well-being of animals.

Possible Objections to Reasons

Karpati includes several objections to his reasons. For instance, in paragraphs 4 and 5, he anticipates that his readers might wonder why humans and computers can't be substituted for animals in research. He responds that experiments on humans will largely fail and computer simulations cannot duplicate complex biological processes.

The End

In the last paragraph, Karpati summarizes his main point: The efforts of radical members of the animal-rights movement to limit the use of animals in research "will bring about a tragedy that will cost many lives." He makes a strong appeal to his readers to take action to prevent just that from happening.

Blueprints for Arguments

Our analysis of Karpati's essay gives some idea of its general organization, but it does not reflect subdivisions or how the various parts are logically connected. That can be done by making an outline. Think of an outline as a blueprint of the argument you're building: It reveals structure and framework but leaves out the materials that cover the frame.

Opinions differ as to the value of making outlines before writing an essay. Some writers need to make formal outlines to organize their thoughts. Others simply scratch down a few key ideas. Still others write essays spontaneously without any preliminary writing. For the beginning writer, an outline is a valuable aid because it demonstrates at a glance how the various parts of an essay are connected, whether the organization is logical and complete, whether the evidence is sequenced properly, and whether there are any omissions or lack of proportion. Your outline need not be elaborate. You might simply jot down your key reasons in a hierarchy from strongest to weakest:

> Introduction
>
> Reason 1
>
> Reason 2
>
> Reason 3
>
> Reason 4
>
> Conclusion

This blueprint might be useful if you want to capture your readers' attention immediately with your most powerful appeal. Or you might use a reverse hierarchy, beginning with your weakest argument and proceeding to your strongest, in order to achieve a climactic effect. The outline will help you build your case.

You might prefer, as do some writers, to construct an outline after, rather than before, writing a rough draft. This lets you create a draft without restricting the free flow of ideas and helps you rewrite by determining where you need to fill in, cut out, or reorganize. You may discover where your line of reasoning is not logical; you may also reconsider whether you should arrange your reasons from the most important to the least or vice versa in order to create a more persuasive effect. Ultimately, outlining after the first draft can prove useful in producing subsequent drafts and a polished final effort. Outlines are also useful when evaluating somebody else's writing. Reducing the argument of the opposition to the bare bones exposes holes in the reasoning process, scanty evidence, and logical fallacies.

The Formal Outline

Some instructors like students to submit *formal outlines* with their papers to show that they have checked their structure carefully. This kind of outlining has several rules to follow:

- Identify main ideas with capital Roman numerals.
- Identify subsections of main ideas with capital letters, indented one set of spaces from the main ideas.
- Identify support for subsections with Arabic numerals, indented two sets of spaces from the main ideas.
- Identify the parts of the support with lowercase Roman numerals, indented three sets of spaces from the main ideas.
- Identify further subdivisions with lowercase letters and then italic numbers, each indented one set of spaces to the right of the previous subdivision.
- Make sure all items have at least two points; it's considered improper informal outlining to have only one point under any subdivision.

To demonstrate what a formal outline can look like, we have outlined Clara Spotted Elk's essay, "Skeletons in the Attic":

I. Hoarding of Indian remains
   A. At Smithsonian
      1. Single Kiowa at Smithsonian
      2. 18,500 others
   B. In other locations
II. Authorities' defense of collections
   A. Refusal to return grave-robbed remains
   B. Maintenance of "specimens"
III. Indians' response
   A. Outrage
      1. Desire to be seen as humans
      2. Desire to have religion accepted by science
      3. Nonacceptance of desecration of graves
      4. Resentment of lack of outcry by public
   B. Accommodation
      1. Limitation in time
      2. Service to Indians and mankind
   C. Demand equality with other religions
IV. "Bones Bill" legislation
   A. Resistance from scientific community
      1. Slick lobbyists
      2. Money

      3. Scientific mystique
      4. Characterization of Indians
         i. Radicals
        ii. Out of touch with culture
       iii. Little appreciation of science
   B. Indian counter-resistance
      1. Few resources
      2. Little money
      3. Moral obligation to ancestors

Keep in mind that an outline should not force your writing to conform to a rigid pattern and, thus, turn your essay into something stilted and uninspired. Follow the model as a map, taking detours when necessary or inspired.

Two Basic Types of Arguments: Position Arguments and Proposal Arguments

Consider the following claims for arguments:

1. Watching television helps to eliminate some traditional family rituals.
2. Pornography poses a threat to women.
3. The rising sea level is a real threat to our way of life in coastal cities.
4. Bilingual education programs fail to help non-English-speaking children become part of mainstream society.
5. Hate crime legislation is intended to allow certain people to have more protection under the law than others.
6. Cigarette advertising should be banned from billboards everywhere.
7. Wall Street should be more tightly regulated.
8. Americans should be required to vote by law.
9. The Ten Commandments ought to be posted in public places, schools, and government offices.
10. Pass/fail grades have to be eliminated across the board if academic standards are to be maintained.

Looking over these statements, you might notice some patterns. The verbs in the first five are all in the present tense: *helps, poses, is, fail, is intended to.* However, each of the last five statements includes "should" words: *should, should not, ought to be, have to be.* These **obligation verbs** are found in almost all claims proposing solutions to a problem. What distinguishes the first group from the second is more than the form of the verb. The first five claims are statements of the writer's stand on a controversial issue. The second group are proposals for what *should* be. Of course, not every kind of argument will fit our classification scheme. However, essentially every argument in this book—and the ones you'll most likely write and read in your careers—falls into one of these two categories or a combination of each, for often a writer states his or her position on an issue, then follows it with proposals for changes. Later in this chapter, we will discuss proposals. For the moment, let's take a look at position arguments.

Position Arguments

A *position argument* scrutinizes one side of a controversial issue. In such an argument, the writer not only establishes his or her stand but also argues vigorously in defense of it. Position arguments are less likely to point to a solution to a problem. Instead, they are philosophical in nature—the kinds of arguments on which political and social principles are founded, laws are written, and business and government policies are established. Position papers also tend to address themselves to the ethical and moral aspects of a controversy. If, for instance, you were opposed to the university's policy of mandatory testing for the AIDS virus, you might write a position paper protesting your school's infringement of individual rights and invasion of privacy.

As indicated by the present tense of the verbs in the first five claims, the position argument deals with the status quo—the way things are, the current state of affairs. Such an argument reminds the audience that something *currently* is good or bad, better or worse, right or wrong. Like all arguments, they tend to be aimed at changing the audience's feelings about an issue—abortion, animal research, health care, the death penalty, and so on. That is why many position papers tend to direct their appeals to the reader's sense of ethics rather than to reason.

By contrast, proposal arguments identify a problem and recommend a solution. That's why their claims contain verbs that *obligate* the readers to take some action. In this sense, they are practical rather than philosophical. For instance, if you were concerned about the spread of AIDS among college students, you might write a paper proposing that condom machines be installed in all dormitories. When you offer a proposal, you're trying to affect the future.

Features to Look for in Position Arguments

What follows are some key features of position arguments. As a checklist, they can help you evaluate someone's stand on an issue and help guide you in writing your own position papers.

The writer deals with a controversial issue. The best kind of position paper is one that focuses on a debatable issue, one in which there is clear disagreement: the war on terrorism, abortion, capital punishment, gay marriage, health care, euthanasia, civil liberties, gun control, separation of church and state, censorship, sex in advertising, freedom of speech, homelessness, gun control. These are issues about which people have many different perspectives.

The writer clearly states a position. Readers should not be confused about where an author stands on an issue. Although the actual issue may be complex, the claim should be stated emphatically and straightforwardly. Don't waffle: "Using the death penalty in some situations and with some rights of appeal probably doesn't do much to lower crime anyway"; far better is an emphatic "Capital punishment is no deterrent to crime." In formulating your claim, be certain that your word choice is not ambiguous. Otherwise the argument will be muddled and, ultimately, unconvincing.

The writer recognizes other positions and potential objections. For every argument there are bound to be numerous other perspectives. Such is the nature of controversy.

As a writer representing a position, you cannot assume that your readers are fully aware of or understand all the disagreement surrounding the issue. Nor can you make a persuasive case without anticipating challenges. So, in your argument, spell out accurately and fairly the main points of the opposition and objections that might arise. We offer six reasons for doing this:

1. *You reduce your own vulnerability.* You don't want to appear ill-informed or naive on an issue. Therefore, it makes sense to acknowledge opposing points of view to show how well you've investigated the topic and how sensitive you are to it. Suppose, for instance, you are writing a paper arguing that "anyone who commits suicide is insane." To avoid criticism, you would have to be prepared to answer objections that fully rational people with terminal illnesses sometimes choose to take their own lives so as to avoid a painful demise and curtail the suffering of loved ones. Even if you strongly disagree, recognizing views from the other side demonstrates that you are a person of responsibility and tolerance—two qualities for which most writers of argument strive.

2. *You distinguish your own position.* By citing opposing views, you distinguish your own position from that of others. This not only helps clarify the differences but also lays out the specific points of the opposition to be refuted or discredited. Some writers do this at the outset of their arguments. Consider, for instance, how Ron Karpati sums up the views of the opposition in the opening paragraphs of his essay "I Am the Enemy": "I am the enemy! One of those vilified, inhumane physician-scientists involved in animal research." (page 123):

3. *You can respond to opposing views.* A good response can challenge an opponent's ideas and examine the basis for the disagreement—whether personal, ideological, or moral. For instance, when Michael Kelley, in "Arguing for Infanticide" (page 204), responds to Steven Pinker's "Why They Kill Their Newborns" (page 196), he points out that Pinker's very logical argument for neonaticide ignores the moral and ethical values of our society regarding the relationship between mothers and their children. Kelley does not suggest that Pinker's reasons are incorrect; instead he challenges the basis for Pinker's argument.

4. *You might also challenge an opponent's logic, demonstrating where the reasoning suffers from flaws in logic.* For instance, the argument that Ms. Shazadi must be a wonderful mother because she's a great office manager does not logically follow. While some qualities of a good manager might bear on successful motherhood, not all do. In fact, it can be argued that the very qualities that make a good manager— leadership, drive, ruthlessness, determination—might damage a parent–child relationship. This logical fallacy, called a false analogy, erroneously suggests that the two situations are comparable when they are not.

5. *You might challenge the evidence supporting an argument.* If possible, try to point out unreliable, unrealistic, or irrelevant evidence offered by the opposition; question the truth of counterarguments; or point to distortions. The realtor who boasts oceanside property is vulnerable to challenge if the house in question is actually half a mile from the beach. Look for instances of stacking the deck. For example, a writer might argue that supporting the building of a new sports complex will benefit the community by

providing new jobs. However, if she fails to mention that workers at the old sports facility will then lose their jobs, she is misleading the audience about the benefits of this change. Challenge the evidence by looking for hasty generalizations. For example, a business degree from state university may indeed guarantee a well-paying job after graduation, but the writer will need more than a few personal anecdotes to convince the reader that this is the case.

6. *You can gain strength through concessions.* Admitting weaknesses in your own stand shows that you are realistic and that you don't suffer from an inflated view of the virtues of your position. It also lends credibility to your argument while helping you project yourself as fair-minded. A successful example of this strategy is Ron Karpati's acknowledgment in paragraph 9 of "I Am the Enemy" (page 123) that the animal-rights movement has sensitized scientists to the needs of animals.

The writer offers a well-reasoned argument to support the position. A position paper must do more than simply state your stand on an issue. It must try to persuade readers to accept your position as credible and convince them to adjust their thinking about the issue. Toward those ends, you should make every effort to demonstrate the best reasons for your beliefs and support the positions you hold. That means presenting honest and logically sound arguments.

Persuaders use three kinds of appeal: to *reason,* to *emotions,* and to readers' sense of *ethics.* You may have heard these described as the appeals of *logos, pathos,* and *ethos.* Although it is difficult to separate the emotional and ethical components from a logical argument, the persuasive powers of a position argument may mean the proper combination of these three appeals. Not all arguments will cover all three appeals. Some will target logic alone and offer as support statistics and facts. Others centering around moral, religious, or personal values will appeal to a reader's emotions as well as reason. Arguments based on emotion aim to reinforce and inspire followers to stand by their convictions. However, relying too heavily on an emotional appeal can result in an ad misericordiam argument, one that attempts to exploit the readers' pity. The most successful arguments are those that use multiple strategies to appeal to readers' hearts and minds.

When the issue centers on right-or-wrong or good-or-bad issues, position arguments make their appeals to the audience's ethical sense. In such papers, your strategy has two intentions: one, to convince the reader that you are a person of goodwill and moral character—thus enhancing your credibility—and, two, to suggest that any decent and moral readers will share your position.

The writer's supporting evidence is convincing. A position paper does not end with an incontrovertible proof such as the demonstration of a scientific law or mathematical theorem. No amount of logic can prove conclusively that your functional judgment is right or wrong; if that were the case, there would be few arguments. It is also impossible to prove that your aesthetic judgments are superior to another's or that a particular song, movie, or book is better than another. But your arguments have a greater chance of being persuasive if you can present convincing evidence that your argument is valid.

We'll say more about evidence in Chapter 6, but for now remember that a strong argument needs convincing evidence: facts, figures, personal observations, testimony of outside authorities, and specific examples. In general, the more facts supporting a position, the more reason there is for the reader to accept that position as valid. The same is true when refuting another position. An author needs to give reasons and hard evidence to disprove or discredit an opponent's stand.

The writer projects a reasonable persona. Whenever we read an argument, we cannot help but be aware of the person behind the words. Whether it's in the choice of expressions, the tenacity of opinion, the kinds of examples, the force of the argument, the nature of the appeal, or the humor or sarcasm, we hear the author's voice and form an impression of the person. That impression, which is projected by the voice and tone of the writing, is the writer's *persona*.

Persona is communicated in a variety of ways: diction or the choice of words (formal, colloquial, slang, jargon, charged terms), the sentence style (long or short, simple or complex), and the kinds of evidence offered (from cool scientific data to inflammatory examples). As in face-to-face debates, a full range of feelings can be projected by the tone of a written argument: anger, irony, jest, sarcasm, seriousness.

Persona is the vital bond linking the writer to the reader. In fact, the success or failure of an argument might be measured by the extent to which the reader accepts the persona. If you like the voice you hear, then you have already begun to identify with the writer and are more likely to share in the writer's assumptions and opinions. If, however, that persona strikes you as harsh, distant, or arrogant, you might have difficulty subscribing to the argument even if it makes logical sense.

A good position argument projects a reasonable persona, one that is sincere and willing to consider opposing views. Steer clear of ad hominem arguments, which make personal attacks on those with whom you disagree rather than on their views. Although readers may not be convinced enough to change their stand or behavior, a writer with a reasonable persona can at least capture their respect and consideration. Remember, the success of your argument will largely depend on your audience's willingness to listen.

A word of warning. Not every persona has to be reasonable or pleasant, although for a beginner this works best. If an arrogant persona is fortified by wit and intelligence, readers

Checklist for Writing a Position Argument

Have you:
- ■ Chosen a controversial issue?
- ■ Clearly stated a position?
- ■ Recognized other positions and possible objections?
- ■ Developed a well-reasoned argument?
- ■ Provided convincing supporting evidence?
- ■ Projected a reasonable persona?

may find it stimulating, even charming. A persona—whether outrageous, humorous, or sarcastic—can be successful if executed with style and assurance. Some of the best arguments in Part Two of this book have biting edges.

When you read an argument with a memorable persona, jot down in your argument journal the details of how the writer created it; that way, you can turn back to this information when you're trying to create personas for the arguments you write.

SAMPLE POSITION ARGUMENT FOR ANALYSIS

Following is an example of a position argument whose title suggests the issue and the author's stand on it: "Is Anything Private Anymore?" In a digital world where highly personal information appears in a multitude of databases and where security cameras are everywhere, the author wonders if privacy still exists. Written by Sean Flynn, this essay first appeared in *Parade* magazine in September 2007.

"Is Anything Private Anymore?"
Sean Flynn

1   Kevin Bankston was a closet smoker who hid his habit by sneaking cigarettes outside his San Francisco office. He expected anonymity on a big city street. But in 2005, an online mapping service that provided ground-level photographs captured him smoking—and made the image available to anyone on the Internet. This year, Google's Street View project caught him again.

2   Coincidence? Absolutely. Yet Bankston's twice-documented smoking highlights a wider phenomenon: Privacy is a withering commodity for all of us.

3   What you buy, where you go, whom you call, the Web sites you visit, the e-mails you send—all of that information can be monitored and logged. "When you're out in public, it's becoming a near certainty that your image will be captured," says (the newly nonsmoking) Bankston.

4   Should you care? I've interviewed numerous people on all sides of the privacy debate to find out just how wary we should be.

5   One thing is clear: In today's world, maintaining a cocoon of privacy simply isn't practical. Need a mortgage or a car loan? A legitimate lender is going to verify a wealth of private information, including your name and address, date of birth, Social Security number and credit history. We all make daily trade-offs for convenience and thrift: Electronic tollbooths mean you don't have to wait in the cash-only lane, but your travel habits will be tracked. The Piggly Wiggly discount card saves you $206 on your annual grocery bill, but it counts how many doughnuts and six-packs you buy. MySpace posts make it easy to keep in touch with friends, but your comments live on.

6   So how do you live in a digital world and still maintain a semblance of privacy? Experts say it's crucial to recognize that those bits of data are permanent—a trail of electronic crumbs that is never swept away, available to anyone with the skills and inclination to sniff it out.

7   Privacy may not feel like much of an issue for those in their teens and 20s. They've grown up chronicling their lives on popular social networking sites like MySpace or Facebook for easy retrieval by friends and strangers alike. But some young people don't realize that what was funny to college buddies might not amuse a law-firm recruiter. Employers regularly research job applicants on the Internet. Some colleges are helping students prepare: Duke University hosts seminars on how to clean up a Facebook account. "You learn why posting pictures of you riding the mechanical bull at Shooters is a bad idea," says Sarah Ball, a senior whose own page is secure and clean.

8   Amy Polumbo, 22, restricted her page on Facebook to 100 or so people who knew her password. "It was a way for me to keep in touch with friends all over the country," she says. But after she was crowned Miss New Jersey in June, someone downloaded pictures of her and threatened blackmail. She thwarted the attempt by releasing the photos herself (they're quite innocent) but suffered weeks of embarrassment.

9   "I know how easy it is for someone to take advantage of you on the Internet," says Polumbo. "The Web is a place where people can destroy your reputation if you're not careful."

10   In fact, all kinds of transgressions now are easily retrievable. An employee at a New York City bank watched his reputation shrink when his colleagues pulled up an article from a small-town newspaper about his drunk-driving arrest two years earlier. Divorce lawyers have been issuing subpoenas for electronic tollbooth records to use in custody cases. (You say you're home at 6 p.m. to have dinner with the kids, but Fast Lane says you're getting off the Massachusetts Turnpike at 7 p.m.) Abbe L. Ross, a divorce lawyer in Boston, finds a gold mine in computers: financial data, e-mails, what Web sites a soon-to-be-ex spouse looks at and for how long. "I love to look through hard drives," she says.

11   Details about you already are stashed in enormous databases. Unless you pay cash for everything, data brokers almost certainly have compiled a profile of you that will be bought and sold dozens of times to marketers and direct-mail firms. "There's almost nothing they can't find out about you," says Jack Dunning, who worked in the junk-mail business for 35 years. Right now, there are roughly 50,000 such lists for sale in a $4 billion a year industry. Now junk mail is going digital: Companies can use personal profiles and records from Internet search engines to tailor advertising—both what you see and pre-cisely when you see it—to individual consumers.

12   And new databases are being created all the time. Most of the major proposals for health-care reform, for example, include compiling medical records into easily and widely accessible digital files. In July, the FBI requested $5 million to pay the major phone com-panies to maintain logs of your calls—information the Feds can't legally stockpile them-selves but might find useful later.

13   Surveillance cameras are increasingly ubiquitous in our post-9/11 world. Indeed, New York City plans to ring the financial district with them, as central London did several years ago.

14   Of course, there are upsides. London's network of cameras helped capture failed car bombers in June. And streamlined electronic medical records would make health care safer and more efficient.

15   Still, most experts say we need to be vigilant about the increasing encroachments on our privacy.

16   The ability to collect information and images has outpaced the security available to protect them. Since January 2005, nearly 160 million personal records have been stolen or inadvertently posted online.

17   And even if information stays secure, the big question remains: Who should be allowed to access these databases? The FBI might find evidence against a few bad guys in millions of phone records, but the government could track all of your calls too. (President Bush has acknowledged that the National Security Agency tapped phone calls, though whose and how many is unknown.)

18   Even more disturbing: All of those data files can be linked and cross-referenced. At the 2001 Super Bowl in Tampa, fans were scanned with cameras linked to facial-recognition software in a hunt for suspected terrorists. Some privacy advocates worry that police could videotape anti-war marches and create a library of digital faces or start mining Web pages for personal information.

19   Kevin Bankston was only caught smoking, but he's worried about larger implications: "The issue isn't whether you have anything to hide," he says. "The issue is whether the lack of privacy would give the government an inordinate amount of power over the populace. This is about maintaining the privacy necessary for us to flourish as a free society."

Analysis of Sample Position Argument

The writer deals with a controversial issue. Most people assume that personal privacy is an inherent right. But is that a realistic expectation in today's world? Few people realize that almost every electronic transaction, whether a bank deposit or store purchase, leaves a permanent digital record. Nor do they realize that every phone call, e-mail, grocery store purchase, or Facebook entry becomes part of huge data systems accessible to others. Controversy arises because such personal information can be used by businesses to track spending habits and, thus, target customers. Also controversial is how the government can keep tabs on its citizenry. That issue is even more controversial since some forms of surveillance—at airports, on highways, and in commercial and financial areas—are considered essential in the fight against terrorism. Of course, to many people, such surveillance constitutes an infringement on individual privacy and, thus, a diminishing of civil liberties. In his essay, Flynn clearly addresses the controversy that in our digital world it may be impossible to protect personal information.

The writer clearly states a position. The title of Flynn's essay implies the author's stand: that personal privacy no longer exists. He begins with the anecdote of a closet smoker who thought that cigarette breaks outside his office gave him anonymity. But an "online mapping service . . . captured him smoking—and made the image available to anyone on the Internet." He concludes this anecdote with a blunt generalization, "Privacy is a withering commodity for all of us" (paragraph 2)—a clear statement of his position. Flynn reiterates his position following other examples of privacy violations—for example, his statement regarding the ready availability of telephone and health records: "Still, most experts say we need to be vigilant about the increasing encroachments on our privacy" (paragraph 15). And in paragraph 16: "The ability to collect information and images has outpaced the security available to protect them." Clearly, he has surveyed the many ways privacy is compromised and concludes that it is rapidly eroding.

The writer recognizes other positions and possible objections. Flynn creates a balanced essay by citing other points of view. At the end of paragraph 5, for example, he cites the consumer perks built into some everyday transactions: "We all make daily trade-offs for convenience and thrift: Electronic tollbooths mean you don't have to wait in the cash-only lane, but your travel habits will be tracked. The Piggly Wiggly discount card saved you $206 on your annual grocery bill, but it counts how many doughnuts and six-packs you buy. MySpace posts make it easy to keep in touch with friends, but your comments live on." Later, when discussing terrorism, he acknowledges "upsides": "London's network of cameras helped capture failed car bombers in June" (paragraph 14). And referring to "easily and widely accessible" health care files, he concedes, "streamlined electronic medical records would make health care safer and more efficient."

As the author explores the topic, his tone remains matter-of-fact and objective. His most emotionally potent comment comes at his conclusion when he refers back to the young smoker. Here his tone approaches a warning regarding surveillance in public places: "Kevin Bankston was only caught smoking . . . This is about maintaining the privacy necessary for us to flourish as a free society."

The writer offers well-developed reasons to support the position. Flynn offers concrete, concise, and convincing evidence to support his position that personal privacy is greatly compromised today. He describes virulent threats and documents these with examples to which the general public can relate. One of his claims is that in today's world of commerce, it is almost impossible to maintain personal privacy—that nearly every transaction is recorded electronically and leaves a permanent trail available to anyone skilled "to sniff it out" (paragraph 6). And he gets specific: "Need a mortgage or a car loan? A legitimate lender is going to verify a wealth of private information, including your name and address, date of birth, Social Security number and credit history" (paragraph 5). Later, he argues that because of the enormous databases, "Companies can use personal profiles and records from Internet search engines to tailor advertising—both what you see and precisely when you see it—to individual consumers" (paragraph 11). For support, Flynn quotes an authority in the field of direct-mail and marketing: "'There's almost nothing they can't find out about you,' says Jack Dunning, who worked in the junk-mail business for 35 years."

Another threat Flynn names is the social networking sites that make personal information available to everyone, including potential employers as well as thieves and sexual predators. He supports his position with reference to students who naively chronicle their lives on MySpace or Facebook. Young people may not know that "employers regularly research job applicants on the Internet," Flynn writes. What may amuse college pals "might not amuse a law-firm recruiter" (paragraph 7). He further supports his position with more anecdotal evidence, a reference to the newly crowned Miss New Jersey, whose Facebook page contained photographs that were used as blackmail. Flynn even quotes her directly: "'The Web is a place where people can destroy your reputation if you're not careful'" (paragraph 9).

Another argument Flynn makes supporting his claim of a diminishing privacy is the ubiquitous use of surveillance cameras in public places. In paragraph 18, he offers the powerful example of the 2001 Super Bowl where "fans were scanned with cameras linked to facial-recognition software in a hunt for suspected terrorists." Flynn's logical concern is that "police could videotape anti-war marches and create a library of digital faces or start mining Web pages for personal information." Building on all his specific concerns, Flynn concludes with larger implications: that the increased lack of privacy could "'give the government an inordinate amount of power over the populace.'"

The writer's supporting evidence is convincing. Flynn's evidence is very convincing. He supports his position in a variety of ways, using anecdotes that the average person can identify with—references to smoker Kevin Bankston or young people using Facebook. He makes use of expert opinion, quoting, for instance, Jack Dunning, who worked for 35 years in the direct-mail business. Throughout the piece, he also cites numerous examples of our compromised privacy.

The writer projects a reasonable persona. Flynn's tone is reasonable and balanced, as his purpose is to alert the general public to the ways personal data are part of public or available records. His tone is friendly as his intention is not to alarm but to enhance awareness so that people can take sensible precautions. Thus, he gives numerous examples but does not inflate them or create a sense of panic.

Proposal Arguments

Position arguments examine existing conditions. *Proposal arguments,* however, look to the future. They make recommendations for changes to the status quo—namely, policy, practice, or attitude. Essentially, what every proposal writer says is this: "Here is the problem, and this is what I think should be done about it." The hoped-for result is a new course of action or way of thinking.

Proposals are the most common kind of argument. We hear them all the time: "There ought to be a law against that"; "The government should do something about these conditions." We're always making proposals of some kind: "Van should work out more"; "You ought to see that movie"; "We should recycle more of our trash." As pointed out earlier in this chapter, because proposals are aimed at correcting problems, they almost always make their claims in obligation verbs such as *ought to, needs to be,* and *must.*

Sometimes proposal arguments take up local problems and make practical recommendations for immediate solutions. For instance, to reduce the long lines at the photocopy machines in your campus library, you might propose that the school invest in more copiers and station them throughout the building. Proposal arguments also seek to correct or improve conditions with more far-reaching consequences. If, for example, too many of your classmates smoke, you might write a proposal to your school's administration to remove all cigarette machines from campus buildings or to limit smoking areas on campus.

Still other proposals address perennial social issues in an effort to change public behavior and government policy. A group of physicians might recommend that marijuana be legalized for medical use. An organization of concerned parents might ask the federal government to require the testing of toys and to ban toys that might contain toxic or flammable materials. Everyone has ideas about things that should be changed; proposals are the means we use to make those changes happen.

Features to Look for in Proposal Arguments

Proposals have two basic functions: (1) They inform readers that there is a problem, and (2) they make recommendations about how to correct those problems. To help you sharpen your own critical ability to build and analyze proposal arguments, we offer some guidelines.

The writer states the problem clearly. Because a proposal argument seeks to change the reader's mind and/or behavior, you first must demonstrate that a problem exists. You do this for several reasons. Your audience may not be aware that the problem exists or they may have forgotten it or think that it has already been solved. Sympathetic audiences may need to be reinspired to take action. It is crucial, therefore, that proposals clearly define the problem and the undesirable or dangerous consequences if matters are not corrected.

For both uninformed and sympathetic audiences, writers often try to demonstrate how the problem personally affects the reader. An argument for greater measures against shoplifting can be more convincing when you illustrate how petty thefts inevitably lead to higher prices. A paper proposing the elimination of pesticides might interest the everyday gardener by demonstrating how carcinogenic chemicals can contaminate local drinking water. To make the problem even more convincing, the claim should be supported by solid evidence—statistics, historical data, examples, testimony of witnesses and experts, and maybe even personal experience.

The writer clearly proposes how to solve the problem. After defining the problem clearly, you need to tell your readers how to solve it. This is the heart of the proposal, the writer's plan of action. Besides a detailed explanation of what should be done and how, the proposal should supply reliable supporting evidence for the plan: testimony of others, ideas from authorities, statistics from studies.

The writer argues convincingly that this proposal will solve the problem. Perhaps the first question readers ask is "How will this solution solve the problem?" Writers usually address this question by identifying the forces behind the problem and demonstrating how their plan will counter those forces. Suppose, for instance, you propose putting condom machines in all college dorms as a means of combating the spread of AIDS. To build a convincing case, you would have to summon evidence, documenting how condoms significantly reduce the spread of AIDS. To make the connection between the problem and your solution even stronger, you might go on to explain how readily available machines leave students little excuse for unsafe sex. Students cannot complain that they jeopardized their health because they couldn't make it to a drugstore.

The writer convincingly explains how the solution will work. Generally readers next ask how the plan will be put into action. Writers usually answer by detailing how their plan will work. They emphasize their plan's advantages and how efficiently (or cheaply, safely, conveniently) it can be carried out. For the condom-machine proposal, that might mean explaining how and where the machines will be installed and how students can be encouraged to use them. You might cite advantages of your proposal, such as the easy installation of the machines and the low price of the contents.

The writer anticipates objections to the proposed solution. Writers expect disagreement and objections to proposal arguments: Proposals are aimed at changing the status quo, and many people are opposed to or are fearful of change. If you want to persuade readers, especially hostile ones, you must show that you respect their sides of the argument too. Most proposal writers anticipate audience response to fortify their case and establish credibility. (See Chapter 4 for more discussion of audience response.)

The writer explains why this solution is better than the alternatives. Although you may believe that your solution to the problem is best, you cannot expect readers automatically to share that sentiment. Nor can you expect readers not to wonder about other solutions. Good proposal writers investigate other solutions that have been tried to solve this problem so they can weigh alternative possibilities and attempt to demonstrate the superiority of their plan and the disadvantages of others. If you are knowledgeable about ways the problem has been dealt with in the past, you might be able to show how your plan combines the best features of other, less successful solutions. For instance, in the condom-machine proposal you might explain to your readers that universities have attempted to make students more aware that unsafe sex promotes the spread of AIDS; however, without the easy availability of condom machines, students are more likely to continue to engage in unsafe sex. The promotion of AIDS awareness and the presence of condom machines might significantly reduce that problem.

The writer projects a reasonable persona. As in position arguments, your persona is an important factor in proposals, for it conveys your attitude toward the subject and the audience. Because a proposal is intended to win readers to your side, the best strategy is to project a persona that is fair-minded. Even if you dislike somebody else's views on an

Checklist for Writing a Proposal Argument

Have you:
- Stated the problem clearly?
- Proposed a solution clearly?
- Explained why the solution will work?
- Demonstrated how the solution will work?
- Addressed possible objections?
- Shown why the solution is better than alternatives?
- Projected a reasonable persona?

issue, projecting a reasonable and knowledgeable tone will have a more persuasive effect than a tone of belligerence.

If you are arguing for condom machines in dormitories, you would be wise to recognize that some people might object to the proposal because availability might be interpreted as encouragement of sexual behavior. So as not to offend or antagonize such readers, adopting a serious, straightforward tone might be the best mode of presenting the case.

SAMPLE PROPOSAL ARGUMENT FOR ANALYSIS

The following argument was written by Amanda Collins, a first-year English composition student, whose assignment was to write a proposal argument. In her paper, she argues for the implementation of foreign language teaching in American elementary schools, focusing in particular on her own home town of East Bridgewater, Massachusetts. Read her essay and respond to the questions that follow. Note that she used research to support her ideas and documentation to acknowledge her sources. The style of documentation used in this paper is MLA, which we discuss in detail in the Documentation Guide.

Collins 1

Amanda Collins
Professor Ingram
ENG 1350
15 December 2013

Bring East Bridgewater Elementary into the World

1   According to a survey of ten European countries and Russia, the average age of students beginning foreign language instruction is eight (Bergentoft 13). In Sweden, ninety-nine percent of the students in primary school study English. One hundred percent of the students study English in secondary schools (Bergentoft 19). However, "across the United States, only about one in three elementary schools offers its students the opportunity to gain some measure of skill in another language" (Met 37). The United States falls drastically short of the standards being set by the rest of the world.

2   The Commonwealth of Massachusetts is no exception. According to a report from the Center for Applied Linguistics (CAL), only forty-four schools across the state offer foreign language programs in primary school (Branaman, Rhodes, and Holmes). Schools not offering foreign language study leave their students at a disadvantage. Foreign language needs to be considered as vital to a child's education as are math, science and reading. Parents would not be happy if their children began math or English studies in high school. So why shouldn't parents be outraged that second languages do not hold much significance in the Massachusetts curriculum? (Brown 166).

East Bridgewater must take steps to change this and open Central Elementary School to foreign language learning.

3   The world is changing as are the skills one needs to succeed. Globalization brings us together. People around the world are connected to each other more than ever before, whether through international communication, travel, or commerce. In a world today that is constantly crossing borders "there is a need for linguistically and culturally competent Americans" (Brown 165). And learning languages is one way to reach such competency. America's students need to be prepared for entrance into this ever-merging world where they will compete with their international peers who are fluent in two or three languages. It is time to adopt a plan like those proven successful elsewhere in America and abroad. It's time to give East Bridgewater's students an advantage. In order to do this, East Bridgewater must live up to the school system's motto, "There is no better place to learn," and mandate foreign language education in the elementary curriculum for every child.

4   Although the Massachusetts Department of Education adopted a curriculum framework in August 1999 that includes foreign language in the requirements for elementary schools, it is still a recommendation, not yet a requirement (Massachusetts Dept. of Educ.). Massachusetts's new Curriculum Framework for World Languages states that "students should graduate from high school able to read, write, and converse in a world language in order to participate in the multilingual, interdependent communities of the twenty-first century . . . to develop proficiency, this framework recommends a sequence of language learning that starts in kindergarten and continues through grade twelve and beyond . . . the World Languages discipline is about making connections" (Massachusetts Dept. of Educ.). The framework places the same value on learning a foreign language as is placed on mathematics, reading and science. Despite the framework's passing, foreign language is not mandated in the elementary curriculum. There is a real need not only to finalize the benefits that students gain by learning languages at an early age, but also to work toward advancing our schools' curricula to include Foreign Language in Elementary School (FLES).

Why Should Children Learn Foreign Languages?

5   Language is an important aspect of the education of students of all ages. It is becoming more important for citizens to be well versed in a language other than their own. The United States was basically a self-sufficient and self-contained country before the World Wars. "Rapid and widespread political, economic, and military changes after World War II gave rise to issues that were global in scope, and many people became aware of the impact that events outside U.S. borders had on domestic affairs" (Smith 38). The United States was learning just how fundamental foreign languages are.

6   One reason is that transcontinental communications have become essential to everyday life in the world. With so much cross-cultural interaction, we must prepare

American children to grow into adults capable of interacting with other cultures. The future of the United States depends on continued and constant communication with countries that speak languages other than our own. There are only about 45 other countries outside the United States where English is spoken. So, in order to maintain the status that this country now enjoys, we must train American children to comprehend changes in the global community. Students must learn foreign languages.

7   In 1999 a study titled *Exploring the Economics of Language* found that "multilingual societies have a competitive advantage over monolingual societies in international trade" (Met 36). The study went on to point out that businesses that had people with the proper language skills to negotiate and carry out commerce with foreign enterprises were at a distinct advantage over those that lacked such talent. So it stands to reason that giving America's students the opportunity to learn a foreign language increases their chances of succeeding in the business world. Likewise, the country benefits because successful businesses on the world level only help the American economy. As Andrew Smith asserts, there is a need to "prepare our students to meet the challenges of our increasingly, sometimes dangerously, interconnected world. It is not likely that the United States will exert global leadership for long with a citizenry that is globally deaf, dumb, and blind" (41).

8   Besides the business industry, other jobs require expertise in a second language. The State Department, the Central Intelligence Agency, and the National Security Agency are among more than 70 government agencies that require proficiency in foreign languages (Met 36). The non-profit service industries need employees to interact with other cultures and speak other languages. The Red Cross, for example, not only aids victims in the United States but throughout the world. Additionally, the Internet and other electronic communications, though originally English-based, are becoming more linguistically diverse, making proficiency in other languages indispensable. Again, we must not deprive students of the opportunity to advance in such career paths; we must provide them language training to make possible career success.

Other Benefits to Learning a Language Early

9   While most people have the ability to learn a foreign language at any age, there are benefits to starting that process when students are young (Lipton 1115). In 1959 neurologist Wilder Penfield claimed that the brain was best able to learn a foreign language before the age of ten. Later research by scientists Chugani and Phelps resulted in the same conclusion: the ideal time to begin studying a foreign language is before puberty (Lipton 1114). Thompson et al. discovered in the year 2000 that the area of the brain associated with language learning grew the most rapidly from age six to thirteen and then slowed. Another researcher suggested that children learning a language before the age of twelve will develop a more authentic accent (Lipton 1114). So this scientific evidence makes a strong case that foreign language learning must begin at a young age. But there are other studies that make the case even stronger.

10   In 1987, a Connecticut test of twenty-six thousand students revealed that children who began foreign language education before grade four did significantly better on speaking, listening, reading, writing and cultural understanding tests than students who started language learning in seventh grade or after (Brown 165). This and other similar studies initiated further investigation into the academic benefits of early foreign language learning.

11   Numerous studies have been conducted to evaluate the ways in which learning a language will enhance the simultaneous learning of other subjects. "Learning [foreign] languages . . . provides a unique conduit to higher-order thinking skills. From the early stages of learning, students move from a representational knowledge base to comparison, synthesis, and hypothesis, all elements of higher-order thinking skills" (Brown 167). Students can gain better understanding of the grammar of their native language when they study the grammar of a foreign tongue, and students who can speak another language can develop stronger reading skills (Met 38). On the national level, there is a call for improved literacy, which is why it is important for parents and educators to recognize how FLES helps students learn to read and write (Bruce 608). FLES students scored higher on the 1985 Basic Skills Language Arts Test than non-FLES students. Foreign language study has helped improve standardized test scores in mathematics and reading for students from a variety of backgrounds. Bilingualism also improves "cognitive functioning, such as metalinguistic skills and divergent thinking" (Met 38). It has even been suggested that students gain more creativity. Foreign language study helps students become more academically successful overall.

12   Additionally, because the world is full of many cultures, studying a foreign language helps prepare students for the cultural understanding that is necessary for the acceptance of such diversity. Brown states, "no other subject matter in the elementary school prepares students for the realization that there are other languages and cultures beyond their own" (167). This in turn aids in teaching students geography, history, and social studies because they will have something to build on, knowing that the United States is not the only country of consequence. Researchers Carpenter and Torney found that younger students studying languages are more open to other cultures and develop more positive attitudes toward foreign cultures and languages (Lipton 1114). From brain functions to academics to character development, learning foreign languages in elementary school is proven to be profitable.

Optimal Solution for East Bridgewater

13   There is no doubt that East Bridgewater must adopt some version of a FLES program. Based on the current circumstances at the Central Elementary School, I recommend that the East Bridgewater School Committee adopt a Sequential FLES program in which students study a language no more than thirty minutes per session up to five times a week.

Collins 5

14 As for the specific language, that decision can be left up to the School Committee. However, it is suggested that only one language be taught for the first year, or at least until the program is underway and running smoothly. And it makes sense to recommend Spanish since that language is used more often than other foreign languages in the United States.

15 Language instruction should take place at least three times a week for thirty minutes. Each school day is six hours long, minus time for lunch and recess. In order to arrange for the addition of a language program, the length of other lessons per day would have to be shortened slightly, but never by more than ten minutes each. This should not be a problem. Foreign languages are as equally important to a child's education as math, reading or science, and, therefore, would advance students' education in the long run. Since it has been proven that the study of a second language enhances students' performances in other subjects, the amount of time shaved from each subject's session would be more than made up for in the students' overall success.

16 To fund this undertaking, East Bridgewater should apply to the Federal Language Assistance Program (FLAP). As of the year 2000, Springfield and Medford were the only two towns to receive FLAP grants. Funds are also available through Goals 2000: Educate America Act of 1994. Under the Improving America's Schools Act of 1994, Title VII grants are given out for foreign language assistance. In the year 2001, the Massachusetts Board of Education received two, and Newton, Malden, Medford, Salem, and Springfield Public Schools each received a grant. East Bridgewater has the opportunity to apply for all of these grants.

17 Meetings should be scheduled with parents to discuss the importance of foreign language education. Brochures outlining fundraising activities should be distributed. The costs of the meetings and printed materials would be minimal, and they would be more than paid for with the benefits of the program. When parents and communities join together, fundraisers can bring in large revenues. East Bridgewater can hold benefits similar to the concert and art auction held by parents in Athens, Georgia. These grants and locally raised money can also help defray the cost of adding teachers to the staff and carrying out the proper training. Books and other teaching materials can be purchased from grant funds as well. There really is no shortage of money available. Once a town or district realizes the advantages of foreign language learning and expresses a desire to include it in their elementary school, the government and private agencies could offer funds to help get those programs underway.

18 Teaching foreign language to students is a necessity. Linguistic and national borders are becoming a thing of the past as the result of globalization. It is a school's responsibility and a student's right to have every opportunity afforded them to become globally aware and literate citizens. East Bridgewater's School Committee shares that responsibility as educators of this country's future leaders. Now is the time to act and close the gap on the foreign language deficiency that exists in East Bridgewater's Central Elementary School.

Collins 6

Works Cited

Bergentoft, Rune. "Foreign Language Instruction: A Comparative Perspective." *Annals of the American Academy of Political and Social Science* 532 (1994): 8–34. Print.

Branaman, Lucinaa, Nancy Rhodes, and Annette Holmes. "National Directory of Early Foreign Language Programs." Center for Applied Linguistics. CAL, 1999. Web. 4 Dec. 2004.

Brown, Christine L. "Elementary School Foreign Language Programs in the United States." *Annals of the American Academy of Political and Social Science* 532 (1994): 164–76. Print.

Bruce, Anita. "Encouraging the Growth of Foreign Language Study." *Modern Language Journal* 86 (2002): 605–09. Print.

Lipton, Gladys C. "The FLES Advantage: FLES Programs in the Third Millennium." *French Review* 74 (2001): 1113–24. Print.

Massachusetts Dept. of Educ. "World Languages Curriculum Framework." Massachusetts Dept. of Educ., Jan. 1996. Web. 1 Dec. 2009.

Met, Myriam. "Why Language Learning Matters." *Educational Leadership* 59 (2001): 36–40. Print.

Smith, Andrew F. "How Global Is the Curriculum?" *Educational Leadership* 60 (2002): 38–41. Print.

QUESTIONS FOR ANALYSIS AND DISCUSSION

Briefly summarize the main points of Amanda Collins's essay. Then answer the following questions about the essay to see how it fulfills our guidelines for a proposal argument:

1. Where does Collins identify the problem? Explain how she demonstrates that the problem is significant. Does she explain how today's young students can be affected? Where does she do this?

2. What solution does Collins propose? Where is it stated?

3. Does Collins explain how her solution will work? Where does she do this? Does she provide enough detail to understand how it will work?

4. Has Collins anticipated objections to her solution? In which paragraphs? How does she respond to the objection?

5. Does Collins seem aware of other attempts to solve the problem? Where does she refer to them?

6. What attitude about her subject does Collins convey to her readers? Does she seem reasonable and balanced? Where exactly?

Analyzing the Structure

The Beginning

Amanda Collins has already divided her paper into four parts: "Introduction," "Why Should Children Learn Foreign Language?" "Other Benefits to Learning a Language Early," and "Optimal Solution for East Bridgewater." Her "Introduction" constitutes the beginning of the essay. The middle includes those paragraphs grouped under her next two parts ("Why Should Children Learn Foreign Language?" and "Other Benefits to Learning a Language Early"). The end corresponds to those paragraphs under "Optimal Solution for East Bridgewater."

In paragraph 1, Amanda introduces the problem: Compared to several foreign countries, only about a third of American elementary schools offer foreign language teaching. And this creates a disadvantage not only for children who are preparing for a global world but for America. Then in paragraph 2, she tightens her focus to the state of Massachusetts, which, characteristic of the rest of the country, offers a paltry response: Only 44 schools statewide offer foreign language programs at the primary level. She concludes that paragraph with a point-blank proposal that "East Bridgewater must take steps to change this and open Central Elementary School to foreign language learning."

We get a sense of Amanda from these introductory paragraphs. We hear both concern and sincerity in her tone. We are also clear on her positions. Equating foreign language learning with math and writing, she projects a sense of urgency if American young people are to grow up to function successfully in a world that is linguistically and culturally interconnected and competitive. She appeals to both reason and emotion when she states: "It is time to adopt a plan like those proven successful elsewhere in America and abroad. It's time to give East Bridgewater's students an advantage." She also appeals to a sense of ethics, reminding authorities of their responsibility and duty to live up to the school system's motto, "There is no better place to learn." And she concludes this part of the argument insisting that East Bridgewater mandate that foreign language be taught at Central Elementary so students can begin to share in the benefits to come.

The Middle

The next eight paragraphs Amanda has divided into two sections: "Why Should Children Learn Foreign Language?" and "Other Benefits to Learning a Language Early." These represent the middle of Amanda's essay, where she makes her case and where she does the real arguing for her proposal.

Background Information Paragraphs 1, 2, and 4 set the context for Amanda's complaint and the basis for her proposal. In paragraph 1, she says how America "falls drastically short of the standards being set by the rest of the world." In the next paragraph she says that Massachusetts is characteristic of the larger problem with only 44 schools statewide— a small percentage—offering foreign language programs at the primary level. Paragraph 4 focuses on how despite an adopted curriculum that includes a foreign language requirement in Massachusetts schools, it has still not been mandated, leaving East Bridgewater students deprived.

Reasons in Support of the Claim Paragraphs 5 through 12 make up the heart of Amanda's essay. Here she supports her claim that it's important for children to learn foreign languages. And she offers several reasons. One key point is the competition in international business that American students will eventually face in the multilingual world of commerce. As evidence, she cites a source (paragraph 6) that claims how only 45 countries besides the United States speak English, implying that most of the rest of the 160 or so countries do not. So in a majority of the world's nations, commerce is conducted in foreign tongues.

She also refers to a study that supports her claim that "monolingual societies" are at a distinct disadvantage over those where other languages are spoken. She summons the support of Andrew Smith (paragraph 7) who also sees a need to prepare our children for an increasing global economy and culture. In the next paragraph, she points out that besides business, other careers require expertise in a second language—e.g., nonprofit organizations as well as some 70 government agencies, including the CIA, that require proficiency in foreign languages. She concludes that with the Internet and other electronic communications, once English-based, the world is becoming more linguistically diverse, making proficiency in other languages indispensable. Again, she argues, we must not deprive students the opportunity to advance in such career paths.

In paragraphs 9 through 12, Amanda offers other benefits to early language learning besides career success, thus bolstering her claim. Because children best learn foreign languages at a young age, she argues they will develop more authentic accents. Second, foreign language learning also helps children perform better in speaking, writing, and even mathematics. For support, she cites numerous studies, allowing her to conclude: "From brain functions, to academics, to character development, learning foreign languages in elementary school is proven to be profitable."

Response to Other Points of View Although Amanda cites no specific opposing views, she implies that America may be slow to develop language programs at the primary level because of a general apathy and/or the belief that speaking English is good enough. She hints at this when she mentions America's pre–World Wars sense of self-sufficiency and self-containment. And even though Americans had learned "how fundamental foreign languages" were following World War II, vigorous implementation, especially on the primary school level, has been lacking.

Anticipates Possible Objections to Reasons Amanda indirectly anticipates opposition to early language training: that if people need to learn a foreign language for their careers they can take courses as adults. With considerable supporting evidence, she argues that the earlier children learn foreign languages the better. And she cites scientific studies that confirm how young children absorb foreign languages faster and more efficiently than adolescents or adults.

The End

The final five paragraphs constitute the end of Amanda's argument. Here she returns to the problem in East Bridgewater and offers specific proposals on implementing foreign language training in Central Elementary. She recommends a program of half-hour sessions three to five times a week; she suggests Spanish since it is the second most-spoken language in America; she suggests various means of funding the program; and she recommends that parents get involved. She concludes with reaffirmations of her argument that it is important for young students to learn foreign languages and that it is a school's responsibility to provide students that opportunity. Her final sentence rounds out her argument and nicely returns to the home front: "Now is the time to act and close the gap on the foreign language deficiency that exists in East Bridgewater's Central Elementary School."

Narrative Arguments

Sometimes position and proposal arguments do not take on the familiar shapes as just discussed. Sometimes the author's position on an issue is implied rather than straightfor-wardly stated. Sometimes instead of a well-reasoned argument bound by a hierarchy of supporting details, the evidence is incorporated in a dramatic illustration of the issue. So is the author's stand. What we're talking about is argument in the form of a *narrative*.

Instead of spelling out the claims and making explicit points, the narrative argument relies on a scene, a series of episodes, or a story to advocate a change of behavior or way of thinking. Whether true or hypothetical, a narrative may serve as the body of an argument or it may be used at the beginning as a springboard to the central claim and discussion. Either way, a narrative can be a powerful strategy for winning the sympathy of an audience by describing experiences that evoke emotional responses. Following is an argument aimed at getting people to protest a governmental proposal to remove grizzly bears from list of animals protected by the Endangered Species Act. It begins with a student's personal narrative, an account that is emotionally appealing and that leads into an explicit appeal:

> We'd been hiking for three hours east of Yellowstone's Slough Creek when our guide motioned us to stop. "Bears," he whispered. We heard a piercing sound—more like a wailing cry than a roar. We cut through some sage and over a rise when we saw a grizzly bear mother and two yearling cubs. From about a hundred yards we watched in hushed fascination as the adorable cubs romped and wrestled in the grass while the mother watched from a short distance. They were seemingly unaware of our presence and continued to cavort, one cub trying to engage the mother in play by nudging her with his nose. This went on for several minutes until the mother made a sound and stood erect, sniffing the air. She must have sensed danger because she bellowed for the cubs to follow. In a moment they tumbled down a ravine and out of sight.
>
> To see that mother grizzly and her young at such close range was not just a rare experience but an eye-opener. It was a reminder that these magnificent, elusive crea-tures are in a constant struggle to survive. They reproduce only every three years and spend at least that time rearing their cubs. They are vulnerable to hunters, traffic, and male grizzlies which will kill their own cubs in order to render nursing mothers fer-tile again. While their numbers have increased over the past decades, these bears are threatened once again.
>
> The current administration has recently proposed taking grizzlies off the Endangered Species list, thus stripping them of the kind of protection from hunters that could push them to the edge of extinction once again. We must do everything in our power

to make people aware of the continuing struggle to save these iconic vestiges of frontier America.

The appeal here makes a case for protecting the grizzlies by re-creating an encounter with a mother bear and her cubs, thus invoking in the reader identification with the author's sympathy for the creatures. Even if the reader has never encountered grizzly bears in the wild, the narrative at least evokes in readers yearnings for such. To anyone who has ever visited a zoo or seen wildlife movies, the description of the cubs at play has a strong emotional appeal.

While this strategy—the use of a story—differs from the standard position and proposal argument, the narrative argument still has three basic parts—a beginning, middle, and end—and, here, a paragraph for each. The first is the actual narrative, the "story" in which the author invites the reader to partake in the experience. Here we read the author's observations of the animals "cavorting"; the final sentence concludes with the animals' sensing danger and eventually departing. In essence, this opening paragraph is the author's invitation to share in the emotional experience of the encounter. The second paragraph shifts to an appreciation of that experience and an evaluation of the vulnerability of the animals. Here the author reminds us that these "magnificent" creatures are threatened by a variety of forces, and the author names specifics—hunters, vehicular traffic, and other grizzlies. The third paragraph states the specific problem that could further endanger the animals—the then-current administration's proposal to remove them from the Endangered Species list. And it concludes with a proposal for people who care to "do everything in . . . [their] power to make people aware of the continuing struggle to save" the grizzlies.

A narrative can also constitute other peoples' experiences as in the following third-person account of a teenager's death by drug overdose. Like the earlier first-person narrative, the Web log entry that follows is constructed on a timeline, moving from the deeper to the more recent past.

Megan B. started smoking marijuana and drinking alcohol at the age of thirteen. But when those didn't work for her she decided she needed to step it up a level. So by fourteen she began using cocaine as well as taking prescription drugs including Ritalin, Xanax, and Percocet. There was no need to go to a doctor for prescriptions. Friends got them from their parents' medicine cabinets. Like so many kids, she regarded prescription drugs as "safer" than other drugs. She figured that since people took them legally all the time, she'd be fine with them. By the time she was sixteen, she had graduated to heroin, sniffing it with friends to calm herself and get sleep. The stuff was easy to get and only a few dollars a bag. But then her heroin use started spiraling out of control. She missed curfews. She missed school; she didn't come home nights, saying she was staying at friends' homes. When her parents asked if she was taking drugs, she, of course, lied. For some time they believed her. Then two months before her seventeenth birthday, she died from an overdose. Her parents had missed the warning signs—the erratic behavior, her bouts of depression, restlessness, angry denials—discounting them as teenage rebelliousness. By the time they tried to intervene, to get professional help, Megan was dead.

What makes this narrative so effective is its objective tone, its matter-of-fact chronicling of Megan B.'s sad demise. Nowhere in the passage does the author take on an admonishing or threatening tone; nor does she cite a lot of dry statistics about drugs and young people's deaths. Instead, the author creates a growing sense of inevitability that climaxes in the stark final announcement, "By the time they tried to intervene, to get professional help, Megan was dead." The Internet has hundreds of Websites with narratives of the accidental deaths of drug victims. Likewise, there are dedicated sites with stories of deaths due to drunk driving, guns, house poisons, suicide, and other tragedies.

Features to Look for in Narrative Arguments

For a narrative argument to be successful, it should tell a story that clearly dramatizes a controversial issue. It should also meet some of the following basic criteria, which we offer as a checklist to evaluate your own or other writers' narratives.

The writer's narrative illustrates a controversial issue. Like either a position or a proposal argument, the narrative should tell a story that dramatizes an experience or series of experiences relevant to a controversial issue.

The narrative is a scene, a series of episodes, or a story that advocates a change of behavior or way of thinking. A narrative is more than just the citation of personal evidence—yours or someone else's—in support of your stand on an issue. It is a running account of events, usually arranged in chronological order, that illustrate someone's experience with aspects of the issue being debated. Even if your audience is aware of the problem and may even be sympathetic, framing your argument as a narrative has the potential to invite the reader to identify personally with the character or characters in the discourse and, as a result, move them to action. A paper proposing stricter laws against drunk drivers, for instance, might be especially persuasive if it is cast as a real-life account of someone who experienced injury in an automobile accident caused by a drunk driver.

The narrative should be credible. Whether your narrative is based on your own personal experience or someone else's, it should have credibility if it is going to win the sympathy of an audience. If because of inaccuracies, contradictions, or unbelievable exaggeration the story strains for validity, your narrative will lose its power to persuade.

The narrative should be representative. No matter how credible, your narrative should be *representative* of the issue. Say, for instance, you were stopped for exceeding the speed limit by 30 miles per hour in a town you passed through infrequently. In your narrative, you describe how the police officer not only reprimanded you but also put you under arrest, escorting you to the police station where you were put in a jail cell overnight. No matter how harrowing that narrative may be, no matter how unpleasant the police reaction was, your case would be weak if you argued that the town's police force was out of control and should be investigated by the district attorney's office. Unless you had other evidence that police overreaction was standard in that town, your narrative would not be symptomatic of a real problem. In contrast, the tragic story of Megan B. whose drug abuse was not dealt with in time is representative of hundreds of young people who annually fall victim to drug overdoses.

The narrative must avoid sentimentality. Opening an argument with a strong narrative has the potential of snagging the readers' attention and sympathy from the start. But you should be careful not to let your appeal become too emotional or sink into melodrama, otherwise your argument will lose sympathy. Choose your words and present facts and details carefully. Avoid words and expressions that are emotionally too loaded, too forceful.

SAMPLE NARRATIVE ARGUMENT

Narratives can have a greater impact on readers than other kinds of arguments because narratives appeal to values and emotions common to most people and, thus, have more persuasive power than cool logic and dry statistics. What follows is an appeal for people to be open-minded about physician-assisted suicide. It's an argument that is fashioned on a narrative and, thus, structured on a timeline—and one that is particularly poignant since much of it chronicles the author's grappling with his own terminal medical condition. Jerry Fensterman is the former director of development for Fenway Community Health in Boston, Massachusetts. This article appeared as a guest editorial in the *Boston Globe* on January 31, 2006, a few months before Mr. Fensterman's death.

I See Why Others Choose to Die

Jerry Fensterman

1   The U.S. Supreme Court's recent decision to let stand Oregon's law permitting physician-assisted suicide is sure to fuel an ongoing national debate. Issues of life and death are deeply felt and inspire great passions. It would be wonderful, and unusual, if all those joining the fray would do so with the humility and gravity the matter deserves.

2   I am approaching 50, recently remarried, and the father of a terrific 13-year-old young man. By every measure I enjoy a wonderful life. Or at least I did until April 2004, when I was diagnosed with kidney cancer. Surgery was my only hope to prevent its spread and save my life. The discovery of a new lump in December 2004 after two surgeries signaled that metastasis was underway. My death sentence had been pronounced.

3   Life may be the most intense addiction on earth. From the moment I first heard the words "you have cancer" and again when I was told that it was spreading out of control, I recognized my addiction to life almost at the cellular level. I have tried since then, as I did before, to live life to the fullest. I also committed myself to doing everything within my power to extend my life.

4   Toward that end I am participating in my third clinical trial in a year. I have gained some small benefit from it. I am, however, one of the first people with my cancer to try this drug. Its median benefit seems to be only on the order of three months. So my expectations are modest. The side effects of these drugs are significant, as are the symptoms of the cancer's gallop through my body. All things considered, I believe I have earned my merit badge for "doing all one can in the face of death to stay alive."

5   That the experience has changed me is obvious. I have a few scars, have lost 50 pounds, and my hair is thinner. I rely on oxygen nearly all the time, can no longer perform the job I loved, and have difficulty eating. More profoundly, my universe has contracted. Simply leaving home has become an enormous task, and travel is essentially out of the question. I can no longer run, swim, golf, ski, and play with my son. I haven't yet learned how to set goals or make plans for a future that probably consists of weeks or months, not years. I am also nearing a point where I will not be able to take care of my most basic needs.

6   Mine has been a long, difficult, and certain march to death. Thus, I have had ample time to reflect on my life, get my affairs in order, say everything I want to the people I love, and seek rapprochement with friends I have hurt or lost touch with. The bad news is that my pain and suffering have been drawn out, the rewarding aspects of life have inexorably shrunk, and I have watched my condition place an increasingly great physical and emotional burden on the people closest to me. While they have cared for me with great love and selflessness, I cannot abide how my illness has caused them hardship, in some cases dominating their lives and delaying their healing.

7   Perhaps the biggest and most profound change I have undergone is that my addiction to life has been "cured." I've kicked the habit! I now know how a feeling, loving, rational person could choose death over life, could choose to relieve his suffering as well as that of his loved ones a few months earlier than would happen naturally.

8   I am not a religious person, but I consider myself and believe I have proved throughout my life to be a deeply moral person. Personally I would not now choose physician-assisted suicide if it were available. I do not know if I ever would. Yet now, I understand in a manner that I never could have before why an enlightened society should, with thoughtful safeguards, allow the incurably ill to choose a merciful death.

9   The Supreme Court's ruling will inflame the debate over physician-assisted suicide. Besides adding my voice to this debate, I ask you to carefully search your soul before locking into any position. If you oppose physician-assisted suicide, first try to walk a mile in the shoes of those to whom you would deny this choice. For as surely as I'm now wearing them, they could one day just as easily be on your feet or those of someone you care deeply about.

Analysis of Sample Narrative Argument

Unlike the Megan B. and grizzly bear examples, Fensterman does not begin with a story and conclude with his claim. Instead, he opens with an acknowledgment of the U.S. Supreme Court's ruling to let stand the law permitting physician-assisted suicide. He then follows with seven paragraphs that personalize his coming to terms with his "death sentence." These paragraphs constitute the body of the piece and, like most narratives, the contents are structured on a timeline. In this case, the narrative begins in April 2004 when the author was diagnosed with kidney cancer and then relates events occurring in the next year and a half. In his final two paragraphs, he refers back to the controversy, saying that he would not choose physician-assisted suicide at this time and does not know if he ever would. But he has learned through his own experience of terminal illness why the option should be available.

Analyzing the Structure

The Beginning

Paragraph 1 constitutes the beginning of Fensterman's narrative argument—where he names the controversy, which his following narrative dramatizes. Here he specifically cites the U.S. Supreme Court's recent ruling "to let stand Oregon's law permitting physician-assisted suicide." Acknowledging how this will only fuel the ongoing national debate, he asks, because the issue is a matter of life and death, that people enter it "with the humility and gravity the matter deserves," thus anticipating his own personal story.

The Middle

Paragraphs 2 through 7 constitute Fensterman's personal narrative of his "death sentence." He immediately identifies himself as a 50-year-old recently remarried man and a father who "enjoys a wonderful life" and who clearly has a lot to live for. But in April 2004, he was diagnosed with cancer of the kidney. Over the next five paragraphs (3–7), he chronicles the events of the next two years. In December 2004, a new lump was discovered following two surgeries, signaling the cancer had spread. That "death sentence" announcement made Fensterman recognize his "addiction to life almost at the cellular level" (paragraph 3). As he says, since then he has dedicated himself to prolonging his life including participating in another clinical trial. But the benefits were short-lived and the side effects were significant—scars, weight loss, thinning of his hair. Worse, his universe "was contracted." He could no longer work, travel, "run, swim, golf, ski, and play" with his son. In paragraphs 6 and 7, as he approaches death, he says that he is reflecting on his life, getting his affairs in order, and contacting family members and friends. But what pains him the most is how his condition has become "an increasingly great physical and emotional burden on the people" to whom he is closest. And this hardship is what he "cannot abide" (paragraph 6). He concludes that he has become "cured" of his "addiction to life." As a result, he says he now understands "how a feeling, loving, rational person could choose death over life, could choose to relieve his suffering as well as that of his loved ones a few months earlier than would happen naturally" (paragraph 7).

The End

The final two paragraphs (8 and 9) make up the end of Fensterman's piece. Here he returns to the present tense and to his request for open-mindedness. Even after all the anguish he has undergone and the hardship no doubt assumed by his loved ones, Fensterman surprisingly announces that he "would not now choose physician-assisted suicide if it were available." That statement makes even stronger his appeal that "an enlightened society . . . allow the incurably ill to choose a merciful death." At the end of paragraph 9, he shifts to a powerful personal appeal, asking those who might be opposed to physician-assisted suicide to "walk a mile in the shoes of those to whom you would deny this choice." And he concludes with a reminder that he is wearing shoes that could one day "be on your feet or those of someone you care deeply about."

Analyzing the Narrative Features

The writer's narrative dramatizes a controversial issue. In the opening paragraph of Fensterman's piece, he cites the topic he will ultimately be addressing through his narrative argument, namely, the recent U.S. Supreme Court's decision to let stand Oregon's law, permitting physician-assisted suicide. But his focus is a plea for open-minded debate, informed by an appreciation of the experience of a person suffering with a terminal illness. He recognizes that the passage of this law will provoke debate about the rightness or wrongness of physician-assisted suicide. But he wants to argue that one should be acutely aware of the feelings and circumstances of patients suffering a terminal illness before denying them the right to end their lives through physician-assisted suicide.

The writer's narration is credible. Fensterman's narrative is highly credible. In paragraph 2, he forthrightly identifies himself and his plight: "I am approaching 50, recently remarried, and the father of a terrific 13-year-old young man. By every measure I enjoy a wonderful life. Or at least I did until April 2004, when I was diagnosed with kidney cancer." He is an ordinary man, leading an ordinary life, and grateful for ordinary things. However, like everyone else's, his life is fragile, and it nearly crashed down around him when he was diagnosed with cancer. This is a situation everyone can identify with and one everyone secretly fears. At the same time, anyone who knows of the ravages of cancer or knows someone who has suffered from it can identify intensely with the piece.

The writer's narrative is representative of the issue. Fensterman's narrative could not be more representative of the issue. His reflection on the various stages of cancer diagnosis and treatment represent what so many people go through. In paragraph 3, he says that he recognizes that "Life may be the most intense addiction on earth. From the moment I first heard the words 'you have cancer' and again when I was told that it was spreading out of control, I recognized my addiction to life almost at the cellular level." He acknowledges the physical toll the disease takes: "I have a few scars, have lost 50 pounds, and my hair is thinner. I rely on oxygen nearly all the time, can no longer perform the tasks I love . . . Simply leaving home has become an enormous task" (paragraph 5). The specific details reflect what many cancer victims feel. He also acknowledges the burden of his illness on those he loves: "While they have cared for me with great love and selflessness, I cannot abide how my illness has caused them hardship, in some cases dominating their lives and delaying their healing" (paragraph 6). Such a painful sentiment can be widely shared.

The writer's narrative avoids sentimentality. A subject such as imminent death is difficult to discuss without being emotional. Yet Fensterman manages to do just that while avoiding sentimentality. He is straightforward in his description of his own physical and emotional suffering. And in the proclamation that concludes the various stages he has gone through, he dispassionately states, "Perhaps the biggest and most profound change I have undergone is that my addiction to life has been 'cured.' I've kicked the habit" (paragraph 7).

Checklist for Writing a Narrative Argument

- Does your narrative dramatize a controversial issue?
- Is your narrative credible?
- Is your narrative representative of the issue?
- Does your narrative avoid sentimentality?
- Does your narrative advocate a change of behavior or a way of thinking?

The writer's narrative advocates a change of behavior or a way of thinking. Clearly, Fensterman has used the story of his personal struggle with cancer to influence the debate over the appropriateness of physician-assisted suicide. Every aspect of his narrative does that—from the diagnosis of the disease (paragraph 2), to his awareness of the toll cancer treatment is taking on his body and on the family and friends he loves (paragraphs 4, 5, and 6), to his realization that "I now know how a feeling, loving, rational person could choose death over life, could choose to relieve his suffering as well as that of his loved ones a few months earlier than would happen naturally." Although he admits that he personally would not choose physician-assisted suicide, the entire point of his narrative is to illustrate that in the face of terminal suffering a person should have a choice. As he so powerfully concludes, "If you oppose physician-assisted suicide, first try to walk a mile in the shoes of those whom you would deny this choice. For as surely as I'm now wearing them, they could one day just as easily be on your feet or those of someone you care about deeply" (paragraph 9).

EXERCISES

1. Look online or in current issues of a local or national newspaper for essays about controversial issues. Make a list in your journal of the strategies different writers use to begin their arguments. Bring your examples to class and work in a group to share your findings. Photocopy your examples so that each member has a "catalogue" of good introductions to consider.

2. Repeat exercise 1, but this time collect examples of conclusions from argument essays. Your goal here is to compile a catalogue of endings to consult.

3. Construct a formal outline for one of the essays other than "Skeletons in the Attic" in this chapter. Compare it with another student's. If there are places where your outlines differ, analyze how your readings are different.

4. Go back to the examples you found for exercise 1. Divide the essays you and the members of your group found into position and proposal arguments.

5. In your journal, respond to the ideas in Amanda Collins's, Sean Flynn's, or Jerry Fensterman's essay. With which of their reasons do you agree? How would you refute any of their reasons? Make a pro/con checklist that lists their reasons and points you might use to debate them.

6. Through the Internet or your library resources, do some reading on either Karpati's or Fensterman's subject to find out how others view the issue. Create a dialogue among the various positions on the issue and explore their points of view to find common or shared concerns or values. With this knowledge, deliberate about how you stand on the issue.

7. If you were to write an argument essay of your own on either subject, how would you begin your essay? Experiment with a few introductions. Next, write a first draft.

8. Write a narrative argument on some debatable issue with which you have had personal experience.

Using Evidence: Thinking Like an Advocate

LEARNING OBJECTIVES

After studying this chapter, you should be able to:

1. Recognize the five basic types of evidence. (p. 159)
2. Explain how evidence can have very different interpretations. (p. 173)
3. Apply an eight-point checklist to determine if your evidence will work for your argument. (p. 177)

Because the United States is a democracy, a widespread conviction in our society holds that having opinions is our responsibility as citizens—a conviction supported by our fast-forward multimedia culture. You see opinions expressed on the nightly news every time a reporter sticks a microphone in the face of somebody on the street, or whenever Oprah Winfrey moves into the studio audience. It's the heart of talk radio and television programs. In newspapers and magazines, it comes in the form of "opinion polls" that tally up our positions on all sorts of weighty issues:

"Should the use of marijuana for medical purposes be legalized throughout the nation?"

"Is the economy this year in better shape than it was last year at this time?"

"Do you think that the American judicial system treats people equally whether they are rich or poor?"

"Is the U.S. government doing enough to prevent acts of domestic terrorism?"

"Do men and women have the same opportunities for promotions and raises in the workplace?"

"Should people be allowed to purchase assault rifles?"

All this on-the-spot opinion-making encourages people to take an immediate stand on an issue, whether or not they have sufficient understanding and information about it. However, holding an opinion on a matter does not necessarily mean that you have investigated the issue or that you have carefully considered the views of others or that you have gathered enough information to support your position. If you want to make successful arguments, you need more than a gut reaction or simple reliance on yourself for the "truth."

This means thinking of yourself as an *advocate*—a prosecutor or defense attorney, if you like. You need a case to present to the jury of your readers, one that convinces them that your interpretation of an issue is plausible. Like an advocate, when you're constructing an argument you look for support to put before your readers: facts, statistics, people's experiences—in a word, *evidence*. The jury judges your argument both on the evidence you bring forth and on your interpretation of that evidence. So, like an advocate, to write successful arguments you need to understand and weigh the value of the *supporting evidence* for your case.

How Much Evidence Is Enough?

Like any advocate, you need to decide *how much* evidence to present to your readers. Your decision will vary from case to case, although with more practice you'll find it easier to make a judgment. Common sense is a good predictor: If the evidence is enough to persuade you, it's probably enough to persuade like-minded readers. Unsympathetic readers may need more proof. The more unexpected or unorthodox your claim, the more evidence you will need to convince skeptical readers. It's often as much a case of the *right* evidence as it is the *right amount* of evidence. One fact or statistic, if it touches on your readers' most valued standards and principles, may be enough to swing an argument for a particular group. Here's where outlining (Chapter 5) can help; an outline helps you make sure you present evidence for every assertion you make.

It's easier to gather too much evidence and winnow out the least effective than to have too little and try to expand it. One of our instructors used to call this the "Cecil B. DeMille strategy," after the great Hollywood producer. DeMille's theory was that if audiences were impressed by five dancers, they would be overwhelmed by five hundred—but just to be sure, he'd hire a thousand. That's a good strategy to have when writing arguments; you can always use a sentence such as "Of the 116 explosions in GMC trucks with side-mounted fuel tanks, four cases are most frequently cited" and then go on to discuss those four. You've let your readers know that another 112 are on record so they can weigh this fact when considering the four you examine in particular. You may never need a thousand pieces of evidence—or dancers—in an argument, but there's no harm in thinking big!

Why Arguments Need Supporting Evidence

Evidence is composed of facts and their interpretations. As we said in Chapter 1, facts are pieces of information that can be verified—that is, statistics, examples, testimony, historical details. For instance, it is a fact that SAT verbal scores across the nation have gone up for the last ten years. One interpretation might be that students today are spending more time reading and less time watching television than students in the last decade. Another interpretation might be that secondary schools are putting more emphasis on language skills. A third might be that changes in the test or the prevalence of test-preparation courses have contributed to the higher scores.

In everyday conversation, we make claims without offering supporting evidence: "Poverty is the reason why there is so much crime"; "The president is doing a poor job handling the economy"; "Foreign cars are better than American cars." Although we may have good reasons to back up such statements, we're not often called upon to do so, at least not in casual conversation. In written arguments, however, presenting evidence is critical, and a failure to do so is glaring. Without supporting data and examples, an argument is hollow. It will bore the reader, fail to convince, and collapse under criticism. Moreover, you'll be in danger of making a hasty generalization by drawing a conclusion with too little evidence. Consider the following paragraph:

> Video games are a danger to the mental well-being of children. Some children play video games for hours on end, and the result is that their behavior and concentration are greatly affected. Many of them display bad behavior. Others have difficulty doing other, more important things. Parents with young children should be stricter about what video games their children play and how long they play them.

Chances are this paragraph has not convinced you that video games are a threat to children. The sample lacks the details that might persuade you. For instance, exactly what kind of bad behavior do children display? And what specific video games out of the hundreds on the market are the real culprits? How is concentration actually affected? What "more important things" does the author mean? And how many hours of video consumption need to occur before signs of dangerous behavior begin to manifest themselves?

Consider how much sharper and more persuasive the following rewrite is with the addition of specific details, facts, and examples:

> Video games may be fun for children, but they can have detrimental effects on their behavior. They encourage violent behavior. A steady dose of some of the more violent games clearly results in more aggressive behavior. One study by the Department of Psychology at State University has shown that after two hours of "Urban Guerrilla," 60 percent of the 12 boys and 20 percent of the 12 girls tested began to mimic the street-fighting gestures—punching, kicking, karate-chopping each other. The study has also shown that such games negatively affect concentration. Even half an hour after their game playing had lapsed, the boys had difficulty settling down to read or draw. Since my parents restricted my little brother's game playing to weekends, he concentrates when completing his homework and has fewer fights with his best friend.

The statistics from the academic study, as well as the concrete case of the writer's own brother, give readers something substantial to consider. Presenting supporting evidence puts meat on the bones of your argument. (In Chapter 9, we will go into greater depth about how to gather research evidence, particularly from the library and the Internet.)

Forms of Evidence

We hope that when you begin to develop an argument, you utilize debate, dialogue, and deliberation, as we suggested in Chapter 1. As you do this, you need to expand and deepen your understanding of the issue by collecting useful evidence from both sides of the issue. Don't neglect this critical step: Remember, the bulk of your argument is composed of material supporting your claim.

Writers enlist four basic kinds of evidence to support their arguments: personal experience (theirs and others'), outside authorities, factual references and examples, and statistics. We'll examine each separately, but you'll probably want to use combinations of these kinds of evidence when building your arguments in order to convince a wide range of readers.

Personal Experience—Yours and Others'

The power of personal testimony cannot be underestimated. Think of the number of movies that have failed at the box office in spite of huge and expensive ad campaigns simply because word-of-mouth trashed it. Or, conversely, think of the number of times you've read a book on the recommendation of friends—or taken a certain course or shopped at a particular store. You might have chosen the college you're attending based on the recommendation of someone you know. Many people find the word-of-mouth judgments that make up personal testimony the most persuasive kind of evidence.

In written arguments, the personal testimony of other people is used to affirm facts and support your claim. Essentially, their experiences provide you with eyewitness accounts of events that are not available to you. Such accounts may prove crucial in winning over an audience. Suppose you are writing about the rising abuse of alcohol among college students. In addition to statistics and hard facts, your argument can gain strength from quoting the experience of a first-year student who nearly died one night from alcohol poisoning. Or, in an essay decrying discrimination against minorities in hiring, consider the authenticity provided by an interview of neighborhood residents who felt they were passed over for a job because of race or ethnic identity.

Your own eyewitness testimony can be a powerful tool of persuasion. Suppose, for example, that you are writing a paper in which you argue that the big teaching hospital in the city provides far better care and has a lower death rate than the small rural hospital in your town. The hard facts and statistics on the quality of care and comparative mortality rates you provide will certainly have a stark persuasiveness. But consider the dramatic impact on those figures were you to recount how your own trip to the rural emergency room nearly cost you your life because of understaffing or the lack of critical but expensive diagnostic equipment.

Personal observation is useful and valuable in arguments. However, you should be careful not to draw hasty generalizations from such testimony. The fact that you and three of your friends are staunchly in favor of replacing letter grades with a pass/fail system does not support the claim that the entire student body at your school is in favor of the conversion. You need a much greater sample. Likewise, the dislike most people in your class feel for a certain professor does not justify the claim that the university tenure system should be abolished. On such complex issues, you need more than personal testimony to make a case.

You also have to remember the "multiple-perspective" rule. As any police officer can tell you, there are as many versions of the "truth" of an incident as there are people who saw it. The people involved in a car accident see it one way (or more), yet witnesses in a car heading in the other direction may interpret events differently, as will people in an apartment six stories above the street on which the accident took place. Your job is to sort out the different testimonies and make sense of them. Personal experience—yours and that of people you know—is valuable. However, on major issues you need statistics and data, as well as the evidence provided by outside authorities. But before we turn to outside authorities here is an example of a position argument based on personal experience.

This position argument, based on personal experience, is written by Kari Peterson, an English major at the University of Hawaii in Honolulu. Using her own personal experience to make a convincing case, she argues for the need for society to alter its perceptions of individuals with disabilities and to redefine such individuals not in terms of limitations but a range of talents and competencies.

Peterson 1

Kari Peterson

Professor Larson

English 101

April 15, 2013

My Body, My Closet: A Personal History of Passing, Coming Out,
and Grappling with Identity and Disability in America

1   The average person will not notice the slight barrel shape of my chest or the mild clubbing of my fingertips. They probably will not hear the faint crackle when I exhale, or even think much of my persistent coughing. They will not see me as "different"; at worst I might be categorized as a chronic cold sufferer. A pulmonologist, however, will recognize these subtle physical attributes as classic signs of a very specific and lethal congenital disorder. A sweat test, chest x-rays, and breathing tests will subsequently confirm my status as a woman with cystic fibrosis, and as a woman with a disability. Despite looking decidedly "normal," I am, in fact, a de facto member of the "other."

2   Luckily, once removed from the damning light of the biomedical realm, and placed into the context of everyday interaction, I am allowed to be just another human being. Other than my phenotype, that pronounces my Caucasian heritage (replete with pale skin, blonde hair, and blue eyes), the rest of my social identity is mine to carve out. My choices in education, employment, hobbies, and participation in various group activities will construct what social roles, perceptions, and expectations are projected

on to me. The result is a wide swath of labels: from the broad "student,"
"intern," "employee," feminist," to the more specific "metalwork artist,"
"Latin dance enthusiast," "dog lover" . . . and so forth. My disability status
is notably absent.

3   Until recently, "individual with a disability" was not a label I
openly embraced. Instead, it was one I actively shunned. Because cystic
fibrosis does not result in decreased mobility, use of a mobility assistive
device, physical deformities, involuntary spasms or seizures, difficulty in
producing speech, the reduced or complete inability to see or hear, or
manifest in any other obvious (external) way associated with disability,
I have had, unlike many in the disability community, the choice to be
"seen" as a "person with a disability" or to "pass" as an able-bodied
individual.

4   For most of my life, the choice was simple: I elected to "pass."
My healthy looking body made a convenient closet. Why hide? Why deny
such an intrinsic, and in my case permanent, part of my identity? The
answer lies in the inevitably narrow depictions of disability in the news,
media, and entertainment outlets. Or in the readily available statistics
profiling the disparities between the able-bodied and the disabled in
areas such as completion of higher education, unemployment, employment discrimination, and even the increased likelihood of being a victim
of rape. The answer may even be found in you, dear reader. What is your
internal reaction to "seeing" disability? Do you perhaps feel pity? A tinge
of resentment? General discomfort or maybe awkwardness? Nothing? Dig
deeper. Would you hire someone with a disability for a demanding job?
Or award a business grant? How about a loan for a personal mortgage?
Still nothing? Now let's put your skin in the game—literally. Would you
have sex with someone with a disability? Date one? Marry?

5   My point is, look for the place in your own thinking where the water
gets murky, because that insidious space is where the decision to "pass"
or "come out" is rooted. It is also the space that must be collectively

transformed to promote equality for the disability community. It will not be enough to alter policy at the state or even Federal level; the change has to occur at the level of cultural perception.

6   Somewhere between recognition of my own internalized ableism and a waning ability to "pass" as my cystic fibrosis worsened, I came out. My experiences as a newly outed person with a disability have both made it abundantly clear that the status quo is not acceptable, but also hopeful that there is genuine possibility for change.

7   How does one go about a task as Herculean as changing a cultural perception, especially about something as deeply entrenched as disability? It begins with addressing culture's definition of disability itself, namely dismantling the core idea that disability is defined as a poor health outcome. Instead, ability and disability should be viewed as demographic variables, and disability as only a difference of ability. Essentially, a view of disability as a demographic variable is one that accepts disability as a "normal" status in lieu of situating disability in opposition to normality. In the same way that society has largely recognized and accepted a wider spectrum of sexual desire and sexual orientation as natural and variant, the same must be done for disability. Furthermore people with disabilities must be defined not in terms of limitations but rather defined in terms of the wide range of skills, talents, capabilities and competencies, energies and gifts that these individuals possess. This shift in definition does not preclude a desire to seek medical treatment, nor does it suggest that poor health is not a component part of some disabilities. It simply creates a more inclusive definition to fit all disability statuses, including those that are temporary or episodic, and describes a spectrum of ability rather than a pathologizing of inability.

8   If this sounds impossible, simply recall social views on sexual orientation even within the past few decades. The Stonewall riots took place in just 1969. In stark contrast, a Gallup poll taken in 2011 demonstrated that a majority of Americans (53%) were in favor of gay marriage (gallup.com).

Cultures therefore can and do experience dramatic shifts, though it often takes brave trailblazers and the energy of grassroots advocacy.

9   Why is the view of disability as a poor health outcome problematic? This definition is not only narrow and inaccurate, but also damaging because it cements disability as being mutually exclusive from associations with "health," "vitality," "endurance," "vibrancy," "productivity," "sexuality" and ability in any form. The net result of this fixed dichotomy is a proliferation of negative stereotypes of disability that range from people with disabilities as objects of pity to social burdens. Even "positive" portrayals of people with disabilities as medical miracles still focus on the struggle caused by disability. The result of all of these narrow portraits is a monolithic and reductionist view of disability that fails to capture either the actual disability experience or the people who have them.

10   One of the most powerful platforms for both challenging current disability stereotypes and constructing a new view of disability is the media. Film, novels, broadcast news, even an Internet meme or a seemingly innocuous video on YouTube, has the ability to direct the social narratives we project onto our understanding of the world. Yes, even an Internet meme. On November 18th, 2011 the University of California, Davis made headlines after a photo was published of university police officer Lt. John Pike spraying a group of seated student demonstrators with pepper spray. The photo subsequently spawned a wide range of Photoshop manipulations, including the cop spraying the signers of declaration of independence and the presidents on Mount Rushmore. The meme images focus on both the absurdity of the act as well as highlight the disparate power dynamics at play. The viewer is directed to see injustice.

11   There are a multitude of memes that involve disability. Some mock disabled statuses, others celebrate it, and some that capture the uncomfortable space in between, the uncomfortable place that people with disability fall into society's tendency to place populations into false paradigms. Many of the memes feature pop culture references or characters and are not specific

to disability, but have been captioned to reflect on disability. For example two popular memes, one featuring a still from the television show *Futurama* and one featuring a still and dialogue from *The Lord of the Rings*, have had a number of captions applied to them, including caption relating to disability. The disability meme from *Futurama* simply reads, "Can't tell if disabled, or just faking." Captions applied to the LOTR meme include "One does not simply go on a night out when in a wheelchair" and "One does not simply justify disabilities expenses." Both of these memes therefore clearly subscribe to negative stereotypes about disability.

12   On the other, inspirational side of the aisle are the memes that celebrate disability, or more specifically those that demonstrate the power to overcome adversity. One meme depicts a man and a young girl, both fitted with prostheses legs, both running, both full of joy; the caption reads "The only disability in life is a bad attitude." Although none of these memes is likely to be the deciding factor in determining how disability is viewed, it is clear that we use memes (and other forms of media) as a forum to dissect, evaluate, and reevaluate our own social views.

13   In a nutshell, all media matters. As Michael Real writes in his text, *Exploring Media Culture: A Guide*, "what connects the individual person to media and culture is consciousness. We direct our consciousness to media texts, and the texts impress our consciousness"(Real, pg. 12), further noting that "it is a mistake to conceive of media and communication as simply ways of moving information." (Real, pg. 14) The relationship we have with the media, as Real points out, is oddly reciprocal; despite the fact that media is a social construction of our own making it also works to construct our social views. The issue with contemporary depictions of disability is that there are too few and that they reaffirm and reinforce marginalizing views about disability.

14   So where does one find fictional characters or stories about people with disabilities? Good question. Go ahead and compile a mental list,

see if you can come up with more than twenty. Now whittle down the list to exclude characters that are villains, passive repositories for their disabilities, or redemptive foils for other characters. Chances are your list is significantly shorter, and herein lies the problem. Characters with disabilities are rare, often one dimensional caricatures, or simply props for their disabilities.

15　　One of the most extreme examples of media's (specifically Hollywood) tendency to caricaturize disability is the preponderance of villains with disabilities, specifically the type that are driven to their villainy and madness because of disability. This particular character type is a regular feature in many action, fantasy, and science fiction novels and films; a few notable examples of the evil cripple trope include arch villains such as Dr. No (*James Bond*), Obesandjo (*District 9*), Dr. Connor (*The Amazing Spider Man*), Darth Vader (Star *Wars* Trilogy) Captain Hook (*Peter Pan*), Leigh Teabing (*The Da Vinci Code*), The Joker (*Dark Knight*), and Mason Verger (*The Silence of the Lambs*).

16　　On the other end of the spectrum is the person with a disability whose primary function is to serve as a redemptive foil for the main character. For example, in the film *Walk to Remember*, the main character Landon Carter is shown to be a broken, damaged, and thoroughly self destructive person until he is redeemed by his love for the virginal Jamie Sullivan who ultimately succumbs to leukemia. The issue with the film is not the plot, but the respective characterizations of Landon and Jamie. The character of Landon Carter is allowed room to be complex, flawed, and demonstrate growth whereas Jamie's character is confined to not only her disability but her role as Landon's salvation. She cannot escape her archetypal obligations of purity and grace, even as she discovers that she is dying. Jamie's body undergoes tremendous change, but her character development remains stagnant. Other films that follow a similar trajectory in terms of disability as a precursor to discovery or redemption are *P.S. I Love You, Life as a House, My Sister's Keeper*, and *Here on Earth*.

17   This critique is not meant to suggest that villains should never have disabilities, or that a disability cannot serve as a powerful plot device. But it is an issue if the representation of disability is limited to these formats.

18   Disability narratives also face hurdles in non-fiction. In his text, *Disability and Media: Prescriptions for Change,* Charles Riley dissects what he refers to as the disability industrial complex, or the gross commercialization of disability narratives that follow a structure of loss, dramatic breakthrough, and recovery or fall into the medical miracle category. Referring to the Chicken Soup for the Soul Series (a series of books containing inspirational short stories and essays, many of which focus on disability and recovery), he notes " . . . the Chicken Soup machine alone buoyed the quarterly sales of Amazon, Border and Barnes and Noble". But he goes on to ask, "Did it bring any benefit to the disability community besides royalty checks?" Riley's conclusion is a proverbial double edged sword. On the one hand he notes that the commercialization of disability has lead to a larger audience for stories about disability and, therefore, the subsequent ability to build greater public awareness of disability issues. Comparing the ability of former celebrity Lance Armstrong, who battled testicular cancer on the public stage, and a specifically medical publication to draw attention to cancer, he writes "there is a substantial difference between the impact on public awareness of a book such as Lance Armstrong's *It's Not About the Bike* (700,000 copies and massive press coverage) and an article on testicular cancer even in the *New England Journal of Medicine* (circulation 200,000)." However he laments "the narrative that sells preempts the narrative that empowers in a trade-off that perpetuates the stereotypes that satisfy the nondisabled readers that economically support the books." In other words, the stories about disability that get told are the ones that sell. Thus the stories that have made it into public consciousness are those with blockbuster recovery or achievement in spite of incredible hurdles. There is no room for the "every" person in the world of the commercial disability narrative.

19   Why does any of this matter? Because, to put it bluntly, the disability community is still actively being marginalized. Here are the numbers. The Department of Labor's March 2013 Labor report showed only a 20.7% labor force participation rate of people with disabilities versus a 68.7% rate of people without disabilities. The unemployment rate for people with disabilities is 13% versus 7.4% for people without disabilities. 26,379 charges were filed (under the Americans with Disabilities Act and/or Title VII) with the Equal Employment Opportunities Commission. The National Council on Disability report indicates that although the enrollment of people with disabilities at post secondary institutions has increased by over 50%, their graduation rate is still less than half of their able-bodied peers. According to the Bureau of Justice, the rate of violent crime for "females with disabilities, the rate of violence was 53 per 1,000 in 2011, compared to 17 per 1,000 for females without disabilities." In other words, we have a serious issue of inequity.

20   These dire statistics do not occur in a vacuum. Could it be that cultural misconceptions about "disability" are in part responsible for the economic and social marginalization of people with disabilities? Does the misapprehension of a "disability" place unnecessary obstacles in the path of people with disabilities?" I think it does. It wasn't too long ago when women in the workplace were viewed with suspicion and contempt; after all, the woman's "natural" place was in the home caring for children and tending to the domestic. When this view predominated, fewer women attended or completed college, joined the workforce, or left childcare to men. Today the dialogue has shifted to increasing the number of female CEOs and women in senior executive positions. Women now earn the majority of bachelor college degrees. More men are choosing to stay at home with children, while women return to work. It is only the social dinosaur that still believes that women should be relegated to the domestic sphere.

21

Peterson 9

In spite of a great deal of personal trepidation and the very real stigma of being disabled, I came out. Why? Because it is my small contribution towards changing the status quo. Because I can help to challenge the stereotypes and stigma that suppress the disability community on a daily basis. Because I can prove that my disability does not define me. Because hopefully my willingness to be "out" will give others the courage to do the same. Obviously, it will take more than me, more than every person with a disability living openly. It will take our able bodied allies standing with us, demanding that our differences do not make us less than equal.

Peterson 10

Works Cited

"Americans with Disabilities Act of 1990 (ADA) Charges (includes Concurrent Charges with Title VII, ADEA, and EPA) FY 1997–FY 2012." *ADA.* N.p., n.d. Web. 5 Apr. 2013.

"Bureau of Justice Statistics (BJS)." *Bureau of Justice Statistics (BJS).* N.p., n.d. Web. 5 Apr. 2013.

"For First Time, Majority of Americans Favor Legal Gay Marriage." *For First Time, Majority of Americans Favor Legal Gay Marriage.* N.p., n.d. Web. 5 Apr. 2013.

"ODEP—Office of Disability Employment Policy." *U.S. Department of Labor.* N.p., n.d. Web. 14 Apr. 2013.

"Persons with a Disability: Labor Force Characteristics Summary." *U.S. Bureau of Labor Statistics.* U.S. Bureau of Labor Statistics, 08 June 2012. Web. 5 Apr. 2013.

Real, Michael R. *Exploring Media Culture: A Guide.* Thousand Oaks, CA: Sage Publications, 1996. Print.

Riley, Charles A. *Disability and the Media: Prescriptions for Change.* Hanover, NH: University of New England, 2005. Print.

Outside Authorities

Think of the number of times you've heard statements such as these:

"Scientists have found that . . ."

"Scholars inform us that . . ."

"According to his biographer, President Lincoln decided that . . ."

What these statements have in common is the appeal to outside authorities—people recognized as experts in a given field, people who can speak knowledgeably about a subject. Because authoritative opinions are such powerful tools of persuasion, you hear them all the time in advertisements. Automobile manufacturers quote the opinions of professional race car drivers; the makers of toothpaste cite dentists' claims; famous basketball players push brand-name sneakers all the time. Similarly, a good trial lawyer will almost always rely on forensic experts or other such authorities to help sway a jury.

Outside authorities can provide convincing evidence to support your ideas. However, there are times when expert opinion can be used inappropriately. This faulty use of authority can undermine the effectiveness of your argument. For the most part, experts usually try to be objective and fair-minded when asked for opinions. But, an expert with a vested interest in an issue might slant the testimony in his or her favor. The dentist who has just purchased a huge number of shares in a new toothpaste company would not be an unbiased expert. You wouldn't turn for an unbiased opinion on lung cancer to scientists working for tobacco companies, or ask an employee facing the loss of his or her job to comment on the advisability of layoffs. When you cite authorities, you should be careful to note any possibility of bias so your readers can fairly weigh the contributions. (This is often done through *attribution*; see Chapter 9.) Knowing that Professor Brown's research will benefit from construction of the supercollider doesn't make her enthusiasm for its other potential benefits less credible, but it does help your readers see her contributions to your argument in their proper context.

You should also check the credentials of those experts you are citing as evidence. Certainly claims supported by the research of reliable authorities in the field can add to the validity of your argument. But research is often debated, and evidence often disputed. So you should evaluate the credentials of the expert or experts who conducted the studies—what organizations, institutions, and universities they are affiliated with; their educational background; the books and/or journals where they may have published their results. It would also be wise to familiarize yourself with the actual research to be certain that it looks like valid and convincing support for your argument.

Another faulty use of authority is the use of an expert to provide evidence in a subject area in which he or she possesses no expertise. If you are going to cite authorities, you must make sure that they are competent; they should have expertise in their fields. You wouldn't turn to a professional beekeeper for opinions on laser surgery any more than you would quote a civil engineer on macroeconomic theory. And yet, just that is done all the time in advertising. Although it makes better sense to ask a veterinarian for a professional opinion about what to feed your pet, advertisers hire known actors to push dog food (as well as yogurt and skin cream). Of course, in advertising, celebrity sells. But that's not the case in most written arguments. It would not impress a critical reader to cite Tom Cruise's views on the use of fetal tissue or the greenhouse effect. Again, think about the profile of your audience. Whose expertise would they respect on your topic? Those are the experts to cite.

Factual References and Examples

Facts do as much to inform as they do to persuade, as we mentioned in Chapter 1. If somebody wants to sell you something, they'll pour on the details. For instance, ask the used-car salesperson about that black 2012 Ford Explorer in the lot, and he or she will hold forth about what a "creampuff" it is: only 18,400 original miles, mint condition, five-speed transmission with overdrive, all-black leather interior, and loaded—AC, power brakes, cruise control, CD player, premium sound system, captain's chair, and so on. Or listen to how the cereal manufacturers inform you that their toasted Os now contain "all-natural oat bran, which has been found to prevent cancer." Information is not always neutral. The very selection process implies intent. By offering specific facts or examples about your claim, you can make a persuasive argument.

The strategy in using facts and examples is to get readers so absorbed in the information that they nearly forget they are being persuaded to buy or do something. So common is this strategy in television ads that some have been given the name "infomercials"—ads that give the impression of being a documentary on the benefits of a product. For instance, you might be familiar with the margarine commercial narrated by a man who announces that at 33 years of age he had a heart attack. He then recounts the advice of his doctor for avoiding coronary disease, beginning with the need for exercise and climaxing with the warning about cutting down on cholesterol. Not until the very end of the ad does the narrator inform us that, taking advantage of his second chance, the speaker has switched to a particular brand of margarine, which, of course, is cholesterol free.

In less blatant form, this "informational" strategy can be found in newspaper columns and editorials, where authors give the impression that they are simply presenting the facts surrounding particular issues when in reality they may be attempting to persuade readers to see things their way. For instance, suppose in an apparently objective commentary a writer discusses how history is replete with people wrongfully executed for first-degree murder. Throughout the piece, the author cites several specific cases in which it was learned too late that the defendant had been framed or that the real killer had confessed. On the surface, the piece may appear to be simply presenting historical facts, but the more subtle intention may be to convince people that capital punishment is morally wrong. The old tagline from *Dragnet*, "Just the facts, ma'am," isn't quite the whole picture. How those facts are used is also part of their persuasive impact.

Often facts and examples are used to establish cause-and-effect relationships. It's very important, when both writing and reading arguments, to test the links the facts forge. While one event may indeed follow another, you can't automatically assume a causal relationship. This can result in a logical fallacy, in this case post hoc, ergo propter hoc. For instance, it may rain the day after every launch of the space shuttle, but does that prove that shuttle launches affect the weather in Florida? Similarly, we are all familiar with politicians who claim credit for improvements in the economy that have little to do with the legislation they have proposed. They hope to gain votes by having the public believe that there is a direct causal relationship between their actions and the economic improvement. Often this strategy backfires when opponents point out the lack of any actual connection.

Sometimes even experts disagree; one might see the rise in prostate cancer rates for vasectomy patients as reason to abolish the surgery; another might point to other contributing causes (diet, lack of exercise, hormonal imbalance). If you don't have the expertise to determine which of the conflicting experts is correct, you'll probably decide based on the *weight of the evidence*—whichever side has the most people or the most plausible reasons supporting it. This, in fact, is how most juries decide cases.

Statistics

People are impressed by numbers. Saying that 77 percent of the student body at your school supports a woman's right to choose is far more persuasive than saying that a lot of people on campus are pro-choice. **Statistics** have a special no-nonsense authority. Batting averages, medical statistics, polling results (election and otherwise), economic indicators, the stock market index, unemployment figures, scientific ratings, FBI statistics, percentages, demographic data—they all are reported in numbers. If they're accurate, statistics are difficult to argue against, though a skillful manipulator can use them to mislead.

The demand for statistics has made market research a huge business in America. During an election year, weekly and daily results on voters' opinions of candidates are released from various news organizations and TV networks, as well as independent polling companies such as the Harris and Gallup organizations. Most of the brand-name products you buy, the TV shows and movies you watch, or the CDs you listen to were made available after somebody did test studies on sample populations to determine the potential success of these items. Those same statistics are then used in promotional ads. Think of the number of times you've heard claims such as these:

"Nine out of ten doctors recommend Zappo aspirin over any other brand."

"Our new Speed King copier turns out 24 percent more copies per minute."

"Sixty-eight percent of those polled approve of women in military combat roles."

Of course, these claims bear further examination. If you polled only ten doctors, nine of whom recommended Zappo, that's not a big enough sample to imply that 90 percent of *all* doctors do. To avoid drawing a hasty generalization from too small a sample, avoid using sweeping words such as *all, always, never,* or *none.* Either be straightforward about the statistics supporting your claim or limit your claim with qualifiers such as *some, many, often,* or *few.* As Mark Twain once observed, "There are lies, damned lies, and statistics."

Numbers don't lie, but they can be manipulated. Sometimes, to sway an audience, claim makers will cite figures that are inaccurate or dated, or they will intentionally misuse accurate figures to make a case. If, for instance, somebody claims that 139 students and professors protested the invitation of a certain controversial guest to your campus, it would be a distortion of the truth not to mention that another 1,500 attended the talk and gave the speaker a standing ovation. Providing only those numbers or statistics that support the writer's claim and ignoring or concealing figures that might indicate otherwise is one way of stacking the deck. While this practice might deceive—at least temporarily—an uninformed audience, the writer risks damaging his or her credibility once the true figures are revealed.

Be on guard for the misleading use of statistics, a technique used all too frequently in advertising. The manufacturer that claims its flaked corn cereal is 100 percent cholesterol free misleads the public because no breakfast cereal of any brand contains cholesterol (which is found only in animal fats). French fries prepared in pure vegetable oil are also cholesterol free, but that doesn't mean that they're the best food for your health. Manufacturers that use terms like *cholesterol-free, light,* and *low fat* are trying to get you to buy their products without really revealing the basis for their nutritional claims. Although it's tempting to use such crowd-pleasing statistics, it's a good idea to avoid them in your own arguments because they are deceptive. If your readers discover your deception, your chances of persuading them to accept your position or proposal become unlikely.

Different Interpretations of Evidence

As we already said, evidence consists of solid facts, scientific studies and data, historical analysis, statistics, quotations from accepted authorities, and pertinent examples, as well as personal narratives that your audience will find relevant and compelling.

But not all evidence is of equal worth or value; not all evidence makes an argument valid. And not all scientific facts have a single interpretation. This is why different people can look at the same scientific data and have completely different interpretations. Although they may not argue over facts or the data, they will strenuously debate the interpretations of facts. In fact, some of the most hotly contested issues in society and politics revolve around the interpretation of the evidence. And the reason that people disagree about interpretation is that people hold fundamental differences in underlying beliefs, values, and assumptions.

Different Definitions

People will disagree based on different definitions of terms and concepts. If your parents say to be home at a "reasonable" hour, does that mean 11 P.M. or 2 A.M.? What might be deemed "reasonable" to your parents may not be the same to you, especially if you showed up at 3 A.M. But if they specified to be home no later than 1 A.M., then you have precision, which means a 3 A.M. arrival would not be "reasonable."

The point is that arguments over the definition of a subjective term such as *reasonable* will never resolve the argument. The same is true when critics declare that this book or movie is the "best of the year." There will always be dissenters, even people who may think the selection or award winner was far worse than its competition. Criteria differ from person to person. For instance, what is "violent" to a 16-year-old video game fan is not the same as what is violent to an acknowledged pacifist. What is pornography to some is erotic art to others. In fact, for decades the U.S. Supreme Court could not come up with a clear definition of *pornography* in order to determine laws and regulations and eventually gave up, deciding that any regulation of such—with the exception of child pornography, which is prohibited under law—was an infringement on rights of free speech. Such avoidance by the courts essentially freed itself from the decades-long trap of wordplay.

The point is that language is relative; it is difficult for people to agree completely on the definition of any complex word. And adding to their complexity are the different connotations of words—connotations that signal different emotional reactions in an audience. Consider such charged words as *evil, racist, liberal, Nazi, religious extremist,* even *terrorist.* Often arguments are made in which such terms are employed beyond their dictionary definitions for the purpose of arousing strong reactions. With the proper audience, the effect can be powerful.

Different Interpretations of Tradition and Past Authority

It can be said that evidence sometimes lies in the eyes of the beholder. That is, what is evidence to some people may not be evidence to others. The reason is that writers often appeal to authority and traditions that for them have special weight. This is especially evident in arguments based on moral values and beliefs, such as those regarding the death penalty, euthanasia, abortion, same-sex marriages, and animal rights. Such appeals may be persuasive to those who believe in the authority of tradition, but not persuasive to others who don't share in those beliefs.

Sometimes people will claim that something is right because it has always been practiced. Consider, for instance, the following statements:

"When we were kids, we walked to school. So, you're not taking the car."

"Women have always taken their husband's last name in marriage, so why should we change now?"

"The ancient Greeks and Romans practiced euthanasia in order to end a patient's unnecessary suffering, so why shouldn't we?"

Each of these claims is a familiar appeal to tradition. Of course, such appeals raise the question that because something is an old practice does not necessarily mean it should be continued today. The logical fallacy is that behavior is never necessarily right simply because it has always been done.

Tradition is often used as evidence of a higher authority. But even such a fixed piece of evidence can actually be interpreted in different ways by different audiences as different sets of beliefs and assumptions may prevail. For instance, the dominant argument against gun control is the Second Amendment of the U.S. Constitution guarantee: "A well regulated militia, being necessary to the security of a free state, the right of the people to keep and bear arms, shall not be infringed." For the National Rifle Association and others, those words represent the highest legal authority in preserving and protecting the rights of law-abiding citizens to have guns in our American democracy. If your audience is highly traditional and interprets the Second Amendment straightforwardly, this is an argument to which they would be open. But another audience might reject that strict interpretation. That audience might not question people's right to bear arms but the interpretation of that amendment regarding the regulation of guns. While many people would agree that hunters, sportspeople, and collectors have the right to own guns, nearly everybody would argue that the Second Amendment does not give individuals the unlimited right to own any weapons they like, such as military assault weapons with large magazines that were used in shooting sprees in a movie theatre in Aurora, Colorado, in 2012 and then in an elementary school in Newtown, Connecticut, that same year. And that is where the debates become heated—on the question of just how much governmental restriction is too much. When tackling controversial issues, you must be aware of your audience's attitude toward your evidence.

Similarly, the First Amendment is often enlisted as the highest authority regarding an individual's right to free speech in America. But like gun control, that right is limited by the court's interpretation. In the eyes of the law, you cannot intentionally publish lies about a public figure, claiming, for instance, that a local politician sells illegal drugs on the side. Such a claim is libelous and an abridgment of your free-speech rights—and, of course, grounds for a lawsuit. Nor, in the eyes of the law, can you get away with crying "Fire!" in a crowded theater if there is no fire, because the ensuing panic could lead to injury.

While there are some restraints on the rights to free speech, the powerful First Amendment has been invoked to protect flag burning, nude dancing, Internet pornography, Nazi party parades, and Ku Klux Klan rants, to varying degrees of success. And although such claims may seem to undermine the guarantee by protecting dubious and malicious intentions, restriction of the principle could give way to even greater dangers—the tyrannical abuse by government. In several other free and democratic societies, censorship laws empower governments legally to prohibit certain kinds of speech that are protected by the U.S. Constitution.

Religious tradition is another powerful authority that is invoked in arguments about major social issues. References to biblical or Koranic prohibitions are often presented as evidence against arguments in favor of certain public practices. For instance, consider same-sex marriages. Because of scriptural laws against homosexuality, many people argue that gay and lesbian couples should not be allowed to wed under the eyes of the law. The same is true regarding capital punishment. The Sixth Commandment from the Old Testament of the Bible says, "Thou shall not kill." For years, people opposed to legalized abortion have employed such "evidence." The same Sixth Commandment has also been referenced by others in opposition to capital punishment and euthanasia. But the problem with strict appeal to such authority for evidence is that, like tradition, interpretation of religious taboos can be ambiguous and contradictory. For instance, the Old Testament of the Bible also argues, "An eye for an eye, and a tooth for a tooth"—thus, "evidence" that can be enlisted in an argument in favor of the death penalty. Once again, familiarity with your audience should help you determine just the kind of authority and tradition you enlist as evidence. If, for instance, you knew you were addressing religiously conservative readers, summoning the moral import of the scriptures could be very persuasive on some of these public issues.

Different Interpretations of Scientific Data

As we said earlier, scientific data are a persuasive form of evidence. In fact, in most arguments scientific evidence is universally perceived as valid and acceptable. But not everybody interprets scientific evidence in the same way, nor do they draw the same conclusions. For example, one of the most talked about issues of our times is global warming. Over the last several decades, scientific data point to rising average temperatures of the earth's atmosphere and oceans. The data also cite the rise in carbon dioxide in the atmosphere, one of the components of the so-called greenhouse gas. These are the hard facts. Many scientists have looked at the data and determined that there is a direct relationship—namely, that the rise in CO_2 has caused the rise in oceanic and atmospheric temperatures; they blame the effect on human consumption of fossil fuels. These scientists warn that unless something drastic is done, the world's weather will change for the worse for many populated areas, while polar caps will continue to melt and raise sea levels to catastrophic proportions, leading to global coastal flooding.

However, not everybody draws the same conclusion from the data. Not everybody blames the global warming phenomenon on human activity. Nor do they warn of catastrophic climate changes and serious effects on life. Nor do they offer the same political responses.

Some Tips About Supporting Evidence

Because, as argument writers, you'll be using evidence on a routine basis, it will help you to develop a systematic approach to testing the evidence you want to use. Here are some questions to ask yourself about the evidence you enlist in an argument.

Do You Have a Sufficient Number of Examples to Support Your Claim?

You don't want to jump to conclusions based on too little evidence. Suppose you want to make the case that electric cars would be better for the environment than motor vehicles. If all you offer as evidence is the fact that electric vehicles don't pollute the air, your argument would be somewhat thin. Your argument would be much more convincing if you offered the following evidence: that in addition to zero emission at the tailpipe—which is good for the atmosphere—electric cars do not use engine fluids or internal combustion parts, all of which constitute wastes that contaminate our landfills and water supplies. Furthermore, because electric vehicles don't use gasoline or oil, the hazards associated with storage of such fluids are eliminated.

Likewise, you should avoid making hasty generalizations based on your own experience as evidence. For instance, if your Acme Airlines flight to Chattanooga was delayed last week, you shouldn't conclude that Acme Airlines always leaves late. However, were you to consult airline industry records to demonstrate that over the last six months 47 percent of the frequent flyers interviewed complained that Acme flights left late, you would have a persuasive case.

Is Your Evidence Detailed Enough?

The more specific the details, the more persuasive your argument. Instead of generalizations, cite figures, dates, and facts; instead of paraphrases, offer quotations from experts. Remember that your readers are subconsciously saying, "Show me! Prove it!" If you want to tell people how to bake bread, you wouldn't write, "Mix some flour with some yeast and water"; you'd say, "Dissolve one packet of yeast in 1 cup of warm water and let it sit for ten minutes. Then slowly mix in 3 cups of sifted whole wheat flour." Or, as in our electric car example quoted earlier, instead of simply asserting that there would be none of the fluid or solid wastes associated with internal combustion vehicles, specify that in electric vehicles there would be no motor oil, engine coolants, transmission fluid or filters, spark plugs, ignition wires, and gaskets to end up in landfills. What your readers want are specifics—and that's what you should give them.

Is Your Evidence Relevant to the Claim You Make or Conclusion You Reach?

Select evidence based on how well it supports the point you are arguing, not on how interesting, novel, or humorous it is or how hard you had to work to find it. Recall that using evidence that is unrelated or irrelevant is a logical fallacy called a non sequitur. For instance, if you are arguing about whether John Lennon was the most influential songwriter in rock-and-roll history, you wouldn't mention that he had two sons or that he owned dairy cattle; those are facts, but they have nothing to do with the influence of his lyrics. Historian Barbara Tuchman relates that in writing *The Guns of August,* she discovered that the Kaiser bought his wife the same birthday present every year: 12 hats of his choosing, which he required her to wear. Tuchman tried to use this detail in Chapter 1, then in Chapter 2, and so on, but was finally obligated to relegate the detail to a stack of notecards marked "Unused." It just didn't fit, even though for her it summarized his stubborn selfishness. (She did work it into a later essay, which is why we know about it.) Learn her lesson: Irrelevant evidence distracts an audience and weakens an argument's persuasive power.

Does Your Conclusion (or Claim) Exceed the Evidence?

Don't make generalizations about entire groups when your evidence points to select members. Baseball may be the national pastime, but it would be unwise to claim that *all* Americans love baseball. Experience tells you that some Americans prefer football or basketball, while others don't like any sports. Claims that are out of proportion to the evidence can result in a fallacy called the **bandwagon appeal.** The bandwagon appeal suggests to the audience that they should agree with the writer because everyone else does, rather than because the writer has supplied compelling evidence to support the reasons and claim. This is a favorite strategy of advertisers, who work to convince us that we should buy a certain product because everyone else is doing so. While this strategy is in itself fallacious, these salespeople are often unable to produce adequate evidence to support their sweeping claims of nationwide popularity for their product.

Is Your Evidence Up-to-Date and Verifiable?

You want to be sure that the evidence you enlist isn't so dated or vague that it fails to support your claim. For instance, figures demonstrating an increase in the rate of teen pregnancy will not persuade your audience if the numbers are ten years old. Similarly, it wouldn't be accurate to say that candidate Nakamura fails to support the American worker because 15 years ago he purchased a foreign car. His recent and current actions are far more relevant.

When you're citing evidence, your readers will expect you to be specific enough for them to verify what you say. A writer supporting animal rights may cite the example of rabbits whose eyes were burned by pharmacological testing, but such tests have been outlawed in the United States for many years. Another writer may point to medical research that appears to abuse its human subjects, but not name the researchers, the place where the testing took place, or the year in which it occurred. The readers have no way of verifying the claim and may become suspicious of the entire argument because the factual claims are so difficult to confirm.

Is Your Evidence Appropriate for Your Audience?

As discussed in Chapter 3, before you write, it is important to spend some time identifying the audience you will address in your argument. Knowing your audience helps you determine the slant of your argument as well as your language and voice. Likewise, it will influence the evidence you choose to present, the sources of information you use, and the kind of authorities or experts in the field you cite to support your point of view. And that evidence could help make the difference between a convincing argument and one that fails.

Imagine that you are writing an argument against the use of steroids by college students. If you are writing a paper for your biology professor and are discussing the damaging effect of steroids on the body, you would use highly technical evidence— evidence most likely from medical journals aimed at scientists and medical professionals or from your biology textbook. If, however, you are writing an article for your college newspaper, your audience would be your peers, young adults both male and female who may be experimenting or tempted to experiment with steroids. Your focus might be on issues of peer pressure to look good or to succeed in athletics. Therefore the evidence you select might include quotations from known health professionals published in psychology journals or specialized Websites, or from newspaper articles addressing the impact of steroids on one's mental and emotional health. Such evidence would not be highly technical.

Let's take another example. Assume that you decided to write a paper, arguing that healthier food should be served in your student cafeteria. If you were addressing your peers, the evidence you cite might come from general publications devoted to nutrition or you might quote one of the many health and diet gurus published widely today. Your evidence would be geared to convince your peers that a healthier diet would lead to healthier and trimmer bodies and possibly better frames of mind. In contrast, if your goal was to convince the university's trustees, your argument would focus on the obligation of the university to provide a healthy diet. You might argue that doing so not only enhances the well-being of the student body but also the reputation of the university. And this enhancement translates into more student applications for admission. To support these arguments, you would use evidence based on your own personal experience as well as experiences of your peers. Additionally, evidence taken from publications geared to university administrators would be convincing.

Keep in mind that whether your audience is a peer group, a professor, or a college administrator, you must document your evidence—you must let your reader know where you got your support material. You must document the source of any idea you *summarize* or *paraphrase or quote* directly from. The most widely used forms of documentation used in colleges and universities are the Modern Language Association (MLA) style, used widely in the humanities, and the American Psychological Association (APA) style, used widely in the social sciences. These are explained in greater detail in Chapter 9, Researching Arguments.

Is Your Evidence Slanted?

Sometimes writers select evidence that supports their case while ignoring evidence that does not. Often referred to as stacking the deck, this practice makes for an unfair argument, and one that could be disastrous for the arguer. Even though some of your evidence has merit, your argument will be dismissed if your audience discovers that you slanted or suppressed evidence.

For example, suppose you heard a friend make the following statements: "If I were you, I'd avoid taking a course with Professor Gorman at all costs. He gives surprise quizzes, he assigns 50 pages a night, and he refuses to grade on a curve." Even if these reasons are true, that may not be the whole truth. Suppose you learned that Professor Gorman is, in fact, a very dynamic and talented teacher whose classes successfully stimulate the learning process. By holding back that information, your friend's argument is suspect.

To Test Your Evidence for Logical Fallacies, Ask These Questions

Stacking the deck	Did I present evidence that only supports my point of view? Have I withheld evidence that might contradict it?
Non sequitur	Is my evidence related and relevant to the reasons or claim it is supporting?
Hasty generalization	Have I provided sufficient evidence to support my conclusions?
Dicto simpliciter	Does my evidence cover exceptions to any generalizations that I've made?
Red herring	Does all of my evidence pertain to the true issue? Have I tried to distract my audience's attention with irrelevant concerns?
Bandwagon appeal	Can my evidence stand on its own? Have I argued that my audience should support my ideas because they reflect a popular viewpoint?
Faulty use of authority	Are the authorities I cite actually experts in my subject area? Could my authorities be biased because of their background or their professional or political associations?

Sometimes writers will take advantage of their readers' lack of information on a topic and offer evidence that really doesn't support their claims. Recently several newspapers reported that a study written up in the *Archives of Internal Medicine* proved that eating nuts prevents heart attacks. According to the study, some thirty thousand Seventh-Day Adventists were asked to rate the frequency with which they ate certain foods. Those claiming to eat nuts five or more times a week reported fewer heart attacks. What the newspapers failed to report was that most Seventh-Day Adventists are vegetarians, and that those who ate more nuts also ate fewer dairy products (which are high in cholesterol and saturated fat, both of which contribute to heart disease) and eggs (also high in cholesterol) than others in the study. Newspapers have failed to report that all the subsequent pro-nut publicity was distributed by a nut growers' association.[1]

---

[1]Mirkin, Gabe, and Diana Rich. *Fat Free Flavor Full*. Boston: Little, Brown, 1995, 51.

It is to your benefit to present all relevant evidence so that you clearly weigh both sides of an issue. As we discussed in Chapter 4, you want to demonstrate to your readers that you have made an effort to consider other perspectives and that your conclusions are fair and balanced. Otherwise your argument might not be taken seriously. Let's return to the argument that electric cars are more beneficial to the environment than cars with internal combustion engines. Your key evidence is the fact that electric cars do not use petroleum products and various motor parts that contribute to the pollution of air, land, and waterways. If you left your argument at that, you would be guilty of suppressing an important concern regarding electric vehicles: the disposal of the great amounts of lead in the huge electric vehicles' lead-acid batteries and even the lighter lead-carbon alternatives. Failure to acknowledge that opposing point reduces your credibility as a writer. Readers would wonder either about your attempt at deception or about your ignorance. Either way, they would dismiss your argument.

A much better strategy would be to confront this concern and then try to overcome it. While acknowledging that lead is a dangerous pollutant, you could point out that more than 95 percent of battery lead is recycled. You could also point out that progress is being made to improve battery technology and create alternatives such as lithium ion batteries used in recent concept cars.[2] The result is a balanced presentation that makes your own case stronger.

In summary, using evidence means putting yourself in an advocate's place. You'll probably do this while building your argument, and certainly when you revise; then you should see yourself as an advocate for the other side and scrutinize your evidence as if you were going to challenge it in court. As a reader, you need to keep that "show me!" attitude in mind at all times. A little healthy skepticism will help you test the information you're asked to believe. The next chapter will help you do so.

SAMPLE ARGUMENT FOR ANALYSIS

The following is a paper written by a student, Arthur Allen. In it, Allen considers the high rate of recidivism in America—that is, convicts committing more crimes after they've been released from prison. In his paper, he argues that religion might be a better form of rehabilitation than just more harsh punishment. Read the essay carefully and take notes about it in your argument journal. Then, either individually or in your peer group, answer the questions that follow. Notice the style is MLA, which is discussed in the documentation guide.

---

[2]Jim Motavalli, "Axion's New Lead-Carbon Batteries May Help Usher in Electric Cars," thedailygreen.com//living-green/blogs, April 14, 2009.

Allen 1

Arthur Allen

Professor Capobianco

English 097

2 March 2009

Prayer in Prison: Religion as Rehabilitation

1 Prisons don't work if the prisoners are released only to commit more crimes. Unfortunately, that happens all too frequently. In fact, the phenomenon is known as recidivism—that is, a convict re-offends after having been released from confinement. The challenge faced within prisons across America is how best to minimize recidivism in order to ensure that the convicts do not commit more crimes. There are two main schools of thought regarding the prevention of recidivism: increasing the harshness of the punishment (most often by increasing time in prison) or offering convicts rehabilitation programs.

2 The Canadian crime-reduction research group Canada Safety Council found that "there is little evidence that harsh penalties are the best way to prevent further offences" ("Crime"). The council cites studies in Australia, Canada, and America, all pointing to this conclusion. In fact, the group finds that "long prison sentences without other remedial programs may actually increase the chances of re-offending after release" ("Crime"). However, a seemingly more effective method of reducing recidivism, while largely controversial, is rehabilitation, more often than not using a religious basis.

3 The obvious concern with religion-based rehabilitation is the perceived clash with the Constitution, which prohibits the government from making any "law respecting an establishment of religion or forbidding free exercise thereof" (O'Connor 531). There are no questions, however, about its effectiveness: In Texas, about 40% of parolees who do not participate in any form of rehabilitation program return to prison within

Allen 2

three years; in the same amount of time, less than 5% of those who participated in a rehabilitation program were rearrested (Bradley). Other implementations of these types of programs have been comparably successful in Louisiana (Van Wel) as well as in Iowa, Kansas and Minnesota (Alter).

4   One of the major rehabilitation programs nationally is the Interchange Freedom Initiative (IFI) Program, a third-party rehabilitation program based on offering religion to inmates. Sam Dye, director of the Interchange program in Iowa, says,

> The only true lasting change that is worth anything is change that comes from the inside out, change from the heart. You can coerce a person, from the outside, to do what you want them to do; but once that external pressure is gone, typically people go back to act the way they did before. So if you really want to change a person, you have to get a ahold of their heart. (Bradley)

This seems to make sense: The prisoner must be changed from the inside out in order to keep that prisoner from committing a future crime. That is to say, prisoners will not change simply because they have been told they were wrong or because they were punished severely. Recidivism occurs when there is no change in the status quo of the life of the criminal. If a person is pushed to the point where he or she needs to sell drugs and rob stores in order to pay the bills, a harsh prison life will not change that situation.

5   However, the question surrounding rehabilitation programs is not about their effectiveness but about their constitutionality. Les Nester, a lawyer and critic of the IFI program, says, "the concerns would be that the state is actually promoting and advancing Christianity. If you look at

the programming, it is very sectarian, very evangelical programming. . . .
I think the IFI program is a brainwash tactic" (Neary). He argues that
because the state government is promoting the use of rehabilitation programs that use Christianity as a way to rehabilitate criminals, the state is
declaring affiliation with a specific religion. However, the IFI is not purely
a Christian program. It incorporates many faiths, including Judaism and
Islam, in its treatment of prisoners. One graduate of the program states,
"I think Islam has everything to do with my growth and development
and my transformation that I have accomplished, in the sense that Islam
taught me for the first time what it is to take responsibility for my actions"
(Neary).

6   The argument for inclusion of any religion rather then exclusion
of all religions is summed up succinctly in an article by William Bennett,
who states, "The First Amendment does not require the government
to be neutral on the subject of religion. It requires it to be neutral only
on any one particular form of religion" (Bennett 54). In other words,
while the government should not show favoritism toward one particular religion, it also does not have the obligation of pretending religion
does not exist. Thus, this distinction allows the government to sponsor
religious programs in the context of furthering the social good (reduction of crime) as long as it does not promote one religious program over
another.

7   In another article, John Swomley argues that the government
could not give funding to one religious group without giving funding
to all religious groups; this argument then implies that the government could not provide any funding to religious rehabilitation programs
in prisons if it did not give funding to all 300-plus religious groups
(Swomley 62). This argument is backwards: The government is free to

Allen 4

give money to any religious group it sees fit. It is prohibited, however, from denying one group funding in the same situation where it would grant another group that same funding. To say that the government is responsible for giving "all or none" to religious groups would be like saying the government is required to either employ all races in government positions or employ none of them. If a religion-based rehabilitation program wants to operate, it should not be denied fund but should be funded equally as all other religion-based rehabilitation programs representing different faiths.

8   Furthermore, civil liberties groups have actually held back from suing the IFI program because it provides a number of unique services including a support community both for convicts in prison and for those who have been released. As one graduate of the IFI program puts it, "Now I have someone I can call, even in the middle of the night. And when I start feeling bad . . . who you gonna call? You call your brother, he uses drugs. You call your sister, she's using drugs. Mom's upset with you. Dad's gone. Whereas, with IFI, I was given a family." In other words, because it is a third-party nonprofit program, the IFI is not only able to reach prisoners in a way government officials can't by offering spiritual growth and continuity, but also it provides follow-through support after prison by offering a new family to which the convicts feel a sense of loyalty and responsibility (Bradley).

9   As an alternative to harsher punishments, rehabilitation is clearly superior. When prison is the necessary evil in a person's life, the harshness of it will make little difference. The change must truly come from the inside out. And faith-based rehabilitation programs have proven successful.

Allen 5

Works Cited

Alter, Alexandra. "Study Touts Faith-Based Prison Rehabilitation Program." The Pew Forum on Religion and Public Life. Pew Forum, 19 June 2003. Web. 28 Feb. 2009.

Bennett, William. "America's Indentity Is Rooted in Religion." *Religion in America: Opposing Viewpoints*. Ed. William Dudley et al. San Diego: Greenhaven p, 2001. Print.

Bradley, Barbra. *God Pods*. NPR News. Iowa, 2001. Radio.

"Crime, Punishment, Safety." *Canada Safety Council*. Canada Safety Council, 2009. Web. 27 Feb. 2009.

Neary, Lynn. *Sing Sing Studies*. NPR News, Washington DC. 1998. Radio.

O'Connor, Karen, and Larry J. Sabato. *American Government: Continuity and Change*. New York: Pearson Education, 2004. Print.

Swomley, John. "TK." Religion in America: Opposing Viewpoints. Ed. William Dudley et al. San Diego: Greenhaven p, 2001. Print.

Van Wel, Alex. "US Prison Rehabilitation through Faith." BBC News. BBC, 2 Oct. 2002. Web. 27 Feb. 2009.

QUESTIONS FOR ANALYSIS AND DISCUSSION

1. What claim (Chapter 1) is Allen arguing? What are the reasons for his claim? What do you think the pros and cons he listed in developing this argument might have been?

2. Who is Allen's target audience? What clues does he give you? What values and prejudices might the readership hold?

3. What different forms of evidence (personal, outside authorities, factual references, statistics) does Allen provide? Which form(s) of evidence does he rely on most?

4. Evaluate the supporting evidence that Allen provides. Is it relevant? Is it detailed enough? Does it seem dated and verifiable? Does his claim exceed his evidence? Does his evidence strike you as slanted? If you were his reader, would you be persuaded by his reasons? What changes (if any) in evidence would you recommend to help him make his argument more persuasive?

5. Use debate, dialogue, and deliberation to respond to Allen's essay in your journal. See Chapter 1 to review this process.
   a. Create a dialogue to help you understand and respond productively to Allen's ideas.
   b. Given what you've learned through debate and dialogue, write at least a page in which you deliberate about the conflicting issues that Allen raises in his essay. How does your understanding of Allen's position change or modify your own viewpoint? Is there a way to reconcile conflicting concerns about this subject?

EXERCISES

1. Either online or in your library, locate the opinion pages in the editorial section of five different local or national newspapers. From these, collect three pieces that deal with separate controversial topics. In your journal, evaluate each piece according to the kinds of evidence used: personal experience, outside authority, factual references, examples, and statistics. Photocopy the one essay that to you makes the most appropriate and convincing use of evidence. Annotate that essay, and bring copies to class to share your findings with your work group.

2. In a small group, make a list of three statements that you might want to argue for or against in an essay. In your journal, list each of your classmate's two strongest pieces of evidence that might be used. As a group, consider which of the four categories of evidence seem most fitting for the subjects at hand.

3. Carefully read the essay by Kari Peterson entitled "My Body, My Closet" on page 161. In your journal, identify the thesis statement of this piece. Then list and identify the various kinds of evidence Peterson uses to prove her point. As a group determine the following: (a) Did Peterson use a sufficient number of examples? (b) Is the evidence relevant to the claim made in the piece? (c) Is the evidence up-to-date and verifiable? (d) Did Peterson convince you of her opinion? Why or why not?

4. In your group, take a controversial issue of your own choice (i.e., "Should the sale of automatic assault weapons be banned in the United States?" or "Should the use of marijuana for medical purposes be legalized?" or "Is security at our college adequate?") Then as a group, brainstorm an unedited list of reasons for or against the issue. Make the list as extensive and freewheeling as possible. Then go through the list and pick the three strongest reasons to support a particular point of view. The three strongest reasons to oppose that point of view. What kinds of reasons worked best given the issue? Which were the least effective?

5. Listen to conversations among your peers or people you overhear in a coffee shop or elsewhere. In your journal, make a list of any arguable topics you hear and the kinds of evidence people tend to use as support. Do most people have convincing

reasons backing up their opinions? Do they rely on outside authorities? Are these outside authorities credible in your estimation? Do people tend to quote newspaper articles, television or radio talk shows, gossip they heard in the office? Do they quote statistics? Does this exercise make you think differently about the way you argue or express your opinion in casual conversation? Share these findings with your group.

Establishing Claims: Thinking Like a Skeptic

LEARNING OBJECTIVES

After studying this chapter, you should be able to:

1. Identify and describe the six parts of the Toulmin model of argument. (p. 190)
2. Use the Toulmin model to analyze written arguments. (p. 199)
3. Distinguish between qualifiers and warrants. (p. 201)

You have decided the issue you're going to argue. With the aid of debate and dialogue, you've sharpened your ideas and considered alternative perspectives and common concerns. You've thought about your audience and determined what you have in common, where you might agree, and where you might disagree. After deliberating, you have formulated a working claim, and you have gathered solid evidence to support it. Now it's time to establish the logical structure of your argument and decide how best to arrange this material to persuade your readers.

If you've ever tried handing in a paper made up of slapped-together evidence and first-draft organization, you've probably discovered a blueprint for disaster. Perhaps you didn't test your work, didn't revise it, or didn't think about how it would appeal to a reader. You assumed that because *you* understood how the parts fit together, your readers would as well. To help you detect and correct these problems, this chapter focuses on thinking like a *skeptic*—a skeptical building inspector, to be exact—because a skeptical attitude works best.

To construct a persuasive argument, one that has a chance of convincing your readers, you have to pay careful attention to the logical structure you are building. You can't take anything for granted; you have to question every step you take, every joist and joint. You have to ask yourself if you're using the right material for the right purpose, the right tool at the right time. In other words, you have to think like a building inspector examining a half-built two-story house—one whose builder is notoriously crafty at compromising quality. A healthy skepticism—and a logical system—helps uncover flaws before they create a disaster.

The Toulmin Model

Stephen Toulmin, a British philosopher and logician, analyzed hundreds of arguments from various fields of politics and law.[1] He concluded that nearly every argument has certain patterns and parts. The best arguments, Toulmin found, are those addressed to a

---

[1]Toulmin, Stephen. *The Uses of Argument.* Cambridge: Cambridge UP, 1958.

skeptical audience, one eager to question the reasoning where it seems faulty, to demand support for wobbly assumptions, and to raise opposing reasons.

The slightly retooled version of the Toulmin model we describe later encourages you to become a skeptical audience. It also gives you the tools to write persuasive arguments aimed to win over a skeptical reader. It provides useful everyday terms to help you unearth, weigh, and, if necessary, fix an argument's logical structures. It lets you verify that the major premises in your argument or those of your opposition are clear and accurate, and helps you determine whether repairs to your claims are needed and whether counterarguments are addressed. It shows you where supporting evidence may be needed and helps you avoid logical fallacies. And, since Toulmin's terms are designed to be broadly practical, they allow you to present your case to a wide variety of readers.

Toulmin's Terms

According to Toulmin, a fully developed argument has six parts. They are the *claim*, the *grounds*, the *warrant*, the *backing*, the *qualifiers*, and the *rebuttals*.

The Claim

The **claim** is the assertion you are trying to prove—the same term as discussed in Chapter 1. It is the position you take in your argument, often as a proposal with which you are asking your reader to agree. In a well-constructed argument, each part makes its ultimate claim, its conclusion, seem inevitable. For example, *you should stay home from school if you have the flu.* This sounds like a reasonable claim, but some people may challenge it. You need to explain why your audience should agree with you.

The Grounds

Just as every argument contains a claim, every claim needs supporting evidence. The **grounds** are the hard data—statistics, research studies, facts, and examples that bolster your claim and that your audience accepts without requiring further proof. Grounds are the "truth" on which you base your claim. For example, *The influenza virus is highly contagious. According to the Centers for Disease Control, every season, an average of 11,000 people die in the United States from complications connected to the flu.* While some readers may accept the grounds as enough proof to accept your claim, others will require more information. This is where the warrant comes in.

The Warrant

The claim is usually stated explicitly. However, underlying the claim are a number of assumptions and principles that are also critical to the success of your argument. These are the **warrants** that implicitly support your argument by connecting your claim to the grounds. They enable your audience to follow the reasoning in your argument. They explain why the hard evidence supports your claim. So the success of your argument depends on whether the audience accepts these often half-buried assumptions, commonly held values, legal or moral principles, laws of nature, commonsense knowledge, or shared beliefs. Warrants tend to be based on values shared by the population. They may be true or mere presumptions based on emotion, rather than hard facts. For example, *The flu is easily passed from person to person, and it is inconsiderate to make other people sick. The responsible thing to do is to stay home until you feel better.*

Let's look at a few more examples. We are all familiar with the advertiser that promises that its shampoo will eliminate dandruff. The basic **claim** here is that you should shampoo your hair with this manufacturer's product. And as **grounds**, the manufacturer says that studies have shown that 60 percent of those people who use their shampoo no longer have dandruff. One underlying **warrant** here is that people don't want dandruff—a commonly held assumption that you share with your audience. Another is that we assume 60 percent to be a sufficient proportion to accept the claim. Because warrants are based on commonly held values or patterns of reasoning, they are not easily detected. Here's another example:

Claim: Cigarette smoking is harmful to your health.

Grounds: The U.S. Surgeon General has warned that cigarettes cause a number of diseases including cancer, heart trouble, and injury to fetuses in pregnant women.

Warrant: The Surgeon General is a medical authority we can trust.

At times, warrants can be a challenge to determine since they are often based on unstated but commonly held assumptions. And that is why it is important to find them. More on that follow.

The Backing

Because your warrant is an assumption, you cannot be certain that it will always be accepted by your readers. So you must provide reasons to back it up. These reasons, called **backing,** indicate that the warrant is reliable in a particular argument, though it doesn't have to be true in all cases at all times. For example, *The flu can lead to other serious conditions such as pneumonia. In fact, over 200,000 people end up hospitalized because of flu-related complications. It is better to stay home when you have the flu, rather than risk getting even more sick and missing more time at work or school.* The backing provides additional support to the warrant by addressing other facets of the claim; in this case, the risk of complications.

The Qualifiers

Qualifiers provide a way to indicate when, why, and how your claim and warrant are reliable. They're words or phrases such as *often, probably, possibly, almost always;* verbs like *may* and *might, can* and *could;* or adjectives and adverbs that yoke your claim to some condition. The subtlest kind of qualifier is an adjective that acknowledges that your claim is true to a degree: *Complications from the flu often make it harder to go back to school. Usually it takes longer for you to feel better.* The qualifiers *often* and *harder* and *usually* imply that the statement is conditional and not absolute. They allow for exceptions.

You need to consider a few guidelines about using qualifiers; like antibiotics, they're too powerful to use unwisely. Using too many qualifiers can indicate that you're exaggerating your argument's validity. As we've mentioned in previous chapters, common fallacies, such as *hasty generalizations,* are often potentially valid arguments that go astray by not qualifying their claims enough, if at all. Using *no* qualifiers can result in a claim that is too general and sweeping. Although many students think a qualified claim is a weak claim, in fact, the qualified claim is often the most persuasive. Few truths are *completely* true; few claims are *always* right. A well-qualified claim, then, shows that the writer respects both the difficulty of the issue and the intelligence of the reader.

Nevertheless, qualifiers alone cannot substitute for reasoning your way to the tough, subtle distinctions on which the most persuasive arguments depend. An example could be "Innocent people have an inviolable right to life." It's wisely qualified with the word "innocent" since just saying "People have an inviolable right to life" wouldn't hold up. Hitler, after all, was human. Did he too have "an inviolable right to life"? But even *innocent* is not qualification enough. It raises too many tough, troubling questions. "Innocent" of what? "Innocent" by whose judgment, and why? What if killing a few innocent people were the only way to end a war that is killing *many* innocent people?

Using a lot of qualifiers, therefore, is no guarantee that your argument is carefully reasoned. In fact, strongly qualifying your argument's claim may be a sign that you doubt your argument's validity. But such doubt can itself be encouraging. Misusing or overusing qualifiers can indicate that your instinct of anxiety is right—that you've discovered better reasons to doubt your initial argument than to defend it. In fact, acknowledging the appeal of a flawed claim—and describing how you only discovered its flaws once you tried trumpeting its strengths—is an effective way of earning the reader's respect. It shows you to be an honest arguer capable of learning from errors—and thus worth learning *from.*

Deciding what to state and what to imply is a large part of writing any good argument. Just as a building's crossbeams don't have to be visible to be working, not everything important in an argument has to be stated. For example, if someone were to claim that winters in Minnesota are "mostly long and cold," we probably wouldn't stop the flow of argument to ask him to define the qualifier *mostly.* We'd instead keep the qualifier in mind, and let the Minnesotan's definition of *mostly* emerge, implied, from the rest of the story. Similarly, it's sometimes wise to leave your argument's qualifiers implied.

Still, it's often better to risk belaboring the obvious. To minimize the chances that your reader will misunderstand (or altogether miss) your meaning, qualify your claims as clearly and explicitly as possible. "Reading" the argument you're writing like a skeptical reader will help you decide which qualifiers are needed, where they are needed, and how explicitly they need to be stated.

The Rebuttals

Reading your argument skeptically also allows you to participate, answer, and even preempt rebuttals. **Rebuttals** represent the exceptions to the claim. There are many different kinds of rebuttals, and any persuasive argument ought to acknowledge and incorporate the most important ones. Rebuttals are like large-scale qualifiers. They acknowledge and explain the conditions or situations in which your claim would not be true—while still proving how your claim *is* true under other conditions. It's wise, then, to anticipate such rebuttals by regularly acknowledging all your argument's limits. This acknowledgment will prompt you to craft your claims more carefully. For example, look at the claim that you should stay home from school if you have the flu. One could argue that if you are coughing and sneezing, you *probably* will give the flu to people sitting around you. Then again, you might not. You might sit in the back of the room, away from other people. Or you could take medication that reduces your sneezing. A challenger might argue that while it is inconsiderate to expose classmates to the flu, if one has an exam that one thinks cannot be missed or face failure, it may be in one's personal best interest to go to class. You would need to persuasively convince your reader that your claim holds true despite these challenges. You might anticipate the challenge and write: *Rather than expose your classmates to dangerous strains of flu, such as H1N1, go to your student health service and request a letter explaining your absence. This will protect your classmates and allow you the time to get better so that you can focus on the test later.*

Let's look at another example. Say that a sportswriter argues that allowing big-market baseball teams to monopolize talent ruins competition by perpetuating dynasties. Your rebuttal might be to cite the overlooked grounds of ignored evidence—grounds that complicate, if not contradict, the writer's claim: "Then why have small-market teams won four of the last ten World Series?" Had the sportswriter anticipated and integrated this rebuttal, she could have improved the argument—from her warrant on up. Her argument could have taken into account this rebuttal in the form of more careful qualifications. "While the rule of money doesn't guarantee that the richer teams will always win the World Series, it does make it more difficult for hard-pressed teams to compete for available talent." This is now, of course, a less sweeping claim—and, therefore, more precise and persuasive.

Of course, no writer can anticipate his or her readers' every rebuttal, nor should the writer even try. But you should test your argument by trying to rebut it yourself or working with classmates in small groups. Then revise your arguments with those rebuttals in mind.

Review: Six Parts of an Argument

Claim	The assertion you are trying to prove
Grounds	The supporting evidence for the claim
Warrant	A generalization that explains why the evidence, also known as the grounds, supports the claim
Backing	Reasons that show the warrant is reliable
Qualifiers	Words that show when, how, and why your claim is reliable
Rebuttal	Exceptions to the claim

Finding Warrants

Finding your warrants in order to explicate your argument can help you in several ways: You persuade your reader more effectively, detect flaws in your own argument, and identify the cause of otherwise confusing debates more quickly.

For example, let's say you want to argue the claim that all students in American schools should be taught in English rather than in the students' native or family languages. The grounds supporting this claim are results of research showing a high correlation between English fluency and socioeconomic success.

For your audience to accept the connection between your claim and your grounds, you and they must agree on several warrants that underlie it. (Remember that warrants are underlying assumptions or common knowledge.) The first might be the assumption that schools prepare students for socioeconomic success in U.S. society. Since one of the purposes of education is to develop skills such as reading, writing, and thinking critically, skills that are considered basic requirements for success, most of your audience would likely accept this assumption. Therefore, it can be left implied and unstated.

The second warrant implied by your claim may not be as readily acceptable to your audience as the previous one and will need to be explicitly supported in your essay: that our English language skills affect whether we are successful. The third warrant, implied by the second, is that individuals who are not fluent in English will not be successful members of society. These warrants will need considerable backing to show that they are reliable. How do English language skills enable individuals to attain socioeconomic success? How are individuals who lack fluency in English adversely affected? You will want to provide additional backing in the form of evidence, examples, and statistics to demonstrate that English language skills have a significant impact on an individual's chances for social and economic success.

Your fourth and final warrant is particularly important because it establishes a critical link between your claim that all students should be taught in English and the need for fluency to succeed. This warrant assumes nonnative-speaking students will achieve greater fluency in English in the English-only classroom. You will need additional backing to prove this warrant, especially when you take into account possible rebuttals. For instance, what about students who enter U.S. schools with no English skills at all? How can they learn the required curriculum with no fluency in English? Will English-only classrooms fail to teach them language skills as well as subject matter? Will this approach alienate them from the American educational system and, thus, from success in our society? Making your responses to these rebuttals explicit will strengthen your argument.

Using Toulmin's approach to analyze your argument allows you to dig beneath the surface of your claim to find the underlying assumptions that form its foundation. It also allows your audience to see that even if they disagree with your claim, they may agree with many of the principles and assumptions that support it. Revealing this common ground, however hidden it lies, can provide opportunities to begin a dialogue that emerges from the recognition of shared values and beliefs. For instance, take the notoriously divisive issue of capital punishment. Those who support capital punishment say, in essence, "A human life is so precious that anyone who is guilty of depriving another of it should forfeit his or her own life." Those who oppose capital punishment say, in effect, "Human life is so precious that we have no right to deprive another of it no matter what the cause." By digging down to the warrants that underlie these positions, we may be surprised to find that the two sides have much in common: a respect for and appreciation of the value of human life. This discovery, of course, is no guarantee that we can reconcile dramatically opposing views on a particular issue. But the recognition of commonality might provide a first step toward increasing understanding—if not consensus—between opposing sides.

Digging deeply to excavate your warrants can also help you avoid two common logical fallacies: post hoc, ergo propter hoc and slippery slope arguments. A post hoc, ergo propter hoc fallacy occurs when the writer mistakenly draws a causal relationship between two or more events or situations that are unrelated or simply coincidental. Similarly, a slippery slope argument is based on an assumption that a particular outcome is inevitable if certain events happen or if a situation is allowed to continue. In both cases, the writer fails to identify and support the underlying warrants that would create a convincing logical link.

SAMPLE ARGUMENTS FOR ANALYSIS

Now let's turn to two sample arguments to see how our version of the Toulmin model can help you test your own arguments more effectively. The first piece, originally published in *The New York Times Magazine,* provides a very logical but highly provocative argument about a crime that always receives considerable media attention: infanticide. The second article appeared a few days later in *The New York Times.* And while these essays relate events that happened several years ago, the issue of infanticide is still a national problem. In fact, statistically, the United States ranks high on the list of countries whose inhabitants kill their babies. For infants under the age of 1 year, the American homicide rate is eleventh in the world. The author of the first essay, Steven Pinker, wrote this piece while director of the Center for Cognitive Neuroscience at Massachusetts Institute of Technology. Pinker is currently the Johnstone Family Professor of Psychology in the Department of Psychology at Harvard University. He is the author of *How the Mind Works* (1997) and most recently *The Stuff of Thought* (2007). Following Pinker's essay is a point-by-point counterargument (page 204) by Michael Kelley.

To Avoid Errors in Logic, Check for These Logical Fallacies

Post hoc, ergo propter hoc	Be certain to demonstrate a cause–effect relationship between events by uncovering all warrants that underlie your claim.
Slippery slope argument	Make explicit the chain of events that link a situation to its possible outcome. Provide proof that this progression will inevitably occur.

Warrants

Notice the many layers of warrants that can underlie a single claim:

Claim	All students in American public schools should be taught in English-only classrooms.
Grounds	Research shows high correlation between English fluency and socioeconomic success in America.
Warrant	Schools prepare students for success in our society.
Warrant	Success in American society can be determined by our English language skills.
Warrant	Individuals who are not fluent in English will not succeed in our society.
Warrant	Teaching classes only in the English language will ensure that students will be fluent in English.

Why They Kill Their Newborns
Steven Pinker

1   Killing your baby. What could be more depraved? For a woman to destroy the fruit of her womb would seem like an ultimate violation of the natural order. But every year, hundreds of women commit neonaticide: They kill their newborns or let them die. Most neonaticides remain undiscovered, but every once in a while a janitor follows a trail of blood to a tiny body in a trash bin, or a woman faints and doctors find the remains of a placenta inside her.

2   Two cases have recently riveted the American public. Last November, Amy Grossberg and Brian Peterson, 18-year-old college sweethearts, delivered their baby in a motel room and, according to prosecutors, killed him and left his body in a dumpster. They will go on trial for murder next year and, if convicted, could be sentenced to death. In June, another 18-year-old, Melissa Drexler, arrived at her high-school prom, locked herself in a bathroom stall, gave birth to a boy and left him dead in a garbage can. Everyone knows what happened next: she touched herself up and returned to the dance floor. In September, a grand jury indicted her for murder.

3   How could they do it? Nothing melts the heart like a helpless baby. Even a biologist's cold calculations tell us that nurturing an offspring that carries our genes is the whole point of our existence. Neonaticide, many think, could be only a product of pathology. The psychiatrists uncover childhood trauma. The defense lawyers argue temporary psychosis. The pundits blame a throwaway society, permissive sex education and, of course, rock lyrics.

4   But it's hard to maintain that neonaticide is an illness when we learn that it has been practiced and accepted in most cultures throughout history. And that neonaticidal women do not commonly show signs of psychopathology. In a classic 1970 study of statistics of child killing, a psychiatrist, Phillip Resnick, found that mothers who kill their *older* children are frequently psychotic, depressed or suicidal, but mothers who kill their newborns are usually not. (It was this difference that led Resnick to argue that the category infanticide be split into neonaticide, the killing of a baby on the day of its birth, and filicide, the killing of a child older than one day.)

5   Killing a baby is an immoral act, and we often express our outrage at the immoral by calling it a sickness. But normal human motives are not always moral, and neonaticide does not have to be a product of malfunctioning neural circuitry or a dysfunctional upbringing. We can try to understand what would lead a mother to kill her newborn, remembering that to understand is not necessarily to forgive.

6   Martin Daly and Margo Wilson, both psychologists, argue that a capacity for neonaticide is built into the biological design of our parental emotions. Mammals are extreme among animals in the amount of time, energy and food they invest in their young, and humans are extreme among mammals. Parental investment is a limited resource, and mammalian mothers must "decide" whether to allot it to their newborn or to their current and future offspring. If a newborn is sickly, or if its survival is not promising, they may cut their losses and favor the healthiest in the litter or try again later on.

7   In most cultures, neonaticide is a form of this triage. Until very recently in human evolutionary history, mothers nursed their children for two to four years before becoming fertile again. Many children died, especially in the perilous first year. Most women saw no more than two or three of their children survive to adulthood, and many did not see any survive. To become a grandmother, a woman had to make hard choices. In most societies documented by anthropologists, including those of hunter-gatherers (our best glimpse into our ancestors' way of life), a woman lets a newborn die when its prospects for survival to adulthood are poor. The forecast might be based on abnormal signs in the infant, or on bad circumstances for successful motherhood at the time—she might be burdened with older children, beset by war or famine or without a husband or social support. Moreover, she might be young enough to try again.

8   We are all descendants of women who made the difficult decisions that allowed them to become grandmothers in that unforgiving world, and we inherited that brain circuitry that led to those decisions. Daly and Wilson have shown that the statistics on neonaticide in contemporary North America parallel those in the anthropological literature. The women who sacrifice their offspring tend to be young, poor, unmarried and socially isolated.

9   Natural selection cannot push the buttons of behavior directly; it affects our behavior by endowing us with emotions that coax us toward adaptive choices. New mothers have always faced a choice between a definite tragedy now and the possibility of an even greater tragedy months or years later, and that choice is not to be taken lightly. Even today, the typical rumination of a depressed new mother—how will I cope with this burden?—is a legitimate concern. The emotional response called bonding is also far more complex than the popular view, in which a woman is imprinted with a lifelong attachment to her baby if they interact in a critical period immediately following the baby's birth. A new mother will first coolly assess the infant and her current situation and only in the next few days begin to see it as a unique and wonderful individual. Her love will gradually deepen in ensuing years, in a trajectory that tracks the increasing biological value of a child (the chance that it will live to produce grandchildren) as the child proceeds through the mine field of early development.

10   Even when a mother in a hunter-gatherer society hardens her heart to sacrifice a newborn, her heart has not turned to stone. Anthropologists who interview these women (or their relatives, since the event is often too painful for the woman to discuss) discover that the women see the death as an unavoidable tragedy, grieve at the time and remember the child with pain all their lives. Even the supposedly callous Melissa Drexler agonized over a name for her dead son and wept at his funeral. (Initial reports that, after giving birth, she requested a Metallica song from the deejay and danced with her boyfriend turned out to be false.)

11   Many cultural practices are designed to distance people's emotions from a newborn until its survival seems probable. Full personhood is often not automatically granted at birth, as we see in our rituals of christening and the Jewish bris. And yet the recent neonaticides will seem puzzling. These are middle-class girls whose babies would have been kept far from starvation by the girl's parents or by any of thousands of eager adoptive couples. But our emotions, fashioned by the slow hand of natural selection, respond to the signals of the long-vanished tribal environment in which we spent 99 percent of our evolutionary history. Being young and single are two bad omens for successful motherhood, and the girl who conceals her pregnancy and procrastinates over its consequences will soon be disquieted by a third omen. She will give birth in circumstances that are particularly unpromising for a human mother: alone.

12   In hunter-gatherer societies, births are virtually always assisted because human anatomy makes birth (especially the first one) long, difficult and risky. Older women act as midwives, emotional supports and experienced appraisers who help decide whether the infant should live. Wenda Trevathan, an anthropologist and trained midwife, has studied pelvises of human fossils and concluded that childbirth has been physically torturous, and therefore probably assisted, for millions of years. Maternal feelings may be adapted to a world in which a promising newborn is heralded with waves of cooing and clucking and congratulating. Those reassuring signals are absent from a secret birth in a motel room or a bathroom stall.

13   So what is the mental state of a teenage mother who has kept her pregnancy secret? She is immature enough to have hoped that her pregnancy would go away by itself, her maternal feelings have been set at zero and she suddenly realizes she is in big trouble.

14   Sometimes she continues to procrastinate. In September, 17-year-old Shanta Clark gave birth to a premature boy and kept him hidden in her bedroom closet, as if he were E.T., for 17 days. She fed him before and after she went to school until her mother discovered him. The weak cry of the preemie kept him from being discovered earlier. (In other cases, girls have panicked over the crying and, in stifling the cry, killed the baby.)

15   Most observers sense the desperation that drives a woman to neonaticide. Prosecutors sometimes don't prosecute; juries rarely convict; those found guilty almost never go to jail. Barbara Kirwin, a forensic psychologist, reports that in nearly 300 cases of women charged with neonaticide in the United States and Britain, no woman spent more than a night in jail. In Europe, the laws of several countries prescribed less-severe penalties for neonaticide than for adult homicides. The fascination with the Grossberg-Peterson case comes from the unusual threat of the death penalty. Even those in favor of capital punishment might shudder at the thought of two reportedly nice kids being strapped to gurneys and put to death.

16   But our compassion hinges on the child, not just on the mother. Killers of older children, no matter how desperate, evoke little mercy. Susan Smith, the South Carolina woman who sent her two sons, 14 months and 3 years old, to watery deaths, is in jail, unmourned, serving a life sentence. The leniency shown to neonaticidal mothers forces us to think the unthinkable and ask if we, like many societies and like the mothers themselves, are not completely sure whether a neonate is a full person.

17   It seems obvious that we need a clear boundary to confer personhood on a human being and grant it a right to life. Otherwise, we approach a slippery slope that ends in the disposal of inconvenient people or in grotesque deliberations on the value of individual lives. But the endless abortion debate shows how hard it is to locate the boundary. Anti-abortionists draw the line at conception, but that implies we should shed tears every time an invisible conceptus fails to implant in the uterus—and, to carry the argument to its logical conclusion, that we should prosecute for murder anyone who uses an IUD. Those in favor of abortion draw the line at viability, but viability is a fuzzy gradient that depends on how great a risk of an impaired child the parents are willing to tolerate. The only thing both sides agree on is that the line must be drawn at some point before birth.

18   Neonaticide forces us to examine even that boundary. To a biologist, birth is as arbitrary a milestone as any other. Many mammals bear offspring that see and walk as soon as they hit the ground. But the incomplete 9-month-old human fetus must be evicted from the womb before its oversized head gets too big to fit through its mother's pelvis. The usual

primate assembly process spills into the first years in the world. And that complicates our definition of personhood.

19   What makes a living being a person with a right not to be killed? Animal-rights extremists would seem to have the easiest argument to make: that all sentient beings have a right to life. But champions of that argument must conclude that delousing a child is akin to mass murder; the rest of us must look for an argument that draws a small circle. Perhaps only the members of our own species, *Homo sapiens*, have a right to life? But that is simply chauvinism; a person of one race could just as easily say that people of another race have no right to life.

20   No, the right to life must come, the moral philosophers say, from morally significant traits that we humans happen to possess. One such trait is having a unique sequence of experiences that defines us as individuals and connects us to other people. Other traits include an ability to reflect upon ourselves as a continuous locus of consciousness, to form and savor plans for the future, to dread death and to express the choice not to die. And there's the rub: our immature neonates don't possess these traits any more than mice do.

21   Several moral philosophers have concluded that neonates are not persons, and thus neonaticide should not be classified as murder. Michael Tooley has gone so far as to say that neonaticide ought to be permitted during an interval after birth. Most philosophers (to say nothing of nonphilosophers) recoil from that last step, but the very fact that there can be a debate about the personhood of neonates, but no debate about the personhood of older children, makes it clearer why we feel more sympathy for an Amy Grossberg than for a Susan Smith.

22   So how do you provide grounds for outlawing neonaticide? The facts don't make it easy. Some philosophers suggest that people intuitively see neonates as so similar to older babies that you couldn't allow neonaticide without coarsening the way people treat children and other people in general. Again, the facts say otherwise. Studies in both modern and hunter-gatherer societies have found that neonaticidal women don't kill anyone but their newborns, and when they give birth later under better conditions, they can be devoted, loving mothers.

23   The laws of biology were not kind to Amy Grossberg and Melissa Drexler, and they are not kind to us as we struggle to make moral sense of the teenagers' actions. One predicament is that our moral system needs a crisp inauguration of personhood, but the assembly process for Homo sapiens is gradual, piecemeal and uncertain. Another problem is that the emotional circuitry of mothers has evolved to cope with this uncertain process, so the baby killers turn out to be not moral monsters but nice, normal (and sometimes religious) young women. These are dilemmas we will probably never resolve, and any policy will leave us with uncomfortable cases. We will most likely muddle through, keeping birth as a conspicuous legal boundary but showing mercy to the anguished girls who feel they had no choice but to run afoul of it.

An Analysis Based on the Toulmin Model

Clearly Steven Pinker has taken a controversial stance on a disturbing social issue. In fact, in light of civilized society's attitudes toward the sacredness of the mother–infant bond, his position is one that many people might find shocking and repugnant. How could he propose that neonaticide, the murder of one's newborn infant, be viewed as an acceptable form of behavior, one that we have inherited from our evolutionary ancestors? As Pinker readily admits in the first three paragraphs, neonaticide seems alien to most of the values we as civilized people cherish. Nevertheless, Pinker argues that while it may be regarded as immoral, neonaticide is not necessarily the act of a mentally deranged woman, but rather a difficult decision guided by an instinct for survival handed down to a mother by generations of women before her. While he does not condone or endorse this practice, Pinker urges his readers to try to understand a context that might drive women to commit such an act.

No matter how repugnant an idea may be, it cannot be repudiated unless it is understood. Therefore it is important to be detached and put aside emotion when confronted with ideas that are unacceptable. Genocide, child slavery, and child prostitution, for example, are topics most people would rather avoid. But to understand the forces underlying these practices, and to eradicate them, one must be knowledgeable about them. This might require digesting material that is disturbing and contrary to all the values held by a civilized society.

So, while your first reaction to Pinker's ideas may be to dismiss them as outrageous and unworthy of serious consideration, a close analysis of his argument using the Toulmin method may demonstrate how carefully Pinker has crafted his argument to challenge many of our assumptions about human behavior and, in particular, motherhood.

Claims and Grounds

Pinker presents the first part of his claim in paragraph 4 of his essay: Neonaticide is not an abnormal behavior but one that has been practiced "in most cultures throughout history." This statement seems to contradict the popular notion of neonaticide. Because our society regards neonaticide as an immoral act, many people likely assume that it is a rare occurrence. However, Pinker anticipates this assumption in paragraph 1 by reminding us that neonaticide *does* occur in our own society. It is, he claims, more common than we realize, since most murders of newborn babies go undetected. Only "every once in a while" do we discover that this act has taken place because some physical evidence is found. While Pinker offers no grounds for his assertion that "every year, hundreds of women commit neonaticide," his audience's familiarity with newspaper accounts of newborns abandoned in dumpsters and public restrooms lends credibility to his statement. This point is important because it establishes a link between contemporary women's behavior and the practices of our "long-vanished tribal environment."

Pinker develops this idea further in paragraphs 6 through 8 by suggesting that this behavior has been programmed into our "biological design" through human evolutionary development. He provides the grounds to support this part of his claim by citing two scholarly sources: Philip Resnick's study of child-killing statistics, which indicates that women who kill their newborn babies are typically not mentally ill, and research by Martin Daly and Margo Wilson that suggests neonaticide may be an intrinsic part of our "biological design," a necessity for human beings with limited resources to invest in their offspring. Relying on these grounds, Pinker goes on to argue in paragraph 9 that neonaticide is an "adaptive choice," one that is preferable to nurturing an infant whose continued survival is in doubt because of either the physical condition of the child or environmental difficulties for the mother.

So far, then, we have found two of the essential parts of the Toulmin model in Pinker's essay:

Claim   Neonaticide is not a pathologic behavior but can be, rather, the result of evolutionary development.

Grounds Various anthropological studies indicate that neonaticide is a common and accepted practice in many contemporary societies; studies by psychologists argue that neonaticide is a normal part of our parenting emotions; research by psychologists demonstrates that women who commit neonaticide are not mentally ill.

Warrants, Backing, and Rebuttals

Now let's move on to Pinker's warrants, which work to support his claim. Pinker never directly states, yet he strongly implies as a *warrant,* that "biology is destiny." It is clear from his claim and the grounds used to support it that Pinker believes the biological impulses of a new mother who commits neonaticide may overwhelm her civilized sense of what is morally or even emotionally right. Human beings, according to Pinker, are at the mercy of their neurological programming. Pinker offers *backing* for this *warrant* in paragraph 10 when he relates interviews by anthropologists with women who have killed their newborn babies and who appear to grieve sincerely for their children, regarding their actions as "an unavoidable tragedy." These women, according to Pinker, were compelled to make a difficult choice, which each did in spite of her maternal feelings toward the newborn. Pinker reinforces this point later in the essay when he states in paragraph 23 that "the laws of biology were not kind to Amy Grossberg and Melissa Drexler," two young women who killed their infants just after birth. Pinker strongly implies that biological forces were at work when these women made their decisions.

Pinker's warrant provides plenty of opportunity for *rebuttal* because even if the reader accepts the idea that human beings, despite the teachings of civilized society, are still subject to the dictates of more primitive and instinctive urges, Pinker asserts that the urge to kill one's baby is stronger than, say, the maternal instinct to nurture that infant. We have all heard of situations in which a mother has risked or sacrificed her own life to save that of her child. Why, we might ask, wouldn't this emotion dominate the behavior of a new mother? Pinker acknowledges this rebuttal in paragraph 11 when he points out that the neonaticides we read about in newspapers are often committed by middle-class girls who have the resources to support a child or the option to give the baby up for adoption.

Pinker responds to this rebuttal in two ways: First, he reiterates his claim that the internal forces of our evolutionary background are stronger than the individual's own sense of right and wrong. These young women are responding to the "signals of the long-vanished tribal environment in which we spent 99 percent of our evolutionary history." Moreover, Pinker goes on to suggest, neonaticide is triggered by environmental and social factors, specifically the age, marital status, and isolation of the new mother, that work to suppress more positive maternal responses. As he explains in paragraph 12, maternal feelings are more likely to emerge in an atmosphere of "cooing and clucking and congratulating" than in a "motel room or bathroom stall."

Pinker goes on to support his argument with several additional layers of warrants: If human behavior is controlled by deeply ingrained biological forces, then we can't be held legally responsible for these actions. In other words, while we may deeply deplore the act of neonaticide, we cannot fault these women for acting on an impulse they may not completely understand or feel able to control. In paragraph 15, Pinker provides backing for this claim by observing that few women in the United States are actually incarcerated for this crime and several European countries treat neonaticide less severely than other forms of homicide. Thus, although the killing of one's baby generates strong moral outrage in our society, we treat it less severely than most other offenses in the same category.

Logically, then, the next question must be "Why is this the case?" When older children are murdered by their mothers, as in Pinker's example of Susan Smith in paragraph 16, we waste little sympathy on the plight of the mother. We can agree with Pinker that "our compassion hinges on the child." Why do we react, according to Pinker, in a very different way to the death of a newborn? Pinker has very carefully brought us to his next warrant, which even he admits is the "unthinkable": Our reaction to the killing of a newborn and the killing of an older child is different because a newborn is not yet a "full person."

Pinker provides backing for his warrant in paragraphs 18 through 20. In paragraph 18, he points out a fact most readers would agree with: Unlike other mammals, human babies are helpless at birth. They are "incomplete." It will take an infant several years to achieve the level of physical development that some mammals enjoy at birth. Thus, a newborn baby cannot claim its rights as a person based on its physical completeness. Then, Pinker asks, on what basis can a newborn be seen as possessing "a right not to be killed"? By what traits do we define a person with a right to life? In paragraph 20, Pinker calls on the-*backing* of "moral philosophers" who describe the traits human beings must possess to be considered fully human. Pinker concludes that newborn babies "don't possess these traits any more than mice do."

Anticipating that most readers will have a strong negative response to these ideas, Pinker acknowledges several rebuttals to this warrant. In paragraph 17, he recognizes that neither side of the abortion debate would agree with his assertion that birth should not be a marker to determine when a human being is given a right to life. To anti-abortionists, who maintain that "personhood" begins at conception, Pinker responds that if we adopt this viewpoint, the destruction of any fertilized human egg would be considered murder. To those in favor of abortion rights, who consider personhood to begin when the baby is capable of living outside the protection of the mother's body, Pinker counters that this depends on the condition of the infant and the willingness of the parents to accept the risks inherent in a premature birth. In paragraph 19, Pinker also rejects the position that all life deserves to be preserved. If this were practiced, Pinker reasons, then "delousing a child is akin to mass murder." Pinker's stance forces us to reexamine how we define a "person" and how we can determine at what point the right to live unharmed begins.

We can briefly summarize Pinker's warrants and backing as follows:

Warrant 1   Biology is destiny. We are at the mercy of our neurological programming, which has been handed down from our evolutionary ancestors.

Backing   Examples of women who grieve for the newborns they killed; references to Melissa Drexler and Amy Grossberg, who killed their newborn infants.

Warrant 2	If human behavior is controlled by deeply ingrained biological forces, then women can't be held legally responsible for following their natural impulses.
Backing	Examples of lenient criminal treatment of women who commit neonaticide; examples of less severe penalties for women who kill newborns, as opposed to those given for the murder of older children or adults.
Warrant 3	A newborn infant is not a full person. Neonates do not yet possess those human qualities that bestow on them the right to life.
Backing	A description of a newborn infant's physical helplessness; a definition of a "full person" according to some moral philosophers; a comparison of the intellectual and moral awareness of a newborn infant with that of a mouse.

Qualifiers

Throughout his essay, Pinker is careful to use *qualifiers* that limit and clarify his claim. There are many examples of these; we will point out a few that appear early in the essay along with our emphasis and comments:

Paragraph 4	"But it's *hard* [difficult but not impossible] to maintain that neonaticide is an illness when we learn that it has been practiced and accepted in *most* [but not all] cultures throughout history. And that neonaticidal women do not *commonly* [typical but not in all cases] show signs of psychopathology."
Paragraph 5	"But normal human motives are *not always* [happens some of the time] moral, and neonaticide *does not have to be* [but it could be] a product of malfunctioning neural circuitry or a dysfunctional upbringing."

By using qualifiers, Pinker demonstrates his awareness that his claim may not always be true under all circumstances and accounts for the differing experiences of his audience.

As we stated at the beginning of this chapter, to construct a persuasive argument, you must pay careful attention to the logical structure you are building. As the Toulmin method illustrates, unless your claim is supported by a firm foundation (your warrants) and well buttressed by convincing grounds and backing, your structure will not withstand the rebuttals that will test its strength.

Pinker's view on neonaticide is disturbing, to say the least. For his essay to be persuasive, the reader must be willing to accept each of his warrants and the backing he uses to support them. Four days after Pinker's essay appeared in *The New York Times,* the following article was published in *The Washington Post.* As you read the article, notice how author Michael Kelley, a senior writer at the *National Journal,* attacks Pinker's claim by questioning each of his warrants and their backing. Calling Pinker's premise one of the "most thoroughly dishonest constructs anyone has ever attempted to pass off as science,"

Kelley also levels severe criticism at one of Pinker's sources, Michael Tooley. Kelley comments that Pinker's citation of Tooley's radical views, even though he may not directly agree with them, makes him "guilty by association." Kelley's accusation demonstrates why you should choose your sources carefully. Your audience will associate your views with the company they keep.

Arguing for Infanticide
Michael Kelley

1   Of all the arguments advanced against the legalization of abortion, the one that always struck me as the most questionable is the most consequential: that the widespread acceptance of abortion would lead to a profound moral shift in our culture, a great devaluing of human life. This seemed to me dubious on general principle: Projections of this sort almost always turn out to be wrong because they fail to grasp that, in matters of human behavior, there is not really any such thing as a trendline. People change to meet new realities and thereby change reality.

2   Thus, for the environmental hysterics of the 1970s, the nuclear freezers of the 1980s and the Perovian budget doomsayers of the 1990s, the end that was nigh never came. So, with abortions, why should a tolerance for ending human life under one, very limited, set of conditions necessarily lead to an acceptance of ending human life under other, broader terms?

3   This time, it seems, the pessimists were right. On Sunday, Nov. 2, an article in the *New York Times*, the closest thing we have to the voice of the intellectual establishment, came out for killing babies. I am afraid that I am sensationalizing only slightly. The article by Steven Pinker in the *Times Magazine* did not go quite so far as to openly recommend the murder of infants, and printing the article did not constitute the *Times'* endorsement of the idea. But close enough, close enough.

4   What Pinker, a professor of psychology at the Massachusetts Institute of Technology, wrote and what the *Times* treated as a legitimate argument, was a thoroughly sympathetic treatment of this modest proposal: Mothers who kill their newborn infants should not be judged as harshly as people who take human life in its later stages because newborn infants are not persons in the full sense of the word, and therefore do not enjoy a right to life. Who says that life begins at birth?

5   "To a biologist, birth is as arbitrary a milestone as any other," Pinker breezily writes. "No, the right to life must come, the moral philosophers say, from morally significant traits that we humans happen to possess. One such trait is having a unique sequence of experiences that defines us as individuals and connects us to other people. Other traits include an ability to reflect upon ourselves as a continuous locus of consciousness, to form and savor plans for the future, to dread death and to express the choice not to die. And there's the rub: our immature neonates don't possess these traits any more than mice do."

6   Pinker notes that "several moral philosophers have concluded that neonates are not persons, and thus neonaticide should not be classified as murder," and he suggests his

acceptance of this view, arguing that "the facts don't make it easy" to legitimately outlaw the killing of infants.

7   Pinker's casually authoritative mention of "the facts" is important, because Pinker is no mere ranter from the crackpot fringe but a scientist. He is, in fact, a respected explicator of the entirely mainstream and currently hot theory of evolutionary psychology, and the author of *How the Mind Works*, a widely read and widely celebrated book on the subject.

8   How the mind works, says Pinker, is that people are more or less hard-wired to behave as they do by the cumulative effects of the human experience. First cousins to the old Marxist economic determinists, the evolutionary psychologists are behavioral determinists. They believe in a sort of Popeye's theory of human behavior: I do what I do because I yam what I yam because I wuz what I wuz.

9   This view is radical; it seeks to supplant both traditional Judeo-Christian morality and liberal humanism with a new "scientific" philosophy that denies the idea that all humans are possessed of a quality that sets them apart from the lower species, and that this quality gives humans the capacity and responsibility to choose freely between right and wrong. And it is monstrous. And, judging from the writings of Pinker and his fellow determinists on the subject of infanticide, it may be the most thoroughly dishonest construct anyone has ever attempted to pass off as science.

10   Pinker's argument was a euphemized one. The more blunt argument is made by Michael Tooley, a philosophy professor at the University of Colorado, whom Pinker quotes. In this 1972 essay "Abortion and Infanticide," Tooley makes what he calls "an extremely plausible answer" to the question: "What makes it morally permissible to destroy a baby, but wrong to kill an adult?" Simple enough: Personhood does not begin at birth. Rather, "an organism possesses a serious right to life only if it possesses the concept of a self as a continuing subject of experiences and other mental states, and believes that it is itself such a continuing entity."

11   Some would permit the killing of infants "up to the time an organism learned how to use certain expressions," but Tooley finds this cumbersome and would simply establish "some period of time, such as a week after birth, as the interval during which infanticide will be permitted."

12   And Tooley does not bother with Pinker's pretense that what is under discussion here is only a rare act of desperation, the killing of an unwanted child by a frightened, troubled mother. No, no, no. If it is moral to kill a baby for one, it is moral for all. Indeed, the systematic, professionalized use of infanticide would be a great benefit to humanity. "Most people would prefer to raise children who do not suffer from gross deformities or from severe physical, emotional, or intellectual handicaps," writes eugenicist Tooley. "If it could be shown that there is no moral objection to infanticide the happiness of society could be significantly and justifiably increased."

13   To defend such an unnatural idea, the determinists argue that infanticide is in fact natural: In Pinker's words, "it has been practiced and accepted in most cultures throughout history." This surprising claim is critical to the argument that the act of a mother killing a child is a programmed response to signals that the child might not fare well in life (because of poverty, illegitimacy or other factors). And it is a lie.

14   In fact, although millions of mothers give birth every year under the sort of adverse conditions that Pinker says trigger the "natural" urge to kill the baby, infanticide

is extremely rare in all modern societies, and is universally treated as a greatly aberrant act, the very definition of a moral horror. The only cultures that Pinker can point to in which infanticide is widely "practiced and accepted" are those that are outside the mores of Western civilization: ancient cultures and the remnants of ancient cultures today, tribal hunter-gatherer societies.

15   And so goes the entire argument, a great chain of dishonesty, palpable untruth piled upon palpable untruth. "A new mother," asserts Pinker, "will first coolly assess the infant and her situation and only in the next few days begin to see it as a unique and wonderful individual." Yes, that was my wife all over: cool as a cucumber as she assessed whether to keep her first-born child or toss him out the window. As George Orwell said once of another vast lie, "You have to be an intellectual to believe such nonsense. No ordinary man could be such a fool."

QUESTIONS FOR ANALYSIS AND DISCUSSION

1. Briefly outline the basic Toulmin components of Kelley's argument: What is his claim? What grounds does he use to support it? Then find and identify Kelley's warrants and the backing he provides to demonstrate their reliability.

2. To what aspects of Pinker's claim and warrants does Kelley object? On what grounds does he object?

3. Pinker limits his discussion of neonaticide to the behavior of "depressed new mothers" (paragraph 9). Does Kelley ignore this distinction in his response to Pinker? How does Kelley shift the discussion from Pinker's "anguished girls" (paragraph 23) to "millions of mothers" (paragraph 14 in Kelley)? Do you think this is a fair interpretation of Pinker's intent?

4. Kelley begins his essay with a reference to the legalization of abortion. On what basis does he suggest a link between the "widespread acceptance of abortion" and Pinker's theories about neonaticide?

5. In paragraph 3 of his essay, Kelley states that Pinker "did not go quite so far as to openly recommend the murder of infants." Discuss the implications of Kelley's use of the qualifiers *quite* and *openly*. What do you think he intends to imply about Pinker's objectives?

6. In paragraph 10, what does Kelley mean by describing Pinker's argument as "euphemized"? What connection does Kelley make between Pinker's views and the theories expressed by Michael Tooley in his 1972 essay? Does your analysis of Pinker's claim and warrants lead you to believe that Pinker endorses Tooley's theories, as Kelley asserts?

7. In your journal, discuss your own response to Kelley's essay. Which reasons do you find particularly persuasive? With which reasons do you disagree, and why?

8. In paragraph 9, Kelley criticizes Pinker's attempt to take a "scientific" approach to a serious moral issue by suggesting that humans lack "the capacity and responsibility to choose freely between right and wrong." In your journal, consider how Pinker might respond to that statement. Would he agree with Kelley's interpretation of his ideas? How would Pinker suggest that society should deal with the problem of neonaticide?

The previous two essays focused on parental love becoming grossly dysfunctional as the possible result of tragic neurological wiring. What follows is a paper about the effects of parental love on children of divorce. Given the fact that half of all children will see their parents' marriage terminate by the time they turn 18, divorce has become an American way of life. While society may shake its collective head at such a statistic, lamenting the loss of the traditional family, not all children of divorce see it as a problem. In the following essay, an introductory writing student explores the effect of his parents' divorce on his development, arguing that divorce should not be a taboo topic and that children of broken homes are not always damaged.

This student, who chooses to remain anonymous, wrote this essay when he was a college freshman. When he is not living on campus, he splits his time between his mother's home in New York and his father's home in Massachusetts.

Read through this essay and make notes in your journal. Notice whether and how its parts work together—and, if possible, where some of the parts may need to be reworked. Then respond to the questions that follow.

Student Essay 1

Anonymous
Professor Ramos
English 201
5 March 2013

Did I Miss Something?

1　　The subject of divorce turns heads in our society. It is responsible for bitten tongues, lowered voices, and an almost pious reverence saved only for life-threatening illness or uncontrolled catastrophe. Having grown up in a "broken home," I am always shocked to be treated as a victim of some social disease. When a class assignment required that I write an essay concerning my feelings about or my personal experiences with divorce, my first reaction was complete surprise. An essay on aspects of my life affected by divorce seems completely superfluous because I cannot differentiate between the "normal" part of my youth and the supposed angst and confusion that apparently come with all divorces. The separation of my parents over sixteen years ago (when I was three years old) has either saturated every last pore of my developmental epidermis to a point where I cannot sense it or it has not affected me at all. Eugene Ehrlich's *Highly Selective Dictionary for the Extraordinarily Literate* (1997) defines divorce as a "breach"; however, I cannot sense any schism in my life resulting from the event to which other people seem to attribute so much importance. My parents' divorce is a ubiquitous part of who I am, and the only "breach" that could arrive from my present familial arrangement would be to tear me away from what I consider my normal living conditions.

Student Essay 2

2   Though there is no doubt in my mind that many unfortunate people have had their lives torn apart by the divorce of their parents, I do not feel any real sense of regret for my situation. In my opinion, the paramount role of a parent is to love his or her child. Providing food, shelter, education, and video games are of course other necessary elements of successful child rearing, but these secondary concerns stem from the most fundamental ideal of parenting, which is love. A loving parent will be a successful one even if he or she cannot afford to furnish his or her child with the best clothes or the most sophisticated gourmet delicacies. With love as the driving force in a parent's mind, he or she will almost invariably make the correct decisions. When my mother and father found that they were no longer in love with each other after nine years of marriage, their love for me forced them to take the precipitous step to separate. The safest environment for me was to be with one happy parent at a time, instead of two miserable ones all the time. The sacrifice that they both made to relinquish control over me for half the year was at least as painful for them as it was for me (probably even more so), but in the end I was not deprived of a parent's love, but merely of one parent's presence for a few weeks at a time. My father and mother's love for me has not dwindled even slightly over the past fifteen years, and I can hardly imagine a more well-adjusted and contented family.

3   As I reread the first section of this essay, I realize that it is perhaps too optimistic and cheerful regarding my life as a child of divorced parents. In all truthfulness, there have been some decidedly negative ramifications stemming from our family separation. My first memory is actually of a fight between my mother and father. I vaguely remember standing in the end of the upstairs hallway of our Philadelphia house when I was about three years old, and seeing shadows moving back and forth in the light coming from under the door of my father's study, accompanied by raised voices. It would be naïve of me to say that I have not been at all affected by divorce, since it has permeated my most primal and basic memories; however, I am grateful that I can only recall one such incident, instead of having parental conflicts become so quotidian that they leave no mark whatsoever on my mind. Also, I find that having to divide my time equally between both parents leads to alienation from either side of my family. Invariably, at every holiday occasion, there is one half of my family (either my mother's side or my father's) that has to explain that "Junior is with his [mother/father] this year," while aunts, cousins, and grandparents collectively arch eyebrows or avert eyes. Again, though, I should not be hasty to lament my distance from loved ones, since there are many families with "normal" marriages where the children never even meet their cousins, let alone get to spend every other Thanksgiving with them. Though divorce has certainly thrown some proverbial monkey wrenches into some proverbial gears, in general my otherwise strong familial ties have overshadowed any minor blemishes.

Student Essay 3

4   Perhaps one of the most important reasons for my absence of "trauma" (for lack of a better word) stemming from my parents' divorce is that I am by no means alone in my trials and tribulations. The foreboding statistic that sixty percent of marriages end in divorce is no myth to me, indeed many of my friends come from similar situations. The argument could be made that "birds of a feather flock together" and that my friends and I form a tight support network for each other, but I strongly doubt that any of us need or look for that kind of buttress. The fact of the matter is that divorce happens a lot in today's society, and as a result our culture has evolved to accommodate these new family arrangements, making the overall conditions more hospitable for me and my broken brothers and shattered sisters.

5   I am well aware that divorce can often lead to issues of abandonment and familial proximity among children of separated parents, but in my case I see very little evidence to support the claim that my parents should have stayed married "for the sake of the child." In many ways, my life is enriched by the division of my time with my father and my time with my mother. I get to live in New York City for half of the year, and in a small suburb of Boston for the other half. I have friends who envy me, since I get "the best of both worlds." I never get double-teamed by parents during arguments, and I cherish my time with each one more since it only lasts half the year.

6   In my opinion, there is no such thing as a perfect life or a "normal" life, and any small blips on our karmic radar screen have to be dealt with appropriately but without any trepidation or self-pity. Do I miss my father when I live with my mother (and vice versa)? Of course I do. However, I know young boys and girls who have lost parents to illness or accidental injury, so my pitiable position is relative. As I look back on the last nineteen years from the relative independence of college, I can safely say that my childhood has not been at all marred by having two different houses to call home.

QUESTIONS FOR ANALYSIS AND DISCUSSION

1. Identify the author's claim. Where does he state it in his essay? From your experience, do you agree with him? Do you agree that people discuss divorce "in an almost pious reverence saved only for life-threatening illness"?

2. On what grounds does the author base his claim? Find specific evidence he presents to support his claim. Do you find it convincing and supportive?

3. Do you agree with the author's definition of what makes a good parent?

4. The author has several warrants, some of them stated explicitly and some implied. In paragraph 2, he states: "A loving parent will be a successful one even if he or she cannot afford to furnish his or her child with the best clothes or the most sophisticated gourmet delicacies." Do you agree with his warrant? On what commonly shared values or beliefs does he base this warrant? Are there any aspects of his warrant with which you disagree? What backing does the author provide to support his warrant? Is it sufficient?

5. What other warrants underlie the author's claim? In a small peer group, identify several layers of warrants and discuss whether these need additional backing to be convincing.

6. Notice the qualifier the author uses in paragraph 3 when he says, "In all truthfulness, there have been *some* decidedly negative ramifications stemming from our family separation" (emphasis added). What limitations does this qualifying statement put on his argument? Does this limitation weaken his argument at all?

7. Does the author acknowledge and address anticipated rebuttals to his argument? Can you locate any in his essay? What rebuttals can you make in response to his argument?

8. If you are a child of divorced parents, write about the experience as it affected your emotional and psychological outlook. How did it impact your life growing up, and how did it affect your adult view of marriage? Answer the same questions if your parents remained married, considering in your response how your life may have been different if your parents had divorced while you were young.

9. In your peer group, discuss the effects of divorce on children. Further develop the author's idea that it is just another way of life. Compare notes with classmates to assemble a complete list. Based on this list, develop your own argument about the effects of divorce on children.

EXERCISES

1. In your work group, work out a concise and clear definition of the following three Toulmin terms: the claim, the grounds, and the warrant. As a group, create a statement that is a claim. Then using that claim, write a statement functioning as grounds to support your claim. Write a statement that functions as a warrant to support your claim.

2. As in exercise 1, write a definition of the following terms: *the backing, the qualifiers,* and *the rebuttals.* Then using the same claim as in exercise 1, write a statement of backing to support you claim, of qualifiers to support your claim, and of rebuttals to support your claim.

3. In the discussion of qualifiers on page 191, the author writes, "Few truths are *completely* true; few claims are *always* right. A well-qualified claim, then, shows that the writer respects both the difficulty of the issue and the intelligence of the reader." Explain this statement. Why is it so important to qualify a claim? Give your own example.

4. What is the difference between a qualifier and a rebuttal? Listen to a radio or television news program where there is a debate between two opposing sides on some timely issue. Do you feel qualifiers or rebuttals are part of the discussion? Or do broad generalizations dominate the discussion? Which would you prefer: a conversation dominated by broad generalizations or a conversation containing qualifiers and rebuttals? Why?

5. In your group or in your journal, study each claim listed next. Note that each is a very broad based generalization. Rewrite each claim using one or two qualifiers that make your claim more credible:
   a. Right to die legislation is a godsend to the elderly.
   b. Winter in New England is a beautiful season.
   c. A good football helmet will prevent concussions or serious injuries to the head.
   d. Making the purchase and possession of automatic assault weapons illegal will reduce the death rate due to gun violence.

6. In your group or in your journal, study each claim listed next. Then write two rebuttals that you would need to address in order to make your claim convincing:
   a. The sentence for anyone convicted of murder should be life in prison without parole.
   b. Failure to check the organ donation box on your driver's license is an act of selfishness.
   c. To be considered an educated person, one should play at least one musical instrument proficiently.
   d. Surrendering one's right to privacy is worth it in the fight against terrorism.
   e. Obese people should pay higher health insurance premiums than thin people.

8

Using Visual Arguments: Thinking Like an Illustrator

LEARNING OBJECTIVES

After studying this chapter, you should be able to:

1. Apply the basic tools of critical reading to the analysis of visual arguments in art, advertising, editorial cartoons, and news photos. (p. 213)
2. Explain how the persuasive elements in advertising work. (p. 221)
3. Explain how the persuasive elements in editorial cartoons create an argument. (p. 225)
4. Explain how the various elements in news photographs create arguments. (p. 231)
5. Explain how graphics (tables, charts, and graphs) can enhance a written argument. (p. 235)

Ours is a visual world. From the earliest cave paintings of prehistoric Spain to the complicated photomosaic posters that adorn dormitory walls today, we are inspired, compelled, and persuaded by visual stimuli. Everywhere we look images vie for our attention—magazine ads, T-shirt logos, movie billboards, artwork, traffic signs, political cartoons, statues, and storefront windows. Glanced at only briefly, visuals communicate information and ideas. They project commonly held values, ideals, and fantasies. They relay opinion, inspire reaction, and influence emotion. And because competition for our attention today is so great and the time available for communication is so scarce, images must compete to make an impression or risk being lost in a blur of visual information.

Because the goal of a calculated visual is to persuade, coax, intimidate, or otherwise subliminally influence its viewer, it is important that its audience can discern the strategies or technique it employs. In other words, to be a literate reader of visuals, one must be a literate reader of arguments.

Consider the instant messages projected by brand names, company logos, or even the American flag. Such images may influence us consciously and unconsciously. Some visual images, such as advertisements, may target our emotions, while others, such as graphics, may appeal to our intellect. Just as we approach writing with the tools of critical analysis, we should carefully consider the many ways visuals influence us.

Common Forms of Visual Arguments

Visual arguments come in many different forms and use many different media. Artists, photographers, advertisers, cartoonists, and designers approach their work with the same intentions that authors of written material do—they want to share a point of view, present an idea, inspire, or evoke a reaction. Think back to when you had your high school yearbook photo taken. The photographer didn't simply sit you down and start snapping pictures. More likely, the photographer told you how to sit, how to tilt your head, and where to gaze. You selected your clothing for the picture carefully and probably spent extra time on your hair that day. Lighting, shadow, and setting were also thoughtfully considered. You and your photographer crafted an image of how you wanted the world to see you—an image of importance because it would be forever recorded in your yearbook, as well as distributed to family and friends as the remembrance of a milestone in your life. In effect, you were creating a visual argument.

While there are many different kinds of visual arguments, the most common ones take the form of artwork, advertisements, editorial cartoons, and news photos. These visuals often do not rely on an image alone to tell their story, although it is certainly possible for a thoughtfully designed visual to do so. More often, however, advertisements are accompanied by ad copy, editorial cartoons feature comments or statements, and news photos are placed near the stories they enhance.

Ancillary visuals—that is, tables, graphs, and charts—have great potential for enhancing written arguments and influencing the audience. They provide snapshots of information and provide factual support to written information. We will discuss these types of visuals, and how you can use them to enhance your own written arguments, later in this chapter. But now, let us examine some powerful visual images and the ways they capture our attention, impact our sensibilities, and evoke our responses.

Analyzing Visual Arguments

As critical readers of written arguments, we do not take the author simply at face value. We consider the author's purpose and intent, audience, style, tone, and supporting evidence. We must apply these same analytical tools to "read" visual arguments effectively. As with written language, understanding the persuasive power of "visual language" requires a close examination and interpretation of the premise, claims, details, supporting evidence, and stylistic touches embedded in any visual piece. We should ask ourselves the following four questions when examining visual arguments:

- Who is the target *audience?*
- What are the *claims* made in the images?
- What shared history or cultural *assumptions*—or warrants—does the image make?
- What is the supporting *evidence?*

Like works of art, visuals often employ color, shape, line, texture, depth, and point of view to create their effect. Therefore, to understand how visuals work and to analyze the way visuals persuade, we must also ask questions about specific aspects of form and design. For example, some questions to ask about print images such as those in newspaper and magazine ads include the following:

- What in the frame catches your attention immediately?
- What is the central image? What is the background image? Foreground images? What are the surrounding images? What is significant in the placement of these images? Their relationship to one another?

- ■ What verbal information is included? How is it made prominent? How does it relate to the other graphics or images?
- ■ What specific details (people, objects, locale) are emphasized? Which are exaggerated or idealized?
- ■ What is the effect of color and lighting?
- ■ What emotional effect is created by the images? Pleasure? Longing? Anxiety? Nostalgia?
- ■ Do the graphics and images make you want to know more about the subject or product?
- ■ What special significance might objects in the image have?
- ■ Is there any symbolism embedded in the images?

Considering these questions helps us to survey a visual argument critically and enables us to formulate reasoned assessments of its message and intent. In the next pages of this chapter, we will analyze in greater detail some visual arguments presented in art, advertising, editorial cartoons, and photographs. Part Two of this book continues the investigation of visual arguments as they connect to the topics of each chapter.

Art

The French artist Georges Braque (1882–1963) once said, "In art, there can be no effect without twisting the truth." While not all artists would agree with him, Braque, who with Pablo Picasso originated the cubist style, "saw" things from a different perspective than the rest of us, and he expressed his vision in his paintings. All art is an interpretation of what the artist sees. It is filtered through the eyes of the artist and influenced by his or her own perceptions.

Throughout history, artists have applied their craft to advance religious, social, and political visual arguments. Portraits of kings and queens present how the monarchs wanted their people to see them, with symbolic tools of power such as scepters, crowns, and rich vestments. Art in churches and cathedrals was used as a means of visual instruction for people who could not read. Much of modern art reveals impressions, feelings, and emotions without remaining faithful to the actual thing depicted. While entire books are written about the meaning and function of art, let's examine how one particular artist, Pablo Picasso (1881–1973), created a visual argument.

Pablo Picasso's *Guernica*

Pablo Picasso, with fellow artist Georges Braque, invented a style of painting known as **cubism.** Cubism is based on the idea that the eye observes things from continually changing viewpoints, as fragments of a whole. Cubism aims to represent the essential reality of forms from multiple perspectives and angles. Thus, cubist paintings don't show reality as we see it. Rather, they depict pieces of people, places, and things in an unstable field of vision.

Picasso's painting *Guernica* (Figure 8.1, page 215) represents the essence of cubism. During the Spanish Civil War, the German air force bombed the town of Guernica, the cultural center of the Basque region in northern Spain and a Loyalist stronghold. In only a few minutes on April 26, 1937, hundreds of men, women, and children were massacred in the deadly air strike. Two months later, Picasso expressed his outrage at the attack in a mural he titled simply, *Guernica.*

Figure 8.1

Picasso, Pablo (1881–1973) © ARS, NY. Guernica, 1937. Museo Nacional Centro de Arte Reina Sofia, Madrid, Spain. Art Resource, NY.

The mural is Picasso's statement about the horror and devastation of war. The painting is dynamic and full of action, yet its figures seem flat and static. It is balanced while still presenting distorted images and impressions. It is ordered while still evoking a sense of chaos and panic. To better understand Picasso's "statement," let's apply some of the questions about visual arguments described earlier in the chapter to this painting.

Who Is Picasso's Target Audience?

Knowing the history of the painting can help us understand whom Picasso was trying to reach. In January 1937, Picasso was commissioned to paint a mural for the 1937 Exposition Internationale des Arts et Techniques dans la Vie Moderne, an art exhibition to open in France in May of that same year. Although he had never been a political person, the atrocity of Guernica in April compelled him to express his anger and appeal to the world.

Before the mural went on display, some politicians tried to replace it with a less "offensive" piece of art. When the picture was unveiled at the opening of the expo, it was received poorly. One critic described it as "the work of a madman." Picasso had hoped that his work would shock people. He wanted the outside world to care about what happened at Guernica. However, Picasso may have misjudged his first audience. In 1937, Europe was on the brink of world war. Many people were in denial that the war could touch them and preferred to ignore the possibility that it was imminent. It was this audience who first viewed *Guernica*—an audience that didn't want to see a mural about war, an audience that was trying to avoid the inevitable. Years later, the mural would become one of the most critically acclaimed works of art of the twentieth century.

What Claims Is Picasso Making in the Images?

Picasso's painting comprises many images that make up an entire scene. It depicts simultaneously events that happened over a period of time. The overall claim is that war itself is horrible. The smaller claims address the injustice of Guernica more directly. A mother wails in grief over her dead infant, a reminder that the bombing of Guernica was a massacre of innocents. Picasso also chose to paint his mural in black and white, giving it the aura of a newspaper, especially in the body of the horse. He could be saying, "This is news" or "This is a current event that you should think about."

It should be mentioned that Picasso created many versions of the images in the mural, carefully considering their position, placement, and expression, sometimes drawing eight or nine versions of a single subject. He thoughtfully considered how the images would convey his message before he painted them in the mural.

What Shared History or Cultural Assumptions Does Picasso Make?

The assumptions in any argument are the principles or beliefs that the audience takes for granted. These assumptions implicitly connect the claim to the evidence. By naming his mural *Guernica,* Picasso knew that people would make an immediate connection between the chaos on the wall and the events of April 26, 1937. He also assumed that the people viewing the painting would be upset by it. In addition, there are symbols in the painting that would have been recognized by people at the time—such as the figure of the bull in the upper-left-hand corner of the mural, a long-time symbol for Spain.

What Is Picasso's Supporting Evidence?

Although Picasso was illustrating a real event, cubism allowed him to paint "truth" rather than "reality." If Picasso was trying to depict the horror of Guernica and, by extension, the terror and chaos of war, all the components of his mural serve as supporting evidence. The wailing figures, panicked faces, the darkness contrasted by jumbled images of light, all project the horror of war. Even the horse looks terrified. Overall, *Guernica* captures the emotional cacophony of war. Picasso wasn't just trying to say, "War is hell." He was also trying to impress upon his audience that such atrocities should never happen again. In essence, Picasso was making an appeal for peace by showing its opposite, the carnage of war.

QUESTIONS FOR ANALYSIS AND DISCUSSION

Referring to the more specific questions regarding visual arguments discussed earlier in the chapter, apply them to Picasso's painting.

1. What images in the painting catch your attention, and why?
2. What is the central image? Is there a central image? What appears in the foreground? What is significant about the placement of the images? How do they relate to one another?
3. What verbal information, if any, is included, and why? (Remember that Picasso did title his painting *Guernica*. What might have happened if he had named it something more abstract?)
4. What specific details are emphasized? What is exaggerated or idealized?
5. What is the effect of color and light?
6. Does the image make you want to know more?
7. What symbolism is embedded in the image?

Norman Rockwell's *Freedom of Speech*

Picasso's mural was designed to be displayed in a large hall at the World Exposition and later, presumably, in a museum. Other artists had less grand aspirations for their work. Norman Rockwell (1894–1978) was an artist who featured most of his work on the covers of magazines, most notably the *Saturday Evening Post,* a publication he considered "the greatest show window in America." In 47 years, Rockwell contributed 321 paintings to the magazine and became an American icon.

On January 6, 1941, President Franklin Delano Roosevelt addressed Congress, delivering his famous "Four Freedoms" speech. Against the background of the Nazi domination of Europe and the Japanese oppression of China, Roosevelt described the four essential human freedoms—freedom of speech, freedom of worship, freedom from want, and freedom from fear. Viewing these freedoms as the fundamental basis on which our society was formed, Roosevelt called upon Americans to uphold these liberties at all costs. Two years later, Rockwell, inspired by Roosevelt's speech, created his famous series of paintings on these "Four Freedoms," reproduced in four consecutive issues of the *Saturday Evening*

Post. So popular were the images that they were used by the U.S. government to sell war bonds, to inspire public support for the war effort, and to remind people of the ideals for which they were fighting. The paintings serve as an example of how art can sometimes extend into advertising.

Let's take a closer look at one of the four paintings, *Freedom of Speech* (Figure 8.2). When the war department adopted the painting for the war bond effort, it added two slogans to the image. The command "Save Freedom of Speech" was printed at the top of the painting in large, capital letters and, in even larger typeface, "Buy War Bonds" was printed at the bottom. As we analyze this painting, we will also make references to its later use as part of the effort to sell war bonds.

Figure 8.2

Before he took a brush to his canvas, Rockwell consciously or unconsciously asked himself some of the same questions writers ask when they stare at a blank piece of paper while preparing to create a written argument. After determining that he would use the American small-town vehicle of democracy, the town meeting, as the means to express the theme of freedom of speech, he then painted his "argument."

Who Is Rockwell's Audience?

The *Saturday Evening Post* was widely read in America in the 1930s and 1940s. Rockwell would have wanted his work to appeal to a wide audience, readers of the magazine. If we examine the people in the painting—presumably based on Rockwell's Arlington, Vermont, friends and neighbors—we can deduce the kind of audience the artist was hoping to touch: small-town citizens from a middle-income, working-class environment. Like the language of an argument written for a "general audience," the figures represent what Rockwell considered all-American townsfolk.

The venue is a meetinghouse or town hall because people are sitting on benches. The figures represent a generational cross-section of men and women, from the elderly white-haired man to the left of the central standing figure to the young woman behind him. Style of dress reinforces the notion of class diversity, from the standing man in work clothes to the two men dressed in white shirts, ties, and suit jackets. The formality of the seated figures also opens audience identity to life beyond a small, rural community. That is, some of the men's formal attire and the woman in a stylish hat broaden the depiction to include white-collar urban America. While diversity in age and class is suggested, diversity of race is not. There are no Asians, African Americans, or other nonwhites in the scene. This exclusion might be a reflection of the times and, perhaps, the popular notion of what constituted small-town America 70 years ago. While such exclusion would be unacceptable today, it should be noted that in the years following this painting's completion, Rockwell used his considerable talent and fame to champion the civil rights struggle.

What Is Rockwell's Claim?

When the government adopted Rockwell's painting for its World War II effort campaign to sell war bonds, it added the caption: "Save Freedom of Speech. Buy War Bonds." When we consider the poster as an advertising piece, this essentially becomes the poster's claim. And we know the artist's intention, to illustrate the theme of freedom of speech. Rockwell's challenge was in how he makes his claim—how he dramatizes it on canvas. Just as a writer uses words to persuade, the artist makes his claim in symbolic details of the brush.

It has been said that Norman Rockwell's paintings appeal to a dreamy-eyed American nostalgia and at the same time project a world where the simple acts of common folk express high American ideals. In this painting, we have one of the sacred liberties dramatized by a working-class man raised to the figure of a political spokesperson in the assembly of others. Clearly expressing his opinion as freely as anybody else, he becomes both the illustration and defender of the democratic principles of freedom and equality.

What Are Rockwell's Assumptions?

As with written arguments, the success of a visual argument depends on whether the audience accepts the assumptions (the values, legal or moral principles, commonsense knowledge, or shared beliefs) projected in the image. One assumption underlying Rockwell's illustration is that freedom of speech is desirable for Americans regardless of gender, class, or position in society. We know this instantly from the facial expressions and body language of the figures in the canvas. For example, the face of the man standing seems more prominent because it is painted against a dark blank background and is brighter than any others, immediately capturing our attention. His face tilts upward with a look of pride, lit as if by the inspiration of the ideals he represents—freedom of expression. One might even see suggestions of divine inspiration on his face as it rises in the light and against the night-blackened window in the background. The lighting and man's posture are reminiscent of religious paintings of past centuries. Additionally, the man's body is angular and rough, while his facial characteristics strongly resemble those of a young Abraham Lincoln—which suggests a subtle fusion of the patriotic with the divine. The implied message is that freedom of speech is a divine right.

As for the surrounding audience, we take special note of the two men looking up at the speaker. The older man appears impressed and looks on with a warm smile of approval, while the other man on the right gazes up expectantly. In fact, the entire audience supports the standing man with reasonable, friendly, and respectful gazes. The speaker is "Everyman." And he has the support and respect of his community. Rockwell's audience, subscribers of the *Saturday Evening Post,* saw itself in this image—an image that mirrored the values of honest, decent, middle America.

What Is Rockwell's Supporting Evidence?

The key supporting image in Rockwell's painting is the sharp contrast between the standing man and those sitting around him. Not only is he the only one on his feet, but he is the only working-class person clearly depicted. He stands out from the others in the room; and it is significant that they look up to him—a dramatic illustration of what it means to give the common man his say. Were the scene reversed—with the central figure formally dressed and those looking up approvingly attired in work clothes—we would have a completely different message: that is, a representative of the upper class perhaps "explaining" higher concepts to a less-educated people. The message would be all wrong. In the painting, class barriers are transcended as the "common man" has risen to speak his mind with a face full of conviction, while upper-class people look on in support. That's the American ideal in action.

Because this is a painting instead of a newspaper photograph, every detail is selected purposely and, thus, is open to interpretation. One such detail is the fold of papers sticking out of the man's jacket pocket. What might those papers represent? And what's the point of such a detail? What associations might we make with it? There are words printed on the paper, but we cannot read them, so we're left to speculate. The only other paper in the painting is in the hand of the man on the right. The words *report* and *town* are visible. So, we might conclude that the speaker's pocket contains the same pamphlet, perhaps a summary report of the evening's agenda or possibly a resolution to be voted on. Whatever the documentation, the man clearly doesn't need it because his remarks transcend whatever is on that paper. And here lies more evidence of Rockwell's claim and celebration of the unaided articulation of one man's views out of many—the essence of freedom of speech.

Referring to the more specific questions regarding visual arguments discussed earlier in the chapter, apply them to Rockwell's painting.

1. What images in the painting catch your attention, and why?
2. What is the central image? Is there a central image? What appears in the foreground? What is significant about the placement of the images? How do they relate to one another?
3. What verbal information, if any, is included, and why?
4. What specific details are emphasized? What is exaggerated or idealized?
5. What is the effect of color and light?
6. Does the image make you want to know more?
7. What symbolism is embedded in the image?

Advertisements

Norman Rockwell sought to embody a concept through his art; and, as a result, his painting tries to prompt reflection and self-awareness. In other words, his visuals serve to open the mind to a new discovery or idea. Advertising also selects and crafts visual images. However, advertising has a different objective. Its goal is not to stimulate expansive and enlightened thought but to direct the viewer to a single basic response: Buy this product!

Images have clout, and none are so obvious or so craftily designed as those from the world of advertising. Advertising images are everywhere—television, newspapers, the Internet, magazines, the sides of buses, and highway billboards. Each year, companies collectively spend more than $150 billion on print ads and television commercials (more than the gross national product of many countries). Advertisements comprise at least a quarter of each television hour and form the bulk of most newspapers and magazines. Tapping into our most basic emotions, the appeal of advertisements goes right to the quick of our fantasies: happiness, material wealth, eternal youth, social acceptance, sexual fulfillment, and power.

Yet, most of us are so accustomed to the onslaught of such images that we see them without looking and hear them without listening. But if we stopped to examine how the images work, we might be amazed at their powerful and complex psychological force. And we might be surprised at how much effort goes into the crafting of such images—an effort solely intended to make us spend our money.

Like a written argument, every print ad or commercial has *an audience, claims, assumptions,* and *evidence.* Sometimes these elements are obvious; sometimes they are understated; sometimes they are implied. They may boast testimonials by average folk or celebrities, or cite hard scientific evidence. And sometimes they simply manipulate our desire to be happy or socially accepted. But common to every ad and commercial, no matter what the medium, is the *claim* that you should buy this product.

Print ads are potentially complex mixtures of images, graphics, and text. So in analyzing an ad, you should be aware of the use of photography, the placement of those images, and the use of text, company logos, and other graphics such as illustrations, drawings, sidebar boxes, and so on. You should also keep in mind that every aspect of the image has been thought about and carefully designed. Let's take a look at how a recent magazine ad for Fresh Step cat litter uses some of these elements including social appeal, the use of color, light, and setting to convince us to buy this product.

Fresh Step Cat Litter Ad

When analyzing a print ad, we should try to determine what first captures our attention. In the Fresh Step ad (Figure 8.3), it is the huge and arresting image of the cat. In particular, the cat's worried facial expression, its paws tucked between its legs, and the curved tail. This order seems logical considering the purpose of the ad. The cat's posture clearly and comically suggests that it is in serious need of kitty litter. We then notice the room's décor, the furniture, and decorations. At the bottom, the Fresh Step logo jumps out at us, directing our eyes to the fine print: "Cats everywhere are having a hard time smelling their litter boxes."

Who Is the Audience for the Ad?

The ad could appeal to anyone who has a cat. It could be argued that based on the details of the interior, the audience might be older individuals, people with expensive, traditional taste—perhaps an elderly couple who loves cats. On the other hand, the ad is comically appealing to anyone who purchases cat litter. The humor of the ad—the visual joke of a cat's urgent need to locate its litter box—draws in a wide audience.

What Is the Claim?

Because advertisers are vying for our attention, they must project their claim as efficiently as possible in order to discourage us from turning the page. The stated or implied claim of all advertising is that the product will make life better for us. Of course, most ads aren't so bald in their claims. But the promise is there by inference. The claim of this ad is that if you own a cat and want to have an odor-free home, buy Fresh Step. Further, by purchasing this brand of cat litter, you become part of a community of tasteful, savvy cat owners.

What Is the Evidence?

The evidence for the desirability of Fresh Step is in the visuals and the text. The visuals suggest that people with taste buy Fresh Step. Likewise, the cat's need for a litter box is made all the more urgent by the orderly, dainty, old-fashioned, and neatly appointed room the cat is placed in. The furniture, walls, and decorative touches suggest an occupant who is most likely elderly, very particular, traditional, and fussy. The furniture is of another era. The combination of French provincial table and chair, colonial wainscoting, stenciled

Figure 8.3

wallpaper, a Currier-and-Ives type painting, Victorian lighting, and neatly arranged Russian dolls all suggest an occupant whom the cat could easily offend. And the text tells us why: because Fresh Step is so good at eliminating odors, that even cats—noted for their keen sense of smell—"have a hard time smelling their litter boxes."

What Are the Assumptions?

The creators of this ad made several assumptions about us, the audience: (1) that many cat-owners need litter boxes for their pets, (2) that most people value odor-free rooms, and (3) that people associate an expensive decor with people of discriminating preferences. Thus, most people will be satisfied purchasing Fresh Step cat litter.

Sample Ads for Analysis

Apply the principles of critical analysis described in the previous section on advertising, as well as the elements of form and design discussed earlier in the chapter, to the ads that appear in the following pages.

1. Who is featured in the picture in Figure 8.4? How does this ad play upon expectations already created by the product in past advertisements?

Figure 8.4

2. This ad is promoting a candy product. What connection, if any, do the characters have to the product? In your opinion, does the ad effectively market the product?

3. Who do you think is the target audience for this advertisement? How do you think a young adult would respond to it? A politician or government worker? A child? An older adult? Explain.

4. After viewing this ad, would you be more inclined to purchase the product it is advertising? Why or why not?

5. What do you need to know about pop culture to understand the ad and the characters depicted in it?

Victoria's Dirty Secret

QUESTIONS FOR ANALYSIS AND DISCUSSION

1. In what ways does the model in Figure 8.5 look like the typical Victoria's Secret model? Be specific. In what ways does this model differ? Consider her attire, the wings, hair styling, expression, body posture, shoes, and so on. If you see any differences, how would you explain them? How do the similarities and/or differences contribute to the ad's criticism of the catalogue production of Victoria's Secret?

2. Consider the chain saw. What is the effect of having the model holding a sketched chain saw instead of a real one? And what do you make of the style of the drawing? Why not have a more realistic drawing than this roughly drawn one?

3. After reading the text of the ad, consider some of the characteristics of its argument. What is the basic claim? Locate specific evidence. Are opposing points of view presented? Where specifically?

4. Is this ad a proposal or a position argument? Explain your answer.

5. Visual arguments should inspire or provoke a reaction. On a scale of one to ten, how persuasive is this ad? Are you inspired to take action—specifically to contact the CEO of Victoria's Secret's parent company? Does it inspire you to get involved with ForestEthics' campaign?

6. Consider the small photograph insert. What is depicted, and how well does it illustrate the argument being made in the ad? How does it relate to the image of the model? Explain in detail.

Editorial or Political Cartoons

Editorial cartoons have been a part of American life for over a century. They are a mainstay feature on the editorial pages in most newspapers—those pages reserved for columnists, contributing editors, and illustrators to present their views in words and pen and ink. As in the nineteenth century when they first started to appear, such editorial cartoons are political in nature, holding up political and social issues for public scrutiny and sometimes ridicule.

Figure 8.5

A stand-alone editorial cartoon—as opposed to a strip of multiple frames—is a powerful and terse form of communication that combines pen-and-ink drawings with dialogue balloons and captions. They're not just visual jokes, but visual humor that comments on social/political issues while drawing on viewers' experience and knowledge.

The editorial cartoon is the story of a moment in the flow of familiar current events. And the key words here are *moment* and *familiar*. Although a cartoon captures a split instant in time, it also infers what came before and, perhaps, what may happen next—either in the next moment or in some indefinite future. And usually the cartoon depicts a specific moment in time. One of the most famous cartoons of the last 50 years is the late Bill Mauldin's Pulitzer Prize–winning drawing of the figure of Abraham Lincoln with his head in his hands. It appeared the morning after the assassination of President John Kennedy in 1963. There was no caption nor was there a need for one. The image represented the profound grief of a nation that had lost its leader to an assassin's bullet. But to capture the enormity of the event, Mauldin brilliantly chose to represent a woeful America by using the figure of Abraham Lincoln as depicted in the sculpture of the Lincoln Memorial in Washington, DC. In so doing, the message implied that so profound was the loss that it even reduced to tears the marble figure of a man considered to be our greatest president, himself assassinated a century before.

For a cartoon to be effective, it must make the issue clear at a glance and it must establish where it stands on the argument. In the Mauldin illustration, we instantly recognize Lincoln and identify with the emotions. We need not be told the circumstances, since by the time the cartoon appeared the next day, all the world knew the horrible news that the president had been assassinated. To convey less obvious issues and figures at a glance, cartoonists resort to images that are instantly recognizable, that we don't have to work hard to grasp. Locales are determined by giveaway props: An airplane out the window suggests an airport; a cactus and cattle skull, a desert; an overstuffed armchair and TV, the standard living room. Likewise, human emotions are instantly conveyed: Pleasure is a huge toothy grin; fury is steam blowing out of a figure's ears; and love is two figures making goo-goo eyes with floating hearts overhead. People themselves may have exaggerated features to emphasize a point or an emotion.

In his essay "What Is a Cartoon?" Mort Gerberg says that editorial cartoons rely on such visual clichés to convey their messages instantly. That is, they employ stock figures for their representation—images instantly recognizable from cultural stereotypes like the fat-cat tycoon, the mobster thug, and the sexy female movie star. And these come to us in familiar outfits and props that give away their identities and profession. The cartoon judge has a black robe and gavel; the prisoner wears striped overalls and a ball and chain; the physician dons a smock and holds a stethoscope; the doomsayer is a scrawny long-haired guy carrying a sign saying, "The end is near." These are visual clichés known by the culture at large, and we instantly recognize them.

The visual cliché may be what catches our eye in the editorial cartoon, but the message lies in what the cartoonist does with it. As Gerberg observes, "The message is in twisting it, in turning the cliché around."

Mike Luckovich's "Let's Be Responsible" Cartoon

Consider Mike Luckovich's cartoon (from *The Atlanta Journal-Constitution*) in Figure 8.6 that addresses the issue of texting while driving. The visual cliché is a group of friends gathering in a very ordinary bar. We know that from the familiar props: the ubiquitous signage identifying the setting as a bar, the single dangling light fixture, bottles of alcohol, draft pulls, and the broad back of the bartender. Even the patrons are familiar figures—four casually dressed, slightly unkempt, individuals who look neither prosperous nor polished but slightly down on their luck. Note the dark-haired young man wears a T-shirt with a cartoon figure on it; another male sports unconventionally messy hair and the suggestion of beads around his neck. The woman has over-styled blond hair, and the bald man wears a plain white shirt. The twist, of course, is that instead of clasping a martini or a beer, the patrons of this bar are all regarding their cell phones. There is not a drink on the table (though we can assume that they have had or will be having considerable alcohol since they are concerned about who will be driving). Maybe not.

The issue, of course, is the debate about driving while texting. The cartoon addresses the numerous deadly accidents caused by drivers who were texting rather than paying attention to the road, thus causing accidents, which fill the news. A public debate still rages about outlawing texting while driving, fueled by the increased number of text messages being sent as well as the number of resulting accidents. (In 2012, 2011, seven trillion text

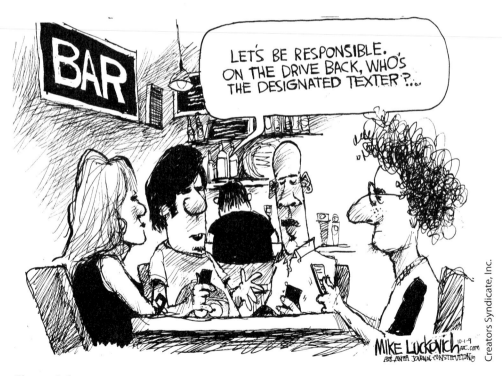

Figure 8.6

messages were sent. A year later, the number rose to 8 trillion worldwide.) According to a recent *New York Times*/CBS news poll (NYTimes.com/polls), nearly all Americans say sending a text message while driving should be illegal; and half of all Americans say texting behind the wheel should be punished at least as harshly as drunk driving. This concern is reflected in some legislation: It is now illegal in at least 41 states to text while driving, and the federal government is exerting pressure to ban it in all states.

The cartoon's joke is in the twist—the gap between the familiar and the unexpected. The familiar is the bar scene; the unexpected is the fact that the patrons are not holding alcoholic drinks but texting devices. What is important is a sober texter not a sober driver. Thus, the caption: "Let's be responsible. On the drive back, who's the designated texter?"

What Is the Cartoon's Claim?

The claim in this cartoon is that driving while texting is as dangerous and possibly more dangerous than driving while drinking. This claim is implicit in the satirical image of the bar patrons holding their cell phones and concentrating on texting. And it is implicit in the comment, "Let's be responsible. On the drive back, who's the designated texter?"

What Are the Cartoon's Assumptions?

This cartoon makes the assumption that people are preoccupied with texting and that they recognize that texting while driving is irresponsible and dangerous. It also presumes that readers are aware of the spate of serious accidents caused by "texters" and that they equate such behavior with drunk driving. Furthermore, the cartoon assumes familiarity with the campaign to designate a sober driver if other passengers are drinking. Part of the humor of the cartoon is based on the substitution of texting devices for alcohol.

What Is the Cartoon's Evidence?

The cartoon presents the ironic and humorous notion that its bar patrons are not even thinking about drinks. None are present. Instead, they are preoccupied with text messaging. This is the vice they go to the bar to indulge. They are so consumed with texting, that they want to be certain they can continue on the drive home. The implication is that they will not be able to restrain themselves from texting and must appoint a "designated texter" so texting will not be interrupted.

QUESTIONS FOR ANALYSIS AND DISCUSSION

Apply the principles of critical analysis described in the previous section on editorial cartoons, as well as the elements of form and design discussed earlier in the chapter, to the cartoons. First take a look at Figure 8.7, cartoon by Pat Bagley.

1. What is the claim or claims embodied in the visual elements of this political cartoon? What constitutes the evidence of the claim or claims? Cite the specific pieces of evidence.
2. Consider the audience for this cartoon. What groups of citizens would be most likely to have a strong reaction? Does the cartoon suggest a solution to the problems depicted? Are the problems interrelated?

"BACK IN AUGHT-FIVE WE HAD TO CHOOSE BETWEEN HIGHWAYS AND EDUCATION..."

Courtesy of Pat Bagley

Figure 8.7

3. What is the tone of the cartoon? Would you describe it as comical? Satirical? Facetious? Overstated? Amusing? Disturbing?

4. This cartoon originally appeared on the editorial page in *The Salt Lake City Tribune*. Is the cartoon particular to the Salt Lake City area? Why or why not? What could you change in the piece so that it applied to a different city or area?

5. What is the grill-like tray on the top of the cars? And what is the bumper extension jutting off each car? How do they fit into the ad? What is the significance of the insignia on the vehicle on the lower right corner that says "SUV2020"?

6. What might "back in aught-five we had to choose" most likely refer to?

7. Based on the cartoonist's "argument," what do you think he is advocating? Is he for or against highway improvement? For or against education? Can you tell? Does it matter?

QUESTIONS FOR ANALYSIS AND DISCUSSION

Refer to Figure 8.8, cartoon by Daryl Cagle.

1. What is happening in this cartoon? Whom does the first kid "hate"? Does the cartoon make more sense when we know that it appeared shortly after September 11, 2001? Why or why not?

2. Consider the comment made by the middle kid in the cartoon, who agrees at first, but then asks a clarifying question. Is this significant? Why doesn't the first kid ask the same thing?

Daryl Cagle/Cagle Cartoons, Inc.

Figure 8.8

3. What is the cartoonist's claim in this cartoon? What evidence does he provide? Explain.
4. Although this cartoon was drawn in the context of the events following September 11, 2001, would it have been equally effective ten years ago? Ten years into the future? Would the previous cartoon be as timeless? Explain.

News Photographs

Although editorial cartoons can stand on their own, they are frequently featured on editorial pages in newspapers that include commentary on the topic they depict. Photographs are another vehicle used to augment commentary in newspapers, journals, and magazines. Indeed, sometimes the photograph *tells* the story better than words ever could, because it has the ability to touch our deepest emotions instantly.

At first glance, you may think that photos are simply snapshots of an event or a moment. But most photographs presented in leading newspapers and journals are the result of effort and planning. Photojournalists are constantly making editorial decisions when they take a picture. They think about where to take the photo, the right moment, whom to include, the angle, the lighting, and depth of field. They consider the subject matter and how it might affect an audience. In some cases, they think about why they are taking the picture and what argument they want to present on film. Some of the most compelling photographs in history come from photojournalists capturing one moment. These photos are not posed, but they still tell a story. Some famous photos include the shot of a sailor kissing a nurse in New York City's Times Square when victory was declared at the end of World War II. Or, who can forget the photo of young American gymnast, Gabrielle Douglas, on the balance beam in the women's individual final of the London 2012 Olympic Games? Although we might not recall the names of the people involved, the image itself remains stamped on our memory.

As a unit, the news story and the photo work together to tell a story. The best photos often tell a story without using any words. But knowing the context in which the photo was taken is important as well. At the very least, the date and location establish the circumstances. Consider Figure 8.9, a photograph of the aftermath of Hurricane Sandy, a formidable storm that slammed into the northeast coast of the United States on October 29, 2012, destroying entire neighborhoods in New York, New Jersey, and Rhode Island. This hurricane, like Hurricane Katrina that devastated New Orleans in the fall of 2005, was of historic proportions with winds up to 90 miles per hour and destructive sea surges. Sandy left behind billions of dollars of destruction, decimating homes and entire communities. Flooding, lack of electrical power, a gasoline shortage,

Figure 8.9

and a profound sense of isolation contributed to people's misery. This photograph was taken on November 2, 2012 (four days after storm hit) in the heavily damaged Rockaway neighborhood in Queens by Spencer Platt of Getty Images. The image captures the human toll of the destruction, and tries to make storm statistics regarding the fury, duration, wind speeds, and surging water levels mean more than numbers. Here that toll is evidenced by the immediate material consequences: battered homes, streets clogged with sand and debris, a destroyed car, and a damaged community. And notice the absence of people in the photograph. Prior to the storm, this street could have been an icon of American success for the average man and woman. But this image prompts the viewer to think beyond immediate material loss. For instance, note the American flag and its placement at the center of the photograph. That core symbol evokes several responses. On one hand, it suggests the unity and resilience of a people and a country in the face of a natural disaster proclaiming the "can do" spirit of America and Americans who have triumphed over disaster countless times. On the other hand, the flag evokes the idea of the American Dream—the conviction that with hard work everyone can achieve prosperity: a home, a car, a neighborhood. Sadly Hurricane Sandy for some had dashed that dream and, at least momentarily, destroyed the components of the American Dream.

It is clear that the photographer carefully eyed every element of this scene: the homes in the background, the street incongruously covered in debris, the car with its gutted frame and blasted-out windows. The composite evokes a war zone. Through the careful selection and placement, the photographer created an evocative image, stirring many reactions, some hopeful, some discouraging. The image transcends a snapshot and becomes a work of art, forcing the viewer to contemplate the scene from many perspectives. One sees the personal cost of a storm, the possibility of resilience, the erosion of the American Dream. Like all good art, the questions the photograph raises are many and complex.

Who Is the Target Audience?

This photograph is an outstanding example of the many powerful images to come out of the year 2012 because it is newsworthy, powerful, and artful. The photograph targets a general audience likely to be concerned with social and economic issues and open to the exploration of the human consequences of such. The cost of Hurricane Sandy's destruction is not just the loss of a home, but the loss of a dream as well.

What Is the Purpose of the Image?

The image captures a moment in time—one that the photographer felt was important to underscore. It shows the devastation of a storm: home, a neighborhood, and personal achievement. The iconic symbols of the American Dream—a home, a car, a neighborhood—are jeopardized. But at the same time, the American flag suggests the strength and resilience to recover. Despite the fact that no people are shown in the photograph, the plight of hundreds of nameless individuals is highlighted.

What Are the Claims Made in the Image?

Although no people are shown, this photograph humanizes the many statistics from Hurricane Sandy by dramatizing something of the human toll. Given the context of

Hurricane Sandy and its destruction of property, the viewer can draw a number of claims from the image. Foremost is the claim that a home offers a family security and membership in a community. Another is that a car affords status, the freedom to navigate one's environment on one's own terms, and signifies another level of achievement. Rich or poor, being a home owner, possessing a car, and being part of a community are part of the American Dream. Another claim is that such a natural disaster turns one's valued possessions into damaged goods. Yet another embedded claim rests in the American flag, which reaffirms one's resilience as an American citizen, while embodying the notion that together as a people we can conquer any adversity.

What Assumptions Does the Image Make?

The photographer assumes that most people will find this image arresting. Given the context, a natural disaster, it is assumed that the photograph is emotionally charged.

QUESTIONS FOR ANALYSIS AND DISCUSSION

Consider the photograph in Figure 8.10 taken by *Boston Globe* photojournalist Suzanne Kreiter. It shows two panhandlers on a Boston street. The photograph accompanied an article, "A Street to Call Home," which reports on how some homeless people panhandle on the very spot where they live.

1. This photograph accompanied an article about homelessness in an urban area of the Northeast. What assumptions about the audience does the photographer make?
2. What details in the photograph convey homelessness to the viewer? Consider objects, location, and background.
3. A close examination of the two main figures in this photograph makes a strong statement about their character. Consider their position, posture, relationship to one another, the direction of their gazes, the facial expressions, and their clothing, and describe the character of these individuals.
4. Would you describe these people as heroic? Downtrodden? Defiant? Helpless victims? Noble survivors? Explain why.
5. What argument about homelessness is embedded in this photograph? In other words, what is the claim?
6. Does the background of the photograph detract from or add to the meaning of the photograph?
7. How do you expect to see the homeless depicted? Is this expectation based on stereotype? Does this image of the homeless reinforce or contradict the stereotypical view of the homeless? Explain your answer. Does this photograph change your idea of urban poverty? Why or why not?
8. Do you see any similarities in style or content between this photograph and Norman Rockwell's *Freedom of Speech*?

Figure 8.10

Ancillary Graphics: Tables, Charts, and Graphs

Art, advertisements, editorial cartoons, and news photos all present interesting visual ways to persuade, and knowing how they do this improves your critical thinking and analytical skills. Ancillary graphics, however, such as tables, charts, and graphs, are some visual tools you can use in your own persuasive essays. In Chapter 6, we discussed how numerical data and statistics are very persuasive in bolstering an argument. But a simple table, chart, or graph can convey information at a glance while conveying trends that support your argument. In fact, such visuals are preferable to long, complicated paragraphs that confuse the reader and may detract from your argument.

Ancillary graphics usually take the form of tables, charts, graphs (including line, bar, and pie graphs), and illustrations such as maps and line drawings (of a piece of equipment, for example).

Numerical Tables

There are many ways of representing statistical data. As you know from courses you've taken in math or chemistry, the simplest presentation of numerical data is the table. Tables are useful in demonstrating relationships among data. They present numerical information arranged in rows or columns so that data elements may be referenced and compared. Tables also facilitate the interpretation of data without the expense of several paragraphs of description.

Suppose you are writing a paper in which you argue that part-time faculty at your institution teach more hours, but are underpaid and undersupported when it comes to benefits. Your research reveals that most part-time faculty receive less than $4,000 per course, and nearly one-third earn $3,000 or less per course—which is little more than the minimum wage. You also discover that the treatment of part-timers at your own school reflects a national trend—faced with rising enrollments and skyrocketing costs, colleges and universities have come to rely more on part-time instructors. Moreover, while they may carry heavier teaching loads, these part-time faculty do not receive the same benefits as professors. Your claim is that such lack of support is not only unfair to the instructors but also that it compromises the nature of higher education since low compensation drives instructors to take on other jobs to meet the cost of living.

Presenting this information in a table will allow you to demonstrate your point while saving space for your discussion. The following tables provide the results of a survey conducted by the Coalition on the Academic Workforce (CAW), describing how history faculty are facing this situation.

As the title indicates, the table reproduced in Table 8.1 shows the percentage of history courses taught by full- and part-time faculty. The table intends to help readers understand how much institutions have come to depend on part-time instructors, especially graduate teaching assistants and part-time nontenure-track teachers—people who are paid the least and often denied the benefits enjoyed by full-time faculty. The horizontal rows break down faculty types into five discrete categories—from "Full-Time Tenure Track" at the top to "Graduate Teaching Assistants" at the bottom. The three vertical columns tabulate the percentages according to categories: "Intro Courses," "Other Courses," and "All Courses," which is the median—the calculated halfway point between the other two categories.

Percentage of History Courses Taught, by Faculty Type

	Intro Courses	Other Courses	All Courses
Full-Time Tenure Track	49%	72%	59%
Full-Time Nontenure Track	9%	5%	7%
Part-Time Tenure Track	1%	1%	1%
Part-Time Nontenure Track	23%	15%	19%
Graduate Teaching Assistants	17%	8%	13%
Percentage of All Courses Taught	55%	45%	
Number of Courses Taught	5,825	4,759	10,584

Source: AHA Surveys.

Table 8.1

Reading from left to right along the first row, we see that 49 percent of the introductory history courses and 72 percent of the "other courses" were taught by full-time tenure-track faculty. This compares with 41 percent of the introductory courses taught by part-timers (part-time tenure track [1%] + part-time nontenure-track faculty [23%] + graduate teaching assistants [17%]). The last column, which represents the median percentage of intro and other courses, tells us that part-timers taught 33 percent or a third of all history courses. That is a compelling figure when tabulated for comparison to full-time faculty.

The second table (Table 8.2) presents the reported benefits for nontenure-track and part-time faculty. Here nine categories of benefits are tabulated according to three categories of faculty. (Presumably nearly 100 percent of history departments provide full-time tenure-track faculty the kinds of support and benefits listed.) The first line shows the comparative institutional support for travel to professional meetings for the three categories of instructors: 76.9 percent for full-time nontenure track, 46.4 for part-time faculty paid a fraction of full-time salary, and 15.2 for part-time faculty paid by the course.

The fifth line down tabulates the copaid health plan for the three categories of faculty. As we can see at a glance, 72 percent of the institutions with full-time nontenure-track faculty and 63 percent of the departments with part-time faculty paid a fraction of full-time salaries and provided some kind of health plan copaid by the school and faculty member. This compares with just 13 percent of institutions providing such a benefit to part-time faculty paid on a per-course basis. Similarly, 32 percent of the institutions with full-time nontenure-track faculty provided a health plan paid for by the

History Departments, Benefits

	% for Full-Time Nontenure-Track Faculty	% for Part-Time Faculty (Paid by semester)	% for Part-Time Faculty (Paid by course)
Support Travel to Prof. Mtgs.	76.9	46.4	15.2
Support Attendance at Prof. Mtgs.	41.0	28.6	22.9
Provide Regular Salary Increases	68.4	53.6	28.1
Access to Research Grants	52.1	39.3	13.3
Health Plan Paid by Both	72.17	62.96	12.99
Health Plan Paid by School	32.17	22.22	2.26
Health Plan Paid by Employee	1.74	7.41	3.95
Retirement Plan	73.91	55.56	10.17
Life Insurance	76.52	44.44	5.65

Source: AHA Surveys.

Table 8.2

school, as compared to 2.26 percent of those with faculty paid by the course. Reading across the other benefits categories reveals how much more generous institutions were to full-time nontenure-track faculty than to part-timers—including retirement plans and insurance.

As the previous paragraphs demonstrate, explaining all this information in the body of your text can be complicated and confusing. And when you are trying to prepare a compelling argument, simplicity of style and clarity of text are essential. Using tables helps you clearly depict data while you move forward with your discussion.

Line Graphs

Line graphs show the relationship between two or more sets of numerical data by plotting points in relation to two axes. The vertical axis is usually used to represent amounts, and the horizontal axis normally represents increments of time, although this is not always the case. Line graphs are probably easier for most people to read than tables, and they are especially useful when depicting trends or changes over time. Consider the graph in Table 8.3.

This graph plots the comparative increase and decrease of full- and part-time faculty over a 30-year period (based on data from American Historical Association [AHA] surveys). The vertical or *y*-axis represents the percentage of part-time faculty, and the horizontal or *x*-axis represents the time starting from 1980. There are two lines on the graph: The upper line represents the decreasing percentage of full-time history faculty of the colleges and universities surveyed, while the lower line represents the increase in part-time history faculty over the same 30-year period. The declining slope of the upper line instantly captures the decreasing dependence on full-time faculty, whereas the rising slope of the lower line illustrates the increasing dependence on part-time hires. Because the data are plotted on the same graph, we understand how the two are interrelated.

We also notice that neither line is straight but slightly curving. The upper line (full-time faculty) curves downward, while the lower line (part-time faculty) curves upward. Around the year 2005, these lines cross just below the 50th percentile level on the *y*-axis—that is, more than half the college history courses surveyed are currently being taught by part-timers. Also, if we extrapolate both lines toward the right along the curves they are defining, we will eventually arrive at some hypothetical future date when 100 percent of all history courses are taught by part-time faculty and none by full-timers.

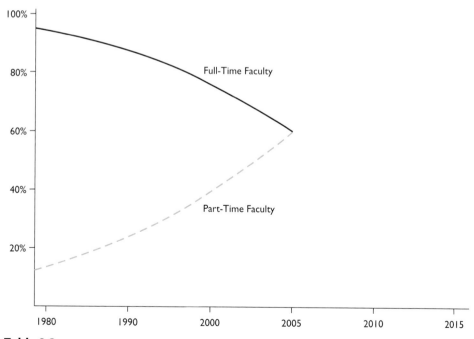

Table 8.3

While we presume that most colleges and universities would not allow this to happen, the trend suggests just how the increased dependence on part-timers is changing the nature of higher education, as fewer courses are taught by full-time faculty. The graphs indeed make a persuasive argument.

Bar Graphs

Bar graphs are often used to compare parts and enable readers to grasp complex data and the relationships among variables at a glance. A bar graph uses horizontal or vertical bars and is commonly used to show either quantities of the same item at different times, quantities of different items at the same time, or quantities of the different parts of an item that make up the whole. They are usually differentiated by contrasting colors, shades, or textures, with a legend explaining what these colors, shades, or textures mean.

The bar graph in Table 8.4 shows the increase of part-time and adjunct faculty in history departments over a 33-year period as broken down by type of employment and gender (based on data from the AHA survey of the historical profession and unpublished data from AHA departmental surveys). As indicated, the graph demonstrates a dramatic increase in that time period. In 1980, only 4.3 percent of male and 2.0 percent of female history faculty were part-time—a total of 6.3 percent. Nearly three decades later, part-time male and female faculty increased to over 46 percent. This number could be even larger if graduate teaching assistants were included. As this graph shows, bar graphs take comparative amounts of data and transform them into instant no-non-sense images.

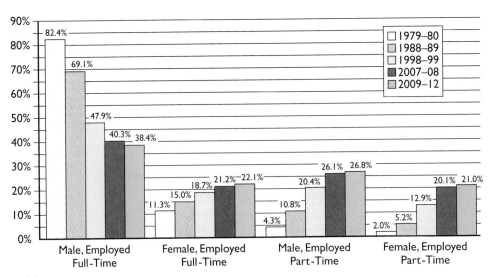

Table 8.4

Pie Charts

Pie charts present data as wedge-shaped sections of a circle or "pie." The total amount of all the pieces of the pie must equal 100 percent. They are an efficient way of demonstrating the relative proportion of the whole something occupies—an instant way to visualize "percentages" without thinking in numbers. But when using pie charts, it is best to include six or fewer slices. If more pieces than that are used, the chart becomes messy and its impact is muted. Table 8.5 dramatically demonstrates the portion of all history courses in the CAW survey that were taught by part-time faculty, including graduate students.

This pie chart clearly reveals that the combined wedges of graduate teaching assistants and part-time instructors form a substantial portion of the pie. In fact, they comprise almost half of the teaching population. This image quickly and powerfully demonstrates the point of your argument that part-time faculty make up a disproportionately large part of history faculty while receiving a disproportionately small percentage of the benefits. The chart allows readers to visualize the information as they read it. In the student sample in Chapter 9, Shannon O'Neill includes a pie chart along with an editorial cartoon to bolster her written argument, "Literature Hacked and Torn Apart: Censorship in Public Schools" (see page 285–290).

Used together, these visuals can play an invaluable role in bolstering a written argument on behalf of part-time faculty. Instead of blinding readers with reams of raw data, these visuals organize confusing numbers, and at a glance bring their significance to life. Comparative benefits and changing dependencies are transformed into memorable and easy-to-understand tables, graphs, and charts.

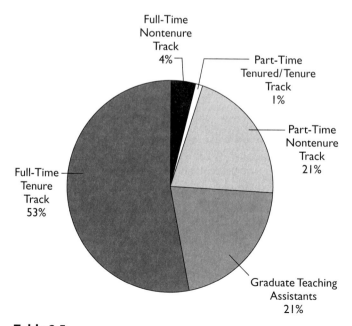

Table 8.5

Tips for Using Ancillary Graphics

While understanding the types of ancillary graphics at your disposal is important, it is also important to know how to use them properly. Here are a few guidelines to consider when using graphics in your persuasive essays:

- Include only the data you need to demonstrate your point.
- Make a reference to the chart or graphic in the body of your text.
- Try to keep the graphic on the same page as your discussion.
- Present only one type of information in each graph or chart.
- Label everything in your graph and provide legends where appropriate.
- Assign a figure number to each graphic for easy reference.
- Don't crowd your text too closely around the graphic.
- Remember to document the sources used to create the graphics.

As you begin to incorporate visuals into your own papers, consider the discussion provided earlier in this chapter regarding visual arguments. Consider why you wish to use the graphic and what you want it to do. Think about your audience's needs.

SAMPLE STUDENT ARGUMENT FOR ANALYSIS

Lee Innes, a first-year business major, was interested in the subject of women in sports—an enormous topic that he needed to narrow down. He began by asking why male athletes dominate the world of sports. What the impact of sex-role stereotyping is on women's athletics? What is Title IX and what is its impact on college athletics? Is scholarship money unfairly distributed to male athletes? In what major sports do women excel? In what major sports do women receive the most attention or the highest salaries or the most product endorsement fees? Why is it that tennis, volleyball, and soccer are among the sports in which women receive the most attention? Why does a sport like women's beach volleyball attract a large and enthusiastic audience?

Although each question presented an interesting issue to explore, he decided to narrow the focus to one that he could cover in a paper of reasonable length. While anticipating the 2012 Summer Olympics in London, he thought back on the 2008 summer games in Bejing, an event he had followed closely. He recalled feeling conflicted as he watched the women's beach volleyball. The athletic skill and strength of the women was dazzling. But their athletic feats attracted less attention than their scant bikinis. Reflecting on this, Lee realized he had a narrowly defined a specific topic: women's volleyball uniforms. His essay would consider the controversial issue of women as sexy spectacles in the Olympics—in particular, if the selection of their uniforms was a case of sexism in sport. He arrived at a *working* claim that both limited the range of his topic and very clearly expressed his point of view about it:

> Women in all sports, including Olympic beach volleyball, should be judged and promoted on their skill as athletes not on how they look in bikinis.

This claim helped him concentrate his research on those areas pertinent to his ideas. In addition to referencing expert views from magazines, newspapers, and Websites,

Lee bolstered his claim—and argument—by including a photo of a woman in Olympic uniform and a comparative schematic of men's versus women's uniforms. The visuals clearly enhanced his written argument.

Lee Innes
Professor Khoury
Writing 122
19 February, 2013

A Double Standard of Olympic Proportions

1 During the London Olympics held in 2012, I found myself considering the pressing issues facing this international event. Would the U.S. host the Olympics again in the near future? When will performance-enhancing drugs cease to taint the games? Will French judges ever favor anyone but the French? And what happened to the women's volleyball skimpy bikini uniforms?

2 Admittedly, the last question may carry less weight than the others, but as a stereotypical heterosexual male, I certainly appreciated the, er, aesthetic value of the women's volleyball competition. In 2012, some women sported bikinis, and others wore more modest, albeit still body-hugging, spandex uniforms. I have to admit, in past years of competition, the display—and it indeed sometimes seemed to be just that—did trouble me a little. If I had been reading a popular magazine targeting young males, *Maxim* or *FHM* for example, ogling young women in bikinis would have felt more acceptable. But these women were representing my country in the Olympics, in an athletic competition. What is with the bikinis?

3 It may come as a surprise to some people that until March of 2012, our female athletes *had* to wear bikini uniforms. They were actually required. The U.S. Volleyball Team does not pick the uniforms; they were *forced* to wear them by the International Volleyball Federation. I, personally, was shocked—both by the idea that an official sports organization would require such a uniform, and by the fact that women had not reacted with more outrage. As an American, I cannot imagine being told that I must wear an article of clothing that held me out for public display.

4 A little history may be useful here. In 1999, the International Volleyball Federation (FIVB), based in Switzerland, decided volleyball uniforms should be standardized. It was this organization that chose the bikini uniform worn by the Olympic athletes. Interestingly, there was only one woman on the committee when they designed and implemented the uniform. Kristine Drakich, in a 1997 interview with the Canadian Association for the Advancement of Women and Sport and Physical Activity, commented that she was the only female athlete representative for the International Volleyball Federation's Beach Volleyball World Council at that time. The council, she observed, was "an intimidating place for anybody . . . this is a place

Innes 2

with about 50 members, all men, except for my position" (Robertson). One can surmise that a predominantly male committee was responsible for voting in favor of adopting the bikini uniform for women for beach volleyball competition. (It makes one wonder if Hugh Heffner sat in on the meetings.)

5   Perhaps more at issue and culturally significant is that the men's beach volleyball uniform was nowhere near as revealing. The men's uniform featured a tank top and lose fitting shorts. The women's uniform, in addition to the bikini top, sports a brief with a waistline that falls below the belly button. And the women's uniform bottoms must be two and a half inches wide on the sides, providing very little coverage, even for the toned glutes of these women. That's only *five* inches wide. Jeanne Moos reported on the decision in a *CNN Online* article: "Women's volleyball uniforms will be standardized in order to banish t-shirts and shorts." Moos expressed her own viewpoint bluntly, "Beach volleyball has now joined go-go girl dancing as perhaps the only two professions where a bikini is the required uniform."

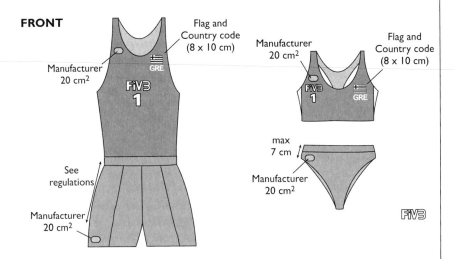

Fig. 1. Men's volleyball uniforms are shown on the left and
        women's volleyball uniforms are on the right.

Figure 1

6   Even men noticed the inequality. Blogger Sean P. Aune observed that photos of beach volleyball players were "little more than soft-porn." "There is no doubt

these women work just as hard as any other athletes to get where they are, and all you ever see or hear about them is just these blasted outfits. How many people know that Misty May-Treanor and Kerri Walsh are on a run of nearly 100 consecutive wins as a team? Does that matter? Oh, who cares, slap some more butt shots up there!" Aune also noted that the country of origin of each player is written across their rear ends. Something I hadn't noticed before.

7   Opponents of the uniform seemed to become more vocal as the extensive television coverage of the Olympic beach volleyball matches brought the issue to the public eye. Jeneé Osterheldt reported in the August 20, 2004, *Kansas City Star* that the required uniform was upsetting some sports officials and players. "[Female] players can't cover up, even if they want to . . . Donna Lopiano, executive director of the Women's Sports Foundation, [says] 'It's like telling a swimmer she has to wear a bikini instead of a high-performance suit, when the material has been shown to increase speed. Elasticized attire on leg muscles, especially larger muscles like the thigh, has been proven to reduce fatigue. If you are looking for performance enhancement, you wouldn't choose bikini bottoms' " (Osterheldt).

8   But Lopiano's statement addressed what seems to be an irrelevant detail to the IFVB board. Official commentary on the "performance enhancement" of the uniforms was absent from the literature. It would appear that performance had little, if anything, to do with the decision at all. The uniforms, it seems, were designed not for functionality but for marketing purposes. In a *Business Week* article addressing the "comeback" of beach volleyball as a legitimate sport, Leonard Armato, the marketing man responsible for getting volleyball on NBC as an athletic event, was quoted admitting, "[Beach volleyball is] an incredibly sexy sport. We're not embarrassed that the women [wear] bikinis"(Khermouch).

9   Based on ticket sales for beach volleyball, it seems like the IFVB had the right idea. In fact, some athletes admit that they like the attention the bikinis garner for the sport. British star Denise Johns told the *Sunday Times* in 2008, "The people who own the sport [the Fédération Internationale de Volleyball] want it to be sexy. I used to play in shorts and a T-shirt and was reluctant to change. But if it gets volleyball attention, so be it."

10   One could also argue that media attention helps out both the sport and the athletes. Since their victory in Athens, Kerri Walsh and Misty May-Treanor enjoyed tremendous popularity. One could argue that their cute bikinis certainly didn't hurt their careers. Donning bikinis long before their foray into Olympic glory, the pair was in a Visa ad during the 2004 Super Bowl, playing beach volleyball in the snow and ice. Their likenesses have been displayed on McDonald's wrappers and boxes. And after their Olympic win, they were featured on the front page of practically every sports section of every newspaper in the country.

Innes 4

11   But just because the uniforms garnered a lot of attention doesn't mean they are right. Even the Australian Sports Commission, part of the Australian government, recognized that the uniform was really designed to put women on display. In 2011, it published a fact sheet on "sexploitation" in sports, stating that in their view, "Women's beach volleyball . . . has introduced uniforms intentionally to focus attention on the athletes' bodies rather than for any technological, practical or performance-enhancing reasons." Clearly, the winds of change were blowing.

12   So over the past decade, the women's uniform elicited public outcry, partially due to publicity, and partially because women themselves were beginning to challenge the uniforms. Then, just before the 2012 Olympic Games in London, a weighty decision was handed down by the Olympic committee. Women would no longer be required to wear bikinis for beach volleyball competition. The International Volleyball Federation announced that female competitors in Olympic volleyball would be permitted to wear shorts and sleeved tops out of respect for the cultural beliefs of some participating countries. "Many of these countries have religious and cultural requirements, so the uniform needed to be more flexible," said International Volleyball Federation spokesman Richard Baker to The Associated Press. The new guidelines now permit shorts of a maximum length of three centimeters (1.18 inches) above the knee, and sleeved or sleeveless tops.

13   Interestingly, some women, including Kerri Walsh, defended the bikini uniform. All of which then leads me to my next question: If women want to wear the bikini uniform, is there anything wrong here? Or, perhaps acknowledging the Australian Sports Commission's statement that bikini uniforms encourage "sexploitation," should the uniforms be banned, even if some female athletes prefer them?

14   And now that women have a choice—bikini or no bikini—another question looms: *What about the men?* At a press conference held in August of 2012, men's beach volleyball athlete Phil Dalhausser noted that he felt just fine about his lack of choices. "I'm OK with this. They're way prettier than us." Todd Rogers, a medalist in 2008, agreed saying, that he thought that men wearing Speedos would draw attention to the game, but "I don't think it would be a positive effect."

15   But note that even the men admit that the point of women's bikini uniforms is for purely aesthetic (beauty) reasons, and not for performance. Rogers further noted, "I've practiced in Brazil where the Brazilians are wearing Speedos and it just doesn't look good. To see a guy's package is just not the same."

Innes 5

Works Cited

Aune, Sean P. "Olympic Beach Volley Ball Uniforms. SeanPAune.com. 13 Aug. 2008.
Web. 2 Feb. 2010.

Khermouch, Gerry. "Son of a Beach Volleyball." *Business Week*. 20 Apr. 2002. Print.

Krupnick, Ellie. "Olympic Volleyball Uniforms: Bikinis No Longer Required for
Women" *The Huffington Post*. 28 Mar. 2012

Moos, Jeanne. "Bikini Blues—Beach Volleyball Makes the Swimsuit Standard." *CNN
Online*. CNN, 13 Jan. 1999. Web. 5 Feb. 2010.

Osterheldt, Jeneé. "Olympic Athletes Prance Chic to Cheek." *Kansas City Star*.
20 Aug. 2004, late ed.: A1. Print.

Robertson, Sheila. "Insight Into an Activist." ACTION Canadian Association for the
Advancement of Women and Sport and Physical Activity. CAAWS, n.d. Web.
4 Feb. 2010.

QUESTIONS FOR ANALYSIS AND DISCUSSION

1. Do you agree with Lee Innes's working claim here? What are your thoughts about the role of male and female athletic attire? About the use of attire to promote or popularize a sporting event? In your journal, respond to Innes's ideas by exploring your own views on the media's promotion of women athletes and whether or not the promotion is based on talent or appearance.

2. Consider the effectiveness of the author's use of the visuals—the photograph of the female player's bikini uniforms and the comparative uniform schematics for men and women. Do the illustrations bolster Innes's argument? Do the visuals convince you of an inequity if not sexual exploitation in uniform guidelines? Explain your answers.

3. Even if you didn't watch the 2012 Olympic women's beach volleyball competition or don't follow the sport, do you think that most fans are concerned with what Innes and others see as "sexploitation"? Why or why not?

4. What do you make of the fact some female athletes defended the bikini uniform? Does that weaken Innes's argument? Or as suggested by Innes, do you think that the lack of complaints suggests more deeply rooted gender issues in our culture?

5. In your journal, write an entry as if done by a member of either the men's or women's U.S. Olympic Volleyball Team after the first day of competition. In it, explore how he or she feels about their uniform options.

1. As the opening paragraph of this chapter points out, "[W]e are inspired, compelled, and persuaded by visual stimuli. Everywhere we look images vie for our attention." Reflecting on this statement, make a list in your journal of some of the visual stimuli you experienced in a typical day, considering everything from magazine ads to T-shirt logos to editorial cartoons. Then in a group discuss each member's findings. Are you surprised at the number of stimuli? Have each group member describe the impact, if any, of these on mood, thinking, state of mind, self-perception, and values. Was the impact greater or less than anticipated?

2. Identify one particularly controversial issue currently being debated in the media. On the Internet, do a keyword search to find editorial cartoons addressing this issue. Select one that you consider most affecting, persuasive, or compelling, then write an analysis in your journal. Using your knowledge of visual arguments, discuss in a paper the cartoon's claim, assumptions, and evidence used as well as the tone. Make a copy of that cartoon and share it with your group for analysis.

3. Do the same as exercise 2, but this time find a news photograph that speaks of a current controversial issue or event. In your journal, be sure to examine the target audience, the purpose of the image, its claims, and its assumptions. Again, the group should share findings.

4. Paging through a favorite magazine, find an ad that you find interesting and effective. Then imagine that you are the creative director of the team who will put this ad together. Write a memo to your staff describing the ad you wish to see created. Explain the persuasive function of each element in the ad and why you think it will work to sell the product you are advertising.

5. In the periodical section of your library, select a newspaper or a magazine of interest to you and try to categorize the ads according to the kind of product being sold. For example, vacuum cleaners would classify as housewares, shampoo as personal grooming, jeans as articles of clothing, and so on. Based on the ads, determine the demographics of the audience for the publication. How does the categories of ads correspond to the audience the magazine is marketed to?

Researching Arguments:
Thinking Like an Investigator

LEARNING OJBECTIVES

After studying this chapter, you should be able to:

1. Explain the primary research sources for writing arguments. (p. 250)
2. Describe how to prepare, conduct, and process interviews of experts in researching debate issues. (p. 251)
3. Determine which secondary research materials will best suit your needs in researching different sides of an argument. (p. 251)
4. Explain how to locate print, electronic, and online research sources. (p. 255)
5. Explain how to compile a working bibliography. (p. 253)
6. Explain how to evaluate research sources. (p. 260)
7. Describe how and when to summarize and how and when to quote secondary sources. (p. 266)
8. Explain how to avoid plagiarism. (p. 272)
9. Recognize and explain the difference between MLA and APA documentation styles. (p. 275)

Most arguments derive their success from the evidence they contain, so good argumentative writers learn to find evidence in many sources and present the best evidence to support their claims. In the academic world, much of that evidence is gathered through *research,* either conducted in a lab or field or through examination of the previously published work of other investigators and scholars. The research paper you may be asked to write challenges you to learn how more experienced writers find and present evidence that meets the standards of the academic community.

In the previous chapters, we've stressed the importance of finding evidence that will impress readers of your argument's merits. To review, researched evidence plays an important role in convincing readers of the following:

- Expert, unbiased authorities agree with your position in whole or in part, adding to your credibility.
- Your position or proposal is based on facts, statistics, and real-life examples, not mere personal opinion.
- You understand different viewpoints about your subject as well as your own.
- Your sources of information are verifiable because researched evidence is always accompanied by documentation.

A good analogy to use, once again, is that of the lawyer presenting a case to a jury. When you write a researched argument, you're making a case to a group of people who will make a decision about a subject. Not only do you present your arguments in the case but also you call on witnesses to offer evidence and expert opinion, which you then interpret and clarify for the jury. In a researched argument, your sources are your witnesses.

Writing an argumentative research paper isn't different from writing any other kind of argument, except in scale. An argument research paper is not a different species from the essays you have been writing; but it is usually longer than nonresearched papers; and the formal presentation (including documentation) must be addressed in more detail.

Sources of Information

There are two basic kinds of research sources, and depending partly on the type of issue you've picked to research, one may prove more helpful than the other. The first is *primary sources,* which include firsthand accounts of events (interviews, diaries, court records, letters, manuscripts). The second is *secondary sources,* which interpret, comment on, critique, explain, or evaluate events or primary sources. Secondary sources include most reference works and any books or articles that expand on primary sources. Depending on whether you choose a local or a more global issue to write about, you may decide to focus more on primary or more on secondary sources; but in most research, you'll want to consider both.

Primary Sources

If you choose a topic of local concern, your chief challenge will be finding enough research material. Very current controversies or issues won't yet have books written about them, so you may have to rely more heavily on electronic databases, which you can access through a computer, or interviews and other primary research methods to find information. If you choose a local issue to argue, consider the following questions:

- Which experts on campus or in the community might you interview for the pros and cons of the debated issue? An administrator at your college? A professor? The town manager? Think of at least two local experts who could provide an overview of the issue from different perspectives.
- What local resources—such as a local newspaper, radio station, TV station, or political group—are available for gathering print or broadcast information? If one of your topics is a campus issue, for example, the student newspaper, student committees or groups, university online discussion groups, and the student government body might be places to search for information.

Once you determine the several possible sources of information, your next step is to set up interviews or make arrangements to read or view related materials. Most students find that experts are eager to talk about local issues and are willing to be interviewed. However, you'll need plenty of time to gather background information, phone for interviews, prepare questions, and write up your notes afterward. If you're depending on primary research for the bulk of your information, get started as soon as the paper is assigned.

Preparing for Interviews

A few common courtesies apply when preparing for interviews. First, be ready to discuss the purpose of your interview when setting up an appointment. Second, go into the interview with a list of questions that shows you have already thought about the issue. Be on time and have a notebook and pen or recorder, especially if you decide to quote people directly. But first ask their permission to do so.

Conducting Interviews

Be prepared to jot down only key words or ideas during the interview, reserving time afterward to take more detailed notes. Keep the interview on track by asking focused questions if the interviewee wanders while responding. When leaving, ask if it would be okay to call should you have follow-up questions.

Writing Up Interviews

As soon as possible after the interview, review your notes (or recording) and flesh out the details of the conversation. Think about what you learned. How does the information you gathered relate to your main topic or question? Did you learn anything that surprised or intrigued you? What questions remain? Record the date of your interview; you will need to document your source when you write the paper.

Secondary Sources

Many primary sources—published interviews, public documents, results of experiments, and first-person accounts of historical events, for example—are available in your library, which is also a vast repository of secondary source material. If your topic is regional, national, or international in scope, you'll want to consider both of these kinds of sources. For example, if your topic is proposed changes to the Social Security system, you might find information in the *Congressional Record* on committee deliberations, a primary source, and also read articles on the op-ed page of *The New York Times* for interpretive commentary, a secondary source.

Preparing Interview Questions

Consider the following guidelines as you prepare questions for an interview:

■ Find out as much information as you can about the issue and about the expert's stand on the issue before the interview. Then you won't waste interview time on generating details you could have found in the newspaper or on the local TV news.

■ Ask open-ended questions that allow the authority to respond freely, rather than questions requiring only yes or no answers.

■ Prepare more questions than you think you need and rank them in order of priority according to your purpose. Using the most important points as a guide, sequence the list in a logical progression.

Preview: A Search Strategy

- Choose your topic.
- Get an overview of your topic.
- Compile a working bibliography.
- Locate sources.
- Evaluate sources.
- Take notes.

A Search Strategy

Because the sheer amount of information in the library can be daunting, plan how you will find information before you start your search. Always consult a reference librarian if you get stuck in planning your search or if you can't find the information you need.

Choosing Your Topic

Your argument journal may remind you of potential topics, and Chapter 3 covered how to develop a topic. But what if you still can't think of one? You might try browsing through two print sources that contain information on current issues:

Facts on File (1940 to the present). A weekly digest of current news.

Editorials on File (1970 to the present). Selected editorials from U.S. and Canadian newspapers reprinted in their entirety.

Or go online to the *Political Junkie* Website, which will provide you with ideas from the latest news stories in national and regional newspapers and magazines, columnists' viewpoints on current issues, up-to-the-minute reports on public figures, and links to the Websites of numerous political and social organizations. You can access this site at http://www.politicaljunkie.com. Also, think about which subjects you find interesting from the essays in Part Two of this book. These four sources should give you a wealth of ideas to draw on.

Getting an Overview of Your Topic

If you don't know a lot about your topic, encyclopedias can give you general background information. Just as important, encyclopedia articles often end with bibliographies on their subjects—bibliographies prepared by experts in the field. Using such bibliographies can save you hours in the library.

Your library, no doubt, houses in print generalized and specialized encyclopedias. Your library should also allow you access to online general and specialized encyclopedia databases related to your topic. What follows are a few of the dozens of major online encyclopedias that you may find helpful:

Some General and Specialized Online Encyclopedias

Academic American Encyclopedia

New Encyclopedia Britannica

Cambridge Histories Outline
Encyclopedia of Life Sciences
Gale Encyclopedia of Medicine
International Encyclopedia of Social and Behavioral Sciences
Oxford Art Online
Oxford Encyclopedia of American Literature
Oxford Encyclopedia of British Literature
Oxford Music Online

This is just a brief listing of the many encyclopedias available in areas that range widely. It is worth discussing the value of online encyclopedias, such as the ever popular Wikipedia (en.wikipedia.org). *Wikipedia* has been described as a sort of "collective brain" of information that is provided by anyone who wants to share knowledge about a subject. Hundreds of thousands of people have contributed to *Wikipedia* entries, and thousands more have edited and amended them. *Wikipedia*'s strengths include its currency, the vast quantity of information available, and the fact that entries may be amended and challenged. Within seconds of breaking news, *Wikipedia*'s entries will reflect new information, provided someone wishes to add it. Many entries will feature source material at the end of the page. Review these sources with the same critical eye that you evaluate the *Wikipedia* entry. While the information on *Wikipedia* is expected to be correct, it is not guaranteed; and be aware that there is no central editorial authority who confirms the accuracy of the entries. Likewise, source material may sometimes be questionable. Our recommendation is to use *Wikipedia* as a resource, but not the *only* resource in your research arsenal. Note any challenges or disputes to the entry (which will appear in a block above the entry), and use the information only if you feel confident that the information is accurate.

Compiling a Working Bibliography

Because you don't know at the beginning of your search which sources will prove most relevant to your narrowed topic, keep track of every source you consult. Record complete publication information about each source in your notebook, on index cards, or on printouts of online sources. The list that follows describes the information you'll need for particular kinds of sources.

For a Book

- Authors' and/or editors' names
- Full title, including subtitle
- Place of publication (city, state, country)
- Date of publication (from the copyright page)
- Name of publisher
- Volume or edition numbers
- Library call number

For an Article

- ■ Authors' names
- ■ Title and subtitle of article
- ■ Title of periodical (magazine, journal, newspaper)
- ■ Volume number and issue number, if any
- ■ Date of the issue
- ■ Page numbers on which the article appears
- ■ Library location

For an Electronic Source

- ■ Authors' names, if given
- ■ Title of material accessed
- ■ Name of periodical (if applicable)
- ■ Volume and issue numbers (if applicable)
- ■ Date of material, if given
- ■ Page numbers or numbers of paragraphs (if indicated)
- ■ Title of the database
- ■ Publication medium (e.g., CD-ROM, diskette, microfiche, online)
- ■ Name of the vendor, if relevant
- ■ Electronic publication date
- ■ Date of your access to the material
- ■ Path specification for online media (e.g., FTP information, directory, file name). APA also asks for DOI (digital object identifier). If none is available, provide a URL.

Note that for electronic sources, which come in many different formats, you should record all the information that would allow another researcher to retrieve the documents you used. This will vary from source to source, but it's important to give as much information as you can.

Your instructor may ask you to prepare an *annotated bibliography,* in which you briefly summarize the main ideas in each source and note its potential usefulness. You will also want to evaluate each source for accuracy, currency, or bias.

Sample Entries for an Annotated Bibliography

Shannon O'Neill, a journalism major, decided to write her argument essay on book banning in the public schools. Here are some sample entries from her annotated bibliography. (Shannon O'Neill's paper can be found on pages 285–290 in the Documentation Guide.)

Barnhisel, Greg, ed. *Media and Messages: Strategies and Readings in Public Rhetoric.* New York: Longman, 2005. This book contains many useful essays, editorials, and articles examining contemporary issues in the media and presents a balanced view of a large variety of topics. Barnhisel draws useful summaries and conclusions based on information in each chapter. The book is unbiased because it presents criticisms from all angles. In my paper, I used an article and an editorial because they give interesting perspectives on censorship of the written word; one focused on student newspapers; the other criticized censorship as the result of "politically correctness." Both pieces oppose censorship. While the text as a whole is balanced, there aren't any useful pieces advocating for censorship of the written word; rather, they focused on censorship of the visual media or Internet.

"Challenging a Book in Your School." *Gateways to a Better Education*. **1998. 5 Oct. 2009** http://www.gtbe.org. This Website is for a national organization that promotes the spread of Christian values. While it does not advocate censorship or removal of specific works, it encourages parents to challenge their children's curriculum and take an active part in deciding what should or should not be taught in public schools—all with a Christian agenda. This site is clearly biased, but it is an important and useful source for the presentation of the religious argument for book censorship.

"Challenged and Banned Books." *American Library Association*. **2009. 5 Oct. 2009** http://www.ala.org/advocacy/banned/frequentlychallenged/21stcenturychallenged/2009 This organization's Website is extremely useful because it gives background information on the banning and censoring of books and lists recently and frequently banned books and authors. It also gives statistics on reasons for challenges, which I used for a pie chart. The site could be considered biased, though, because it encourages the idea of free speech and discourages censorship based on the premise of the First Amendment. It also encourages people to read banned books and coined Banned Book Week, which celebrates books that have been banned or challenged.

A working bibliography (as opposed to an annotated bibliography) would include the complete publication information for each source, but not the evaluation of its usefulness to the paper.

Locating Sources

Your college library offers a range of methods and materials for finding the precise information you need. Here is a brief guide to locating periodicals, books, and electronic sources.

Finding Periodicals

Instead of going to the periodicals room and leafing page by page through magazines, journals, and newspapers for information pertinent to your topic, use periodical indexes to locate articles you need. Your library will have these indexes available in print, CD-ROM, or online databases. The form you choose will depend on what is available and how current your information must be. When deciding whether to use the printed or electronic versions, carefully note the dates of the material the indexes reference. For example, you cannot use the CD-ROM version of *The Readers' Guide to Periodical Literature* to find a source from 1979. However, for a more current source (from 1983 to the present), use the CD-ROM version since it provides abstracts of articles. It will allow you to decide whether locating the full article is worth your time and effort. Here is a list of some of the periodical indexes often available in college libraries. If your library does not have these indexes, ask the reference librarian about the best way to find periodical articles in your library.

Periodical Indexes

General

Readers' Guide to Periodical Literature. 1915 to present. Print. Indexes popular journals and magazines and some reviews of movies, plays, books, and television.

Readers' Guide Abstracts. 1983 to present. Same content as *Readers' Guide* but with abstracts.

Newspaper Abstracts. 1985 to present. Abstracts of articles in national and regional newspapers.

New York Times. 1851 to present. Extensive coverage of national and international news.

Periodical Abstracts. 1986 to present. Abstracts and full-text articles from more than 950 general periodicals.

ABI/Inform. August 1971 to present. About 800,000 citations to articles in 1,400 periodicals. Good source for business-related topics. Complete text of articles from 500 publications since 1991.

LexisNexis Universe. Full-text access to newspapers, magazines, directories, legal and financial publications, and medical journals.

Specialized

Applied Science and Technology Index/Applied Science and Technology Abstracts. 1913 to present. Covers all areas of science and technology.

Art Index/Art Abstracts. 1929 to present. Wide coverage of art and allied fields.

Business Periodicals Index. 1958 to present. Covers all areas of business.

Education Index/Education Abstracts. 1929 to present. Covers elementary, secondary, and higher education.

PAIS International in Print/PAIS Database (formerly *Public Affairs Information Service Bulletin*). 1915 to present. Excellent index to journals, books, and reports in economics, social conditions, government, and law.

Ethnic Newswatch. 1990 to present. Indexes news publications by various ethnic groups. Includes full texts of most articles.

Social Sciences Index (*International Index* 1907–1965; *Social Sciences and Humanities* 1965–1974; *Social Sciences Index* 1974 to present). 1907 to present. Indexes scholarly journals in political science, sociology, psychology, and related fields.

Humanities Index. (See *Social Sciences Index* entry for name changes.) 1907 to present. Covers scholarly journals in literature, history, philosophy, folklore, and other fields in the humanities.

America: History and Life. 1964 to present. Index and abstracts to articles in more than 2,000 journals. Covers the histories and cultures of the United States and Canada from prehistory to the present.

SPORT Discus. 1975 to present. Covers sports, physical education, physical fitness, and sports medicine.

Social Issues Researcher (SIRS). Full-text articles from newspapers, journals, and government publications related to the social sciences.

Congressional Universe. Offers a legislative perspective on congressional bills, hearings, public laws, and information on members of Congress.

Sociofile. 1974 to present. Coverage includes family and socialization, culture, social differentiation, social problems, and social psychology.

Essay and General Literature Index. 1900 to present. Indexes essays and chapters in collected works. Emphasis is on social sciences and humanities.

Finding Books

Your library catalog—whether in print (card), electronic, or microform format—indexes the books your library holds. Books are listed in three basic ways: by author, title, and general subject. If the catalog is electronic, you can also use keyword searches to locate books. On a computer terminal, you type in a word related to your topic, and the catalog lists all the sources that include that word.

To make keyword searching more efficient, you can often combine two or more search terms. For example, if you know that you want information on "violence" and can narrow that to "violence and music not rap music," the catalog will give you a much shorter list of sources than if you had typed only *violence,* a very broad topic. This is called Boolean searching, and the typical ways you can combine terms are to use *and* to combine search terms, *or* to substitute search terms (e.g., "violent crime" or "assault"), and *not* to exclude terms. For example, suppose you are looking for information on cigarette smoking by teenagers. In a Boolean search, you could use the search phrase: "teenager or youth and smoking not marijuana."

If you are searching by subject rather than author or title, it's useful to know that libraries organize subject headings according to the *Library of Congress Subject Headings (LCSH).* These are large red books, usually located near the library's catalog. You will save time and be more successful if you look up your subject in the *LCSH.* For example, if you search the catalog using the term *movies,* you won't find a single source. If you look up "movies" in the *LCSH,* it will tell you that the subject heading is "motion pictures." Type in *motion pictures,* and you'll find the sources you need.

Following are other useful sources of information:

Biographies

There are so many different biographical sources it is difficult to know which one has the information you need. The following titles will save you a lot of time:

Biography and Genealogy Master Index. (Spans from B.C. to the present.) Index to more than one million biographical sources.

Biographical Index. 1947 to present. International and all occupations. Guide to sources in books, periodicals, letters, diaries, and so on.

Contemporary Authors. 1962 to present. Contains biographical information about authors and lists of their works.

Almanacs

World Almanac and Book of Facts. 1968 to present. Facts about government, business, society, and so on. International in scope.

Statistical Abstract of the United States. 1879 to present. Published by the U.S. Census Bureau. Good source for statistics about all aspects of the United States including economics, education, society, and politics.

Statistical Masterfile. 1974 to present. State and national government statistics and data, private and international.

Reviews, Editorials

Book Review Digest. 1905 to present. Index to book reviews with excerpts from the reviews.

Book Review Index. 1965 to present. Indexes to more books than the *Book Review Digest* but doesn't have excerpts from reviews.

Bibliographies

Look for bibliographies in journal articles, books, encyclopedia articles, biographical sources, and so on.

Finding Internet Sources

The Internet offers countless possibilities for research using government documents, newspapers and electronic journals, Websites, business publications, and much more. You may have access to the Internet through campus computer labs, your own computer, or your handheld device.

To make your search easier and more efficient, you can rely on several of the powerful search engine databases available for exploring the Internet. Search engine databases are built by computer robot programs called "spiders" that "crawl" the Web. Each of the search engines we've listed next uses keyword searches to find material on your topic. These words can specify your topic, supply the title of a book or article about your topic, name a person associated with your topic, and so on. It's important to try out a number of keyword combinations when you are searching for resources. For instance, if your topic is assisted suicide, you might also search under "euthanasia" and "physician-assisted suicide." By adding additional terms such as *terminal illness, legalization,* and *patient's rights,* you may be able to both narrow your search and find material filed under different topic headings that are related to your subject. And you'll get a more accurate response if you use quotation marks around key search phrases.

Here is a list of the more popular search engines. You'll find them useful for locating information on the Internet:

Google

This search engine is the first line for searching and the most popular. It will give you a lot of options, including blog posts, wiki pages, group discussion threads, and various document formats such as PDFs. Keywords can be used for subject searches or to find a phrase that appears in the sources. You may also supply the name of a person or a title to prompt your search. It will search for each of your keywords separately or as a unit. You can also limit or expand the time parameters of your search from the current date to up to 2 years. A word of caution: Information found on Google may not always be appropriate or credible, and advertisers pay to appear higher up in the search results. Thus, you may receive some recommendations that have little or nothing to do with your search. (See following section on evaluating sources.)

Yahoo!

Yahoo! works just like Google. It will also expand your search by linking you to two other search engines if you request them.

Exalead.com

Although not as useful for academic research as are Google and Yahoo! this search engine provides thumbnail preview pages.

About.com

Although not as useful for academic research as are Google, Dogpile, and Yahoo! this search engine connects users to a network of experts or "guides" who offer practical solutions to common problems spanning a wide field of topics.

In addition to the traditional search engines, there are others that conduct "meta searches"; that is, they allow you to leverage the power of many popular search engines at the same time. Combined, these engines cover more of the Internet than a single search engine can cover. Here is a list of some of the most popular and powerful meta-search engines:

Dogpile

This is a popular meta-search engine that combines the power of several other major search engines including Google, Yahoo! Search, Bing, Ask.com, and LookSmart. It displays results from each different search engine.

Ixquick.com

This meta-search engine ranks results based on the number of "top 10" rankings a site receives from the various search engines.

Wikipedia

Wikipedia is an online multilingual encyclopedia (see description on page 253). It is not a search engine, but it can provide you with both information and links to more information. *Wikipedia* covers a vast range of topics with articles that are useful and current and that offer links to related pages and additional information. Because entries are created by anyone who registers and are constantly being revised, material is subject to error and misinformation.

When you are using any search engine, be sure to check the instructions so you can use it as effectively as possible. Also, don't rely on only one search engine. Use several to give yourself access to the broadest range of materials.

Three additional Websites that may help you if you are searching for information related to government, politics, legislation, or statistics are the following:

Library of Congress

This Website provides information about the U.S. Congress and the legislative process. It will search for past legislative bills by topic, bill number, or title; allow you to read the *Congressional Record* from the current and past years' Congresses; find committee reports by topic or committee name; and provide full-text access to current bills under consideration in the House of Representatives and the Senate.

U.S. Census Bureau

You can find facts, figures, and statistics derived from the last census at this site. There is also some information about world population.

White House

At this site, you can find current and past White House press briefings and news releases, as well as a full range of statistics and information produced by federal agencies for public use.

Remember that the Internet is constantly changing, so no book will be completely up to date on how to access its information. Check to see if your college has workshops or courses on using the Internet—it's an important research tool, and it's worth your time to learn how to navigate in cyberspace.

Evaluating Sources

The first examination of your sources is a preliminary assessment to help you decide whether the material is *relevant* and *reliable* for your purposes.

Print Sources

You can often sense a print source's relevance by skimming its preface, introduction, table of contents, conclusion, and index (for books) or abstract and headings (for articles) to see whether your topic appears and how often. Many students mark their bibliography cards with numbers (1 = most relevant, 2 = somewhat relevant, 3 = not very relevant) to help them remember which sources they most want to examine. If a source contains no relevant material, mark the bibliography card "unusable" but don't discard it; if you refine your topic or claim later, you may want to go back to that source.

The reliability of a printed source is judged in a number of ways:

- Check the date: Is it recent or timely for your topic?
- Look at the citations: Is the author's evidence recent or timely?
- Is the author an expert in the field? To find out, use the biographical sources listed earlier in this chapter or find book reviews in the reference section.

■ Where does the author work? A source's credentials may influence your readers. You may also find out what biases the author may have; for example, if the author is the founder of Scientists Against Animal Research, you'll have a good idea about his or her personal beliefs on that subject.

Electronic Sources

Using Internet material presents special challenges in determining the value of a source. Unlike most printed journal and newspaper articles and books, online materials are not necessarily reviewed by editors or professional colleagues to determine whether facts are correct and conclusions reliable. Anyone with the technical skills can develop a Website and post opinions for the world to read. So it's difficult to determine whether such information is worth using. But here are a few suggestions that will help you determine if a source is credible:

■ **Domain address** Each Internet host computer is assigned a domain indicating the type of organization that created the site. This domain indicator appears at the end of the address. Most sites will be labeled one of the following:

edu for an educational site

gov for a government site

com for a commercial site

org for an organizational site

While we can't vouch for the quality of all the material at these different domains, it is more likely that sites affiliated with an educational institution or a government office will provide information that has been carefully researched and prepared. Although commercial and organizational sites may also provide valid information, it is important to check carefully for bias or misinformation that might be made available to further the interests of the business or organization.

■ **Author of the site** Try to identify the author or authors of the material published at the site. Is the author a professional or an authority in a field relevant to the topic? The director of a public health clinic may have opinions worth considering on the medical use of marijuana; he may or may not have the same level of credibility in a discussion about punishment for juvenile criminals.

■ **Identity of the organization** If the site is maintained by an organization, find out what interests the organization represents. Who created the organization? A government-appointed committee investigating public support of family planning will have a very different agenda from a committee organized by private interest groups. While both groups may be scrupulously honest in their presentation of the facts, each may interpret those facts with a particular bias. Your awareness of their "slant" will help you decide how to use the information. The reference section of most libraries can provide directories of associations and organizations.

■ **Date of posting** Check the date when the site was posted. Has the site been updated recently? If not, is the material still current and relevant?

■ **Quality of references** Are sources provided to support the information posted on the site? Most credible sites will document their facts, research studies, and statistics. Many articles and essays will be followed by a bibliography. It's always a good idea to double-check these references to determine whether the information is accurate. The absence of any references to support statements of fact and statistics may indicate that the site is unreliable.

■ **Quality of material** Look for indications that the material has been written or assembled by an educated, well-informed individual who offers a balanced and thoughtful perspective on the issue. Is the written text free of obvious grammatical mistakes, spelling errors, problems with sentence structure, and so on? Does the author indicate awareness and respect for other views even while disagreeing with them? Is the coverage of material thorough and well supported? Although poorly written Websites can indicate low reliability, don't be fooled by slick, attractive presentations. You need to investigate beneath the surface to determine whether the content of the site meets academic standards of fairness and thoroughness.

■ **Intended use** Consider how you will use the material at the site. If you are looking for reliable statistics and factual information, then checking the author's credentials and the status of the organization or company will be important to maintaining your own credibility. However, sometimes personal examples and experiences of individuals who are not professionally qualified may still be of value. For example, a student writing a paper on Alzheimer's disease came across a site in which an Alzheimer's patient kept a diary of the progression of her illness. Even though she was not qualified to give expert medical opinion on the disease itself, her diary provided a unique insight into the feelings and perceptions of someone experiencing the loss of her intellectual capabilities. In her paper, the student writer was able to incorporate some of this compelling personal testimony.

Let's see how this advice works in practice. Shannon O'Neill decided to do an Internet search to find background information for her argument essay on book banning in the public schools. (Sample entries from her annotated bibliography appear earlier in this chapter.) Using several search engines and a keyword search, Shannon had no trouble finding a large number of sites concerned with this subject. However, before relying on the information at the sites, Shannon had to determine which sites were reliable. To do this, she examined several features of each site, as recommended earlier.

The first site Shannon found was the Online Books Page: Banned Books Online at http://onlinebooks.library.upenn.edu/banned-books.html. Using the criteria from the list we've provided, Shannon made the following evaluation of the site :

■ **Domain address** As Shannon noted, the domain address identified the Website as being based at the University of Pennsylvania, a well-known and reputable school.

■ **Author of the site** At the end of the site, the author identified himself by name. Using the home page link "About Us" under "The Inside Story" (see Figure 9.1), Shannon found information about the author who identified himself as a computer scientist who works in a library at the University of Pennsylvania and who received

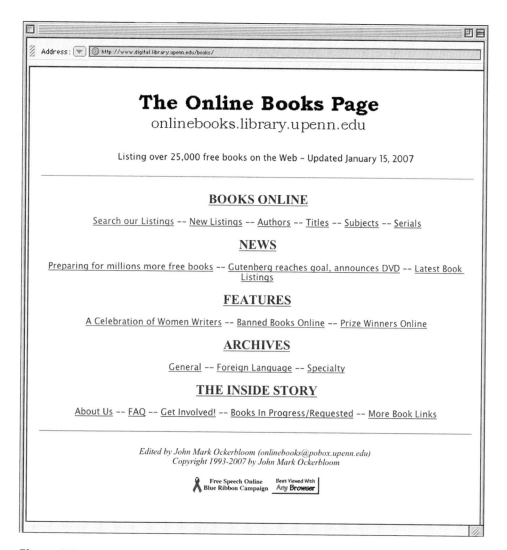

Figure 9.1

a PhD in computer science at Carnegie Mellon University. But since this description didn't indicate any special expertise on the subject of banned books, Shannon returned to the home page and clicked on the link "Banned Books."

■ **Identity of the organization** The link provided on the home page allowed Shannon to gather more information about the Online Books Page and its author. Shannon found a number of links that provided her with considerable information on banned books including classics by Geoffrey Chaucer and John Milton. Another link specified the criteria used to determine which books were placed on the banned book list. Still other links provided further background information about the goals of the site and its association with the Library of Congress. This information and the support of well-known and credible organizations and projects made Shannon feel confident about the value of this site.

■ **Date of posting** Shannon noted that the material on the Website was current, having last been updated in the very month in which she was doing her research. The site itself contained information about both recent attempts to limit public library Internet access and historical accounts of book banning.

■ **Quality of references** The author provided frequent references to other Websites on banned books, as well as to printed books on censorship. Checking through the Internet and the college library, Shannon confirmed that these references were used reliably and even decided to incorporate some of them into her research.

■ **Quality of material** Shannon found the text well written and the entire site organized and thorough. To evaluate whether the author's perspective was balanced, Shannon checked to see if books from the full range of the political spectrum were included in the list. She discovered that the list included a group of diverse books, from the Bible to the Qur'an to works of nineteenth-century poetry to contemporary books that had been criminalized under "hate speech" laws in other countries. Although it was clear to Shannon that the author of the site did not approve of book banning, this bias did not seem to distort the information he provided.

■ **Intended use** Shannon was interested in finding out the titles of books that were banned, those responsible for the banning, and the reasons behind the decisions. She found the Online Books Page very useful. Shannon was particularly impressed by its range of titles. The site's list covered classic and historical works, as well as more modern ones. The explanations that accompanied each listing briefly explained the circumstances surrounding the book's censorship and provided specific dates and information about it.

After carefully evaluating the Online Books Page: Banned Books Online, Shannon concluded that it was a reliable source that might supply her with valuable information for her argument essay.

Shannon found three other Websites that were also concerned with the issue of banned books. However, after using the criteria outlined earlier to evaluate the three, Shannon decided not to use them. Here are some of the reasons why:

■ **Domain address** Two of the sites had addresses that indicated that they had no association with any educational institution, government, business, or organization; the Websites were developed by individuals for their own personal use. Shannon decided that the materials on these sites were more likely to reflect personal opinion than careful research. The third site was maintained by an organization that Shannon decided to investigate further.

■ **Author of the site** By using the links provided in each site, Shannon discovered that one author was a student writing a paper for an Internet course; another was an individual who supplied some personal information about his life (as well as family photographs) but nothing that indicated expertise on book banning; and the third was identified as a news editor for a newspaper published in California. Shannon needed more information before she could conclude that any of these authors was a reliable source.

- **Identity of the organization** Only the site authored by the newspaper editor indicated an association with an organization. Using links in the site, Shannon found that he was affiliated with a religious group that strongly advocated the elimination of different races and religions in American life. After reading several articles on the group's Website, Shannon concluded that the material contained strong political and racial bias that made her question the reliability of the newspaper editor.
- **Date of posting** None of the sites had been updated within the past year. Although Shannon was interested in both historical and current information on book banning, she was concerned that the authors had made no attempts to keep the information in the sites current and timely.
- **Quality of references** Only one site contained a list of related readings, and none of the sites used references to support statements of fact or opinion.
- **Quality of material** Shannon immediately noticed the poor writing quality of the student paper. It was filled with misspellings and grammatical errors and was poorly organized. The second site demonstrated better quality writing, but the author did not develop or support his ideas sufficiently. For instance, he based much of his claim on an "informal survey" without specifying the details of how the survey was conducted. The site authored by the newspaper editor did not reflect respect for other viewpoints or any attempt to present a balanced perspective on the issue of book banning.
- **Intended use** Shannon wanted to be sure that the information she used in her argument essay was accurate. The absence of information about two of the authors and the political affiliations of the third caused her to doubt that any of these sites could be relied on for accuracy.

As Shannon discovered, the Internet can offer a wide array of source material to research, but it does take additional effort to determine which sources will meet the standards required for academic research. If you remember to think like an investigator and examine your findings carefully, you'll discover reliable and valuable information and ideas for your argument essays.

Taking Notes

There are as many different styles of note-taking as there are writers. Some people like to use index cards, recording one idea on each card. This is useful because you can easily shift cards around as you change your outline; you don't have to recopy material as often. Other students take notes in a journal or on sheets of paper so they can make notes or copy bibliographic references in the margins. If you decide to use note cards, we offer two words of advice: First, mark every note card in some way to identify the source. You might want to use the author's name, an abbreviation of the title, or a numbering system tying your note cards and bibliography together. Don't neglect this or you'll find yourself desperately searching for a reference at 2 a.m. on the day your paper is due, with no way to track it down. Second, on each note card indicate whether it's a summary, paraphrase, or direct quote; some people use different colored cards, pens, or highlighters to distinguish the three kinds of notes. Other people use the initials *S, P,* and *Q* to mark the cards. This designation proves useful when deciding how and when to *document* your sources (see the Documentation Guide).

Most research notes fall into one of three categories: summary, paraphrase, and quotation.

You may also make use of online note-taking. The Internet offers several sites that help students to take, manage, and store their notes and documents—including images and audio data—securely online. Most of these services offer easy systems for organizing notes according to categories just as you would with index cards or file folders as well as search engines for finding old notes. You can also create as many folders as you like, while assigning as many notes as desired to each folder. Because these services are Web applications rather than desktop programs, you can access material from any computer.

Some of these services require a fee; one is NoodleTools (http://www.noodletools .com), which offers students innovative software that searches, accesses, records, and organizes information using online note cards. It also formats your bibliography in MLA or APA style. (NoodleTools is included in Pearson Longman's MyCompLab. If this book was packaged with an access code to MyCompLab, you will have free access to Noodle-Tools.) In spite of the fee, NoodleTools is an excellent resource that might be worth the money for all the conveniences offered. Other online services are free, such as mynoteit .com, Google Docs, WordPress.com, and Yahoo! Notepad, which is accessible upon opening a free e-mail account with Yahoo!

A word of caution: You can lose track of sources if the particular research link goes down. To avoid such pitfalls, always make copies of your information on CDs, discs, and/ or data sticks. You should also make hard copies and print notes with particularly important information.

Summary

Summary is most useful for recording an author's main idea without the background or supporting evidence. To summarize accurately, condense an extended idea into a sentence or more in your own words. Your goal is to record the *essence* of the idea as accurately as possible in your own words.

Here's Shannon's summary of a passage from one of her sources:

Original
In Mark Twain's lifetime, his books *Tom Sawyer* and *Huckleberry Finn* were excluded from the juvenile sections of the Brooklyn Public Library (among other libraries), and banned from the library in Concord, MA, home of Henry Thoreau. In recent years, some high schools have dropped *Huckleberry Finn* from their reading lists, or have been sued by parents who want the book dropped. In Tempe, Arizona, a parent's lawsuit attempted to get the local high school to remove the book from a required reading list and *went as far as a federal appeals court* in 1998. (The court's *decision in the case*, which affirmed Tempe High's right to teach the book, has some interesting comments about education and racial tensions.) The Tempe suit, and recent others, were concerned with the use of the word "nigger," a word that also got *Uncle Tom's Cabin* challenged in Waukegan, Illinois. (From Ockerbloom, John Mark. The Online Books Page: Banned Books Online. http://digital.library.upenn.edu/books/ banned-books.html.)

Shannon's Summary

Mark Twain's *Huckleberry Finn* is one of the most infamously banned books, as some say it promotes racism by using the "n" word. In 1998, parents in Arizona filed a lawsuit attempting to remove the book from a high school reading list, and the suit went all the way to the federal appeals court. The court's decision returned the book to the reading list.

For more on writing summaries, see Chapter 2.

Paraphrase

Paraphrasing is useful when you want to preserve an author's line of reasoning or specific ideas but don't want or need to use the original words. When you paraphrase, you restate the original as accurately as possible using your own words and sentence structure.

Here is an excerpt from another source that Shannon used in her paper:

Original

Textbook publishers are sensitive to the often right-wing committees and boards of education that purchase books for large states like Texas and California, and will also delete references to evolution or the scientifically hypothesized age of the Earth. (From Barnhisel, Greg, ed. *Media and Messages: Strategies and Readings in Public Rhetoric*, p. 422.)

Shannon's Paraphrase

When they prepare their book lists, publishers put their business at risk if they forget that states with large, expensive, book-consuming school systems—Texas, for example—often have unyielding opinions about a number of sensitive topics. Evolution, for example, is not discussed in some of the science textbooks students use in school—an inappropriate move that denies students exposure to an important scientific theory.

Quotation

Direct quotation should be used only when the author's words are particularly memorable or succinct, or when the author presents factual or numerical evidence that can't be easily paraphrased. You must copy the author's *exact* wording, spelling, capitalization, and punctuation *as you find it* (even if it contains an obvious mistake). Proofread every direct quotation at least twice; it's easier than you think to leave something out, change a verb tense, or add a word or two. If you want to add words for grammatical completeness or clarity, put them in square brackets such as these [ ]. If you want to eliminate words, mark the omission with three spaced periods, called *ellipsis points* (if the omission comes at the end of a sentence, the ellipsis is typed with four spaced periods). If you find a source you are certain to quote from, it might be worthwhile to photocopy it to avoid errors when rewriting the words.

Here is an example of the effective use of quotation, based on another of Shannon's sources:

Original

Congress shall make no law respecting an establishment of religion, or prohibiting the free exercise thereof; or abridging the freedom of speech, or of the press; or the right of the people peaceably to assemble, and to petition the Government for a redress

of grievances. ("About the First Amendment." *First Amendment Center.* http://www
.firstamendmentcenter.org/about.aspx?item=about_firstamd.)

Shannon's Effective Use of Quotation

According to the First Amendment, citizens of the United States are guaranteed the
right to freedom of speech, which also includes the freedoms of thought and expression: "Congress shall make no law respecting an establishment of religion, or prohibiting the free exercise thereof; or abridging the freedom of speech, or of the press [. . .]."

Drafting Your Paper

Sometimes the sheer size of a researched argument paper can be intimidating. As a result, some
writers suffer from "writer's block" at the outset. Here are strategies for starting your draft:

1. **Write a five-minute summary.** Write a quick, one- or two-paragraph description of
   what your final paper will say—that is, a thumbnail sketch of the paper to clarify in
   your own mind how it will come together. The summary doesn't have to be formal;
   some people don't even use complete sentences. Almost always, these summaries dispel writer's block and get your creativity flowing.
2. **Divide the paper into sections.** Dividing the paper into sections makes the task of
   writing a long paper more manageable. Most writers divide a paper, as we did in
   Chapter 5, into beginning, middle, and end, and further subdivide the middle.
3. **First, draft the sections you're confident about.** Drafting first the sections you
   feel most confident about builds momentum for drafting other parts of the paper.
   As reported by many students, this strategy might also lead you to alter the slant or
   emphasis of the final paper, thereby resulting in a better outcome.
4. **Use a simple code to indicate sources.** Using a simple code to indicate sources will
   save you a great deal of time in revising your paper. As you write your draft, you may
   not want to interrupt the flow of your ideas to copy quotations or summaries from
   note cards; instead, you can insert into your draft the author's or source's name and a
   quick reference to the content so that you'll know on a later draft what you intended
   to include. Here's an example of how Shannon used coded references in her first draft:

   Attempts to ban books in public schools is on the rise. [People, Attacks 6] John
   Steinbeck's *Of Mice and Men* is a frequent target of protest for parents. [Mitchell,
   NYT B17]

   Here you can see Shannon's code at work as she refers to notes from a report published by People for the American Way and an article from page B17 of the *New York
Times.* Later, she will have to incorporate these sources into her first draft and provide
parenthetical citations; for the time being, she simply lists in shorthand the evidence to
support her general statements.

Incorporating Your Research

Because the effort made in finding sources and taking notes is so time-consuming, some
writers think that their work will be "wasted" if they don't somehow cram all the notes
they've taken into their final papers. Unfortunately, the results of such cramming often

look less like a paper and more like note cards stapled together with an occasional sentence wedged between to provide transitions. Every successful writer ends up gathering more research data than are needed for a paper. But it's better to have a lot of material to choose from than not enough to make a persuasive case. The five tests at the end of Chapter 6 (sufficiency, detail, relevance, avoidance of excess, and appropriateness) should help you determine which notes to incorporate into the final draft. Here, too, the flexibility of having one note per card may help because you can shuffle and change the sequence of sources to see which order of presentation will have the most impact on your readers. If you are working on a computer, you may mark and move blocks of text around as you judge the arrangement of your evidence. The first arrangement may not always be the best, so allow yourself some flexibility.

When incorporating sources into your paper, you don't want the "seams" to show between your own writing and the summaries, paraphrases, and quotations from your sources. So it's worth the effort to write sentences and phrases that smoothly introduce sources into the text. Consider two examples:

Awkward   The Anaheim school board decided to ban *Beloved,* and this was "not an example of censorship, but an isolated incident."

Revised   The school board in the Anaheim, California, school system stated that its decision to ban *Beloved* was "not an example of censorship, but an isolated incident."

Remember that while *you,* the writer, may understand how a particular source supports your points, your *readers* may miss the connections unless you provide them. Again we fall back on the analogy of making a case to a jury: A good attorney not only presents a witness's testimony but also helps the jury understand what that testimony means.

Attribution

Many students fail to understand the importance of introducing their sources when incorporating them into a paper. This introduction is called **attribution,** and it is an important part of the process of documentation. Attribution shows your readers that your evidence comes from identifiable, reliable sources. When the attribution contains the name of a book or the author's professional affiliation or other credentials, it also suggests to your readers how reliable the source may be. For instance, if you present a statistic on divorce and attribute it to the book *How to Pick Up Women,* your readers are less likely to respect that statistic than if it came from the U.S. Census Bureau. Likewise, if you cite evidence that eating rutabagas prevents colon cancer, your readers will treat the evidence differently if it comes from an unbiased researcher at the Mayo Clinic rather than from one at the American Rutabaga Institute. In neither case is the evidence less likely to be true, but the attribution in both cases makes the difference in plausibility.

Many students have only one phrase in their repertoires for attribution: "According to . . ." This works, but it is not very informative. By choosing a more connotative argumentative verb, as you do when you state a position or proposal, you can signal to your readers the source's attitude toward the statement. For instance, consider this sentence:

Senator Smith _____ that the change is needed.

Attribution Verbs

Source Is Neutral

comments	observes	says
describes	points out	sees
explains	records	thinks
illustrates	reports	writes
notes		

Source Implies or Suggests but Doesn't Actually Say

analyzes	asks	assesses
concludes	considers	finds
predicts	proposes	reveals
shows	speculates	suggests
supposes	infers	implies

Source Argues

alleges	claims	contends
defends	disagrees	holds
insists	maintains	argues

Source Agrees with Someone/Something Else

admits	agrees	concedes
concurs	grants	allows

Source Is Uneasy or Disagrees

belittles	bemoans	complains
condemns	deplores	deprecates
derides	laments	warns

Using the following list of attribution verbs, look at how selecting a verb can determine the way your audience regards Smith's position (not all these verbs will work in this sentence structure).

If you're not sure of the connotations of any of these verbs, or you're not sure that the sentence you created works with a particular choice, consult an unabridged dictionary or your instructor. Clumsy attribution can distract readers in the same way typos and grammatical errors can; so you want to make your attributions as smooth as possible. (For placement of a bibliographic reference after attributed material, see the next section on documentation.)

Revising and Editing Your Paper

After you have worked your source material into a draft, it's time to look at your writing skeptically, as your readers will. Start by testing all the parts of your argument. This may not be easy to do because you've been living with this topic for some time and may have lost your objectivity and ability to see the gaps. (If you're working in writing groups, ask another member to read your paper and offer you some feedback on it.) Then change, delete, add, or reorganize material to make your case more effective.

To help you revise your argument, we recommend making an outline of the draft *as you've written it*—not as you intended to write it. This will serve as an X-ray of the paper, helping you detect any holes or imbalances. Moreover, it will show you the actual order in which points are presented so that you can consider reorganizing or changing your argumentative strategy. The strategies explained in Chapter 6 and Chapter 7 for assessing evidence and considering claims ought to help you at this stage; apply them as stringently to your own writing as you would to an essay you're reading.

If you made notes in your journal about connections you wanted to make in your final paper, now is the time to include those connections if, in fact, they still fit. You might also consider other kinds of evidence to include. Can you think of personal experiences—yours or others'—to support the evidence of your outside authorities? Have you found facts and statistics to buttress the opinions you present? What are your readers' criteria for judging an issue? Have you presented claims that meet those criteria and phrased them in that manner? It's also time to make sure that all transitions between points are included and are accurate. For instance, if you switch points around, make sure that the point you call "second" is actually the second, not the third or fourth. Also, check that you've included documentation for all your sources and that you have bibliographic note cards or other records of documentation information to prepare the notes in your final copy. Then polish your prose so that your sentences are smooth, your paragraphs are complete, and your grammar and punctuation are precise. Many students let down their efforts when they sense their papers are nearing completion; as a result, their final grades suffer. The revising and editing stage requires sharp attention. Don't undercut all your hard research efforts by presenting your argument in anything but its best form.

Preparing and Proofreading Your Final Manuscript

Once you have polished the draft to your satisfaction, it is time to attend to the presentation of your paper. Flawless presentation is important in research, not only because of the appreciation it will win from your instructor and readers, but also because it will reinforce your credibility with your readers. A sloppy paper with typographical or grammatical errors, missing documentation, or illegible print makes your readers think that your argument might be sloppy as well. A well-prepared paper suggests to your readers that you have taken care to ensure that everything is correct—not only the presentation, but the content as well. This good impression may make readers more inclined to accept your arguments.

Most instructors expect research papers to be neatly and legibly typed with clear titles, double spacing, standard margins (1 inch) and type sizes (10 or 12 points), and minimal handwritten corrections. Your last name and the page number should appear in the upper-right-hand corner of every page after the title page. For English courses, the standard guide to manuscript format is the *MLA Handbook for Writers of Research Papers,* 7th edition. MLA requirements are spelled out in most college composition handbooks and illustrated in Shannon's final paper (see the Documentation Guide). Before you submit your paper, proofread it carefully for typographical errors, misspellings, omitted words, and other minor errors. If possible, let several hours elapse before your final proofreading so you can see what you've actually typed instead of what you *think* you typed.

Plagiarism

Plagiarism is a crime in the academic community. The scholarly world operates by exchanging information and acknowledging its sources. If you fail to acknowledge your sources or let it appear that someone else's work is your own, you are sabotaging the exchange of scholarly information. You're blocking the channels. And plagiarism has very serious consequences: It can earn you a failing grade on an assignment or a suspension or even expulsion from school for a course, and/or a permanent notation on the transcript that future employers and graduate schools will see.

Plagiarism falls into two categories: intentional and accidental. Intentional plagiarism includes copying a phrase, a sentence, or a longer passage from a source and passing it off as your own; summarizing or paraphrasing someone else's ideas without acknowledgment; and buying or borrowing a paper written by someone else and submitting it as your own. Accidental plagiarism includes forgetting to place quotation marks around someone else's words and not acknowledging a source because you were ignorant of the need to document it. Carelessness and ignorance are not defenses against plagiarism.

Many questions about plagiarism involve the tricky subject of *common knowledge*— that is, standard information in a field of study as well as commonsense observations and proverbial wisdom. Standard information includes the major facts in a discipline—for example, the chemical formula for water is H_2O or the Seneca Falls Convention for Women's Rights took place in 1848. If most of your sources accept such a fact without acknowledgment, you can assume it is common knowledge to readers in that field. However, if you're dealing with lesser-known facts (the numbers of soldiers at the Battle of Hastings), interpretations of those facts (assessments of the importance of the Seneca Falls meeting), or a specialist's observation (a scholar's analysis of Susan B. Anthony's rhetoric), you'll need to provide documentation.

Commonsense information, such as the notions that politicians are concerned with getting votes and that icy roads make driving dangerous, need not be documented. Proverbs and clichés don't need documentation either, although proverbs taken from recognized poems or literary works do. (Thus, "A stitch in time" needs no documentation, but "To be or not to be" should carry a reference to *Hamlet.*)

Here are four simple rules to help you avoid plagiarism:

1. *Take your research notes carefully.* Write down (or print out) a full bibliographical reference for each source (the forms appear in the Documentation Guide). Also, note whether you are quoting, paraphrasing, or summarizing what you find in your source (see earlier discussion in this chapter). If your notes are clear and thorough, you'll never have to worry about which words and ideas are yours and which come from your sources.

2. *Always introduce your source carefully so that your audience know to whom they're listening.* Proper attribution is a signal to your readers that you're switching from your own work to someone else's. It is also a signal to you to check that a source is represented accurately (with no exaggeration) and that a bibliographic citation appears in your list of works cited or references.

3. *When in doubt, document.* While it is possible to overdocument, it is not an intellectual crime to do so. Rather, it reveals a lack of self-confidence in your own argument or your determination to prove to your instructor and readers that you've seen every source ever published on your subject. However, overdocumenting is a less serious academic sin than plagiarizing!

4. *Enter the documentation right after the use of the source; it doesn't "carry over" between paragraphs or pages.* It is tempting, especially when using one source for an extended period, to leave all the documentation until the end of a large passage of text (which might be several paragraphs or several pages in length). But even if you weave attribution skillfully throughout the whole passage, the convention in academics is that you document a source in each paragraph in which you use it. If another source intervenes, it is twice as important that the main source be documented on every use. So if you use the same article in four successive paragraphs, each of those paragraphs must have some parenthetical source reference. With skillful attribution, the parenthetical reference can be reduced to a simple page number, which won't interrupt the flow of your text.

To understand how plagiarism works, let's look at some of the ways writers might handle, or mishandle, this passage from Dennis Baron's article "English in a Multicultural Society," which appeared in the Spring 1991 issue of *Social Policy.* Here's the original passage from page 8:

> The notion of a national language sometimes wears the disguise of inclusion: we must all speak English to participate meaningfully in the democratic process. Sometimes it argues unity: we must speak one language to understand one another and share both culture and country. Those who insist on English often equate bilingualism with lack of patriotism. Their intention to legislate official English often masks racism and certainly fails to appreciate cultural difference; it is a thinly veiled measure to disenfranchise anyone not like "us."

Plagiarized Use

Supporters of U.S. English argue we must all speak one language to understand one another and share both culture and country. But Dennis Baron argues that "[t]heir intention to legislate official English often masks racism and certainly fails to appreciate cultural difference" (8). English-only legislation really intends to exclude anyone who is not like "us."

This is plagiarism because the writer has copied Baron's words in the first sentence and paraphrased them in the last, but made it appear as though only the middle sentence was actually taken from Baron's article.

Plagiarized Use

Calls for a national language sometimes wear the disguise of inclusion, according to linguist Dennis Baron. When U.S. English argue that we must all speak English to participate meaningfully in the democratic process, or that we must speak one language to understand one another and share both culture and country, Baron says they are masking racism and failing to appreciate cultural difference (8).

Here the plagiarism comes in presenting Baron's actual words without quotation marks, so it looks as if the writer is paraphrasing rather than quoting. Even with the attribution and the citation of the source, this paragraph is still an example of plagiarism because the direct quotations appear as the writer's paraphrase.

Acceptable Use

Linguist Dennis Baron argues that supporters of official English legislation use the reasons of inclusion, unity, and patriotism to justify these laws, but that their efforts may hide racist and culturally intolerant positions. Baron says that sometimes English-only laws are "thinly veiled measure[s] to disenfranchise anyone not like 'us'" (8).

Here the source is properly handled. The writer paraphrases most of the original text in the first sentence, then skillfully incorporates a direct quotation in the second (note the use of square brackets to make the noun agree in number with the verb, and the conversion of double quotation marks from the original into single quotation marks in the quote). The attribution clearly says that both points are taken from Baron, but the quotation marks show where Baron's own words, rather than the writer's, are used.

Documentation Guide:

MLA and APA Styles

The two most common systems of documentation used in colleges and universities are the Modern Language Association (MLA) style, used widely in the humanities, and the American Psychological Association (APA) style, used widely in the social sciences. We will explain them in detail in this chapter. (Some of your courses may also require you to use the Council of Science Editors, or CSE, style; *The Chicago Manual of Style,* which you might know as Turabian style; or a journalistic style guide such as *The Associated Press Style Book.*) Your instructor will tell you which rules to follow.

Where Does the Documentation Go?

Both MLA and APA styles call for parenthetical citations within the paper and a source list at the end of the paper. In both styles, you use a brief reference or attribution to your source in parentheses within the body of the paper and a full bibliographical citation in a list of works cited (MLA) or references (APA). (These are the equivalents of what you probably called a "bibliography" in high school.) Documenting your sources, if performed properly, will help you avoid plagiarism. The shape that citations take in the two systems, however, is a little different, so make sure you observe the forms carefully.

Documentation Style

Let's look at how both systems handle documentation for some of the most commonly used information sources. Suppose you want to quote from Matt Bai's article "The New Boss," which appeared in the January 30, 2005, issue of the *New York Times Magazine.* Here's how it would appear in your list of sources or bibliography:

MLA Bai, Matt. "The New Boss." *The New York Times Magazine*, 30 Jan. 2005: 38+. Print.

APA Bai, M. (2005, January 30). The new boss. *The New York Times Magazine*, 38–45, 62, 68, 71.

As you can see, each style orders information differently.

Likewise, both styles use a parenthetical reference in the paper to show where the evidence comes from, but again they do it differently.

MLA One author talks about giving "added value" to employers, some of whom have come to view him, warily, as a partner (Bai 42).

If the author's name appears in your attribution, only the page number needs to go in the parentheses:

MLA   Matt Bai talks about giving "added value" to employers, some of whom have come to view him, warily, as a partner (42).

Both references tell your readers that they can find this source in your works cited list, alphabetized by the last name *Bai*. If you had more than one reference to Bai in your works cited list, then you would add a shortened form of the title in the parentheses so readers would know to which Bai article you were referring (Bai, "New Boss" 42).

The APA style references for the same situations would be

APA   One author talks about giving "added value" to employers, some of whom have come to view him, warily, as a partner (Bai, 2005, p. 42).

or

APA   Bai (2005) talks about giving "added value" to employers, some of whom have come to view him, warily, as a partner (p. 42).

When you use more than one work by an author in your paper, APA style distinguishes them by date of publication. For example, if you cited two Bai articles from 2005, the earlier one would be designated 2005a, and the second as 2005b.

Using parenthetical citations for electronic sources can be much trickier because such sources typically have no page numbers. If your source uses paragraph numbers, provide the paragraph number preceded by *par.* or *para.* If you need to include the author's name or a brief title, place a comma after the name or title. If another type of designation is used in the source to delineate its parts (such as *screens* or *Part II*), write out the word used for that part:

MLA   Between 2000 and 2004, the message delivered by political advertisements changed dramatically (Edwards, par. 15).

APA   Between 2000 and 2004, the message delivered by political advertisements changed dramatically (Edwards, 2005, para. 15).

If your source has no numbering, no page or paragraph numbers should appear in your parenthetical reference unless your instructor indicates that you should do otherwise. Some instructors ask students to number the paragraphs of electronic sources to make references easier to locate.

A Brief Guide to MLA and APA Styles

The handbooks for MLA and APA documentation are available in most college libraries. If you don't find the information you need in this brief guide, look for these books or Websites:

MLA   *MLA Handbook for Writers of Research Papers.* 7th ed. New York: MLA, 2009. Print.

The Modern Language Association also has a Website.

APA   *Publication Manual of the American Psychological Association* (2009). (6th ed.) Washington, DC: American
Psychological Association.

The American Psychological Association does not provide a guide to documentation on its Website; however, the Purdue University Online Writing Lab provides a useful
guide to APA documentation.

Books

MLA   Author. *Title*. Edition. City of Publication: Publisher, Year. Medium of Publication.

APA   Author. (Year of Publication). *Title*. City of Publication, State: Publisher.

One Author

MLA   Krakauer, Jon. *Where Men Win Glory: The Odyssey of Pat Tillman*. New York: Random, 2009. Print.

APA   Krakauer, J. (2009). *Where men win glory: The odyssey of Pat Tillman*. New York, NY:
Random House.

MLA uses the author's full first name plus middle initial, whereas APA uses the initial of the first name (unless more initials are needed to distinguish among people with
the same initials). APA capitalizes only first words and proper nouns in titles and subtitles; MLA capitalizes all words except prepositions, conjunctions, and articles. MLA
lists only the city; APA lists the city but also includes the state. MLA shortens certain
publishers' names, whereas APA just drops unnecessary words such as *Co., Inc.*, and
Publishers. Lastly, MLA includes the medium of the publication consulted, which is
"Print" in this case.

Two or More Authors

MLA   Reinhart, Carmen M., and Kenneth S. Rogoff. *This Time Is Different: Eight Centuries of Financial Folly*. Princeton:
Princeton UP, 2009. Print.

APA   Reinhart, C. M., & Rogoff, K. S. (2009). *This time is different: Eight centuries of financial folly*. Princeton, NJ:
Princeton University Press.

In MLA style, only the first author's name is given in inverted form. In APA style, the
ampersand (&) is used to join authors' names. The ampersand is also used in parenthetical
references in text, for example "(Reinhart & Rogoff, 2009, p. 63)," but not in attributions,
for example, "According to Pyles and Algeo." In MLA style, for works with more than
three authors you may replace all but the first author's name by the abbreviation *et al*. In
APA style, list the names of up to seven authors, followed by an ellipsis (…), and provide
the last author's name.

More Than One Book by an Author

MLA   Gladwell, Malcolm. *Outliers*. New York: Little, 2008. Print.

            —. *What the Dog Saw and Other Adventures*. New York: Little, 2009. Print.

In MLA style, if you cite more than one work by a particular author, the individual works are listed in alphabetical order. For the second and any additional entries, type three hyphens and a period instead of the author's name; then skip a space and type the title in italics.

In APA style, when you cite more than one work by an author, the author's name is repeated for each work. The order of the entries is based on the publication dates of the titles, with the earliest-published given first, instead of alphabetical order. If two works by one author are published in the same year, alphabetization is done by title and the letters *a*, *b*, and so on are placed immediately after the year.

Book with an Editor

MLA   Haynes, Kenneth, ed. *Geoffrey Hill: Collected Critical Writings*. New York: Oxford UP, 2008. Print.

APA   Haynes, K. (Ed.). (2008). *Geoffrey Hill: Collected critical writings*. New York, NY: Oxford University Press.

Essay in a Collection or Anthology

MLA   Fisher, M. F. K. "Gare de Lyon." *Americans in Paris: A Literary Anthology*. Ed. Adam Gopnik. New York: Library of America, 2004. 581–91. Print.

APA   Fisher, M. F. K. (2004). Gare de Lyon. In A. Gopnik (Ed.), *Americans in Paris: A literary anthology* (pp. 581–591). New York, NY: Library of America.

Book in a Later Edition

MLA   Janaro, Richard, and Thelma Altshuler. *The Art of Being Human*. 10th ed. New York: *Longman*, 2012.

APA   Janaro, R., & Altshuler, T. (2012). *The art of being human* (10th ed.). New York, NY: Longman.

Multivolume Work

MLA   Doyle, Arthur Conan. *The New Annotated Sherlock Holmes*. Ed. Leslie S. Klinger. 2 vols. New York: Norton, 2004. Print.

APA   Doyle, A. C. (2004). *The new annotated Sherlock Holmes* (L. S. Klinger, Ed.). (Vols. 1–2). New York, NY: Norton.

Book with a Group or Corporate Author

MLA   American Medical Association. *Handbook of First Aid and Emergency Care.* New York. Random, 2009. Print.

APA   American Medical Association. (2009). *Handbook of first aid and emergency care.* New York, NY: Random House.

Begin the entry with the corporate or group name alphabetized by the first letter of the main word (not including *a, an,* or *the*).

Article from a Reference Work

MLA   Bragg, Michael B. "Aircraft Deicing." *The McGraw-Hill Concise Encyclopedia of Science and Technology.* 6th ed. 2009. Print.

APA   Bragg, M. (2009). Aircraft deicing. In *The McGraw-Hill concise encyclopedia of science and technology* (Vol. 1, pp. 339–342). New York, NY: McGraw-Hill.

If the reference book is widely available (such as a major encyclopedia or bibliography), a short bibliographic form as shown here is acceptable in MLA; APA recommends including more information rather than less. For a less widely known reference book, MLA recommends using the form for a book, multiple-authored book, or series, depending on what the book is.

Editor's Preparation of a Previous Work

MLA   Lovecraft, H. P. *Tales.* Ed. Peter Straub. New York: Library of America, 2005. Print.

APA   Lovecraft, H. P. (2005). *Tales* (P. Straub, Ed.). New York, NY: Library of America.

Translated Work

MLA   Pamuk, Orhan. *The Museum of Innocence.* Trans. Maureen Freely. New York: Knopf, 2009. Print.

APA   Pamuk, O. (2009). *The museum of innocence* (M. Freely, Trans.). New York, NY: Alfred A. Knopf. (Original work published 2008)

In APA style, the date of the translation is placed after the author's name. The date of the original publication of the work appears in parentheses at the end of the citation. This text would be cited in a paper as "(Pamuk, 2008/2009)."

Anonymous Work

MLA   *The Chicago Manual of Style: The Essential Guide for Writers, Editors, and Publishers.* 16th ed. Chicago: U of Chicago P, 2010. Print.

APA   *The Chicago manual of style: The essential guide for writers, editors, and publishers* (16th ed.). (2010). Chicago, IL: University of Chicago Press.

Periodicals

MLA format and APA format for articles in journals, periodicals, magazines, newspapers, and so on are similar to the formats for books. One of the few differences concerns the volume number of each issue. Volume numbers for magazines or journals found in a library or acquired by subscription (these usually appear six times a year or less frequently) should be included in your entry. If a journal appears monthly or more frequently, or can be acquired on newsstands, you can usually omit the volume number. If the journal has continuous pagination (i.e., if the January issue ends on page 88 and the February issue begins on page 89), you don't need to include the month or season of the issue in your citation. If the journal starts over with page 1 in each issue, then you must include the month or season in your citation.

Magazines and newspapers (unlike scholarly journals) often carry articles on discontinuous pages (e.g., pages 35–37 and then 114–115). MLA permits the use of the form "35+" instead of giving all the pages on which such articles appear. With APA style, all page numbers must be noted.

Most journals and many periodicals contain a DOI. In APA, if a DOI has been assigned to your source, include it at the end of the citation, regardless of whether you used the print or electronic version of the source.

MLA	Author. "Article Title." *Journal or Magazine Title* volume number (Date): inclusive pages. Medium of publication.

APA	Author. (Date). Article title. *Journal or Magazine Title, volume number,* inclusive pages. doi:

Scholarly Journal

MLA	Spandler, Helen, and Tim Calton. "Psychosis and Human Rights: Conflicts in Mental Health Policy and Practice." *Social Policy and Society* 8 (2009): 245–6. Print.

APA	Spandler, H., & Calton, T. (2009). Psychosis and human rights: Conflicts in mental health policy and practice. *Social Policy and Society, 8*(2), 245–256. doi:10.1017/S1474746408004764

Magazine Article

MLA	Wallace, Amy. "An Epidemic of Fear." *Wired* Nov. 2009: 128+. Print.

APA	Wallace, A. (2009, November). An epidemic of fear. *Wired,* 128–135, 166, 168, 170.

This is the form for a magazine that appears monthly. For a magazine that appears bimonthly or weekly, provide the complete date.

MLA	Mahr, Krista. "Tuna: The Hidden Cost of the World's Priciest Fish." *Time* 16 Nov. 2009: 38–43. Print.

APA	Mahr, K. (2009, November 16). Tuna: The hidden cost of the world's priciest fish. *Time,* 38–43.

Review

MLA	Vaill, Amanda. "Brooklyn Bohemians." Rev. of *February House,* by Sherill Tippins. *New York Times Book Review* 6 Feb. 2005: 8. Print.

APA	Vaill, A. (2005, February 6). Brooklyn bohemians [Review of the book *February house,* by S. Tippins]. *The New York Times Book Review,* p. 8.

When newspapers designate sections with identifying letters (e.g., *A*, *B*), that information is included in the reference. With MLA style, "4+" indicates that the review begins on page 4 and continues on other nonadjacent pages in the newspaper. APA includes initial articles such as "The" in a newspaper title; MLA omits them. If the reviewer's name does not appear, begin with "Rev. of *Title*" in the MLA system or "[Review of the book *Title*]" in the APA system. If the reviewer's name does not appear but the review has a title, begin with the title of the review in both systems.

Newspaper Article

MLA   Barnes, Brooks. "The Quiet Force Behind DreamWorks," *New York Times,* 15 July 2013. B1. Print.

APA   Barnes, B. (2013 July 15). The quiet force behind DreamWorks," *The New York Times*, B1.

Newspaper Editorial

MLA   Judge, Michael. "Epitaph on a Tyrant." Editorial. *Wall Street Journal* 7 Feb. 2005: A19. Print.

APA   Judge, M. (2005, February 7). Epitaph on a tyrant [Editorial]. *The Wall Street Journal*, A19.

Letter to the Editor of a Magazine or Newspaper

MLA   Rafferty, Heather A. Letter. "The Other 'CIA.'" *Weekly Standard* 7 Feb. 2005: 5. Print.

APA   Rafferty, H. (2005, February 7). The other "CIA" [Letter to the editor]. *The Weekly Standard, 5.*

If the newspaper or magazine doesn't give a title to the letter, for MLA style use the word *Letter* followed by a period after the author's name. Do not underline the word or enclose it in quotation marks. For APA style, skip that information and use the rest of the citation form.

Internet Sources

Web Page

MLA   Redford, Robert. "Common Sense for the Clean Energy and Climate Debate." *OnEarth.* Natural Resources Defense Council, 11 Nov. 2009. Web. 12 Nov. 2009.

APA   Redford, R. (2009, November 11). Common sense for the clean energy and climate debate. Retrieved from http://www.onearth.org/node/1603

For MLA, begin with the name of the individual who created the Website. Follow with the title of the work in quotation marks (if you are citing a smaller work within a larger site), then the title of the entire Website in italics. Then write the name of the organization associated with the site, if available; the date of publication, if available; the medium of publication, which is the "Web" in this case, and the date of access.

MLA does not require a URL in the citation. However, if your source is difficult to locate, you can provide the complete URL in angle brackets after the date of access. If the URL is long, you can break it onto the next line after a single or double slash.

For APA, begin with the last name of the author followed by initials and period. Follow with the date of publication or latest update. Use "(n.d.)" if no date is available. If there is no author, begin with the title of the site, and then the date of publication or update. Close with the electronic address, whether it is the URL or DOI.

Online Magazine Article

MLA   Upbin, Bruce, and Dan Bigman. "The Carbon Question." *Forbes Magazine.* Forbes.com, 15 Oct. 2009. Web. 12 Nov. 2009.

APA   Upbin, B., & Bigman, D. (2009, October 15). The carbon question. *Forbes Magazine.* Retrieved from http://www.forbes.com/forbes/2009/1102/opinions-steve-forbes-climate-change-lets-get-real.html

MLA gives the date of access for electronic sources, and this date of access appears right after *Web.* APA provides the date of publication and lists this date after the author.

Online Article in Electronic Journal

MLA   Knypstra, Syste. "Teaching statistics in an Activity Encouraging Format." *Journal of Statistics Education,* 17.2 (2009): n. pag. Web. 23 Oct. 2009.

APA   Knypstra, S. (2009). Teaching statistics in an activity encouraging format. *Journal of Statistics Education, 17*(2). Retrieved from www.amstat.org/publications/jse/v17n2/knypstra.html

Online Article Retrieved from a Database

MLA   Thompson, Ayanna. "Introduction: Shakespeare, Race, and Performance." *Shakespeare Bulletin* 27.3 (2009): 359–61. *Project Muse.* Web. 7 Nov. 2009.

APA   Thompson, A. Introduction: Shakespeare, race, and performance. *Shakespeare Bulletin, 27*(3), 359–361. doi:10.1353/shb.0.0109

To document material from a database in MLA, italicize the database service, indicate the medium of publication, that is, Web, and the date of access. For APA, provide the DOI if available. Otherwise, you can list the database after *Retrieved from.*

Online Book

MLA   Bacon, Jono. *The Art of Community: Building the New Age of Participation.* Sebastopol: O'Reilly, 2009. *Art of Community.* Web. 4 Nov. 2009.

APA   Bacon, J. (2009). *The art of community: Building the new age of participation.* Retrieved from http://www.artofcommunityonline.org/get/

CD-ROM

MLA   "Electrometer." *The McGraw-Hill Encyclopedia of Science and Technology.* 9th ed. CD-ROM. New York: McGraw, 2002.

APA   Electrometer. (2002). In *The McGraw-Hill encyclopedia of science and technology (9th ed.).* [CD]. New York, NY: McGraw-Hill.

E-Mail

MLA   Mendez, Michael R. "Re: Solar power." E-mail to Edgar V. Atamian. 13 Sept. 2013.

In APA, electronic correspondence via e-mail typically does not appear in the reference list. It is cited only in an in-text reference: (M. Mendez, personal communication, September 13, 2013).

Miscellaneous Sources

Film, Filmstrip, Slide Program, Videotape, DVD

MLA   Nair, Mira. *Amelia*. Perf. Hilary Swank, Richard Gere, and Ewan McGregor. Fox Searchlight Pictures, 2009. Film.

APA   Forster, M. (Director). Bellflower, Nellie (Producer) (2004). *Finding neverland* [Motion picture]. United States: Miramax.

To cite a filmstrip, slide program, videotape, or DVD in MLA style, include the name of the medium after the distributor and year of release. If you are citing the work as a whole rather than the work of one of the creative artists involved in the project, start with the title instead. For instance:

MLA   *Harry Potter and the Half-Blood Prince*. Dir. David Yates. Warner Bros., 2009. DVD.

APA   Heyman, D. (Producer), & Yates, D. (Director). (2009). *Harry Potter and the half-blood prince* [Motion picture]. United States: Warner Bros.

Television or Radio Program

MLA   Burns, Ken, dir. *The National Parks: America's Best Idea*. PBS. KCTS, Seattle. 28 Sept. 2–Oct. 2009. Television.

APA   Burns, K., and Duncan, D. (Producers). (2009). *The national parks: America's best idea* [Television series]. Seattle: KCTS.

In MLA, include the network as well as the call letters and city of the local station, if available. Then, add the broadcast date and medium of reception. For a radio broadcast, substitute *Radio*.

In APA, list the producer for an entire television series. To cite an individual episode in a series, list the writer and director instead, and substitute "Television series episode."

Interview

MLA   Pennington, Linda Beth. Personal interview. 20 Apr. 2012.

In APA, personal communications including interviews do not appear in the reference list. They are cited only in an in-text reference: "(L. Pennington, personal interview, April 20, 2012)."

The APA doesn't offer forms for "nonrecoverable" materials such as personal letters, e-mail messages, lectures, and speeches, and these sources are not included in reference listings. However, in college writing assignments, most instructors will ask you to include them. You may, therefore, have to design a hybrid citation form based on the standard forms. Remember that the APA encourages you to provide more, rather than less, information in your citations. The MLA has forms for almost any kind of communication, even nonrecoverable ones. Consult the *MLA Handbook for Writers of Research Papers,* 7th edition, to find additional forms.

SAMPLE RESEARCH PAPERS

Following are two sample student research papers, the first in MLA format and the second in APA format. As you read them, notice the margins and other format requirements of the two styles, such as the use of running heads, the placement of titles, and the different citation forms. We have added marginal annotations to highlight special features and to demonstrate the structural elements of the arguments.

As these research papers demonstrate, the researched argument is different from the other arguments you've written only in quantity and format, not in quality. You must still make a claim and find evidence to support it, tailor your presentation to your readers, and use a logical structure that considers the various sides of an issue. As you progress in your academic life and, later, in your professional life, you will find that variations on the researched argument can become successful senior projects, theses, sales proposals, journal articles, grant proposals, and even books—so mastering the skills of argumentative writing will serve you well.

O'Neill 1

Shannon O'Neill

Professor Martinez

English 111

13 November 2013

Literature Hacked and Torn Apart:

Censorship in Public Schools

During the 2008 Summer Olympic Games in Beijing, international journalists covering the event found their access to certain Websites restricted by the Chinese government—something that the country's citizens deal with every day. But even in America, where we wouldn't dream of a government that told us what sites we could not browse, an industry of censorship is lurking in the fine print: the banning of books in public schools.

According to the First Amendment, citizens of the United States are guaranteed the right to freedom of speech, which also includes the freedom of expression: "Congress shall make no law respecting an establishment of religion, or prohibiting the free exercise thereof; or abridging the freedom of speech, or of the press. . . ." Although rooted in the Constitution, these rights are considered inconvenient by some who would censor the voices of others in order to promote a private agenda.

Greg Barnhisel of Duquesne University observes that book banning is nothing new. Since the advent of the printing press, "society has bemoaned how information or entertainment corrupts the youth and coarsens the intellectual atmosphere." He says that in the early 1800s, "parents fretted about the craze for rebellious Romantic writers like Byron and Goethe that resulted in a rash of faddish suicides of young men imitating the melancholy heroes of literature" (465).

Two centuries later, parents are still the loudest advocates for book censorship. Taking the authority of schools into their own hands, they arrogantly assert that what they think is best for *their* children to read is what is best for *all* children. According to the American Library Association's (ALA) Website, 10,220 challenges to books were reported between 1990 and 2008. They estimate, however, that for every challenge that is reported, four or five are not. Seventy percent of those challenges were to literature in schools or school libraries, and parents were the initiators fifty-seven percent of the time. The reasons for the challenges ranged from homosexuality to a religious viewpoint.

Gateways to a Better Education, a national organization devoted to promoting Christian values in public schools, envisions them as "learning communities enriched by the appropriate

1" margin on each side and bottom

Heading appears on first page

Double-space between title and first line and throughout

Introduces general topic and position

Ellipsis indicates words omitted from quotation

Use of authority

Narrows topic to book banning

Gives sense of history

Identifies opposition and cites statistics

and lawful expression of Christian values and ideas." Their Website continues, "We are making the case that implementing our vision is culturally appropriate, academically legitimate, legally permitted, and morally imperative. ("Our Mission")" But their case is "imperative" only if you share their vision of using the classroom to advocate Christian beliefs. If unchecked, such efforts can blur the separation of church and state, imposing religious ideals on students and parents who may not share those beliefs.

In an article on the group's Website, Gateways spokesperson Eric Buehrer asserts that parents and teachers have the moral obligation to censor the material presented to students: "There are many educators who believe that when parents question something being taught in the classroom, it's meddling. When parents ask to have something removed . . . it's censorship! But, is it? To hear certain groups tell it, you'd conclude that Hitler is alive and well and lurking in the wings of Hooterville High School." While Beuhrer does not advocate the banning of a specific book in his article, he supports and encourages parents who wish to challenge books on a local level.

Denying students access to literature that does not support one individual's religious or moral beliefs is detrimental to the learning process. By questioning the authority of schools, parents are questioning the art of learning itself. Books should be selected based on established academic principles and not on the fulfillment of religious or moral agendas. Censors have criticized many classic, exemplary literary works. John Mark Ockerbloom of *"The Online Books Page"* reports that Mark Twain's *Adventures of Huckleberry Finn,* an infamously banned book, is controversial because it contains the "n" word. In 1998, parents in Arizona filed a lawsuit attempting to remove the book from a high school reading list, and the suit went all the way to the federal appeals court. The court's decision returned the book to the reading list.

Sometimes, in their zeal to protect young readers from offense, even well-intended people miss the point. Literature is created in a context, reflecting the fears and prejudices of the time. Twain did not intend to ridicule African Americans. To the contrary, his work reflected the dialect and prejudice of the book's period. Reading the book, we join Huck Finn on a moral journey that leads him to question and finally reject the accepted—and hypocritical—social institutions of his time. Today we consider the "n" word brutal and insulting, but without it, the book would be less effective in helping us understand our sad history of racism and tolerance for slavery. Excising the word to avoid offense is an odd sort of denial, a way to pretend that people of the time spoke respectfully to those whom they brutalized. When we remove the word, we are reaching back in time and altering the record of what people said.

O'Neill 3

The human body is often the target of challenges and bans. Robert Lipsyte's novel *One Fat Summer,* about an overweight boy who gains self-confidence, was removed from a seventh-grade class in New York because one parent complained about its mention of adolescent sexuality. The teachers in the district, however, praised the book for addressing the difficulties of growing up, and claimed that students enjoyed reading it (Vinciguerra). In fighting to have the book removed, the critic confronted reality and ignored it, asserting in effect that adolescents are unaware of sex—a preposterous notion. Where students benefited from the book's lessons, others peeked beneath the covers and saw something dangerous.

Similarly, *It's Perfectly Normal,* by Robie H. Harris, has made the ALA's top ten list of most frequently challenged books three times since 2003, topping the list once. The association's Website gives "homosexuality, nudity, sex education, religious viewpoint, abortion, and being unsuited to age group" as the reasons. The message sent by parents who criticize this book is that what their kids are going through during puberty is *not* normal, but is shameful and embarrassing.

My Sister's Keeper, by Jodi Picoult, in which a young girl sues her parents over the right to control her own body when they want her to donate an organ to her dying sister, was banned in 2008 in a Michigan school district ("Book Is Banned"). Perhaps parents were threatened by the novel's strong-willed protagonist. Clearly the message being sent is that anything that has to do with our bodies is off limits and inappropriate.

Also under attack are books that have encouraged kids to read—J. K. Rowling's *Harry Potter* series. Number two on the ALA's list of the most frequently challenged books of 2003, the series has also climbed the ladder of success. The fifth in the series, *Harry Potter and the Order of the Phoenix,* had the largest first printing of any work of fiction—8.5 million copies (Rutten). The ALA states that the series has been challenged because of "Satanism."

An article on the Christian Website "*Surf-in-the-Spirit*" cites the Bible and claims that the Harry Potter series persuades children to enjoy the "ungodly practice" of magic. The author asserts that the books promote Satan's goals, which are to "destroy [our children's] lives and condemn their souls. He will surely succeed if parents fall into the trap of believing that these books 'are only a story' and are just innocent evil. . . . This is the worst kind of evil, because it has deceived so many . . . into accepting it" (Smith). People have the right to believe that wizardry is Satan's work, but banning the popular series is yet another way of imposing personal beliefs on those who may have a different opinion about magic.

Acknowledges specific objections

Responds to objections

Specific evidence

Specific evidence

Acknowledges opposition with direct quotation

Parenthetical reference

O'Neill 4

Conservatives are not alone in promoting censorship; liberals share the affliction. The art of deciding what is politically correct has become its own industry. The English language has been hacked and torn apart in the effort to promote equality, but the result is a disconnection from reality. It seems like nothing is acceptable enough for literature, since both political spectrums endure a conflicting battle.

In her essay "Cut on the Bias," education scholar Diane Ravitch says that the educational publishing industry adheres to specific guidelines that prevent the exposure of controversial words or topics, notably those involving gender, race, religion, or sex. Ravitch compiled a list of over five hundred words that have been banned by publishers, including "landlord," "senior citizen," "yacht," and "actress" (428). "Founding Fathers" is avoided because it is supposedly sexist, and a story about animals living in a rotted tree trunk was criticized because it could be offensive to people who live in low-income apartments (Barnhisel 422). It cannot be denied that the country's Founding Fathers were men; the sad fact is that during the establishment of the United States, women were not *considered* capable of running a revolution. Ravitch correctly asserts that the enforcement of politically correct—but historically inaccurate—language promotes denial and ignorance: "Bowdlerization is not only dishonest, it leads to the dumbing down of language and ideas. And . . . I'm convinced: The widespread censorship of language and ideas in education caused by the demands of advocacy groups will not end unless it is regularly exposed to public review and ridicule" (429).

But for some, censoring books is not enough; they want to destroy them. In 2004, officials at a high school in New York ripped certain pages, deemed inappropriate because of sexuality, from tenth-grade students' copies of Susan Kaysen's *Girl, Interrupted* (Staino). The destruction of books is insulting to anyone who has any respect for literature. In Wisconsin in 2009, a fight between a town library and a group of locals ensued over eighty-two "sexually explicit" books in the young-adult section. When the library refused to move the books in question to the adult section, four disgruntled men filed a suit, asked for financial damages, and called for a novel about a homosexual teenager to be publicly burned because it was "explicitly vulgar, racial and anti-Christian" and it "damaged" their "mental and emotional well-being" (Hanna).

Students at a high school in Florida came close to being denied access to literature that would not only teach them about life in Afghanistan and the impact of war, but also about redemption and forgiveness (Denis). *The Kite Runner,* a highly acclaimed novel by Khaled Hosseini, made the ALA's top ten list of most frequently challenged books of 2008. Their Website explains that the blame was placed on having "offensive language" and being "sexually explicit" and "unsuited to age group." That year, a parent from the Florida school questioned the novel's appropriateness, but the school board voted to keep the book in the curriculum ("Board Rejects" 2). A sophomore from the school said of the book, "This is . . . the real word. This is what goes on in other countries and it really opens your eyes . . ." (Denis).

Response to opposition

Acknowledges other sources of censorship liberals

Use of authority

Specific evidence

Quotes authority

Claim with evidence

Specific evidence

O'Neill 5

Appallingly, students' writing is subject to censorship as well. Jill Rosen explains in her article "High School Confidential" that:

> Yanked newspaper stories, disappointed student journalists and resolute administrators are an unfortunately common part of the high-school experience. Censorship occurs so consistently, so ubiquitously that it's almost clichéd, no more eyebrow-raising than the cafeteria serving mystery meat or a nerd getting books smacked out of his arms in the hallway. (498)

Rosen claims that school administrators can do this because of the Supreme Court's 1988 decision in *Hazelwood School District vs. Kuhlmeier*. Before that case, "papers operated under the premise that a student's right to free speech should only be limited in cases where it could disrupt school or invade the rights of others" (498).

Barnhisel states that censorship is an especially complicated issue in a country as diverse as the United States: "For every George W. Bush fighting for 'family values'. . . there is a Madonna . . . seeking to expand the bounds of what's permissible." He says that standards are "handled by thousands of different people and groups with thousands of different agendas and values and hundreds of ways of enforcing their desires" (471).

If we ban everything that might offend anyone, what is left to write? Books that discuss diversity, our bodies, and the struggles of minorities expose children to life's truths. Senseless and gratuitous violence is woven into television shows, video games, and movies to enhance their popularity, but literature chosen by educators with the intention of making students think is at the center of a crossfire.

Censorship denies reality and creates false worlds in which certain words or actions do not exist. U.S. Supreme Court Justice Louis D. Brandeis put it perfectly that "Fear of serious injury alone cannot justify oppression of free speech. . . . Men feared witches and burnt women. It is the function of speech to free men from the bondage of irrational fears" ("Schools and Censorship").

Should parents be concerned about what their children are reading? Of course. The issue is not about parental supervision; it is about efforts to censor reading material to advance a narrow and not necessarily shared agenda. If unchecked, we could find ourselves in a time when it's acceptable for books, like "witches," to be burned.

Marginal annotations:

Long quotation (more than four lines): left margin indented 1" (10 spaces double-space)

Cites authority to support claim

Cites authority to support claim

Cites evidence to support claim

O'Neill 7

Works Cited

ALA.org. American Library Association, 2009. Web. 5 Oct. 2013.

Barnhisel, Greg, ed. *Media and Messages: Strategies and Readings in Public Rhetoric.* New York: Longman, 2005. Print.

"Board Rejects Book Ban." *Brechner Report* 33.4 (2009): 2. Web. 14 Oct. 2013.

"Book Is Banned by Clawson School District." *WXYZ.com.* Scripps TV Station Group, 18 Dec. 2008. Web. 10 Oct. 2013.

Buehrer, Eric. "Challenging a Book in Your School." *Gtbe.org.* Gateways to a Better Education, 1998. Web. 5 Oct. 2013.

Denis, Alex. "Parent's Complaint May Get Novel Banned in Schools." *WJHG.com.* Gray Television, 17 Nov. 2008. Web. 8 Oct. 2013.

Hanna, Jason. "Library Fight Riles Up City, Leads to Book-Burning Demand." CNN.com. Cable News Network, 22 July 2009. Web. 8 Oct. 2013.

Ockerbloom, John Mark, ed. "Banned Books Online." *The Online Books Page.* U Pennsylvania, 2009. Web. 10 Oct. 2013.

"Our Mission." *Gtbe.org.* Gateways to a Better Education, 2006. Web. 6 Oct. 2013.

Ravitch, Diane. "Cut on the Bias." Barnhisel. 428–429.

Rosen, Jill. "High School Confidential." Barnhisel. 496–503.

Rutten, Tim. "It's All Hillary and Harry." *Los Angeles Times.* Los Angeles Times, 18 June 2003. Web. 6 Oct. 2013.

"Schools and Censorship: Banned Books." *Pfaw.org.* People for the American Way, n.d. Web. 11 Oct. 2013.

Smith, Kathy A. "Harry Potter: Seduction into the Dark World of the Occult, Part One." *Surf-in-the-Spirit.* Fill the Void Ministries, 2000. Web. 6 Oct. 2013.

Staino, Rocco. "NY High School Interrupts 'Girl, Interrupted.'" *School Library Journal.* Reed Business Information, 12 Dec. 2008. Web. 8 Oct. 2013.

Twain, Mark. *Adventures of Huckleberry Finn.* Ed. Susan K. Harris. Boston: Houghton Mifflin, 2000. Print.

Vinciguerra, Thomas. "A 1977 Novel Comes under Scrutiny." *New York Times* 8 June 1997, LI ed., sec. 1:3:8. Print.

List is alphabetical by author's last name. Use title if no author. Double-space throughout

Title of books, journals, and newspapers are italicized

Websites are constantly updated. Include date of access.

Website with individual author

1/2"

Running head: TAPPED OUT   1

Tapped Out: Bottled Water's Detrimental Side
Dan Hoskins
Roger Williams University
Professor Goodfellow
ENG 102
November 20, 2013

Abbreviated
title and
number appear
on each page,
including the
title page.

If your
instructor
requires an
abstract of your
paper, locate it
on the second
page of your
paper.

Tapped Out: Bottled Water's Detrimental Side

Less than a generation ago, getting a drink of water was as simple as turning on the kitchen faucet. Over the last two decades, however, bottled water has emerged as a healthier and environmentally friendly alternative. Whether this perception is accurate is a matter currently being scrutinized. But it can be argued that bottled water is not, in fact, more pure than tap water. Furthermore, the disposal of the bottles poses a threat to the environment. Therefore steps should be taken to discourage the use of bottled water.

The rise in the use of bottled water can be attributed to a national health movement that began in the late 1970s. The bottled water conglomerate Nestle Waters claims on its Website that bottled water products emerged in the late 1970s as "the refreshing alternative to sugary drinks" (Nestle-Waters NA, 2009).

Federal and state legislation passed in the late 1970s and 1980s to ensure the purity of public water sources reflected a growing sense that tap water was polluted and unsafe. In *H20: The Guide to Quality Bottled Water,* Arthur von Wiesenberger (1988) cites acts such as the Resource Conservation and Recovery Act of 1976 and California's Safe Drinking Water and Toxic Enforcement Act of 1986 as significant initiatives aimed at cleaning up public water supplies. While these acts did contribute to the protection of public water, Wiesenberger claims that they also created the impression that tap water was inherently unsafe, thus paving the way for bottled water as a healthy alternative.

Since the passage of such legislation, bottled water consumption has risen. According to *The Washington Post,* bottled water has replaced juice as America's third most popular drink of choice behind soda and milk (Mui, 2009). Now a staple of the American household, bottled water has over the last 20 years become a multibillion dollar industry, as shown in Figure 1 (Fiberwater, 2009).

This industry has grown primarily on the idea that bottled water is safer and healthier than tap water. The difference in price between bottled water and tap water implies a gap in quality: if it cost more, it must be better, right? Generally, bottled water sells for about one to four dollars per gallon. By comparison, tap water costs 0.003 dollars per gallon (San Francisco Public Utility Commission, 2004). Also suggestive of superiority are marketing images of refreshing streams or picturesque mountain ranges, promoting images of natural wholesomeness and environmental friendliness. In spite of such images, bottled water companies stretch the truth.

Double-space between title and first line and throughout paper.

States proposal

1" margins

Quotes authority

Author is not cited in text, so name and date appear in parentheses

Cites supporting evidence with price comparison

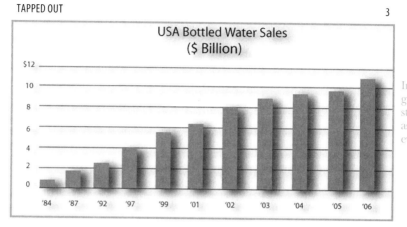

Figure 1. Bottled water: The brightest star in the beverage universe. Adapted from Fiberwater.com (2009, October 25).

Governmental agencies regulate both tap and bottled water. The Environmental Protection Agency (EPA) (as well as state and local governments) controls tap water consumption, while the Food and Drug Administration (FDA) handles the safety of bottled water. But it is clear that the EPA, which controls tap water, is a stronger regulatory body than the FDA, which, unfortunately, is limited to inspecting only products that are sold over state borders. Since bottled water conglomerates have distilleries in different states, many a bottled water can slip through the cracks of inspection. Tap water, on the other hand, has no such luxury and thus is held to higher standards than bottled water (San Francisco Public Utility Commission, 2004).

Obviously, a difference in inspectors does not necessarily mean that bottled water is contaminated. However, the Website *Food and Water Watch* (2009) cites a Natural Resources Defense Council investigation of bottled waters that found many to contain bacteria not allowed under the safety guidelines of most United States legislatures. The article, "Bottled Water: Illusions of Purity," states that the investigation tested "more than 1,000 bottles of water of 103 brands" to find that "nearly one in five brands contained, in at least one sample, more bacteria than allowed under microbiological-purity guidelines adopted by some states, the industry, and the European Union" (Food and Water Watch, 2009).

In case contaminants in the water are not bad enough, there's the second part of the *bottled* water equation: the bottle. Bottle plastics often contain harmful chemicals, such as

Includes graph of statistical data as supporting evidence

Use of authority as support

Use of authority as support

TAPPED OUT   4

phthalates, that can contaminate the contents. According to "Bottled Water: Illusions of Purity,"
when heated, "Phthalates can cause reproductive difficulties, liver problems and increased risk of
cancer" (Food and Water Watch, 2009).

        Another false charge is that tap water contains dangerous levels of lead. Most often cited
as the source is the piping through which the water travels. However, frequent EPA field testing
shows that the lead content in tap water is not potentially harmful. Bottled water, on the other
hand, it has been shown, can carry harmful compounds such as phthalate in both its water and the
bottle carrying it.

        Even more damaging than bottled water's effects on the human body are the cumulative
effects on the environment by the production and disposal of billions of water bottles. In "Message in a
Bottle: What a Waste," M. F. Epstein notes the large number of discarded water bottles littering Boston's
Charles River. He writes that while picking up trash along the river, "the 112 bottles that I picked up
are a minute portion of the 3 billion plastic bottles of water that Americans buy and discard annually"
(Epstein, 2009).

        If this one section of Boston can have such an epidemic of bottle littering, one can only imagine
the impact on a global scale. While bottled water does use recyclable plastic, the San Francisco Public
Utility Commission points out that "not all of the containers are recycled and a portion inevitably end up
in the land fill" (2004).

        The improper disposal of bottles is one detrimental effect on the environment. Another
is the bottle's actual production. While the plastic used is of high quality and can be recycled, an
article on the Website lighterfootsteps.com, "Five Reasons Not to Drink Bottled Water," claims that
the 1.5 million tons of plastic used for bottled water each year "requires up to 47 million gallons of
oil per year to produce" (Baskind, 2008). Many brands, such as Fiji, claim their water comes from an
exotic location where the water is natural and untouched by human hands. While this claim may be a
promotional gimmick, the actual transport of bottled water over thousands of miles from those exotic
locations, if a reality, is detrimental in itself. A great deal of carbon dioxide and other greenhouse
gasses are released in the process.

        A number of solutions exist for stopping the rising tide of bottled water and its impact on our
health and the environment. The simplest and most obvious, of course, is to stop buying bottled water.
On an individual level, we each can make a difference by refraining from purchasing the product and by
helping to recycle and pick up discarded bottles when we see them.

Use of authority
as support

Presents other
position

Refutes other
position

Cites supporting
evidence with
statistics

Reasons
supporting
proposal

Reusable aluminum containers, which allow for portable water without the threat of waste, can be purchased at most retailers. If consumers still feel threatened by the rumors surrounding tap water, these aluminum containers can be refilled with water from a household filter. Currently, there are many different types of filters on the market, some of which can be attached to a sink faucet. Aluminum containers and household filters create the same benefits of bottled water—portability and pureness—without the littering.

Of course, this personal boycott may only have minor results. But there are larger solutions that can stop bottled water use on a national level. Many Websites and environmental advocates suggest federal legislation aimed at limiting the sale of bottled water. Short of a national ban, which is highly improbable, the only governmental option to discourage consumption is to legislate a sales tax on bottles.

But how do we address the other problems posed by bottled water—the litter of plastic bottles and carbon emissions? To accomplish these, something larger than expanded FDA regulations would be needed. In conjunction with a sales tax on bottled water there should be a national campaign against bottled water similar to campaigns against tobacco use.

Since a number of Websites, books, and newspaper articles are already discrediting America's dependency on bottled water, this process may have already begun informally. Furthermore, there is at least one film, *Tapped,* that speaks out against the use of bottled water. Some Websites have propagated a "No Bottled Water Pledge" with signers pledging themselves to end the use of bottled water.

Is there hope for significant change? Is a campaign against bottled water enough to make Americans forgo the convenience and overcome the notion that tap water is unhealthy? Recent reports suggest there is. While an article in *The Washington Post* suggests decreased sales of bottled water is a result of the current economic recession, other articles note this trend is caused by a backlash against bottled water itself. Robinson-Jacobs (2008) suggests that one of the reasons bottled water sales are suffering is because "Environmentalists are making inroads in their efforts to get consumers back to the tap."

Bottled water sales originally grew out of fears about tap water and an inclination to become healthier. If these motivations to become healthier drove Americans away from the tap, they can certainly drive them back there. Most Americans who drink bottled water are unaware of the negative consequences. But as this message is distributed, bottled water sales are more than likely going to decrease. As such, it is important to do our part by spreading the word that bottled water is not good for our health or our environment.

Proposes solution to problem

Acknowledges weakness of proposal

Implementation of proposal

Cites other solutions to problem

Cites authorities

Cites solution to problem

TAPPED OUT   6

Cites solution
to problem

     One Website, fakeplasticfish.com, goes so far to suggest that readers write to President Obama asking him to set an example as our nation's leader and stop his consumption of bottled water. The Website has even dug up some rather unglamorous shots of him drinking bottled water at a press conference (Terry, 2009). An Obama-supported boycott on bottled water could be quite effective in diminishing bottled water sales.

Conclusion

     However, whether you are the president of the United States or just a lowly undergraduate student like myself, you too can aid in the fight against bottled water. Remember that tap water, while dirt cheap, is not necessarily dirty. Keeping these ideas in mind, small steps can be taken to help protect our health.

TAPPED OUT   7

References

Begin first line
of each citation
at left margin.

Indent all
subsequent
lines five spaces
from left
margin.

Capitalize the
first letter of
titles and
subtitles.

Baskind, C. (2008, May 11). Five reasons not to drink bottled water. Lighter
     Footsteps. Retrieved from http://lighterfootstep.com/2008/05/
     five-reasons-not-to-drink-bottled-water/

Robinson-Jacobs, K. (2008, October 31). Bottled water sales growth slow to trickle. *Dallas*
     Morning News. Retrieved from http://www.dallasnews.com/

Epstein, M. F. (2009, October 7). Message in a bottle: What a waste. *The Boston Globe.*
     Retrieved from http://www.boston.com

Fiberwater. (2009, October 25). Bottled water: The brightest star in the beverage universe.
     Retrieved from http://www.fiberwater.com/industry_bwi.php

Food and Water Watch. (2009, October 24). Bottled water: Illusions of purity.
     Retrieved from http://www.foodandwaterwatch.org/water/bottled/
     bottled-water-illusions-of-purity

TAPPED OUT   8

Mui, Y. Q. (2009, August 13). Bottled water boom appears tapped out. *Washington Post*.
      Retrieved from http://www.washingtonpost.com

Nestle-Waters NA. (2009, October 25). *History of bottled water*. Retrieved from http://
      www.nestle-watersna.com/popup.aspx?w=600&h=400&f=/NR/rdonlyres/
      E40D0A10-2D3F-415A-A8E4-7503B9DBBF27/693/timeline.swf

San Francisco Public Utility Commission. (2004, April). Bottled water vs. tap water: Making a
      healthy choice. Retrieved from http://www.dph.sf.ca.us/phes/water/FactSheets/
      bottled_water.pdf

Terry, B. (2009, July 9). Bottled water problem: It's not just the bottle. *Fake
      Plastic Fish*. Retrieved from http://fakeplasticfish.com/2009/07/
      bottled-water-problem-its-not-just/

Wiesenberger, A. von. (1988). *H20: The guide to quality bottled water*. Santa Barbara, CA:
      Woodbridge Press.

PART TWO

Thematic Readings

Advertising and Consumerism

The clock radio wakes us, blaring advertisements for vitamins, banks, and automobiles. Our coffee cups announce the brand we drink, and the logos on our clothing reveal the psychology of our fashion choices. As we wait for the bus or drive our cars, billboards display lounging vacationers in exotic locations. As we read a magazine, clothing ads tell us what we should wear, cigarette ads depict a life of clean refreshment, and alcohol ads warn us to drink their product responsibly. We open the newspaper and shuffle through pages of department store advertisements. And as we sit down at our desks to work, the Internet browser flashes a banner for a camcorder, and it's not even 9:00 a.m.!

Every single day of our lives, we are bombarded with advertising images and messages. Advertising is so pervasive that few of us really notice it or consider its enormous influence on our lives. This chapter examines the many different ways advertising weaves its web of influence—how it hooks consumers, how it creates feelings of need, and how it manipulates us through words and symbols, convincing us to buy.

While most of us know advertising is everywhere, we may not be aware of how marketers target us. Hours of market research on the demographic structure, geographic area, age, gender, and cultural background of a consumer group are devoted to each and every product before it hits the shelf. Marketers really get to know us, and what they know may surprise us. The language marketers use to appeal to consumers focuses on images and fantasies. Advertisers often twist words that carry no true meanings yet still convince us that their product is better or more desirable. And they use images to manipulate our most basic instincts to get us to believe that we need their product.

Advertising is effective because it taps into our psychology. With so many products and services offering similar products, advertisers have a limited amount of time to convince us that their product is not only better, but also that we truly need it to be happy. Consumer psychology addresses why we want what we want. The essays in this chapter encourage us to take a closer look at our consumer habits and the cultural and social forces that drive our desire to acquire more things.

The Daily You

Joseph Turow

Advertisers do not target their campaigns to universal audiences. Rather, they target specific audiences to market specific products. Communications professor Joseph Turow explains how the Internet is being leveraged against the consumer by providing online experiences that presume to target the user but instead severely limit choices, while collecting more data in the guise of "tailoring" the online experience. Now not just ads but also news and entertainment are being customized by newly powerful media agencies on the basis of data we don't know they have collected and compiled into profiles of who we are and what we want to see. Are you, for example, a "socially liberal organic eater," "a diabetic individual in the household," or "single city struggler"? And, if so, how does that affect what you see and do online?*

BEFORE YOU READ

The following essay discusses how marketers use target marketing, based on demographic profiling, to sell specific products to particular groups of people. How would you describe the consumer target group to which you belong? What values define your group, and why?

AS YOU READ

How can exploiting information about where we live help advertisers market their products? Is there anything unethical about this approach?

1   At the start of the twenty-first century, the advertising industry is guiding one of history's most massive stealth efforts in social profiling. At this point you may hardly notice the results of this trend. You may find you're getting better or worse discounts on products than your friends. You may notice that some ads seem to follow you around the internet. Every once in a while a Website may ask you if you like a particular ad you just received. Or perhaps your cell phone has told you that you will be rewarded if you eat in a nearby restaurant where, by the way, two of your friends are hanging out this very minute.

2   You may actually like some of these intrusions. You may feel that they pale before the digital power you now have. After all, your ability to create blogs, collaborate with others to distribute videos online, and say what you want on Facebook (carefully using its privacy settings) seems only to confirm what marketers and even many academics are telling us: that consumers are captains of their own new media ships.

3   But look beneath the surface, and a different picture emerges. We're at the start of a revolution in the ways marketers and media intrude in—and shape—our lives. Every day

---

*Joseph Turow, *The Daily You* (excerpt), January 10, 2012.

most if not all Americans who use the internet, along with hundreds of millions of other users from all over the planet, are being quietly peeked at, poked, analyzed, and tagged as they move through the online world. Governments undoubtedly conduct a good deal of snooping, more in some parts of the world than in others. But in North America, Europe, and many other places companies that work for marketers have taken the lead in secretly slicing and dicing the actions and backgrounds of huge populations on a virtually minute-by-minute basis. Their goal is to find out how to activate individuals' buying impulses so they can sell us stuff more efficiently than ever before. But their work has broader social and cultural consequences as well. It is destroying traditional publishing ethics by forcing media outlets to adapt their editorial content to advertisers' public-relations needs and slice-and-dice demands. And it is performing a highly controversial form of social profiling and discrimination by customizing our media content on the basis of marketing reputations we don't even know we have.

4   Consider a fictional middle class family of two parents with three children who eat out a lot in fast-food restaurants. After a while the parents receive a continual flow of fast-food restaurant coupons. Data suggest the parents, let's call them Larry and Rhonda, will consistently spend far more than the coupons' value. Additional statistical evaluations of parents' activities and discussions online and off may suggest that Larry and Rhonda and their children tend toward being overweight. The data, in turn, result in a small torrent of messages by marketers and publishers seeking to exploit these weight issues to increase attention or sales. Videos about dealing with overweight children, produced by a new type of company called content farms, begin to show up on parenting Websites Rhonda frequents. When Larry goes online, he routinely receives articles about how fitness chains emphasize weight loss around the holidays. Ads for fitness firms and diet pills typically show up on the pages with those articles. One of Larry and Rhonda's sons, who is fifteen years old, is happy to find a text message on his phone that invites him to use a discount at an ice cream chain not too far from his house. One of their daughters, by contrast, is mortified when she receives texts inviting her to a diet program and an ad on her Facebook page inviting her to a clothing store for hip, oversized women. What's more, people keep sending her Twitter messages about weight loss. In the meantime, both Larry and Rhonda are getting ads from check-cashing services and payday-loan companies. And Larry notices sourly on auto sites he visits that the main articles on the home page and the ads throughout feature entry-level and used models. His bitterness only becomes more acute when he describes to his boss the down-market Web he has been seeing lately. Quite surprised, she tells him she has been to the same auto sites recently and has just the opposite impression: many of the articles are about the latest German cars, and one home-page ad even offered her a gift for test-driving one at a dealer near her home.

5   This scenario of individual and household profiling and media customization is quite possible today. Websites, advertisers, and a panoply of other companies are continuously assessing the activities, intentions, and backgrounds of virtually everyone online; even our social relationships and comments are being carefully and continuously analyzed. In broader and broader ways, computer-generated conclusions about who we are affect the media content—the streams of commercial messages, discount offers, information, news, and entertainment—each of us confronts. Over the next few decades the business logic

that drives these tailored activities will transform the ways we see ourselves, those around us, and the world at large. Governments too may be able to use marketers' technology and data to influence what we see and hear.

6   From this vantage point, the rhetoric of consumer power begins to lose credibility. In its place is a rhetoric of esoteric technological and statistical knowledge that supports the practice of social discrimination through profiling. We may note its outcomes only once in a while, and we may shrug when we do because it seems trivial—just a few ads, after all. But unless we try to understand how this profiling or reputation-making process works and what it means for the long term, our children and grandchildren will bear the full brunt of its prejudicial force.

7   The best way to enter this new world is to focus on its central driving force: the advertising industry's media-buying system. Media buying involves planning and purchasing space or time for advertising on outlets as diverse as billboards, radio, Websites, mobile phones, and newspapers. For decades, media buying was a backwater, a service wing of advertising agencies that was known for having the lowest-paying jobs on Madison Avenue and for filling those jobs with female liberal arts majors fresh out of college. But that has all changed. The past twenty years have seen the rise of "media agencies" that are no longer part of ad agencies, though they may both be owned by the same parent company. Along with a wide array of satellite companies that feed them technology and data, media agencies have become magnets for well-remunerated software engineers and financial statisticians of both sexes.

8   In the United States alone, media-buying agencies wield more than $170 billion of their clients' campaign funds; they use these funds to purchase space and time on media they think will advance their clients' marketing aims. But in the process they are doing much more. With the money as leverage, they are guiding the media system toward nothing less than new ways of thinking about and evaluating audience members and defining what counts as a successful attempt to reach them. Traditionally, marketers have used media such as newspapers, magazines, radio, billboards, and television to reach out to segments of the population through commercial messages. These advertisers typically learned about audience segments from survey companies that polled representative portions of the population via a variety of methods, including panel research. A less prestigious direct-marketing business has involved contacting individuals by mail or phone. Firms have rented lists of public data or purchase information that suggests who might be likely customers.

9   The emerging new world is dramatically different. The distinction between reaching out to audiences via mass media and by direct-response methods is disappearing. Advertisers in the digital space expect all media firms to deliver to them particular types of individuals—and, increasingly, particular individuals—by leveraging a detailed knowledge about them and their behaviors that was unheard of even a few years ago. The new advertising strategy involves drawing as specific a picture as possible of a person based in large part on measurable physical acts such as clicks, swipes, mouseovers, and even voice commands. The strategy uses new digital tracking tools like cookies and beacons as well as new organizations with names like BlueKai, Rapleaf, Invidi, and eXelate. These companies track people on Websites and across Websites in an effort to learn what they do, what they care about, and who their friends are. Firms that exchange the information often

do ensure that the targets' names and postal addresses remain anonymous—but not before they add specific demographic data and lifestyle information. For example:

10 ■ Rapleaf is a firm that claims on its Website to help marketers "customize your customers' experience." To do that, it gleans data from individual users of blogs, internet forums, and social networks. It uses ad exchanges to sell the ability to reach those people. Rapleaf says it has "data on 900+ million records, 400+ million consumers, [and] 52+ billion friend connections." Advertisers are particularly aware of the firm's ability to predict the reliability of individuals (for example, the likelihood they will pay their mortgage) based on Rapleaf's research on the trustworthiness of the people in those individuals' social networks.

11 ■ A company called Next Jump runs employee discount and reward programs for about one-third of U.S. corporate employees. It gets personal information about all of them from the human relations departments of the companies and supplements that information with transactional data from the manufacturers it deals with as well as from credit companies. Armed with this combination of information, Next Jump can predict what people want and what they will pay for. It also generates a "UserRank" score for every employee based on how many purchases a person has made and how much he or she has spent. That score plays an important role in determining which employee gets what product e-mail offers and at what price.

12 ■ A firm called The Daily Me already sells an ad and news personalization technology to online periodicals. If a *Boston Globe* reader who reads a lot of soccer sports news visits a *Dallas Morning News* site, the Daily Me's technology tells the *Dallas Morning News* to serve him soccer stories. Moreover, when an ad is served along with the story, its text and photos are instantly configured so as to include soccer terms and photos as part of the advertising pitch. A basketball fan receiving an ad for the same product will get language and photos that call out to people with hoop interests.

13 These specific operations may not be in business a few years from now. In the new media-buying environment companies come and go amid furious competition. The logic propelling them and more established firms forward, though, is consistent: the future belongs to marketers and media firms—publishers, in current terminology—that learn how to find and keep the most valuable customers by surrounding them with the most persuasive media materials. Special online advertising exchanges, owned by Google, Yahoo!, Microsoft, Interpublic, and other major players, allow publishers to auction and media agencies to "buy" individuals with particular characteristics, often in real time. That is, it is now possible to buy the right to deliver an ad to a person with specific characteristics at the precise moment that that person loads a Web page. In fact, through an activity called cookie matching, which I discuss in detail later, an advertiser can actually bid for the right to reach an individual whom the advertiser knows from previous contacts and is now tracking around the Web. Moreover, the technology keeps changing. Because consumers delete Web cookies and marketers find cookies difficult to use with mobile devices, technology companies have developed methods to "fingerprint" devices permanently and allow for persistent personalization across many media platforms.

14   The significance of tailored commercial messages and offers goes far beyond whether or not the targeted persons buy the products. Advertisements and discounts are status signals: they alert people as to their social position. If you consistently get ads for low-priced cars, regional vacations, fast-food restaurants, and other products that reflect a lower-class status, your sense of the world's opportunities may be narrower than that of someone who is feted with ads for national or international trips and luxury products. Moreover, if like Larry and Rhonda you happen to know that your colleague is receiving more ads for the luxury products than you are, and more and better discounts to boot, you may worry that you are falling behind in society's estimation of your worth.

15   In fact, the ads may signal your opportunities actually are narrowed if marketers and publishers decide that the data points—profiles—about you across the internet position you in a segment of the population that is relatively less desirable to marketers because of income, age, past-purchase behavior, geographical location, or other reasons. Turning individual profiles into individual evaluations is what happens when a profile becomes a reputation. Today individual marketers still make most of the decisions about which particular persons matter to them, and about how much they matter. But that is beginning to change as certain publishers and data providers—Rapleaf and Next Jump, for example— allow their calculations of value to help advertisers make targeting decisions. In the future, these calculations of our marketing value, both broadly and for particular products, may become routine parts of the information exchanged about people throughout the media system.

16   The tailoring of news and entertainment is less advanced, but it is clearly under way. Technologies developed for personalized advertising and coupons point to possibilities for targeting individuals with personalized news and entertainment. Not only is this already happening, the logic of doing that is becoming more urgent to advertisers and publishers. Advertisers operate on the assumption that, on the internet as in traditional media, commercial messages that parade as soft (or "human interest") news and entertainment are more persuasive than straightforward ads. Publishers know this too, and in the heat of a terrible economic downturn even the most traditional ones have begun to compromise long-standing professional norms about the separation of advertising and editorial matter.

17   And in fact many of the new online publishers—companies, such as Demand Media, that turn out thousands of text and video pieces a day—never really bought into the old-world ideas about editorial integrity anyway. What this means is that we are entering a world of intensively customized content, a world in which publishers and even marketers will package personalized advertisements with soft news or entertainment that is tailored to fit both the selling needs of the ads and the reputation of the particular individual.

18   The rise of digital profiling and personalization has spawned a new industrial jargon that reflects potentially grave social divisions and privacy issues. Marketers divide people into targets and waste. They also use words like anonymous and personal in unrecognizable ways that distort and drain them of their traditional meanings. If a company can follow your behavior in the digital environment—an environment that potentially includes your mobile phone and television set—its claim that you are "anonymous" is meaningless. That is particularly true when firms intermittently add off-line information such as shopping patterns and the value of your house to their online data and then simply strip the name and

address to make it "anonymous." It matters little if your name is John Smith, Yesh Mispar, or 3211466. The persistence of information about you will lead firms to act based on what they know, share, and care about you, whether you know it is happening or not.

19   All these developments may sound more than a little unsettling; creeped out is a phrase people often use when they learn about them. National surveys I have conducted over the past decade consistently suggest that although people know companies are using their data and do worry about it, their understanding of exactly how the data are being used is severely lacking. That of course shouldn't be surprising. People today lead busy, even harried, lives. Keeping up with the complex and changing particulars of data mining is simply not something most of us have the time or ability to do. There are many great things about the new media environment. But when companies track people without their knowledge, sell their data without letting them know what they are doing or securing their permission, and then use those data to decide which of those people are targets or waste, we have a serious social problem. The precise implications of this problem are not yet clear. If it's allowed to persist, and people begin to realize how the advertising industry segregates them from and pits them against others in the ads they get, the discounts they receive, the TV-viewing suggestions and news stories they confront, and even the offers they receive in the supermarket, they may begin to suffer the effects of discrimination. They will likely learn to distrust the companies that have put them in this situation, and they may well be incensed at the government that has not helped to prevent it. A comparison to the Financial industry is apt. Here was an industry engaged in a whole spectrum of arcane practices that were not at all transparent to consumers or regulators but that had serious negative impact on our lives. It would be deeply unfortunate if the advertising system followed the same trajectory.

20   Despite valiant efforts on the part of advocacy groups and some federal and state officials, neither government rulings nor industry self-regulation has set policies that will address these issues before they become major sources of widespread social distress. Part of the reason for the lack of action may be that neither citizens nor politicians recognize how deeply embedded in American life these privacy-breaching and social-profiling activities are. Few individuals outside advertising know about the power of the new media-buying system: its capacity to determine not only what media firms do but how we see ourselves and others. They don't know that that system is working to attach marketing labels to us based on the clicks we make, the conversations we have, and the friendships we enjoy on Websites, mobile devices, iPads, supermarket carts, and even television sets. They don't know that the new system is forcing many media firms to sell their souls for ad money while they serve us commercial messages, discounts, and, increasingly, news and entertainment based on our marketing labels. They don't realize that the wide sharing of data suggests that in the future marketers and media firms may find it useful to place us into personalized "reputation silos" that surround us with worldviews and rewards based on labels marketers have created reflecting our value to them. Without this knowledge, it is hard to even begin to have broad-based serious discussions about what society and industry should do about this sobering new world: into the twenty-first century the media-buying system's strategy of social discrimination will increasingly define how we as individuals relate to society—not only how much we pay but what we see and when and how we see it.

1. What are the broader cultural and social consequences of social profiled marketing tactics? How can they harm consumers?

2. Turow posits that in a few decades, the business logic used by online data mining will "transform the way we see ourselves, those around us, and the world at large." How can the ads you see every day influence the way you view yourself and the people around you? Explain.

3. Turow uses the example of a typical American family that uses the Internet. How does this example help support the points he raises in his essay? Is it an effective way to explain to his audience what data mining could do/is doing? Explain.

4. How does packaging individuals or groups of people make them "useful targets" for advertisers? Can you think of examples of how advertisers package people or groups of people?

5. Evaluate Turow's tone in this essay. What phrases or words reveal his tone? Who is his audience? How does this tone connect to his intended audience?

6. Turow notes that data mining should "creep out" people who think that they are in control of technology, or even know about it, but think it won't have an impact on them. Why does he feel this way? Are you creeped out? Why or why not?

7. Turow once commented that "new approaches to marketing make it increasingly worthwhile for . . . media companies to separate audiences into different worlds according to distinctions that ad people feel make the audiences feel secure and comfortable." What types of ads appeal to you and why? Do you feel that online advertisements that actively target you as part of a particular segment of society work more effectively on you as a consumer? Explain your perspective in a well-considered essay. Cite specific ads in your response to support your view.

It's All in the Details

Jennifer Baumgartner

Many of us deliberately purchase brand-name products emblazoned with logos because we feel that we are buying both quality and image. On some level, we either identify with the brand, or wish to identify ourselves with others who we know also wear that brand. Brand-name products target groups of consumers—Pepsi and Levi's appeal to large, diverse populations, while Fendi or Gucci appeal to very elite ones. Brands depend on image—the image the brand promotes and the image the consumer believes will be projected by the product. For many people, brands can announce membership in a particular group, value systems, personality, and personal style. In this next essay, psychologist Jennifer Baumgartner explains that logos are just price tags on clothes, and when we wear them, we serve as human billboards, branding ourselves.*

BEFORE YOU READ

Do you have particular brands to which you are most loyal? What cultural and social influences, if any, contribute to your desire for a particular brand?

AS YOU READ

What can a brand tell you about the person who uses it? Do brands "define" people? How do brands "identify" people as members of a particular group, social level, or lifestyle?

1   In fashion, who you are wearing is an opportunity to advertise who you are. Articles of clothing—shirts, scarfs, dresses—are neutral stimuli; they have no inherent capacity to generate a response from us. We learn to associate meaning with these items through classical conditioning. What brand advertisers do is pair neutral stimuli with provocative images that do elicit a response. Eventually, we respond to brands even in the absence of the original stimulus.

2   For example, imagine walking into an Abercrombie store and staring into the eyes of a hot naked man on a horse. This stimulus elicits an emotional response . . . oh, I don't know . . . let's say *lust*! Eventually, you associate Abercrombie clothing with sexiness. Eventually you don't even need pictures of naked models in compromising positions to equate Abercrombie with sexiness—just seeing the label or the name is enough. Abercrombie hopes that you will want to feel sexy and will want others to associate you with sexiness, and so will buy its clothing.

3   Designers and advertisers depend on and profit from our emotional experiences with our clothing and our desire to elicit the same emotional experiences from others. When you buy designer clothing, you are no longer buying mere pieces of fabric—you are buying everything associated with the brand. You are buying into the "feel" of the brand experience. And in turn, you are buying the opportunity to convey that this brand represents a part of you.

4   So how is the "feel" created? Advertisements, whether in the glossy pages of *Town and Country* or flashing onto our plasma screens, feature the brand, not the product, as the central part of the experience. If advertisers have done their job, we feel something after viewing these ads: aroused, relaxed, joyful, invigorated.

5   Another technique is to use a representative for the brand, which can be a person, place or thing. A movie star, dripping with pearls and sequins, at the Eiffel Tower. A polo field in Spain dotted with thoroughbreds and sun hats. A white Rolls-Royce with cashmere blankets and caramel suede driving gloves on monogramed leather seats. The psychology of social influence tells us that it is members of our *reference group*—which often

---

*Jennifer Baumgartner, *You Are What You Wear* (excerpt), March 27, 2012.

includes people we admire who are featured in advertisements—who persuade us to buy their belongings.

6 These forms of enticements do not stop with the advertisements, but continue throughout the store. The music, the lights, the flowers, the champagne. What was once a room filled with shelving and racks of clothing has now been converted into a posh dressing salon. These items are used to enhance not only the shopping experience, so that you will stay longer and buy, but the brand identity. These atmospheric and decorative elements—the soundtrack, the level of illumination, the room temperature, and the décor—are not randomly chosen but carefully selected by a highly trained staff. Nothing is left to chance.

7 Even the people working in the stores are simply an extension of the brand. From my retail experience with both high- and low-end stores, I can tell you that every detail—from the greetings I used to answer the phone to the color of my nail polish—was carefully monitored. In one store, I was not allowed to wear black clothing or jewelry of any kind, and I was encouraged to ignore customers unless spoken to. At another store, I was told to always "look busy" on the floor so that customers would believe that merchandise was "going fast." At yet another store, I spent a day learning nothing but how to package a purchase, give the purchase to the customer, and return the method of payment.

8 The store and its employees become part of the selling point, part of the brand. The unspoken words resounding form sales associates are: *If you buy our clothes, this experience can be yours too.*

Tell Me About Yourself

9 We become our own billboards, sometimes literally. From the sublime to the ridiculous, statements on your clothing send clear messages. You think BOYS ARE CUTE, and you support St. Jude's Children's Hospital. You tell the world I VOTED TODAY or I KISS COWBOYS. Perhaps you ran the TURKEY TROT 2000 or play COED NAKED LACROSSE. Everyone who sees you learns that you were the president of the debate club at SQUIRREL TOOTH UNIVERSITY and that while you were there you pledged DELTA DELTA DELTA. These messages are bumper stickers for the body. The world gets a glimpse of your interests, likes, dislikes, causes and activities.

10 Whether the message is from stamped tees or designer names, examining why you have chosen to tell the world about yourself in this way can lead to fruitful self-analysis. Do you wear these items just because you like them? Do you wear them because you're insecure in who you are without them? Do you wear them because you're trying to hide behind them? Do you wear them hoping to spark conversation? Do you wear them to tell the world of your accomplishments?

The Logo

11 Advertisements are certainly not limited to television, magazines and storefronts. You, the customer, become the walking talking billboard for the brand you love when you wear its logo. Have you ever seen the guy dressed in a banana suit dancing along a main road enticing you to come into his store for a closer look? Well, guess what? You are that guy.

12 Logos are incredibly powerful symbols that companies use in order to sell their products and acquire loyal clientele. Whether it is the iconic Burberry plaid or the interlocking

C's of Chanel, logos become the watermark for a certain standard of living as established by the brand. If we wear logos, we are saying that we support the label as well as the lifestyle that goes along with it. Logos are especially effective when used to establish a status hierarchy. The message of these logos is loud and clear: I can afford this brand and the glamorous lifestyle associated with it.

13   Like any trend, the importance of logos changes throughout the fashion cycle. I recall a particularly lean financial year in grad school when logos were *it*. Forced to choose between food and logos, I Carrie Bradshaw-ed it and chose to go hungry. At the end of the year I had so many plaids, symbols, and letters in my wardrobe that I actually had difficulty dressing. If I stared at myself long enough in the mirrored elevator on my way to class, I could see dolphins swimming or fields of flowers in the patterns. I think I was cured of the logo obsession when I realized that cows have brands on their backsides too.

14   The logo obsession has become one of the most prevalent fashion errors of our time. The desire to emulate reality television stars, celebrities, and socialites begins with wardrobe, specifically the logo-laden items. Although this desire seems externally based, the message you wear tells everyone who sees you so much more than you like Goyard.

15   From the comfort of our family rooms, we watch the famous, fabulous, and foolish wear beautiful designers clothes that we covet. Whether we looking at the latest reality star or the newest nominee on the red carpet, we catch a bit of reflected glamour even as we sit in front of our TVs in our bathrooms or curled up in our beds. But watching beautiful people wearing beautiful things in such an accessible way plays tricks on the brain. The more we see television and film stars and celebrities, the more we believe that we can have what they have—or at least, that we ourselves should have what they have. Even though our bank accounts and lifestyles don't match the designer outfits, we buy them anyway. The old if-she-can-have-it-so-should-I trick.

16   When you use a brand to make up for what you think you lack, your logo obsession has deeper roots. Using brands this way never works. You experience the initial high of your latest acquisition, but then comes the financial low. And unfortunately, your disappointment does not end with your wallet. You're in for an emotional low as well. In our efforts to shore ourselves up internally by building ourselves up externally, we ultimately let ourselves down and disappointment sets in.

17   All of us have gotten caught up in the "right" brand, the "right" color, the "right" style that will contribute to our image. In addition to putting a hole in our pocket, choices made according to this criterion may lead us to buy things we don't really want. Having nice things is, well, nice. But seeking out nice things to make you better has the opposite effect. If you know who you are, the latest Birkin bag or Gucci dress won't become a measure of your worth. If you know who you are, then you can sit among people clad in designer duds while wearing a Target top, Old Navy shorts, and Walmart shoes and still feel totally comfortable.

QUESTIONS FOR ANALYSIS AND DISCUSSION

1. How does Baumgartner support her argument? Evaluate her use of supporting sources. Are there any gaps in her article? If so, identify areas where her essay could be stronger. If not, identify some of the essay's particular strengths.

2. How would you define your personal style and the image you wish to project? What products and/or brands contribute to that image? Explain.

3. Baumgartner notes that when you purchase brand-name products for the status you think they confer, "it never works." You are bound for financial and emotional disappointment. Do you agree? How do you feel when you sport a brand that you admire? Do you find yourself soon regretting the purchase? Why or why not?

4. What does Baumgartner mean when she says she "Carrie Bradshaw-ed" it? Have you ever found yourself in a similar situation? Explain.

5. Are your fashion choices influenced by what you see on television? Explain.

6. Evaluate Baumgartner's conclusion. Do you agree that if you are "comfortable with yourself" brands do not matter? Respond with your own point of view.

Branded World: The Success of the Nike Logo
Michael Levine

You have probably heard the expression "the clothes make the man." The previous essay explored the ways we seek to define ourselves with logos and brands. Consciously or unconsciously, we reveal something about ourselves through our clothing choices. Marketing companies pay big bucks for athletes, screen stars, and musicians to sport their logos on clothing, at events, even on their cars. Why are logos so powerful?

Logos are graphic designs that represent and help market a particular brand or company. Some logos are instantly recognizable, needing no words to explain what they represent. A good example of a logo with international recognition is the image of the Olympic rings. Other logos may be more obscure and specific to particular countries or demographic groups. Chances are most senior citizens wouldn't recognize the Lugz logo or know what product was associated with it. Sometimes a logo can simply be the initial or name of the brand. Chanel is famous for its interlocking C design, and Kate Spade's name serves as her logo. Spade's logo is distinctive because of the font face used to spell her name, which is written in lowercase letters. The next piece, by public relations guru Michael Levine, examines why the brand Nike is such a successful logo.*

BEFORE YOU READ

What makes you want to buy a product? Is it peer influence, cultural pressure, or social status? Do generational marketing techniques influence you?

---

*Michael Levine, *A Branded World: Adventures in Public Relations and the Creation of Superbrands* (excerpt), 2003.

AS YOU READ

Consider the influence of an athlete's endorsement for products: from sports equipment and apparel to soft drinks, watches, and automobiles. What image does the athlete project about the product? How much does the brand's logo factor into the product promotion? Do athletes sell products, or do athletes wearing brand logos sell products? Explain.

1   There are few branding tales as epic and impressive as that of Nike. Before Phil Knight made the swoosh a universally known symbol, a soft shoe you wore to play sports or run in was called a sneaker. There weren't separate sneakers for basketball, running, walking, cross-training, and tennis; there were just sneakers. They were made by companies like Keds and PF Fliers, and they were usually worn by children. Professional athletes wore shoes made for their individual sports, which were either not available to the general public or were not identifiable by brand. A few companies, like Adidas, were making "tennis shoes," which adults wore when they played a sport on the weekends.

2   Now, there are "athletic shoes." They are very specific to their tasks and can be found in stores like Foot Locker and Sports Authority, classified by usage: Cross-trainers are not the same as shoes for walking, which are different from running shoes, which are not to be confused with basketball shoes. And much of that distinction can be attributed to Nike and the awe-inspiring job it has done in defining not only its own brand but the very category of product the brand helped to create.

3   "The way you build a brand is by creating a new category you can be first in," says branding guru Al Ries. "I have yet to hear anybody ever refer to Nike as a sneaker. It's only the older people who used to buy Keds who refer to Nike as a sneaker. There is an enormous difference between an athletic shoe and a sneaker. You can look at the two and say they look alike, they smell alike, they sound alike. I say no: Your typical inner-city kid isn't going to wear Keds and call it a sneaker. They want a Nike; it's a different deal." How did Nike transform the category of sports footwear into the massive $14 billion business it is today? And how did it manage to grab an astounding 45 percent of the market by the year 2000? Was it just such an obviously superior product that the public couldn't help but notice and respond to? Or was the branding of Nike so well considered and crafty that it outshone all the rest of the brands in its category, using every possible branding tactic almost perfectly?

4   Once it was associated with the active, aggressive, powerful brand Nike had assigned itself, the swoosh become an incredibly articulate mark . . .

5   I am inclined to state that the latter was the prevailing condition. Nike took what was, for its category, a revolutionary product (the waffle sole) and transformed what could have been a niche product into something that every kid in the street playing basketball had to have. Beyond that, however, Nike expanded its brand into other market segments, appealing to adults, to women, to nonathletes. And it extended its brand into products other than shoes: apparel, signature hats, shirts, shorts, and many other products that bore the suddenly familiar Nike symbol.

6   "[Nike] figured out a very simple brand visually, and they didn't deviate from it at all. They kept that message very well defined," says Howard Rubenstein, president of

Rubenstein Associates, a New York publicity firm. "If you just glance at [Nike's] logo, you know what the message is."

7   The swoosh, Nike's squiggly symbol, has no intrinsic meaning in our lexicon; before the company developed it, it did not exist as a symbol communicating anything. But once it was associated with the active, aggressive, powerful brand Nike had assigned itself, the swoosh become an incredibly articulate mark, communicating the continued thrust forward of anyone who had the wherewithal to don a piece of apparel that bore the symbol.

8   Still, the swoosh wasn't the only way that Nike differentiated itself from other athletic shoe companies, and it certainly wasn't the main tool in developing that brand's identity. More than anything else, the company was probably best known in its early years for its associations with well-known sports celebrities, who never, ever appeared in public without a swoosh on at least one visible article of clothing.

9   Tiger Woods, Derek Jeter, and especially Michael Jordan were routinely seen wearing the Nike logo, and while they never necessarily said a word in a Nike advertisement, it was clear their endorsement was meant to relay a message to consumers: "Be like (fill in the extremely famous sports celebrity). Wear Nike." The copy might not have read "Just Do It," but the message was loud and clear.

10   "Nike was successful in making that [swoosh] synonymous with performance," says *Variety* publisher Charlie Koones. "Not just the performance of their shoe, but performance on a larger scale." By allying themselves with great athletes, by building a bit of a jock attitude. It's interesting to ask yourself what is the feeling that comes out of your brand promise."

11   The road for Nike has not been entirely bump free, however. Allegations that the company's products were manufactured overseas in sweatshops have dogged the brand, and there have been declines in the athletic shoe market generally in the past few years. But Nike continues on, and even if its brand is a tiny bit diminished, it is still head and shoulders above the rest of the industry.

12   "At one time, I think Nike truly was a genuine brand," says Duane Knapp, author of *The Brand Mindset.* "In others words, they were perceived by the customer as one of a kind. Maybe in some customers' minds, that's true today. They're not perfect. At this point in time, you'd have to ask their customers what's the difference between Nike and Adidas. It really doesn't matter what the executives think; it matters what the customers think. When Phil Knight invented the waffle sole, they were a genuine brand. Now that they've gotten into different things, my feeling is they've probably moved from right to left on that continuum in the customer's mind. They are not a one-of-a-kind brand anymore. That doesn't mean they're a bad brand. But every brand is moving toward being a commodity unless the company does something continually, every single day, and that is where the public relations comes in."

13   Nike's position in the athletic shoe and apparel industry is without peer, but it is true that the brand is not as strong as it once was, partially due to increased competition and partially because nothing could stay that hot. Allegations that the company used overseas sweatshops to assemble $120 athletic shoes didn't help.

14   Through it all, Nike's public relations professionals emphasized that the company was doing its best to improve conditions in its worldwide facilities, and, as it addressed the

problem, it continued to thrive. While the situation is not yet completely resolved, it has not crippled Nike by any stretch of the imagination.

15   Knapp brings up two important points: First, the company has to have a strong sense of its identity from the consumer's point of view. The image company executives have is irrelevant if the consumer sees the product and the brand in a different light. Second, the brand identity and brand integrity must be reinforced in the consumer's mind every day. Not once a week, not whenever there's a sales downturn: every day. If the mission of the company is not to satisfy the customer's expectations and exceed them every time, the brand might never become a true household name, and it certainly won't last for decades like Coca-Cola, Disney, and McDonald's—and even those brands have had major stumbling points.

QUESTIONS FOR ANALYSIS AND DISCUSSION

1. Levine notes that Nike's swoosh logo has no "intrinsic meaning" beyond what it has come to represent: Nike products. Examine the clothing you are wearing and the personal items within 10 feet of you right now. How many items bear a logo? What are they? Do they have any "intrinsic meaning"? Explain.

2. What brands do you tend to purchase and why? Are there particular logos that are associated with the brands you prefer? Explain.

3. Are you more likely to purchase a product with a prominent or prestigious logo than a "no-name" brand? Why or why not?

4. What is your college or university's logo? Is it a shield? A phrase? A mascot? How does the symbol chosen by your school reflect its values and identity? Explain.

5. Levine quotes Duane Knapp on the shifting of the Nike brand, "At one time, I think Nike truly was a genuine brand." Why does Knapp feel that Nike is not a "genuine" brand anymore? What changed? Do you agree with his assessment?

Disturbing Trends in Junk Food Advertising for Children
Laura Gottesdiener

According to the Centers for Disease Control (CDC), obesity in children has tripled since 1980. In 2013, the CDC reported that 17 percent (12.5 million) children were obese in the United States. From 1998 through 2003, the prevalence of extreme obesity increased among low-income children aged 2–4 years, with the greatest average annual increase presenting among 4-year-olds. Once quite rare, young children are increasingly developing adult-type diabetes and other diseases once seen only in their elders. While pediatricians grapple with the issue, fast-food restaurants continue to be more plentiful than supermarkets in urban areas. In the next essay, writer Laura Gottesdiener explores some of the possible reasons America's kids are falling victim to the obesity crisis.*

Have you ever wanted to purchase a food product because of the way it was advertised to you? Were you influenced by commercials or fast-food gimmicks such as the promise of a free toy or gift? Explain.

Who is responsible for addressing the issue of childhood obesity? Parents? Schools? The government? The restraunt industry? Public media? Explain.

1 Ever wonder why one-third of all children in the United States are overweight, if not dangerously obese? According to a slew of recent reports, the cornucopia of junk food advertising to children plays a substantial role in creating this public health crisis. From bribing children with toys and sweepstakes to convincing them to eat a "fourth meal," the industry is glutted with examples of perverse, profit-chasing schemes to capitalize on children's appetites at the expense of their long-term health. Here are seven of the most perverse trends in junk food advertising to children.

1. Bombarded!

2 Junk food marketing to children and adolescents has become billion-dollar industry. According to 2006 data, the most recent numbers available, kids experience at least $1.6 billion worth of food advertising a year—the vast majority of the ads geared toward pushing high-calorie and low-nutrition snacks down kids' throats. According to data [4] compiled by the nonprofit health organization Food & Water Watch, children see nearly 5,000 TV food ads every year, and teenagers get bombarded by almost 6,000 annually.

3   The vast majority of these ads are specifically geared toward children, using tricks like cartoon characters and sweepstakes prizes to make the sugary cereals and fatty hamburgers all the more attractive. As children's online activity has risen, massive corporations like McDonald's have also designed child-focused Websites, complete with video games that teach children brand recognition, that are getting hundreds of thousands of young visitors a month. In the month of February 2011, for example, 350,000 children under the age of 12 visited McDonald's two main Websites, HappyMeal.com and McWorld.com.

---

*Laura Gottesdiener, AlterNet, published in partnership with GlobalPossibilities.org, November 29, 2012.

4   Most disturbingly, the amount of this advertising is steadily increasing. According to a report from Yale University's Rudd Center for Food Policy & Obesity, the advertising increased dramatically in only two years, between 2007 and 2009. Children between the ages of 6 and 11 saw a staggering 56 percent more ads for Subway [5], and 26 percent more ads for McDonald's. African American children were disproportionately targeted by this advertising, seeing 50 percent more advertisements for fast food than white children of the same age.

2. The ads, not the TV, are what's making kids fat

5 While many have complained that sedentary television culture is causing the childhood obesity crisis, new studies suggest that the real culprit may be the constant ads for junk food that children are viewing during commercial break—not the television programs themselves.

6   A 2006 Institute of Medicine government report stated, [4] "It can be concluded that television advertising influences children to prefer and request high-calorie and low-nutrient foods and beverages." Even clearer evidence comes from a long-term study in Quebec, where fast food advertising geared specifically toward children has been banned both online and in-print for the last 32 years. There, researchers discovered that the province has the least childhood obesity of anywhere in Canada, and that the ban decreased children's consumption by an estimated two to four billion calories. [6] In Britain, the president of the Royal College of Pediatrics and Child Health, has also advocated for the state to ban junk food advertisements [7] on television until after 9 pm, when the majority of children are already asleep.

3. Ten extra pounds a year

7 How fat are these television advertisements making kids? According to one recent study, their effects are surprisingly heavy. The experiment compared [4] children's food consumption while watching television programs with food commercials, versus programs that ran straight through without any ads. It concluded that kids consumed almost 50 percent more calories while watching the 30-minute program with commercials—a total of almost 100 calories in only a half an hour. Over the course of a year, that would lead to a 10-pound weight gain.

4. Children clueless while industry cashes in

8 One of the biggest problems with child-specific advertising is that young kids aren't even able to recognize the commercials for what they are: short segments intended to sell them things. As the *Food and Water Watch Report* explains [4], children under the age of four can't even recognize the difference between a television show and the commercials—the line between content and advertising is completely invisible to them. Children between four and eight may understand that advertisements are different from the T.V. program, but they still don't recognize that ads are paid commercials intended to convince them to buy something.

9   However, just because children can't recognize the ads for what they are doesn't mean that these commercials don't affect them. Studies show toddlers are able to accurately identify brand logos and that young children prefer food wrapped in McDonald's packaging.

5. A fourth meal?

10 A study of one child-geared advertising campaign, launched by Taco Bell, demonstrates how perverse this marketing really is. In 2006, Taco Bell launched a campaign to convince children to eat a "Fourth Meal," which is after dinner and before breakfast. (Essentially, the fourth meal is at the time of night when children should be sleeping or doing their homework.)

11   The campaign kicked off [8] with a Website showing children in their pajamas wandering around outside and eating nachos, tacos and other late-night snacks offered by Taco Bell. The foods being marketed often had more than 400 calories, placing them squarely in the meal category. But the goal isn't just to sell more tacos; it's actually to carve out an entire new post-dinner market where the consumer base is young children.

6. Holding schools hostage

12 Increasingly, these types of ads aren't only on television and online; they are also in schools where the child-marketing focus is even more obvious. As budget cuts and austerity measures have swept the nation, schools are increasingly relying on money from vending machine contracts and corporate partnerships. These revenue streams rely on how much food the students buy, meaning that the school earns more money if it stocks these machines with junk food.

7. Industry's idea of self-regulation: Happy meals with apple slices

13 Due to increasing criticism from the public health community and the federal government, the fast food industry undertook the ambitious task of self-regulation in 2006, launching the Children's Food and Beverage Advertising Initiative. Under this initiative, companies pledged to market "better-for-you" foods to children. Here are selections from the menu they came up with:

■ Burger King Kids Meals with "Fresh Apple Slices" and fat-free milk or apple juice
   Assuming the meal is a plain hamburger, the offering has nearly 400 calories
■ McDonald's Happy Meals with fries, apple slices and fat-free chocolate milk
   Assuming the meal is a plain hamburger, the offering has more than 550 calories
■ Kid Cuisine Meals Primo Pepperoni Double Stuffed Pizza *480 calories, with 15 grams of fat*
■ Chef Boyardee Pepperoni Pizza Ravioli *290 calories*

Sometimes the industry's definition of regulation is the best argument for government intervention.

Links:
[1] http://www.alternet.org
[2] http://www.alternet.org/authors/laura-gottesdiener

[3] http://globalpossibilities.org/

[4] http://documents.foodandwaterwatch.org/doc/FoodWaterWatchReportFoodMktgKids
.pdf

[5] http://articles.latimes.com/2010/nov/08/news/la-heb-fast-food-20101108

[6] http://parenting.blogs.nytimes.com/2012/07/13/ban-on-advertising-to-children
-linked-to-lower-obesity-rates/

[7] http://www.telegraph.co.uk/health/children_shealth/9521993/Adverts-for-junk-food
-should-be-banned-before-9pm-says-childrens-doctor.html

[8] http://www.thefix.com/content/marketing-munchies-stoner-foods-taco-bell-rob
-dyrdek7677

QUESTIONS FOR ANALYSIS AND DISCUSSION

1. What tricks do advertisers use to make their products "attractive" to children? Cite some examples from your own experience.

2. Gottesdiener states that "ads, not the TV, are what's making kids fat." How can ads make children fat? How do they influence kids and the choices they make?

3. Why are children particularly vulnerable to advertising? Explain.

4. Gottesdiener explains that the fast-food chain Taco Bell is now encouraging a "fourth meal"—a meal eaten after dinner, but before bedtime. What is your own opinion of this trend? Do many people already eat a fourth meal? Explain.

5. Gottesdiener ends her piece with the statement, "Sometimes the industry's definition of regulation, is the best argument for government intervention." What does she mean? Is government regulation necessary to address the issue? Why or why not?

Reading the Visual

Bump

Adbusters magazine is a nonprofit, reader-supported, 120,000-circulation journal that provides critical commentary on consumer culture and corporate marketing agendas. Articles and issues from the magazine have been featured on MTV and PBS, *The Wall Street Journal, Wired,* and in hundreds of other newspapers, magazines, and television and radio shows around the world. Articles in *Adbusters* are "dedicated to examining the relationship between human beings and their physical and mental environment," striving to create a "world in which the economy and ecology resonate in balance." This "ad" appeared in both its magazine and on its Website, at www.adbusters.org.

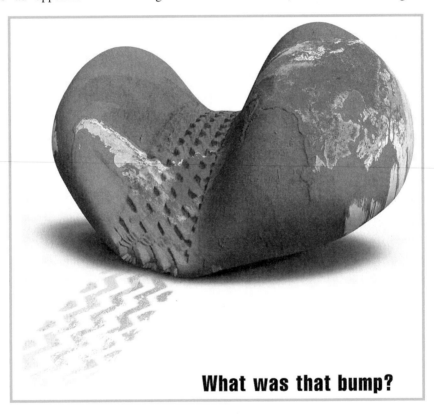

What was that bump?

QUESTIONS FOR ANALYSIS AND DISCUSSION

1. What message is *Adbusters* trying to convey with this ad? Explain.
2. What is your impression of this ad? Does it appeal to you? Why or why not? Who do you think is the intended audience?
3. Visit the http://adbusters.org/spoofads/ Website and view some of the other "ads" it has posted online. Select one and explain how *Adbusters* twists the original ad to make a point.

The Language of Advertising
Charles A. O'Neill

In this essay, marketing executive Charles A. O'Neill disputes much of the criticism concerning dubious advertising language advertising doublespeak. While admitting to some of the craftiness of his profession, O'Neill defends the huckster's language—both verbal and visual—against claims that it distorts reality. Examining some familiar television commercials and magazine ads, he explains why the language may be charming and seductive but far from brainwashing.*

BEFORE YOU READ

O'Neill makes several generalizations that characterize the language of advertising. Think about ads you have recently seen or read and make a list of your own generalizations about the language of advertising.

AS YOU READ

Does the fact that O'Neill is a professional advertising consultant influence your reception of his essay? Does it make his argument more or less persuasive?

1 In 1957, as the world continued its long recovery from World War II, people had good reason to be concerned about Science. On the one hand, giant American corporations offered the promise of "Better Living Through Chemistry."[1] Labs and factories turned out new "miracle" fabrics, vaccines, and building materials that were readily put to use in our consumer driven society.

2 But World War II American Science had also yielded The Bomb, the most terrible weapon yet conceived. Then, in 1957, the Soviets launched the first manmade object to orbit the earth. Sputnik was visible as a glimmer of light moving across the night sky, evidence of the USSR's lead in space and science. The Arms Race had begun. Families were encouraged to build bomb shelters in the yard, and millions of school children learned to "Duck and Cover" while at cocktail parties their parents discussed the ethics of barring their shelter doors to their less well prepared neighbors.

3 So when Vance Packard wrote his seminal book, *The Hidden Persuaders*,[2] about a dark alliance of social scientists with product marketers, he struck a resonant chord. He explained how scientists were using market research and psychology to gain a better understanding of "people's subsurface desires, needs and drives," to "find their points of vulnerability." By applying the principles of laboratory experimentation and scientific reasoning to learn about the fears, habits and aspirations of John and Mary Public, they would help businesses create products whose sales would be fueled by ever-more powerful advertising.

4 The post World War II era offered numerous examples of consumer excess. Cars sported tail fins stretched to new extremes, for no practical purpose. They began to look

---

*This essay first appeared in the textbook *Exploring Language* in 1998 and was updated in 2011.

like airplanes or rocket ships. It is hard to miss the overtly sexual reference in the jutting chrome bumpers of the era's most flamboyant road machines. It was a time when big was best, in starlets as well as the family car.

5   Mr. Packard is certainly not alone as a critic of advertising. Every decade has brought a new generation of critics. Just as in his time, we recognize the value of advertising, but on some level we can't quite fully embrace it as a "normal" part of our experience. At best, we view it as distracting. At worst, we view it as a pernicious threat to our health, wealth and social values.

6   How does advertising work? Why is it so powerful? Why does it raise such concern? What case can be made for and against the advertising business? In order to understand advertising, you must accept that it is not about truth, virtue, love, or positive social values. It is about selling a product. Ads play a role in moving customers through the sales process. This process begins with an effort to build awareness through the clutter of competitive messages. By presenting product benefits, or by creating differences in packaging when real differences don't exist, ads convince the customer to buy the product. Once prospects have become purchasers, advertising is used to sustain brand loyalty, reminding customers of all the good reasons for their original decision to buy.

7   Advertisements derive their power from a purposeful, directed combination of words, images and symbols. The combination is the language of advertising, a language unlike any other.

8   The historic context and technologies have changed since Mr. Packard's day, and so, too, have consumer tastes. Nonetheless, research-based advertising techniques are alive and well and appearing in newspapers, magazines, flat screen displays, billboards and mobile devices in your very own neighborhood.

9   Everyone who grows up in the Western world soon learns that advertising language is different from other languages. We may have forgotten the sponsors, but we certainly know these popular slogans "sound like ads."

10   "Where's the beef?" (Wendy's restaurants)

11   "Please, don't squeeze the Charmin." (Charmin bathroom tissue)

12   "M'm! M'm! Good!" (Campbell's Soup)

13   "I've fallen, and I can't get up!" (Lifecall)

14   "Where do you want to go today? (Microsoft)

15   "The Real Thing" (Coca Cola)

16   "Fifteen minutes could save you fifteen percent or more on car insurance." (GEICO)

Edited and Purposeful

17 Slogans work through repetition. They may seem casual, but in fact they are carefully engineered. Slogans and all other types of advertising messages have a clear purpose; they are intended to trigger a specific response.

18   The response may be as utterly simple as "Say, I *am* hungry. Let's pull right on up to the drive-through window and order a big, juicy Wendy's burger!" Sometimes our reactions are more complex.

19   A two minute television ad broadcast in the fourth quarter of Super Bowl XLVI,[3] is a case in point, and it was memorable for several reasons. In marketing terms, it was a notable success.

13   One purpose of Super Bowl ads is to create "buzz," and this ad scored at the top of the charts in You Tube's ratings competition.[4] A stark departure from what we've come to expect in the typical Super Bowl ad, it was neither cute nor funny. It did not feature talking dogs, frogs, pigeons, cats, monkeys, deer, or lizards, and its one female character was fully dressed.

14   It began with a shot of a cow on a snow covered field, not some fanciful graphic display. There was no complex sound track, only the mellifluous voice of Paul Harvey, an American broadcaster, reading a poem he had recorded at a convention of the Future Farmers of America.

15   Excerpts follow:[5]

"SO GOD MADE A FARMER"
And on the 8th day God looked down on his planned paradise and said, "I need a caretaker!" So, God made a farmer!
God said I need somebody willing to get up before dawn, milk cows and work all day in the fields, milk cows again, eat supper and then go to town and stay past midnight at a meeting of the school board. So, God made a farmer!
It had to be somebody who'd plow deep and straight . . . and not cut corners. Somebody to seed and weed, feed, breed . . . and rake and disc and plow and plant and tie the fleece and strain the milk. Somebody who'd bale a family together with the soft strong bonds of sharing, who'd laugh and then sigh . . . and then respond with smiling eyes, when his son says he wants to spend his life "doing what dad does." So, God made a farmer!

16   The ad was sponsored by Chrysler to promote a pickup truck, the Ram.

17   Before we dismiss this as little more than an affectionate paean to the hard working American Farmer, it would be useful to review a basic fact about farms and farmers, courtesy of the United States Environmental Protection Administration.[6] Consider that among the 315,000,000 people living in America, less than one percent work as farmers, meaning that this Super Bowl ad that is essentially a two minute long presentation about hardly anyone. Now of course 960,000 persons are "someones," but certainly not a sufficiently large slice of the American demographic pie as to directly justify such expensive time on the biggest television presentation of the year.

18   In advertising terms, however, that fact is beside the point; so far from the point that if the ad had depicted a more demographically significant population—say office workers or children of families that had lost their homes to foreclosure—it would have been far less interesting.[7] Its power lies not in a foundation of hard facts or in a particular place and time; it is actually timeless and not just about farmers but about Americans: hard workers all, not working for the trappings of wealth or to enjoy the view from the corner office, but doing work because the work needs to be done. It says: "Fields must be planted. Cows must be milked. That's why we work."

19   Although the brand name of the truck does not appear in the ad, it is also shown at work in a field. By the suggestive power of association we see that the truck is just like a farmer. No corners cut here! Gentle enough, but firm when firm is needed; a solid, reliable companion, strong and flexible, suited to any task, ready to get to work in the fields—or on the street where you live.

20   We feel an emotional connection to the characters in this ad. It takes us back to a simpler time in America, to our agrarian roots. It gives us a poignant glimpse of the past. The ad moves along slowly, almost lovingly, through several still photos of a church, a farmhouse at dawn, tractors and fields, but most prominently, farmers. The characters are subdued, pensive, pleased enough to have us stop by for a visit, so long as we remember that they need to get back to work soon.

21   Brent Snavely, a business writer for *The Detroit Free Press*, noted that the ad immediately generated goodwill for the brand. In an article, he described the reaction of a Texan who drives a GMC pickup, but will now consider a Ram.[8] "That was the No. 1 commercial," the man said. "It was just good, clean-cut, good all-American stuff." Mr. Snavely said, "This ad stands for something; it tells a story that resonates with a large portion of America, especially in a time of economic uncertainty."[9] The ad was a pretty powerful bit of marketing, especially when you consider that Mr. Harvey had recorded the poem more than 30 years earlier and had passed away in 2009.

Rich and Arresting

22 Advertisements cannot succeed unless we notice them, even if only on the fringes of our consciousness. We notice few of the hundreds of advertising messages to which we are exposed each day. Ad creators accept this as a fact of life.

23   How to breach the awareness barrier? Running an ad that stands out from the usual Super Bowl fare is one way to do it, but in the history of advertising the hands-down, favorite technique is to take advantage of everyone's desire to be attractive. Put more plainly, the answer is Sex. Flip through any popular magazine, and you will find it packed with ads that are unabashedly, unapologetically sexual. Victoria's Secret, Calvin Klein and every other clothing and fragrance marketer uses sex to sell. Popular media is a veritable playground of titillation, abounding with images of barely clothed men and women in poses suggesting that if only you would wear one of our little padded brassieres or spray our product behind your ears, a world a sexual adventure will reveal itself to you—even if, like many Americans these days, your Body Mass Index places you squarely in the rippling embrace of Obesity, a disease some attribute to mass market advertising for fat-laden, fast food.

24   Every successful advertisement uses a creative strategy based on an idea intended to attract and hold the attention of the targeted consumer audience. The strategy may include strong creative execution or a straightforward presentation of product features and customer benefits or even something as simple as mind-numbing repetition. And some ads—the most artful in many respects—don't even mention the product, let alone list its benefits. Looking back at the Ram ad, for example, there is no mention of horse power, the manufacturer's warranty, its durability, the type and style of wheels, and accessories. And promoting fuel economy? Forget that, too. The ad works by creating an emotional connection between the viewer and traditional Mid-American values.

25   Looking at an ad as distinctive and yet as simple as "So God Made a Farmer" may create the impression that marketers roll out of the bed in the morning, go to the office, and spout slogans on demand. Possible, but unlikely. Ads do not often emerge like Botticelli's Venus from the sea, flawless and fully grown. Most often, the creative strategy is developed only after extensive research, just as Mr. Packard suspected. "Who will be interested in our product? How old are they? Where do they live? How much money do they earn?

What problem will our product solve?" In this case, "What is there about a truck that appeals to so many people?" Answers to these questions provide the foundation on which the creative strategy is built.

Involving

26 We have seen that the language of advertising is carefully engineered; we have discovered a few of the devices it uses to get our attention. The marketer's next task is to show us how the product fulfills a need and why it does that better than the competition. It is the copy-writer's responsibility to express, exploit, and intensify such product differences. Often, there are not any real differences, in which case superficial differences are amplified. As long as the ad is working to get our attention, the "action" is mostly in the ad itself, in the words and visual images. But as we read an ad or watch it on television, we become more deeply involved. The action starts to take place in us. Our imagination is set in motion, and our individual fears and aspirations, quirks, and insecurities come into play.

27 All advertising is about exploitation: the systematic, deliberate identification of our needs and wants, followed by the delivery of a carefully constructed promise that Brand X will satisfy them.

28 Symbols offer an important tool for involving consumers in advertisements, not so much because they carry meanings of their own, but because we bring meaning to them. There is nothing objectively appealing about the gritty photos in the Ram ad and nothing inherently unique or compelling about a picture of a cow in a field or a farm house at dawn. But assemble these images together in the right sequence with an arresting poem delivered in the right cadence and magic happens. Suddenly, in our minds, trucks aren't just for farmers any more.

29 Another common device used to engage our attention is old but still effective: the use of famous or notorious personalities as product spokespeople or models. Advertising writers did not invent the human tendency to admire or seek to identify with famous people. Once we have seen a famous person in an ad, we associate the product with the person: "Britney Spears drinks milk. She's a hottie. I want to be a hottie, too! 'Hey Mom, Got Milk?' " William Shatner pitches Priceline, a gecko lizard pitches GEICO. Anonymous half naked men and women pose seductively. The logic is faulty, but we all want to be sexy, confident, poised, and either thin, rich or both. The ads bring the words, sounds and pictures. We bring the chemistry and the money.

A Simple Language

30 Advertising language differs from other types of language in another important respect; it is a simple language. Try this exercise: Clip a typical story from the publication you read most frequently. Calculate the number of words in an average sentence. Count the number of words of three or more syllables in a typical 100-word passage, omitting words that are capitalized, combinations of two simple words, or verb forms made into three-syllable words by the addition of *–ed* or *–es*. Add the two figures (the average number of words per sentence and the number of three-syllable words per 100 words), then multiply the result by 4. According to Robert Gunning[10] the result is the approximate grade level required to understand the content. He developed this formula, the "Fog Index," to determine the comparative ease with which any given piece of written communication can be read.

31   Let's apply the Fog Index to the complete text of **an ad that was part of the California Milk Processor Board's** "Got Milk?" advertising campaign, one featuring pop star Britney Spears.[11]

32   *"Baby, one more time isn't enough. 9 out of 10 girls don't get enough calcium. It takes about 4 glasses of milk every day. So when I finish this glass, fill it up, baby. Three more times."*

33   The average sentence in this ad is 7.4 words. There is only one three-syllable word, *calcium*. Counting *isn't* and *don't* as two words each, the ad is 40 words in length. The average number of three syllable words per hundred is 2.5.

7.4 words per sentence

+2.5 three syllable words/100

9.9

3.4

3.96

34   According to Gunning's scale, this ad is about as hard to read as a comic book, requiring the reading skill of a fourth grader. But the text is only part of the message. The rest is the visual; in this case, a photo of Britney sprawled across a couch, legs in the air, while she talks on the phone. A plate holding cookies and a glass of milk is set next to her.

35   Why do advertisers generally favor simple language? Today's consumer cannot take the time to focus on anything for long. Every aspect of modern life runs at a frenzied pace. With mobile devices everywhere, the world is always awake, switched on, feeding our hunger for more information, and more contact, now. Time generally, and TV-commercial time in particular, is experienced in increasingly smaller segments. Fifteen-second commercials are no longer unusual. The two minute Ram ad is an effective exception.

36   Advertising language is simple; in the engineering process, difficult words or images—which in other forms of communication may be used to lend color or fine shades of meaning—are edited out and replaced by simple words or images not open to misinterpretation. You don't need to be a college scholar to grasp the deliberate double entendre in "Baby, one more time isn't enough."

Who Is Responsible?

37 Advertising mirrors the fears, quirks, and aspirations of the society that creates it (and is, in turn, sold by it). This factor alone exposes advertising to parody and ridicule. The overall level of acceptance and respect for advertising is also influenced by the varied quality of the ads themselves. Some ads are deliberately designed to provoke controversy. But this is only one of the many charges frequently levied against advertising. Others include:

1. Advertising encourages unhealthy habits.
2. Advertising feeds on human weaknesses and exaggerates the importance of material things, encouraging "impure" emotions and vanities.
3. Advertising sells daydreams—distracting, purposeless visions of lifestyles beyond the reach of the majority of the people who are most exposed to advertising.
4. Advertising warps our vision of reality, implanting in us groundless fears and insecurities.

5. Advertising downgrades the intelligence of the public.
6. Advertising debases English.
7. Advertising perpetuates racial and sexual stereotypes.

38   What can be said in advertising's defense? First and foremost, advertising is only a reflection of society.

39   Those who say that advertising debases the intelligence of the public would perhaps do well to ask themselves another question: Exactly how intelligent is the public? Sadly, evidence abounds that "the public" at large is not particularly intelligent, after all. Johnny can't read. Susie can't write. And the entire family spends the night in front of the television, watching one mindless reality show after another. Ads are effective because they sell products. They would not succeed if they did not reflect the values and motivations of the real world. Advertising both reflects and shapes our perception of reality.

40   Advertising can encourage positive social change. It stimulates markets for useful new consumer products. It sustains economic activity and fuels growth.[12] As in the case of the Ram ad, it can celebrate the best of America and in so doing give us reason to believe that the virtues that served us well in the past will protect and nurture us in the future. The problem is that advertising, like any form of mass communication, can be a force for "good" or "bad." It can just as readily reinforce or encourage irresponsible behavior, ageism, sexism, ethnocentrism, racism, homophobia—you name it—as it can encourage support for diversity and social progress. People living in society create advertising. Society isn't perfect. Like it or not, it's here to stay.

41   Perhaps, by learning how advertising works, we can become better equipped to sort out content from hype, enduring values from emotions, and progressive ideas from propaganda.

Sources

1. "Better Living Through Chemistry" is the name of an album by Fatboy Slim, but as used here it is a variant of a DuPont advertising slogan, "Better Things for Better Living . . . Through Chemistry." Source: Wikipedia, http://en.wikipedia.org/wiki /Better_Living_Through_Chemistry
2. Vance Packard, *The Hidden Persuaders* (D. Mackay & Co, 1957).
3. To see the commercial, visit http://www.ramtrucks.com/en/keepplowing/ In addition to the advertisement, the site contains information about the Future Farmers of America. The ad was made in cooperation with the FFA and the National FFA Foundation.
4. The company donated $1,000,000 to the foundation based on the number of times the ad was viewed on You Tube Source: Wikipedia. See http://en.wikipedia.org/wiki /So_God_Made_a_Farmer#The_speech
5. Excerpts are reproduced here. For the complete text, and an informative discus -sion about the ad, see *The Atlantic*'s web site, http://www.theatlantic.com/politics /archive/2013/02/paul-harveys-1978-so-god-made-a-farmer-speech/272816/
6. Source: www.epa.gov/ag101/demographics.html as last updated 6/27/2012
7. Loans.org: 2.3 million children were involved in home foreclosures. See http://loans .org/mortgage/infographics/america-nation-underwater
8. *"Automakers score big on game day,"* by Brent Snavely, Detroit Free Press, 2/5/2013.

9. Conversation with Brent Snavely, 3/6/2013.
10. Curtis D. MacDougall, *Interpretive Reporting* (New York: Macmillan, 1968), p. 94. Also see Wikipedia, http://en.wikipedia.org/wiki/Gunning_fog_index
11. The Website, creativecriminals.com, has a compilation of 300 print ads from the "Got Milk?" campaign. See http://creativecriminals.com/celebrities/got-milk-most-complete-compilation/
12. In the United States, consumer spending accounted for 72% of gross domestic product in 2011. GDP is the market value of all goods and services produced by a country. Data from The World Bank. See http://data.worldbank.org/indicator/NE.CON.PETC.ZS

QUESTIONS FOR ANALYSIS AND DISCUSSION

1. O'Neill says that advertisers create in consumers a sense of need for products. Do you think it is ethical for advertisers to create such a sense when their products are "generic" and do not differ from the competition? Consider ads for gasoline, beer, and coffee.

2. O'Neill anticipates potential objections to his defense of advertising. What are some of these objections? What does he say in defense of advertising? Which set of arguments do you find stronger?

3. O'Neill describes several ways that advertising language differs from other kinds of language. Briefly list the ways he mentions. Can you think of any other characteristics of advertising language that set it apart?

4. Do you think it is ethical for advertisers to create a sense of product difference when there really isn't any? Again, consider advertisements for products such as gasoline, beer, or coffee.

5. O'Neill is an advertising professional. How does his writing style reflect the advertising techniques he describes? Cite examples to support your answer.

Sample Ads and Study Questions

The next section features recent magazine and billboard advertisements. Diverse in content and style, some ads use words to promote the product, while others depend on emotion, name recognition, visual appeal, or association. They present a variety of sales pitches and marketing techniques.

Corresponding to each ad is a list of questions to help you analyze how the ad works its appeal to promote a product. When studying the advertisements, approach each as a consumer, an artist, a social scientist, and a critic with an eye for detail.

M&MS

1. Who is featured in the picture? How does this ad play upon expectations already created by the product in past advertisements?
2. This ad is promoting a candy product. What connection, if any, do the characters have to the product? In your opinion, does the ad effectively market the product?
3. Who do you think is the target audience for this advertisement? How do you think a young adult would respond to it? A politician or government worker? A child? An older adult? Explain.
4. After viewing this ad, would you be more inclined to purchase the product it is advertising? Why or why not?
5. What do you need to know about pop culture to understand the ad and the characters depicted in it?

THE LONGER YOU LIVE ON THE STREET
THE HARDER IT IS TO GET OFF IT **samusocial**

SUPPORT US AT WWW.SAMUSOCIAL.FR

SAMUSOCIAL

1. Examine these advertisements carefully. What is happening in them? What is being "sold"?
2. How do the settings contribute to the images?
3. Would you know what these ads were "selling" if there were no company name mentioned in them? Explain.
4. If you were leafing through a magazine and saw these ads, would you stop to read them? Why or why not?
5. How do these ads make a point? What cultural and social issue do they raise? In your opinion, are they an effective way to raise awareness? Money? Explain.

OMEGA

1. What is happening in this ad? How does the person in the ad "sell" the product? Does he have any relationship to the product? Explain.
2. Does the use of the image of the man in this ad surprise you? Are you intrigued enough to read the ad? Why or why not? Explain your reaction to the ad.
3. Who is the audience for this ad? What might you need to know to understand it?
4. If you were leafing through a magazine and saw this ad, would you stop to examine it? Why or why not? In what sort of magazine would you expect to see this ad?
5. Review the quote featured in the ad "We chose to go to the moon." What are the multiple interpretations of this line? Where does the quote appear? Would the quote work as well if it were placed elsewhere in the ad? Why or why not?

UNITED COLORS OF BENETTON

1. Benetton is a clothing company. How does the image of the waterfowl connect with the product it sells? In your opinion, is this effective marketing? Why or why not?
2. What is the meaning of the dot on the duck? Why is it there?
3. What is happening in this photo? Why do you think Benetton chose this photo to market its product line?
4. If you were reading a magazine or walking by a billboard and saw this ad, would you stop to look at it? Would the ad encourage you to buy Benetton clothing? Why or why not?

TIDE

1. What is happening in this ad? What makes you stop and look at it? What happened first, and what will happen next?
2. Who is the likely target audience for this ad? In what magazines would you expect to see it? Is it an effective ad? Explain.
3. How does the tagline "Because stains love your clothes" connect with the product and what is happening in the ad?
4. Would this ad be as effective if the coffee and shirt had their "mouths" closed rather than open? Explain.

1. Is it clear what this billboard is promoting? Is there any ambiguity about that is being "sold" in the advertisement? Explain.
2. How does the ad use humor to convey a message? Does this tactic make you more or less interested in agreeing with the message of the ad?
3. This ad targets kids. What message is it telling them? How does this message differ from others kids are told about smoking?
4. This ad promotes a nonprofit campaign that seeks to promote children's health. Visit the website njbreathes.org that explains the project. After viewing the site and viewing more ads that comprise the campaign, explain why you this this billboard and others on the site will or will not encourage children to avoid smoking cigarettes.

Advertisers: Men Are Not Idiots

*Glenn Sacks and Richard Smaglick**

This next essay addresses how television—especially advertising—can promote damaging sexism, in this case, against men. Because television reaches a broad and diverse audience, it can influence culture and social opinion. As a conduit for social persuasion, could television harm one group of people as much as it may help another? In the next editorial, Glenn Sacks and Richard Smaglick question the depiction of men as lazy, incompetent, insensitive, or simply stupid in commercials. Although such depictions may seem funny, stereotypical "male bashing," they argue, hurts men and society as a whole. Why is it acceptable, they wonder, to make men look so stupid in ads?

BEFORE YOU READ

Think about the ways men and women are portrayed on television commercials. Are there certain gender-based stereotypes that seem common? What makes a male character interesting and engaging? What makes a female character noteworthy and interesting? Are the criteria different?

AS YOU READ

This editorial notes that two reasons why men are ridiculed in commercials is because they are, overall, still privileged and that it is "their turn" to be mocked. What do you think? Is it ok to mock a group of people if society as a whole views them as "privileged"? Why or why not?

"It is difficult to get a man to understand something when his salary depends on his not understanding it." —Upton Sinclair

1   The way the advertising industry portrays men has been drawing increasing scrutiny by both the trade press and the mainstream media. Defenders of the status quo—in which men are depicted as irresponsible fathers and lazy, foolish husbands—are starting to feel outnumbered. It's an understandable feeling.

2   According to United Press International, J. Walter Thompson (JWT), one of America's top advertising agencies, "has decided to stop portraying men as testosterone-soaked fools." Bob Jeffery, Chairman of JWT, explains: "[JWT is developing] smart, positive portrayals of the modern man . . . Men have faded into a collective 'boob-dom,' a sort of 'Jackass' meets 'The Man Show' meets 'The Simpsons.' As a result, the way we approach the men's market is ripe for reinvention."

3   Mark Tungate, author of *Branded Male: Marketing to Men*, explains, "The important thing is not to make dads look like bungling idiots. Marketing needs to empower fathers

*Glenn Sacks and Richard Smaglick, *Advertising Age*, April 14, 2008 (updated March 15, 2013).

because that's where we feel our job is—we want to protect." Tungate criticizes "Lazy ad agencies [who] love gags" and then pick on men because "men are the safest victims."

4   Other outspoken critics of anti-male ads include: Marian Salzman, vice-president of JWT (men have become an "easy target" for ridicule); Syndicated columnist Kathleen Parker, whose weekly columns appear in 300 newspapers ("On television, men are depicted as boors or buffoons . . . they've had enough"); TV host Bill Maher; CBS News' anchor Charles Osgood; nationally syndicated radio talk show host Dr. Laura Schlessinger; syndicated advice columnist Amy Alkon; nationally syndicated military columnist Jacey Eckhart; *Chicago Tribune* columnist Ross Werland: Law professor/author/blogger Glenn Reynolds of Instapundit; Dr. Christine B. Whelan, author of *Why Smart Men Marry Smart Women*; major market talk show hosts Mike McConnell, Ron Smith, and Joe Elliott; and numerous others.

5   The evidence is clear—"man as idiot" isn't going over very well these days.

6   Defenders of the advertising status quo generally put forth two arguments: males are "privileged" and "it's men's turn," so it's OK to portray them this way; and men simply don't care how they're portrayed. Both of these arguments are highly questionable.

7   Young males certainly aren't privileged. The vast majority of learning-disabled students are boys, and boys are four times as likely to receive a diagnosis of attention-deficit hyperactivity disorder as girls. Girls get better grades than boys and are much more likely than boys to graduate high school and enter college. According to the National Center for Education Statistics, women earn 60% of all bachelor's degrees and 60% of all Master's Degrees.

8   That adult men are "privileged" over women is also questionable. Yes, men do make up the majority of CEOs, politicians, and powerbrokers. They also make up the majority of the homeless, the imprisoned, the suicide victims, and those who die young.

9   The "Great Recession" has made claims of blanket male privilege even more suspect. As Reihan Salam noted in *Foreign Policy*, "Consider, to start, the almost unbelievably disproportionate impact that the current crisis is having on men—so much so that the recession is now known to some economists . . . as the 'he-cession.' More than 80 percent of job losses in the United States . . . have fallen on men, according to the U.S. Bureau of Labor Statistics."

10   How fathers are portrayed is of particular importance. Fatherlessness is one of the greatest threats our children face. Syndicated columnist Leonard Pitts Jr. explains, "Twenty-eight percent of American kids . . . are growing up in fatherless homes, heir to all the struggle and dysfunction that condition portends . . . who can deny those [are] appalling numbers[?]"

11   Among the many ills fatherlessness portends are much higher rates of teen drug abuse, crime, pregnancy, and school drop-outs.

12   While the advertising industry's dad-as-idiot depiction of fathers certainly isn't the cause of fatherlessness, it's part of the problem. Examples include:

   ■ Kimberly-Clark's Huggies "Dad Test" ad campaign which, according to *Marketing Week*, "featured an unflattering portrayal of five dads caring for their babies for five days, with the premise that if Huggies could survive five days with the somewhat idiotic dads, then they could survive anything."

- T-Mobile's "Smart Guys" commercial, where a daughter tells her mother that the man she married—her father—is an idiot.
- Fiber One's ad wherein the wife (guess what?) outsmarts her dumb husband, tricking him into eating a Fiber One bar, which he thinks are cookies.
- Hanes' "Paste Socks," where an idiot dad cleverly tells mom of his new footwear invention (dipping socks in glue to avoid skidding around), only to be scolded and humiliated in front of their son.

13   In a television culture like ours, how can the endless parade of dad as buffoon ads not negatively influence young people's perceptions of fathers?

14   For young men, it makes it less likely they'll aspire to be fathers, see their own value as fathers or, as Pitts explains, want to do the "hard, but crucial work of being dad." For young women, it means they'll be more likely to be misled into thinking that their children's fathers aren't important, that divorce or separation from them is no big deal, or that they will, as is the increasing trend, simply dispense with dad altogether and have children on their own.

15   Is it true that men really don't care how they're portrayed? Evidence strongly suggests otherwise. According to a study conducted by Leo Burnett Worldwide, four out of five men believe media portrayals of men are inaccurate. The study found that men care more about the way they are viewed than was generally believed.

16   When Kate Santich of the *Orlando Sentinel* did a feature on "men as idiots" advertising in 2004, she says she was "astounded" at the amount of mail she received, almost all of it critical of the way men are portrayed in ads. In a *Washington Times* article in January, advertising industry journalist Todd Wasserman describes getting the exact same reaction to a recent article he wrote on anti-male ads.

17   This sentiment was reflected in the popularity of the highly-publicized campaigns we've launched against advertising which is hostile to males. Several thousand protesters participated in both our campaign against Verizon's anti-father ad "The Elliotts: Homework" and our campaign against Arnold Worldwide as it vied for Volvo's account. Kimberly-Clark's Huggies ad was so widely criticized that Kimberly-Clark decided to pull it.

18   These campaigns have drawn widespread support from women, who generally do not like to see their sons, husbands, and fathers put down. Leo Burnett executive Rose Cameron explains: "One of the great markers [society] looks to about the intelligence of a woman is her choice of husband. So if advertisers position men as idiots in the husband scenario, then you're commenting on her smarts. Women have told us, 'If you want to get on my good side, you do not show my husband as the idiot.'"

19   We have three suggestions for the advertising industry:

20   First, create more ads that are father-positive. Some recent examples include: LEGO's father-son ad "Road Trip"; Kellogg's "Weathering Rain Together"; Google's Search App ad "Smart Dad"; Tropicana's "Squeeze"; and the UK supermarket chain Sainsbury's father-daughter ad "Let's Go Fly A Kite."

21   Second, as we consider whether it's wise to make men the butt of every joke, we should also consider the joke itself. Many see the '60s as the "Golden Age of Advertising." Those who crafted the ads of that era created work of superb quality, seldom if ever resorting to the forms of contempt, shame, and aggressive ridicule of today's ads.

22   Third, when an ad does need to poke fun at somebody, stop automatically defaulting to men-as-fools.

23   Is bashing men a good way to sell products? The ad world has learned, for the most part, to respect womanhood. Given the rising level of media, ad industry, and public disgust with anti-male ads, it's clear that good, respectful humor is a much healthier approach to advertising.

1. The authors conclude with the question, "Is bashing men a good way to sell products?" Answer their question with your own perspective. Reference, if possible, ads mentioned in the essay as well as ones you have viewed yourself.

2. Evaluate how the authors support the thesis of their essay. First, identify their thesis. Then, analyze each supporting element they use to prove their point. Do the authors allow for alternative points of view? Do they try to see multiple sides of the issue? Explain.

3. Consider the contrast between male characters in ads and men in real life. Do male characters in commercials mirror men in the real world? Do the characters in commercials influence your perception of men in general?

4. Some critics have observed that the portrayal of women as generally unintelligent in commercials would never be acceptable if the tables were turned. Respond to this view in your own words. Support your response with examples from the essay and your television viewing experience.

5. Using online video resources research a few commercials, including the ones cited in this essay, that depict men as "idiots." Summarize your impressions of each commercial and why you feel that they do, or do not, demean men.

WRITING ASSIGNMENTS

1. You are an advertising executive. Select one of the products featured in the sample ads section and write a new advertising campaign for it. Do you tap into popular consciousness? Do you use "weasel words"? How do you hook your audience, and how do you create a need for the product? Defend your campaign to your supervisors by explaining the motivation behind your creative decisions.

2. Write a paper in which you consider advertising strategies. Support your evaluation with examples of advertising campaigns with which you are familiar. Make an argument for or against particular campaigns. Are they appropriate? Do they exploit emotions? Are they opportunistic? You may draw support from the articles in this chapter.

3. Identify some commercials or advertisements that especially annoyed you. Why exactly did they bother you? Try to locate any cultural, linguistic, social, or intellectual reasons behind your annoyance or distaste. How do these commercials compare to the marketing criticisms expressed in essays featured in this section?

4. Write an essay in which you explore the connection between social diversification, product targeting, and audience packaging. Explore some of the reasons why the

"divide and conquer" method of marketing works, and whether or not it is an ethical approach to advertising.

5. Teens and young adults covet certain brand-name clothing because they believe it promotes a particular image. What defines brand image? Is it something created by the company, or by the people who use the product? How does advertising influence the social view we hold of ourselves and the brands we use? Write an essay on the connection among advertising, image, and cultural values of what is "in," or popular, and what is not.

6. Laura Baumgartner notes that the roots of consumerism are deeply connected to our personal desire to express and define ourselves. Write an essay in which you defend our inherent desire to define ourselves through what we wear and "who" we wear. Conversely, you may write an essay that questions this behavior and explain why it is harmful to both the individual and society as a whole.

7. *Adbusters* addresses the unethical ways advertisers manipulate consumers to "need" products. However, if we study ads long enough, we can determine for ourselves the ways we may be manipulated. Select several print or television advertisements and analyze how they manipulate consumers to increase their "quest for stuff." Is there anything wrong with this manipulation? Why or why not?

8. Consider the ways the advertising industry influences our cultural perspectives of gender and identity. Write an essay exploring the influence, however slight, television commercials have had on your own perceptions of gender. If you wish, interview other students for their opinions on this issue, and address some of their points in your essay.

11

Gender Matters

In the past century, we have witnessed enormous changes in the roles of women and men at home, in the workplace, and in society. Traditional ways of defining the self in terms of gender have been challenged and irrevocably altered. The essays in this chapter examine how these changes have affected men and women as they continue to redefine themselves, their relationships with each other, and their relationships with society.

Perceptions of gender begin at an early age, and it seems as if children face social and cultural pressures their parents' generation never experienced. Several essays in this chapter take a look at the way society influences our perceptions of gender and our expectations of ourselves and of the opposite sex. We live in a society obsessed with image—a society seemingly more driven by the cultivation of the body and how we clothe it than in personal achievement. In fact, so powerful is the influence of image that other terms of self-definition are difficult to identify. Men and women confront challenges related to body image and self-perception daily. From where does all the body-consciousness pressure come? Why are so many young people seemingly at war with their bodies? And how do cultural perceptions of beauty influence our view of what it means to be male or female?

Most college-age men and women were born after the "sexual revolution" and the feminist movements of the 1960s and 1970s. But it is these movements that have shaped the way men and women behave today and how they view themselves and each other, evaluate opportunity, and envision the future. Some people claim that things have become more complicated, and not for the better. Others take for granted a culture where a woman can pursue a business or medical career without facing tremendous obstacles, or a society in which a man staying at home to raise his children is considered normal. There has even been a recent feminist backlash where young women who rise to the level of CEO of a major company may assert they are not "feminists." In addition to exploring cultural influences on gender, this chapter also addresses how cultural changes of gender roles has—or has not—changed the way men and women perceive themselves and their role in the world.

Saplings in the Storm

Mary Pipher

> With the onset of adolescence, children are faced with a multitude of gender-related issues. In addition to dealing with physical and emotional changes, many adolescents must try to adapt to shifting social roles. Changing social expectations can be overwhelming, says psychologist Mary Pipher, especially for girls.

In this excerpt taken from the introduction to her best-selling book *Reviving Ophelia* (1995), Pipher's special area of interest is how American culture influences the mental health of its people. In this essay, she explains why she is concerned that girls may be losing their true selves in an effort to conform to what they believe society expects from them.*

BEFORE YOU READ

Did the way you fit into your social groups change when you reached adolescence? If so, in what ways? What do you think accounts for such changes?

AS YOU READ

According to Pipher, what social constraints do girls alone face with the onset of adolescence? Why do these cultural pressures exist?

1   When my cousin Polly was a girl, she was energy in motion. She danced, did cartwheels and splits, played football, basketball and baseball with the neighborhood boys, wrestled with my brothers, biked, climbed trees and rode horses. She was as lithe and as resilient as a willow branch and as unrestrained as a lion cub. Polly talked as much as she moved. She yelled out orders and advice, shrieked for joy when she won a bet or heard a good joke, laughed with her mouth wide open, argued with kids and grown-ups and insulted her foes in the language of a construction worker.

2   We formed the Marauders, a secret club that met over her garage. Polly was the Tom Sawyer of the club. She planned the initiations, led the spying expeditions and hikes to haunted houses. She showed us the rituals to become blood "brothers" and taught us card tricks and how to smoke.

3   Then Polly had her first period and started junior high. She tried to keep up her old ways, but she was called a tomboy and chided for not acting more ladylike. She was excluded by her boy pals and by the girls, who were moving into makeup and romances.

4   This left Polly confused and shaky. She had temper tantrums and withdrew from both the boys' and girls' groups. Later she quieted down and reentered as Becky Thatcher. She wore stylish clothes and watched from the sidelines as the boys acted and spoke. Once again she was accepted and popular. She glided smoothly through our small society. No one spoke of the changes or mourned the loss of our town's most dynamic citizen. I was the only one who felt that a tragedy had transpired.

5   Girls in what Freud called the latency period, roughly age six or seven through puberty, are anything but latent. I think of my daughter Sara during those years—performing chemistry experiments and magic tricks, playing her violin, starring in her own plays, rescuing wild animals and biking all over town. I think of her friend Tamara, who wrote a 300-page novel the summer of her sixth-grade year. I remember myself, reading every children's book in the library of my town. One week I planned to be a great doctor like

---

*Mary Pipher, *Reviving Ophelia* (excerpt), 1995.

Albert Schweitzer. The next week I wanted to write like Louisa May Alcott or dance in Paris like Isadora Duncan. I have never since had as much confidence or ambition.

6   Most preadolescent girls are marvelous company because they are interested in everything—sports, nature, people, music and books. Almost all the heroines of girls' literature come from this age group—Anne of Green Gables, Heidi, Pippi Longstocking and Caddie Woodlawn. Girls this age bake pies, solve mysteries and go on quests. They can take care of themselves and are not yet burdened with caring for others. They have a brief respite from the female role and can be tomboys, a word that conveys courage, competency and irreverence.

7   They can be androgynous, having the ability to act adaptively in any situation regardless of gender role constraints. An androgynous person can comfort a baby or change a tire, cook a meal or chair a meeting. Research has shown that, since they are free to act without worrying if their behavior is feminine or masculine, androgynous adults are the most well-adjusted.

8   Girls between seven and eleven rarely come to therapy. They don't need it. I can count on my fingers the girls this age whom I have seen: Coreen, who was physically abused; Anna, whose parents were divorcing; and Brenda, whose father killed himself. These girls were courageous and resilient. Brenda said, "If my father didn't want to stick around, that's his loss." Coreen and Anna were angry, not with themselves, but rather at the grown-ups, whom they felt were making mistakes. It's amazing how little help these girls needed from me to heal and move on.

9   A horticulturist told me a revealing story. She led a tour of junior-high girls who were attending a math and science fair on her campus. She showed them side oats grama, bluestem, Indian grass and trees—redbud, maple, walnut and willow. The younger girls interrupted each other with their questions and tumbled forward to see, touch and smell everything. The older girls, the ninth-graders, were different. They hung back. They didn't touch plants or shout out questions. They stood primly to the side, looking bored and even a little disgusted by the enthusiasm of their younger classmates. My friend asked herself, What's happened to these girls? What's gone wrong? She told me, "I wanted to shake them, to say, 'Wake up, come back. Is anybody home at your house?'"

10   Recently I sat sunning on a bench outside my favorite ice-cream store. A mother and her teenage daughter stopped in front of me and waited for the light to change. I heard the mother say, "You have got to stop blackmailing your father and me. Every time you don't get what you want, you tell us that you want to run away from home or kill yourself. What's happened to you? You used to be able to handle not getting your way." The daughter stared straight ahead, barely acknowledging her mother's words. The light changed. I licked my ice-cream cone. Another mother approached the same light with her preadolescent daughter in tow. They were holding hands. The daughter said to her mother, "This is fun. Let's do this all afternoon."

11   Something dramatic happens to girls in early adolescence. Just as planes and ships disappear mysteriously into the Bermuda Triangle, so do the selves of girls go down in droves. They crash and burn in a social and developmental Bermuda Triangle. In early adolescence, studies show that girls' IQ scores drop and their math and science scores plummet. They lose their resiliency and optimism and become less curious and inclined to take risks. They lose their assertive, energetic and "tomboyish" personalities and

become more deferential, self-critical and depressed. They report great unhappiness with their own bodies.

12   Psychology documents but does not explain the crashes. Girls who rushed to drink in experiences in enormous gulps sit quietly in the corner. Writers such as Sylvia Plath, Margaret Atwood and Olive Schreiner have described the wreckage. Diderot, in writing to his young friend Sophie Volland, described his observations harshly: "You all die at 15."

13   Fairy tales capture the essence of this phenomenon. Young women eat poisoned apples or prick their fingers with poisoned needles and fall asleep for a hundred years. They wander away from home, encounter great dangers, are rescued by princes and are transformed into passive and docile creatures.

14   The story of Ophelia, from Shakespeare's *Hamlet*, shows the destructive forces that affect young women. As a girl, Ophelia is happy and free, but with adolescence she loses herself. When she falls in love with Hamlet, she lives only for his approval. She has no inner direction; rather she struggles to meet the demands of Hamlet and her father. Her value is determined utterly by their approval. Ophelia is torn apart by her efforts to please. When Hamlet spurns her because she is an obedient daughter, she goes mad with grief. Dressed in elegant clothes that weigh her down, she drowns in a stream filled with flowers.

15   Girls know they are losing themselves. One girl said, "Everything good in me died in junior high." Wholeness is shattered by the chaos of adolescence. Girls become fragmented, their selves split into mysterious contradictions. They are sensitive and tenderhearted, mean and competitive, superficial and idealistic. They are confident in the morning and overwhelmed with anxiety by nightfall. They rush through their days with wild energy and then collapse into lethargy. They try on new roles every week—this week the good student, next week the delinquent and the next, the artist. And they expect their families to keep up with these changes.

16   My clients in early adolescence are elusive and slow to trust adults. They are easily offended by a glance, a clearing of the throat, a silence, a lack of sufficient enthusiasm or a sentence that doesn't meet their immediate needs. Their voices have gone underground—their speech is more tentative and less articulate. Their moods swing widely. One week they love their world and their families, the next they are critical of everyone. Much of their behavior is unreadable. Their problems are complicated and metaphorical—eating disorders, school phobias and self-inflicted injuries. I need to ask again and again in a dozen different ways, "What are you trying to tell me?"

17   Michelle, for example, was a beautiful, intelligent seventeen-year-old. Her mother brought her in after she became pregnant for the third time in three years. I tried to talk about why this was happening. She smiled a Mona Lisa smile to all my questions. "No, I don't care all that much for sex." "No, I didn't plan this. It just happened." When Michelle left a session, I felt like I'd been talking in the wrong language to someone far away.

18   Psychology has a long history of ignoring girls this age. Until recently adolescent girls haven't been studied by academics, and they have long baffled therapists. Because they are secretive with adults and full of contradictions, they are difficult to study. So much is happening internally that's not communicated on the surface.

19   Simone de Beauvoir believed adolescence is when girls realize that men have the power and that their only power comes from consenting to become submissive adored objects. They do not suffer from the penis envy Freud postulated, but from power envy.

20   She described the Bermuda Triangle this way: Girls who were the subjects of their own lives become the objects of other's lives. "Young girls slowly bury their childhood, put away their independent and imperious selves and submissively enter adult existence." Adolescent girls experience a conflict between their autonomous selves and their need to be feminine, between their status as human beings and their vocation as females. De Beauvoir says, "Girls stop being and start seeming."

21   Girls become "female impersonators" who fit their whole selves into small, crowded spaces. Vibrant, confident girls become shy, doubting young women. Girls stop thinking, "Who am I? What do I want?" and start thinking, "What must I do to please others?" This gap between girls' true selves and cultural prescriptions for what is properly female creates enormous problems. To paraphrase a Stevie Smith poem about swimming in the sea, "they are not waving, they are drowning." And just when they most need help, they are unable to take their parents' hands.

22   This pressure disorients and depresses most girls. They sense the pressure to be someone they are not. They fight back, but they are fighting a "problem with no name." One girl put it this way: "I'm a perfectly good carrot that everyone is trying to turn into a rose. As a carrot, I have good color and a nice leafy top. When I'm carved into a rose, I turn brown and wither."

23   Adolescent girls are saplings in a hurricane. They are young and vulnerable trees that the winds blow with gale strength. Three factors make young women vulnerable to the hurricane. One is their developmental level. Everything is changing—body shape, hormones, skin and hair. Calmness is replaced by anxiety. Their way of thinking is changing. Far below the surface they are struggling with the most basic of human questions: What is my place in the universe, what is my meaning?

24   Second, American culture has always smacked girls on the head in early adolescence. This is when they move into a broader culture that is rife with girl-hurting "isms," such as sexism, capitalism and lookism, which is the evaluation of a person solely on the basis of appearance.

25   Third, American girls are expected to distance from parents just at the time when they most need their support. As they struggle with countless new pressures, they must relinquish the protection and closeness they've felt with their families in childhood. They turn to their none-too-constant peers for support.

26   Parents know only too well that something is happening to their daughters. Calm, considerate daughters grow moody, demanding and distant. Girls who loved to talk are sullen and secretive. Girls who liked to hug now bristle when touched. Mothers complain that they can do nothing right in the eyes of their daughters. Involved fathers bemoan their sudden banishment from their daughters' lives. But few parents realize how universal their experiences are. Their daughters are entering a new land, a dangerous place that parents can scarcely comprehend. Just when they most need a home base, they cut themselves loose without radio communications.

27   Most parents of adolescent girls have the goal of keeping their daughters safe while they grow up and explore the world. The parents' job is to protect. The daughters' job is to explore. Always these different tasks have created tension in parent-daughter relationships, but now it's even harder. Generally parents are more protective of their daughters than is corporate America. Parents aren't trying to make money off their daughters by selling

them designer jeans or cigarettes, they just want them to be well adjusted. They don't see their daughters as sex objects or consumers but as real people with talents and interests. But daughters turn away from their parents as they enter the new land. They befriend their peers, who are their fellow inhabitants of the strange country and who share a common language and set of customs. They often embrace the junk values of mass culture.

28   This turning away from parents is partly for developmental reasons. Early adolescence is a time of physical and psychological change, self-absorption, preoccupation with peer approval and identity formation. It's a time when girls focus inward on their own fascinating changes.

29   It's partly for cultural reasons. In America we define adulthood as a moving away from families into broader culture. Adolescence is the time for cutting bonds and breaking free. Adolescents may claim great independence from parents, but they are aware and ashamed of their parents' smallest deviation from the norm. They don't like to be seen with them and find their imperfections upsetting. A mother's haircut or a father's joke can ruin their day. Teenagers are furious at parents who say the wrong things or do not respond with perfect answers. Adolescents claim not to hear their parents, but with their friends they discuss endlessly all parental attitudes. With amazing acuity, they sense nuances, doubt, shades of ambiguity, discrepancy and hypocrisy.

30   Adolescents still have some of the magical thinking of childhood and believe that parents have the power to keep them safe and happy. They blame their parents for their misery, yet they make a point of not telling their parents how they think and feel; they have secrets, so things can get crazy. Most parents feel like failures during this time. They feel shut out, impotent and misunderstood. They often attribute the difficulties of this time to their *daughters* and their own failings. They don't understand that these problems go with the developmental stage, the culture and the times.

31   Parents experience an enormous sense of loss when their girls enter this new land. They miss the daughters who sang in the kitchen, who read them school papers, who accompanied them on fishing trips and to ball games. They miss the daughters who liked to bake cookies, play Pictionary and be kissed good-night. In place of their lively, affectionate daughters they have changelings—new girls who are sadder, angrier and more complicated. Everyone is grieving.

32   Fortunately adolescence is time-limited. By late high school most girls are stronger and the winds are dying down. Some of the worst problems—cliques, a total focus on looks and struggles with parents—are on the wane. But the way girls handle the problems of adolescence can have implications for their adult lives. Without some help, the loss of wholeness, self-confidence and self-direction can last well into adulthood. Many adult clients struggle with the same issues that overwhelmed them as adolescent girls. Thirty-year-old accountants and realtors, forty-year-old homemakers and doctors, and thirty-five-year-old nurses and schoolteachers ask the same questions and struggle with the same problems as their teenage daughters.

33   Even sadder are the women who are not struggling, who have forgotten that they have selves worth defending. They have repressed the pain of their adolescence, the betrayals of self in order to be pleasing. These women come to therapy with the goal of becoming even more pleasing to others. They come to lose weight, to save their marriages or to rescue their children. When I ask them about their own needs, they are confused by the question.

34   Women often know how everyone in their family thinks and feels except themselves. They are great at balancing the needs of their coworkers, husbands, children and friends, but they forget to put themselves into the equation. They struggle with adolescent questions still unresolved: How important are looks and popularity? How do I care for myself and not be selfish? How can I be honest and still be loved? How can I achieve and not threaten others? How can I be sexual and not a sex object? How can I be responsive but not responsible for everyone?

35   Before I studied psychology, I studied cultural anthropology. I have always been interested in that place where culture and individual psychology intersect, in why cultures create certain personalities and not others, in how they pull for certain strengths in their members, in how certain talents are utilized while others atrophy from lack of attention. I'm interested in the role cultures play in the development of individual pathology.

36   For a student of culture and personality, adolescence is fascinating. It's an extraordinary time when individual, developmental and cultural factors combine in ways that shape adulthood. It's a time of marked internal development and massive cultural indoctrination.

37   An analysis of the culture cannot ignore individual differences in women. Some women blossom and grow under the most hostile conditions while others wither after the smallest storms. And yet we are more alike than different in the issues that face us. The important question is, Under what conditions do most young women flower and grow?

38   Adolescent clients intrigue me as they struggle to sort themselves out. But these last few years my office has been filled with girls—girls with eating disorders, alcohol problems, posttraumatic stress reactions to sexual or physical assaults, sexually transmitted diseases (STDs), self-inflicted injuries and strange phobias, and girls who have tried to kill themselves or run away. A health department survey showed that 40 percent of all girls in my midwestern city considered suicide last year. The Centers for Disease Control in Atlanta reports that the suicide rate among children age ten to fourteen rose 75 percent between 1979 and 1988. Something dramatic is happening to adolescent girls in America, something unnoticed by those not on the front lines.

39   At first I was surprised that girls were having more trouble now. After all, we have had a consciousness-raising women's movement since the sixties. Women are working in traditionally male professions and going out for sports. Some fathers help with the housework and child care. It seems that these changes would count for something. And of course they do, but in some ways the progress is confusing. The Equal Rights Amendment was not ratified, feminism is a pejorative term to many people and, while some women have high-powered jobs, most women work hard for low wages and do most of the "second shift" work. The lip service paid to equality makes the reality of discrimination even more confusing.

40   Many of the pressures girls have always faced are intensified in the 1990s. Many things contribute to this intensification: more divorced families, chemical addictions, casual sex and violence against women. Because of the media, which Clarence Page calls "electronic wallpaper," girls all live in one big town—a sleazy, dangerous tinsel town with lots of liquor stores and few protected spaces. Increasingly women have been sexualized and objectified, their bodies marketed to sell tractors and toothpaste. Soft- and hard-core pornography are everywhere. Sexual and physical assaults on girls are at an all-time high. Now girls are more vulnerable and fearful, more likely to have been traumatized and less free to roam about alone. This combination of old stresses and new is poison for our young women.

41   Parents have unprecedented stress as well. For the last half-century, parents worried about their sixteen-year-old daughters driving, but now, in a time of drive-by shootings and car-jackings, parents can be panicked. Parents have always worried about their daughters' sexual behavior, but now, in a time of date rapes, herpes and AIDS, they can be sexphobic. Traditionally parents have wondered what their teens were doing, but now teens are much more likely to be doing things that can get them killed.

42   I am saying that girls are having more trouble now than they had thirty years ago, when I was a girl, and more trouble than even ten years ago. Something new is happening. Adolescence has always been hard, but it's harder now because of cultural changes in the last decade. The protected place in space and time that we once called childhood has grown shorter. There is an African saying, "It takes a village to raise a child." Most girls no longer have a village.

QUESTIONS FOR ANALYSIS AND DISCUSSION

1. What does Pipher mean when she says that girls "disappear mysteriously into the Bermuda Triangle" in early adolescence? Why do you think she uses this analogy repeatedly?

2. How do girls change with the onset of adolescence? To what extent are these changes physical and to what extent are they cultural? Do you think girls must make sacrifices to "fit in"? Explain.

3. What is the benefit of androgyny to girls? Can the same benefits be applied to boys?

4. Pipher's essay focuses on what happens to girls when they reach adolescence. Do you think she feels boys face similar issues? Do you think Pipher thinks society is harder on girls than on boys? Explain.

5. Is audience important to the success of this essay? Why or why not? How could this essay apply to issues that face both men and women?

6. Place Pipher's essay in different historical contexts. For example, do you think the problems she describes faced girls in the 1930s or the 1950s? Are the underlying social pressures facing teenage girls the same today? Explain.

Muscular Body Image Lures Boys into Gym, and Obsession

Douglas Quenqua*

The expression goes "vanity, thy name is woman," and most people think of body-obsessive behavior as a female trait. Women still account for 90 percent of cosmetic surgical procedures, and roughly the same number is true for teenagers being treated for eating disorders. But boys can be just as obsessed with their bodies, and

---

*Douglas Quenqua, *New York Times*, November 19, 2012.

pressure from athletics, sports, and the media can add to pressures boys must deal with. Tempted by steroids, cajoled by coaches, and encouraged by peers, some boys, explains journalist Douglas Quenqua, are playing a very dangerous game.

BEFORE YOU READ

What is the "perfect" male physique? What does it look like? Is your image influenced by outside forces, such as the media, your gender, or your age? How do the real men you know compare to the image you have in your mind?

AS YOU READ

The young man featured in this article, David, comments that people judge others on physical appearance. What do you want people to notice about you? How do your feelings compare to those David expresses in this article?

1   t is not just girls these days who are consumed by an unattainable body image.

2   Take David Abusheikh. At age 15, he started lifting weights for two hours a day, six days a week. Now that he is a senior at Fort Hamilton High School in Brooklyn, he has been adding protein bars and shakes to his diet to put on muscle without gaining fat. "I didn't used to be into supplements," said Mr. Abusheikh, 18, who plans on a career in engineering, "but I wanted something that would help me get bigger a little faster."

3   Pediatricians are starting to sound alarm bells about boys who take unhealthy measures to try to achieve Charles Atlas bodies that only genetics can truly confer. Whether it is long hours in the gym, allowances blown on expensive supplements or even risky experiments with illegal steroids, the price American boys are willing to pay for the perfect body appears to be on the rise.

4   In a study to be published in the November 2012 journal *Pediatrics*, more than 40 percent of boys in middle school and high school said they regularly exercised with the goal of increasing muscle mass. Thirty-eight percent said they used protein supplements, and nearly 6 percent said they had experimented with steroids. Over all, 90 percent of the 1,307 boys in the survey—who lived in the Minneapolis-St. Paul area, but typify what doctors say is a national phenomenon—said they exercised at least occasionally to add muscle.

5   "There has been a striking change in attitudes toward male body image in the last 30 years," said Dr. Harrison Pope, a psychiatry professor at Harvard who studies body-building culture and was not involved in the study. The portrayal of men as fat-free and chiseled "is dramatically more prevalent in society than it was a generation ago," he said.

6   While college-age men have long been interested in bodybuilding, pediatricians say they have been surprised to find that now even middle school boys are so absorbed with building muscles. And their youth adds an element of risk. Just as girls who count every calorie in an effort to be thin may do themselves more harm than good, boys who chase an illusory image of manhood may end up stunting their development, doctors say, particularly when they turn to supplements—or, worse, steroids—to supercharge their results.

7   "The problem with supplements is they're not regulated like drugs, so it's very hard to know what's in them," said Dr. Shalender Bhasin, a professor of medicine at Boston University School of Medicine and chief of endocrinology, diabetes and nutrition at Boston Medical Center. Some contain anabolic steroids, and even high-quality protein supplements might be dangerous in large amounts, or if taken to replace meals, he said. "These things just haven't been studied very well," he said.

8   Anabolic steroids pose a special danger to developing bodies, Dr. Bhasin said. Steroids "stop testosterone production in men," he said, leading to terrible withdrawal problems when still-growing boys try to stop taking them. Still, the constant association of steroids with elite athletes like Lance Armstrong and Barry Bonds perpetuates the notion that they can be managed successfully.

9   Online, in bodybuilding forums for teenagers, boys barely out of puberty share weight-lifting regimens and body fat percentages, and judge one another's progress. On Tumblr and Facebook, teenagers post images of ripped athletes under the heading "fitspo" or "fitspiraton," which are short for "fitness inspiration." The tags are spinoffs of "thinspo" and "thinspiration" pictures and videos, which have been banned from many sites for promoting anorexia. "Lifted b4 school today felt good but was weak as hell," wrote one boy who said he was 15 and from Tallahassee, Fla., on a message board on Bodybuilding.com in September, saying he bench-pressed 245 pounds. "Barely got it."

10   Many of these boys probably see themselves in Mike Sorrentino, "The Situation" from the "Jersey Shore" series on MTV, or the Adam Sackler character, on the HBO series "Girls," who rarely wears a shirt or takes a break from his crunches. Mr. Abusheikh, for instance, has a Facebook page full of photos of himself shirtless or showing off his six-pack abs. At his high school, participation in the annual bodybuilding competition hit an all-time high of 30 students this year.

11   "They ask us about everything," said Peter Rivera, a physical education teacher at Fort Hamilton High School who helps oversee the competition. "How do I lose weight? How do I gain muscle? How many times a week should I work out?" Some boys want to be stronger for sports, Mr. Rivera said, but others "want to change their body type."

12   Compared with a sedentary lifestyle of video games and TV, an obsession with working out may not quite qualify as a health hazard. And instructors like Mr. Rivera say most boys are eager for advice on the healthiest, drug-free ways to get in shape.

13   With so little known about supplements, it can be difficult, particularly for teenagers, to make wise decisions. Alonso Huizar, 16, of Tucson, could not say for sure which creatine supplements he takes. "I bounce around," he said. "I get, like, some type of chocolate flavor, depending on the price." Alonso started lifting weights at 15 because he wanted to get bigger for soccer, "but I was also just trying to gain weight in general," he said. Cristiano Ronaldo, the Portuguese soccer player, is the man with the body he would like to have, he said. His mother, Ana, said she would have preferred that Alonso hold off on weight training until he was older, but the pressure from coaches and peers made compromise impossible. "It's pushed on them—if you're going to play soccer, you have to lift weights," she said.

14   A majority of girls in the Minnesota study said they, too, had changed eating or exercise habits to build muscle, with 21 percent using protein supplements and nearly 5 percent using steroids. "The model of feminine beauty is now more toned and fit and sculpted

than it was a generation ago," said Marla Eisenberg, assistant professor of pediatrics at the University of Minnesota, the lead author of the Pediatrics study. "It's not just being thin. It's being thin and toned." Indeed, visitors to the "Fitspo" Facebook page are greeted by a sinewy model wearing a tank top that reads "Strong is the new skinny."

15   Paradoxically, the emphasis on weight lifting among adolescents may be depleting the number of contestants in teenage bodybuilding meets, because many children cannot pass a drug test. "You used to get a lot of teenage bodybuilders, but you don't get them as much anymore," said Andrew Bostinto, president of the National Gym Association. "A lot of these kids are juiced, so they're not entering natural shows." "You get these kids now, they're 5 feet 6 inches, 5 feet 7 inches, weighing 265 pounds with two percent body fat," he said. "Give me a break. You can't put on 30 pounds in a month."

16   Mr. Abusheikh, who stands 5 feet tall and weighs 125 pounds, said he steered clear of steroids and would prefer not to use supplements. But because of his small stature, he needed the extra bulk to compete in his school's bodybuilding contest. "I'm mostly trying to get into engineering," he said, "but if something gets in the way I figure I can always be a personal trainer."

QUESTIONS FOR ANALYSIS AND DISCUSSION

1. According to Quenqua, what is influencing the bodybuilding trend in teen boys? What is "troubling" about this trend? Explain.
2. The male physique as it appears in toys and video games has been blamed by some psychologists as influencing male body image. In your opinion, do the "jacked-up" muscles on action figures influence the way boys feel about their own bodies.
3. What cultural messages tell boys that steroid use is permissible? Describe some of the ways children receive these messages.
4. Analyze the author's use of statistics, facts, and supporting information to reinforce the points he makes in his essay. Do his conclusions seem reasonable based on the data he cites? Why or why not?
5. Compare the pressure on teen males to be fit and muscular to the pressure on teen females to be thin. In what ways are the two situations similar, and in what ways are they different?

Reading the Visual

NEDA Ad and BOSS Ad

Adolescence can be a period of great self-consciousness and insecurity. Some young people—especially teenage girls—may suffer from eating disorders such as anorexia nervosa or bulimia due to distorted self-perception. The person they see in the mirror is drastically different from physical reality. In 2004, the National Eating Disorders Association (NEDA) launched the "Get Real" awareness campaign to portray how distorted the self-image of someone suffering from an eating disorder can be. The campaign ran ads in several fashion and popular magazines, including *InStyle* and *People*. This print ad was created for NEDA by Porter Novelli, a public relations firm known for health care promotional campaigns.

The second ad is for BOSS cologne, a popular men's fragrance. The ad, aimed at the youth market, implies that the wearer of this cologne is a desirable sex object wanted for his lean, muscled and athletically toned physique. Rather than depicting a normal male, the ad features an idealized Adonis-like man clearly excelling in the world of athletics.

FRAGRANCE FOR MEN

BOSS IN MOTION

OFFICIAL PARTNER OF THE ENGLAND CRICKET TEAM

ENGLAND CRICKET

QUESTIONS FOR ANALYSIS AND DISCUSSION

1. These two ads are aimed at different genders. What does each ad assume about the viewer? How does each ad use social constructions of body image to promote its product? Explain.

2. What social and cultural influences could the BOSS ad have on young men? Do you think that men envision themselves to be like the man in the photograph if they use BOSS?

3. Both of these ads use untypical depictions of the body to get their point across. Evaluate how each tries to reach its audience and take action based on what viewers see.

4. If you were leafing through a magazine and saw either one of these ads, would you stop to read it or examine it? If so, why? What catches your eye?

5. What is happening in the NEDA photo? What is the young woman thinking? What does she see, and what do we, as the audience, see? Explain.

6. We have heard the expression "sex sells." How does sex "sell" BOSS cologne? Explain.

In the Combat Zone

Leslie Marmon Silko

Safety experts warn women not to walk alone at night, to park where it is well-lit, and to avoid areas that could conceal muggers or rapists. Self-defense classes for women stress avoidance tactics rather than ways to confront violence actively. This approach, says the Native American best-selling author Leslie Marmon Silko, creates a cultural consciousness of women as victims and targets. In this essay, Silko relates how her childhood hunting experiences helped empower her in a society that tends to view women as prey.*

BEFORE YOU READ

Have you ever found yourself planning your activities based on personal safety? For example, did you do without something because you were afraid of going to the store at night by yourself? Or have you skipped taking a shortcut when it was dark out? If not, why don't you fear these situations?

AS YOU READ

Note Silko's references to hunting throughout the essay. How does the theme of hunting unify the piece?

1   Women seldom discuss our wariness or the precautions we take after dark each time we leave the apartment, car, or office to go on the most brief errand. We take for granted that we are targeted as easy prey by muggers, rapists, and serial killers. This is our lot as women in the United States. We try to avoid going anywhere alone after dark, although economic necessity sends women out night after night. We do what must be done, but always we are alert, on guard and ready. We have to be aware of persons walking on the sidewalk behind us; we have to pay attention to others who board an elevator we're on. We try to avoid all staircases and deserted parking garages when we are alone. Constant vigilance requires considerable energy and concentration seldom required of men.

2   I used to assume that most men were aware of this fact of women's lives, but I was wrong. They may notice our reluctance to drive at night to the convenience store alone, but they don't know or don't want to know the experience of a woman out alone at night. Men who have been in combat know the feeling of being a predator's target, but it is difficult for men to admit that we women live our entire lives in a combat zone. Men have the power to end violence against women in the home, but they feel helpless to protect women from violent strangers. Because men feel guilt and anger at their inability to shoulder responsibility for the safety of their wives, sisters, and daughters, we don't often discuss random acts of violence against women.

---

*Leslie Marmon Silko, *In the Combat Zone*, 1996.

3   When we were children, my sisters and I used to go to Albuquerque with my father. Sometimes strangers would tell my father it was too bad that he had three girls and no sons. My father, who has always preferred the company of women, used to reply that he was glad to have girls and not boys, because he might not get along as well with boys. Furthermore, he'd say, "My girls can do anything your boys can do, and my girls can do it better." He had in mind, of course, shooting and hunting.

4   When I was six years old, my father took me along as he hunted deer; he showed me how to walk quietly, to move along and then to stop and listen carefully before taking another step. A year later, he traded a pistol for a little single shot .22 rifle just my size. He took me and my younger sisters down to the dump by the river and taught us how to shoot. We rummaged through the trash for bottles and glass jars; it was great fun to take aim at a pickle jar and watch it shatter. If the Rio San Jose had water running in it, we threw bottles for moving targets in the muddy current. My father told us that a .22 bullet can travel a mile, so we had to be careful where we aimed. The river was a good place because it was below the villages and away from the houses; the high clay riverbanks wouldn't let any bullets stray. Gun safety was drilled into us. We were cautioned about other children whose parents might not teach them properly; if we ever saw another child with a gun, we knew to get away. Guns were not toys. My father did not approve of BB guns because they were classified as toys. I had a .22 rifle when I was seven years old. If I felt like shooting, all I had to do was tell my parents where I was going, take my rifle and a box of 12 shells and go. I was never tempted to shoot at birds or animals because whatever was killed had to be eaten. Now, I realize how odd this must seem; a seven-year-old with a little .22 rifle and a box of ammunition, target shooting alone at the river. But that was how people lived at Laguna when I was growing up; children were given responsibility from an early age.

5   Laguna Pueblo people hunted deer for winter meat. When I was thirteen I carried George Pearl's saddle carbine, a .30–30, and hunted deer for the first time. When I was fourteen, I killed my first mule deer buck with one shot through the heart.

6   Guns were for target shooting and guns were for hunting, but also I knew that Grandma Lily carried a little purse gun with her whenever she drove alone to Albuquerque or Los Lunas. One night my mother and my grandmother were driving the fifty miles from Albuquerque to Laguna down Route 66 when three men in a car tried to force my grandmother's car off the highway. Route 66 was not so heavily traveled as Interstate 40 is now, and there were many long stretches of highway where no other car passed for minutes on end. Payrolls at the Jackpile Uranium Mine were large in the 1950s, and my mother or my grandmother had to bring home thousands from the bank in Albuquerque to cash the miners' checks on paydays.

7   After that night, my father bought my mother a pink nickel-plated snub-nose .22 revolver with a white bone grip. Grandma Lily carried a tiny Beretta as black as her prayer book. As my sisters and I got older, my father taught us to handle and shoot handguns, revolvers mostly, because back then, semiautomatic pistols were not as reliable—they frequently jammed. I will never forget the day my father told us three girls that we never had to let a man hit us or terrorize us because no matter how big and strong the man was, a gun in our hand equalized all differences of size and strength.

8   Much has been written about violence in the home and spousal abuse. I wish to focus instead on violence from strangers toward women because this form of violence terrifies

women more, despite the fact that most women are murdered by a spouse, relative, fellow employee, or next-door neighbor, not a stranger. Domestic violence kills many more women and children than strangers kill, but domestic violence also follows more predictable patterns and is more familiar—he comes home drunk and she knows what comes next. A good deal of the terror of a stranger's attack comes from its suddenness and unexpectedness. Attacks by strangers occur with enough frequency that battered women and children often cite their fears of such attacks as reasons for remaining in abusive domestic situations. They fear the violence they imagine strangers will inflict upon them more than they fear the abusive home. More than one feminist has pointed out that rapists and serial killers help keep the patriarchy in place.

9   An individual woman may be terrorized by her spouse, but women are not sufficiently terrorized that we avoid marriage. Yet many women I know, including myself, try to avoid going outside of their homes alone after dark. Big deal, you say; well yes, it is a big deal since most lectures, performances, and films are presented at night; so are dinners and other social events. Women out alone at night who are assaulted by strangers are put on trial by public opinion: Any woman out alone after dark is asking for trouble. Presently, for millions of women of all socioeconomic backgrounds, sundown is lockdown. We are prisoners of violent strangers.

10   Daylight doesn't necessarily make the streets safe for women. In the early 1980s, a rapist operated in Tucson in the afternoon near the University of Arizona campus. He often accosted two women at once, forced them into residential alleys, then raped each one with a knife to her throat and forced the other to watch. Afterward the women said that part of the horror of their attack was that all around them, everything appeared normal. They could see people inside their houses and cars going down the street—all around them life was going on as usual while their lives were being changed forever.

11   The afternoon rapist was not the only rapist in Tucson at that time; there was the prime-time rapist, the potbellied rapist, and the apologetic rapist all operating in Tucson in the 1980s. The prime-time rapist was actually two men who invaded comfortable foothills homes during television prime time when residents were preoccupied with television and eating dinner. The prime-time rapists terrorized entire families; they raped the women and sometimes they raped the men. Family members were forced to go to automatic bank machines, to bring back cash to end the ordeal. Potbelly rapist and apologetic rapist need little comment, except to note that the apologetic rapist was good looking, well educated, and smart enough to break out of jail for one last rape followed by profuse apologies and his capture in the University of Arizona library. Local papers recounted details about Tucson's last notorious rapist, the red bandanna rapist. In the late 1970s this rapist attacked more than twenty women over a three-year period, and Tucson police were powerless to stop him. Then one night, the rapist broke into a midtown home where the lone resident, a woman, shot him four times in the chest with a .38 caliber revolver.

12   In midtown Tucson, on a weekday afternoon, I was driving down Campbell Avenue to the pet store. Suddenly the vehicle behind me began to weave into my lane, so I beeped the horn politely. The vehicle swerved back to its lane, but then in my rearview mirror I saw the small late-model truck change lanes and begin to follow my car very closely. I drove a few blocks without looking in the rearview mirror, but in my sideview mirror I saw the compact truck was right behind me. OK. Some motorists stay upset for two

or three blocks, some require ten blocks or more to recover their senses. Stoplight after stoplight, when I glanced into the rearview mirror I saw the man—in his early thirties, tall, white, brown hair, and dark glasses. This guy must not have a job if he has the time to follow me for miles—oh, ohhh! No beast more dangerous in the U.S.A. than an unemployed white man.

13   At this point I had to make a decision: do I forget about the trip to the pet store and head for the police station downtown, four miles away? Why should I have to let this stranger dictate my schedule for the afternoon? The man might dare to follow me to the police station, but by the time I reach the front door of the station, he'd be gone. No crime was committed; no Arizona law forbids tailgating someone for miles or for turning into a parking lot behind them. What could the police do? I had no license plate number to report because Arizona requires only one license plate, on the rear bumper of the vehicle. Anyway, I was within a block of the pet store where I knew I could get help from the pet store owners. I would feel better about this incident if it was not allowed to ruin my trip to the pet store.

14   The guy was right on my rear bumper; if I'd had to stop suddenly for any reason, there'd have been a collision. I decide I will not stop even if he does ram into the rear of my car. I study this guy's face in my rearview mirror, six feet two inches tall, 175 pounds, medium complexion, short hair, trimmed moustache. He thinks he can intimidate me because I am a woman, five feet five inches tall, 140 pounds. But I am not afraid, I am furious. I refuse to be intimidated. I won't play his game. I can tell by the face I see in the mirror this guy has done this before; he enjoys using his truck to menace lone women.

15   I keep thinking he will quit, or he will figure that he's scared me enough; but he seems to sense that I am not afraid. It's true. I am not afraid because years ago my father taught my sisters and me that we did not have to be afraid. He'll give up when I turn into the parking lot outside the pet store, I think. But I watch in my rearview mirror; he's right on my rear bumper. As his truck turns into the parking lot behind my car, I reach over and open the glove compartment. I take out the holster with my .38 special and lay it on the car seat beside me.

16   I turned my car into a parking spot so quickly that I was facing my stalker who had momentarily stopped his truck and was watching me. I slid the .38 out of its holster onto my lap. I watched the stranger's face, trying to determine whether he would jump out of his truck with a baseball bat or gun and come after me. I felt calm. No pounding heart or rapid breathing. My early experience deer hunting had prepared me well. I did not panic because I felt I could stop him if he tried to harm me. I was in no hurry. I sat in the car and waited to see what choice my stalker would make. I looked directly at him without fear because I had my .38 and I was ready to use it. The expression on my face must have been unfamiliar to him; he was used to seeing terror in the eyes of the women he followed. The expression on my face communicated a warning: if he approached the car window, I'd kill him.

17   He took a last look at me and then sped away. I stayed in the car until his truck disappeared in the traffic of Campbell Avenue.

18   I walked into the pet store shaken. I had felt able to protect myself throughout the incident, but it left me emotionally drained and exhausted. The stranger had only pursued me—how much worse to be battered or raped.

19   Years before, I was unarmed the afternoon that two drunken deer hunters threatened to shoot me off my horse with razor-edged hunting crossbows. I was riding a colt on a national park trail near my home in the Tucson Mountains. These young white men in their late twenties were complete strangers who might have shot me if the colt had not galloped away erratically bucking and leaping—a moving target too difficult for the drunken bow hunters to aim at. The colt brought me to my ranch house where I called the county sheriff's office and the park ranger. I live in a sparsely populated area where my nearest neighbor is a quarter-mile away. I was afraid the men might have followed me back to my house so I took the .44 magnum out from under my pillow and strapped it around my waist until the sheriff or park ranger arrived. Forty-five minutes later, the park ranger arrived— the deputy sheriff arrived fifteen minutes after him. The drunken bow hunters were apprehended on the national park and arrested for illegally hunting; their bows and arrows were seized as evidence for the duration of bow hunting season. In southern Arizona that is enough punishment; I didn't want to take a chance of stirring up additional animosity with these men because I lived alone then; I chose not to make a complaint about their threatening words and gestures. I did not feel that I backed away by not pressing charges; I feared that if I pressed assault charges against these men, they would feel that I was challenging them to all-out war. I did not want to have to kill either of them if they came after me, as I thought they might. With my marksmanship and my .243 caliber hunting rifle from the old days, I am confident that I could stop idiots like these. But to have to take the life of another person is a terrible experience I will always try to avoid.

20   It isn't height or weight or strength that make women easy targets; from infancy women are taught to be self-sacrificing, passive victims. I was taught differently. Women have the right to protect themselves from death or bodily harm. By becoming strong and potentially lethal individuals, women destroy the fantasy that we are sitting ducks for predatory strangers.

21   In a great many cultures, women are taught to depend upon others, not themselves, for protection from bodily harm. Women are not taught to defend themselves from strangers because fathers and husbands fear the consequences themselves. In the United States, women depend upon the courts and the police; but as many women have learned the hard way, the police cannot be outside your house twenty-four hours a day. I don't want more police. More police on the street will not protect women. A few policemen are rapists and killers of women themselves; their uniforms and squad cars give them an advantage. No, I will be responsible for my own safety, thank you.

22   Women need to decide who has the primary responsibility for the health and safety of their bodies. We don't trust the State to manage our reproductive organs, yet most of us blindly trust that the State will protect us (and our reproductive organs) from predatory strangers. One look at the rape and murder statistics for women (excluding domestic incidents) and it is clear that the government FAILS to protect women from the violence of strangers. Some may cry out for a "stronger" State, more police, mandatory sentences, and swifter executions. Over the years we have seen the U.S. prison population become the largest in the world, executions take place every week now, inner-city communities are occupied by the National Guard, and people of color are harassed by police, but guess what? A woman out alone, night or day, is confronted with more danger of random violence from strangers than ever before. As the U.S. economy continues "to downsize," and

the good jobs disappear forever, our urban and rural landscapes will include more desperate, angry men with nothing to lose.

23   Only women can put a stop to the "open season" on women by strangers. Women are TAUGHT to be easy targets by their mothers, aunts, and grandmothers who themselves were taught that "a women doesn't kill" or "a woman doesn't learn how to use a weapon." Women must learn how to take aggressive action individually, apart from the police and the courts. . . . Those who object to firearms need trained companion dogs or collectives of six or more women to escort one another day and night. We must destroy the myth that women are born to be easy targets.

QUESTIONS FOR ANALYSIS AND DISCUSSION

1. Why, according to Silko, do women live in a state of fear? What measures must they take to prevent personal harm? What effect does this mentality have on society as a whole?

2. How does a gun equalize the differences between men and women? Do you agree with Silko's father's comment that she and her sisters should never be afraid because a gun "equalized all differences of size and strength" (paragraph 7)?

3. Silko points out that "more than one feminist has pointed out that rapists and serial killers help keep the patriarchy in place" (paragraph 8). How do acts of violence against women maintain the "patriarchy"? What is the patriarchy?

4. Crime experts say that most rapes are motivated by a desire for power and not really for sex. Apply this fact to the rapists Silko describes in paragraphs 10 and 11.

5. In paragraph 21, Silko comments that in many cultures, "women are not taught to defend themselves from strangers because fathers and husbands fear the consequences themselves." What does she mean? Does this statement apply to American society? Explain.

6. How does Silko's story of her trip to the pet store support her argument? Explain.

7. Throughout the essay, Silko makes references to hunting. Explore the multifaceted levels of this hunting theme.

Child-Man in the Promised Land
Kay S. Hymowitz

Many social critics agree that adolescence has been extended. Only 40 years ago, many men and women were married and starting families by the time they were 24 years old. Today, however, the average age of marriage and family has been bumped back, in some cases *way* back. Today's single young men hang out in a hormonal limbo between adolescence and adulthood argues writer and social critic Kay S. Hymowitz. Men are in no hurry to grow up, and the trend has some interesting consequences.*

BEFORE YOU READ ————————————————————————————

Why are young adults waiting longer than ever to get married and have children? What are your own plans for marriage and family? For life five to ten years after graduation?

AS YOU READ ————————————————————————————

Is Hymowitz supportive or critical of the "child-man" she describes? Identify areas in her essay that reveal her point of view on this topic.

1   It's 1965 and you're a 26-year-old white guy. You have a factory job, or maybe you work for an insurance broker. Either way, you're married, probably have been for a few years now; you met your wife in high school, where she was in your sister's class. You've already got one kid, with another on the way. For now, you're renting an apartment in your parents' two-family house, but you're saving up for a three-bedroom ranch house in the next town. Yup, you're an adult!

2   Now meet the twenty-first-century you, also 26. You've finished college and work in a cubicle in a large Chicago financial-services firm. You live in an apartment with a few single guy friends. In your spare time, you play basketball with your buddies, download the latest indie songs from iTunes, have some fun with the Xbox 360, take a leisurely shower, massage some product into your hair and face—and then it's off to bars and parties, where you meet, and often bed, girls of widely varied hues and sizes. They come from everywhere: California, Tokyo, Alaska, Australia. Wife? Kids? House? Are you *kidding*?

3   Not so long ago, the average mid-twentysomething had achieved most of adulthood's milestones—high school degree, financial independence, marriage, and children. These days, he lingers—happily—in a new hybrid state of semi-hormonal adolescence and responsible self-reliance. Decades in unfolding, this limbo may not seem like news to many, but in fact it is to the early twenty-first century what adolescence was to the early twentieth: a momentous sociological development of profound economic and cultural import. Some call this new period "emerging adulthood," others "extended adolescence"; David Brooks recently took a stab with the "Odyssey Years," a "decade of wandering."

4   But while we grapple with the name, it's time to state what is now obvious to legions of frustrated young women: the limbo doesn't bring out the best in young men. With women, you could argue that adulthood is in fact emergent. Single women in their twenties and early thirties are joining an international New Girl Order, hyperachieving in both school and an increasingly female-friendly workplace, while packing leisure hours with

———————————————

*Kay S. Hymowitz, *City Journal*, Winter 2008.

shopping, traveling, and dining with friends [see "The New Girl Order," Autumn 2007]. Single Young Males, or SYMs, by contrast, often seem to hang out in a playground of drinking, hooking up, playing *Halo 3*, and, in many cases, underachieving. With them, adulthood looks as though it's receding.

5   Freud famously asked: "What do women want?" Notice that he didn't ask what men wanted—perhaps he thought that he'd figured that one out. But that's a question that ad people, media execs, and cultural entrepreneurs have pondered a lot in recent years. They're particularly interested in single young men, for two reasons: there are a lot more of them than before; and they tend to have some extra change. Consider: in 1970, 69 percent of 25-year-old and 85 percent of 30-year-old white men were married; in 2000, only 33 percent and 58 percent were, respectively. And the percentage of young guys tying the knot is declining as you read this. Census Bureau data show that the median age of marriage among men rose from 26.8 in 2000 to 27.5 in 2006—a dramatic demographic shift for such a short time period.

6   That adds up to tens of millions more young men blissfully free of mortgages, wives, and child-care bills. Historically, marketers have found this group an "elusive audience"— the phrase is permanently affixed to "men between 18 and 34" in adspeak—largely immune to the pleasures of magazines and television, as well as to shopping expeditions for the products advertised there. But by the mid-1990s, as SYM ranks swelled, marketers began to get their number. One signal moment came in April 1997, when *Maxim*, a popular British "lad magazine," hit American shores. *Maxim* strove to be the anti-*Playboy*-and-*Esquire*; bad-boy owner Felix Dennis sniffed at celebrity publishers with their tired formulas. Instead, he later observed, the magazine's creators adopted the "astonishing methodology of asking our readers what they wanted . . . and then supplying it."

7   And what did those readers—male, unmarried, median age 26, median household income $60,000 or so—want? As the philosophers would say, duh. *Maxim* plastered covers and features with pouty-lipped, tousled-haired pinups in lacy underwear and, in case that didn't do the trick, block-lettered promises of sex! lust! naughty! And it worked. More than any men's magazine before or since, *Maxim* grabbed that elusive 18- to 34-year-old single-college-educated-guy market, and soon boasted about 2.5 million readers—more than *GQ, Esquire*, and *Men's Journal* combined.

8   Victoria's Secret cover art doesn't fully explain the SYM's attraction to *Maxim*. After all, plenty of down-market venues had the sort of bodacious covers bound to trigger the young male's reptilian brain. No, what set *Maxim* apart from other men's mags was its voice. It was the sound of guys hanging around the Animal House living room—where put-downs are high-fived; gadgets are cool; rock stars, sports heroes, and cyborg battles are awesome; jobs and Joni Mitchell suck; and babes are simply hot—or not. "Are there any cool jobs related to beer?" a reader's letter asks in a recent issue. Answer: brand manager, beer tester, and brewmaster.

9   *Maxim* asked the SYM what he wanted and learned that he didn't want to grow up. Whatever else you might say about *Playboy* or *Esquire*, they tried to project the image of a cultured and au courant fellow; as Hefner famously—and from today's cultural vantage point, risibly—wrote in an early *Playboy*, his ideal reader enjoyed "inviting a female acquaintance in for a quiet discussion of Picasso, Nietzsche, jazz, sex." Hearing this, the *Maxim* dude would want to hurl. He'd like to forget that he ever went to school.

10   *Maxim* happily obliges. The editors try to keep readers' minds from wandering with articles like "Confessions of a Strip Club Bouncer." But they rely heavily on picture-laden features promoting the latest skateboards, video games, camcorders, and other tech products, along with an occasional Q-and-A with, say, Kid Rock—all with the bare minimum of print required to distinguish a magazine from a shopping catalog or pinup calendar. *Playboy*'s philosophy may not have been Aristotle, but it was an attempt, of sorts, to define the good life. The *Maxim* reader prefers lists, which make up in brevity what they lose in thought: "Ten Greatest Video Game Heroes of All Time," "The Five Unsexiest Women Alive," "Sixteen People Who Look Like They Absolutely Reek," and so on.

11   Still, *Maxim* is far from dumb, as its self-mockery proves. The *Maxim* child-man prides himself on his lack of pretense, his unapologetic guyness. The magazine's subtext seems to be: "We're just a bunch of horny, insensitive guys—so what?" What else to make of an article entitled "How to Make Your Girlfriend Think Her Cat's Death Was an Accident"? "The only thing worse than a show about doctors is a show about sappy chick doctors we're forced to watch or else our girlfriends won't have sex with us," the editors grumble about the popular (with women) *Grey's Anatomy*.

12   The *Maxim* child-man voice has gone mainstream, which may explain why the magazine's sales were flat enough for Dennis to sell it last summer. You're that 26-year-old who wants sophomoric fun and macho action? Now the culture has a groaning table of entertainment with your name on it. Start with the many movies available in every guy-friendly genre: sci-fi flicks like *Transformers*, action and crime movies like *American Gangster*, comedies like *Superbad*, and the seemingly endless line of films starring Adam Sandler, Jim Carrey, and the "Frat Pack," as *USA Today* dubbed the group of young male comedians that includes Will Ferrell, Ben Stiller, Vince Vaughn, Owen and Luke Wilson, Jack Black, and Steve Carell.

13   With a talent for crude physical comedy, gleeful juvenility, and self-humiliation, the Frat Packers are the child-man counterparts to the more conventional leads, like George Clooney and Brad Pitt, whom women and *Esquire* editors love. In *Old School* (2003), three guys in their thirties decide to start a college fraternity. Frank the Tank (the moniker refers to his capacity for alcohol), played by Ferrell, flashes his saggy white derriere streaking through the college town; the scene is a child-man classic. In 2005's *The 40-Year-Old Virgin*, Carell plays a middle-aged nerd with a large action-figure collection but no action. In one guy-favorite scene, a beautician painfully waxes Carell's hirsute chest; as Carell pointed out later, this was a "guy thing, this sadistic nature that men have to see other men in non-life-threatening pain."

14   Even though the networks must be more restrained, television also has plenty of "stupid fun" (as *Maxim* calls a regular feature), gross-out humor, and even low-level sadism for child-man viewers. This state of affairs is newer than you might think. Apart from sports programming and *The Simpsons*, which came along in the early 1990s, there wasn't a lot to make young men pick up the remote. Most prime-time television appealed to women and families, whose sensibilities were as alien to dudes as finger bowls.

15   Today, the child-man can find entire networks devoted to his interests: Spike TV runs wrestling matches, *Star Trek* reruns, and the high-tech detective drama *CSI*; Blackbelt TV broadcasts martial arts around the clock; sci-fi is everywhere. Several years ago, the Cartoon Network spied the potential in the child-man market, too, and introduced Adult

Swim, late-night programming with "adult" cartoons like *Family Guy* and *Futurama*, a cult favorite co-created by Matt Groening of *The Simpsons* fame. Adult Swim has cut into the male Letterman and Leno audience, luring gold-plated advertisers Saab, Apple, and Taco Bell; child-men, it should come as no surprise, eat lots of fast food.

16   One can also lay the success of cable giant Comedy Central at the child-man's sneakered foot. In its early-nineties infancy, Comedy Central had old movie comedies, some stand-up acts, and few viewers. The next several years brought some buzz with shows like *Politically Incorrect.* But it was in 1997—the same year that *Maxim* arrived in America— that the network struck gold with a cartoon series starring a group of foul-mouthed eight-year-old boys. With its cutting subversion of all that's sacred and polite, *South Park* was like a dog whistle that only SYMs could hear; the show became the highest-rated cable series in that age group.

17   In 1999, the network followed up with *The Man Show*, famous for its "Juggies" (half-naked women with exceptionally large, well, juggies), interviews with porn stars, drinking songs, and a jingle that advised, "Quit your job and light a fart / Yank your favorite private part." It was "like *Maxim* for TV," one network executive told Media Life. Comedy Central's viewers, almost two-thirds of them male, have made both *The Daily Show* and *The Colbert Report* cultural touchstones and launched the careers of stars like Bill Maher, Jimmy Kimmel, Dave Chapelle, and, most notably, Daily Show anchor Jon Stewart—who has already hosted the Academy Awards and is set to do so again, a perfect symbol of the mainstreaming of the SYM sensibility.

18   Nothing attests more to the SYM's growing economic and cultural might than video games do. Once upon a time, video games were for little boys and girls—well, mostly little boys—who loved their Nintendos so much, the lament went, that they no longer played ball outside. Those boys have grown up to become child-man gamers, turning a niche industry into a $12 billion powerhouse. Men between the ages of 18 and 34 are now the biggest gamers; according to Nielsen Media, almost half—48.2 percent—of American males in that age bracket had used a console during the last quarter of 2006, and did so, on average, *two hours and 43 minutes per day.* (That's 13 minutes longer than 12- to 17-year-olds, who evidently have more responsibilities than today's twentysomethings.) Gaming—online games, as well as news and information about games—often registers as the top category in monthly surveys of Internet usage.

19   And the child-man's home sweet media home is the Internet, where no meddling censors or nervous advertisers deflect his desires. Some sites, like MensNewsDaily.com, are edgy news providers. Others, like AskMen.com, which claims 5 million visitors a month, post articles like "How to Score a Green Chick" in the best spirit of *Maxim*-style self-parody. "How is an SUV-driving, to-go-cup-using, walking environmental catastrophe like yourself supposed to hook up with them?" the article asks. Answer: Go to environmental meetings, yoga, or progressive bookstores ("but watch out for lesbians").

20   Other sites, like MenAreBetterThanWomen.com, TuckerMax.com, TheBestPage InTheUniverse.com, and DrunkasaurusRex.com, walk *Maxim's* goofiness and good-natured woman-teasing over the line into nastiness. The men hanging out on these sites take pride in being "badasses" and view the other half bitterly. A misogynist is a "man who hates women as much as women hate each other," writes one poster at MenAreBetterThanWomen. Another rails about "classic woman 'trap' questions—Does

this make me look fat? Which one of my friends would you sleep with if you had to? Do you really enjoy strip clubs?" The Fifth Amendment was created because its architects' wives "drove them ape-shit asking questions that they'd be better off simply refusing to answer."

21   That sound you hear is women not laughing. Oh, some women get a kick out of child-men and their frat/fart jokes; about 20 percent of *Maxim* readers are female, for instance, and presumably not all are doing research for the dating scene. But for many of the fairer sex, the child-man is either an irritating mystery or a source of heartbreak. In Internet chat rooms, in advice columns, at female water-cooler confabs, and in the pages of chick lit, the words "immature" and "men" seem united in perpetuity. Women complain about the "Peter Pan syndrome"—the phrase has been around since the early 1980s but it is resurgent—the "Mr. Not Readys," and the "Mr. Maybes." *Sex and the City* chronicled the frustrations of four thirtysomething women with immature, loutish, and uncommitted men for six popular seasons.

22   Naturally, women wonder: How did this perverse creature come to be? The most prevalent theory comes from feminist-influenced academics and cultural critics, who view dude media as symptoms of backlash, a masculinity crisis. Men feel threatened by female empowerment, these thinkers argue, and in their anxiety, they cling to outdated roles. The hyper-masculinity of *Maxim* et al. doesn't reflect any genuine male proclivities; rather, retrograde media "construct" it.

23   The fact that guys cheer on female heroines like Buffy the Vampire Slayer as much as they do Chuck Norris tells against this theory somewhat. But there's an ounce of truth to it. The men of the new media are in backlash mode, largely because they believe that feminists have stood in their way as media gatekeepers—that is, agents, editors, producers, and the like—who don't understand or accept "men acting like men." They gleefully stick their thumbs in the eyes of politically correct tsk-tskers. In one *South Park* episode, the Sexual Harassment Panda, a mascot who teaches schoolkids the evils of sexual harassment, is fired after his little talks provoke a flood of inane lawsuits. In *Maxim*, readers can find articles like "How to Cure a Feminist," one of whose recommendations is to "pretend you share her beliefs" by asking questions like, "Has Gloria Steinem's marriage hurt the feminist agenda?"

24   Insofar as the new guy media reflect a backlash against feminism, they're part of the much larger story of men's long, uneasy relationship with bourgeois order. The SYM with a taste for *Maxim* or *South Park* may not like Gloria Steinem, but neither does he care for anyone who tells him to behave—teachers, nutritionists, prohibitionists, vegetarians, librarians, church ladies, counselors, and moralists of all stripes. In fact, men have always sought out an antisocial, even anarchic, edge in their popular culture. In a renowned essay, the critic Barbara Ehrenreich argued that the arrival of *Playboy* in 1953 represented the beginning of a male rebellion against the conformity of mid-century family life and of middle-class virtues like duty and self-discipline. "All woman wants is security," she quotes an early *Playboy* article complaining. "And she is perfectly willing to crush man's adventurous freedom-loving spirit to get it." Even the name of the magazine, Ehrenreich observed, "defied the convention of hard-won maturity."

25   Ehrenreich was right about the seditious impulse behind *Playboy*, but wrong about its novelty. Male resistance to bourgeois domesticity had been going on since the bourgeoisie

went domestic. In *A Man's Place*, historian John Tosh locates the rebellion's roots in the early nineteenth century, when middle-class expectations for men began to shift away from the patriarchal aloofness of the bad old days. Under the newer bourgeois regime, the home was to be a haven in a heartless world, in which affection and intimacy were guiding virtues. But in Tosh's telling, it didn't take long before men vented frustrations with bourgeois domestication: they went looking for excitement and male camaraderie in empire building, in adventure novels by authors like Robert Louis Stevenson, and in going to "the club."

26   By the early twentieth century, the emerging mass market in the U.S. offered new outlets for the virile urges that sat awkwardly in the bourgeois parlor; hence titles like *Field and Stream* and *Man's Adventure*, as well as steamier fare like *Escapade* and *Caper*. When television sets came on the market in the late 1940s, it was the airing of heavy-weight fights and football games that led Dad to make the big purchase; to this day, sports events—the battlefield made civilized—glue him to the Barcalounger when he should be folding the laundry.

27   But this history suggests an uncomfortable fact about the new SYM: he's immature because he can be. We can argue endlessly about whether "masculinity" is natural or con-structed—whether men are innately promiscuous, restless, and slobby, or socialized to be that way—but there's no denying the lesson of today's media marketplace: give young men a choice between serious drama on the one hand, and Victoria's Secret models, bat-tling cyborgs, exploding toilets, and the NFL on the other, and it's the models, cyborgs, toilets, and football by a mile. For whatever reason, adolescence appears to be the young man's default state, proving what anthropologists have discovered in cultures everywhere: it is marriage and children that turn boys into men. Now that the SYM can put off family into the hazily distant future, he can—and will—try to stay a child-man. Yesterday's pater-familias or Levittown dad may have sought to escape the duties of manhood through fan-tasies of adventures at sea, pinups, or sublimated war on the football field, but there was considerable social pressure for him to be a mensch. Not only is no one asking that today's twenty- or thirtysomething become a responsible husband and father—that is, grow up—but a freewheeling marketplace gives him everything that he needs to settle down in pig's heaven indefinitely.

28   And that heaven can get pretty piggish. Take Tucker Max, whose eponymous web-site is a great favorite among his peers. In a previous age, Max would have been what was known as a "catch." Good-looking, ambitious, he graduated from the University of Chicago and Duke Law. But in a universe where child-men can thrive, he has found it more to his liking—and remarkably easy—to pursue a different career path: professional "asshole." Max writes what he claims are "true stories about my nights out acting like an average twentysomething"—binge drinking (UrbanDictionary.com lists Tucker Max Drunk, or TMD, as a synonym for "falling down drunk"), fighting, leaving vomit and fecal detritus for others to clean up, and, above all, hooking up with "random" girls galore—sorority sisters, Vegas waitresses, Dallas lap dancers, and Junior Leaguers who're into erotic asphyxiation.

29   Throughout his adventures, Max—like a toddler stuck somewhere around the oedipal stage—remains fixated on his penis and his "dumps." He is utterly without conscience—"Female insecurity: it's the gift that keeps on giving," he writes about his efforts to

undermine his prey's self-esteem in order to seduce them more easily. Think of Max as the final spawn of an aging and chromosomally challenged Hugh Hefner, and his website and best-selling book, *I Hope They Serve Beer in Hell,* as evidence of a male culture in profound decline. *Playboy*'s aspirations toward refinement still hinted at the call of the ego and a culture with limits on male restiveness; Max, the child-man who answers to no one except his fellow "assholes," is all id—and proud of it.

30   Now, you could argue that the motley crew of *Maxim*, Comedy Central, *Halo 3*, and even the noxious Tucker Max aren't much to worry about, and that extended adolescence is what the word implies: a temporary stage. Most guys have lots of other things going on, and even those who spend too much time on TuckerMax.com will eventually settle down. Men know the difference between entertainment and real life. At any rate, like gravity, growing up happens; nature has rules.

31   That's certainly a hope driving the sharpest of recent child-man entertainments, Judd Apatow's hit movie *Knocked Up*. What sets *Knocked Up* apart from, say, *Old School*, is that it invites the audience to enjoy the SYM's immaturity—his T-and-A obsessions, his slobby indolence—even while insisting on its feebleness. The potheaded 23-year-old Ben Stone accidentally impregnates Alison, a gorgeous stranger he was lucky enough to score at a bar. He is clueless about what to do when she decides to have the baby, not because he's a "badass"—actually, he has a big heart—but because he dwells among social retards. His roommates spend their time squabbling about who farted on whose pillow and when to launch their porn website. His father is useless, too: "I've been divorced three times," he tells Ben when his son asks for advice about his predicament. "Why are you asking me?" In the end, though, Ben understands that he needs to grow up. He gets a job and an apartment, and learns to love Alison and the baby. This is a comedy, after all.

32   It is also a fairy tale for guys. You wouldn't know how to become an adult even if you wanted to? Maybe a beautiful princess will come along and show you. But the important question that Apatow's comedy deals with only obliquely is what extended living as a child-man does to a guy—and to the women he collides with along the way.

33   For the problem with child-men is that they're not very promising husbands and fathers. They suffer from a proverbial "fear of commitment," another way of saying that they can't stand to think of themselves as permanently attached to one woman. Sure, they have girlfriends; many are even willing to move in with them. But cohabiting can be just another Peter Pan delaying tactic. Women tend to see cohabiting as a potential path to marriage; men view it as another place to hang out or, as Barbara Dafoe Whitehead observes in *Why There Are No Good Men Left*, a way to "get the benefits of a wife without shouldering the reciprocal obligations of a husband."

34   Even men who do marry don't easily overcome child-manhood. Neal Pollack speaks for some of them in his 2007 memoir *Alternadad*. Pollack struggles with how to stay "hip"—smoking pot and going to rock concerts—once he becomes a father to Elijah, "the new roommate," as he calls him. Pollack makes peace with fatherhood because he finds that he can introduce his toddler to the best alternative bands, and also because he has so many opportunities to exercise the child-man's fascination with "poop." He is affectingly mad for his little boy. Yet his efforts to turn his son into a hip little Neal Pollack—"My son and I were moshing! Awesome!"—reflect the self-involvement of the child-man who resists others' claims on him.

35   *Knocked Up* evokes a more destructive self-involvement in a subplot involving Alison's miserably married sister Debbie and her husband, Pete, the father of her two little girls. Pete, who frequently disappears to play fantasy baseball, get high in Las Vegas, or just go to the movies on his own, chronically wields irony to distance himself from his family. "Care more!" his wife yells at him. "You're cool because you don't give a shit."

36   And that "coolness" points to what may be the deepest existential problem with the child-man—a tendency to avoid not just marriage but any deep attachments. This is British writer Nick Hornby's central insight in his novel *About a Boy*. The book's antihero, Will, is an SYM whose life is as empty of passion as of responsibility. He has no self apart from pop-culture effluvia, a fact that the author symbolizes by having the jobless 36-year-old live off the residuals of a popular Christmas song written by his late father. Hornby shows how the media-saturated limbo of contemporary guyhood makes it easy to fill your days without actually doing anything. "Sixty years ago, all the things Will relied on to get him through the day simply didn't exist," Hornby writes. "There was no daytime TV, there were no videos, there were no glossy magazines. . . . Now, though, it was easy [to do nothing]. There was almost too much to do."

37   Will's unemployment is part of a more general passionlessness. To pick up women, for instance, he pretends to have a son and joins a single-parent organization; the plight of the single mothers means nothing to him. For Will, women are simply fleshy devices that dispense sex, and sex is just another form of entertainment, a "fantastic carnal alternative to drink, drugs, and a great night out, but nothing much more than that."

38   As the title of his 2005 novel *Indecision* suggests, Benjamin Kunkel also shows how apathy infects the new SYM world. His hero, 28-year-old Dwight Wilmerding, suffers from "abulia"—chronic indecisiveness—so severe that he finds himself paralyzed by the Thanksgiving choices of turkey, cranberry sauce, and dressing. His parents are divorced, his most recent girlfriend has faded away, and he has lost his job. Like Will, Dwight is a quintessential slacker, unable to commit and unwilling to feel. The only woman he has loved is his sister, who explains the attraction: "I'm the one girl you actually got to know in the right way. It was gradual, it was inevitable." Like Hornby, Kunkel sees the easy availability of sex as a source of slacker apathy. In a world of serial relationships, SYMs "fail to sublimate their libidinal energies in the way that actually makes men attractive," Kunkel told a dismayed female interviewer in *Salon*. With no one to challenge them to deeper connections, they swim across life's surfaces.

39   The superficiality, indolence, and passionlessness evoked in Hornby's and Kunkel's novels haven't triggered any kind of cultural transformation. Kunkel's book briefly made a few regional bestseller lists, and Hornby sells well enough. But sales of "lad lit," as some call books with SYM heroes, can't hold a candle to those of its chick-lit counterpart. The SYM doesn't read much, remember, and he certainly doesn't read anything prescribing personal transformation. The child-man may be into self-mockery; self-reflection is something else entirely.

40   That's too bad. Men are "more unfinished as people," Kunkel has neatly observed. Young men especially need a culture that can help them define worthy aspirations. Adults don't emerge. They're made.

41   What messages do these magazines project about women, and how do they influence men's personal identities and how they relate to the opposite sex?

1. According to Hymowitz, what does the popularity of men's magazines such as *Maxim* and *FHM* reveal about men and masculinity today? Why are these magazines so popular? Do you think they would have found a market if they had been introduced 20 or 30 years ago? Why or why not?

2. Evaluate Hymowitz's comparison of a man from 1965 and a man today. What differences exist? Why does she think things have not changed for the better? Do you agree? Explain.

3. Hymowitz noted that psychologist Sigmund Freud famously asked, "What do women want?" Based on your personal experience and information provided in this essay, answer this question from your own perspective. If you are male, what do you think women want? If you are female, what do you think men want?

4. How are men's magazines, television media, the Internet, and the movie industry influencing men's personal self-image and how they relate to women, personal responsibility, and the world today? Explain.

5. Based on the detail provided in this essay, provide a definition of the modern "child-man" in America today.

6. What are the social and cultural implications of the "child-man" ethic? How could it affect both men and women today, and the next generation? Explain.

Strong Enough

Wendy Shanker

Sometimes the pressure to conform to media-driven body images can sneak up on us in unexpected ways. When others expect people to look and act a certain way, nonconformists may find themselves in an unwanted spotlight, the subject of ridicule. Wendy Shanker, author of *The Fat Girl's Guide to Life*, describes one such incident, and how the experience led to much soul searching. Why do so many people—even strong ones—still do backflips to try and look like someone they are not?*

In what ways does the fashion and motion-picture industry influence our perception of body-image, self-worth, and social acceptance?

---

*Strong Enough, *The Body Politic,* Feminist.com.

AS YOU READ

Do you know someone who spends a lot of time on his or her appearance ("sweating and cutting and spritzing and waxing and sucking and shooting and plucking")? Do you agree with Shanker that such practices to look a certain way are inherently flawed and doomed to failure? Why or why not?

1   "Are you a lez?" he asked.

2   "What?" I asked, taken aback.

3   "ARE. YOU. A. LEZ." he repeated, enunciating each word as if I was deaf instead of confused.

4   I didn't know what to say. I pulled away.

5   "Well, you must be." He got up from our not-so-secluded spot behind my cabin and snuck back across the lake.

6   That's how a 14-year old boy responded to me at summer camp, a 14-year old girl, when I said I didn't want to have sex with him. Couldn't be that I didn't want to. Wasn't ready to. Or worse, wanted to . . . just not with HIM.

7   I assume his pride was injured. I'm sure he felt rejected (though possibly relieved). Maybe he was expected to come back to his crew with a story that he wasn't going to be able to tell. So he lobbed what was at that time the teen girl equivalent of "fag" at me: lesbian.

8   By the next day, no one in my cabin would talk to me. 'Cause everyone at camp knew I was a LEZ.

9   I'm not gay. But as a fat girl, lots of people assume I am. My theory is that most people are confused by a fat woman who is not on a diet. If I am fat, I'm not doing my evolutionary job, which is to make myself attractive enough for men to want to have sex with me. Being fat is an insult to male egos. It makes dating and mating difficult. I've even met fat guys who have the audacity to share that resentment. So why would I choose to be fat? I must be gay!

10   My straight girl friends with short haircuts tell me they often get the same treatment. By not keeping their hair long and straight (and blond), some men sense it's their subtle way of saying no to our current beauty standard. "How dare you pull a Mia Farrow!" Short hair isn't sexy to a certain kind of man, or to the woman who desires that dude.

11   I believe the same issue was at the heart of the Don Imus controversy. We now know the words by heart, but the subtext got lost. Sure, his comments about the Rutgers women's basketball team were another example of racist, sexist insults from a white dude with a microphone. On a more subtle layer, I saw it as "lez" thinking: "Here's a group of talented, successful, strong young women who seem to have other priorities in life than making them-selves attractive enough for me to want to have sex with them. How dare they? Ah, I know a way to bring them down to size, to collectively voice the thoughts of other men who may feel threatened just like me." Voila, Nappy Headed Ho-Gate broke loose on the airwaves.

12   What I heard was two mouthy men talking like they were scared of the Rutgers play-ers, threatened by their physical appearance. Were they trying to make a guarded statement about the players' sexual preferences? The word "ho" is used in a sexually promiscu-ous context, yet their conversation inferred that they did not deem these women sexu-ally appealing, especially when comparing their "nappy" hairstyles to the long, straight (Caucasian) do's worn by players on the competing team.

13   Look at male ballers and you'll see that many have braided hair and earrings. They wear big, baggy clothes on the court. Unlike their cheerleaders who let it all hang out, the only balls on display are being shot into baskets. Dennis Rodman dyed his hair pink and pierced his nose. Would anyone lob sexual insults at him, or doubt his masculinity?

14   Black women have spoken and written eloquently about hair and identity. Judgments are made inside and outside of the African-American community with something as simple as a hairstyle. Same with fat. The size of the pants I wear seems to say something about my sexual appeal and sexual preference. In the 70s, long hair was a way to stand out. In the 00s, hair is a way to fit in. No wonder the main character in *Hairspray* is a fat girl.

15   Athletic women are taunted about their sexuality in the same way fat women are, the same way women with short haircuts are. It cuts through their threat factor. "What if that chick is stronger than me? What if that chick can run faster, hit harder, and lift more?" Women are expected to be strong and muscular, with cut biceps and ripped abs, but for ogling purposes only. Don't use those muscles to shoot free throws. Don't use them to run marathons. Unless you're wearing a tiny tennis skirt over a thong, it's hard to be strong and look "feminine" at the same time.

17   We don't owe anyone an explanation when it comes the choices we make about appearance. Yet here we are, dieting and sweating and cutting and spritzing and waxing and sucking and shooting and plucking, hoping to look less like ourselves and more like Halle Berry or Angelina Jolie or Anna Kournikova, thinking our problems will be solved. I'll never understand why some men fear fat and strength and pixie cuts; it has nothing to do with them. Wait—maybe that's exactly the problem.

18   I appreciate beauty. I love feeling beautiful. And there are many ways for me to do that. Trust me, Sephora has no better customer. I do my hair, put on makeup, wear sexy clothes, show off my rack and my booty. Whether I'm a size 8 or a size 18 doesn't matter. It's not beauty that's the problem; it's our limited definition of beauty that's a problem. It's why Imus's insult hit so hard. With three little words, he managed to insult our looks and our sexuality, reinforcing our fears that we aren't good enough, pretty enough, or strong enough.

19   Beauty is how YOU see it. Eye of the beholder, remember?

20   That's why the Case of the Nappy-Headed Hos resonated so hard with women of all colors across this country. When I was 14, I didn't have the self-possession or confidence to properly respond to that loser boy behind the cabin. If he asked me now, I'd tell him: "I don't want to have sex with you. And it's not because I like girls. It's because I don't like YOU. When it comes to my sexual preference, I'm strong enough for a woman, but I happen to be made for a man."

QUESTIONS FOR ANALYSIS AND DISCUSSION

1. Try to picture your version of the perfect female body. What does it look like? Is your image influenced by outside forces, such as the media, your gender, or your age? How do real women you know compare to the image in your mind?

2. In your opinion, what made Don Imus's comments so unacceptable? Was it racism? Sexism? Both? Explain.

3. What role does sex appeal and the media play in defining men and women and how they are treated by society at large?

4. Who does Shanker blame for the cultural influences women experience that drive them to "dieting and sweating and cutting and spritzing and waxing and sucking and shooting and plucking"? Explain.

5. Evaluate how well Shanker supports her viewpoint in this essay. Does she provide supporting evidence? Is she biased? Does she provide a balanced perspective, or does she slant her data? Explain.

6. Shanker is the author of *The Fat Girl's Guide to Life*. Does the fact that she is a published author who defends her large size influence your opinion of her essay or her points? Why or why not?

7. Write a personal narrative describing an incident in which a comment made about your appearance caused you discomfort. How old were you? What was the comment? How did it make you feel? In hindsight, what do you think motivated the comment and what did it reveal about the person who said it to you? Explain.

Reading the Visual: Women in Combat*

Early in 2013, the outgoing defense secretary Leon Panetta announced that women would officially be allowed to assume ground combat roles for the first time in our nation's history. Not long after, Chuck Hagel, then President Obama's nominee for defense secretary, said, "I will work with the service chiefs as we officially open combat positions to women, a decision I strongly support." Old arguments resurfaced, and new ones emerged. During the weeks following the announcement, political cartoons reflecting the debate appeared in newspapers across the nation. The one here appeared in the *Buffalo News* on January 27, 2013.

QUESTIONS FOR ANALYSIS AND DISCUSSION

1. What cultural icon is the soldier in the cartoon mirroring? If you are uncertain, Google the phrase she is saying. What visual clichés does the soldier employ so that we know exactly who she "is"?

2. Why do you think Zyglis chose to depict the issue of women in the military in this fashion? Explain.

3. Research the current debate on women in combat roles. What arguments are made for and against women in ground combat? What is your view?

4. In an editorial to *The New York Times*, former army captain Tanya Domi noted that lifting the combat ban is an important step to the continued success of America's military. She also noted "the military's high standards for mental acuity and physical fitness should not be diminished to integrate women into combat units." Why do you think she makes this point? Why is it important? Respond to this statement with your own view.

*Adam Zyglis, *Buffalo News*, January 27, 2013.

The End of Men?

*Hanna Rosin**

In 2010, women became the majority of the workforce for the first time in U.S. history. For every two men who get a college degree in 2013, three women will do the same. For years, women's progress has been cast as a struggle for equality. But what if equality isn't the end point? Could modern, postindustrial society be simply better suited to women? What happens to men and their roles? To traditional family structures? In this next abridged essay, journalist Hanna Rosin reports on the unprecedented role reversal that is now under way—and its possible cultural consequences.

BEFORE YOU READ

Do you feel your behavior is influenced by sex-role expectations? If so, in what ways? Has it influenced your choice of a college major, or your career focus? Is there a difference between the "real" you and the person you present to the world? If there is a difference, is it the result of cultural pressure? Explain.

AS YOU READ

Who is the Marlboro Man? What did he represent? How do stereotypes influence our view of what it means to be male or female? Can you think of other famous stereotypes that influence our cultural perceptions of gender and career choice?

1   In the 1970s the biologist Ronald Ericsson came up with a way to separate sperm carrying the male-producing Y chromosome from those carrying the X. He sent the two kinds of sperm swimming down a glass tube through ever-thicker albumin barriers. The sperm with the X chromosome had a larger head and a longer tail, and so, he figured, they would get bogged down in the viscous liquid. The sperm with the Y chromosome were leaner and faster and could swim down to the bottom of the tube more efficiently. Ericsson had grown up on a ranch in South Dakota, where he'd developed an Old West, cowboy swagger. The process, he said, was like "cutting out cattle at the gate." The cattle left flailing behind the gate were of course the X's, which seemed to please him.

2   In the late 1970s, Ericsson leased the method to clinics around the U.S., calling it the first scientifically proven method for choosing the sex of a child. Instead of a lab coat, he wore cowboy boots and a cowboy hat, and doled out his version of cowboy poetry. In 1979, he loaned out his ranch as the backdrop for the iconic "Marlboro Country" ads because he believed in the campaign's central image—"a guy riding on his horse along the river, no bureaucrats, no lawyers," he recalled when I spoke to him this spring. "He's the boss."

3   Feminists of the era did not take kindly to Ericsson and his Marlboro Man veneer. To them, the lab cowboy and his sperminator portended a dystopia of mass-produced boys. "You have to be concerned about the future of all women," Roberta Steinbacher,

---

*Hanna Rosin, *Atlantic*, July/August 2010.

a nun-turned-social-psychologist, said in a 1984 *People* profile of Ericsson. "There's no question that there exists a universal preference for sons." Steinbacher went on to complain about women becoming locked in as "second-class citizens" while men continued to dominate positions of control and influence.

4 Ericsson, now 74, laughed when I read him these quotes from his old antagonist. Seldom has it been so easy to prove a dire prediction wrong. In the '90s, when Ericsson looked into the numbers for the two dozen or so clinics that use his process, he discovered, to his surprise, that couples were requesting more girls than boys. In some clinics, Ericsson has said, the ratio is now as high as 2 to 1. Polling data on American sex preference is sparse, and does not show a clear preference for girls. But the picture from the doctor's office unambiguously does. A newer method for sperm selection, called MicroSort, is currently completing Food and Drug Administration clinical trials. The girl requests for that method run at about 75 percent.

5 Even more unsettling for Ericsson, it has become clear that in choosing the sex of the next generation, he is no longer the boss. "It's the women who are driving all the decisions," he says—a change the MicroSort spokespeople I met with also mentioned. At first, Ericsson says, women who called his clinics would apologize and shyly explain that they already had two boys. "Now they just call and [say] outright, 'I want a girl.'"

6 Why wouldn't you choose a girl? That such a statement should be so casually uttered by an old cowboy like Ericsson—or by anyone, for that matter—is monumental. For nearly as long as civilization has existed, patriarchy—enforced through the rights of the firstborn son—has been the organizing principle, with few exceptions. Men in ancient Greece tied off their left testicle in an effort to produce male heirs; women have killed themselves (or been killed) for failing to bear sons. In her iconic 1949 book, *The Second Sex*, the French feminist Simone de Beauvoir suggested that women so detested their own "feminine condition" that they regarded their newborn daughters with irritation and disgust. Now the centuries-old preference for sons is eroding—or even reversing. "Women of our generation want daughters precisely because we like who we are," breezes one woman in *Cookie* magazine. Even Ericsson, can sigh and mark the passing of an era. "Did male dominance exist? Of course it existed. But it seems to be gone now. And the era of the firstborn son is totally gone."

7 Ericsson's extended family is as good an illustration of the rapidly shifting landscape as any other. His 26-year-old granddaughter—"tall, slender, brighter than hell, with a take-no-prisoners personality"—is a biochemist and works on genetic sequencing. His niece studied civil engineering at the University of Southern California. His grandsons, he says, are bright and handsome, but in school "their eyes glaze over. I have to tell 'em: 'Just don't screw up and crash your pickup truck and get some girl pregnant and ruin your life.'" Recently Ericsson joked with the old boys at his elementary-school reunion that he was going to have a sex-change operation. "Women live longer than men. They do better in this economy. More of 'em graduate from college. They go into space and do everything men do, and sometimes they do it a whole lot better. I mean, hell, get out of the way—these females are going to leave us males in the dust."

8 Man has been the dominant sex since, well, the dawn of mankind. But for the first time in human history, that is changing—and with shocking speed. Cultural and economic changes always reinforce each other. And the global economy is evolving in a way that is eroding the historical preference for male children, worldwide. Over several centuries, South Korea, for instance, constructed one of the most rigid patriarchal societies

in the world. Many wives who failed to produce male heirs were abused and treated as domestic servants; some families prayed to spirits to kill off girl children. Then, in the 1970s and '80s, the government embraced an industrial revolution and encouraged women to enter the labor force. Women moved to the city and went to college. They advanced rapidly, from industrial jobs to clerical jobs to professional work. The traditional order began to crumble soon after. In 1990, the country's laws were revised so that women could keep custody of their children after a divorce and inherit property. In 2005, the court ruled that women could register children under their own names. As recently as 1985, about half of all women in a national survey said they "must have a son." That percentage fell slowly until 1991 and then plummeted to just over 15 percent by 2003. Male preference in South Korea "is over," says Monica Das Gupta, a demographer and Asia expert at the World Bank. "It happened so fast. It's hard to believe it, but it is." The same shift is now beginning in other rapidly industrializing countries such as India and China.

9   Up to a point, the reasons behind this shift are obvious. As thinking and communicating have come to eclipse physical strength and stamina as the keys to economic success, those societies that take advantage of the talents of all their adults, not just half of them, have pulled away from the rest. And because geopolitics and global culture are, ultimately, Darwinian, other societies either follow suit or end up marginalized. In 2006, the Organization for Economic Cooperation and Development devised the Gender, Institutions and Development Database, which measures the economic and political power of women in 162 countries. With few exceptions, the greater the power of women, the greater the country's economic success. Aid agencies have started to recognize this relationship and have pushed to institute political quotas in about 100 countries, essentially forcing women into power in an effort to improve those countries' fortunes.

10   In feminist circles, these social, political, and economic changes are always cast as a slow, arduous form of catch-up in a continuing struggle for female equality. But in the U.S., the world's most advanced economy, something much more remarkable seems to be happening. American parents are beginning to choose to have girls over boys. As they imagine the pride of watching a child grow and develop and succeed as an adult, it is more often a girl that they see in their mind's eye.

11   What if the modern, postindustrial economy is simply more congenial to women than to men? For a long time, evolutionary psychologists have claimed that we are all imprinted with adaptive imperatives from a distant past: men are faster and stronger and hardwired to fight for scarce resources, and that shows up now as a drive to win on Wall Street; women are programmed to find good providers and to care for their offspring, and that is manifested in more-nurturing and more-flexible behavior, ordaining them to domesticity. This kind of thinking frames our sense of the natural order. But what if men and women were fulfilling not biological imperatives but social roles, based on what was more efficient throughout a long era of human history? What if that era has now come to an end? More to the point, what if the economics of the new era are better suited to women?

12   Once you open your eyes to this possibility, the evidence is all around you. It can be found, most immediately, in the wreckage of the Great Recession, in which three-quarters of the 8 million jobs lost were lost by men. The worst-hit industries were overwhelmingly male and deeply identified with macho: construction, manufacturing, high finance. Some of these jobs will come back, but the overall pattern of dislocation is neither temporary nor

random. The recession merely revealed—and accelerated—a profound economic shift that has been going on for at least 30 years, and in some respects even longer.

13   Earlier this year, for the first time in American history, the balance of the workforce tipped toward women, who now hold a majority of the nation's jobs. The working class, which has long defined our notions of masculinity, is slowly turning into a matriarchy, with men increasingly absent from the home and women making all the decisions. Women dominate today's colleges and professional schools—for every two men who will receive a B.A. this year, three women will do the same. Of the 15 job categories projected to grow the most in the next decade in the U.S., all but two are occupied primarily by women. Indeed, the U.S. economy is in some ways becoming a kind of traveling sisterhood: upper-class women leave home and enter the workforce, creating domestic jobs for other women to fill.

14   The postindustrial economy is indifferent to men's size and strength. The attributes that are most valuable today—social intelligence, open communication, the ability to sit still and focus—are, at a minimum, not predominantly male. In fact, the opposite may be true. Women in poor parts of India are learning English faster than men to meet the demands of new global call centers. Women own more than 40 percent of private businesses in China, where a red Ferrari is the new status symbol for female entrepreneurs. Iceland elected Prime Minister Johanna Sigurdardottir, the world's first openly lesbian head of state, who campaigned explicitly against the male elite she claimed had destroyed the nation's banking system, and who vowed to end the "age of testosterone."

15   Yes, the U.S. still has a wage gap, one that can be convincingly explained—at least in part—by discrimination. Yes, women still do most of the child care. And yes, the upper reaches of society are still dominated by men. But given the power of the forces pushing at the economy, this setup feels like the last gasp of a dying age rather than the permanent establishment. Dozens of college women I interviewed for this story assumed that they very well might be the ones working while their husbands stayed at home, either looking for work or minding the children. Guys, one senior remarked to me, "are the new ball and chain." It may be happening slowly and unevenly, but it's unmistakably happening: in the long view, the modern economy is becoming a place where women hold the cards.

16   Men dominate just two of the 15 job categories projected to grow the most over the next decade: janitor and computer engineer. Women have everything else—nursing, home health assistance, child care, food preparation. Many of the new jobs, says Heather Boushey of the Center for American Progress, "replace the things that women used to do in the home for free." None is especially high-paying. But the steady accumulation of these jobs adds up to an economy that, for the working class, has become more amenable to women than to men.

17   The list of growing jobs is heavy on nurturing professions, in which women, ironically, seem to benefit from old stereotypes and habits. Theoretically, there is no reason men should not be qualified. But they have proved remarkably unable to adapt. Over the course of the past century, feminism has pushed women to do things once considered against their nature—first enter the workforce as singles, then continue to work while married, then work even with small children at home. Many professions that started out as the province of men are now filled mostly with women—secretary and teacher come to mind. Yet I'm not aware of any that have gone the opposite way. Nursing schools have tried hard

to recruit men in the past few years, with minimal success. Teaching schools, eager to recruit male role models, are having a similarly hard time. The range of acceptable masculine roles has changed comparatively little, and has perhaps even narrowed as men have shied away from some careers women have entered. As Jessica Grose wrote in *Slate*, men seem "fixed in cultural aspic." And with each passing day, they lag further behind.

18   As we recover from the Great Recession, some traditionally male jobs will return—men are almost always harder-hit than women in economic downturns because construction and manufacturing are more cyclical than service industries—but that won't change the long-term trend. When we look back on this period, argues Jamie Ladge, a business professor at Northeastern University, we will see it as a "turning point for women in the workforce."

19   The economic and cultural power shift from men to women would be hugely significant even if it never extended beyond working-class America. But women are also starting to dominate middle management, and a surprising number of professional careers as well. According to the Bureau of Labor Statistics, women now hold 51.4 percent of managerial and professional jobs—up from 26.1 percent in 1980. They make up 54 percent of all accountants and hold about half of all banking and insurance jobs. About a third of America's physicians are now women, as are 45 percent of associates in law firms—and both those percentages are rising fast. A white-collar economy values raw intellectual horsepower, which men and women have in equal amounts. It also requires communication skills and social intelligence, areas in which women, according to many studies, have a slight edge. Perhaps most important—for better or worse—it increasingly requires formal education credentials, which women are more prone to acquire, particularly early in adulthood. Just about the only professions in which women still make up a relatively small minority of newly minted workers are engineering and those calling on a hard-science background, and even in those areas, women have made strong gains since the 1970s.

20   Office work has been steadily adapting to women—and in turn being reshaped by them—for 30 years or more. Joel Garreau picks up on this phenomenon in his 1991 book, *Edge City*, which explores the rise of suburbs that are home to giant swaths of office space along with the usual houses and malls. Companies began moving out of the city in search not only of lower rent but also of the "best educated, most conscientious, most stable workers." They found their brightest prospects among "underemployed females living in middle-class communities on the fringe of the old urban areas."

21   Near the top of the jobs pyramid, of course, the upward march of women stalls. Prominent female CEOs, past and present, are so rare that they count as minor celebrities, and most of us can tick off their names just from occasionally reading the business pages: Meg Whitman at eBay, Carly Fiorina at Hewlett-Packard, Anne Mulcahy and Ursula Burns at Xerox, Indra Nooyi at PepsiCo; the accomplishment is considered so extraordinary that Whitman and Fiorina are using it as the basis for political campaigns. Only 3 percent of Fortune 500 CEOs are women, and the number has never risen much above that.

22   But even the way this issue is now framed reveals that men's hold on power in elite circles may be loosening. In business circles, the lack of women at the top is described as a "brain drain" and a crisis of "talent retention." And while female CEOs may be rare in America's largest companies, they are highly prized: last year, they out-earned their male counterparts by 43 percent, on average, and received bigger raises.

23   "Women are knocking on the door of leadership at the very moment when their talents are especially well matched with the requirements of the day," writes David Gergen in the introduction to *Enlightened Power: How Women Are Transforming the Practice of Leadership*. What are these talents? Once it was thought that leaders should be aggressive and competitive, and that men are naturally more of both. But psychological research has complicated this picture. In lab studies that simulate negotiations, men and women are just about equally assertive and competitive, with slight variations. Men tend to assert themselves in a controlling manner, while women tend to take into account the rights of others, but both styles are equally effective, write the psychologists Alice Eagly and Linda Carli, in their 2007 book, *Through the Labyrinth*.

24   Over the years, researchers have sometimes exaggerated these differences and described the particular talents of women in crude gender stereotypes: women as more empathetic, as better consensus-seekers and better lateral thinkers; women as bringing a superior moral sensibility to bear on a cutthroat business world. In the '90s, this field of feminist business theory seemed to be forcing the point. But after the latest financial crisis, these ideas have more resonance. Researchers have started looking into the relationship between testosterone and excessive risk, and wondering if groups of men, in some basic hormonal way, spur each other to make reckless decisions. The picture emerging is a mirror image of the traditional gender map: men and markets on the side of the irrational and overemotional, and women on the side of the cool and levelheaded.

25   It could be that women boost corporate performance, or it could be that better-performing firms have the luxury of recruiting and keeping high-potential women. But the association is clear: innovative, successful firms are the ones that promote women. The same Columbia-Maryland study ranked America's industries by the proportion of firms that employed female executives, and the bottom of the list reads like the ghosts of the economy past: shipbuilding, real estate, coal, steelworks, machinery.

26   It is fabulous to see girls and young women poised for success in the coming years. But allowing generations of boys to grow up feeling rootless and obsolete is not a recipe for a peaceful future. Men have few natural support groups and little access to social welfare; the men's-rights groups that do exist in the U.S. are taking on an angry, anti-woman edge. Marriages fall apart or never happen at all, and children are raised with no fathers. Far from being celebrated, women's rising power is perceived as a threat.

27   What would a society in which women are on top look like? We already have an inkling. This is the first time that the cohort of Americans ages 30 to 44 has more college-educated women than college-educated men, and the effects are upsetting the traditional Cleaver-family dynamics. In 1970, women contributed 2 to 6 percent of the family income. Now the typical working wife brings home 42.2 percent, and four in 10 mothers—many of them single mothers—are the primary breadwinners in their families. The whole question of whether mothers should work is moot, argues Heather Boushey of the Center for American Progress, "because they just do. This idealized family—he works, she stays home—hardly exists anymore."

28   The terms of marriage have changed radically since 1970. Typically, women's income has been the main factor in determining whether a family moves up the class ladder or stays stagnant. And increasing numbers of women—unable to find men with a similar income and education—are forgoing marriage altogether. In 1970, 84 percent of women

ages 30 to 44 were married; now 60 percent are. In 2007, among American women with-out a high-school diploma, 43 percent were married. And yet, for all the hand-wringing over the lonely spinster, the real loser in society—the only one to have made just slight financial gains since the 1970s—is the single man, whether poor or rich, college-educated or not. Hens rejoice; it's the bachelor party that's over.

29   The sociologist Kathryn Edin spent five years talking with low-income mothers in the inner suburbs of Philadelphia. Many of these neighborhoods, she found, had turned into matriarchies, with women making all the decisions and dictating what the men should and should not do. "I think something feminists have missed," Edin told me, "is how much power women have" when they're not bound by marriage. The women, she explained, "make every important decision"—whether to have a baby, how to raise it, where to live. "It's definitely 'my way or the highway,' " she said. "Thirty years ago, cultural norms were such that the fathers might have said, 'Great, catch me if you can.' Now they are desperate to father, but they are pessimistic about whether they can meet her expectations." The women don't want them as husbands, and they have no steady income to provide.

30   Over the years, researchers have proposed different theories to explain the erosion of marriage in the lower classes: the rise of welfare, or the disappearance of work and thus of marriageable men. But Edin thinks the most compelling theory is that marriage has disappeared because women are setting the terms—and setting them too high for the men around them to reach. "I want that white-picket-fence dream," one woman told Edin, and the men she knew just didn't measure up, so she had become her own one-woman mother/father/nurturer/provider. The whole country's future could look much as the present does for many lower-class African Americans: the mothers pull themselves up, but the men don't follow. First-generation college-educated white women may join their black counterparts in a new kind of middle class, where marriage is increasingly rare.

31   In fact, the more women dominate, the more they behave, fittingly, like the domi-nant sex. Rates of violence committed by middle-aged women have skyrocketed since the 1980s, and no one knows why. In Roman Polanski's *The Ghost Writer*, the traditional political wife is rewritten as a cold-blooded killer at the heart of an evil conspiracy. In her recent video *Telephone*, Lady Gaga, with her infallible radar for the cultural edge, rewrites *Thelma and Louise* as a story not about elusive female empowerment but about sheer, ruthless power. Instead of killing themselves, she and her girlfriend (played by Beyoncé) kill a bad boyfriend and random others in a homicidal spree and then escape in their yel-low pickup truck, Gaga bragging, "We did it, Honey B."

32   The Marlboro Man, meanwhile, master of wild beast and wild country, seems too far-fetched and preposterous even for advertising. His modern equivalents are the stunted men in the Dodge Charger ad that ran during this year's Super Bowl in February. Of all the days in the year, one might think, Super Bowl Sunday should be the one most dedicated to the cinematic celebration of macho. The men in Super Bowl ads should be throwing balls and racing motorcycles and doing whatever it is men imagine they could do all day if only women were not around to restrain them.

33   Instead, four men stare into the camera, unsmiling, not moving except for tiny blinks and sways. They look like they've been tranquilized, like they can barely hold themselves

up against the breeze. Their lips do not move, but a voice-over explains their predicament—how they've been beaten silent by the demands of tedious employers and enviro-fascists and women. Especially women. "I will put the seat down, I will separate the recycling, I will carry your lip balm." This last one—lip balm—is expressed with the mildest spit of emotion, the only hint of the suppressed rage against the dominatrix. Then the commercial abruptly cuts to the fantasy, a Dodge Charger vrooming toward the camera punctuated by bold all caps: MAN'S LAST STAND. But the motto is unconvincing. After that display of muteness and passivity, you can only imagine a woman—one with shiny lips—steering the beast.

QUESTIONS FOR ANALYSIS AND DISCUSSION

1. What concerns did Ronald Ericsson's research and method raise? Why did these concerns turn out to be largely unfounded?
2. How does Ronald Ericsson's work set up the rest of Rosin's essay? How does it frame the issue Rosin is raising?
3. Rosin points out that for most of human history, cultures have preferred having boys to girls. What reasons does she provide for the shift in many cultures to now prefer having girls? How well does she support her argument and with what data?
4. According to Rosin, why are women dominating in the workplace? How is this competitive edge connected to the recession? Is it likely to continue for the next decade? Beyond? Explain.
5. Why haven't men embraced the highly employable "nurturing professions"? What reasons does Rosin give? What reasons, if any, can you offer based on your knowledge of American culture? Explain.
6. What are some of the drawbacks of having women dominate the workforce? How are men being affected by this cultural shift?
7. How has marriage been impacted by the shift of women dominating the employment and educational landscape? Explain.

Still a Man's World

Philip N. Cohen*

In the previous essay, Hanna Rosin explained why opportunities that have opened for women over the last 30 years are now allowing them to seemingly outpace men in the economic, educational, and social arenas. In this essay, Philip N. Cohen, a professor of sociology at the University of Maryland, argues that this simply isn't the case. Authors such as Kay Hymowitz, Hanna Rosin, and Liza Mundy present a world in which men do not matter, and seem to be quite satisfied with the idea.

*Philip N. Cohen, *Boston Review*, January–February 2013.

Cohen points out that not only is Rosin incorrect, but he fears that promoting such a notion is harmful to both men and women.

BEFORE YOU READ

When you hear the term *gender gap*, what do the words mean to you? Is it a difference in point of view? Wage earnings? Equality in political and economic arenas? Explain.

AS YOU READ

Does it matter who earns more—men or women? Does greater economic success mean that one gender holds more "power" than the other? In your own relationships, does it matter how much money your significant other makes (more or less)? Explain.

1   The notion that women are outpacing men in economic achievement is becoming a post-feminist rallying cry. A legion of authors laments the man-children whom today's successful, focused career women are forced to date, coddle, and ultimately dump.

2   Two recent books, Hanna Rosin's *The End of Men* and Liza Mundy's *The Richer Sex*, collect the many strands of this tale of women ascendant. These authors are motivated by the same basic facts: women's attainment of college degrees has surpassed that of men; in early 2010 it briefly appeared that women would be the majority of the American labor force; the proportion of married couples in which the wife earns more than the husband has increased and now approaches 30 percent; unmarried, childless young women who work full time have high earnings relative to similarly situated men; and finally, a majority of workers in the fastest-growing occupations are women.

3   Together, these facts contribute to an important story that is well established among gender inequality researchers, but which remains a matter of confusion for some journalists and readers. Gender inequality in the economic realm has in fact narrowed dramatically since the mid-twentieth century, even as the overwhelming weight of evidence shows that men as a group maintain systematic advantages over women. However, the relative status of men and women is not built from singular data points, but rather from giant moving orbs of data with wide distributions around central tendencies. As the gender gap, then, has grown smaller overall—as the distributions have grown closer together—naturally there are circumstances in which women are doing better than men. The question is how to extrapolate from those circumstances.

4   Both Rosin and Mundy match selected statistics with compelling anecdotes to form narratives in which women not only are drawing even with men, but also are heading for inevitable economic dominance. But despite their assertions—and the progressive direction of change—there is no reason to expect their projections to come to pass in the foreseeable future. Their skillful writing and anecdotal reporting appear to provide convincing support for a narrative that is fundamentally untrue. And that is not a compliment to contemporary journalism.

5   That is not to say that Rosin and Mundy are simply replicating each other's mistakes. The two books diverge considerably despite their shared commitment to a similar over-reaching economic forecast. Rosin's distortion, exaggeration, and carelessness are so ubiquitous as to undermine the reader's confidence in her reporting, which mostly reads as a series of shallow caricatures. Mundy's stories, on the other hand, which seem to draw from a larger pool of interviews, often are interesting descriptions of how modern women, men, and couples navigate the (relatively unusual) situation in which women have more financial clout than their potential or actual partners.

6   In this sense, Mundy is describing a possible future reality. The question is, will it come to pass on its own, as the inevitable product of economic rationality? Both books suggest an affirmative answer. But has the battle for equality been virtually won already? Or does equality still require concerted action?

7   For Rosin and Mundy, women's rise to the top of the economic heap begins with school. There is some justification for this view. Women earn the majority of college degrees in the United States, and they are the majority of college students, having established better academic records in high school. To both authors this trend signals a major shift. But women surpassed men as the majority of BA earners in the early 1980s, and that advantage has only marginally increased since then, to 57 percent. Moreover, women continue to earn less at every level of education, and not merely as a function of time spent on family obligations and occupational choices. A recent study by the American Association of University Women, for example, found that even among full-time workers just one year after college graduation, women earn 82 percent of men's average earnings.

8   For college graduates, fields of study are a big part of the pay-gap story, and a reason not to focus exclusively on overall graduation rates. In the 1970s and 1980s, the segregation of men and women into different major fields decreased markedly, as women began majoring in psychology, biology, communications, and business in greater numbers. But health, education, and English are as predominately female as ever—and math and engineering remain stubbornly resistant to change.

9   In any event, when it comes to gender, proportional growth in educational programs is no guarantee of commensurate increase in labor market clout. In law and medical schools, for example, women peaked at almost half of graduates in the last decade, but women are still less than 40 percent of doctors and lawyers in the 35- to 44-year-old age range, where they earn 72 percent and 81 percent of male counterparts' pay, respectively. The main reason for these gaps is that more women have dropped out of these professions, and more remain in specialties, such as pediatrics and family law, that pay less.

10   Women have improved their relative status in these high-value fields, but there is no sign of their dominance on the horizon. In the face of such stubbornness on the part of the data, both Rosin and Mundy single out women's greater progress in the fields of pharmacy and veterinary medicine. These occupations are much smaller and less well paid than medicine, and neither is a steppingstone to physician jobs. Rather than seeing veterinarians and pharmacists as harbingers of future female dominance, then, it might be more accurate to describe them as inadequate safety valves for highly capable and well-educated women. The large number of women in those fields reflects not their upper hand, but rather frustrated opportunities for success in more lucrative and powerful fields.

11   So women are getting more education, with limited results in the labor market. How do we go from there to a new day in gender relations? Here the transition to a postindustrial, service- and knowledge-based economy—in conjunction with declining gender discrimination driven by managerial rationalization—is important. It might seem to be leading inevitably to women's economic dominance. This deterministic story is intuitively appealing: the demands of the economy are shifting dramatically in women's favor, brains have superseded brawn, and social skills have become increasingly important, all of which favors women over men.

12   In support of this view, both authors use projections by the U.S. Bureau of Labor Statistics showing that the occupations with the largest expected growth in the next decade are dominated by women. But that description is superficial—misleading, even.

13   According to Mundy, nine out of ten occupations with the largest projected growth in the next decade—registered nurses, home health aides, customer service representatives, food preparation and service workers, personal care aides, retail personnel, office staff, accountants, nursing aides, and postsecondary teachers—are majority female. For Rosin it is twelve out of the top fifteen. This is impressive, except that there are hundreds of occupations overall, and with women almost half the labor force, many of those occupations are close to majority female. In fact, the employees of Mundy's top-ten occupations made up just 15 percent of the workforce in 2010, and are projected to make up only 17 percent by 2020. The top 15 are projected to increase from 22 percent to just 23 percent of the workforce. The growth in these jobs doesn't represent much of a change on an economy-wide scale. The bottom line is that women are projected to increase their share of the labor force by no more than 1 percent in the next decade.

14   This should not be that surprising. After the 1960s it was not change in the occupational structure that drove increases in women's employment, but rather the integration of existing occupations. However, integration has been stalled since the mid-1990s, and economic development since then barely favors women over men. Yes, there are more nurses and home health aides today than there were in the 1960s, but there are also fewer maids and domestic servants. And although blue-collar manufacturing jobs have declined, truck driving and construction have not. The decline of manufacturing is no longer shaping our gender story—the industry represents only 8.3 percent of workers. Ostensibly gender-neutral processes of economic transformation are not the sources of women's progress they once were.

15   So many people continue to be so attached to this narrative of women's rapid advance in the labor force that they haven't noticed there has been no advance in almost two decades: women occupied between 46 and 47 percent of the labor force every year from 1994 through 2011, the last year for which we have data. This stagnation undermines Rosin's and Mundy's accounts, in which continuous and fast-paced change is not just taking us toward equality but beyond it.

16   And that's the real danger in their exaggerated stories: creating the impression that women's progress is inevitable and unstoppable. Mundy and Rosin assume that incomes favor young, single women and that this distribution holds up among married couples, too. Increasing numbers of married women are in fact out-earning their husbands—which is important—but both authors exaggerate the claim.

17   Women's higher rates of college completion are not turning into a landslide of female-breadwinner marriages. That is because the majority of couples marry on the same side of

the college/non-college divide, on each side of which men's earnings are systematically higher. And after they marry, couples, with the cooperation of employers, tend to move very efficiently in the direction of male economic dominance. Childbearing, division of labor, and career-balancing practices all favor male breadwinning.

18 At present, a little more than a quarter of wives in their prime working years earn more than their husbands do, though the numbers are higher if you follow Mundy and Rosin, who restrict the pool to couples with working wives. Mundy calls the imagined impending majority of such families the "Big Flip," and devotes much of her book to how American men and women fail or succeed at adjusting to it. In this construction, any couple in which the wife earns more than her husband has already undergone the Big Flip, and the rest of the country is sliding rapidly down that path.

19 However, even when wives earn more, they almost always earn only a little more— which does not quite give them the authority to establish a "matriarchy" (Rosin's term) or qualitatively overturn gender relations, as implied by Mundy's flipping terminology. It's true that only 7 percent of wives out-earned their husbands in 1970, so we have seen a real change in gender relations. If change continues at that pace, women really will be the majority earners in more than half of married couples by midcentury. Also, if world population growth keeps increasing at the rate it has in the past century, the earth will eventually become a ball of human flesh expanding at the speed of light. Neither of these outcomes is a sure bet; predicting the future is not as simple as extending the line on a graph.

20 Rapid change in the direction of equality has not produced equality. The biggest trend in the income distribution of married couples has been the decline of the zero-earning wife. In 1970, 44 percent of wives earned nothing. Today that figure is 21 percent. However, it is still almost three times more common for the husband than for the wife to be the only earner in the couple. As for the idea of female-dominant newlywed couples, this is rarer than the authors assume. Rosin, to create her illustrations, conducts an online survey looking specifically for such couples and, not surprisingly, finds some. Mundy focuses on Atlanta, writing, "Of all the major cities where young women out-earn young men, Atlanta is number one."

21 But marriage markets aren't as simple as pairing eligible men and women together at random. Even in places where the average earnings are a little higher among unmarried women, a few simple sorting preferences produce (straight) couples that overwhelmingly lean male-dominant. The most important preferences are for race/ethnicity and education: most couples match up along these lines. Within racial/ethnic and education groups, men earn more at every level. On top of that, the male partner is usually a few years older. With those parameters set, men will earn more in most couples. If you add an additional preference for higher-earning men within a couple—which is still what most people appear to want, whether they say it explicitly or not—then the male-dominant skew in the resulting marriages is even stronger.

22 Take Atlanta. Among childless full-time workers there, unmarried young women earn more than unmarried young men, but Census data confirm that just-married men's incomes are higher than just-married women's. Three-quarters of Atlanta couples marry on the same side of the college/non-college divide, and in cases where both spouses have college degrees, women earn more in just one-third of couples. Overall, only 38 percent

of newlywed Atlanta couples have a higher-earning wife. As these couples advance along their careers, that percentage is unlikely to rise.

23   The growing prevalence of breadwinning wives is an important phenomenon, but it is not the end of gender inequality as we know it, and that prevalence is not irreversibly increasing. Mundy has argued that her critics, including me, are institutionally wedded to a glass-half-empty form of feminism, which is sliding toward irrelevance as women's progress gains steam. And we have indeed made much progress, as I've outlined above. But there is a lot of room for interpretation and speculation about what will—and should—happen next.

24   Mundy overreaches and oversells her interpretation. But at least enough of her facts are true that we can have a reasonable debate based on them. The same cannot be said of Rosin. In a blog post defending herself, she writes, "I hesitate to get drawn into data wars. . . . I've learned over the course of my research that data can support many different stories." But many of Rosin's errors are not matters of interpretation, the inevitable collateral damage from a data free-for-all in which we all focus on different bits of the larger story. Rather, they are factual claims that happen to be clearly and demonstrably untrue. Here are three examples:

25   1) The unsourced claim that "in Asia"—unqualified by any further detail, such as the name of a country or countries—"the average age of marriage for women is thirty-two." This is false not only for women across Asia as a whole, but also for every country in Asia, where women in the biggest countries mostly marry at or before age twenty (Indonesia, India); in their early twenties (China); or, at the high end, in their late twenties (Korea, Japan).

26   2) The description of sexual assault rates as "so low in parts of the country—for white women especially—that criminologists can't plot the numbers on a chart," which is nonsensical as well as untrue. Not only are U.S. rates of sexual assault plottable, they are not even low by the standards of wealthy countries.

27   3) "Women are now lead TV anchors, Ivy League College heads, bank presidents, corporate CEOs, movie directors, scatologically savvy comedians, presidential candidates—all unthinkable even twenty years ago." With one exception, each of those milestones not only was thinkable but had *already occurred* twenty years before she wrote, most of them long before. (The exception is a female Ivy League president, which wasn't recorded until nineteen years earlier, in 1993.)

28   Rosin also has an affinity for sweeping proclamations that do the work of facts without being testable. Thus, "Our vast and struggling middle class . . . is slowly turning into a matriarchy"; women are "taking over the middle class"; and Auburn, Alabama, of all places, has "turn[ed] itself into a town dominated by women."

29   And, for the careful reader, Rosin presents an exhausting parade of exaggerations, which are obvious if one consults her endnotes for verification. Some of these are simply aggravating stretches, such as referring to the health and education sectors as adding "about the same number" of jobs as were shed by the manufacturing sector in the 2000s, when the former number was 4.5 million and the latter was 5.7 million, a difference of 26 percent. Others are distorted to the point of falsehood. She wants us to believe that "young women" are earning more than "young men," but what she really has in mind is a much narrower group: single, childless, female full-time workers ages 22–30. That list of qualifications is indeed awkward, but without it, the fact is not a fact. Elsewhere Rosin reports, "Nearly a third of Brazilian women now make more money than their husbands,"

but her citation refers to only 28 percent, and then only among college-educated female full-time workers—a far cry from all Brazilian women. This is an abbreviated list.

30   Even if we do continue to advance toward gender equality, it might not accompany, or cause, fundamental transformation of gender patterns in those arenas that have been most resistant to change: male dominance of the highest echelons of political, economic, and institutional power; the cultural devaluation of work associated with women; the persistent difference-based gender socialization of the sexes from the earliest moments of childhood; the political domination of women's bodies by men; and the gendered division of labor, especially that which is unpaid.

31   Mundy and Rosin miss all this because they embrace mechanical and deterministic narratives of change. There is little apparent role for an active agenda promoting equality beyond the assumption that anti-discrimination laws and practices will advance continuously, driven, one supposes, by the inherent economic rationality of gender egalitarianism. And in these books there is no discussion of organized resistance on the part of men in positions of power and authority.

32   The economic, political, and cultural changes that motivate Rosin and Mundy are real. For example, there is a competitive price to pay for an old-fashioned attachment to sexism. Modern rationality exerts pressure in the direction of universalism, as the sociologist Robert Max Jackson argues in *Destined for Equality: The Inevitable Rise of Women's Status* (1998). But these changes also are old news. More pressing now is the question of how to unlock the door between the stalled present and further progress toward equality.

33   Feminist action on law and policy may now be as important as ever. In the legal realm, gender discrimination suits are very hard to win unless a man and woman are being paid differently for doing exactly the same job for the same employer, as in the famous Lilly Ledbetter case. In policy, the United States lags atrociously on vital matters of work-family integration. Specifically, paid family leave might reduce the career consequences of unpaid care-work obligations. Universal preschool education would smooth women's reentry into the labor force after childbirth while reducing the inequalities in childcare that help reproduce class inequality. And we might even stretch our imaginations to consider a shorter workweek, which besides reducing unemployment could help dislodge the hyper-present "ideal worker" image many hold dear, thereby shaking loose a more gender-balanced family life.

34   And in the mainstream culture, we need to challenge the crushing norm of intensive parenting and combat the resurgence of highly polarized gender socialization for children. The stalled progress that has become apparent since the mid-1990s arguably reflects a weakened feminist movement—its transformation into an inward-looking program of self-improvement under the mantra of empowerment and choice. Sitting back to watch the tide of women's dominance roll in will not help.

35   To these authors, feminism—rarely mentioned—is a cultural trend running as a bit player in the background, integrated into the stream of progress. (Mundy has described institutional feminist actors as a "fempire" of dour naysayers unwilling to accept a future of positive change.) Meanwhile, the men who would stand to lose their privileged positions thanks to feminism's success actually are resisting change. At the low end, many blue-collar men have blocked the entrance of women into their trades, passively or actively. At the high end, the board rooms and executive suites of corporate America are monuments to sexism's perseverance, with annual progress in women's representation measured in the fractions of

a percent. Active gender discrimination—especially based on women's status as mothers—continues to plague working women. We cannot assume a future of continuous, inexorable change in the direction of gender equality, the satiating lullaby of these tall tales.

QUESTIONS FOR ANALYSIS AND DISCUSSION

1. Why does Cohen feel that both Rosen and Mundy have made mistakes in their extrapolation of labor and education statistics? Explain.

2. Why does Cohen argue that Rosen's and Mundy's arguments are fundamentally untrue? What faults does he find with the conclusions they have drawn? Explain.

3. Read more about Liza Mundy's book and viewpoint at the New America Foundation or in the *New York Times* article "Breadwomen" by Rachel Shteir. Why does Mundy envision a future in which women hold more economic and political sway? Is her vision likely? Why does Cohen question the likelihood of such a future?

4. Cohen notes that despite closing the educational gap, women still earn less than men—sometimes much less than men, such as in the fields of medicine and law, where equal numbers graduate. What accounts for this disparity?

5. After reading Cohen's essay, write a response expressing your own viewpoint. Reference points from both Hanna Rosin's and Philip Cohen's essays in your response.

6. Cohen points out that even if women do earn more than men in the future, it will not create a "matriarchy" (Rosin) or "flip" (Mundy) gender roles. Why does he challenge their vision for the future? What is your view?

7. In your view, who makes the more valid argument—Rosin or Cohen—and why?

WRITING ASSIGNMENTS

1. Write an essay exploring the effects of the perception of women as homemakers and mothers in the media. Some of the areas of your exploration might draw from television, film, art, advertising, newspapers, music, and other popular media. How do media representations of women enforce (or refute) the perception of women as mothers and homemakers rather than professionals?

2. Consider the ways Hollywood influences our cultural perspectives of gender and identity. Write an essay exploring the influence, however slight, film and television have had on your own perceptions of gender. If you wish, interview other students for their opinion on this issue, and address some of their points in your essay.

3. Thirty years ago, men were expected to earn more than women. Do we still hold such beliefs? Poll your classmates to find out their opinions regarding income status. Do men feel that they should earn more? Would they feel less masculine if their girlfriends or wives earned more then they did? Do women look for higher incomes when they consider a partner? Analyze your results and write an argument that draws conclusions from your survey and its connection to feminism in the twenty-first century.

4. In your own words, define the terms *masculine* and *feminine*. You might include library research on the origins of the words or research their changing implications over the years. Develop your own definition for each word, and then discuss with the rest of the class how you arrived at your definitions.

5. Several of the authors in this section attribute youth's desire to act, dress, and look a certain way to media pressure. Write an essay discussing whether this is true or not true. Support your perspective using examples from the authors, and your own experiences and observations.

6. Is it harder to grow up male or female in America today? Using information from the articles in this chapter, as well as outside resources, write an essay explaining which gender faces the greatest and most daunting challenges, and why. Will this situation grow worse? Offer suggestions to help ease the gender-related challenges children face growing up in today's culture.

7. Write an essay in which you consider your own sense of cultural conditioning. Do you feel your behavior has been conditioned by sex-role expectations? In what ways? Is there a difference between the "real" you and the person you present to the world? If there is a difference, is it the result of cultural pressure? Explain.

8. Write an essay examining the role television and entertainment media has had on our perceptions of male and female social roles and how we fit in as men and as women in society today.

9. In her essay, Hanna Rosin observes that men, in general, have failed to embrace the "nurturing professions" including teaching, nursing, and secretarial roles. What influence, if any, do perceptions of gender have on our employment expectations of men and women? What are "men's jobs" and "women's jobs"? What stigma is connected to a woman having a traditionally male job, such as in construction work, or a man having a female one, such as in nursing? Discuss your results with the class as part of a broader discussion about perceptions of contemporary gender roles.

12

Moral Quandaries in Medicine

Modern medicine has ushered in a medical world of which our great-grandparents could only dream. Today, in wealthy societies, human health has reached new heights, as medicine and surgery extend our life spans and allow us to lead more productive lives. But new medicines, surgical interventions, diagnostic tools, and life-extending procedures generate new problems and new ethical questions. One cannot leaf through a newspaper or turn on the television without confronting weighty debates on issues concerning reproductive technology, organ transplantation, health care reform, and the right to die.

While our health overall has improved, obesity rates even among the very young continue to soar, undermining medicine's best efforts to keep us healthy. We know that obesity can lead to a myriad of illnesses and health conditions from diabetes to joint issues to heart problems, and can tax a health system with limited resources. And buzzing behind all the progress is the hard truth that health care is expensive and that medical marvels cost money—sometimes a lot of money.

On another front, consider that 50 years ago organ transplant was available only to identical twins. Today, with the help of donor matching and anti-rejection drugs, organ transplantation enables thousands of people every year to have a second chance at life. But the need for organs is greater than the supply, leaving many people on long waitlists with time running out. How do we grow organ donor lists? And why isn't everyone an organ donor?

For the past several decades, infertile couples have achieved a healthy pregnancy through reproductive technology. Sperm and egg donation make it possible for women who would have had no options a generation before to achieve a healthy pregnancy. With this technology come questions. What rights do children of sperm (or egg) donors have to their biological heritage? Should egg and sperm donors have a right to anonymity? Or, like children of adoption, should children born of sperm donation be able to locate their fathers?

Reproductive technology has moved beyond test-tube babies into a brave new world of genetic testing. We can prevent some babies from carrying on the gene for certain deadly diseases, including Huntington's disease and Duchenne muscular dystrophy, and we are on the brink of "cosmetic genetics" that could allow us to opt for certain physical traits for our future offspring. But all this miracle science brings words of caution from ethicists: Are we taking the idea of "designer babies" too far?

From questions about creating life, we are also dealing with tough issues connected to the end of life. Should the terminally ill be able to end their lives on their own terms?

Although some states have passed "death with dignity" laws, many ethical considerations remain. As right-to-die laws continue to appear on ballots across the country, we must consider the multiple issues connected to assisted suicide. Could patients be "coerced" to end their lives? Pressured into taking the lethal dose? Could they die at the hands of an impatient heir? Or are these concerns minor when considering the rights of individuals to make life and death decisions?

Ethical and moral issues of right and wrong have challenged people throughout history. Many of these issues are deeply connected to questions concerning life itself—when it begins, how it begins, and when it ends. This chapter explores a few of the controversial medical subjects that Americans are wrestling with today.

The Quagmire

Daniel Callahan and Sherwin B. Nuland

> Most of us depend on modern medicine. It is probable that many of us would not be alive today if it were not for antibiotics, life-saving surgery, or even more radical medical intervention. Advances in medicine are viewed as remarkable and essential, but have we come to expect too much from medicine? Do we try to extend lives without considering the costs? Are we funding research that is taking too long to produce results? And are we pouring too much money into keeping the sickest people alive? In this article, octogenarians and retired professors Daniel Callahan and Sherwin Nuland argue that today's medical advances should be balanced against another factor: the insupportable, unsustainable economic cost of this sort of success. To make things right, they contend, will take nothing less than a sweeping culture shift on the part of both society and the medical profession.*

BEFORE YOU READ

How has our view of medicine changed over the last 50 years? What do we expect of medical treatment?

AS YOU READ

The authors argue that we must be persuaded to lower our expectations of medicine to inspire a new medical model based on harsh economic realities. In your view, should research focused on advancing medicine be scaled back for economic reasons? Or can you put a price tag on medicine?

1 In 1959, the great biologist René Dubos wrote a book called *Mirage of Health*, in which he pointed out that "complete and lasting freedom from disease is but a dream remembered from imaginings of a Garden of Eden." But, in the intervening decades,

*Daniel Callahan and Sherwin Nuland, *New Republic*, June 9, 2011.

his admonition has largely been ignored by both doctors and society as a whole. For nearly a century, but especially since the end of World War II, the medical profession has been waging an unrelenting war against disease—most notably cancer, heart disease, and stroke. The ongoing campaign has led to a steady and rarely questioned increase in the disease-research budget of the National Institutes of Health (NIH). It has also led to a sea change in the way Americans think about medicine in their own lives: We now view all diseases as things to be conquered. Underlying these changes have been several assumptions: that medical advances are essentially unlimited; that none of the major lethal diseases is in theory incurable; and that progress is economically affordable if well managed.

2   But what if all this turns out not to be true? What if there are no imminent, much less foreseeable cures to some of the most common and most lethal diseases? What if, in individual cases, not all diseases should be fought? What if we are refusing to confront the painful likelihood that our biological nature is not nearly as resilient or open to endless improvement as we have long believed?

3   Let us begin by pointing to some unpleasant realities, starting with infectious disease. Forty years ago, it was commonly assumed that infectious disease had all but been conquered, with the eradication of smallpox taken as the great example of that victory. That assumption has been proved false—by the advent, for example, of HIV as well as a dangerous increase in antibiotic-resistant microbes. Based on what we now know of viral disease and microbial genetics, it is reasonable to assume that infectious disease will never be eliminated but only, at best, become less prevalent.

4   Then there are chronic diseases, now the scourge of industrialized nations. If the hope for eradication of infectious disease was misplaced, the hopes surrounding cures for chronic diseases are no less intoxicated. Think of the "war on cancer," declared by Richard Nixon in 1971. Mortality rates for the great majority of cancers have fallen slowly over the decades, but we remain far from a cure. No one of any scientific stature even predicts a cure for heart disease or stroke. As for Alzheimer's, not long before President Obama recently approved a fresh effort to find better treatments, a special panel of the NIH determined that essentially little progress has been made in recent years toward finding ways to delay the onset of major symptoms. And no one talks seriously of a near-term cure.

5   One of the hardiest hopes in the chronic-disease wars has been that of a compression of morbidity—a long life with little illness followed by a brief period of disability and then a quick death. A concept first introduced by James Fries in 1980, it has had the special attraction of providing a persuasively utopian view of the future of medicine. And it has always been possible to identify very old people who seemed to have the good fortune of living such a life—a kind of end run on medicine—and then dying quickly. But a recent and very careful study by Eileen Crimmins and Hiram Beltran-Sanchez of the University of Southern California has determined that the idea has no empirical support. Most of us will contract one or more chronic diseases later in life and die from them, slowly. "Health," Crimmins and Beltran-Sanchez write, "may not be improving with each generation" and "compression of morbidity may be as illusory as immortality. We do not appear to be moving to a world where we die without experiencing disease, functioning loss, and disability."

6   Average life expectancy, moreover, steadily increasing for many decades, now shows signs of leveling off. S. Jay Olshansky, a leading figure in longevity studies, has for some years expressed skepticism about the prospect of an indefinite increase in life expectancy.

He calls his position a "realist" one, particularly in contending that it will be difficult to get the average beyond 85. He also writes that it is "biased" to assume that "only positive influences on health and longevity will persist and accelerate." That view, he notes, encompasses a belief that science will surely keep moving on a forward track—a projection that is not necessarily true. Simply look at the "breakthroughs" that have been predicted for such scientific sure things as stem-cell technology and medical genetics—but have yet to be realized. These breakthroughs may eventually happen, but they are chancy bets. We have arrived at a moment, in short, where we are making little headway in defeating various kinds of diseases. Instead, our main achievements today consist of devising ways to marginally extend the lives of the very sick.

7   There are many ways of responding to this generally pessimistic reading of medical innovation in recent years. The most common is simply to note all the progress that has been made: useful new drugs, helpful new devices and technologies, decreased disability, better ways of controlling pain, and so on. And it is certainly true that some aspects of medicine have made enormous strides over the past few decades. Some of these strides, in fact, have taken place in the very areas—such as cardiac and infectious diseases (for instance, treatment of HIV)—in which so much of the outlook remains otherwise unpromising. One of us was the beneficiary of a life-saving heart operation at age 78, of a kind that did not exist a decade ago (and both of us celebrated our eightieth birthdays this past year). Americans do live longer, by eight to nine years since 1960; a great range of treatments are available for our illnesses, mild or severe; our pain is better relieved; and our prospects for living from youth to old age have never been greater.

8   It might also be said that there is no reason to believe that cures for infectious and chronic diseases cannot eventually be found; it is just taking longer than expected and the necessary knowledge for breakthroughs seems to be slowly accumulating. Or it might be said that more people living longer, though sick, is a not inconsiderable triumph.

9   These advances, however, should be balanced against another factor: the insupportable, unsustainable economic cost of this sort of success. Twenty years from now, the maturation of the baby boom generation will be at flood tide. We will have gone from 40 million Americans over the age of 65 in 2009 to 70 million in 2030. This will put enormous pressure on the health care system, regardless of whether Obama's reform efforts, or even Paul Ryan's, prove successful. The chronic diseases of the elderly will be the front line. Because we cannot cure those diseases at present, nor reasonably hope for cures over the next few decades, the best we will be able to do in many cases, especially those of the elderly and frail, is extend people's lives for a relatively short period of time—at considerable expense and often while causing serious suffering to the person in question.

10   Consider that a National Cancer Institute study projects a 39 percent increase in cancer costs between 2010 and 2020. That figure represents in great part our success in extending the lives of those already afflicted with the disease. Kidney dialysis also has become an economic quagmire. A 150 percent increase in the number of such patients is expected over the next decade. The cost of Alzheimer's disease is projected to rise from $91 billion in 2005 to $189 billion in 2015 to $1 trillion in 2050 (twice the cost of Medicare expenditures for all diseases now).

11   In a 2006 article, Harvard economist David Cutler and colleagues wrote, "Analyses focused on spending and on the increase in life expectancy beginning at 65 years of age

showed that the incremental cost of an additional year of life rose from $46,800 in the 1970s to $145,000 in the 1990s. . . . If this trend continues in the elderly, the cost-effectiveness of medical care will continue to decrease at older ages." Emory professor Kenneth Thorpe and colleagues, summing up some Medicare data, note that "more than half of beneficiaries are treated for five or more chronic conditions each year." Among the elderly, the struggle against disease has begun to look like the trench warfare of World War I: little real progress in taking enemy territory but enormous economic and human cost in trying to do so.

12   In the war against disease, we have unwittingly created a kind of medicine that is barely affordable now and forbiddingly unaffordable in the long run. The Affordable Care Act might ease the burden, but it will not eliminate it. Ours is now a medicine that may doom most of us to an old age that will end badly: with our declining bodies falling apart as they always have but devilishly—and expensively—stretching out the suffering and decay. Can we conceptualize something better? Can we imagine a medicine that is more affordable—that brings our health care system's current cost escalation, now in the range of 6 percent to 7 percent per year, down to 3 percent, which would place it in line with the annual rise in GDP? Can we imagine a system that is less ambitious but also more humane—that better handles the inevitable downward spiral of old age and helps us through a somewhat more limited life span as workers, citizens, and parents?

13   The answer to these questions is yes. But it will require—to use a religious term in a secular way—something like a conversion experience on the part of physicians, researchers, industry, and our nation as a whole.

14   Vannevar Bush, a scientific advisor to President Franklin D. Roosevelt, famously said that science is an "endless frontier." He was right then and that is still true now. But scientific progress to extend that frontier is not an endlessly affordable venture. Health care, like the exploration of outer space, will always be open to progress, but we understand that putting humans on Mars is not at present economically sensible. We have settled for a space station and the Hubble telescope. We must now comparably scale down our ambitions for medicine, setting new priorities in light of the obstacles we have encountered.

15   We need, first of all, to change our approach to research. A key ingredient of the economic engine of medical progress has been the endless issuing of promissory notes by scientists and the medical industry, which are then amplified by the media. The human genome project, stem-cell research, highly touted "breakthroughs"—all have raised hopes that we are on the verge of saving hundreds of millions of lives. But these promises have not materialized. A more realistic rhetoric is necessary, one that places a heavier emphasis on caring for the sick, not curing them.

16   The traditional open-ended model of medical research, with the war against death as the highest priority, should give way to a new goal: aiming to bring everyone's life expectancy up to an average age of 80 years (already being approached), reducing early death, and shifting the emphasis in the direction of improving the quality of life of those in every age group. The highest priority should be given to children, the next-highest to those in their adult years (the age group responsible for managing society), and the lowest to those over 80.

17   In light of the fact that we are not curing most diseases, we need to change our priorities for the elderly. Death is not the only bad thing that can happen to an elderly person. An old age marked by disability, economic insecurity, and social isolation are also great

evils. Instead of a medical culture of cure for the elderly we need a culture of care, notably a stronger Social Security program and a Medicare program much more heavily weighted toward primary care. Less money, that is, for late-life technological interventions and more for preventive measures and independent living. Some people may die earlier than now, but they will die better deaths.

18   Bringing about these changes would require shifts in the medical profession. Imagine a health care pyramid. At the lowest and broadest level is public health (health promotion and disease prevention). The next level is primary medicine and emergency care. The level above that consists of short-term hospital care for acute illness. And the top, narrowest level is high-technology care for the chronically ill. It is essential that we find ways to push down the ever-expanding kind of care at the highest level to lower levels, and particularly to the public-health and primary-care levels. The standards for access to care at the highest levels should be strict, marked by a decent chance of good outcomes at a reasonable cost.

19   Along these lines, one obvious step is to encourage more medical students to become primary-care physicians rather than specialists. Though there is nothing new or radical in such a proposal, it will not be easy to implement. Medical education must be better subsidized to reduce the debt of young doctors, which discourages many from entering family practice and tempts them toward ever-narrowing and more lucrative specialties.

20   Yet the most difficult shift will have to take place not among doctors, but among the public as a whole. The institution of medicine is enormously popular with the public. None of us likes being sick or threatened with death. Modern technology has brought us many benefits that enhance the prestige and social power of medicine. But the public must be persuaded to lower its expectations. We must have a society-wide dialogue on what a new model of medicine will look like: a model that will be moderate in its research aspirations, and dominated by primary care and neighborhood clinics staffed mainly by family physicians, paramedics and nurses for routine health needs, and organized teams for acute care. If this society-wide dialogue is to be successful, doctors will have to call repeated attention to the economic and social realities of the endless war on disease. They will have to remind the public that this war cannot be won—or can achieve small, incremental victories only—and if we are not careful, we can harm ourselves trying.

21   Finally, we need a health care system that is far more radically reformed than the system envisioned by the Affordable Care Act (ACA). Should the ACA be successful down to the last detail, it is still unlikely to succeed in bringing the annual rise in health care costs down to the annual GDP increase. In their 2011 yearly report, the Medicare program trustees project insolvency by 2024. The only reliable way of controlling costs has been the method used by most other developed countries: a centrally directed and budgeted system, oversight in the use of new and old technologies, and price controls. Medicine cannot continue trying to serve two masters, that of providing affordable health care and turning a handsome profit for its middlemen and providers.

22   Even so, those countries with less costly but more effective health care systems are in trouble as well—not as much as we are, but enough to inspire constant reforms. Every health care system has to cope with aging populations, new technologies, and high patient expectations. However a health care system is organized, the open-ended idea of medical progress is the deepest driver of health care costs. It dooms us to live too much of our later years in poor and declining health, and to die inch by inch from failure of one organ after

another. Is it really a medical benefit, for ourselves or our families, to be doomed by frailty to a life that makes even walking a hazard? Or to spend our last years in and out of doctors' offices and ICUs? Those results are what progress has given us—a seeming benefit that has become a serious economic and personal burden.

23   "All politics," the late and wise Tip O'Neill once said, "is local." It can no less be said that "all medicine is personal." Our own experience in trying to talk about the kind of wholesale reforms we think necessary for medicine's future is that people are far more concerned about what it will mean for themselves and their families than for something as general and abstract as the health care system. Their heads tell them that rationing and limits will probably be necessary, but they reject these ideas if it means that a loved one might not have what is needed to be kept alive, even if in a bad or terminal state. Unhappily, however, some rationing and limit-setting will be necessary. There is no way the Medicare program can survive unless it both sharply cuts benefits and raises taxes. Certain benefits can be cut directly or indirectly—directly by reducing payments for treatments, or indirectly by increasing co-payments and deductibles to a painful level, sufficient to discourage people from insisting on them.

24   But our broader point is not really about policy changes such as rationing. It is, put simply, that substantial shifts will be needed in the way our culture thinks about death and aging. There is good evidence that if physicians talk candidly and with empathy to critically ill patients and their families, telling them what they are in for if they want a full-court press, minds can be changed. That, in turn, means that physicians themselves will have to acknowledge their limits, explore their own motivations, and be willing to face patients with bad news as a way of avoiding even worse treatment outcomes. The ethic of medicine has long been to inspire unbounded hope in the sick patient and the same kind of hope in medical research. Sobriety and prudence must now take their place.

25   The problems we are describing are, of course, hardly the only flaws within the U.S. medical system. Among the spheres of concern most commonly cited for major criticism are: the perception of significant deterioration in the doctor-patient relationship; the state of care at the end of life; maldistribution of health care availability among geographic locations; malpractice and tort law; physician entrepreneurship; emphasis on profit motive by the insurance and pharmaceutical industries; duplication of resources among competing health facilities; multiple tiers of access and care, largely determined by income; wasting of money, resources, and personnel within the system; and costly overspecialization.

26   Sometimes—at all times, actually—the problems seem overwhelming. Not only does the complexity of the issues make them appear insoluble, but so does the way in which each seems to intertwine with all the others, inevitably to exacerbate the whole. The entire web of interconnected, complicating factors has long since reached the bewildering point where no issue can be addressed, or so much as approached, in isolation. The complexities are enough to make every stakeholder in American medicine—namely all of us—throw up our hands in desperation.

27   But there is, in fact, a solution: a top-down, bottom-up study of the entire U.S. health system, with a view toward taking it apart and reconstructing it in a manner adapted to our nation's needs—a multiyear, multidisciplinary project whose aim would be to change the very culture of American medicine. The inadequate, inequitable, and

financially insupportable system that has been jerry-built and constantly band-aided during recent decades will no longer do. Nor will incremental policy reforms, no matter how well-intentioned.

28   There is a historical precedent for such a project. At the turn of the twentieth century, U.S. medical education was a disgrace, and care of the sick, except in a certain few facilities, was almost as bad. Something had to be done. In 1908, the newly founded Carnegie Foundation for the Advancement of Teaching stepped in, hiring a 42-year-old educator named Abraham Flexner to embark on a study of medical education in North America. His report, published two years later, became a clarion call for drastic change. Subsequently, armed with a total of $600 million provided by the Carnegie and Rockefeller philanthropies and other contributors, Flexner visited 35 schools in the United States and Canada, and provided the financial wherewithal for the changes so desperately needed. The result of this remarkable effort was that, within ten years, U.S. medical schools became the prototype upon which all others tried to fashion themselves; our nation's medicine, like the vastly improved institutions that gave it new life, became the gold standard for the world.

29   We can do this kind of thing again. It will take political will; unyielding leadership; vast amounts of money, both from government and private philanthropy; and extreme patience. Above all, it will take the confidence of the American people that a more humane, more affordable kind of medicine is possible.

QUESTIONS FOR ANALYSIS AND DISCUSSION

1. Callahan and Nuland observe that advances in modern medicine have led Americans to "now view all diseases as things to be conquered." In their view, what are the negative consequences of this belief?

2. Callahan and Nuland ask "what if, in individual cases, not all diseases should be fought?" How do they answer this question? What evidence do they offer that we *shouldn't* try to cure all diseases? What reasons do they give for not pursuing medical advances to the utmost?

3. What is morbidity? How does it factor into the debate on the fight against disease? Explain.

4. How old are the authors? Does their age seem surprising, considering the content of their essay? Does it challenge or support the content of their essay? Explain.

5. In your opinion, is it ethical to extend the lives of the very sick and incurable, at great financial cost to the general public? Is it fair to the sufferer? Why or why not?

6. The authors argue that there is a way to make medicine more affordable and humane. What solution do they offer? What culture shift must occur to implement it?

7. Evaluate the ethical implications of the authors' solution to creating affordable health care. Present your own view, referring to specific points raised in the essay.

Survival of the Wrongest

David H. Freedman

Many people rely on media and news to provide the latest health information. But it seems as if every medical recommendation is soon countered with information dictating the exact opposite. One study reports that vitamin E is great for you, and another reports it could cause cancer. One study reports a link between red wine and longevity; another says alcohol shortens the life span. And people closest to the information—reporters—are in the compromising position of contradicting themselves, sometimes in the same week. In this essay, journalist David Freedman reports that health journalists have fallen into a trap. He explains how personal-health journalism ignores the fundamental pitfalls baked into all scientific research and serves up a daily diet of unreliable information. Even when following guidelines of good science reporting, health journalists still manage to write articles that grossly mislead the public, often in ways that can lead to poor health decisions with catastrophic consequences.*

BEFORE YOU READ —————————————————————

Most of us have a vague idea of what is healthy and unhealthy. Where do we learn this information? Where does our knowledge of health and medicine come from?

AS YOU READ —————————————————————

How much do you rely on news media to provide you with timely and accurate health data? Do you follow what recommendations are put forth in the media? Why or why not?

1   In late 2011, in a nearly 6,000-word article in *The New York Times Magazine*, health writer Tara Parker-Pope laid out the scientific evidence that maintaining weight loss is a nearly impossible task—something that, in the words of one obesity scientist she quotes, only "rare individuals" can accomplish. Parker-Pope cites a number of studies that reveal the various biological mechanisms that align against people who've lost weight, ensuring that the weight comes back. These findings, she notes, produce a consistent and compelling picture by "adding to a growing body of evidence that challenges conventional thinking about obesity, weight loss, and willpower. For years, the advice to the overweight and obese has been that we simply need to eat less and exercise more. While there is truth to this guidance, it fails to take into account that the human body continues to fight against weight loss long after dieting has stopped. This translates into a sobering reality: once we become fat, most of us, despite our best efforts, will probably stay fat."

———————————————

*David H. Freedman, *Columbia Journalism Review*, January 2013.

2   But does this mean the obese should stop trying so hard to lose weight? Maybe. Parker-Pope makes sure to include the disclaimer that "nobody is saying" obese people should give up on weight loss, but after spending so much time explaining how the science "proves" it's a wasted effort, her assurance sounds a little hollow.

3   The article is crammed with detailed scientific evidence and quotes from highly credentialed researchers. It's also a compelling read, thanks to anecdotal accounts of the endless travails of would-be weight-losers, including Parker-Pope's own frustrating failures to remove and keep off the extra 60 pounds or so she says she carries.

4   In short, it's a well-reported, well-written, highly readable, and convincing piece of personal-health-science journalism that is careful to pin its claims to published research.

5   There's really just one problem with Parker-Pope's piece: Many, if not most, researchers and experts who work closely with the overweight and obese would pronounce its main thesis—that sustaining weight loss is nearly impossible—dead wrong, and misleading in a way that could seriously, if indirectly, damage the health of millions of people.

6   Many readers—including a number of physicians, nutritionists, and mental-health professionals—took to the blogs in the days after the article appeared to note its major omissions and flaws. These included the fact that the research Parker-Pope most prominently cites, featuring it in a long lead, was a tiny study that required its subjects to go on a near-starvation diet, a strategy that has long been known to produce intense food cravings and rebound weight gain; the fact that many programs and studies routinely record sustained weight-loss success rates in the 30-percent range; and Parker-Pope's focus on willpower-driven, intense diet-and-exercise regimens as the main method of weight loss, when most experts have insisted for some time now that successful, long-term weight loss requires permanent, sustainable, satisfying lifestyle changes, bolstered by enlisting social support and reducing the temptations and triggers in our environments—the so-called "behavioral modification" approach typified by Weight Watchers, and backed by research studies again and again.

7   Echoing the sentiments of many experts, Barbara Berkeley, a physician who has long specialized in weight loss, blogged that the research Parker-Pope cites doesn't match reality. "Scientific research needs to square with what we see in clinical practice," she wrote. "If it doesn't, we should question its validity." David Katz, a prominent physician-researcher who runs the Yale Prevention Research Center and edits the journal *Childhood Obesity*, charged in his *Huffington Post* blog that Parker-Pope, by listing all the biological mechanisms that work against weight loss, was simply asking the wrong question. "Let's beware the hidden peril of that genetic and biological understanding," he wrote. "It can be hard to see what's going on all around you while looking through the lens of a microscope." In fact, most of us know people—friends, family members, colleagues—who have lost weight and kept it off for years by changing the way they eat and boosting their physical activity. They can't all be freaks of biology, as Parker-Pope's article implies.

8   *The Times* has run into similar trouble with other prominent articles purporting to cut through the supposed mystery of why the world keeps getting dangerously fatter. One such piece pointed the finger at sugar and high-fructose corn syrup, another at bacteria. But perhaps the most controversial of the *Times*'s solution-to-the-obesity-crisis articles was the magazine's cover story in 2002, by science writer Gary Taubes, that made the case that high-fat diets are perfectly slimming—as long as one cuts out all carbohydrates.

His article's implicit claim that copious quantities of bacon are good for weight loss, while oatmeal, whole wheat, and fruit will inevitably fatten you up, had an enormous impact on the public's efforts to lose weight, and to this day many people still turn to Atkins and other ultra-low-carb, eat-all-the-fat-you-want diets to try to shed excess pounds. Unfortunately, it's an approach that leaves the vast majority of frontline obesity experts gritting their teeth, because while the strategy sometimes appears to hold up in studies, in the real world such dieters are rarely able to keep the weight off—to say nothing of the potential health risks of eating too much fat. And of course, the argument Taubes laid out stands in direct opposition to the claims of the Parker-Pope article. Indeed, most major *Times* articles on obesity contradict one another, and they all gainsay the longstanding consensus of the field.

9   The problem isn't unique to the *Times*, or to the subject of weight loss. In all areas of personal health, we see prominent media reports that directly oppose well-established knowledge in the field, or that make it sound as if scientifically unresolved questions have been resolved. The media, for instance, have variously supported and shot down the notion that vitamin D supplements can protect against cancer, and that taking daily and low doses of aspirin extends life by protecting against heart attacks. Some reports have argued that frequent consumption of even modest amounts of alcohol leads to serious health risks, while others have reported that daily moderate alcohol consumption can be a healthy substitute for exercise. Articles sang the praises of new drugs like Avastin and Avandia before other articles deemed them dangerous, ineffective, or both.

10   What's going on? The problem is not, as many would reflexively assume, the sloppiness of poorly trained science writers looking for sensational headlines, and ignoring scientific evidence in the process. Many of these articles were written by celebrated health-science journalists and published in respected magazines and newspapers; their arguments were backed up with what appears to be solid, balanced reporting and the careful citing of published scientific findings.

11   But personal-health journalists have fallen into a trap. Even while following what are considered the guidelines of good science reporting, they still manage to write articles that grossly mislead the public, often in ways that can lead to poor health decisions with catastrophic consequences. Blame a combination of the special nature of health advice, serious challenges in medical research, and the failure of science journalism to scrutinize the research it covers.

12   Personal-health coverage began to move to the fore in the late 1980s, in line with the media's growing emphasis on "news you can use." That increased attention to personal health ate into coverage of not only other science, but also of broader healthcare issues. A 2009 survey of members of the Association of Health Care Journalists found that more than half say "there is too much coverage of consumer or lifestyle health," and more than two-thirds say there isn't enough coverage of health policy, healthcare quality, and health disparities.

13   The author of a report based on that survey, Gary Schwitzer, a former University of Minnesota journalism researcher and now publisher of healthcare-journalism watchdog HealthNewsReview.org, also conducted a study in 2008 of 500 health-related stories published over a 22-month period in large newspapers. The results suggested that not only has personal-health coverage become invasively and inappropriately ubiquitous, it is of generally questionable quality, with about two-thirds of the articles found to have major

flaws. The errors included exaggerating the prevalence and ravages of a disorder, ignoring potential side effects and other downsides to treatments, and failing to discuss alternative treatment options. In the survey, 44 percent of the 256 staff journalists who responded said that their organizations at times base stories almost entirely on press releases. Studies by other researchers have come to similar conclusions.

14   Thoughtful consumers with even a modest knowledge of health and medicine can discern at a glance that they are bombarded by superficial and sometimes misleading "news" of fad diets, miracle supplements, vaccine scares, and other exotic claims that are short on science, as well as endlessly recycled everyday advice, such as being sure to slather on sun protection. But often, even articles written by very good journalists, based on thorough reporting and highly credible sources, take stances that directly contradict those of other credible-seeming articles.

15   There is more at stake in these dueling stories than there would be if the topic at hand were, say, the true authorship of Shakespeare's plays. Personal healthcare decisions affect our lifespan, the quality of our lives, and our productivity, and the result—our collective health—has an enormous impact on the economy. Thirty years ago, misleading health information in the press might not have been such a problem, since at the time physicians generally retained fairly tight control of patient testing and treatment decisions. Today, however, the patient is in the driver's seat when it comes to personal health. What's more, it is increasingly clear that the diseases that today wreak the most havoc—heart disease, cancer, diabetes, and Alzheimer's—are most effectively dealt with not through medical treatment, but through personal lifestyle choices, such as diet, exercise, and smoking habits.

16   Consider the potential damage of bad weight-loss-related journalism. Obesity exacerbates virtually all major disease risks—and more than one in 20 deaths in the US is a premature death related to obesity, according to a 2007 *Journal of the American Medical Association* study. Obesity carries an annual price tag of as much as $5,000 a year in extra medical costs and lost productivity, for a total cost to the US economy of about $320 billion per year—a number that could quadruple within 10 years as obesity rates climb, according to some studies. (There is, of course, a lot of uncertainty in cost projections, and this research does not account for the impact of the Affordable Care Act.) On top of these costs are the subjective costs of the aches, discomforts, and compromised mobility associated with obesity.

17   Meanwhile, there's a wide range of convincing-sounding yet wildly conflicting weight-loss-related claims made by prominent science journalists. People who might otherwise be able to lose weight on the sort of sensible, lifestyle-modification program recommended by most experts end up falling for the faddish, ineffective approaches touted in these articles, or are discouraged from trying at all. For example, innumerable articles (including Parker-Pope's *Times* piece) have emphasized the notion that obesity is largely genetically determined. But study after study has shown that obesity tends to correlate to environment, not personal genome, as per the fact that people who emigrate from countries with traditionally low obesity rates, such as China, tend to hew to the obesity rates of their adopted countries. What's more, global obesity rates are rapidly rising year by year, including in China, whereas the human genome barely changes over thousands of years. And studies clearly show that "obesity genes" are essentially neutralized by healthy behaviors such as exercise.

18   It is not encouraging to those trying to muster the focus and motivation to stick to a healthy-eating-and-exercise program to hear that their obesity is largely genetically

determined, suggesting—sometimes explicitly—that the obese are doomed to remain so no matter what they do. A 2011 *New England Journal of Medicine* study (as reported in *The New York Times*) found that people tend to binge after they find out they carry a supposed fat-promoting gene. Other studies have shown—in keeping with common sense—that one of the best predictors of whether someone starting a weight-loss program will stick with it is how strongly the person believes it will succeed. When journalists erode that confidence with misleading messages, the results are easy to predict.

19   When science journalism goes astray, the usual suspect is a failure to report accurately and thoroughly on research published in peer-reviewed journals. In other words, science journalists are supposed to stick to what well-credentialed scientists are actually saying in or about their published findings—the journalists merely need to find a way to express this information in terms that are understandable and interesting to readers and viewers.

20   But some of the most damagingly misleading articles don't stem from the reporter's failure to do this. Rather, science reporters—along with most everyone else—tend to confuse the findings of published science research with the closest thing we have to the truth. But as is widely acknowledged among scientists themselves, and especially within medical science, the findings of published studies are beset by a number of problems that tend to make them untrustworthy, or at least render them exaggerated or oversimplified.

21   It's easy enough to verify that something is going wrong with medical studies by simply looking up published findings on virtually any question in the field and noting how the findings contradict, sometimes sharply. To cite a few examples out of thousands, studies have found that hormone-replacement therapy is safe and effective, and also that it is dangerous and ineffective; that virtually every vitamin supplement lowers the risk of various diseases, and also that they do nothing for these diseases; that low-carb, high-fat diets are the most effective way to lose weight, and that high-carb, low-fat diets are the most effective way to lose weight; that surgery relieves back pain in most patients, and that back surgery is essentially a sham treatment; that cardiac patients fare better when someone secretly prays for them, and that secret prayer has no effect on cardiac patients. (Yes, these latter studies were undertaken by respected researchers and published in respected journals.)

22   Biostatisticians have studied the question of just how frequently published studies come up with wrong answers. A highly regarded researcher in this subfield of medical wrongness is John Ioannidis, who heads the Stanford Prevention Research Center, among other appointments. Using several different techniques, Ioannidis has determined that the overall wrongness rate in medicine's top journals is about two thirds, and that estimate has been well-accepted in the medical field.

23   A frequent defense of this startling error rate is that the scientific process is supposed to wend its way through many wrong ideas before finally approaching truth. But that's a complete mischaracterization of what's going on here. Scientists might indeed be expected to come up with many mistaken explanations when investigating a disease or anything else. But these "mistakes" are supposed to come in the form of incorrect theories—that a certain drug is safe and effective for most people, that a certain type of diet is better than another for weight loss. The point of scientific studies is to determine whether a theory is right or wrong. A study that accurately finds a theory to be incorrect has arrived at a correct finding. A study that mistakenly concludes an incorrect theory is correct, or vice-versa, has arrived at a wrong finding. If scientists can't reliably test the correctness of their theories,

then science is in trouble—bad testing isn't supposed to be part of the scientific process. Yet medical journals, as we've seen, are full of such unreliable findings.

24   Another frequent claim, especially within science journalism, is that the wrongness problems go away when reporters stick with randomized control trials (RCTs). These are the so-called gold standard of medical studies, and typically involve randomly assigning subjects to a treatment group or a non-treatment group, so that the two groups can be compared. But it isn't true that journalistic problems stem from basing articles on studies that aren't RCTs. Ioannidis and others have found that RCTs, too (even large ones), are plagued with inaccurate findings, if to a lesser extent. Remember that virtually every drug that gets pulled off the market when dangerous side effects emerge was proven "safe" in a large RCT. Even those studies of the effectiveness of third-party prayer were fairly large RCTs. Meanwhile, some of the best studies have not been RCTs, including those that convincingly demonstrated the danger of cigarettes, and the effectiveness of seat belts.

25   Why do studies end up with wrong findings? In fact, there are so many distorting forces baked into the process of testing the accuracy of a medical theory, that it's harder to explain how researchers manage to produce valid findings, aside from sheer luck. To cite just a few of these problems:

26   **Mismeasurement**   To test the safety and efficacy of a drug, for example, what researchers really want to know is how thousands of people will fare long-term when taking the drug. But it would be unethical (and illegal) to give unproven drugs to thousands of people, and no one wants to wait 20 years for results. So scientists must rely on animal studies, which tend to translate poorly to humans, and on various short-cuts and indirect measurements in human studies that they hope give them a good indication of what a new drug is doing. The difficulty of setting up good human studies, and of making relevant, accurate measurements on people, plagues virtually all medical research.

27   **Confounders**   Study subjects may lose weight on a certain diet, but was it because of the diet, or because of the support they got from doctors and others running the study? Or because they knew their habits and weight were being recorded? Or because they knew they could quit the diet when the study was over? So many factors affect every aspect of human health that it's nearly impossible to tease them apart and see clearly the effect of changing any one of them.

28   **Publication bias**   Research journals, like newsstand magazines, want exciting stories that will have impact on readers. That means they prefer studies that deliver the most interesting and important findings, such as that a new treatment works, or that a certain type of diet helps most people lose weight. If multiple research teams test a treatment, and all but one find the treatment doesn't work, the journal might well be interested in publishing the one positive result, even though the most likely explanation for the oddball finding is that the researchers behind it made a mistake or perhaps fudged the data a bit. What's more, since scientists' careers depend on being published in prominent journals, and because there is intense competition to be published, scientists much prefer to come up with the exciting, important findings journals are looking for—even if it's a wrong finding. Unfortunately, as Ioannidis and others have pointed out, the more exciting a finding, the more likely it is to be wrong. Typically, something is exciting specifically because it's unexpected, and it's unexpected typically because it's less likely to occur. Thus, exciting findings are often unlikely findings, and unlikely findings are often unlikely for the simple reason that they're wrong.

29   Ioannidis and others have noted that the supposed protection science offers to catch flawed findings—notably peer review and replication—is utterly ineffective at detecting most problems with studies, from mismeasurement to outright fraud (which, confidential surveys have revealed, is far more common in research than most people would suppose).

30   None of this is to say that researchers aren't operating as good scientists, or that journals don't care about the truth. Rather, the point is that scientists are human beings who, like all of us, crave success, status, and funding, and who make mistakes; and that journals are businesses that need readers and impact to thrive.

31   It's one thing to be understanding of these challenges scientists and their journals face, and quite another to be ignorant of the problems they cause, or to fail to acknowledge those problems. But too many health journalists tend to simply pass along what scientists hand them—or worse, what the scientists' PR departments hand them. Two separate 2012 studies of mass-media health articles, one published in *PLoS Medicine* and the other in *The British Medical Journal*, found that the content and quality of the articles roughly track the content and quality of the press releases that described the studies' findings.

32   Given that published medical findings are, by the field's own reckoning, more often wrong than right, a serious problem with health journalism is immediately apparent: A reporter who accurately reports findings is probably transmitting wrong findings. And because the media tend to pick the most exciting findings from journals to pass on to the public, they are in essence picking the worst of the worst. Health journalism, then, is largely based on a principle of survival of the wrongest. (Of course, I quote studies throughout this article to support my own assertions, including studies on the wrongness of other studies. Should these studies be trusted? Good luck in sorting that out! My advice: Look at the preponderance of evidence, and apply common sense liberally.)

33   What is a science journalist's responsibility to openly question findings from highly credentialed scientists and trusted journals? There can only be one answer: The responsibility is large, and it clearly has been neglected. It's not nearly enough to include in news reports the few mild qualifications attached to any study ("the study wasn't large," "the effect was modest," "some subjects withdrew from the study partway through it"). Readers ought to be alerted, as a matter of course, to the fact that wrongness is embedded in the entire research system, and that few medical research findings ought to be considered completely reliable, regardless of the type of study, who conducted it, where it was published, or who says it's a good study.

34   Worse still, health journalists are taking advantage of the wrongness problem. Presented with a range of conflicting findings for almost any interesting question, reporters are free to pick those that back up their preferred thesis—typically the exciting, controversial idea that their editors are counting on. When a reporter, for whatever reasons, wants to demonstrate that a particular type of diet works better than others—or that diets never work—there is a wealth of studies that will back him or her up, never mind all those other studies that have found exactly the opposite (or the studies can be mentioned, then explained away as "flawed"). For "balance," just throw in a quote or two from a scientist whose opinion strays a bit from the thesis, then drown those quotes out with supportive quotes and more study findings.

35   Of course, journalists who question the general integrity of medical findings risk being branded as science "denialists," lumped in with crackpots who insist evolution and climate change are nonsense. My own experience is that scientists themselves are generally supportive of journalists who raise these important issues, while science journalists

are frequently hostile to the suggestion that research findings are rife with wrongness. Questioning most health-related findings isn't denying good science—it's demanding it.

36   Ironically, we see much more of this sort of skeptical, broad-perspective reporting on politics, where politicians' claims and poll results are questioned and fact-checked by journalists, and on business, where the views of CEOs and analysts and a range of data are played off against one another in order to provide a fuller, more nuanced picture.

37   Yet in health journalism (and in science journalism in general), scientists are treated as trustworthy heroes, and journalists proudly brag on their websites about the awards and recognition they've received from science associations—as if our goal should be to win the admiration of the scientists we're covering, and to make it clear we're eager to return the favor. The *New York Times*'s highly regarded science writer Dennis Overbye wrote in 2009 that scientists' "values, among others, are honesty, doubt, respect for evidence, openness, accountability and tolerance and indeed hunger for opposing points of view." But given what we know about the problems with scientific studies, anyone who wants to assert that science is being carried out by an army of Abraham Lincolns has a lot of explaining to do. Scientists themselves don't make such a claim, so why would we do it on their behalf? We owe readers more than that. Their lives may depend on it.

QUESTIONS FOR ANALYSIS AND DISCUSSION

1. What was wrong about the article by Tara Parker Pope that the author refers to in his opening paragraphs. Was she conveying important information? Selling a story likely to resonate with readers? Conveying erroneous information? Explain.
2. Why is personal-health reporting so popular? How much have people come to rely upon it?
3. What damage could "bad weight-loss-related journalism" cause? Explain.
4. What are the most common pitfalls that plague health reporters? What mistakes do they make? Explain.
5. How do health reporters exploit the "wrongness problem" with data from studies? How can this exploitation harm the public?
6. What, if anything, do health reporters owe their reading public? What ethical standards should they adhere to, if any? Explain.

A Father's Day Plea to Sperm Donors

Colton Wooten

Assisted reproductive medicine offers opportunities that were once the stuff of science fiction. Today, donated sperm may be joined with a donated egg and implanted in still another unrelated individual to produce a baby. With artificial insemination, women today no longer need a male partner to become pregnant, and some women have decided to pursue single-parenthood. Although the outcome is usually a positive one for the parent(s), what about the children of these medical miracles? In the following essay, student Colton Wooten, the child of a woman who opted for artificial insemination with the help of an anonymous donor, makes a personal plea to the men who so willingly give up their genetic material in exchange for beer money.*

Are there ethical and unethical reasons for sperm donation? Egg donation? Or is donor motivation irrelevant to the issue?

Wooten notes he knows a little of his biological history from what his mother read about his sperm donor. If biological history is already provided, why would a child produced through sperm donation wish to contact his or her biological father?

1   When I was 5, my mother revealed to me that I had been conceived through artificial insemination. This was before I understood anything about sex or where babies came from—I think I thought they just sprang from their mothers' stomachs at random. Because my understanding of conventional conception was so thin, my mom remained vague about the details of my conception—in all its complexity—until I got older.

2   When that time came, I learned how my mother, closing in on her 40s, found herself unmarried and childless. She had finished graduate school and established a career, but regretted not having a family. And so she decided to take the business of having a baby into her own capable hands. Artificial insemination seemed like a smart idea, perhaps the only idea.

3   She arranged a consultation at the University of North Carolina fertility clinic in early 1992. During the visits that followed she examined the profiles of the sperm bank's donors, compared favorable traits and credentials, and picked one. In the autumn of that year, I was born.

4   My mom's decision intrigued many people. Some saw it as a triumph of female self-sufficiency. But others, particularly her close friends and family, were shocked. "You can't have a baby without a man!" they would gasp.

5   It turns out, of course, you can, and pretty easily. The harder part, at least for that baby as he grows older, is the mystery of who that man was. Or is.

6   I didn't think much about that until 2006, when I was in eighth grade and my teacher assigned my class a genealogy project. We were supposed to research our family history and create a family tree to share with the class. In the past, whenever questioned about my father's absence by friends or teachers, I wove intricate alibis: he was a doctor on call; he was away on business in Russia; he had died, prematurely, of a heart attack. In my head, I'd always dismissed him as my "biological father," with that distant, medical phrase.

7   But the assignment made me think about him in a new way. I decided to call the U.N.C. fertility center, hoping at least to learn my father's name, his age or any minutiae of his existence that the clinic would be willing to divulge. But I was told that no files were saved for anonymous donors, so there was no information they could give me.

8   In the early days of in vitro fertilization, single women and sterile couples often overlooked a child's eventual desire to know where he came from. Even today, despite recent movies like

*Colton Wooten, *New York Times*, June 18, 2011.

The Kids Are All Right, there is too little substantial debate on the subject. The emotional and developmental deficits that stem from an ignorance of one's origins are still largely ignored.

9   I understand why fertility centers chose to keep sperm donation anonymous. They were attempting to prevent extra chaos, like custody battles, intrusion upon happy families (on either party's side), mothers showing up on donors' doorsteps with homely, misbegotten children with runny noses and untied shoelaces to beg for child support. It's entirely reasonable, and yet the void that many children and young adults born from artificial insemination experience from simply not knowing transcends reason.

10   I don't resent my mom; she did the best thing she knew how to do at the time, and found a way to make a child under the circumstances. But babies born of the procedure in the future should have the right to know who their donors are, and even have some contact with them. Sperm donors need to realize that they are fathers. When I was doing college interviews, one of the interviewers told me that he didn't have any children, but that he had donated sperm while in college because he needed the money. He didn't realize that he probably is someone's father, regardless of whether he knows his child.

11   I'm one of those children, and I want to know who my father is. There are some programs like the Donor Sibling Registry that try to connect those conceived through sperm and egg donation with lost half-siblings and sometimes even parents. But I don't have much hope that I'll ever find him.

12   For my eighth grade project, I settled on fabricating the unknown side of my family tree, and not much has changed since then. I'm 18 now, today is Father's Day, and I still hardly know anything about my biological father, just a few vague details that my mother remembers from reading his profile so many years ago. I know that he was a medical student at U.N.C. the year I was born. I know that he had olive skin and brown hair. I know that his mother was Italian and his father Irish.

13   I call myself an only child, but I could very well be one of many siblings. I could even be predisposed to some potentially devastating disease. Because I do not know what my father looks like, I could never recognize him in a crowd of people. I am sometimes overwhelmed by the infinite possibilities, by the reality that my father could be anywhere: in the neighboring lane of traffic on a Friday during rush hour, behind me in line at the bank or the pharmacy, or even changing the oil in my car after many weeks of mechanical neglect.

14   I am sometimes at such a petrifying loss for words or emotions that make sense that I can only feel astonished by the fact that he could be anyone.

QUESTIONS FOR ANALYSIS AND DISCUSSION

1. What excuses does Wooten make to account for his father's nonpresence in his life? What motivates him to make these excuses?
2. How does Wooten feel about his mother's choice to pursue pregnancy through sperm donation?
3. What challenges present themselves for children born of sperm donors? What does Wooten feel was "overlooked"?
4. Wooten states that he understands the principle of anonymity at sperm donor clinics: "They were attempting to prevent extra chaos, like custody battles, intrusion upon happy families (on either party's side), mothers showing up on donors' doorsteps with homely, misbegotten children with

runny noses and untied shoelaces to beg for child support"? Why does he feel that these reasons are not valid? Respond with your own view.

5. Do children created with the assistance of sperm donors have a right to know their biological fathers? Is anonymity unjust? Many recent laws have paved the way for offspring of sperm donation to find their biological fathers. If you donated your sperm or eggs, how would you react if your biological child suddenly contacted you? Explain.

A Baby, Please. Blond, Freckles—Hold the Colic
Gautam Naik

Our understanding of human genetics has grown tremendously over the last decade. Today, scientists have discovered which genes cause diseases such as Huntington's disease, Duchenne muscular dystrophy, and certain breast cancers, and can identify these genes in a human embryo. This knowledge allows fertility doctors to select and implant only embryos which do not carry the the mutated gene, sparing parents and their future children needless suffering and early death from the disease. But other possibilities come with this technology. If scientists can identify embryos to prevent disease, could they also use this science to create kids with more desirable traits, from hair color to intelligence? Are true designer babies the wave of the future? In this article, science journalist Gautam Naik explains how made-to-order babies are no longer the stuff of science fiction.*

BEFORE YOU READ

What attributes, if any, are ethical for parents to select for their unborn children?

AS YOU READ

Some people blame their genes for characteristics they consider undesirable about their bodies—including height, obesity, hair color, nose and ear shape, and even baldness. If your parents could have genetically designed you, what would you have wanted them to influence? Or are you happy with what nature gave you?

1 Want a daughter with blond hair, green eyes and pale skin?

2 A Los Angeles clinic says it will soon help couples select both gender and physical traits in a baby when they undergo a form of fertility treatment. The clinic, Fertility Institutes, says it has received "half a dozen" requests for the service, which is based on a procedure called pre-implantation genetic diagnosis, or PGD.

3 While PGD has long been used for the medical purpose of averting life-threatening diseases in children, the science behind it has quietly progressed to the point that it could potentially be used to create designer babies. It isn't clear that Fertility Institutes can yet deliver on its claims of trait selection. But the growth of PGD, unfettered by any state or federal regulations in the U.S., has accelerated genetic knowledge swiftly enough that pre-selecting cosmetic traits in a baby is no longer the stuff of science fiction.

_____

*Gautam Naik, *Wall Street Journal*, February 12, 2009.

4   "It's technically feasible and it can be done," says Mark Hughes, a pioneer of the PGD process and director of Genesis Genetics Institute, a large fertility laboratory in Detroit. However, he adds that "no legitimate lab would get into it and, if they did, they'd be ostracized."

5   But Fertility Institutes disagrees. "This is cosmetic medicine," says Jeff Steinberg, director of the clinic that is advertising gender and physical trait selection on its Web site. "Others are frightened by the criticism but we have no problems with it."

6   PGD is a technique whereby a three-day-old embryo, consisting of about six cells, is tested in a lab to see if it carries a particular genetic disease. Embryos free of that disease are implanted in the mother's womb. Introduced in the 1990s, it has allowed thousands of parents to avoid passing on deadly disorders to their children.

7   But PGD is starting to be used to target less-serious disorders or certain characteristics—such as a baby's gender—that aren't medical conditions. The next controversial step is to select physical traits for cosmetic reasons.

8   "If we're going to produce children who are claimed to be superior because of their particular genes, we risk introducing new sources of discrimination" in society, says Marcy Darnovsky, associate executive director of the Center for Genetics and Society, a nonprofit public interest group in Oakland, Calif. If people use the method to select babies who are more likely to be tall, the thinking goes, then people could effectively be enacting their biases against short people.

9   In a recent U.S. survey of 999 people who sought genetic counseling, a majority said they supported prenatal genetic tests for the elimination of certain serious diseases. The survey found that 56% supported using them to counter blindness and 75% for mental retardation.

10   More provocatively, about 10% of respondents said they would want genetic testing for athletic ability, while another 10% voted for improved height. Nearly 13% backed the approach to select for superior intelligence, according to the survey conducted by researchers at the New York University School of Medicine.

11   There are significant hurdles to any form of genetic enhancement. Most human traits are controlled by multiple genetic factors, and knowledge about their complex workings, though accelerating, is incomplete. And traits such as athleticism and intelligence are affected not just by DNA, but by environmental factors that cannot be controlled in a lab.

12   While many countries have banned the use of PGD for gender selection, it is permitted in the U.S. In 2006, a survey by the Genetics and Public Policy Center at Johns Hopkins University found that 42% of 137 PGD clinics offered a gender-selection service.

13   The science of PGD has steadily expanded its scope, often in contentious ways. Embryo screening, for example, is sometimes used to create a genetically matched "savior sibling"—a younger sister or brother whose healthy cells can be harvested to treat an older sibling with a serious illness.

14   It also is increasingly used to weed out embryos at risk of genetic diseases—such as breast cancer—that could be treated, or that might not strike a person later in life. In 2007, the Bridge Centre fertility clinic in London screened embryos so that a baby wouldn't suffer from a serious squint that afflicted the father.

15   Instead of avoiding some conditions, the technique also may have been used to select an embryo likely to have the same disease or disability, such as deafness, that affects the parents. The Johns Hopkins survey found that 3% of PGD clinics had provided this service, sometimes described as "negative enhancement." Groups who support this approach argue, for example, that a deaf child born to a deaf couple is better suited to participating in the parents' shared culture. So far, however, no single clinic has been publicly identified as offering this service.

16   Like several genetic diseases, cosmetic traits are correlated with a large number of DNA variations or markers—known as single nucleotide polymorphisms, or SNPs—that work in combination. A new device called the microarray, a small chip coated with DNA sequences, can simultaneously analyze many more spots on the chromosomes.

17   In October 2007, scientists from deCode Genetics of Iceland published a paper in Nature Genetics pinpointing various SNPs that influence skin, eye and hair color, based on samples taken from people in Iceland and the Netherlands. Along with related genes discovered earlier, "the variants described in this report enable prediction of pigmentation traits based upon an individual's DNA," the company said. Such data, the researchers said, could be useful for teasing out the biology of skin and eye disease and for forensic DNA analysis.

18   Kari Stefansson, chief executive of deCode, points out that such a test will only provide a certain level of probability that a child will have blond hair or green eyes, not an absolute guarantee. He says: "I vehemently oppose the use of these discoveries for tailor-making children." In the long run, he adds, such a practice would "decrease human diversity, and that's dangerous."

19   In theory, these data could be used to analyze the DNA of an embryo and determine whether it was more likely to give rise to a baby of a particular hair, skin or eye tint. (The test won't work on other ethnicities such as Asians or Africans because key pigmentation markers for those groups haven't yet been identified.)

20   For trait selection, a big hurdle is getting enough useful DNA material from the embryo. In a typical PGD procedure, a single cell is removed from a six-cell embryo and tested for the relevant genes or SNPs. It's relatively easy to check and eliminate diseases such as cystic fibrosis that are linked to a single malfunctioning gene. But to read the larger number of SNP markers associated with complex ailments such as diabetes, or traits like hair color, there often isn't enough high-quality genetic material.

21   William Kearns, a medical geneticist and director of the Shady Grove Center for Preimplantation Genetics in Rockville, Md., says he has made headway in cracking the

problem. In a presentation made at a November meeting of the American Society of Human Genetics in Philadelphia, he described how he had managed to amplify the DNA available from a single embryonic cell to identify complex diseases and also certain physical traits.

22   Of 42 embryos tested, Dr. Kearns said he had enough data to identify SNPs that relate to northern European skin, hair and eye pigmentation in 80% of the samples. Dr. Kearns' talk attracted the attention of Dr. Steinberg, the head of Fertility Institutes, which already offers PGD for gender selection. The clinic had hoped to collaborate with Dr. Kearns to offer trait selection as well. In December, the clinic's Web site announced that couples who signed up for embryo screening would soon be able to make "a pre-selected choice of gender, eye color, hair color and complexion, along with screening for potentially lethal diseases."

23   Dr. Kearns says he is firmly against the idea of using PGD to select nonmedical traits. He plans to offer his PGD amplification technique to fertility clinics for medical purposes such as screening for complex disorders, but won't let it be used for physical trait selection. "I'm not going to do designer babies," says Dr. Kearns. "I won't sell my soul for a dollar." A spokeswoman for Dr. Steinberg said: "The relationship between them is very amicable, and this center looks forward to working with Dr. Kearns."

24   For trait selection, Dr. Steinberg is now betting on a new approach for screening embryos. It involves taking cells from an embryo at day five of its development, compared with typical PGD, which uses cells from day three. The method potentially allows more cells to be obtained, leading to a more reliable diagnosis of the embryo.

25   Trait selection in babies "is a service," says Dr. Steinberg. "We intend to offer it soon."

QUESTIONS FOR ANALYSIS AND DISCUSSION

1. What is PGD? How has it been used in the past? How can it be used now and in the future?
2. Is there an ethical difference between using PGD to prevent disease and using it to select eye color? Why or why not?
3. What do we traditionally think of as "cosmetic medicine"? Is choosing the hair and eye color of your child "cosmetic medicine"? Why or why not?
4. What is "negative enhancement"? How has it been used? Should parents be allowed to opt for traits in their babies that present perceived disabilities, such as deafness, if they themselves share this trait?
5. If PGD could be used to enhance a child's athletic ability or intelligence, what happens to those members of society who cannot afford this selective process?
6. How could our understanding of genetics change reproduction? Would it be considered irresponsible to not genetically alter our offspring? What about in cases of inherited diseases? Could parents be held criminally accountable for bearing children who have diseases that could have been prevented with PGD?

Reading the Visual

Loving Every Child

http://blogs-images.forbes.com/jonentine/files/2012/11/downs-syndrome.png also at http://www
.spcs.org.nz/2012/loving-every-child-defying-eugenics/

QUESTIONS FOR ANALYSIS AND DISCUSSION

1. What is this poster advocating for? What is eugenics?
2. Some opponents of prenatal screening programs say that it runs counter to nature's process of natural selection, while others protest that it is against God's will. What is your view?
3. Research prenatal screening. What ethical quandaries does it present?
4. Evaluate the effectiveness of this poster. Does it catch your eye? Does it effectively convey its message? Why or why not?

Encourage the Golden Rule for Organ Donations, Transplant Coverage

Joseph S. Roth

Over the last 50 years, organ transplantation has extended the lives of thousands of people who would have otherwise died prematurely. Transplantation today was once the stuff of science fiction—everything from skin and blood vessels to hearts, livers, and even partial body parts have been successfully transplanted. But the number of people needing a transplant continues to rise faster than the number of available donors. Over 4,000 transplant candidates are added to the national waiting list each month. Each day, about 77 people receive organ transplants nationwide. Sadly, an average of 18 people die each day waiting for transplants due to lack of available organs. One would expect that a recipient of an organ transplant would be eager to pay it forward. This is sometimes not the case, explains Joseph S. Roth, president of the New Jersey Organ and Tissue Sharing Network. Here, he argues that patients and their families who are on the organ transplant list should be required to be on the donor registry themselves.*

BEFORE YOU READ

Are you or have you thought about becoming an organ donor? Why or why not?

AS YOU READ

Why would someone refuse to donate the organs of a dying loved one?

1 Caseworkers from our organization recently went to the hospital to visit the family of a woman who suffered a stroke. The woman was dead, but machines continued to keep her organs functioning. She was an ideal candidate to be an organ donor. Her husband, it turns out, was on the waiting list to receive a heart.

2 Our caseworkers asked the husband if he would allow his wife's organs to be donated. The husband, to the shock of our caseworkers, said no. He simply refused. Here was a man willing to accept an organ to save his own life, but who refused to allow a family member to give the gift of life to another person.

3 We have experienced other such cases, including the family of a woman who received a kidney. The donation enhanced and added years to her life. Yet, when she was declared brain dead, the family refused to allow her organs to be used to save others.

4 Cases like this are rare, thankfully, but are nonetheless troublesome. And they point to a larger incongruity. Tell 100 people they are going blind. Then ask how many would accept a cornea transplant to see again. Nearly all would say "yes." Then ask the same people how many are registered organ donors. You will find far different numbers. For instance, just 43 percent of American adults are registered organ donors.

---

*Joseph Roth, *New Jersey Star Ledger*, March 25, 2012.

5   At NJ Sharing Network, we have watched, frustrated, as people in our state die because the organs that could save them are left unused. We are hopeful that policymakers will consider this a crisis worthy of attention—and that they see the need to educate the public and encourage all New Jerseyans to become organ donors.

6   Our proposal—we call it the Golden Rule proposal—would permit health insurers in New Jersey to limit transplant coverage for people who decline to register as organ donors. It would be the first such law in the nation. No one would be denied an organ. But under the proposal, insurers could limit reimbursement for the hospital and medical costs associated with transplants of the kidney, pancreas, liver, heart, intestines and lungs.

7   In addition, the legislation would require insurance companies to provide information at each policy renewal about how their policyholders can register with the Donate Life New Jersey Registry to be organ donors.

8   The Golden Rule proposal would prompt us all to think about our civic responsibility—and our willingness to treat others the way we want to be treated. We believe that when people understand the facts, they will respond generously.

9   Just recently, Israel—a country that ranked among the bottom of Western countries in organ donation—became the first country in the world to incorporate "nonmedical" criteria into the system. A frustrated heart transplant surgeon spearheaded the changes after some of the people whose lives he saved confided they had no intention of ever donating organs themselves. The Israeli system now gives transplant priority to patients who are registered organ donors.

10   As a result, people in that country are now lining up to register.

11   In the United States, we rely on a system of altruism. That would not change under the Golden Rule.

12   Organ donation would remain what it has always been—a lifesaving and generous gift.

13   But the Golden Rule would spark a much-needed conversation that will prompt us all to ask if we are as willing to give as to receive. The law would prompt people to tell their loved ones their wishes. The result would be more registered organ donors and, as a result, more lives saved in New Jersey.

14   And that is an objective we can all agree on.

QUESTIONS FOR ANALYSIS AND DISCUSSION

1. What is the "Golden Rule" proposal? Is it a high-pressure tactic to get people to agree to be on the organ donor list? Or, is it a fair attempt to ensure that organ donation has a level playing field? Explain.

2. In your opinion, would the Golden Rule increase organ donations? Why or why not?

3. What is the Golden Rule after which the proposal is named? How does it apply to the proposal put forth in New Jersey?

4. Roth says that the Golden Rule proposal would "prompt us all to think about our civic responsibility—and our willingness to treat others the way we want to be treated." Is organ donation a "civic responsibility?" Why or why not?

5. Write a response to Roth in which you explain why you are either in favor of, or are against, the Golden Rule proposal. Support your view with reasons.

What You Lose When You Sign That Donor Card
Dick Teresi

Many people agree that organ donation is a selfless act that brings life to those in desperate need, even as someone else's life has ended. But organ donation can be confusing for many families who are faced with the sudden loss of a loved one. Is brain-dead really "dead." Is there a chance of recovery? Are doctors too eager to harvest organs? All these questions can frighten a family in a time of crisis. In this essay, author Dick Teresi says that organ donors and families asked to donate their loved one's organs must demand more control over the process. He argues that doctors don't have to tell you or your relatives what they will do to your body during an organ harvest operation because you'll be dead, with no legal rights. He also fears that doctors may be blurring the line between life and death.*

BEFORE YOU READ

What is the definition of "death" to you? Is it brain death? Are you dead if you cannot survive without the help of a machine? Does "death" have a clear and fixed definition, or does it depend on the situation?

AS YOU READ

Teresi argues that donors, as technically dead people, have no rights over what happens to their bodies during the donation process. Does this deter you from the idea of organ donation? Why or why not?

1   The last time I renewed my driver's license, the clerk at the DMV asked if she should check me off as an organ donor. I said no. She looked at me and asked again. I said, "No. Just check the box that says, 'I am a heartless, selfish bastard.' "

2   Becoming an organ donor seems like a win-win situation. Some 3.3 people on the transplant waiting list will have their lives extended by your gift (3.3 is the average yield of solid organs per donor). You're a hero, and at no real cost, apparently.

3   But what are you giving up when you check the donor box on your license? Your organs, of course—but much more. You're also giving up your right to informed consent. Doctors don't have to tell you or your relatives what they will do to your body during an organ harvest operation because you'll be dead, with no legal rights.

4   The most likely donors are victims of head trauma (from, say, a car or motorcycle accident), spontaneous bleeding in the head, or an aneurysm—patients who can be ruled dead based on brain-death criteria. But brain deaths are estimated to be just around 1% of the total. Everyone else dies from failure of the heart, circulation and breathing, which leads the organs to deteriorate quickly.

5   The current criteria on brain death were set by a Harvard Medical School committee in 1968, at a time when organ transplantation was making great strides. In 1981,

---

*Dick Teresi, *Wall Street Journal*, April 4, 2012.

the Uniform Determination of Death Act made brain death a legal form of death in all 50 states.

6   The exam for brain death is simple. A doctor splashes ice water in your ears (to look for shivering in the eyes), pokes your eyes with a cotton swab and checks for any gag reflex, among other rudimentary tests. It takes less time than a standard eye exam. Finally, in what's called the apnea test, the ventilator is disconnected to see if you can breathe unassisted. If not, you are brain dead. (Some or all of the above tests are repeated hours later for confirmation.)

7   Here's the weird part. If you fail the apnea test, your respirator is reconnected. You will begin to breathe again, your heart pumping blood, keeping the organs fresh. Doctors like to say that, at this point, the "person" has departed the body. You will now be called a BHC, or beating-heart cadaver.

8   Still, you will have more in common biologically with a living person than with a person whose heart has stopped. Your vital organs will function, you'll maintain your body temperature, and your wounds will continue to heal. You can still get bedsores, have heart attacks and get fever from infections.

9   "I like my dead people cold, stiff, gray and not breathing," says Dr. Michael A. DeVita of the University of Pittsburgh Medical Center. "The brain dead are warm, pink and breathing."

10   You might also be emitting brainwaves. Most people are surprised to learn that many people who are declared brain dead are never actually tested for higher-brain activity. The 1968 Harvard committee recommended that doctors use electroencephalography (EEG) to make sure the patient has flat brain waves. Today's tests concentrate on the stalk-like brain stem, in charge of basics such as breathing, sleeping and waking. The EEG would alert doctors if the cortex, the thinking part of your brain, is still active.

11   But various researchers decided that this test was unnecessary, so it was eliminated from the mandatory criteria in 1971. They reasoned that, if the brain stem is dead, the higher centers of the brain are also probably dead.

12   But in at least two studies before the 1981 Uniform Determination of Death Act, some "brain-dead" patients were found to be emitting brain waves. One, from the National Institute of Neurological Disorders and Stroke in the 1970s, found that out of 503 patients who met the usual criteria of brain death, 17 showed activity in an EEG.

13   Even some of the sharpest critics of the brain-death criteria argue that there is no possibility that donors will be in pain during the harvesting of their organs. One, Robert Truog, professor of medical ethics, anesthesia and pediatrics at Harvard Medical School, compared the topic of pain in an organ donor to an argument over "whether it is OK to kick a rock."

14   But BHCs—who don't receive anesthetics during an organ harvest operation—react to the scalpel like inadequately anesthetized live patients, exhibiting high blood pressure and sometimes soaring heart rates. Doctors say these are simply reflexes.

15   What if there is sound evidence that you are alive after being declared brain dead? In a 1999 article in the peer-reviewed journal Anesthesiology, Gail A. Van Norman, a professor of anesthesiology at the University of Washington, reported a case in which a 30-year-old patient with severe head trauma began breathing spontaneously after being declared brain dead. The physicians said that, because there was no chance of recovery, he could still be

considered dead. The harvest proceeded over the objections of the anesthesiologist, who saw the donor move, and then react to the scalpel with hypertension.

16   Organ transplantation—from procurement of organs to transplant to the first year of post-operative care—is a $20 billion per year business. Recipients of single-organ transplants—heart, intestine, kidney, liver, single and double lung and pancreas—are charged an average $470,000, ranging from $288,000 for a kidney transplant to $1.2 million for an intestine transplant, according to consulting firm Milliman. Neither donors nor their families can be paid for organs.

17   It is possible that not being a donor on your license can give you more bargaining power. If you leave instructions with your next of kin, they can perhaps negotiate a better deal. Instead of just the usual icewater-in-the-ears, why not ask for a blood-flow study to make sure your cortex is truly out of commission?

18   And how about some anesthetic? Although he doesn't believe the brain dead feel pain, Dr. Truog has used two light anesthetics, high-dose fentanyl and sufentanil, which won't harm organs, to quell high blood pressure or heart rate during harvesting operations. "If it were my family," he said, "I'd request them."

QUESTIONS FOR ANALYSIS AND DISCUSSION

1. Why does Teresi say that, on the surface, organ donation appears to be a "win-win" situation?
2. Why does Teresi choose not to check the "organ donor" box on his license renewal? What does he say to the clerk at the registry?
3. Teresi describes the tests for determining brain death. What does he think of these tests?
4. Write a response to Teresi in which you either agree or disagree with his viewpoint.
5. What arguments does Teresi give for why he does not wish to be an organ donor? Make a list and respond to each point with your own view.
6. What "bargaining power" is given to families who lose a loved one who has not indicated an organ donor preference?

Chorus of Voices Grows Stronger for "Death with Dignity"

Steve Lopez

Do terminally ill patients have the right to end their own lives when they want to? Do doctors have a moral obligation to help them? For many people who face an untimely death by disease, maintaining control of when and how they die is very important. Some wish to regain some control over their life and their disease. Others wish to avoid needless suffering. And some wish to avoid burdening loved ones financially and emotionally as the end draws near. The issue has received more attention as "right to die" laws have appeared on ballots across the country. In most states, the dying must find their own way of committing suicide, often violently, and secretively. In this essay, journalist Steve Lopez describes such a situation, and the difficult choices families must face*.

BEFORE YOU READ

In your opinion, what are the rights of terminally ill patients? Is there a difference between a dying patient asking to be taken off a respirator and a dying patient asking for a lethal dose of a drug?

AS YOU READ

What does it mean to "die with dignity"? What is dignity? Why is maintaining their dignity important to so many patients?

1   The bullet that Larry Robert Broman used to kill himself went clean through his head and into the wall.

2   No one had expected him to do it. Not his ex-wife, who had remained close to him. And not their two grown daughters.

3   It happened early in the morning.

4   "I heard a noise and ran down the hall," said his oldest daughter, Heather O'Hara, who forced her way into the back bedroom of her Riverside home, where she'd been caring for her terminally ill father. "His hands went limp. The gun was in front of the sofa and he was sideways."

5   Broman, a 65-year-old born-again Christian and former Air Force flight mechanic, had grown increasingly miserable about the indignities he suffered as lung cancer spread through his body. O'Hara suspects he had hidden the 9-millimeter handgun in the folds of the sofa and waited for his moment. A visiting hospice aide, who had stepped into the next room, said Broman's last words were, "Lord, please forgive me."

6   I've learned a lot this year about that appointment that awaits us all, some of it from personal experience. In February of 2012, my father died, and in August I nearly followed. My mortality wake-up call came in a hospital after knee surgery, when I flat-lined because of a heart arrhythmia and was resuscitated by a nurse.

7   In response to columns about those events, stories have streamed in from people who are running out of time themselves, or enduring the pain of watching loved ones fade. The deaths they face are as different as the lives they've lived, but a steady refrain runs through their emails and letters.

8   People want more control in the end. They want to be in charge of one last thing. These people speak a common language, linked by a desire to have lethal, doctor-prescribed medication as a legal option, as do residents of Oregon and Washington. When they can't

---

*Steve Lopez, *Los Angeles Times*, December 18, 2012.

feed and bathe themselves, when all privacy is lost, when they become a burden to loved ones, they want an exit. They live in fear not of death, but of languishing interminably without purpose or joy.

9   I've felt privileged to be let into their lives.

10   The patch job is still faintly visible on the wall of the bedroom where Broman took his life. A company called A-1 Clean the Scene was called in to eliminate the bloodstains. The agony hasn't waned for his daughters and ex-wife, who wish they had sensed the full depth of his desperation. There's anger, too, along with the guilt. Why couldn't the hospice staff have done a better job of easing his pain? And why aren't there humane options when the suffering has become too great?

11   "Why couldn't the doctor here have offered . . . an option saying, 'When you get sick of this, Larry, all you have to do is mix this up and drink it?' " asks Rebecca Beal, Broman's ex-wife. "Part of the horror of all this is thinking of that moment . . . knowing this was his only way out . . . when he actually took the gun and had to pull the trigger."

12   Amy Brackett, Broman's youngest daughter, said that when a pastor visited the house not long before the shooting, he asked her father what his one prayer would be. "I want to go to heaven, and I want to be with God," her father said. "But I don't want to have to go through this to get there."

13   Talking about death with dignity is a charged subject. I've heard criticism from people of faith who say life and death should be left in God's hands. But Larry Broman's daughters and ex-wife, all of them Christians, feel differently. They say they've begun advocating on their Facebook pages and elsewhere for better alternatives to prolonged and painful deaths.

14   O'Hara points out that those who say death should be left in God's hands often take drastic steps to prolong their lives using ventilators or feeding tubes. "They condemn you for taking your life, but they don't condemn you for being artificially kept alive." At the funeral, the pastor told mourners that Broman's last act was not a selfish one. He was in a burning building, and he jumped.

15   "God doesn't judge you on your last act on earth, but on how you lived your life," Beal said.

16   Beal said that Broman's death was particularly hard on her current husband, Sam, a doctor who had grown close to Broman, and has stage four cancer himself. "I don't know what we're facing. I have no idea," a tearful Beal said. "I'm trying to figure it out, but I've learned a lot. I've learned about what I'm not going to go through, and I'm an advocate for people to have a choice at the end."

A house of sorrow

17   "Recipe for death."

18   Those were the words in the subject field of the e-mail from Fran Measley. "Dear Steve, as an 88-year-old caregiver of my husband for many months, I do not want my children going through the same experience with me. Would you send me the name of the concern that sells the recipe for death that you mentioned in your column. . . . My husband and I agreed that when we are old and infirm, death is a friend."

19   By the time I responded, Donald Measley, an Air Force pilot who flew supplies into postwar Germany as part of the Berlin airlift, had died. I apologized for not getting back to Fran sooner and also explained that I hadn't actually written about a specific "recipe for death." I'd written about Compassion & Choices (http://www.compassionandchoices. org), a nonprofit offering end-of-life counseling nationwide. The organization encourages terminally ill, suffering patients to discuss their wishes with their doctors, but in some cases offers advice on possible combinations of legally obtained medication that when properly self-administered, can hasten death.

20   Measley, a retired high school English teacher, clarified something, too. It wasn't her husband she was seeking help for. "I wanted it for me," she said. "I don't want my children going through what I just went through."

21   Her husband lived a good life but did not die a good death, Measley said, explaining how she fed him, cleaned him, picked him up when he fell, and patiently endured his demented outbursts. The last two years were particularly sad, Fran said, and her husband was miserable. Once, he asked Fran who she was. When she said that she was his wife, he called her a liar. "Honey," he said one day, "I'm in the bathroom and I don't know how I got here."

22   Peripheral neuropathy left him shuffling along, leaning against walls and clutching furniture. "He asked our son to shoot him, then said, 'I can't get any better, and this can't go on.' Our son looked at him and said, 'I won't do it.' "

23   When I visited Measley in the Santa Barbara home she shared with her husband, she vividly recalled the day she came upon him, alone in the den. "He had a little pistol about like this," she said, holding her fingers a few inches apart. "He didn't say anything. He looked up at me." Measley hid the gun, but wished there were a clean way out for her husband. If this were Oregon, I asked, would he have asked his doctor for a prescription?

24   "Yes. He would have been happy to."

25   Don Measley died at a hospice center. He was 90. A month later, Fran's 55-year-old son-in-law died in a motorcycle accident. "This is a house of sorrow," Measley said.

A good time to go

26   If Kitti Ford-Scholz, 77, was pretending not to fear death, it was an Oscar-winning performance. We sat on the patio of her red, wood-frame home looking over Oahu's Kaneohe Bay, and she told me about the funeral she'd thrown for herself in late October.

27   "It was a celebration of life," she said. "It was a bunch of people sitting around talking, and it was lot of laughter. Just a happy time. The lady who may be buying my house came in from Washington. A friend of mine who has a titanium spine, and is 85, flew in from Illinois. I got to see all of these people who have been so much a part of my life."

28   The slender and elegant Ford-Scholz was nonchalant about how terribly sick she was.

29   "I just found out that everything [is] shutting down, that I have cancer everywhere. My biggest problem is that the bones are just riddled. . . . It's wrapped around my spine, I've got it in thousands of little nerve endings. My lungs. My ribs. My heart. My brain. And here I am. I'm not supposed to be enjoying life, but I am."

30   It's been a rich life, she said, with three children and an entrepreneurial spirit that led her to start her own skin lotion company. Why end it strapped to a bed or tangled up in wires and tubes?

31 In that spirit, she rose gingerly but bravely, and we walked to a car that was waiting to take her to a pharmacy for a prescription written by Dr. Robert Nathanson. Nathanson and an advisory council of physicians have been pushing for Hawaii—where polling suggests people strongly support death with dignity—to offer more end-of-life choices. They argue that doctors can legally prescribe potentially lethal dosages of morphine in the service of pain relief, so they're prepared to test whether there is enough wiggle-room in the law to allow them to legally offer more direct aid in dying to terminally ill patients who request it.

32 We parked the car and Ford-Scholz walked into the store and up to the pharmacy window alone. It seemed cruel that, in such a moment, she couldn't have a friend or family member with her for support. But she wanted to avoid any chance that someone would be prosecuted for participating in her death.

33 Driving back home, I saw the first hint of hesitation on Ford-Scholz's part as she held the little white bag with sleeping pills inside. "I'm not sure how strong I am, but I think I'm strong enough to take it," she said. We opened the bag and inside were 90 capsules.

34 "I'm supposed to pull 60 of them apart and dump the capsules into applesauce or chocolate pudding or something," she said. "I don't know if I can eat four ounces of something. That bothers me. There are still a lot of ifs."

35 In Oregon and Washington, many people who have met the requirements for aid in dying don't end up using the medication. But they say they're comforted knowing they have the option, and Ford-Scholz said the same. Earlier in the day, she told me she was tired of hearing from people promoting one remedy or another for her health problems.

36 "I keep trying to tell people. . . . I don't want it, leave me alone. I don't want it, and besides, the economy in this country is so bad, and in other countries, too, I'm kind of glad I'm leaving. I think this is a good time to go. I think you guys have your hands full."

37 Ford-Scholz died at home, peacefully, with two daughters at her side. She was too incapacitated in the end to use the prescription.

The most humane option

38 In September 2012, a Northern California man named E. T. Rulison wrote a letter that was passed on to me by a friend of his.

39 "Dear Californians planning to live out your life in this state:

40 "I am a physician. Since the 1940s I have been deeply dedicated to quality of life for my patients and loved ones. I am now 97, and can feel life ebbing away steadily . . .

41 "The majority of people I have cared for at the end of their lives desperately have wanted the dignity of ending their lives as they lived their lives, with some influence over their conditions . . .

42 "I have . . . friends who saw no better choice for themselves in their . . . suffering but to end their lives ungraciously, by suicide. The loved ones left behind were devastated by the consequences . . . I am encouraging you to begin conversations about the end of life choices such as are available for the dignity of citizens in other states."

43 Rulison lives with his wife in Cameron Park, on the eastern flank of Sacramento. Jean is 87.

44 "I robbed the cradle," said Rulison, whose mind is still sharp even as his body gives out. "I don't think he's forgotten anything he ever knew," his wife confirmed.

And there's a lot to remember

45   Rulison worked as an anesthesiologist with the Army Medical Corps in World War II, treating wounded soldiers in the 51st Evacuation Hospital in Europe. He went on to a long career as a general surgeon, then retired and began traveling the world with Jean as a scuba diver and underwater photographer. Together, we watched an old *American Sportsman* episode in which Rulison and *Jaws* author Peter Benchley dive in the Sea of Cortez to study the schooling patterns of hammerhead sharks, and in one scene, Rulison rides a manta ray with an 18-foot wingspan.

46   These days, the big adventures are history, and Rulison gets around the house with a walker and cane. He has survived a triple bypass, and about 20 years ago, oral cancer spread to his neck. Part of his face was removed, chewing became impossible, and he has existed on pureed foods for two decades. But he enjoys reading, loves his wife's company, and he has a new cause. Death with dignity. Legislative and ballot proposals have failed previously in the state, but Rulison hopes Californians can be educated to view the option not as suicide, but as an acceptable personal choice.

47   "I don't want to sit around a nursing home and not know what day it is, or have people come and see me and I don't recognize them," Rulison said. "To me, that's not living." When he decides he's ready, he will open a safe that contains a vial of methadone, a syringe and a needle. He's been holding on to that drug since he shut down his medical practice in 1976. He will squeeze one shot into each hip, he said, find a comfortable place to lie down, and that will be it. If he is too feeble to manage that on his own, he has arranged for someone to help.

48   I asked why he would do it that way rather than starving himself. Not eating or drinking will certainly do the job, Rulison said. But why shouldn't we all have the most humane option available to us? "It's quicker and neater, I think, to do it my way. I'm just eliminating two weeks of starvation. It gets messy toward the end. You get so weak you can't take care of yourself." There is no trace of fear in his voice.

49   "I have a rather pragmatic view of life," Rulison said. "To me, we're born, we live, we die and we're recycled into new life."

50   In his letter to California, Rulison ended with this:

51   "Perhaps these last encouragements before I myself die with dignity will fall on listening ears."

QUESTIONS FOR ANALYSIS AND DISCUSSION

1. What position does Lopez take on the issue of the "death with dignity" debate? Identify places in his essay that reveal his position.

2. Lopez recounts the experiences of several family members and patients who are nearing death. In your opinion, how well do these experiences support the case for assisted suicide?

3. Heather O'Hara, daughter of Larry Brohman, points out, "They condemn you for taking your life, but they don't condemn you for being artificially kept alive." Respond to this viewpoint. How are the two situations similar, and how are they different?

4. What reasons do the people in Lopez's article give supporting the legalization of "death with dignity" assisted suicide for the terminally ill?
5. What plans does Dr. Rulison have for his own death? Does his story influence your view of the issue? Why or why not?
6. What arguments do people usually make for and against assisted suicide for the terminally ill? How do you think someone against assisted suicide would respond to the examples provided in this article?

Suicide by Choice? Not So Fast
Ben Mattlin

Ethical concerns surrounding assisted suicide for the terminally ill abound. While most people agree that it would be ideal for patients to avoid needless suffering, fears over possible abuses are often raised when arguing against ballot measures. What if an heir wished to hasten death? What if a family member, weary of caring for someone during prolonged illness, started pressuring the patient to end it all for everyone's good? What if insurance companies started making it easier to get a lethal prescription, by making it far less expensive than treating the illness? In this following editorial, author and NPR commentator Ben Mattlin explains why assisted suicide would have been all too easy to recommend to him. Years after his grim prognosis, he is still alive and enjoying life. The Massachusetts ballot measure to which Mattlin refers in his editorial was the Massachusetts "Death with Dignity" Initiative, also known as Question 2, an indirect initiated state statute to allow physician-assisted suicide. The measure was voted down by a thin margin, 49 percent of voters for and 51 percent against the statute.*

BEFORE YOU READ

Many people against physician-assisted suicide for the terminally ill cite ways it could be abused. Make a list of the ways assisted suicide could go awry.

AS YOU READ

Consider how Mattlin frames his argument. What examples does he provide to support his view? What is his most compelling reason? Explain.

1   In November 2012, voters in Massachusetts will decide whether to adopt an assisted-suicide law. As a good pro-choice liberal, I ought to support the effort. But as a lifelong disabled person, I cannot.

*Ben Mattlin, *The New York Times,* October 31, 2012.

2   There are solid arguments in favor. No one will be coerced into taking a poison pill, supporters insist. The "right to die" will apply only to those with six months to live or less. Doctors will take into account the possibility of depression. There is no slippery slope.

3   Fair enough, but I remain skeptical. There's been scant evidence of abuse so far in Oregon, Washington and Montana, the three states where physician-assisted death is already legal, but abuse—whether spousal, child or elder—is notoriously underreported, and evidence is difficult to come by. What's more, Massachusetts registered nearly 20,000 cases of elder abuse in 2010 alone.

4   My problem, ultimately, is this: I've lived so close to death for so long that I know how thin and porous the border between coercion and free choice is, how easy it is for someone to inadvertently influence you to feel devalued and hopeless—to pressure you ever so slightly but decidedly into being "reasonable," to unburdening others, to "letting go."

5   Perhaps, as advocates contend, you can't understand why anyone would push for assisted-suicide legislation until you've seen a loved one suffer. But you also can't truly conceive of the many subtle forces—invariably well meaning, kindhearted, even gentle, yet as persuasive as a tsunami—that emerge when your physical autonomy is hopelessly compromised.

6   I was born with a congenital neuromuscular weakness called spinal muscular atrophy. I've never walked or stood or had much use of my hands. Roughly half the babies who exhibit symptoms as I did don't live past age 2. Not only did I survive, but the progression of my disease slowed dramatically when I was about 6 years old, astounding doctors. Today, at nearly 50, I'm a husband, father, journalist and author.

7   Yet I'm more fragile now than I was in infancy. No longer able to hold a pencil, I'm writing this with a voice-controlled computer. Every swallow of food, sometimes every breath, can become a battle. And a few years ago, when a surgical blunder put me into a coma from septic shock, the doctors seriously questioned whether it was worth trying to extend my life. My existence seemed pretty tenuous anyway, they figured. They didn't know about my family, my career, my aspirations.

8   Fortunately, they asked my wife, who knows exactly how I feel. She convinced them to proceed "full code," as she's learned to say, to keep me alive using any and all means necessary.

9   From this I learned how easy it is to be perceived as someone whose quality of life is untenable, even or perhaps especially by doctors. Indeed, I hear it from them all the time— "How have you survived so long? Wow, you must put up with a lot!"—even during routine office visits, when all I've asked for is an antibiotic for a sinus infection. Strangers don't treat me this way, but doctors feel entitled to render judgments and voice their opinions. To them, I suppose, I must represent a failure of their profession, which is shortsighted. I am more than my diagnosis and my prognosis.

10   This is but one of many invisible forces of coercion. Others include that certain look of exhaustion in a loved one's eyes, or the way nurses and friends sigh in your presence while you're zoned out in a hospital bed. All these can cast a dangerous cloud of depression upon even the most cheery of optimists, a situation clinicians might misread since, to them, it seems perfectly rational.

11   And in a sense, it is rational, given the dearth of alternatives. If nobody wants you at the party, why should you stay? Advocates of Death With Dignity laws who say that patients themselves should decide whether to live or die are fantasizing. Who chooses suicide in a vacuum? We are inexorably affected by our immediate environment. The deck is stacked.

12   Yes, that may sound paranoid. After all, the Massachusetts proposal calls for the lethal dose to be "self-administered," which it defines as the "patient's act of ingesting." You might wonder how that would apply to those who can't feed themselves—people like me. But as I understand the legislation, there is nothing to prevent the patient from designating just about anyone to feed them the poison pill. Indeed, there is no requirement for oversight of the ingestion at all; no one has to witness how and when the lethal drug is given. Which, to my mind, leaves even more room for abuse.

13   To be sure, there are noble intentions behind the "assisted death" proposals, but I can't help wondering why we're in such a hurry to ensure the right to die before we've done all we can to ensure that those of us with severe, untreatable, life-threatening conditions are given the same open-hearted welcome, the same open-minded respect and the same open-ended opportunities due everyone else.

QUESTIONS FOR ANALYSIS AND DISCUSSION

1. What is the "slippery slope" to which Mattlin refers in paragraph 2? Explain.
2. In what ways do issues connected to elder abuse apply to "right to die" laws? Explain.
3. Why does Mattlin object to laws supporting physician-assisted suicide for the terminally ill?
4. Mattlin states, "I've lived so close to death for so long that I know how thin and porous the border between coercion and free choice is, how easy it is for someone to inadvertently influence you to feel devalued and hopeless . . ." What does Mattlin fear will happen to people with severe illnesses if the "death with dignity" law is passed?
5. What is "quality of life"? Who decides what it means? Why is it an important consideration when addressing the right-to-die debate?
6. What "invisible forces of coercion" has Ben Mattlin experienced? How does his recounting of these comments contribute to his viewpoint?

WRITING ASSIGNMENTS

1. Imagine that a close friend has informed you that he or she has been diagnosed with a terminal illness and is considering suicide. Write a letter to your friend in which you explain why you either support or are against the plan. Be sure to address your friend's emotions and fears about the illness and death, as well as your own moral standpoint. You may also include in your response any legal ramifications suicide may bring.

2. Write an essay in which you argue for or against a ballot measure that would support physician-assisted suicide. If you support a measure, outline what it would include.

3. Research the issue of "death with dignity" and countries and states that allow physician-assisted suicide. Write an essay evaluating the success and/or failures of such programs in the United States and abroad.

4. The organ transplant list is long, with some patients dying before an organ becomes available. Should the list be "first come first serve"? Should we give priority to the sickest patients? Or should the probability of success be given greater consideration? What about the patient's age or ability to contribute to society matter? Should those who led unhealthy lives, such as smokers or alcoholics, be given less priority?

5. One solution that has been proposed to increase organ donation is to make it an "opt-out" measure rather than an "opt-in." In other words, you would have to indicate that you do not wish to donate your organs. Research this issue and explain why you think it would or would not be a good solution to the organ shortage.

6. Do you think sperm donation is ethical? Should there be limits to how many times a particular donor's sperm is used?

7. Should children of sperm donors be able to contact their fathers if they wish? What restrictions, if any, should be placed on sperm donor's history and personal information?

8. Would you want to know the genetic blueprint of your future child? If so, explain how you would use the knowledge. If no, explain why.

9. Consider the impact on future generations were we able to determine a child's genetic makeup. Besides medical benefits and possible problems, discuss the social ramifications of such power. For example, some countries prefer male children to female, and others find certain physical traits more desirable than others. What could the long-term consequences of genetic control have on the world?

New Issues in Higher Education

For many students, college offers both an opportunity to learn about the world and a chance to exercise the personal freedoms and responsibilities of adulthood, when words and actions matter. The university opens the door to the millennia-old bodies of knowledge that our intellectual history is based upon, as well as the cutting-edge thinking that will shape the future.

Despite the many new freedoms college students enjoy, a college campus is not truly the "real world." Campus policies often aim to control student behavior. Administrators may impose restrictions on students' right to assemble, implement speech codes, and enforce rules of behavior. At the same time, universities pledge to deliver a meaningful education and to prepare students for the challenges of adulthood. This chapter examines issues connected to the role of the university, students' personal rights and responsibilities, and the future of the American campus experience.

What exactly is the role of the university? What does higher education owe to students? From the minute you take your Preliminary Scholastic Aptitude Test (PSAT) as a junior in high school, the questions abound: Does everyone have the right to a college education? Should everyone go to college? Is today's college curriculum preparing students for the real world? Does college prepare students to compete in a new world economy and to think for themselves? Do the liberal arts matter? Do professors matter? And what should students expect after graduation? Great jobs? A lifetime of hard work?

Many students arrive on campus eager to learn and equally eager to party. Some readings in this chapter explore the issue of personal responsibility on campus. If college students are truly adults, do they need college administrators acting in *loco parentis*—controlling what they decide to do outside the classroom? What responsibilities come with independence? Are students expecting college to be an educational experience that will prepare them for the real world, or are they expecting merely a fun time? These readings consider the nuances of college life—what students might expect and what the university expects in return.

Diversity: The Value of Discomfort

Ronald D. Liebowitz

In the next essay, Middlebury College president Ronald D. Liebowitz explains that college is not, and should not be, a sterile environment in which one is never challenged. Diversity of students and diversity of points of view encourage real-world experiences in which people must work together. There is value in discomfort because it encourages us to be critical thinkers and to challenge ourselves and the people around us to reach consensus—even if we don't always agree with each other. What follows is Liebowitz's baccalaureate address to the class of 2007 at Middlebury College on May 26, 2007.*

BEFORE YOU READ

How diverse is your campus population—among both students and faculty? How much is the diversity on campus connected to your regional location and college mission?

AS YOU READ

What were the "culture wars"? Do they still exist, in whole or in part, on college campuses today?

1   Good afternoon. On behalf of the faculty and staff of the College, I extend a warm welcome to the parents and families of our graduating seniors, and of course to members of the class of 2007, as well.

2   Both this baccalaureate service and commencement are joyous occasions celebrating an important transition in the lives of our graduates. Today's service is an occasion to reflect on what our graduating seniors have already done, on the experience and the accomplishments of the past four years, and what those years have meant to them and to this College community.

3   Let me begin, therefore, by telling you a few things about the Middlebury Class of 2007. There are 643 graduates in this class, 287 men and 356 women. Some 365 of you are graduating with honors, and 65 were elected to Phi Beta Kappa. The most popular majors for your class were economics, chosen by 92 students, and English, chosen by 74, and 135 of you majored in two subjects. About 77 percent of you—497 students—studied at least one foreign language, and 62 percent—405 students—studied abroad for at least one semester in 48 countries. Members of your class have earned three Watson Fellowships for research abroad, two Fulbright Scholarships, and a Keasbey Scholarship to study at Oxford University.

4   Your class has been characterized by an exceptional spirit of volunteerism. Collectively, approximately 70 percent of you contributed to the community through volunteer and service-learning projects, as well as through pro bono consulting work. Some of you have served on local fire departments and rescue squads; traveled to New Orleans in the wake of hurricane Katrina to assist in the rebuilding effort; served as Big Brothers or Big Sisters to local children; worked with the John Graham Community Shelter, providing meals and companionship to the homeless; and shared your expertise with local businesses and regional economic development groups based on what you learned in economics and geography courses.

---

*Ronald D. Liebowitz, Baccalaureate Address to Middlebury College, 2007.

5   Largely because of your energy, leadership, and dedication, Middlebury has been recognized by the Carnegie Foundation for its "community engagement" and by the Princeton Review, which named Middlebury as one of its "colleges with a conscience" for fostering social responsibility and public service. I am enormously proud of all that you have done to bring positive changes to our community, our country, and our world.

6   I am also truly impressed by the imagination and scholarship of this class. These qualities were vividly demonstrated last month at our first College-wide symposium recognizing student research and creativity. About 60 members of your class participated in that symposium, where students presented the results of research on subjects ranging from solar power to social entrepreneurship to religious life at Middlebury. This symposium, which is going to be an annual event, exemplifies the spirit of intellectual risk-taking, independent thought, and a passion for learning that should characterize the best of a liberal arts education.

7   You've had impressive success in the arts, as well. For example, a number of members of this class belonged to the cast and crew that staged last year's remarkable production of *The Bewitched*, which was presented at the Kennedy Center in Washington as one of four finalists in the American College Theatre Festival. In addition, a member of your class relied on her work in the arts to become one of the winners of the Kathryn Wasserman Davis 100 Projects for Peace national fellowship program. She will use the study of architecture to analyze the border crossings between Israel and the West Bank and Gaza Strip, exploring how such crossings may be reconceived as points of connection rather than of division.

8   In athletics, too, you have excelled. Your class includes 30 athletes who have earned All American honors in intercollegiate sports and 50 who earned all-NESCAC academic honors. You helped to win 25 NESCAC championships and eight national titles for Middlebury over the past four years in intercollegiate sports, and this spring our rugby club won its first national championship.

9   There is yet one more notable thing about this class that I would like to mention. You have helped to make Middlebury a more diverse and inclusive place than it was four years ago—which brings me to the theme I particularly want to discuss this afternoon. Your class is statistically the most diverse, and the most international, ever to graduate from Middlebury. That has certainly affected—and I would say it has greatly improved—the education you have received here.

10   Why? In a nutshell: since so much of what you learn in college you learn from your fellow students, the broader the range of backgrounds and perspectives those students represent, the broader and richer the education one is likely to receive. Because of the residential and human-intensive nature of your Middlebury education, little of what you do that is related to your studies is done in solitude. You are always bouncing ideas off of classmates, roommates, hall-mates, housemates, teammates, or fellow members of student organizations.

11   The human-intensive nature of learning at liberal arts colleges was energized by the Civil Rights and other social movements of the 1960s. Formerly underrepresented groups began attending American colleges and universities in significantly greater numbers, and the breadth of learning experiences changed radically. The changes, at first, were by dint of the kinds of discussions that were taking place on a meaningful scale in the classroom.

Those discussions, whether about a classical work of literature or an interpretation of some historical event, included new perspectives that had previously been absent from the classroom, and no doubt forced some people to rethink their opinions.

12   Over time, the fruits of a broadened scope of discussion extended to the curriculum and the faculty with similar results: a bigger tent of ideas within which to teach and learn. But that bigger tent brought intellectual conflict and discomfort. The so-called "culture wars" were an expression of the tension created by the challenge and inclusion of new interpretations of the curriculum. Some degree of conflict was inevitable given the new and vastly different perspectives that had been previously excluded from, or were, at best, on the margins of the academy. Through these changes, the academy became a richer, but also a more polarized, environment for learning.

13   Since the 1960s, small, rural liberal arts colleges have not experienced as rapid and extensive a change in the composition of their student bodies as public institutions or schools located in urban areas. Yet, many have changed quite significantly, especially with the arrival, more recently, of international students, many of whom come from the developing world.

14   I cite, for example, the changes that have taken place here at Middlebury since 1980. In 1980, less than 5 percent of the student population was either an American student of color or an international student . . . that is less than 1 in 20 students. Our incoming class, the Class of 2011, will be approximately 32 percent American students of color and international. Twenty-seven years ago it was 1 in 20; today, it is 1 in 3. In addition, the change in the percentage of students on need-based financial aid is noteworthy because a student body with greater socioeconomic diversity is essential to our students' exposure to a variety of perspectives. In 1980, the percentage was 24 percent, while for the incoming class this September, the percentage is 47 percent: the highest ever.

15   This change in the composition of the student body reflects, in part, the changing demographics of the United States. But more than that, it reflects the College's deliberate effort to provide the richest learning environment for students. The College's recently approved strategic plan has as its highest priority increasing access to Middlebury for the very strongest students by continuing to meet the full need of all admitted students, increasing the grant portion of our financial aid packages, and reducing the amount of debt a student will incur during four years at the College.

16   The strategic planning committee believed that, by removing some of the financial barriers to studying at Middlebury, the College would more easily matriculate students from rural areas, from developing countries, and from inner cities. The student body, as a result, would be more ethnically, racially, and socio-economically diverse. There would no doubt be a greater diversity of ideas coming from students with such varied backgrounds, which would once again energize the classroom with frequent exchanges rooted in our students' vastly different life experiences.

17   It is no longer a cliché to say that "the local is the global and the global the local." In fact, it should go without saying that all of you who are graduating tomorrow will no longer be competing with young men and women predominantly from your hometowns, from a particular region of this country, or even from the United States. In all likelihood, the majority of you will be trying to get a job, pursue a project, or secure a spot in a leading graduate or professional school that will bring you in direct competition with young

people from . . . you name it: Shanghai, Tokyo, Madrid, Buenos Aires, Johannesburg, *Delhi*, or Berlin. Even those of you determined to do something independently, outside of official structures or institutions, will soon learn that you are now part of a global network, and the sooner you adapt to what this means, the easier you will discover how to succeed within that network.

18   In other words, it is no longer adequate to understand only one's own culture, no matter how dominant that culture may seem; or one's political and economic system, no matter how much others claim to want to copy it; or a single approach to solving problems, no matter how sure you are that your approach is the best. To succeed in the 21st century— which means to be engaged in the world in a way that allows you to make a difference, to fulfill a sense of achievement, and to allow you to be true to yourself because you know who you are—you need to be multi-cultural, multi-national, and multi-operational in how you think. And you can only be multi-cultural, multi-national, and multi-operational if you feel comfortable with the notion of difference. And that is why we seek diversity.

19   But greater diversity means change, and change on college campuses is almost always difficult. Few 18- to 22-year-olds are skilled in inviting or tolerating perspectives that are vastly different from than their own. Frankly, the same goes for 30-, 40-, and 50-something-year-old academics. Even though a campus may become more diverse in terms of the numbers of underrepresented groups present, the level of engagement can still be inconsequential if those representing different viewpoints are not encouraged and supported to express them. If an institution is not prepared to make space, figuratively speaking, for previously excluded groups, and support their presence on campus, its diversity efforts cannot succeed. And if the wariness about discomfort is stronger than the desire to hear different viewpoints because engaging difference is uncomfortable, then the quest for diversity is hollow no matter what the demographic statistics on a campus reflect.

20   In order for the pursuit of diversity to be intellectually defensible and valuable to those seeking a first-rate education, it needs to result in deliberation. It cannot simply facilitate the exchange of one orthodoxy or point of view for another. The best liberal arts education requires all voices, those of the old order as much as those of the new, and even those in between, to be subjected to the critical analysis that is supposed to make the academy a distinctive institution in society.

21   I know first hand of several incidents during your four years at the College that speak directly to the challenges of ensuring that a diverse spectrum of opinions can be voiced and considered within our academic community. To name just a few: the protest against the College's policy allowing military recruitment on campus; the complaints about the College's judicial procedures that were triggered by the suspension of an African-American student; the reaction to the College's decision to accept an endowed professorship in honor of a conservative former chief justice of the United States Supreme Court; and most recently, the rash of hateful homophobic graffiti and the resulting discussions about offensive stereotyping and free speech on a college campus.

22   Several of these issues were discussed at faculty meetings or in several large forums on campus. Though the depth of engagement at these gatherings may not have reached the level that many who were passionate about the issues would have liked, students and faculty did express themselves in ways that didn't happen on this campus 20, 15, or even 10 years ago. Issues were brought up by students and faculty that raised the collective

consciousness of those in attendance, and, in some cases, had an impact on College policies and procedures.

23   The reaction to one gathering, in particular, was as instructive as the issues about which we learned at the open forum. Following a meeting in McCullough social space that was called to address several racial incidents on campus, I received a number of e-mails from students in which they apologized on behalf of their fellow students, whom the e-mail writers believed were disrespectful in how they engaged me. I found the e-mails—and there were a good number of them—surprising, because I found the meeting, which was attended by 300 students, more civil than I expected it to be, and in no case do I recall any student expressing their concerns in ways that I would consider disrespectful. Was it uncomfortable? Yes, for sure. Were the students disrespectful? I don't think so. But being uncomfortable, as many of us were made to feel that day, is a good thing; it needs to be part of one's education.

24   Similarly, this year's open discussions about homophobic graffiti and other anti-gay acts on campus did not delve as deeply into the root causes of such unacceptable stereotyping and the vicious treatment of individuals as one might expect given the incidents in question. Yet, the reactions to what was said at the open meetings created discomfort among those who were accused of contributing to homophobia on campus. The accusation—stereotyping recruited athletes as homophobic—highlights, once again, the challenges that greater diversity and openness bring to an academic community. Was the stereotyping of a single group a productive way to engage this important topic?

25   What emerged from our discussions of the homophobic incidents, at least thus far, is hardly what one might call neat and tidy. There was, however, much learned beginning with a far greater awareness of the bigotry that exists here as it does in society at-large, and that we have considerable work to do if we truly aspire to be a community that welcomes diversity and wishes to learn from it. We also witnessed how easy it can be for some members of an aggrieved group to fall into the same kind of stereotyping from which they themselves have suffered. Diversity sure can be messy.

26   The controversy surrounding the acceptance by the College of an endowed professorship in American history and culture in honor of William Rehnquist is one more example of the complexities that come with an increasingly diverse community. Because the former chief justice was conservative, and was on the side of several court decisions that ran counter to the positions held by several underrepresented groups on campus, there was a genuine feeling on the part of some that honoring Mr. Rehnquist was a repudiation of their presence on campus and a sign that the College did not value diversity. They felt, in their words, "invisible and disrespected" as a result of the College accepting the professorship. Though one can understand this perspective, especially given the history of underrepresented groups here and on other campuses, it is unfortunate that the Chief Justice's accomplishments and reputation as a brilliant jurist by liberal and conservative constitutional scholars alike were lost in the opposition to his politics.

27   Ironically, the stance taken by those who believed it was wrong to honor the Chief Justice because of his position on particular court cases undermines the very thing the protestors support most passionately—diversity. Some couched their protests in the name of the goals of liberal education, arguing that the ultimate goal should be about "advancing" social change. I do not share in that narrow definition of liberal education, especially

liberal education in and for the 21st century. Rather, liberal education must be first and foremost about ensuring a broad range of views and opinions in the classroom and across campus so that our students can question routinely both their preconceived and newly developed positions on important matters. Such deliberation will serve as the best foundation for enabling our graduates to contribute to the betterment of society.

28　In writing on the College's alumni online listserv about the Rehnquist controversy and the reported opposition of some to President Clinton speaking at tomorrow's Commencement ceremony, an alumnus from the Class of 2001 offered this perspective:

> "I always thought that the benefit of a place like Middlebury was that it opened your mind and helped you become more informed by allowing (or, forcing) you to interact with, listen to, and learn from people [with] different opinions—even if that meant welcoming those you disagree with onto your own turf."

29　I hope those of you in the audience who are graduating tomorrow have given, and will continue to give, this topic some thought. For sure, diversity is intellectually and socially challenging; it forces you to engage issues more broadly than you might otherwise. It often creates unintended consequences; and it surely can make one uncomfortable. But some discomfort, amidst all that is comfortable about college life, is the best preparation for a successful entry into our increasingly complex global world.

30　We have today few if any institutions that can claim a monopoly on how best to make the world a better, more tolerant, and just place. Talented, thoughtful, and well-educated individuals like yourselves, who have been made to feel uncomfortable and understand difference, are more likely than others to figure out how to discern right from wrong, acceptable from unacceptable behavior, and know the difference between ethical and unethical conduct.

31　As you leave college, the most important kind of confidence you must feel is the confidence that your education has prepared you to make sound judgments and to act on them. I believe because you have been exposed to diverse ideas, opinions, and people over the course of the past four years, and have been made to feel uncomfortable at times, you will discover that confidence and draw upon it so that it will serve you well in exercising your judgment and claiming your place in the wider world.

QUESTIONS FOR ANALYSIS AND DISCUSSION

1. According to Middlebury College president Ronald Liebowitz, what value does diversity add to a college education? What challenges does it present as well?
2. Liebowitz cites several examples of issues raised during the graduates' four years at Middlebury. How do these examples support his theme of the importance of diversity on campus? Why is it important to permit and even support the expression of unpopular points of view? Do you agree?
3. Liebowitz notes, "It is no longer a cliché to say that 'the local is the global and the global the local.'" What does he mean? Explain this statement and connect it to your own college experience.

4. Liebowitz begins his speech with a description of the graduates and their accomplishments. How does this introduction connect to the theme of his speech?

5. In October 2006, Middlebury College established the Justice William H. Rehnquist Professorship of American History and Culture—a controversial chair that met with some protest. Who was Rehnquist? Why did some students and faculty object to the creation of the professorship? What does Liebowitz say about the controversy, and the decision to create the professorship, despite the dispute?

6. Compare the points Liebowitz makes in this speech with the welcoming speech made by Glenn Loury in Chapter 14. What points do both men make about perceptions of identity, culture, and diversity? In what ways are their points similar, and in what ways do they differ?

My Struggles With Anti-Intellectualism
Paul Stoller

The word *university* is derived from the Latin *universitas magistrorum et scholarium*, which translates roughly to "community of teachers and scholars." Today, when asked why they attend college, most students answer that they hope it will prepare them to land a job after graduation. Many professors hope that college provides a place where students may develop critical thinking skills, advance their ability to reason and apply logic, and expand their perspective. Many parents, footing large tuition bills, will assert simply that a college should prepare their children to get a good job. In the following essay, Professor Paul Stoller wonders what happened to the importance of critical thinking as part of the academic experience. Are colleges merely job mills, or are they supposed to be something more? And what is lost for both students and society when we no longer value critical thinking and intellectual inquiry?*

BEFORE YOU READ

Why have you gone to college? What do you hope to get out of the experience? What are your expectations from your professors and curriculum, your school, and your student body?

AS YOU READ

Are you encouraged to "think critically" in your college course work? What does the term *critical thinking* mean to you?

---

*Paul Stoller, *Huffington Post*, May 8, 2012.

1 In a recent blog post, "Waging War on Higher Education," I wrote about the need to encourage students to think critically. The piece triggered a flurry of comments from *Huffington Post* readers. Most of the comments took on a populist, no-nonsense tone that I found all too familiar. Even so, I found some of the comments disconcerting. My discomfort stemmed not from the critical nature of the comments, but from their widespread disdain for critical thinking. Many of the commentators suggested that critical thinking was a kind of "pie in the sky" activity, a luxury we can no longer afford. In this sociocultural orientation to the world, thinking about fine points of philosophy, art, or anthropology is often seen as a waste of time. In this narrative, if you go to college, which these days is a major investment of money, you do so to acquire the set of skills to get a good paying job—end of story. Indeed, the root of my discomfort came from the fact that I've been hearing these anti-intellectual narratives my whole life.

2 Many people think that professors are members of the wealthy elite—people who are disconnected from the economic and social trials of "real life." While it is certainly the case that some professors and other "intellectuals" come from privileged backgrounds, many of us grew up in more modest circumstances. I grew up in lower middle-class household in suburban Washington, D.C. My mother and father graduated from high school. Only a few of my maternal and paternal aunts and uncles had studied at a college. Most of my relatives worked—and worked hard—in small family-centered businesses. At family gatherings they would encourage me to go to college to get a good job and find "the good life."

3 If you don't have what it takes to be a doctor or a lawyer, they would tell me, then study accounting —it's a good profession. People always need accountants, they would advise again and again. In my family's view of the world, the world—my world—was filled with limitations. Accordingly, in life it was good to be pragmatic and make choices that would provide for your family. These pragmatic narratives compelled me to study political science with an eye toward law school. By my junior year in college, though, I knew that I wasn't cut out for law or medicine. When I announced to my parents, who only wanted the best for me, that I didn't want to be a lawyer or doctor, my mother cried. My father's unforgettable frown burned into my being.

4 "What are you going to do with yourself?" my father asked.

5 "He can always sell insurance like his cousin Ivan," my mother said reassuringly.

6 "I want to be writer."

7 "What!" My mother exclaimed. "There's no money in that. You're a dreamer," she said shaking her head. She turned to my father. "He could always work with you, I guess."

8 No one in my family could have ever imagined that I would spend seven years of my life in West Africa and learn to speak foreign languages, let alone become a professor who publishes essays and books. That narrative just didn't compute in my family. In my case, a perfect storm of circumstances—the draft, the war in Vietnam, and the potential of a Peace Corps deferment—propelled me to the Republic of Niger and eventually a life as scholar, a person who has spent a lot of time reading books, thinking about what's he's read, and then writing texts about those ideas.

9 "And they pay him for this," my mother would say in wonder. "He could have done better in law or business."

10 Even after I had been teaching for several years, my parents did not understand what I did for a living. I felt—falsely as it turned out—that my career choice had profoundly

disappointed them. Eventually they came to better understand what I did and read every one of my books, proudly showing them off to family and neighbors.

11   So what happened to steer me away from the narrow life path that the circumstances of my birth had shaped. For me, college had a profound impact on my life. I stumbled upon professors who took an interest in me. They became mentors who exposed me to the wonders of the world, who convinced me that my life was full of possibilities, and who told me that I had the potential to teach at a university.

12   You should at least try to follow your dreams, they advised. Maybe things will work out for you. Maybe they won't. But try to follow a different path. Who knows what you'll find?

13   There is a deep tradition of anti-intellectualism in American cultural and political life. It has a long history, spreading its messages into every nook and cranny of American social and political life. We are the "can-do" nation that values "common-sense" solutions to our problems. We are suspicious of "egg heads," dreamers and "pointy-headed" intellectuals who drive Volvos, like French food, and drink frothy cappuccinos. Such notions, of course, are gross fabrications that lead to a dangerous ignorance.

14   In the past, "can do" pragmatism was the fuel of *American* prosperity. But that pragmatism was reinforced with an abiding respect for knowledge and critical thinking. In the past we knew that it was hard to do anything in a place devoid of new ideas, a place where dreamers are discouraged from dreaming. That's why in the present it's important to combat the anti-intellectualism of the public sphere and support enlightened higher education, a space where mentors, to borrow from one of my readers, don't teach students what to think but show them how to think—a skill that prepares them for a productive life in the world, a skill that moves all of us forward.

QUESTIONS FOR ANALYSIS AND DISCUSSION

1. What is Stoller's objective with this essay? What point is he trying to convey?
2. Stoller notes that in the United States, there is a general bias against smart people ("We are suspicious of 'egg heads,' dreamers and 'pointy-headed' intellectuals."). Have you observed this view? As a college student, have you ever experienced this bias?
3. Why does Stoller recount his family background and economic status? How does his story connect to his point? Does it strengthen his argument? Why or why not?
4. Stoller notes that for many people, "if you go to college, which these days is a major investment of money, you do so to acquire the set of skills to get a good paying job—end of story." Respond to his observation. Why do we go to college? What is the goal?
5. Stoller asserts that colleges should not teach students what to think but show them how to think. Why does he feel this is important? What is the difference? Do you agree with him, or do you agree with some of his critics who feel critical thinking is a kind of "pie in the sky" activity "that we can no longer afford"? Explain.

For-Profit Colleges—A Sneaky Scam or Saving Grace?

USA Today and Steve Gunderson

For years, a college education has been viewed as a sure ticket to a good job and steady employment. In fact, many jobs require a college degree. But not everyone can get into a four-year school, and not everyone wishes to embark on the time commitment it entails. Enter the for-profit college—schools that offer flexible schedules, less rigorous entrance requirements, and hundreds of online courses— all for a price. For-profit schools often cost twice as much as traditional schools. But despite their for-profit status, much of a for-profit school's revenue comes from federal grants and loans. Critics argue that these schools are loading students with questionable credentials and debt that they cannot hope to pay back. Advocates counter that for-profit schools provide a valuable education to nontraditional students, including low-income adults, adults with families, and people who don't have time to attend day-schools. *USA Today* explored the issue as an opinion editorial in July of 2012. First, *USA Today* takes the perspective that for-profit colleges are a racket focused on generating a profit rather than on educating students. Then, Steve Gunderson, president of the Association of Private Sector Colleges and Universities, defends the role of for-profits, describing the important role they play for nontraditional students.*

BEFORE YOU READ

What led you to apply to the college you now attend? Was it a choice you made long ago? A decision you made in your senior year of high school? A change-of life decision in adulthood? Explain.

AS YOU READ

For-profit colleges have been criticized for their aggressive recruitment, high marketing budgets, and enrollment practices. What do you think? Do they play an important role, or are they merely another profit-making scam for big business?

For-Profit College. What a Racket.

USA Today editorial

1   Waste in the federal government always generates consternation. Remember the "bridge to nowhere," the $398 million route to a largely unpopulated Alaskan island contained in a 2005 spending bill? Or how about Solyndra, the solar energy company that went bankrupt after receiving $535 million in government loans from the Obama administration?

---

*USA Today and Steve Gunderson, *USA Today*, July 30, 2012.

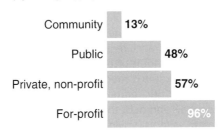

Indebted
Nearly all students at for-profit colleges take out loans.

Percentage of students who borrow (by college type):

Community   13%

Public   48%

Private, non-profit   57%

For-profit   96%

Source: Senate Health, Education, Labor and Pensions Committee By Janet Loehrke, USA TODAY

2   Such programs are as indefensible as they are common, but they aren't the most costly form of federal waste. More troubling is the far greater sums that line the pockets of powerful special interests.

3   The for-profit college racket is a prime example. A Senate committee report released in [July of 2013] adds to the mountain of evidence that some of these schools are more interested in harvesting federal money than they are in educating students.

4   The report found that taxpayers are getting very little from the $32 billion (that's roughly 60 Solyndras) spent each year in grants and loans to students who attend these colleges.

5   Many beneficiaries of this largesse charge as much or more than many of the nation's top universities, which are hardly models of efficiency themselves and which also use easily available student aid as an excuse to avoid cost control. In 2009, the for-profits spent on average just 17.7% of their revenue on instruction and 24.4% on marketing and recruitment. They reported 19.4% in profits. Pay to top executives averaged $7.3 million, well above that received by leaders of traditional schools.

6   The Education Department, using somewhat different calculations, estimates that for-profits spend 20.8% of their money on instruction. For public universities, the equivalent number is 26.7% while at private ones it is 32.9%. And both these numbers are skewed downward by the presence of massive hospitals at some schools.

7   Even more astounding, 54% of the students who enrolled in for-profit colleges in 2008 and 2009 had dropped out by 2010. Many of them, as well as those who did manage to finish, are now drowning in debt. Fully 96% of students at for-profit colleges have taken out loans, compared with about 50% at traditional four-year colleges and just 13% at community colleges.

8   In a real marketplace, this kind of business model would be unsustainable. Students would not pony up such princely sums. Private lenders wouldn't lend for something of such dubious value, and foundations and scholarship funds wouldn't contribute. But for-profit universities are kept afloat by the fact that virtually all their money comes in the form of federal grants and loans. So long as the schools can persuade students to apply

for this government financing, which they do aggressively, and so long as they can lobby Washington to ignore their sky-high dropout and loan default rates, the money will continue to flow. After all, what does it matter to them if a student defaults? Taxpayers take the hit, not the schools.

9   The federal government is attempting to rein in some of the worst abuses by, for example, cutting off loan money to for-profits schools with default rates above 35%. That's way too charitable. A stronger incentive would be to make the schools financially responsible for some of the amount owed by those who drop out.

10   Even so, billions of dollars will still be squandered for little gain. Taxpayer money going into for-profit colleges would be better spent on community colleges. They provide practical training and flexibility, at reasonable prices, for students who need to juggle work and education. They keep their focus on teaching. All they lack is a powerful lobby that throws its weight around in Washington to sustain business models that are too often based on picking taxpayers' pockets.

Counter Point: Private-Sector Colleges Fill a Need
Steve Gunderson

1   Let's start at the beginning. There are good and bad schools in every sector of higher education. We should all be working together to create postsecondary education that provides real access, real education and real skills leading to real jobs. Today, 13 million are unemployed and 90 million are underemployed.

2   Projections suggest we need an additional 20 million workers with postsecondary education skills in this decade. Our only hope to meet this challenge is through the growth of private investments in postsecondary education because we've reached the peak of public dollars.

3   Rather than leading this charge, Sen. Tom Harkin and his staff continue their obsession with just one element of postsecondary education: private-sector colleges. He criticizes private-sector schools for allocating 17% of revenues to instruction—but he doesn't tell you the University of Iowa allocates only 16.2%!

4   He criticizes our schools for serving a disproportionate number of veterans and low-income students. We should be celebrating the fact that we provide academics and schedules in ways that work for adults with real jobs, real families and all the challenges of life. Yes, loan defaults are too high! Let us limit the loans a student receives to the amount needed for education.

5   Rather than leading a bipartisan effort to pursue comprehensive reforms for all of higher education, the senator uses old statistics and mixes apples and oranges in his attempt to make a case for more laws and more regulations. America is at a crossroads in terms of our economy, our education system and the growth of the middle class.

6   Let's set aside ideology. Let's work together to develop one set of common standards for all students in all colleges. Let's develop protocols that accurately calculate the graduation rates and the placement rates of all students at every college. Let's work together

to figure out how we can ensure access to higher education for all, especially the low-income, in an era of deficit reduction.

7   There is so much to do. And there's no time for yesterday's political ideology. It's a new era demanding new forms of innovation and delivery in higher education—for everyone.

QUESTIONS FOR ANALYSIS AND DISCUSSION ──────────────

1. Review *USA Today*'s opening paragraph. How does the paragraph connect to the points the paper makes in its editorial? How does it work to align the audience to the viewpoint it is presenting? Explain.

2. How do federal grants and loans benefit both students and for-profit schools? Why do many graduates find it difficult to repay student loans? Do you feel that for-profit schools that arrange for these loans are partly responsible for the problem? Explain.

3. What is the primary argument *USA Today* makes against for-profit colleges?

4. According to the *USA Today* editorial, over half of all students who enroll in for-profit colleges drop out. What keeps for-profit colleges afloat?

5. What is the primary argument Steve Gunderson makes in his argument in defense of for-profit colleges?

6. What tactics does Gunderson use to defend his position that for-profit colleges fill a vital need? Refer to the first section of the book for some argument tactics used by writers to persuade audiences to their viewpoint.

What's Wrong With Vocational School?
Charles Murray

Are too many Americans going to college? Unlike students in Europe and Asia, over 70 percent of high school graduates intend to pursue some form of higher education, partially because many businesses have made college degree a requirement for even entry-level office jobs. But are too many students trying to go to college? Are we making unreasonable demands of students and undervaluing the "vocational" trades? In the following essay, Charles Murray, a scholar at the conservative think tank the American Enterprise Institute, discusses how the pressure to go to college hurts less gifted students as well as the extremely bright ones. Murray is perhaps best known for his controversial book *The Bell Curve* (1994), coauthored with Richard Herrnstein, which discusses the role of IQ in American society.*

───────────

*Charles Murray, *Wall Street Journal*, January 17, 2007.

BEFORE YOU READ

Much of the argument in this essay hinges on the value of IQ. What is IQ? Do you think one's IQ should influence the decision of whether one should pursue higher education?

AS YOU READ

Is vocational school, as Murray suggests, indeed considered "second class"? What accounts for this judgment? How can this attitude hurt the United States in the long run?

1 My topic yesterday was education and children in the lower half of the intelligence distribution. Today I turn to the upper half, people with IQs of 100 or higher. Today's simple truth is that far too many of them are going to four-year colleges. Begin with those barely into the top half, those with average intelligence. To have an IQ of 100 means that a tough high-school course pushes you about as far as your academic talents will take you. If you are average in math ability, you may struggle with algebra and probably fail a calculus course. If you are average in verbal skills, you often misinterpret complex text and make errors in logic.

2 These are not devastating shortcomings. You are smart enough to engage in any of hundreds of occupations. You can acquire more knowledge if it is presented in a format commensurate with your intellectual skills. But a genuine college education in the arts and sciences begins where your skills leave off.

3 In engineering and most of the natural sciences, the demarcation between high-school material and college-level material is brutally obvious. If you cannot handle the math, you cannot pass the courses. In the humanities and social sciences, the demarcation is fuzzier. It is possible for someone with an IQ of 100 to sit in the lectures of Economics 1, read the textbook, and write answers in an examination book. But students who cannot follow complex arguments accurately are not really learning economics. They are taking away a mishmash of half-understood information and outright misunderstandings that probably leave them under the illusion that they know something they do not. (A depressing research literature documents one's inability to recognize one's own incompetence.) Traditionally and properly understood, a four-year college education teaches advanced analytic skills and information at a level that exceeds the intellectual capacity of most people.

4 There is no magic point at which a genuine college-level education becomes an option, but anything below an IQ of 110 is problematic. If you want to do well, you should have an IQ of 115 or higher. Put another way, it makes sense for only about 15% of the population, 25% if one stretches it, to get a college education. And yet more than 45% of recent high school graduates enroll in four-year colleges. Adjust that percentage to account for high-school dropouts, and more than 40% of all persons in their late teens are trying to go to a four-year college—enough people to absorb everyone down through an IQ of 104.

5 No data that I have been able to find tell us what proportion of those students really want four years of college-level courses, but it is safe to say that few people who are intellectually unqualified yearn for the experience, any more than someone who is athletically

unqualified for a college varsity wants to have his shortcomings exposed at practice every day. They are in college to improve their chances of making a good living. What they really need is vocational training. But nobody will say so, because "vocational training" is second class. "College" is first class.

6   Large numbers of those who are intellectually qualified for college also do not yearn for four years of college-level courses. They go to college because their parents are paying for it and college is what children of their social class are supposed to do after they finish high school. They may have the ability to understand the material in Economics 1 but they do not want to. They, too, need to learn to make a living—and would do better in vocational training.

7   Combine those who are unqualified with those who are qualified but not interested, and some large proportion of students on today's college campuses—probably a majority of them—are looking for something that the four-year college was not designed to provide. Once there, they create a demand for practical courses, taught at an intellectual level that can be handled by someone with a mildly above-average IQ and/or mild motivation. The nation's colleges try to accommodate these new demands. But most of the practical specialties do not really require four years of training, and the best way to teach those specialties is not through a residential institution with the staff and infrastructure of a college. It amounts to a system that tries to turn out televisions on an assembly line that also makes pottery. It can be done, but it's ridiculously inefficient.

8   Government policy contributes to the problem by making college scholarships and loans too easy to get, but its role is ancillary. The demand for college is market-driven, because a college degree does, in fact, open up access to jobs that are closed to people without one. The fault lies in the false premium that our culture has put on a college degree. For a few occupations, a college degree still certifies a qualification. For example, employers appropriately treat a bachelor's degree in engineering as a requirement for hiring engineers. But a bachelor's degree in a field such as sociology, psychology, economics, history or literature certifies nothing. It is a screening device for employers. The college you got into says a lot about your ability, and that you stuck it out for four years says something about your perseverance. But the degree itself does not qualify the graduate for anything. There are better, faster and more efficient ways for young people to acquire credentials to provide to employers.

9   The good news is that market-driven systems eventually adapt to reality, and signs of change are visible. One glimpse of the future is offered by the nation's two-year colleges. They are more honest than the four-year institutions about what their students want and provide courses that meet their needs more explicitly. Their time frame gives them a big advantage—two years is about right for learning many technical specialties, while four years is unnecessarily long.

10   Advances in technology are making the brick-and-mortar facility increasingly irrelevant. Research resources on the Internet will soon make the college library unnecessary. Lecture courses taught by first-rate professors are already available on CDs and DVDs for many subjects, and online methods to make courses interactive between professors and students are evolving. Advances in computer simulation are expanding the technical skills that can be taught without having to gather students together in a laboratory or shop. These and other developments are all still near the bottom of steep growth curves.

The cost of effective training will fall for everyone who is willing to give up the trappings of a campus. As the cost of college continues to rise, the choice to give up those trappings will become easier.

11   A reality about the job market must eventually begin to affect the valuation of a college education: The spread of wealth at the top of American society has created an explosive increase in the demand for craftsmen. Finding a good lawyer or physician is easy. Finding a good carpenter, painter, electrician, plumber, glazier, mason—the list goes on and on—is difficult, and it is a seller's market. Journeymen craftsmen routinely make incomes in the top half of the income distribution while master craftsmen can make six figures. They have work even in a soft economy. Their jobs cannot be outsourced to India. And the craftsman's job provides wonderful intrinsic rewards that come from mastery of a challenging skill that produces tangible results. How many white-collar jobs provide nearly as much satisfaction?

12   Even if forgoing college becomes economically attractive, the social cachet of a college degree remains. That will erode only when large numbers of high-status, high-income people do not have a college degree and don't care. The information technology industry is in the process of creating that class, with Bill Gates and Steve Jobs as exemplars. It will expand for the most natural of reasons: A college education need be no more important for many high-tech occupations than it is for NBA basketball players or cabinet makers. Walk into Microsoft or Google with evidence that you are a brilliant hacker, and the job interviewer is not going to fret if you lack a college transcript. The ability to present an employer with evidence that you are good at something, without benefit of a college degree, will continue to increase, and so will the number of skills to which that evidence can be attached. Every time that happens, the false premium attached to the college degree will diminish.

13   Most students find college life to be lots of fun (apart from the boring classroom stuff), and that alone will keep the four-year institution overstocked for a long time. But, rightly understood, college is appropriate for a small minority of young adults—perhaps even a minority of the people who have IQs high enough that they could do college-level work if they wished. People who go to college are not better or worse people than anyone else; they are merely different in certain interests and abilities. That is the way college should be seen. There is reason to hope that eventually it will be.

QUESTIONS FOR ANALYSIS AND DISCUSSION

1. Why does Murray feel that too many students are going to college? Why does he think this harms many students?
2. Murray's essay generated much controversy. He was accused of being "elitist" and of ignoring the benefits of a wider college-educated society. What do you think? Is he being elitist, or is he stating an uncomfortable truth—we unfairly devalue trade educations while elevating university ones?
3. This essay was written as part of a series for the *Wall Street Journal*. Does the content match the presumed audience? What assumptions based on readership does Murray make? Identify specific words/phrases/ideas in his essay that demonstrate how he writes to his audience.

4. Do you think that colleges are indeed "dumbing down" curricula to accommodate a broader range of students with lower abilities? Why or why not? Refer to your own experience as well as points Murray raises in his essay.

5. How, according to Murray, does government contribute to the problem of college over-enrollment? Explain.

6. Evaluate Murray's tone in paragraph 11 addressing the benefits of craftsmen. Do you agree that more value should be attributed to vocational trades so that students will be enticed to pursue careers in masonry and carpentry? Explain.

Is College a Lousy Investment?

Megan McArdle

Many students feel compelled to earn a college degree out of fear that they will be unemployable if they do not. Parents are encouraged to start saving for junior's college tuition about the same time they get their first ultrasound. In this next essay, Megan McArdle argues that going to college has turned into an American neurosis. College tuition is sending parents to the poorhouse and saddling students with a backpack full of debt that doesn't even guarantee a job in the end. With college debt making national headlines, journalist Megan McArdle asks, is college a bum deal?*

BEFORE YOU READ

Do the benefits of a college education outweigh its significant cost? Was cost a factor for you when you decided which college to apply to and which one to attend? Why or why not?

AS YOU READ

At the end of her essay, McArdle posits, "why am I going to college?" Answer this question with your own viewpoint. What factors contributed to your decision to go to college? Was it the hope of a good job? Pressure from parents? Was it simply presumed you would go? Did you experience anxiety over getting accepted? Choosing the right school? Explain.

---

*Megan McArdle, *Newsweek*, September 9, 2012.

1　Why are we spending so much money on college?

2　And why are we so unhappy about it? We all seem to agree that a college education is wonderful, and yet strangely we worry when we see families investing so much in this supposedly essential good. Maybe it's time to ask a question that seems almost sacrilegious: is all this investment in college education really worth it?

3　The answer, I fear, is that it's not. For an increasing number of kids, the extra time and money spent pursuing a college diploma will leave them worse off than they were before they set foot on campus.

4　For my entire adult life, an education has been the most important thing for middle-class households. My parents spent more educating my sister and me than they spent on their house, and they're not the only ones . . . and, of course, for an increasing number of families, most of the cost of their house is actually the cost of living in a good school district. Questioning the value of a college education seems a bit like questioning the value of happiness, or fun.

5　Donald Marron, a private-equity investor whose portfolio companies have included a student-loan firm and an educational-technology startup, says, "If you're in a position to be able to pay for education, it's a bargain." Those who can afford a degree from an elite institution are still in an enviable position. "You've got that with you for your whole life," Marron pointed out. "It's a real imprimatur that's with you, as well as access to all these relationships."

6　That's true. I have certainly benefited greatly from the education my parents sacrificed to give me. On the other hand, that kind of education has gotten a whole lot more expensive since I was in school, and jobs seem to be getting scarcer, not more plentiful. These days an increasing number of commentators are nervously noting the uncomfortable similarities to the housing bubble, which started with parents telling their children "renting is throwing your money away," and ended in mass foreclosures.

7　An education can't be repossessed, of course, but neither can the debt that financed it be shed, not even, in most cases, in bankruptcy. And it's hard to ignore the similarities: the rapid run-up in prices, at rates much higher than inflation; the increasingly frenetic recruitment of new buyers, borrowing increasingly hefty sums; the sense that you are somehow saving for the future while enjoying an enhanced lifestyle right now, and of course, the mountain of debt.

8　The price of a McDonald's hamburger has risen from 85 cents in 1995 to about a dollar today. The average price of all goods and services has risen about 50 percent. But the price of a college education has nearly doubled in that time. Is the education that today's students are getting twice as good? Are new workers twice as smart? Have they become somehow massively more expensive to educate?

9　Perhaps a bit. Richard Vedder, an Ohio University economics professor who heads the Center for College Affordability and Productivity, notes that while we may have replaced millions of filing clerks and payroll assistants with computers, it still takes one professor to teach a class. But he also notes that "we've been slow to adopt new technology because we don't want to. We like getting up in front of 25 people. It's more fun, but it's also damnably expensive."

10　Vedder adds, "I look at the data, and I see college costs rising faster than inflation up to the mid-1980s by 1 percent a year. Now I see them rising 3 to 4 percent a year over inflation. What has happened? The federal government has started dropping money out of airplanes." Aid has increased, subsidized loans have become available, and "the universities have gotten the money." Economist Bryan Caplan, who is writing a book about education, agrees: "It's a giant waste of resources that will continue as long as the subsidies continue."

11 Promotional literature for colleges and student loans often speaks of debt as an "investment in yourself." But an investment is supposed to generate income to pay off the loans. More than half of all recent graduates are unemployed or in jobs that do not require a degree, and the amount of student-loan debt carried by households has more than quintupled since 1999. These graduates were told that a diploma was all they needed to succeed, but it won't even get them out of the spare bedroom at Mom and Dad's. For many, the most tangible result of their four years is the loan payments, which now average hundreds of dollars a month on loan balances in the tens of thousands.

12 A lot of ink has been spilled over the terrifying plight of students with $100,000 in loans and a job that will not cover their $900-a-month payment. Usually these stories treat this massive debt as an unfortunate side effect of spiraling college costs. But in another view, the spiraling college costs are themselves an unfortunate side effect of all that debt. When my parents went to college, it was an entirely reasonable proposition to "work your way through" a four-year, full-time college program, especially at a state school, where tuition was often purely nominal. By the time I matriculated, in 1990, that was already a stretch. But now it's virtually impossible to conceive of high-school students making enough with summer jobs and part-time jobs during the school year to put themselves through a four-year school. Nor are their financially shaky parents necessarily in a position to pick up the tab, which is why somewhere between one half and two thirds of undergrads now come out of school with debt.

13 In a normal market, prices would be constrained by the disposable income available to pay them. But we've bypassed those constraints by making subsidized student loans widely available. No, not only making them available: telling college students that those loans are "good debt" that will enable them to make much more money later.

14 It's true about the money—sort of. College graduates now make 80 percent more than people who have only a high-school diploma, and though there are no precise estimates, the wage premium for an elite school seems to be even higher. But that's not true of every student. It's very easy to spend four years majoring in English literature and beer pong and come out no more employable than you were before you went in. Conversely, chemical engineers straight out of school can easily make triple or quadruple the wages of an entry-level high-school graduate.

15 James Heckman, the Nobel Prize–winning economist, has examined how the returns on education break down for individuals with different backgrounds and levels of ability. "Even with these high prices, you're still finding a high return for individuals who are bright and motivated," he says. On the other hand, "if you're not college ready, then the answer is no, it's not worth it." Experts tend to agree that for the average student, college is still worth it today, but they also agree that the rapid increase in price is eating up more and more of the potential return. For borderline students, tuition hikes can push those returns into negative territory.

16 Effectively, we've treated the average wage premium as if it were a guarantee—and then we've encouraged college students to borrow against it. The result will be no surprise

to anyone who has made the mistake of setting his or her teenager loose in a shopping mall with a credit card and no spending limit. Eighteen-year-olds demand amenities—high-speed Internet, well-upholstered classrooms, world-class fitness facilities—and in order to stay competitive, college administrators happily provide them. Then they raise the tuition for which the 18-year-olds are obediently borrowing the money.

17   "We have an academic arms race going on," says Vedder. "Salaries have done pretty well. Look at the president of Yale. Compare his salary now with his salary in 2000." In 2000, Richard Levin earned $561,709. By 2009, it was $1.63 million. "A typical university today has as many administrators as faculty."

18   Vedder also notes the decrease in teaching loads by tenured faculty, and the vast increase in nonacademic amenities like plush dorms and intercollegiate athletics. "Every campus has its climbing wall," he notes drily. "You cannot have a campus without a climbing wall."

19   Just as homeowners took out equity loans to buy themselves spa bathrooms and chef's kitchens and told themselves that they were really building value with every borrowed dollar, today's college students can buy themselves a four-year vacation in an increasingly well-upholstered resort, and everyone congratulates them for investing in themselves.

20   Unsurprisingly those 18-year-olds often don't look quite so hard at the education they're getting. In *Academically Adrift*, their recent study of undergraduate learning, Richard Arum and Josipa Roksa find that at least a third of students gain no measurable skills during their four years in college. For the remainder who do, the gains are usually minimal. For many students, college is less about providing an education than a credential—a certificate testifying that they are smart enough to get into college, conformist enough to go, and compliant enough to stay there for four years.

21   When I was a senior, one of my professors asked wonderingly, "Why is it that you guys spend so much time trying to get as little as possible for your money?" The answer, Caplan says, is that they're mostly there for a credential, not learning. "Why does cheating work?" he points out. If you were really just in college to learn skills, it would be totally counterproductive. "If you don't learn the material, then you will have less human capital and the market will punish you—there's no reason for us to do it." But since they think the credential matters more than the education, they look for ways to get the credential as painlessly as possible.

22   There has, of course, always been a fair amount of credentialism in education. Ten years ago, when I entered business school at the University of Chicago, the career-services person who came to talk to our class said frankly, "We could put you on a cruise ship for the next two years and it wouldn't matter."

23   But how much, exactly, does credentialism matter? For years there's been a fierce debate among economists over how much of the value of a degree is credentials and how much the education. Heckman thinks the credentialism argument—what economists call "signaling"—is "way overstated." His work does show that a lot depends on outside factors like cognitive ability and early childhood health. But he says flatly that "no one thinks that schooling has no effect on ability."

24   That debate matters a lot, because while the value of an education can be very high, the value of a credential is strictly limited. If students are gaining real, valuable skills in school, then putting more students into college will increase the productive capacity of

firms and the economy—a net gain for everyone. Credentials, meanwhile, are a zero-sum game. They don't create value; they just reallocate it, in the same way that rising home values serve to ration slots in good public schools. If employers have mostly been using college degrees to weed out the inept and the unmotivated, then getting more people into college simply means more competition for a limited number of well-paying jobs. And in the current environment, that means a lot of people borrowing money for jobs they won't get.

25   But we keep buying because after two decades prudent Americans who want a little financial security don't have much left. Lifetime employment, and the pensions that went with it, have now joined outhouses, hitching posts, and rotary-dial telephones as something that wide-eyed children may hear about from their grandparents but will never see for themselves. The fabulous stock-market returns that promised an alternative form of protection proved even less durable. At least we have the house, weary Americans told each other, and the luckier ones still do, as they are reminded every time their shaking hand writes out another check for a mortgage that's worth more than the home that secures it. What's left is . . . investing in ourselves. Even if we're not such a good bet.

26   Between 1992 and 2008, the number of bachelor's degrees awarded rose almost 50 percent, from around 1.1 million to more than 1.6 million. According to Vedder, 60 percent of those additional students ended up in jobs that have not historically required a degree— waitress, electrician, secretary, mail carrier. That's one reason the past few decades have witnessed such an explosion in graduate and professional degrees, as kids who previously would have stopped at college look for ways to stand out in the job market.

27   It is in that market that students may first, finally, have begun to revolt. For decades, when former English majors wondered how to get out of their dead-end jobs, the answer was "go to law school"—an effect that was particularly pronounced in economic downturns. In 2010 in the *Los Angeles Times*, Mark Greenbaum warned prospective lawyers that "the number of new positions is likely to be fewer than 30,000 per year. That is far fewer than what's needed to accommodate the 45,000 juris doctors graduating from U.S. law schools each year."

28   That was the year that LSAT taking peaked, with 170,000 prospective lawyers signing up for the test. But then students apparently started heeding Greenbaum's warning. Two years later that figure dropped to just 130,000, lower than it had been in more than a decade. Law-school applications also dropped, from 88,000 to 67,000.

29   That's a heartening sign for those of us who believe that we've been graduating too many unemployable lawyers. But as we saw with the housing and dotcom booms, what comes after a bubble is not usually a return to a nice, sustainable equilibrium; it's chaos. Of course, the first thing to do when you're in a hole is stop digging. But that still leaves you in a pretty big hole.

30   Everyone seems to agree that the government, and parents, should be rethinking how we invest in higher education—and that employers need to rethink the increasing use of college degrees as crude screening tools for jobs that don't really require college skills. "Employers seeing a surplus of college graduates and looking to fill jobs are just tacking on that requirement," says Vedder. "De facto, a college degree becomes a job requirement for becoming a bartender."

31   We have started to see some change on the finance side. A law passed in 2007 allows many students to cap their loan payment at 10 percent of their income and forgives any balance after 25 years. But of course, that doesn't control the cost of education; it just shifts it to taxpayers. It also encourages graduates to choose lower-paying careers, which diminishes the financial return to education still further. "You're subsidizing people to become priests and poets and so forth," says Heckman. "You may think that's a good thing, or you may not." Either way it will be expensive for the government.

32   What might be a lot cheaper is putting more kids to work: not necessarily as burger flippers but as part of an educational effort. Caplan notes that work also builds valuable skills—probably more valuable for kids who don't naturally love sitting in a classroom. Heckman agrees wholeheartedly: "People are different, and those abilities can be shaped. That's what we've learned, and public policy should recognize that."

33   Heckman would like to see more apprenticeship-style programs, where kids can learn in the workplace—learn not just specific job skills, but the kind of "soft skills," like getting to work on time and getting along with a team, that are crucial for career success. "It's about having mentors and having workplace-based education," he says. "Time and again I've seen examples of this kind of program working."

34   Ah, but how do we get there from here? With better public policy, hopefully, but also by making better individual decisions. "Historically markets have been able to handle these things," says Vedder, "and I think eventually markets will handle this one. If it doesn't improve soon, people are going to wake up and ask, 'Why am I going to college?' "

QUESTIONS FOR ANALYSIS AND DISCUSSION

1. According to McArdle, what similarities exist between a college education and the recent housing bubble?

2. McArdle wonders if college tuition has doubled over the last decade: "Is the education that today's students are getting twice as good? Are new workers twice as smart? Have they become somehow massively more expensive to educate?" Respond to her questions with information from the article as well as your personal experience.

3. Vedder notes that climbing walls now appear on campuses nationwide. Why does he choose this as an example for campus amenities? What other "extras" have been appearing on college campuses today? Are they necessary? Why or why not?

4. Beyond academics, how important is the quality of a college campus, including the amenities it offers, the condition of its housing, and the extracurricular activities it offers? How did the campus impact your decision to attend your college? Explain.

5. McArdle notes, "for many students, college is less about providing an education than a credential—a certificate testifying that they are smart enough to get into college, conformist enough to go, and compliant enough to stay there for four years." What is "credentialism"? How does

it play into the workforce? What impact does it have on the four years a student spends in college?

6. What impact, if any, does McArdle's article have on your perspective of college, both as a student and as a college graduate.

A's for Everyone!

Alicia C. Shepard

In an era of rampant grade inflation, some college students find it shocking to discover there are five letters in the grading system. It used to be that earning a B in a course was cause for celebration. But across college campuses nationwide, many students argue that an A is now the only acceptable grade. Increasingly, students are arguing with their professors to raise lower grades to higher ones, and urging them to consider their "hard work," rather than skill, talent, and performance, as the reason for an A grade. Today's parents are also putting pressure on their children to achieve high grades, adding to student anxieties. In this next essay, Professor Alicia Shepard describes the trend from the perspective of a teacher and a parent.*

BEFORE YOU READ

What grades do you expect to earn in your college classes? In your opinion, what is a "good grade" and why?

AS YOU READ

Professor Watson notes that many students believe that "working hard" should carry weight when factoring grades. What do you think? Is this a fair system? What is the line between talent and product and effort and earnestness?

1 It was the end of my first semester teaching journalism at American University. The students had left for winter break. As a rookie professor, I sat with trepidation in my office on a December day to electronically post my final grades.

2 My concern was more about completing the process correctly than anything else. It took an hour to compute and type in the grades for three classes, and then I hit "enter." That's when the trouble started.

3 In less than an hour, two students challenged me. Mind you, there had been no preset posting time. They had just been religiously checking the electronic bulletin board that many colleges now use.

4 "Why was I given a B as my final grade?" demanded a reporting student via e-mail. "Please respond ASAP, as I have never received a B during my career here at AU and it will surely lower my GPA."

---

*Alicia C. Shepard, *Washington Post*, June 5, 2005.

5   I must say I was floored. Where did this kid get the audacity to so boldly challenge a professor? And why did he care so much? Did he really think a prospective employer was going to ask for his GPA?

6   I checked the grades I'd meticulously kept on the electronic blackboard. He'd missed three quizzes and gotten an 85 on two of the three main writing assignments. There was no way he was A material. I let the grade mar his GPA because he hadn't done the required work.

7   I wasn't so firm with my other challenger. She tracked me down by phone while I was still in my office. She wanted to know why she'd received a B-plus. Basically, it was because she'd barely said a word in class, so the B-plus was subjective. She harangued me until, I'm ashamed to admit, I agreed to change her grade to an A-minus. At the time, I thought, "Geez, if it means that much to you, I'll change it." She thanked me profusely, encouraging me to have a happy holiday.

8   Little did I know the pressure was just beginning.

9   The students were relentless. During the spring semester, they showed up at my office to insist I reread their papers and boost their grades. They asked to retake tests they hadn't done well on. They bombarded me with e-mails questioning grades. More harassed me to change their final grade. I began to wonder if I was doing something wrong, sending out some sort of newbie signal that I could be pushed around. Then I talked to other professors in the School of Communication. They all had stories.

10   My colleague Wendy Swallow told me about one student who had managed to sour her Christmas break one year. Despite gaining entry into AU's honors program, the student missed assignments in Swallow's newswriting class and slept through her midterm. Slept through her midterm! Then she begged for lenience.

11   "I let her take it again for a reduced grade," Swallow says, "but with the warning that if she skipped more classes or missed more deadlines, the midterm grade would revert to the F she earned by missing it. She then skipped the last three classes of the semester and turned in all her remaining assignments late. She even showed up late for her final."

12   Swallow gave the student a C-minus, which meant she was booted out of the honors program. The student was shocked. She called Swallow at home hysterical about being dropped from the program. To Swallow, the C-minus was a gift. To the student, an undeserved lump of Christmas coal.

13   "She pestered me for several days by phone," says Swallow, who did not relent and suggested the student file a formal grievance. She didn't. "The whole exchange, though, made for a very unpleasant break. Now I wait to post my grades until the last minute before leaving for the semester, as by then most of the students are gone, and I'm less likely to get those instantaneous complaints."

14   Another colleague told me about a student she had failed. "He came back after the summer trying to convince me to pass him because other professors just gave him a C," says Leena Jayaswal, who teaches photography. Never mind that he didn't do her required work.

15   John Watson, who teaches journalism ethics and communications law at American, has noticed another phenomenon: Many students, he says, believe that simply working hard—though not necessarily doing excellent work—entitles them to an A. "I can't tell you how many times I've heard a student dispute a grade, not on the basis of in-class performance," says Watson, "but on the basis of how hard they tried. I appreciate the effort, and it always produces positive results, but not always the exact results the student wants. We all have different levels of talent."

16   It's a concept that many students (and their parents) have a hard time grasping. Working hard, especially the night before a test or a paper due date, does not necessarily produce good grades.

17   "At the age of 50, if I work extremely hard, I can run a mile in eight minutes," says Watson. "I have students who can jog through a mile in seven minutes and barely sweat. They will always finish before me and that's not fair. Or is it?"

18   Last September, AU's Center for Teaching Excellence hosted a lunchtime forum to provide faculty members tips on how to reduce stressful grade confrontations. I eagerly attended.

19   The advice we were given was solid: Be clear upfront about how you grade and what is expected, and, when possible, use a numerical grading system rather than letter grades. If the grade is an 89, write that on the paper rather than a B-plus.

20   "The key," said AU academic counselor Jack Ramsay, "is to have a system of grading that is as transparent as possible."

21   Yet even the most transparent grading system won't eliminate our students' desperate pursuit of A's. Of the 20 teachers who came to the session, most could offer some tale of grade harassment.

22   "Most of the complaints that colleagues tell me about come from B students," said James Mooney, special assistant to the dean for academic affairs in the College of Arts and Sciences. "They all want to know why they didn't get an A. Is there something wrong with a B?"

23   Apparently there is. "Certainly there are students who are victims of grade inflation in secondary school," said Mooney. "They come to college, and the grading system is much more rigorous. That's one of the most difficult things to convey to the students. If you're getting a B, you're doing well in a course."

24   But his interpretation is rarely accepted by students or their parents. And the pressure on professors to keep the A's coming isn't unique to AU. It's endemic to college life, according to Stuart Rojstaczer, a Duke University professor who runs a website called Gradeinflation.com. At Duke and many other colleges, A's outnumber B's, and C's have all but disappeared from student transcripts, his research shows.

25   Last spring, professors at Princeton University declared war on grade inflation, voting to slash the number of A's they award to 25 percent of all grades. At Harvard, where half of the grades awarded are A's, the university announced that it would cut the number of seniors graduating with honors from 91 percent to about 50 percent.

26   Despite those moves, Rojstaczer doesn't think it will be easy to reverse the rising tide of A's. He points out that in 1969, a quarter of the grades handed out at Duke were C's. By 2002, the number of C's had dropped to less than 10 percent.

27   Rojstaczer, who teaches environmental science, acknowledged in an op-ed piece he wrote for the *Post* two years ago that he rarely hands out C's, "and neither do most of my colleagues. And I can easily imagine a time when I'll say the same thing about B's."

28   Arthur Levine, president of Columbia University Teacher's College and an authority on grading, traces what's going on to the Vietnam War. "Men who got low grades could be drafted," Levine says. "The next piece was the spread of graduate schools where only A's and B's were passing grades. That soon got passed on to undergraduates and set the standard."

29   And then there's consumerism, he says. Pure and simple, tuition at a private college runs, on average, nearly $28,000 a year. If parents pay that much, they expect nothing less than A's in return. "Therefore, if the teacher gives you a B, that's not acceptable," says

Levine, "because the teacher works for you. I expect A's, and if I'm getting B's, I'm not getting my money's worth."

30   Rojstaczer agrees: "We've made a transition where attending college is no longer a privilege and an honor; instead college is a consumer product. One of the negative aspects of this transition is that the role of a college-level teacher has been transformed into that of a service employee."

31   Levine argues that we "service employees" are doing students a disservice if we cave in to the demand for top grades. "One of the things an education should do is let you know what you do well in and what you don't," he says. "If everybody gets high grades, you don't learn that."

32   But, as I'd already seen, many students aren't interested in learning that lesson—and neither are their parents. When AU administrator James Mooney polled professors about grade complaints, he was appalled to learn that some overwrought parents call professors directly to complain. "One colleague told me he got a call from the mother of his student and she introduced herself by saying that she and her husband were both attorneys," said Mooney. "He thought it was meant to intimidate him."

33   Though I haven't received any menacing phone calls from parents, Mom and Dad are clearly fueling my students' relentless demand for A's. It's a learned behavior. I know, because I'm guilty of inflicting on my son the same grade pressure that now plays out before me as a university professor.

34   Last fall when my Arlington high school senior finally got the nerve to tell me that he'd gotten a C in the first quarter of his AP English class, I did what any self-respecting, grade-obsessed parent whose son is applying to college would do. I cried. Then I e-mailed his teacher and made an appointment for the three of us to meet. My son's teacher was accommodating. She agreed that if my son did A work for the second quarter, colleges would see a B average for the two quarters, not that ruinous C.

35   There's a term for the legions of parents like me. The parents who make sure to get the teacher's e-mail and home phone number on Back to School Night. The kind who e-mail teachers when their child fails a quiz. The kind who apply the same determination to making sure their child excels academically that they apply to the professional world.

36   We are called "helicopter parents" because we hover over everything our kids do like Secret Service agents guarding the president. (My son refers to me as an Apache attack helicopter, and he's Fallujah under siege.) Only we aren't worried about our kids getting taken out by wild-eyed assassins. We just want them to get into a "good" (whatever that means) college.

37   "Parents today have this intense investment in seeing their kids do well in school," says Peter Stearns, provost at George Mason University and author of *Anxious Parenting: A History of Modern Childrearing in America*. "This translates into teachers feeling direct and indirect pressure to keep parents off their backs by handing out reasonably favorable grades and making other modifications, like having up to 18 valedictorians."

38   High school administrators who haven't made those modifications sometimes find themselves defending their grading policies in court. Two years ago, a senior at New Jersey's Moorestown High School filed a $2.7 million lawsuit after she was told she'd have to share being valedictorian with another high-achieving student. A similar episode occurred in Michigan, where a Memphis High School senior who'd just missed being valedictorian claimed in a lawsuit that one of his A's should have been an A-plus.

39   That hyperconcern about grades and class rankings doesn't disappear when kids finally pack for college. Along with their laptops and cell phones, these students bring along the parental anxiety and pressure they've lived with for 18 years.

40   One of my students, Rachael Scorca, says that her parents have always used good grades as an incentive. And they've continued to do so during college. "In high school, my social life and curfew revolved around A's," explains Scorca, a broadcast journalism major. "I needed over a 90 average in order to go out during the week and keep my curfew as late as it was. Once college came and my parents couldn't control my hours or effort, they started controlling my bank account. If I wasn't getting good grades, they wouldn't put money in my account, and, therefore, I wouldn't have a social life."

41   But most of my students tell me the pressure to get top grades doesn't come from their parents any longer. They've internalized it. "I'd say most of the pressure just comes from my personal standards," says Molly Doyle. "It's also something I take pride in. When people ask me how my grades are, I like being able to tell them that I've got all A's and B's."

42   During my second semester of teaching, I received this e-mail from a student who'd taken my fall class on "How the News Media Shape History" and wasn't satisfied with his grade. He (unsuccessfully) tried bribery.

43   "Professor. I checked my grade once I got here and it is a B," he wrote. "I have to score a grade better than a B+ to keep my scholarship and I have no idea how I ended up with a B. In addition, to that I have brought you something from The GREAT INDIAN CONTINENT."

44   I invited him to come to my office so I could explain why he'd gotten a B, but after several broken appointments, he faded away.

45   Other students were more persistent, particularly a bright young man who'd been in the same class as the briber. He'd gotten an A-minus and made it clear in an e-mail he wasn't happy with it: "I have seen a number of the students from the class, and we inevitably got to talking about it. I had assumed that you are a tough grader and that earning an A-minus from you was a difficult task, but upon talking to other students, it appears that that grade was handed out more readily than I had thought. Not that other students did not deserve a mark of that caliber, but I do feel as though I added a great deal to the class. I feel that my work, class participation, and consistency should have qualified me for a solid A."

46   When I ignored the e-mail, he pestered me a second time: "I know it's a great pain in the ass to have an A-minus student complain, but I'm starting to wonder about the way grades are given. I would be very curious to know who the A students were. While other students may have outdone me with quiz grades, I made up for it with participation and enthusiasm. I really feel that I deserved an A in your class. If I was an A-minus student, I assume that you must have handed out a lot of C's and D's. I don't mean to be a pain— I have never contested anything before. I feel strongly about this, though."

47   I shouldn't have done it, but I offered to change the grade. My student was thrilled. He wrote, "With grade inflation being what it is and the levels of competition being so high, students just can't afford to be hurt by small things. I thought that you did a great job with the course."

48   But when I completed the required paperwork, the grade change was rejected by a university official. Though no one questioned me the first time I did it, grades can be

changed only if they are computed incorrectly. "How fair is it to change his grade?" an assistant dean asked me. "What about other kids who might be unhappy but didn't complain?"

49   I e-mailed my student to let him know that he would have to live with an A-minus. "The gods who make these decisions tell me that they rejected it because it's not considered fair to all the other students in the class," I wrote. "The grade you got was based on a numerical formula, and you can only change a grade if you made a mathematical error. I'm sorry."

50   "That seems illogical to me," he e-mailed back. "If a student feels that a grade was inappropriate and wishes to contest that grade, that student obviously must contact the person who gave it to them. Who was I supposed to contact? What was the process that I was to follow? The lack of logic in all this never fails to amaze me!"

51   I told him whom to contact. I'm not sure if he ever followed through, but I saw him recently and he smiled and stopped to talk. Nothing was mentioned about the grade.

52   The day before this spring semester's grades were due I bumped into another professor racing out of the building. What's the hurry? I asked.

53   She told me she had just posted her grades and wanted to get off campus fast. But she wasn't quick enough. Within eight minutes, a B-minus student had called to complain.

54   A few hours after I entered my final grades, I got an e-mail from a student, at 1:44 a.m. She was unhappy with her B. She worked so hard, she told me. This time, though, I was prepared. I had the numbers to back me up, and I wouldn't budge on her grade. No more Professor Softie.

QUESTIONS FOR ANALYSIS AND DISCUSSION

1. Professor Shepard is shocked that a student would challenge the grade she assigned. Have you ever felt that a grade you received was unfair? If so, did you ask your professor for clarification? Did you challenge the professor to change it? Explain.

2. The author changes one grade after the student challenges the subjective nature of "class participation." In your opinion, should class participation be a factor in grade determination? Why or why not?

3. How has electronic grade posting influenced the issue of grade challenging and grade inflation?

4. What are "helicopter parents"? Does it make Shepard's argument more credible when she admits that she is one?

5. Visit the Grade Inflation website at www.gradeinflation.com and review the data on its site. Discuss the issue of grade inflation with your group, and what it might mean to the value of grades in general. If your school appears on the website, discuss its ranking specifically.

6. Write about an experience you had as a student, connected to a grade you receive in class. It could be about a poor grade you felt you didn't deserve, or the pressure to earn a grade because of parental influence or looming college admissions.

Reading the Visual

Passive Activism Ideal

The Gazette

QUESTIONS FOR ANALYSIS AND DISCUSSION

1. What issue is this cartoon raising? Explain.
2. What visual clichés does this cartoon use to convey its message? Whom do the people in the cartoon represent? Could the characters be reversed? Why or why not?
3. This cartoon appeared in a campus newspaper. Would it be as effective in another publication? Why is context important to this cartoon?
4. What is your own opinion of campus activism? Do you participate in any groups? Do you volunteer for any causes? Why or why not?
5. In the 1960s, students were known for leading protests and pioneering social change. Do we still equate campus life with social change? Has the time for campus groups and activism passed? Why or why not?

The Post-Everything Generation

Nicholas Handler

In July 2007, *The New York Times Magazine* published "What's the Matter With College," an essay by historian Rick Perlstein, and invited college students across the United States to respond. Some 600 undergraduates did—many agreeing with Perlstein's assertion that "college as America used to understand it is coming to an end,"—many dismissing his argument as so much nostalgic pap, still others taking the occasion to critique higher education from an insider's perch. The following essay, by Yale University student Nicholas Handler, won the competition. Handler, who hails from Glen Ridge, New Jersey, graduated in 2009 and plans on pursuing a career in human rights law.*

BEFORE YOU READ

A generation is a group of people who were born around the same time and therefore share a similar cultural experience. Their political and cultural ideas and social perspectives are often different from generations preceding them. What are the defining elements of your generation? What things make your age group fundamentally different in thought and action than, say, your parents' generation?

AS YOU READ

What makes Handler pay attention in his literary theory class? What encourages him to think about his generation and how he fits into a larger worldview?

1   I never expected to gain any new insight into the nature of my generation, or the changing landscape of American colleges, in Lit Theory. Lit Theory is supposed to be the class where you sit at the back of the room with every other jaded sophomore wearing skinny jeans, thick-framed glasses, an ironic tee-shirt and over-sized retro headphones, just waiting for lecture to be over so you can light up a Turkish Gold and walk to lunch while listening to Wilco. That's pretty much the way I spent the course, too: through structuralism, formalism, gender theory, and post-colonialism, I was far too busy shuffling through my iPod to see what the patriarchal world order of capitalist oppression had to do with Ethan Frome. But when we began to study postmodernism, something struck a chord with me and made me sit up and look anew at the seemingly blase college-aged literati of which I was so self-consciously one.

2   According to my textbook, the problem with defining postmodernism is that it's impossible. The difficulty is that it is so. . . . post. It defines itself so negatively against what came before it—naturalism, romanticism and the wild revolution of modernism—that it's sometimes hard to see what it actually is. It denies that anything can be explained

---

*Nicholas Handler, *New York Times Magazine*, September 27, 2009.

neatly or even at all. It is parodic, detached, strange, and sometimes menacing to traditionalists who do not understand it. Although it arose in the post-war west (the term was coined in 1949), the generation that has witnessed its ascendance has yet to come up with an explanation of what postmodern attitudes mean for the future of culture or society. The subject intrigued me because, in a class otherwise consumed by dead-letter theories, postmodernism remained an open book, tempting to the young and curious. But it also intrigued me because the question of what postmodernism—what a movement so post-everything, so reticent to define itself—is spoke to a larger question about the political and popular culture of today, of the other jaded sophomores sitting around me who had grown up in a postmodern world.

3   In many ways, as a college-aged generation, we are also extremely post: post-Cold War, post-industrial, post-baby boom, post-9/11 . . . at one point in his famous essay, "Postmodernism, or the Cultural Logic of Late Capitalism," literary critic Frederic Jameson even calls us "post-literate." We are a generation that is riding on the tail-end of a century of war and revolution that toppled civilizations, overturned repressive social orders, and left us with more privilege and opportunity than any other society in history. Ours could be an era to accomplish anything.

4   And yet do we take to the streets and the airwaves and say "here we are, and this is what we demand"? Do we plant our flag of youthful rebellion on the mall in Washington and say 'we are not leaving until we see change! Our eyes have been opened by our education and our conception of what is possible has been expanded by our privilege and we demand a better world because it is our right'? It would seem we do the opposite. We go to war without so much as questioning the rationale, we sign away our civil liberties, we say nothing when the Supreme Court uses *Brown v. Board of Education* to outlaw desegregation, and we sit back to watch the carnage on the evening news.

5   On campus, we sign petitions, join organizations, put our names on mailing lists, make small-money contributions, volunteer a spare hour to tutor, and sport an entire wardrobe's worth of Live Strong bracelets advertising our moderately priced opposition to everything from breast cancer to global warming. But what do we really stand for? Like a true postmodern generation we refuse to weave together an overarching narrative to our own political consciousness, to present a cast of inspirational or revolutionary characters on our public stage, or to define a specific philosophy. We are a story seemingly without direction or theme, structure or meaning—a generation defined negatively against what came before us. When Al Gore once said "It's the combination of narcissism and nihilism that really defines postmodernism," he might as well have been echoing his entire generation's critique of our own. We are a generation for whom even revolution seems trite, and therefore as fair a target for bland imitation as anything else. We are the generation of the Che Guevara tee-shirt.

6   Jameson calls it "Pastiche"—"the wearing of a linguistic mask, speech in a dead language." In literature, this means an author speaking in a style that is not his own—borrowing a voice and continuing to use it until the words lose all meaning and the chaos that is real life sets in. It is an imitation of an imitation, something that has been re-envisioned so many times the original model is no longer relevant or recognizable. It is mass-produced individualism, anticipated revolution. It is why postmodernism lacks cohesion, why it seems to lack purpose or direction. For us, the post-everything generation, pastiche is the use and reuse of

the old clichés of social change and moral outrage—a perfunctory rebelliousness that has culminated in the age of rapidly multiplying non-profits and relief funds. We live our lives in masks and speak our minds in a dead language—the language of a society that expects us to agitate because that's what young people do.

7   But how do we rebel against a generation that is expecting, anticipating, nostalgic for revolution? How do we rebel against parents that sometimes seem to want revolution more than we do? We don't. We rebel by not rebelling. We wear the defunct masks of protest and moral outrage, but the real energy in campus activism is on the internet, with websites like moveon.org. It is in the rapidly developing ability to communicate ideas and frustration in chatrooms instead of on the streets, and channel them into nation-wide projects striving earnestly for moderate and peaceful change: we are the genera-tion of Students Taking Action Now Darfur; we are the Rock the Vote generation; the generation of letter-writing campaigns and public interest lobbies; the alternative energy generation.

8   College as America once knew it—as an incubator of radical social change—is com-ing to an end. To our generation the word "radicalism" evokes images of al Qaeda, not the Weathermen. 'Campus takeover' sounds more like Virginia Tech in 2007 than Columbia University in 1968. Such phrases are a dead language to us. They are vocabulary from another era that does not reflect the realities of today. However, the technological revolu-tion, the moveon.org revolution, the revolution of the organization kid, is just as real and just as profound as the revolution of the 1960's—it is just not as visible. It is a work in progress, but it is there. Perhaps when our parents finally stop pointing out the things that we are not, the stories that we do not write, they will see the threads of our narrative begin to come together; they will see that behind our pastiche, the post generation speaks in a language that does make sense. We are writing a revolution. We are just putting it in our own words.

QUESTIONS FOR ANALYSIS AND DISCUSSION

1. What is post-modern theory? Why does Handler connect to this theory and believe it represents his generation better than any other? Explain.

2. Handler points out that college students today have the opportunity to make a change in the world but often fail to do so because their post-modern world lacks inspiration. Respond to his idea with your own view.

3. As if you were a judge for the *New York Times* essay contest, identify this essay's strengths and weaknesses.

4. What is Handler's opinion of his generation? Identify words and phrases in his essay that demonstrate his view.

5. Handler's essay won the essay competition, but received a lot of criticism as being un-stimulating and even boring. Read the four runner-up essays posted on *The New York Times* website at http://essay.blogs.nytimes .com/2007/09/26/two-years-are-better-than-four/. Was Handler's essay the best? What distinguished it from the others? In your opinion, was one of the runner-up essays better? Explain.

WRITING ASSIGNMENTS

1. Write an essay on what a college education means to you. Include what skills, knowledge, and abilities you feel a college education should confer after four years of study.

2. Review your student handbook and summarize your student rights and responsibilities. Do you agree with your college's rules and regulations? Write an essay in which you agree or disagree, in whole or in part, with the rules and regulations guiding student conduct.

3. Design a college core curriculum that every student must take before graduation, regardless of their major. Select 12 courses to be taken over the four-year time span of the average bachelor's degree. You may be general in your selection ("Western Civilization I & II") or very specific ("Gender and Power in Modern America"). After compiling your curriculum, share your list with other students in class to see which courses were chosen in common, and which ones were different. If your college or university has a core curriculum, compare your final list with that outlined in your student handbook.

4. Megan McArdle argues that college students today are merely attending school to obtain a piece of paper that proves they were smart enough and tough enough to stick it out four years. In other words, they are only there for the credential, and not really for the education. Answer her assertion with your own view. As a college student, are you there for the piece of paper? Are you planning to just go through the motions? How much effort do you expect to put into your college education, and why?

5. Write your own essay of no more than 1,200 words explaining "why college matters." Alternatively, you can write an essay in which you counter that a college education no longer "matters" outside of the credentials it affords in a competitive job market.

6. Murray argues that technical schools are undervalued in society today. Conversely, Stoller argues that Americans view intellectuals with suspicion. Who is right? Write an essay exploring the perception of college, technical school, and other trade schools in today's society. How do we view the graduates of each? What potential earnings can students attending each type of school anticipate? What about public opinion? Explain.

14

Race and Ethnicity

The United States is a union predicated on shared moral values, political and economic self-interest, and a common language. However, it is also a nation of immigrants—people of different races, ethnic identities, religions, and languages. It is a nation whose motto *e pluribus unum* ("one out of many") bespeaks a pride in its multicultural heritage. In this chapter, we explore some of the issues that arise from the diversity of our cultural and ethnic backgrounds.

This chapter examines the complex ways in which our assumptions about race and construction of stereotypes limit our relationships with others and distort how we define ourselves. By definition, stereotypes are generalizations about people based on characteristics such as race, ethnic origin, social class, religion, gender, or physical appearance. Often, stereotypes can lead one to make assumptions about others that are negative and demeaning. Sometimes even stereotypes that attribute positive qualities to certain groups, such as the assumption that Asian Americans are naturally smart, can deny individuals credit for their achievements.

Several readings in this chapter address the ways race can both unify and divide us. Although the United States has been a multiethnic and multiracial society since its founding, in the last few decades different groups of Americans have reasserted their ethnic and racial identities. And while we may glorify the memory of our own immigrant ancestors, we do not always welcome with open arms new waves of immigrants. But old ways of doing things linger on. For example, if race and ethnicity continue to be a question on employment forms and census data, can we ever really think of defining ourselves differently?

The election of Barack Obama to the nation's highest office raised new questions about racism in America. What does it mean for the United States to have a black president? Some people view Obama's election as proof that Americans have finally overcome institutionalized racism. Others view it as the end of a long struggle for equality and access to power. Still others say we have a long way to go. As you read this chapter, think about how the issue of race touches your daily life, including what Barack Obama's election to the presidency might mean to the dynamics of race in America.

Why Latinas Aren't Allowed to Get Angry
Sara Inés Calderón

Racial stereotypes are often based on misperceptions and a lack of understanding of another group's cultural heritage. In this essay, journalist and the editor of *NewsTaco*, Sara Inés Calderón, explores how racial stereotypes are created by cultural misunderstandings, with often insulting results. She also describes how once stereotypes are established, they can perpetuate degrading popular opinions that, in turn, may damage the self-regard of an entire group of people.*

BEFORE YOU READ

Consider the ways the media perpetuate cultural stereotypes. Think about how various media, such as television and cinema, promote cultural clichés.

AS YOU READ

Calderón comments that certain adjectives, such as "spicy," are often used to describe women from her ethnic background. What is the basis for these adjectives? What other words can you cite that are used to describe the personalities of women and men from other ethnic backgrounds?

1   In a few very tangible ways, Latinas have it rougher than other folks. Not only do we often find ourselves in an ethnic/cultural/linguistic/racial minority, cuing others to pile on stereotypical expectations, but we're also female. Often we might be the only woman in the room, and so we also bear the brunt of an entirely new set of stereotypical expectations.

2   And one of the most well-known and perpetuated stereotypes is that of the spicy Latina, which makes it, in effect, impossible for a Latina to express anger in our society. If she does, her anger is not an emotional problem, but rather a genetic one. Latinas can't help but be angry—it's in our DNA, right? This stereotype strips away any sense of human individuality and replaces it with something less human, and easier to manage. When the gesticulating and raised voice and bright colors and verbal sprints into Spanish surface (in any incarnation), folks no longer have to preoccupy themselves with addressing your actual concerns, but simply have to "handle" you until your "condition" passes.

3   It ends up working out for everyone—unless you happen to be Latina.

4   We end up being the victims of the kind of exoticism that assigns fiery traits to an entire group of women, regardless of individual or personal characteristics. Whether or not there are shy and calm Latinas in the world, we are all viewed as ticking time bombs. I do speak Spanish and I do like bright colors, but that doesn't make me a sex kitten. That doesn't mean that, at any moment, I'll become a Salma Hayek, Sofia Vergara, Carmen Miranda: the sultry, seductive, sex-crazed, quick-to-anger woman who, as we see in the movies, is easily placated with money or sex. But thanks to these stereotypes we buy into, anytime I move my hand, I'm "doing it." If I emphasize my words, I'm raising my voice. If I say anything in Spanish, I'm talking about you.

---

*Sara Inés Calderón, *NewsTaco*, 2012

5   Why is it "okay" for men to be angry, or blow off steam, but when women do it—especially Latinas—somehow, it's just not acceptable? Racism and sexism only go so far as to explain away these stereotypes, what's really at issue is how we buy into them as a culture. The spicy Latina stereotype is attractive in its stereotyping, it's sexy and cute, and so it's an easy purchase. The truth is, though, Latinas are not slaves to their anger, anymore than men or other women.

6   In real life, there are no quirky one-liners that leave everyone content within 23 minutes; these stereotypes have real consequences. It's never as cut-and-dry as when we see the stereotypical process play out with the ridiculous-yet-lovable Sofia Vergara on TV: stimulus, overblown emotional response, earnest and slightly condescending placation, happy resolution.

7   Instead, real women—like yours truly—end up having to continue to bear uncomfortable working conditions, uncooperative co-workers, being passed over for promotions, being ignored when they have good ideas or generally being treated like a thing, not a person. It's like being invisible. When you feel like you have something of value to say, and instead of being taken seriously, are dismissed as someone who doesn't know themselves well enough to have feelings in the first place, you begin to question yourself.

8   Am I overreacting? Was it such a big deal? Maybe he's right and I am getting too emotional. Was my voice that loud? Am I really embarrassing my "race?" Do I have a problem with anger?

9   It seems like the easier it is for others to "deal" with Latinas via their stereotypes, the harder it becomes to simply be a Latina in the first place. You begin to wonder whether it's worth it to stand up for yourself if you're going to get a lecture on bringing it down a notch every single time. When everyone around you is telling you that you need to take a chill pill, it seems incredible that it's not just you. The weight of your own self-doubt can become very heavy on your chest, and you wonder if you are embarrassing just yourself, or also your family, your culture and anyone who's ever been mistaken for a Latino at any given time. Isn't that a lot of pressure for one gal to take on?

QUESTIONS FOR ANALYSIS AND DISCUSSION

1. According to Calderón, what explanation is made for Latina women when they raise their voices, or get upset? How does this explanation hurt them as individuals?

2. How do stereotypes attributed to Latina women negatively impact them? Explain.

3. How have the media promoted the image of the "Latina woman"? Can you think of other examples in the media that have employed such stereotypes?

4. Calderón notes that because Latina stereotypes are "cute," they are more easily downplayed. Can you think of other stereotypes for other ethnicities that fall into this trap?

5. In what ways do stereotypes render their subjects "invisible? Why does Calderón feel invisible? Explain.

Leaving Race Behind

Amitai Etzioni

Caucasian, black, Asian, Hispanic, Native American. . . . official forms ask us to indicate our race. In this next essay, author and sociology professor Amitai Etzioni explains why he hesitates to mark any specific race—why is this information important at all? He then explains why the growing Hispanic population raises troubling questions about why race matters to the government, and why the time has come to stop asking this question on forms. The U.S. Census Bureau estimates that there will be almost 50 million citizens claiming Hispanic origins living in the United States, comprising 15 percent of the total population. It projects that within the next 40 years, Hispanics will represent one-quarter of the total population in the United States. Etzioni explains why this trend creates a golden opportunity to address the ills of racism in America.*

BEFORE YOU READ

Have you ever felt discriminated against because of your race? Have you ever found yourself making stereotypical assumptions about others based on their ethnicity, even inadvertently? Explain.

AS YOU READ

In this next essay, Amitai Etzioni recounts a personal experience in which race made him acutely aware of how disclosing this information can be abused. What role has race played in you life? Have you, like Etzioni, experienced a defining moment that changed or influenced your view of yourself or someone in your family connected to your ethnicity?

1 Some years ago the United States government asked me what my race was. I was reluctant to respond because my 50 years of practicing sociology—and some powerful personal experiences—have underscored for me what we all know to one degree or another, that racial divisions bedevil America, just as they do many other societies across the world. Not wanting to encourage these divisions, I refused to check off one of the specific racial options on the U.S. Census form and instead marked a box labeled "Other." I later found out that the federal government did not accept such an attempt to de-emphasize race, by me or by some 6.75 million other Americans who tried it. Instead the government assigned me to a racial category, one it chose for me. Learning this made me conjure up what I admit is a far-fetched association. I was in this place once before.

2 When I was a Jewish child in Nazi Germany in the early 1930s, many Jews who saw themselves as good Germans wanted to "pass" as Aryans. But the Nazi regime would

---

*Amitai Etzioni, *The American Scholar*, September 1, 2006.

have none of it. Never mind, they told these Jews, we determine who is Jewish and who is not. A similar practice prevailed in the Old South, where if you had one drop of African blood you were a Negro, disregarding all other facts and considerations, including how you saw yourself.

3   You might suppose that in the years since my little Census-form protest the growing enlightenment about race in our society would have been accompanied by a loosening of racial categories by our government. But in recent years the United States government has acted in a deliberate way to make it even more difficult for individuals to move beyond racial boxes and for American society as a whole to move beyond race.

4   Why the government perpetuates racialization and what might be done to diminish the role of race in our lives are topics that have become especially timely as Hispanics begin to take a more important role demographically, having displaced African-Americans as the largest American minority. How Hispanics view themselves and how they are viewed by others are among the most important factors affecting whether or not we can end race as a major social divide in America.

5   Treating people differently according to their race is as un-American as a hereditary aristocracy, and as American as slavery. The American ethos was formed by people who left the social stratification of the Old World to live in a freer, more fluid society. They sought to be defined by what they accomplished, not by what they were born with. As Arthur M. Schlesinger Jr. puts it in his book *The Disuniting of America*, one of the great virtues of America is that it defines individuals by where they are going rather than by where they have been. Achievement matters, not origin. The national ideal says that all Americans should be able to compete as equals, whatever their background. American society has been divided along racial lines since its earliest days.

6   Racial characterizations have trumped the achievement ideal; people born into a non-white race, whatever their accomplishments have been unable to change their racial status. Worse, race has often been their most defining characteristic, affecting most, if not all, aspects of their being.

7   As a result, we have been caught, at least since the onset of the civil rights movement, in ambivalence. On the one hand, we continue to dream of the day when all Americans will be treated equally, whatever their race; we rail against—and sometimes punish—those who discriminate according to race in hiring, housing, and social life. At the same time, we have ensconced in law many claims based on race: requirements that a given proportion of public subsidies, loans, job training, educational assistance, and admission slots at choice colleges be set aside for people of color. Many Americans, including African-Americans, are uneasy about what some people consider reverse discrimination. Courts have limited its scope; politicians have made hay by opposing it; and some of its beneficiaries feel that their successes are hollow because they are unsure whether their gains reflect hard-won achievements or special favors. There must be a better way to deal with past and current injustice. And the rapid changes in American demographics call for a reexamination of the place of race in America.

Enter the Hispanic

8 We have grown accustomed to thinking about America in black and white, and might well have continued to do so for decades to come except that Hispanics complicate this simplistic scheme: they do not fit into the old racial categories. Some Hispanics appear to many Americans to be black (for example, quite a few Cuban-Americans), others as white (especially immigrants from Argentina and Chile), and the appearance of still others is hard for many people to pigeonhole. Anyone seeing the lineup of baseball players honored as Major League Baseball's "Latino Legends Team" would find that the players vary from those who are as fair-skinned as Roger Clemens to those who are as dark-skinned as Jackie Robinson. More important by far, survey after survey shows that most Hispanics object to being classified as either black or white. A national survey conducted in 2002 indicated that 76 percent of Hispanics say the standard racial categories used by the U.S. Census do not address their preferences. The last thing most of those surveyed desire is to be treated as yet another race—as "brown" Americans.

9   Hispanics would have forced the question of how we define one another even if they were just another group of immigrants among the many that have made America what it is. But Hispanics are not just one more group of immigrants. Not only have Hispanic numbers surpassed those of black Americans, who until 2003 made up America's largest minority group, Hispanics have been reliably projected to grow much faster than African-Americans or any other American group. Thus, according to the Census, in 1990 blacks constituted 12 percent of the population and Hispanics 9 percent. By 2000, Hispanics caught up with blacks, amounting to 12.5 percent of the population compared to 12.3 percent for blacks. By 2050, Hispanics are projected to be 24.3 percent of the American population, compared to 14.7 percent for blacks. In many cities, from Miami to Los Angeles, in which African-Americans have been the largest minority group, Hispanics' numbers are increasingly felt. While once Hispanics were concentrated in the areas bordering Mexico, their numbers are now growing in places like Denver, St. Paul, and even New England.

10   Immigration fuels the growth of Hispanics relative to the growth of African-Americans because Latin American immigration, legal and illegal, continues at an explosive pace, while immigration from Africa is minuscule. Hispanics also have more children than African-Americans. During the most recent year for which data is available, 2003–2004, one of every two people added to America's population was Hispanic. And while black Americans have long been politically mobilized and active, Hispanics are just beginning to make their weight felt in American politics.

11   The rapid growth in the number, visibility, and power of Hispanics will largely determine the future of race in America, a point highlighted by Clara E. Rodriguez in her book Changing Race: Latinos, the Census, and the History of Ethnicity in the U.S. If Hispanics are to be viewed as brown or black (and some on the left aspire to color them), and above all if Hispanics develop the sense of disenfranchisement and alienation that many African-Americans have acquired (often for very good reasons), then America's immutable racial categories will only deepen.

12   If, on the other hand, most Hispanics continue to see themselves as members of one or more ethnic groups, then race in America might be pushed to the margins. Racial

categories have historically set us apart; ethnic categories are part of the mosaic that makes up America. It has been much easier for an individual to assimilate from an ethnic perspective than from a racial one. Race is considered a biological attribute, a part of your being that cannot be dropped or modified. Ethnic origin, in contrast, is where you came from. All Americans have one hyphen or another attached to their ethnic status: we're Polish-, or German-, or Anglo-, or Italian-Americans. Adding Cuban-Americans or Mexican-Americans to this collage would create more comfortable categories of a comparable sort.

The Race Trap

13 Many people take it for granted that genes determine race, just as genes determine gender. And we also tend to believe that racial categories are easy to discern (though we all know of exceptions).

14   One way to show how contrived racial divisions actually are is to recall that practically all of the DNA in all human beings is the same. Our differences are truly skin deep. Moreover, the notion that most of us are of one race or another has little basis in science. The Human Genome Project informs us not only that 99.9 percent of genetic material is shared by all humans, but also that variation in the remaining 0.1 percent is greater within racial groups than across them. That is, not only are 99.9 percent of the genes of a black person the same as those of a white person, but the genes of a particular black person may be more similar to the genes of a white person than they are to another black person.

15   This point was driven home to college students in a sociology class at Penn State in April 2005. Following their professor's suggestion, the students took DNA tests that had surprising results. A student who identified himself as "a proud black man" found that only 52 percent of his ancestry traced back to Africa, while the other 48 percent was European. Another student who said she takes flak from black friends for having a white boyfriend found that her ancestry was 58 percent European and only 42 percent African. These two students are not alone: an estimated one-third of the African-American population has European ancestry.

16   Which people make up a distinct race and which are considered dark-skinned constantly changes as social prejudices change. Jewish-, Slavic-, Irish-, and Polish-Americans were considered distinct races in the mid-19th and early 20th centuries—and dark races at that, as chronicled in great detail in Matthew Frye Jacobson's book, *Whiteness of a Different Color: European Immigrants and the Alchemy of Race*; and in a well-documented book by Noel Ignatiev, *How the Irish Became White*. Ignatiev found that in the 1850s, Irish people were considered non-white in America and were frequently referred to as "niggers turned inside out." (Blacks were sometimes called "smoked Irish.")

17   The capriciousness of racial classifications is further highlighted by the way the U.S. Census, the most authoritative and widely used source of social classifications, divides Americans into races. When I ask my students how many races they think there are in America, they typically count four: white, black, Asian, and Native American. The Census says there are 15 racial categories: white, African-American, American Indian/Alaska

Native, Asian Indian, Chinese, Filipino, Japanese, Korean, Vietnamese, "other Asian," Native Hawaiian, Guamanian/Chamorro, Samoan, and "other Pacific Islander," and as of 2000 one more for those who feel they are of some other race. (Hispanic is not on this list because the Census treats Hispanic as an ethnicity and asks about it on a separate question, but immediately following that question, the Census asks, "So what is your race, anyhow?")

18   The arbitrary nature of these classifications is demonstrated by the Census Bureau itself, which can change the race of millions of Americans by the stroke of a pen. The Census changed the race of Indian- and Pakistani-Americans from white in 1970 to Asian in 1980. In 1930 the Census made Mexicans into a different race but then withdrew this category. Similarly, Hindu made a brief appearance as a race in the 1930 and 1940 Censuses but was subsequently withdrawn.

19   Anthropologists have found that some tribes do not see colors the way many of us do; for instance, they do not "see" a difference between brown and yellow. Members of these tribes are not colorblind, but some differences found in nature (in the color spectrum) simply don't register with them, just as young American children are unaware of racial differences until someone introduces them to these distinctions. We draw a line between white and black, but people's skin colors have many shades. It is our social prejudices that lead us to make sharp racial categories.

20   I am not one of those postmodernists who, influenced by Nietzsche and Foucault, claim that there are no epistemological truths, that all facts are a matter of social construction. I disagree with Nietzsche's description of truth as "a mobile army of metaphors, metonyms, and anthropomorphisms—in short a sum of human relations, which have been enhanced, transposed, and embellished poetically and rhetorically and which after long use seem firm, canonical, and obligatory to a people." However, there is no doubt that social construction plays a significant role in the way we "see" racial differences, although our views may in turn be affected by other factors that are less subject to construction, for example, historical differences.

21   Most important is the significance we attribute to race and the interpretations we impose on it. When we are told only that a person is, say, Asian-American, we often jump to a whole list of conclusions regarding that person's looks, intelligence, work ethic, character; we make the same sort of jumps for Native Americans, blacks, and other races. Many things follow from these kneejerk characterizations: whether we will fear or like this person, whether we will wish to have him or her as a neighbor or as a spouse for one of our children—all on the basis of race. In short, we load on to race a great deal of social importance that is not a reflection of the "objective" biological differences that exist. To paraphrase the UNESCO Constitution, racial divisions are made in the minds of men and women, and that is where they will have to be ended.

Defining the Hispanic

22 If racial categories have long been settled, the social characterization of the Hispanic is up for grabs. We still don't know whether Hispanics will be defined as a brown race and align themselves with those in the United States who are or who see themselves as marginalized

or victimized—or if they will be viewed as a conglomerate of ethnic groups, of Mexican-Americans, Cuban-Americans, Dominican-Americans, and so forth, who will fit snuggly into the social mosaic.

23   The term Hispanic was first used in the Census in 1980. Before that, Mexican-Americans and Cuban-Americans were classified as white (except when a Census interviewer identified an individual as the member of a different racial group). Until 1980, Hispanics were part of the great American panorama of ethnic groups. Then the Census combined these groups into a distinct category unlike any other. It was as if the federal government were to one day lump together Spanish-, Italian-, and Greek-Americans into a group called "Southern European" and begin issuing statistics on how their income, educational achievements, number of offspring, and so on compare to those of Northern Europeans.

24   And as we've seen, those who define themselves as Hispanic are asked to declare a race. In the 1980 Census, the options included, aside from the usual menu of races, that ambiguous category "Other." There were 6.75 million Americans, including me, who chose this option in 1980. Most revealing: 40 percent of Hispanics chose this option. (Note that they—and I—chose this category despite the nature of the word "Other," which suggests the idea of "not being one of us." Had the category been accorded a less loaded label, say "wish not to be identified with any one group," it seems likely that many millions more would have chosen this box.)

25   To have millions of Americans choose to identify themselves as "Other" created a political backlash because Census statistics are used both to allocate public funds to benefit minority groups and to assess their political strength. Some African-American groups, especially, feared that if African-Americans chose "Other" instead of marking the "African-American" box, they would lose public allotments and political heft.

26   But never underestimate our government. The Census Bureau has used a statistical procedure to assign racial categories to those millions of us who sought to butt out of this divisive classification scheme. Federal regulations outlined by the Office of Management and Budget, a White House agency, ruled that the Census must "impute" a specific race to those who do not choose one. For several key public policy purposes, a good deal of social and economic data must be aggregated into five racial groups: white, black, Asian, American Indian or Alaska Native, and native Hawaiian or other Pacific Islander. How does the government pick a race for a person who checked the "Other" box? They turn to the answers for other Census questions: for example, income, neighborhood, education level, or last name. The resulting profiles of the U.S. population (referred to as the "age-race modified profile") are then used by government agencies in allotting public funds and for other official and public purposes.

27   But the Census isn't alone in oversimplifying the data. Increasingly, other entities, including the media, have treated Hispanics as a race rather than an ethnic group. This occurs implicitly when those who generate social data—such as government agencies or social scientists—break down the data into four categories: white, black, Asian, and Hispanic, which is comparable to listing apples, oranges, bananas, and yams. In their profile of jail inmates, the Bureau of Justice Statistics lists inmates' origins as "white, black, Hispanic, American Indian/Alaska Native, Asian/Pacific Islander, and more than one race."

The *New York Times* ran a front-page story in September 2005 in which it compared the first names used by whites, blacks, Asians, and Hispanics. Replace the word Hispanics with the name of another ethnic group, say Jews, and the unwitting racial implication of this classification will stand out.

28   Still other studies include Hispanics when they explicitly refer to racial groups. For example, a 2001 paper by Sean Reardon and John T. Yun examines what they call "racial balkanization among suburban schools," where there is increased segregation among black, Hispanic, and Asian students. A 2005 *Seattle Times* story uses racial terminology when it reports "Latinos have the fewest numbers among racial groups in master's-of-business programs nationwide, with about 5,000 enrolling annually." Similarly, the *San Diego Union Tribune* states: "A brawl between Latino and black students resulted in a lockdown of the school and revealed tensions between the two largest racial groups on campus."

29   A handful of others go a step further and refer to Hispanics as a brown race. For example, following the recent Los Angeles mayoral election, the *Houston Chronicle* informed us that "Villaraigosa's broad-based support has analysts wondering whether it is evidence of an emerging black-brown coalition." And, *National Public Radio* reported: "There is no black and brown alliance at a South Central Los Angeles high school."

30   One way or another, all of these references push us in the wrong direction—toward racializing Hispanics and deepening social divisions. America would be best served if we moved in the opposite direction.

A New Taxonomy

31   Thus far, workers at the U.S. Census Bureau, following the White House's instructions, seem determined to prevent any de-emphasis of race. They are testing iterations of the wording for the relevant questions in the 2010 Census—but all of these possibilities continue to require people to identify themselves by race. Moreover, Census bureaucrats will continue to impute race to those who refuse to do so themselves, ignoring the ever-growing number of people, especially Hispanics, who do not fit into this scheme.

32   Imagine if instead the federal government classified people by their country (or countries) of origin. For some governmental purposes, it might suffice to use large categories, such as Africa (which would exclude other so-called black groups, such as Haitians and West Indians that are now included in references to "black" Americans), Asia, Europe, Central America, and South America (the last two categories would not, of course, include Spain). For other purposes, a more detailed breakdown might work better—using regions such as the Middle East and Southeast Asia, for example—and if still more detail was desired, specific countries could be used, as we do for identifying ethnic groups (Irish, Polish, Cuban, Mexican, Japanese, Ethiopian, and so on). Kenneth Prewitt, a former director of the U.S. Census Bureau, has suggested the use of ethnic categories. As we have seen, ethnic origins carry some implications for who we are, but these implications decline in importance over time. Above all, they do not define us in some immutable way, as racial categories do. A category called something like "wish not to be identified with any particular group" should be included for those who do not want to be characterized even by ethnicity or for others who view themselves as having a varied and combined heritage.

33   The classification of Americans who are second-generation, and beyond, highlights the importance of the no-particular-group category. Although a fourth-generation Italian-American might still wish to be identified as Italian, he might not, particularly if he has grandparents or parents who are, say, Greek, Korean, and Native American. Forcing such a person to classify himself as a member of one ethnic group conceals the significance of the most important American development in social matters: out-marriage. Out-marriage rates for all groups other than African-Americans are so high that most of us will soon be tied to Americans of a large variety of backgrounds by the closest possible social tie, the familial one. Approximately 30 percent of third-generation Hispanics and 40 percent of third-generation Asians marry people of a different racial or ethnic origin. Altogether, the proportion of marriages among people of different racial or ethnic origins has increased by 72 percent since 1970. The trend suggests more of this in the future. Even if your spouse is of the same background, chances are high that the spouse of a sibling or cousin will represent a different part of the American collage. At holidays and other family events, from birthdays to funerals, we will increasingly be in close connection with "Others." Before too long most Americans will be "Tiger Woods" Americans, whose parental heritage is black, Native American, Chinese, Caucasian, and Thai. Now is the time for our social categories to reflect this trend—and its capacity for building a sense of one community—rather than conceal it.

Where Do We Go from Here?

34 Changing the way we divide up society will not magically resolve our differences or abolish racial prejudices. Nor does a movement toward a colorblind nation mean that we should stop working for a more just America. A combination of three major approaches that deal with economic and legal change could allow us to greatly downgrade the importance of race as a social criterion and still advance social justice. These approaches include reparations, class-based social programs, and fighting discrimination on an individual basis.

35   To make amends for the grave injustice that has been done to African-Americans by slavery and racial prejudice, as well as to bring to a close claims based on past injustices—and the sense of victimhood and entitlement that often accompanies these claims—major reparations are called for. One possible plan might allot a trillion dollars in education, training, and housing vouchers to African-Americans over a period of 20 years. (The same sort of plan might be devised for Native Americans.)

36   Such reparations cannot make full compensation for the sins of slavery, of course. But nothing can. Even so, if Jews could accept restitution from Germany and move on (Germany and Israel now have normal international relations, and the Jewish community in Germany is rapidly growing), could not a similar reconciliation between black and white Americans follow reparations? A precedent in our own history is the payment of reparations to Japanese-Americans because of their internment in World War II. In 1988, the U.S. government issued a formal apology in the Civil Liberties Act and awarded $20,000 to each living person who had been interned. About 80,000 claims were awarded, totaling $1.6 billion.

37   Part of the deal should be that once reparations are made for the sins against African-Americans in the past, black people could no longer claim special entitlements or

privileges on the basis of their race. Reparations thus would end affirmative action and minority set-asides as we have known them.

38   At the same time, Americans who are disadvantaged for any reason not of their own doing—the handicapped; those who grew up in parts of the country, such as Appalachia, in which the economy has long been lagging; those whose jobs were sent overseas who are too old to be retrained—would be given extra aid in applying for college admissions and scholarships, housing allowances, small-business loans, and other social benefits. The basis for such aid would be socio-economic status, not race. The child of a black billionaire would no longer be entitled to special consideration in college admissions, for instance, but the child of a poor white worker who lost his job to outsourcing and could not find new employment would be.

39   Social scientists differ in their estimates of the extent to which differences in opportunity and upward mobility between blacks and whites are due to racial prejudice and the extent to which they are due to economic class differences. But most scholars who have studied the matter agree that economic factors are stronger than racial ones, possibly accounting for as much as 80 percent of the differences we observe. A vivid example: In recent years, Wake County in North Carolina made sure that its public school classes were composed of students of different economic backgrounds, disregarding racial and ethnic differences. The results of this economic integration overshadowed previous attempts to improve achievement via racial integration. While a decade ago, only 40 percent of blacks in grades three through eight scored at grade level, in the spring of 2005, 80 percent did so.

40   Class differences affect not only educational achievement, health, and job selection, but also how people are regarded or stereotyped. Fifty years ago, a study conducted at Howard University showed that although adjectives used to describe whites and blacks were quite different, that variance was greatly reduced when class was held constant. People described upper-class whites and upper-class blacks in a remarkably similar fashion, as intelligent and ambitious. People also described lower-class whites and lower-class blacks in a similar way, as dirty and ignorant. The author concluded that "stereotypes vary more as a function of class than of race."

41   If race-based discrimination were a thing of the past, and black Americans were no longer subjected to it, then my argument that reparations can lead to closure would be easier to sustain. Strong evidence shows, however, that discrimination remains very much with us. A 1990 Urban Institute study found that when two people of different races applied for the same job, one in eight times the white was offered the job and an equally qualified African-American was not. Another Urban Institute study, released in 1999, found that racial minorities received less time and information from loan officers and were quoted higher interest rates than whites in most of the cities where tests were conducted.

42   The victims of current racial discrimination should be fully entitled to remedies in court and through such federal agencies as the Equal Employment Opportunity Commission. These cases should be dealt with on an individual basis or in a class-action suit where evidence exists to support one. Those who sense discrimination should be required to prove it. It shouldn't be assumed that because a given workplace has more people of race x than race y, discrimination must exist.

A Vision of the Future

43 In the end, it comes down to what Americans envision for our future together: either an open society, in which everyone is equally respected (an elusive goal but perhaps closer at hand than we realize), or an even more racialized nation, in which "people of color" are arrayed in perpetual conflict with white people. The first possibility is a vision of America as a community in which people work out their differences and make up for past injustices in a peaceful and fair manner; the other is one in which charges of prejudice and discrimination are mixed with real injustices, and in which a frustrated sense of victimhood and entitlement on the one hand is met with guilt and rejection on the other.

44 A good part of what is at stake is all too real: the distribution of assets, income, and power, which reparations, class-based reforms, and the courts should be able to sort out. But don't overlook the importance of symbols, attitudes, and feelings, which can't be changed legislatively. One place to start is with a debate over the official ways in which we classify ourselves and the ways we gather social data, because these classifications and data are used as a mirror in which we see ourselves reflected.

45 Let us begin with a fairly modest request of the powers that be: Give us a chance. Don't make me define my children and myself in racial terms; don't "impute" a race to me or to any of the millions of Americans who feel as I do. Allow us to describe ourselves simply as Americans. I bet my 50 years as a sociologist that we will all be better for it.

QUESTIONS FOR ANALYSIS AND DISCUSSION

1. Why does Etzioni decline to indicate his race? What point does he make by recounting his personal experiences?
2. Do you think the government and other institutions should change the "race" category to "ethnicity"? Should there be no section on race or ethnicity at all? Would this make the process of gathering information easier or more confusing?
3. Is Hispanic a "race"? Why does the government want to know this information? What issues connected to race are unique to this population?
4. What is the "race trap"? Why is it harmful? Explain.
5. What are reparations? What opinion does Etzioni have on reparations? Can they help address issues of race in America? In the world? Why or why not?
6. According to Etzioni, what unique opportunity do we now have to think "beyond race"? How are Hispanics connected to this opportunity? Explain.
7. Etzioni notes that "race" information has a history of causing more harm than good. Discuss as a group the ways that racial information on government forms could be abused. Then, discuss whether the time has come to eliminate this question from forms, no matter what good intentions (such as affirmative action) are behind it.

Reading the Visual

Depictions of Native Americans as Sports Mascots

Chief Wahoo is the official mascot of the Cleveland Indians. The team's history states that its name honors a Native American named Louis Sockalexis, who briefly played for the team when it was known as the Cleveland Spiders. Many Native Americans have disputed this claim, calling it "revisionist history." The image of Chief Wahoo has been bitterly disputed by many Native Americans who consider him a highly racist and unflattering stereotype. The blog entry that follows discusses the use of Native American images as mascots. Are we taking things too seriously, or are we ignoring the dignity of a group of people with excuses that "it's all just for fun."*

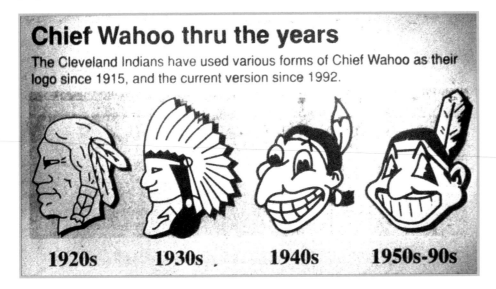

Chief Wahoo thru the years
The Cleveland Indians have used various forms of Chief Wahoo as their logo since 1915, and the current version since 1992.

1920s   **1930s**   **1940s**   **1950s-90s**

1 "Chief Illiniwek" of the University of Illinois will perform for the last time tonight. In fact, as I write this, the student who dances as Chief Illiniwek may have already made history as the last person to do so.

From *YahooSports*:

> The University of Illinois' controversial American Indian mascot was set to perform his last dance, and men who have previously portrayed Chief Illiniwek said they want the tradition to live on in some form.

> The mascot, whose fate was decided by school officials last week, will take center stage at Assembly Hall for one last performance during the men's basketball game between Illinois and Michigan on Wednesday night.

---

*PA Lady, www.palady.wordpress.com, February 22, 2007.

Removing the chief frees the university of NCAA sanctions after the organization deemed Illiniwek—portrayed by buckskin-clad students who dance at home football and basketball games and other athletic events—an offensive use of American Indian imagery and barred the school from hosting postseason athletic events.

2 I applaud the decision of the University of Illinois to comply with NCAA regulations and join the 21st century in ending the use of a stereotype. Now, it's past time for state and regional high school sports leagues to follow the NCAA's lead and mandate an end to "an offensive use of American Indian imagery."

3 My daughter's school calls itself, no kidding, the Redskins.

4 I have a lot of problems with this, and have since we first moved here. Let me give you a few examples of what I find offensive: 1) in the sports section of their website (which I won't link to, for privacy reasons) there are "cute" little caricatures of Indians in feathered headdress and buckskin leggings holding basketballs, pretending to be swimming, performing a split and holding pompoms, 2) their mascot is a chief in feathered headdress, 3) there's a tepee on the track/football field!

5 For one thing, they've mixed up their tribes. The Plains Indians wore the feathered headdress seen on the mascot, not the Susquehannas and/or the Lenni Lenape (Eastern Delaware Nation) which actually lived in my area. Also, the Native tribes of this area lived in longhouses, not tepees.

6 This is important to note because the school is about to celebrate its quasquicentennial (125 years) and thus, was founded about the time of the Indian wars. Back in the early years of the school, people weren't thinking about ethnic stereotypes, they were busy reading about the Bighorn, Sand Creek and Pine Ridge massacres. (Although, back then, they didn't call them massacres. They were "battles" won or lost by the Army.)

7 Second, the administrators, boosters, players, etc., don't seem to understand that the word "Redskin" is an ethnic slur. One of the most offensive phrases used by this school— and its faculty, students, and alumni—is: "Redskin Pride." Literally, this phrase makes me gag.

8 Let's be honest. This is a small school district, 95% or so white. There's little native ancestry here, if only because their ancestors wiped out the native populations with their diseases and their wars. These people have a misguided sense of pride if they can use the word "Redskin" as if it were some type of positive attribute—one to which they have no claim.

9 Over the summer, my mom got into a bit of a verbal tiff with a booster who had the utter audacity to say they weren't demeaning anyone. It was, she said, a way of "honoring" the Native peoples.

10 Huh?

11 How utterly stupid. As a person of Native ancestry, I don't feel "honored." I feel insulted. My Native ancestors were not "Redskins." Those ancestors were of the Bear Clan of the People of the Standing Stone (Oneida Nation) of the Six Nations of the Iroquois.

12 The Six Nations' Articles of Confederacy—creating the oldest known participatory democracy—later inspired the framing of the Constitution of the United States. In fact, the Six Nations' confederation was considered so important to the writing, a delegation of Iroquois were asked to meet with the Continental Congress, and John Hancock was given an Iroquois name: Karanduawn, or the Great Tree.

13   Do you think those whose ancestors were slaves, would feel "honored" if the team was called the "Niggers"? Do you think anyone of Jewish ancestry would feel "honored" if the team was called the "Kikes"? Do you think any of the multitudes in this district who came from Irish and Italian immigrants would feel "honored" if the team was the "Micks" or the "Wops"?

14   Of course not!

15   Those are all derogatory words used to debase another race or belief or ethnic background, and are recognized as such by nearly every sentient being in this country. There is no such recognition for the constant slurs against Native peoples used by sports teams across the nation, professional or otherwise.

16   Let's put it this way, for those still so blind that they continue defending the use of "Redskins" for their high school teams: Would you feel comfortable calling anyone a "Redskin" while you were busy dumping money in a slot machine at a Native-run casino?

17   Ooh! I saw that! Made you a bit uncomfortable, eh? It's one thing to yell "Go Redskins" at a football game, and quite another to actually use it in a place where the owners are "Redskins."

18   It's past time for all sports teams to replace names and mascots which represent "an offensive use of American-Indian imagery."

QUESTIONS FOR ANALYSIS AND DISCUSSION

1. What is the blogger's position on the use of Native Americans as school or sports mascots?
2. The blogger notes that in addition to the stereotypes we perpetuate visually with Native American mascots, the words we use are equally offensive. How does she support this viewpoint? Do you agree?
3. In what ways could Chief Wahoo (see inset) be considered offensive to Native Americans? What does his name mean? What image does the mascot project?
4. Could other ethnic groups be presented as mascots without incident? Why or why not?
5. In your opinion, can the disagreement over the Cleveland Indians' official mascot be resolved? How would you mediate this controversy?

Why Is the NYPD after Me?
Nicholas Peart

Racial profiling relies a great deal on stereotyping—generalized assumptions about groups of people based on characteristics such as race, ethnic origin, social class, religion, gender, or physical appearance. Advocates for racial profiling cite its usefulness in law enforcement, but they often ignore how it marginalizes some groups and even persecutes them because of their ethnic background. The practice of racial profiling has created a sense of social and political distrust, to the extent that some parents give their children the "walking while black" warning, a version of which student Nicholas Peart recounts next. What happens to the social contract when you cannot trust the institutions that profess to uphold the law? What if you are considered guilty of a crime before you even know the charges? In this next essay, Nicholas Peart describes what it means to grow up afraid of the police in a society that stereotypes you as trouble solely because you are young, male, and black.*

BEFORE YOU READ

Have you ever been stopped by the police for any reason? What was the experience like? If not, what would you expect to happen, and how do you think you would react? Explain.

AS YOU READ

What assumptions do you have regarding our legal system? Do you believe that you will be treated fairly? That you are innocent until proven guilty? As you read Peart's essay describing the many times he has been detained by police, consider how your assumptions match his experience. What role, if any, does race play in your personal assumptions of police conduct?

1   When I was 14, my mother told me not to panic if a police officer stopped me. And she cautioned me to carry ID and never run away from the police or I could be shot. In the nine years since my mother gave me this advice, I have had numerous occasions to consider her wisdom.

2   One evening in August of 2006, I was celebrating my 18th birthday with my cousin and a friend. We were staying at my sister's house on 96th Street and Amsterdam Avenue in Manhattan and decided to walk to a nearby place and get some burgers. It was closed so we sat on benches in the median strip that runs down the middle of Broadway. We were talking, watching the night go by, enjoying the evening when suddenly, and out of

*Nicholas K. Peart, *New York Times*, December 17, 2011.

nowhere, squad cars surrounded us. A policeman yelled from the window, "Get on the ground!"

3   I was stunned. And I was scared. Then I was on the ground—with a gun pointed at me. I couldn't see what was happening but I could feel a policeman's hand reach into my pocket and remove my wallet. Apparently he looked through and found the ID I kept there. "Happy Birthday," he said sarcastically. The officers questioned my cousin and friend, asked what they were doing in town, and then said goodnight and left us on the sidewalk.

4   Less than two years later, in the spring of 2008, N.Y.P.D. officers stopped and frisked me, again. And for no apparent reason. This time I was leaving my grandmother's home in Flatbush, Brooklyn; a squad car passed me as I walked down East 49th Street to the bus stop. The car backed up. Three officers jumped out. Not again. The officers ordered me to stand, hands against a garage door, fished my wallet out of my pocket and looked at my ID. Then they let me go.

5   I was stopped again in September of 2010. This time I was just walking home from the gym. It was the same routine: I was stopped, frisked, searched, ID'd and let go.

6   These experiences changed the way I felt about the police. After the third incident I worried when police cars drove by; I was afraid I would be stopped and searched or that something worse would happen. I dress better if I go downtown. I don't hang out with friends outside my neighborhood in Harlem as much as I used to. Essentially, I incorporated into my daily life the sense that I might find myself up against a wall or on the ground with an officer's gun at my head. For a black man in his 20s like me, it's just a fact of life in New York.

7   Here are a few other facts: last year, the N.Y.P.D. recorded more than 600,000 stops; 84 percent of those stopped were blacks or Latinos. Police are far more likely to use force when stopping blacks or Latinos than whites. In half the stops police cite the vague "furtive movements" as the reason for the stop. Maybe black and brown people just look more furtive, whatever that means. These stops are part of a larger, more wide-spread problem—a racially discriminatory system of stop-and-frisk in the N.Y.P.D. The police use the excuse that they're fighting crime to continue the practice, but no one has ever actually proved that it reduces crime or makes the city safer. Those of us who live in the neighborhoods where stop-and-frisks are a basic fact of daily life don't feel safer as a result.

8   We need change. When I was young I thought cops were cool. They had a respectable and honorable job to keep people safe and fight crime. Now, I think their tactics are unfair and they abuse their authority. The police should consider the consequences of a generation of young people who want nothing to do with them—distrust, alienation and more crime.

9   Last May, I was outside my apartment building on my way to the store when two police officers jumped out of an unmarked car and told me to stop and put my hands up against the wall. I complied. Without my permission, they removed my cellphone from my hand, and one of the officers reached into my pockets, and removed my wallet and keys. He looked through my wallet, then handcuffed me. The officers wanted to know if I had just come out of a particular building. No, I told them, I lived next door.

10   One of the officers asked which of the keys they had removed from my pocket opened my apartment door. Then he entered my building and tried to get into my apartment with my key. My 18-year-old sister was inside with two of our younger siblings; later she told me she had no idea why the police were trying to get into our apartment and was terrified. She tried to call me, but because they had confiscated my phone, I couldn't answer.

11   Meanwhile, a white officer put me in the back of the police car. I was still handcuffed. The officer asked if I had any marijuana, and I said no. He removed and searched my shoes and patted down my socks. I asked why they were searching me, and he told me someone in my building complained that a person they believed fit my description had been ringing their bell. After the other officer returned from inside my apartment building, they opened the door to the police car, told me to get out, removed the handcuffs and simply drove off. I was deeply shaken.

12   For young people in my neighborhood, getting stopped and frisked is a rite of passage. We expect the police to jump us at any moment. We know the rules: don't run and don't try to explain, because speaking up for yourself might get you arrested or worse. And we all feel the same way—degraded, harassed, violated and criminalized because we're black or Latino. Have I been stopped more than the average young black person? I don't know, but I look like a zillion other people on the street. And we're all just trying to live our lives.

13   As a teenager, I was quiet and kept to myself. I'm about to graduate from the Borough of Manhattan Community College, and I have a stronger sense of myself after getting involved with the Brotherhood/Sister Sol, a neighborhood organization in Harlem. We educate young people about their rights when they're stopped by the police and how to stay safe in those interactions. I have talked to dozens of young people who have had experiences like mine. And I know firsthand how much it messes with you. Because of them, I'm doing what I can to help change things and am acting as a witness in a lawsuit brought by the Center for Constitutional Rights to stop the police from racially profiling and harassing black and brown people in New York.

14   It feels like an important thing to be part of a community of hundreds of thousands of people who are wrongfully stopped on their way to work, school, church or shopping, and are patted down or worse by the police though they carry no weapon; and searched for no reason other than the color of their skin. I hope police practices will change and that when I have children I won't need to pass along my mother's advice.

QUESTIONS FOR ANALYSIS AND CONSIDERATION ─────────────

1. How do you feel after reading this essay? Are there particular points in Peart's narrative that seem more powerful than others? Do you find yourself becoming emotionally involved with his narrative? Explain.

2. Peart notes that at one point, the police tried to use his key to gain access to his apartment. Is this legal? Does it surprise you? Explain.

3. How is Peart trying to change police behavior toward "blacks and browns" in New York City?

4. Peart believes that he was unfairly judged by the officers involved in multiple detainments based on the color of his skin. What does he feel was most violated by his experiences? How does he appeal to his readers to share his sense of injustice? Explain.

5. Nancy E. Gist, director of the Bureau of Justice Assistance at the U.S. Department of Justice, said, "The guarantee to all persons of equal protection under the law is one of the most fundamental principles of our democratic society. Law enforcement officers should not endorse or act upon stereotypes, attitudes, or beliefs that a person's race, ethnicity, or national origin increases that person's general propensity to act unlawfully. There is no tradeoff between effective law enforcement and protection of the civil rights of all Americans; we can and must have both." Do you agree with her statement that there can be no "tradeoff" between civil protection and civil rights? Can we indeed have both? Why or why not? How do you think Peart would respond to her directive? What about the NYPD?

Arizona's Immigration Law Is Not Racist

Bruce Maiman

Most of us carry a college ID and our license or state ID card. But can you imagine having to carry proof that you are a U.S. citizen everywhere you go? This is the challenge that some people in Arizona are making against Arizona's "Support Our Law Enforcement and Safe Neighborhoods Act," an anti-illegal immigration measure. The 2010 law hinges on the U.S. federal law that requires all aliens over the age of 14 in the United States to register with the U.S. government, and to have registration documents in their possession at all times. The Arizona Act made it a state (in addition to federal) misdemeanor for an alien to be in Arizona without carrying the required documents. State law enforcement officers are allowed to attempt to determine an individual's immigration status during a "lawful stop, detention or arrest" when there is reasonable suspicion that the individual is an illegal immigrant. Critics of the legislation say it encourages racial profiling. While there have been many protests against the law, national polls indicate that the law has majority support in Arizona and in other areas of the United States. Other states have considered adopting similar legislation. In June 2012, the U.S. Supreme Court in *Arizona v. United States* upheld the provision requiring immigration status checks during law enforcement stops. Is the law inherently racist? Or is it an effective step in identifying and reducing the number of illegal immigrants? In this editorial, written before the law was amended in 2012, Bruce Maiman asserts that the law does not encourage racial profiling, because it targets illegal immigrants.*

BEFORE YOU READ

In what ways are issues of race and immigration connected? Does society overall seem to value some immigrants less than others? Is this value system connected to race? Other factors? Explain.

AS YOU READ

Even before the Arizona law was adopted, critics challenged its inherent racism. Why do they feel the law is racist? Does the law target illegal aliens, or illegal aliens of a certain ethnicity? Explain.

1   Since Arizona passed its controversial new immigration bill, it's been nearly impossible to avoid charges by its opponents that the law is racist.

2   It's not racist.

3   That belief that it is racist is born out of what has become that law's most controversial of its several provisions: It gives police the power to question anyone they suspect might be in the country illegally. Immigrants' rights groups say that's racial profiling.

---

*Bruce Maiman, *Populist Examiner*, April 27, 2010.

4   It's a bit irritating to hear that allegation. What do you mean it's profiling? They haven't started enforcing anything yet. Plenty of people in Arizona from the governor on down have made clear there will be no profiling nor will profiling be tolerated; it's against the law in Arizona, just as it was before the current immigration law was passed and just as it will continue to be illegal afterwards.

5   To be racist, the law would have to specifically target one particular race of people. The law would have to specifically say that it is the intention of the legislature of Arizona for police to harass anyone of Latino heritage or brown skin.

6   That's not what the law says. The law is directed at illegal immigrants. It's only by dint of geographic circumstance that almost 100 percent of the illegal immigrants in Arizona come from Mexico.

7   If illegals in Arizona were Swedish or Mongolian, the law would apply to them.

8   Why is this so hard to comprehend: Arizona is a border state with Mexico. It's heavily impacted by illegal immigration. There are nearly half a million illegal immigrants in a state with a relatively small population. They cause a problem for Arizona and Arizona wants to do something about that. I don't see anything in that line of reasoning that is racist. All of those things are legitimate concerns, are they not?

9   Could the law be abused? Of course it could. Any law can be abused. There's a possibility of abuse with every single law we've ever passed.

10   We act as if this law has some special quality about it that invites more abuse than some other law. Any law can be abused and any law enforcement officer can act like a jerk—or worse.

11   If a peace officer, in enforcing this law, indulges in clear racial profiling, violates the Fourth Amendment or goes beyond the intent or language of this law—they have to be disciplined, and if need be, prosecuted. That's not the law being racist but someone carrying out the law being racist by abusing it. It should go without saying that we have to be vigilant to insure the law isn't abused. Our legal system provides abundant recourse in which to conduct such vigilance. We can certainly be more vigilant about any abuse of immigration law than we've been about enforcing the immigration laws currently on the books—not that this would be saying much; we've done almost nothing to enforce the immigration laws currently on the books in this country.

12   In fact, one of the reasons the Arizona legislature is trying to muscle its way out of its immigration problems on its own is because the federal government has dragged its feet on the matter of illegal immigration—so much so that it ignores cotton-headed sanctuary city policies in municipalities all across the country. These are policies that make no secret about their sanctuary laws, which tell their police departments not to enforce the federal immigration laws. Yet, the feds do nothing. That's part of what Arizona is reacting to.

13   Since 1986 when Congress passed the Simpson-Mazzoli Act, the federal government has failed in its responsibility to enforce its own law—looking the other way when employers knowingly hired illegals and treated them shabbily; knowingly looking the other way when the border was being compromised because it provided cheap labor.

14   So it's understandable why Arizona has reacted the way it has.

15   Arizona will have to police this law carefully to ensure that it is not abused, but it is not a racist law. Nor is the act of passing it a racist act. No one can bear the intellectual responsibility of that argument because that's not what the intent of the Arizona

legislature was and that's quite clear. It is an immigration bill, not a brown people bill or a Mexican bill.

16   Suggesting any intent of racial profiling isn't even in consonance with Arizona law enforcement groups which largely opposed the measure. They didn't want to be burdened with such an option, perhaps knowing full well that mistakes might be made, misunderstandings would occur and lawsuits would result. In other words, the police already were reticent about the law. Now that it's passed, they're even more likely to tread carefully.

17   Police officers in Arizona already have enough to do. They're not going to be out there looking for mothers taking their kids to school or motorists minding their business on the way to work.

18   In the normal course of their day, they'll keep a weather eye out for specific red flags—a van packed with individuals that has telltale signs of a coyote situation; a motorist pulled over for running a stop sign who speaks no English, seems to have no license, doesn't seem to comprehend what's going on—that might be a tip off that someone is illegal.

19   But it's not like the police of Arizona have so much free time on their hands they're going to hassle citizens just for driving down the street.

20   To be sure, there will be instances of abuse and there will be bogus allegations of racism by someone who may not have liked that he got stopped because he had a busted tail light. But that has nothing to do with the intention of the law; it has to do with the actions of the individual. To say the law is racist is just inconsistent with both facts and intention. And it's unfair to Arizonans. It imputes to the state of Arizona some sort of mean-spiritedness. That's why some are now calling for economic boycotts of Arizona. The mayor of Phoenix plans to file a lawsuit against the state to block the law.

21   All Arizona is guilty of here is trying to deal with problems within its border, and trying to do so in a country in which the federal government has totally abandoned its responsibility to deal effectively with the subject of illegal immigration.

22   If you can show how this law is racist, or how the legislature of Arizona is racist, or how the people of Arizona are racist because they want to do something about the nearly half-million illegal immigrants in their state, which is costing them money and has caused crime to increase significantly—if you can explain how that gets to be racist, I'm fascinated to hear your logic.

QUESTIONS FOR ANALYSIS AND DISCUSSION

1. Maiman argues that the Arizona law is directed at illegal immigrants, not people of a particular race. Who are the illegal immigrants in Arizona? If most of them are of a particular background, could the law indeed be racist? Why or why not? Refer to points Maiman raises in his editorial.

2. According to the author, what percentage of illegal immigrants in Arizona come from Mexico? Why is this an important consideration in considering the debate over the Arizona law?

3. What "specific red flags" does Maiman believe the police will use to identify illegal immigrants?

4. Maiman points out that if most illegals in Arizona were Swedish or Mongolian, then that would be the group of people most affected by the Arizona law. Respond to this statement with your own viewpoint.

5. In his final paragraph, Maiman says, "If you can show how this law is racist, or how the legislature of Arizona is racist, or how the people of Arizona are racist because they want to do something about the nearly half-million illegal immigrants in their state, which is costing them money and has caused crime to increase significantly, I'm fascinated to hear your logic." Respond to his challenge by either providing a logical argument against the Arizona law (on the grounds that it is racist) or reinforce his argument (on the grounds that it is not).

Welcome to the Dollhouse

Francie Latour

For generations of little girls, Barbie has been a toy both loved and loathed. Most often criticized are Barbie's ridiculous proportions. Still others lament Barbie's lack of varied ethnicity. The release of three new "So-In-Style" African American Barbie dolls was heralded as progress by the toy industry. But many African-American women wondered why Barbie must still have the long flowing tresses sported by all three new dolls. In this essay, journalist Francie Latour challenges that this is not an issue for the toy industry to address, but one for the African-American community as a whole. As the mother of a young daughter, she notes, "It's easy to fill the blogosphere with Barbie commentary, and much more difficult to confront the messages we hand down ourselves. When we complain about how tough our daughters' hair is to comb . . . when we drag them to the swivel chair before they are ready, we tell them how important it is to try to be something besides who they are. Those messages predate Barbie."*

BEFORE YOU READ

Consider our ideal standard of beauty. What is ideal? Is it a westernized image? A multicultural one? Which images of beauty are promoted by the media? How can these images reflect back issues of race?

AS YOU READ

Latour observes that Mattel's new dolls have the hair many African-American women aspire to achieve through long hours at the beauty salon. What position does Latour take on this issue? Does she feel that Mattel is selling out to the status quo? Why or why not?

1   In every black family, there are two kinds of daughters: daughters who have good hair and daughters who don't. For much of my childhood, knowing this was as painful as raking a comb through my own locks, whose strands fell into the "don't" category: stubbornly short, easily broken, at war with the detanglers designed to tame them. And, like most black hair in its natural state, densely coiled and woolly. In the words of my aunties: coarse, bushy, difficult. In the words of history: nappy, picaninny, slave-girl.

2   It's no coincidence that the first black American self-made millionaire, Madame C. J. Walker, made her money turning that kind of hair into straight, shiny, behaving hair. That was 100 years ago, and black women everywhere have been on the same, self-denying quest ever since. Years ago, a cousin of mine perfectly articulated the power of hair over the psyches of black girls. When I told her about a new college boyfriend, who was white,

---

*Francie Latour, *Boston Globe Magazine*, October 25, 2009.

she said, "You're so lucky. If you stay together and get married one day, your daughters will have the best hair." I acted shocked, but I was intimately familiar with the longing and loathing that prompted those words.

3   Now I'm a mother of three with a 2-year-old daughter of my own. (Yes, she's biracial and has smooth curls, but I swear that's a coincidence.) When it comes to cultural clashes over girls, beauty, blackness, and hair, I worry and pay attention. The latest controversy? The arrival of the new "So In Style" Barbie dolls, brought to you by Mattel. Created by an African-American mom and launched in stores last month, Grace, Kara, and Trichelle are black, and they're the new BFFs in Barbie-land. Like their fair-skinned friends, they have long, silky hair that is either bone-straight or loosely wavy.

4   Don't answer yet, there's more. To keep Barbie's new friends in style, Mattel offers a hair-straightening kit, with which girls can fantasize about a ritual of black womanhood most of us would gladly avoid if we could: regular, two-hour sessions at the hair salon to have our woolly manes straightened with harsh chemical straighteners. When that news hit the blogosphere, black mothers, scholars, and childhood experts everywhere got loud, many of them condemning Mattel for reinforcing white standards of beauty. Can't Barbie rock braids or an Afro just once? they cried. The controversy erupted up just as "Good Hair," comedian Chris Rock's new documentary about America's $9 billion black beauty industry, hit theaters.

5   For those of you unfamiliar with the complexities of black hair care, straightening is a process in which a stylist sections your hair and applies a cream that starts out cool but becomes unbearably hot. The cream contains sodium hydroxide, commonly found in drain and oven cleaners, and so corrosive that stylists have to use rubber gloves. When you absolutely can't stand the heat anymore, the stylist rinses it out. Straight hair, and sometimes scabs, result. The longer the cream stays in, the more you burn, but the straighter your hair gets; walk into a black salon and the most common thing you'll see is a woman gripping the armrests of a chair to manage her pain. In other words, hair-straightening is no ride in Ken's convertible or trip to your dreamhouse closet. (I'm not sure if Mattel was giving an ironic wink to the sisters out there, but like the real version of hair-straightening, "So In Style" hair kits are also wildly overpriced, costing more than a pair of the actual dolls.)

6   On the one hand, it seems that Mattel has finally awoken to the Sasha-and-Malia demographic of middle- and upper-class black America: The girls of "So In Style" have wider noses, fuller lips, and a spectrum of realistic skin tones. But one look at these dolls suggests that even in our so-called post-racial world, there are some places America's culture-makers still aren't willing to go. Among them, apparently, is the hair black girls are born with.

7   But is it really fair to expect a toy conglomerate to be at the vanguard of ideas about race and beauty? For that, we would presumably look to real black women leaders. And when we look up to them, what we find is more straight hair. Actually, straight hair with blinding sheen and cascading, otherworldly flow. Beyonce, Tyra, and Oprah all have it. Ditto for black women leaders in politics and business.

8   These are not dolls; these are the living, breathing role models of black America. But they all understand that straight hair is the key to unlocking mainstream success. It's the unspoken, elephant-in-the-room euphemism that remains as true today as it was during slavery: Straight hair is "good hair" because straight hair is white hair. And when blacks

were slaves, straight hair could literally mean survival: Slaves who looked less African were treated better, often lifted from the fields to housework, which meant food, warmth, and maybe even education. Over time, straight hair became synonymous with nonthreatening hair. And that is the black Barbie formula Mattel has counted on going way back.

9   Mattel birthed the Barbie doll in 1959, a period when the notion of a black friend, real or pretend, was unthinkable for many white Americans. It was the same year a white journalist named John Howard Griffin took extreme measures to darken his skin and write about his travels through the deep South passing as a black man. The stories of the intense hatred he experienced were eventually published in the landmark book *Black Like Me*. It's safe to say that when an entire race is struggling for recognition as human beings, nobody quibbles over whether a toy reflects their daughters' self-image.

10   I recently learned, to my amazement, that the first-ever brown-skinned Barbie Mattel dared to put on shelves bears my name. "Colored Francie" made a short-lived appearance in 1967, her dark-ish complexion painted onto a doll with the same features as her white counterpart, including a glistening mane of straight hair. Other versions came later, including the defining "Christie" in 1968 and the nameless "Black Barbie" in 1980. In 1997, Mattel took a turn that left some blacks outraged and others speechless when it teamed up with Nabisco to launch "Oreo Fun Barbie." The African-American version (also short-lived, it turns out) was strangely blue-black, which I'll chalk up to an effort to coordinate with the cookie's electric-blue packaging.

11   When "Black Barbie" arrived on the scene in 1980, I was 9, well within Mattel's target audience. But I never owned her or any other Barbie. I think it had something to do with the dolls I saw at my friends' houses. Whether the dolls were white or any other color, I got a creepy, not so-stylish feeling: Barbie wasn't black like me, or any other black girl or woman I knew. The makers of Grace, Kara, and Trichelle say the new dolls give black girls a truer mirror of themselves. But when I look at them, all these years later, that same feeling comes over me.

12   Here's what I remember about the black girls I knew: They had Mickey Mouse afro puffs tied in giant gumball barrettes or tight cornrow braids, or hair that was bound by nothing at all. For a little while, they had no idea what the word "nappy" meant, until one day they knew exactly what it meant. The black girls I knew marked their entry into womanhood reluctantly, with a first trip to the hair salon that often lived up to their worst fears. Caught in an in-between time when they were too old to sit for their mothers and too young to know what to do themselves, they climbed into swivel chairs and waited for the smell and then the feeling of chemicals that seared their scalps, leaving clumps of hair and Afro-puff innocence to be swept from the salon floor. As time goes on and products improve, many make peace with their unnatural states. Others find their way back to the beginning with locked, coiffed, or otherwise regal crowns. What I call Toni Morrison hair.

13   I haven't heard of anything in the works for a Toni Morrison doll. But I'm not waiting for one, either. Because here's the thing about black girls and hair: Dolls and straightening kits can scar, but so can people. And we do. It's easy to fill the blogosphere with Barbie commentary, and much more difficult to confront the messages we hand down ourselves. When we complain about how tough our daughters' hair is to comb, when we run our fingers through their cousins' smooth tresses and smile, when we drag them to the swivel chair before they are ready, we tell them how important it is to try to be something besides

who they are. Those messages predate Barbie. They were shaped by blacks' need to survive in a white world, but how the messages began matters less than taking responsibility for them now.

14   I still straighten my hair, although I often wet it and let it dry naturally, making it weirdly wavy. For a long time, I believed that while straightening didn't make my hair "good," it made it better. Then one day, a boyfriend (and now husband) perfectly articulated something that was totally new. He described a stray coil of my hair as "helicoptering" across his computer keyboard. I thought: My hair helicopters. My hair helicopters. And it occurred to me that a word of poetry could rewrite painful history. Straight hair may make black women more acceptable in the workplace or the White House. But straight hair can't helicopter.

15   Was I magically healed? Did I go off to my happily-ever-after dreamhouse, never to question my hair (or beauty) again? Well, no. That's for fairy tales. But for several moments, then and afterward, I felt detangled. It was the kind of hair balm you can't get from a bottle.

QUESTIONS FOR ANALYSIS AND DISCUSSION

1. What words does Latour use to describe her own hair? How do these words connect to issues of race and ethnicity in the past, and today?
2. Latour notes that the new Barbie dolls have a deeper meaning in the ways we identify ourselves by race and the ways we think of race within our own communities. How important is race to your own sense of identity? In your opinion, on what criteria do the people you meet judge you? What do you want them to judge you by? By what criteria do you judge yourself?
3. What observations does Latour make about role models for young black America? For young girls? Explain.
4. Latour states "straight hair is 'good hair' because straight hair is white hair." Respond to her assertion with your own viewpoint. Is this a cultural truth, or is it an opinion? Explain.
5. How does Latour's description of her childhood and her feelings about her own hair connect to her argument? What does she hope to change by sharing her memories?

Is He One of Us? Reflections on Identity and Authenticity

Glenn Loury

College is a place where many students begin to grapple with issues of diversity, identity, and the development of one's place in the world. It provides a safe haven where students may consider tough issues. In September 2008, Glenn C. Loury, the Merton P. Stoltz Professor of the Social Sciences at Brown University, addressed the 2,186 new undergraduate, graduate, and medical students during the university's 245th Opening Convocation. Loury encourages students to embrace diversity, while also being mindful of the pitfalls of focusing too much on one's identity and the identity of others. The text of Loury's opening convocation address follows.*

BEFORE YOU READ

Consider your own concept of identity. Who "are" you? In your response, include, if it applies, considerations of race, religion, gender, sexual orientation, ethnicity, political stance, social influence, geography, and intellectual viewpoint.

AS YOU READ

Loury observes, "I have often experienced this dissonance between my self-concept and the socially imputed definition of who I am supposed to be. Many of you, I dare say most, will in one way or another have to confront a similar dilemma." Have you experienced a moment in which your concept of self-identity was challenged, either by others or by your personal experience while at school? Explain.

1   We are all familiar with what I'll call the "identity" reflex—we can all hear the call of some tribe or another. We humans are a variegated lot—differing by race, ethnicity, cultural heritage, religion, political or sexual orientation . . . This is, of course, as it should be. Diversity is a good thing.

2   Still, I am here to tell you that there are times when the "call of the tribe" just might be a siren's call, and when an excessive focus on "identity" just might lead one badly astray. What is more, I firmly believe that this brief sojourn upon which you are embarking as you begin your college careers is just such a time.

3   This, in any event, is the theme I wish to take up here at this Convocation welcoming the Class of 2012, and inaugurating another year of our labors at this great university where you are privileged to study, and where I am blessed to teach.

---

*Glenn Loury, speech, as appears reprinted in *Today at Brown*, September 3, 2008.

4   What is more, as our nation enters the final phase of what by all accounts is a most extraordinary national political campaign, one in which questions of identity have played a huge role, I believe it is important, in a gentle and non-partisan sort of way, to at least raise (if not, in fifteen minutes, to answer!) the question of what role "identity" ought to play in our politics, and in our lives. I want to get us thinking and talking about it. Certainly Rory Stewart's wonderful book, *The Places in Between*, which you all read as part of your preparation for your first year of study here, got me to thinking about it.

5   It is altogether fitting that I raise this question before this audience, as you begin your journey of exploration and discovery—because identity politics has become such a commonplace on our nation's campuses, and in our public life.

6   Now, I must warn you at the outset. I tend to be somewhat curmudgeonly about these matters. (My son Nehemiah, who is in the audience today, can surely vouch for that.) For instance, I hold to the high-minded view that one comes to the university to learn how to think, to gain an awareness of the central questions with which reflective people have struggled over the centuries, and to develop an appreciation for how elusive the answers to such questions can be. That is to say, the university is not the place to come if one expects to be confirmed in one's preconceptions, or comforted and reaffirmed in one's reflexive choices. On the contrary, it is a place to be challenged, to be argued with, and to be confronted with the coherent articulation of ways of looking at the world that are different from one's own.

7   So, let me proceed by telling you a story—one that might help to explain how I became such a curmudgeon on this issue.

8   I grew up on the South Side of Chicago in the 1950s and the 1960s. A formative experience for me occurred during one of those earnest political rallies so typical of the period. Woody, who had been my best friend since boyhood, suggested that we attend. The rally was called by the Black Panther Party to galvanize our community's response to the killing by the Chicago police of party activists Fred Hampton and Mark Clark during an early-morning raid on their apartment in one of the city's many all-black neighborhoods. I can remember even now how agitated about it we all were. And, judging by his demeanor, Woody was amongst the most zealous.

9   Despite this zeal, it took real courage for Woody to attend that meeting. For, although he proclaimed his blackness often, and though he had descended from Negro grandparents on either side of his family, he nevertheless looked to the entire world like your typical white guy. Everyone, on first meeting him, assumed as much. I did, too, when we began to play together a decade earlier, just after I had moved into the middle-class neighborhood called Park Manor where Woody's family had been living for some time. There were a number of white families on our block when we first arrived; within a couple of years they had all been replaced by aspiring black families like our own. Yet, Woody's parents never moved, which puzzled me. Then one day I overheard his mother declare to one of her new neighbors, "We just wouldn't run from our own kind." Somewhat later, while watching the film *Imitation of Life* on TV, my mother explained how someone could be "black" even though they looked "white." She told me about people like that in our own family—second cousins who lived in a fashionable suburb and on whom one would never dare simply to drop in because they were "passing for white." This was my earliest glimpse of the truth that racial identity in America is inherently a social and

cultural, not simply a biological construct—that it necessarily involves an irreducible element of choice.

10   Evidently, Woody's family had been "passing for white" in pre-integration Park Manor. The neighborhood's changing racial composition had confronted them with a moment of truth, and had led them to elect to stay, instead of fleeing as nearly all of their previous neighbors had done, and to raise their children among "their own kind." This was a fateful decision for Woody, who, as he matured, became determined not simply to live among blacks but, perhaps in atonement for what he took to be his parents' sins, unambiguously to become black. The boys in the neighborhood didn't make this easy. Many delighted in teasing him about being a "white boy," and most simply refused to credit his insistent, often repeated claim: "I'm a brother, too!"

11   The fact that some of his relatives were passing made Woody's racial identity claims more urgent for him, but less compelling to others. He desperately wanted to be black, but his peers in the neighborhood would not let him. Because he had the option to be white—an option he radically rejected at the time—those without the option could not accept his claim to a shared racial experience. I knew Woody well. We became good friends, and I wanted to accept him on his own terms. But even I found myself doubting, from time to time, that he fully grasped the pain, frustration, anger, and self-doubt many of us felt upon encountering the intractability of American racism. However much he sympathized with our plight, he seemed to experience it only vicariously.

12   So there we were, at this boisterous, angry political rally. A critical moment came when Woody, seized by some idea, enthusiastically raised his voice above the murmur to be heard. He was cut short in mid-sentence by one of the dashiki-clad brothers-in-charge who demanded to know how a "white boy" got the authority to have an opinion on what black people should be doing. A silence fell over the room. "Who can vouch for this 'white boy,'" asked the "brother," indignantly. More excruciating silence ensued. Now was my moment of truth; Woody turned plaintively toward me, but I would not meet his eyes. To my eternal shame, I failed to speak up for my friend, and he was forced to leave the meeting without a word having been uttered in his defense.

13   That was not exactly a profile in courage on my part, I must confess!

14   This incident of some forty years ago is etched indelibly in my mind, serving as a kind of private metaphor for me, underscoring just how difficult it can be to live in good faith, and how vitally important it is to try. That moment of truth, in that South Side church basement and my failure in the face of it helped me become aware of the depth of my need for the approval of others—particularly co-racialists. The fact is that I willingly betrayed someone whom I loved and who loved me, in order to lessen the risk of being rejected by strangers. In a way, at that moment and often again later in my life, I was "passing" too—that is, hoping to be mistaken for something I was not. I had feared that to proclaim before the radicals in the audience that this supposed "white boy" at my side was in fact our "brother" would have compromised my own chance of being received among them as a genuine colleague. The indignant "brother" who challenged Woody's right to speak was not merely imposing a racial test (only blacks are welcome here), he was mainly applying a loyalty test (you are either with us or against us), and this was a test which anyone present could fail through a lack of conformity with the collectively enforced political norm. I now know that denying one's genuine convictions for the sake

of social acceptance is a price which society often demands of the individual, and all too often this is a price that we are willing to pay.

15   I recall this story about Woody because I think his dilemma (and mine) conveys an important truth about "race" and "identity" in American society—a truth which has wide application outside the bounds of my personal experience. What made Woody's situation so difficult is the fact that, given the expectations and stereotypes held by others, there seemed to be no way for him to avoid living fraudulently—either as a "black" person who was passing for "white," or as a "white" person trying (too hard) to be "black." Actually, it now seems clear to me, he was neither. Woody, like me and like all of us, was a human being trying to make his way in the world, struggling to find himself and seeking recognition on his own terms. As his close friend and frequent companion I had become familiar with, and occasionally shared in, the pitfalls of his situation. People would assume when seeing us together both that he was a white guy and that I was "the kind of Negro who hangs-out with white guys." I resented that assumption.

16   Since then, as an intellectual of African descent, making my living as a teacher and writer during a period of great transformation in our society, I have often experienced this dissonance between my self-concept and the socially imputed definition of who I am supposed to be. Many of you, I dare say most, will in one way or another have to confront a similar dilemma. I have had to face the problem of balancing my desire not to disappoint the expectations of others with a conviction that one must strive to live authentically. This does not make me a heroic figure; I eschew the libertarian ideologue's rhetoric about some glorious individual who, though put-upon by society, nevertheless blazes his own path. I acknowledge that this opposition I am positing between individual and society is ambiguous, in view of the fact that the self is inevitably shaped by the objective world, and by other selves. I know that what one is being faithful to when resisting the temptation to conform to others' expectations by "living authentically" is necessarily a socially determined, if subjectively experienced, version of the self.

17   In his justly famous essay, *On Liberty*, John Stuart Mill offers a radical, passionate defense of the norm of unencumbered public discussion. I urge you, if you have not done so already, to acquaint yourselves with Mill's argument, which holds that individual persons must be allowed to express themselves freely no matter what consequences for society may ensue. Quoting Mill:

18   "Society can and does execute its own mandates, and if it issues wrong mandates instead of right, or any mandates at all in things with which it ought not to meddle, it practices a social tyranny more formidable than many kinds of political oppression, since, though not usually upheld by such extreme penalties, it leaves fewer means of escape, penetrating more deeply into the details of life, and enslaving the soul itself. Protection, therefore, against the tyranny of the magistrate is not enough. We need protection also against the tyranny of the prevailing opinion and feeling, against the tendency of society to impose, by other means than civil penalties, its own ideas and practices as rules of conduct on those who dissent from them."

19   Growing into intellectual maturity has been, for me, largely a process of becoming free of the need to have my choices validated by "the brothers." After many years I have come to understand that until I became willing to risk the derision of the crowd, I had no chance to discover the most important truths about myself or about life—to know my

"calling," to perceive my deepest value commitments and to recognize the goals which I think are most worth striving toward. In a perverse extension of the lesson from *Imitation of Life*, I have learned that one does not have to live surreptitiously as a Negro passing for white in order to deny one's genuine self for the sake of social acceptance. You members of the class of 2012 must not let this happen to you.

20   The most important challenges and opportunities which confront us derive not from our cultural or sexual identities, not from our ethnic or racial conditions, but rather from our human condition. Speaking for myself, I am a husband, a father, a son, a teacher, an intellectual, a citizen. In none of these roles is my race irrelevant, but neither can "identity" alone provide much guidance for my quest to adequately discharge these responsibilities. The particular features of one's social condition, the external givens, merely set the stage of one's life. They do not provide a script. That script must be internally generated; it must be a product of a reflective deliberation about the meaning of this existence for which no political or ethnic program could ever substitute. That is what you have come to the University to learn how to do.

21   Or, to shift the metaphor slightly, the socially contingent features of one's situation— one's racial heritage, family background, or sexual orientation, for instance—and the prevailing views and attitudes about such identity tropes of other people in society—these things are the building blocks, the raw materials, out of which an individual must yet construct the edifice of a life. The authentic expression of a person's individuality is to be found in the blueprint that he or she employs to guide that project of self-authorship. And, the problem of devising such a plan for one's life is a universal problem which confronts all people, whatever their race, class, ethnicity, or other identifying category. By facing and solving this problem we grow as human beings, and we give meaning and substance to our lives. In my view, a personal program wholly dependent on the contingency of identity falls tragically short of its potential, because it embraces too parochial a conception of what is possible and of what is desirable.

22   This is an especially important consideration for those of us who belong to a historically oppressed and stigmatized group. Ironically, to the extent that we blacks see ourselves primarily through a racial lens, we may end up sacrificing possibilities for the kind of personal development that would ultimately further our collective racial interests. We cannot be truly free men and women while laboring under a definition of self derived from the perceptual view of our oppressor and confined to the contingent facts of our oppression. In *A Portrait of the Artist as a Young Man* James Joyce says this about Irish nationalism:

23   "When the soul of a man is born in this country there are nets flung at it to hold it back from flight. You talk to me of nationality, language, religion. I shall try to fly by these nets. . . . Do you know what Ireland is? . . . Ireland is the old sow that eats her farrow."

24   Wearing one's racial identity too heavily can work similarly to hold back young souls from flight into the open skies of American society—or so, at least, it seems to me. Of course there is the constraint of racism that also holds us back. But the trick, as Joyce knew, is to turn such "nets" into wings, and thus to fly by them. One cannot do that if one refuses to see that ultimately it is neither external constraint nor external opportunity, but rather an in-dwelling spirit, which renders such flight possible.

QUESTIONS FOR ANALYSIS AND DISCUSSION

1. What is the "identity" index to which Loury refers? Explain in your own words.

2. Loury references a political campaign at a pivotal moment in the nation's history. To what campaign does he refer? What role did race and identity play in this campaign?

3. Loury tells the story of Woody, a young man from his childhood. He notes that the story "conveys an important truth about 'race' and 'identity' in American society." What did the experience reveal to Loury about himself? About Woody and his place in society? Explain.

4. What are "identity politics"? What role do they play in university life? Why can they be fraught with problems? In society at large?

5. The author identifies himself as "a person of African heritage." Why do you think he chooses these words to describe himself?

6. Loury quotes John Stuart Mill, "We need protection also against the tyranny of the prevailing opinion and feeling, against the tendency of society to impose, by other means than civil penalties, its own ideas and practices as rules of conduct on those who dissent from them." How does this passage connect to the points Loury is making in his speech?

7. Evaluate professor Loury's tone in this speech. How does he appeal to his audience? What is he asking them to do? How effective do you think this speech is in encouraging the audience to heed Loury's appeal?

WRITING ASSIGNMENTS

1. Teenagers often complain that they are watched more closely in stores because it is believed they are more likely to be shoplifters. Write an essay in which you consider the validity of other kinds of profiling, such as that based on age, income, or gender. What assumptions of criminal behavior correspond to these groups? If racial profiling is wrong, is it also wrong to profile on the basis of gender or age? Why or why not?

2. What is the government's official position on racial profiling? Visit the U.S. Department of Justice website and read the "Racial Profiling Fact Sheet." What exceptions does the government make concerning racial profiling, and why? Identify any areas of the document that you find questionable or particularly compelling and explain why.

3. Visit the ACLU's website on racial equality at www.aclu.org and review its information on racial profiling. What are the most pressing issues concerning racial profiling today? Select an issue or case described on the ACLU website and research it in greater depth. Write a short essay summarizing the situation or issue and your position on it.

4. Write a letter to the U.S. government suggesting how race should be considered (or not) on documents, censuses, and other forms. Give concrete examples and detailed support for your point of view.

5. Consider the ways in which Hollywood influences our cultural perspectives of race and ethnicity. Write an essay exploring the influence, however slight, that film and television have had on your own perceptions of race and ethnicity. If you wish, interview other students for their opinions on this issue and address some of their points in your essay.

6. Think about the ways in which the social, intellectual, topographical, and religious histories of an ethnic group can influence the creation of stereotypes. Identify some current stereotypes that are active in American culture. What are the origins of these stereotypes? Write an essay in which you dissect these stereotypes and present ways to dispel them.

7. Write an essay discussing your own family's sense of ethnic or racial identity. What are the origins of some of your family's values, practices, and customs? Have these customs met with prejudice by people who did not understand them? Explain.

8. Visit the U.S. Department of Justice website and read the "Racial Profiling Fact Sheet" posted online at www.justice.gov/opa/pr/2003/June/racial_profiling_fact_sheet.pdf. Review the entire fact sheet and discuss it as a group. What is the government's official position on racial profiling? What exceptions does it make concerning racial profiling, and why? Identify any areas of the document that you find questionable or particularly compelling, and share them with the rest of the class as part of a larger class discussion on the issue of racial profiling and the racism that is connected with it.

9. In his convocation address welcoming Brown University's class of 2012, Glen Loury refers to Rory Stewart's book *The Places in Between*, which was given to all incoming students to read. Do you think this book should be distributed to incoming students at your own school? Why or why not? What message about stereotypes and identity does it convey?

CHAPTER

15

Riding the Economic Roller Coaster

Today's college graduates leave school facing some daunting financial challenges—namely, the toughest labor market the nation has witnessed in over 25 years with an unemployment rate close to 8 percent. While some experts no longer fear another Great Depression, an extended period of unemployment and national debt still looms. College tuition rates are at their highest, the housing market awaits "recovery," and the credit crisis threatens to bankrupt the nation. Many people own homes "under water"—that is, what they owe on their mortgages exceeds the actual resale value of their houses. And while college graduates do have an edge—an unemployment rate of 3.8 percent vs. 7.6 percent for same-age people with only high-school diplomas—many carry a debt greater than their less-educated peers.

To Laura Conaway, former editor of the *Village Voice*, the heirs to this financial crisis have been aptly labeled "Generation Debt." Twentysomethings are facing a complicated future as they transition into adulthood. On the one hand, today's graduates point out that student loans, credit card debt, employment instability, lack of affordable health care, and financial irresponsibility have melded into a foreboding landscape that they have unwillingly inherited. On the other hand, their elders may argue that today's youth have come to expect too many handouts, do not know real struggle, and are unwilling to sacrifice. It's a classic generational argument, but statistics point to a disturbing fact—that today's twentysomethings may be the first generation to be less successful than their parents.

What may the financial landscape look like in the next few years? How did it get this bad? This chapter examines the multifaceted dimensions of the economic crisis young adults now face—from the mortgage meltdown to the credit card crunch. Should we just let the financial sector implode upon itself? Does it really help to bail out floundering businesses? Will things get even worse before they get better? One thing is clear: There are no easy answers as we examine the financial crisis many young Americans—indeed, Americans of every age—are facing today.

Generation Debt

Anya Kamenetz

Many young Americans report that they are trapped by low-end jobs with low wages, few opportunities, high taxes, and huge student loans. Many fear that they are facing a lifetime of recycled debt. Sometime over the last 20 years, something happened: The cost of a college education skyrocketed. It became acceptable for students to carry large debt. People stopped expecting to work in one company for their entire career and started hopping around in search of a better deal. Unable to get on solid financial footing, college graduates started putting off marriage plans and moved in back with their parents. In this excerpt from the book with the same title, Anya Kamenetz explores some of the challenges her generation faces in an economic landscape vastly different from that of her parents' only a generation before.*

BEFORE YOU READ

In this essay, Anya Kamenetz observes that young adulthood is emerging as a "new" distinct phase of life, similar to the recognition of childhood and adolescence in centuries before. What are your expectations from this phase of your life? What challenges do you face, and what benefits might you expect? If you are past young adulthood, compare your experience with the trend now emerging. What might average young adulthood look like 20 years from now?

AS YOU READ

Kamenetz describes the typical college student. Summarize the characteristics she cites, and then describe how you and your fellow classmates compare.

1   The simplest definition of a "generation" is those people who pass through a specific stage of life at the same time. We tend to think of human life stages as natural demarcations of growth, like the rings on a tree. Yet social and economic structures also determine the divisions between infancy and old age. Since 1960, when historian Philippe Aries published the book *Centuries of Childhood*, scholars have been writing about how childhood was "discovered" for sentimental and moralistic reasons in eighteenth- and nineteenth-century Europe. Before this historical turning point, infants were often farmed out to indifferent wet nurses, and seven-year-olds herded sheep.

2   Likewise, for most of human history, sexual maturity occurred just a year or two before marriage, and adolescence, as we know it, didn't exist. As Thomas Hine chronicles in *The Rise and Fall of the American Teenager,* when the United States was industrializing in the nineteenth century, people thirteen and up were the backbone of the semiskilled workforce. Teenagers came to America alone as immigrants. They ran weaving machines, dug mines, herded cattle, picked cotton, and fought wars. If they weren't slaves or indentured servants, they contributed their earnings to their families of origin until they got married and started families of their own.

3   American psychologist G. Stanley Hine popularized the term "adolescent" in 1904, as the rise of compulsory schooling and the move away from an agricultural economy began to lengthen the expected period of youthful preparation. It wasn't until the Great Depression, though, that teenagers' economic life assumed the limits it has today. Hine points out that Roosevelt's New Deal was explicitly designed to take jobs away from young people and give them to heads of households. Teenagers were thus compelled to enroll in

---

*Anya Kamenetz, *Generation Debt* (excerpt), 2007.

high school in much larger numbers than ever before. Young people's secondary economic role has persisted ever since. The affluence and restiveness of postwar America gave new cultural prominence in the 1950s to the modern version of teenhood, a distinct stage of life, a subculture, and a commercial market, funded ultimately by parents. The accepted age of independence for the middle class and above was pushed forward to twenty-one.

4   Now the postmillennial years are bringing in an entirely new life stage: "emerging adulthood," a term coined by developmental psychologist Jeffrey Jensen Arnett in a 2000 article. The Research Network on Transitions to Adulthood at the University of Pennsylvania is a group of a dozen or so experts in various fields: sociologists, policy experts, developmental psychologists, and economists. Their 2005 book, *On the Frontier of Adulthood*, explores emerging adulthood in depth. "More youth are extending education, living at home longer, and moving haltingly, or stopping altogether, along the stepping stones of adulthood," writes Frank F. Furstenberg, chair of the network. "A new period of life is emerging in which young people are no longer adolescents but not yet adults . . . It is simply not possible for most young people to achieve economic and psychological autonomy as early as it was half a century ago." The underlying reason, once again, is an economic shift, this time to a labor market that rewards only the highly educated with livable and growing wages.

5   In 2002, there were 68 million people in the United States aged eighteen to thirty-four. The social and economic upheaval of the past three decades, not to mention that of the past five years, affects us in complex ways. We have all come of age as part of Generation Debt.

6   The Penn researchers use five milestones of maturity: leaving home, finishing school, becoming financially independent, getting married, and having a child. By this definition, only 46 percent of women and 31 percent of men were grown up by age thirty in 2000, compared to 77 percent of women and 65 percent of men of the same age in 1960.

7   "I went from being a child to being a mother," says Doris, now in her fifties. "I was married at twenty. By thirty I had four children and was divorced." Doris completed college and a master's degree while keeping house and raising her children, then supported her family as a medical physicist. Doris' youngest daughter, Miriam, graduated from Southern Connecticut State University in 2000, after six years of work and school, with $20,000 in student loans and $5,000 in credit card debt. Now, at twenty-nine, she is living in Madison, Wisconsin, and training to be a commodities broker, a job she could have pursued with only a high school diploma. Her mother, who bought her first house with her husband in her early twenties, helped Miriam pay off her credit cards and gave her the down payment on the condo she lives in. Miriam earns $28,000 a year and just manages the minimum payments on her loans. She is single. She hasn't passed the five milestones of adulthood; she is barely out to the driveway.

8   Young people are falling behind first of all because of money. College tuition has grown faster than inflation for three decades, and faster than family income for the past fifteen years. Federal aid has lagged behind. An unprecedented explosion of borrowing has made up the difference between what colleges charge and what families can afford. Between 1995 and 2005, the total volume of federal student loans rose 249 percent after inflation, to over $61 billion. Two-thirds of four-year students are graduating with loan debt, an average of up to $19,200 in 2004 and growing every year. Three out of four

college students have credit cards, too, carrying an average unpaid balance of $2,169 in 2005. Nearly a quarter of all students, according to a 2004 survey, are actually putting their tuition directly on plastic.

9   Even as the price has risen, more young people than ever aspire to college. Over 90 percent of high school graduates of all backgrounds say in national surveys that they hope to go on to college. Yet the inadequacy of aid shoots down their hopes. As a direct consequence of the decline in public investment in education at every level, young people today are actually less educated than their parents. The nationwide high school graduation level peaked in 1970 at 77 percent. It was around 67 percent in 2004. According to a recent study cited in the 2004 book *Double the Numbers*, by Richard Kazis, Joel Vargas, and Nancy Hoffman, of every 100 younger people who begin their freshman year of high school, just 38 eventually enroll in college, and only 18 graduate within 150 percent of the allotted time—six years for a bachelor's degree or three years for an *associate's* degree. Only 24.4 percent of the adult population has a B.A., according to the 2000 Census, and those 25 to 34 years old are a little less likely to have one than 45- to 54-year-olds. Sociologists call noncollege youth "the forgotten majority."

10   Statistically, the typical college student is a striving young adult; nearly half are 24 or older. She (56 percent are women) is spending several years in chronic exhaustion splitting her days between a nearly full-time, low-wage job, and part-time classes at a community college or four-year public university. She uses her credit cards to make ends meet—for books, meals, and clothes—and barely manages the minimum payments. Overloaded and falling behind, she is likely to drop out for a semester or for good. Almost one in three Americans in his or her twenties is a college dropout, compared with one in five in the late 1960s.

11   What happens to the three out of four young people who don't get a four-year degree? They are much more likely to remain in the working class than previous generations. Youths eighteen to twenty-four are the most likely to hold minimum wage jobs, giving them a poverty rate of 30 percent in 2000, according to the U.S. Census; that's the highest of any age group. For those aged twenty-five to thirty-four, the poverty rate is 15 percent, compared with 10 percent for older working adults.

12   Policy analyst Heather McGhee, formerly of the think tank Demos, points out, when the Boomers were entering the workforce in 1970, the nation's largest private employer was General Motors. They paid an average wage of $17.50 an hour in today's dollars. The largest employer in the post-industrial economy is Wal-Mart.

13   Their average wage? Eight dollars an hour. The service-driven economy is also a youth-driven economy, burning young people's energy and potential over a deep-fat fryer. McDonalds is the nation's largest youth employer; workers under 24 make up nearly half of the food services, department store, and grocery store workforce nationwide. The working world has always been tough for those starting out, but today's economy relies on a new element—a "youth class." The entire labor market is downgrading toward what was once entry level.

14   For better-off, college-educated sons and daughters, it's the same song, different verse. An astonishing 44 percent of dependent students from families making over $100,000 a year borrowed money for school in 2002. Credit card debt is higher for the middle class than for the poor. Unable to find good jobs with a bachelor's degree, young people are

swelling graduate school classes, only to join the ranks of the unemployed or underemployed, after all.

15   The middle class has been shrinking for two decades. On a family-by-family basis, this means that many people my age who grew up in comfort and security are experiencing a startling decline in their standard of living. Median annual earnings for male workers 25 to 34 sank nearly 20 percent in constant dollars between 1971 and 2002. We start out in the working world with large monthly debt payments but without health insurance, pension benefits, or dependable jobs. It is impossible to predict whether we will be able to make up these deficits with higher earnings later on, but the evidence suggests that most of us will not.

16   In the 1960s the phrase "midlife crisis" captured the malaise of educated middleclass man confronting his mortality and an unfulfilling job or family life. Today "quarter-life crisis" has entered the lexicon for a generation whose unbelievably expensive educations didn't guarantee them success, a sense of purpose, or even a livable income.

When we talk about economics, we are also talking about ambition, responsibility, trust, and family. The new economic realities are distorting the life paths and relationships of the young. We are spending more time moving in and out of school, finding and losing jobs. Some of us move back home, and we put off marriage, children, and home buying. The older generation's response to these changes has been a chorus of disapproval and dismay.

17   The scholars of the Research Network on Transitions to Adulthood, relying on hard data, make the point that economic factors far outweigh psychological ones in explaining what has happened to young adults. "The current changing timetable of adulthood has given rise to a host of questions about whether current generations of young people are more dependent on their parents, less interested in growing up, and more wary of making commitments," they write. Our generation's delay in entering adulthood is often interpreted as a reflection of the narrowed generation gap.

18   In the 1980s, President Ronald Reagan began to dismantle the welfare state and put to rest the liberal dream of ending poverty on a large scale in America. His rhetorical ace was the Cadillac driving, government-cheating "welfare queen." Creating this infamous bogeywoman blamed the poor for their own problems and made taking away their means of support into the morally right thing to do.

19   The lazy, irresponsible, possibly sociopathic "twixter" is this decade's welfare queen, an insidious image obscuring public perception of a real inequity. If you look at where public resources are directed—toward the already wealthy, toward building prisons and expanding the military, away from education and jobs programs—it is easy to see a prejudice against young people as a class.

20   This is not to say that the phenomenon of emerging adulthood in and of itself is exclusively bad. It's a fact of history, like the so-called discoveries of childhood and adolescence before it. This change in the way we experience the life cycle brings upsides and downsides that we may not realize for decades to come. My friends and I overwhelmingly relish the time that we have, as postmillennial young adults, to try out prospective jobs, travel, volunteer, study, and form strong friendships before settling down into career and family responsibilities. Young women, especially, tend to appreciate the way their options have widened, and the chance that medical science gives us to possibly delay motherhood

into our thirties and forties. The more money and education you start out with, the better this time of uncertainty starts to look.

21   The problems arise because our society does not recognize this new state of life, and is instead withdrawing resources from young people. Therefore, the majority of us faces obstacles that make it harder to see the bright side of emerging adulthood. In the past few decades, the trend in the United States has been toward smaller families and looser kinship ties. The bonds of kinship in our national family are weakening too. It's not too dramatic to say that the nation is abandoning its children. In everything from national budget deficits to the rise of household debt to cuts in student aid and public funds for education, Americans are living in the present at the expense of the future.

QUESTIONS FOR ANALYSIS AND DISCUSSION

1. What is the purpose of Kamenetz's recounting of the history of childhood and how childhood has been viewed over the centuries? What point is she trying to support by providing us with this background?

2. Kamenetz observes that the New Deal was largely responsible for our expectations of teenhood today. What factor does she identify as responsible for another shift that marks young adulthood?

3. What are the "five milestones of maturity"? Where are you on the timeline? Have you followed a linear timeline, or have you hopped around, reaching some milestones out of order? At what age would you expect to reach all five milestones? Explain.

4. What reasons does Kamenetz give for why young people are "falling behind"? Explain.

5. Who is the "the forgotten majority"? Why are they forgotten? What does this segment of people represent now and in the future? Explain.

6. What is the author's opinion of low-wage and/or service-driven employment? What does she imply happens to young workers who do not earn college degrees?

Reading the Visual

Food Bank line

Fitzimmons

QUESTIONS FOR ANALYSIS AND DISCUSSION

1. What does the woman mean? What does her statement convey to the viewer?
2. What point is the cartoonist trying to make with this editorial cartoon? Explain.
3. What visual clichés does the cartoonist use to help convey his message?

Millennials' Heads Under a Rock
Ed Schipul

Today's college graduates face one of the toughest labor markets since the Great Depression. Raised as part of the "praise" generation in which they were told they were special and could achieve almost anything, many young adults are left wondering what went wrong. In this next article, blogger and marketing consultant Ed Schipul explains why things are different for this generation's youth, why they need to change their expectations, and why they have reason to be more than a little upset with the Baby Boomers.*

BEFORE YOU READ

What are your expectations of employment after college? Describe your hopes and expectations.

AS YOU READ

How did the spending habits of the Baby Boomers set the stage for the current economic crisis? Why do members of the Millennial generation have reason to be upset with the consumer habits of the Baby Boomers?

1   The GI generation, by all accounts, appears to have raised one of the biggest groups of spoiled kids our country has ever seen. The Baby Boomers. And the Boomers are burying the Millennial generation and their grandkids in debt and chaos. Pretending deficit spending isn't just a deferred tax increase (it is). And that seems wrong to this Gen X'er.

2   In the book *Generations, The History of America's Future*, the authors describe the Boomers as:

The Boomers, who came to college after Eisenhower and before the Carter malaise of 1979. These were the babies of optimism and hubris, Beaver Cleaver and Musketeers, the post-Sputnik high school kids whose SAT scores declined for seventeen straight years, student strikers, flower-child hippies and draft resisters. (30)

3   Much of this can be summed up from the famous line from the musical *Hair* (Australian Cast version because they have cool accents) that goes:

". . . I ain't dying for no one!"

4   Of course that's not exactly true. While some boomers were at Woodstock, many were in Vietnam (including my father who proudly served). And being a complex group of people some Boomers were in both Viet Nam and Woodstock! *But overall they are divided. They don't like each other.*

---

*Ed Schipul, *The List*, August 8, 2009.

5   Let's be blunt. The Baby Boomers as a group have been divided and the conservatives and the liberals in this generation will NEVER agree. Ever. Except on one thing they
agree—that their generation is somehow special and warrants deficit spending. They will
slide into home plate at the end of life having spent every penny and lived life to the fullest. Whoohoo!

6   Yet can you imagine Andrew Carnegie spending every penny on the way out the door?
Or any parent from the 50s? The values changed from "build a legacy," "provide for the
family" to "have a helluva ride!" A generation that proudly says "Spending My Children's
Inheritance" on the bumper sticker of their RV. Towing their jeep.

7   Or rather, they did have that bumper sticker. Until the economy went to hell in a hand
basket built on no-money-down mortgages (because everyone has a right to a house!?
Baroo?) that were then securitized (translation: no accountability). And it all blew up.
Oooops. This has been documented in thousands of ways in the media. OK, let's have a
moment:

8   "Transcendental meditation . . . on the ocean of reality . . . is LOVE!" (Again from
Hair of course.)

9   Gah. Checking the deficit clock as I type this, we are at 11,174,021,379,855. I had to
type that because the online clock was going too fast for me to copy-paste. Really. And
according to the *Urban Dictionary*, the Federal Deficit/Debt is defined as:

> The perpetual and perpetually increasing debt that the United States of America has
> due to the federal government's unlimited debting power with the Federal Reserve.

10   So what does this have to do with the Millennials? Well, they don't see what is happening yet. They haven't quite figured out they are being HOSED! With their internal
focus they haven't looked up from their uber cool sushi twitter meetup at the storms on
the horizon yet. (Photos posted on Facebook later!) *Yes, there are clouds there my friends.*
And they are owned by the Chinese. And I love the Chinese, especially the food, but we
don't get to elect their leaders (does anyone?) and this is influence without representation,
right?

11   Megan K. Scott wrote a recent AP article titled "A bitter pill for 20-somethings" in
which the subject asks:

> "Why don't they want to hire me?" she asked of the companies not responding to
> the resumes she sends out. "I went through four years of college, graduated. You get
> praised while you are working and then all the sudden you are not employable."

12   Because this isn't Fun-Fair-Positive-Work where there is no-score-keeping and an
everyone-gets-a-trophy award dinner at the end. Companies have REAL competitors.
It's called capitalism and it is tough! Why hire a 39.5-hour-per-week-I'm-doing-you-a-
favor-if-I-show-up employee when you can hire an experienced 40 year old? The article
continues:

> "In previous recessions, companies tended to let go of more senior workers because
> of their high salaries, said Andrew Sum, director of the Center for Labor Market Studies
> at Northeastern University. But he said younger workers are faring worse this time around
> as *employers hold on to the workers who have knowledge, experience and better work
> habits.*"

13   Ouch. So when the Millennials figure out that the world is in fact not their oyster. And that they have been sold into debt by the Baby Boomers. Will they get mad? Probably not. Because as Ellen Goodman points out in "Meltdown stoking fears of generational conflict" (originally called "The Virtue of Working Longer"), people don't think in generations. She says:

> The folks revving up generational conflict overlook the fact that most of us do not live or think in age cohort groups. We belong to families. If public money is transferred upward from younger workers to older retirees, private money flows downward from older parents to adult children and grandchildren. In this economy, some older workers are clinging to their jobs to keep the younger employed members of their own families afloat.

14   In summary, the Baby Boomers, in self-congratulations, deficit-spent to have a good life. They bought the house in Florida on money stolen from the future in the form of deficits. And their politicians call it "deficit spending" instead of "a future tax increase" so they can be reelected. And while the deficit isn't going away, the Millennials have stolen the money back from the boomers because the Boomer's Florida house is worth 40 cents on the dollar. But as a family and a tribe everyone has less money and less time.

15   It's like two fishermen fighting over money on the way back to shore, only to have it fall over board lost forever. They spend the rest of the ride back to shore mad at each other, but it doesn't change the fact that the money is GONE. Truly neither won. The Boomers are going to have to keep working. ("Wah! I was promised I wouldn't have to!!") And the Millennials are going to have to work much harder. ("Not fair! I should get a trophy even if I work less than everyone else!") And everyone is mad at everyone. Just friggin' great.

16   Another line from *Hair*: What do we want? PEACE! When do we want it? NOW!

17   I suspect the Boomers will continue to act in their own self-interest. Which won't get us to the desired "peace." When exactly will the Millennials figure out what is going on? And what will they do about it?

QUESTIONS FOR ANALYSIS AND DISCUSSION

1. How are the Baby Boomers "burying their grandkids"? How does Schipul twist this phrase to apply to his overarching point that the Baby Boomers have created a mess for the younger generation to clean up?
2. Why does Schipul reference the 1970s' musical *Hair*? How does this musical apply to the points he raises? If necessary, look up the theme and context of the musical online before you answer this question.
3. What is Schipul's opinion of the Baby Boomers? Of Gen-Y and the Millennial generation? What generation do you think he is from and how does his age help shape his view of the generations he cites?
4. What response does Schipul give the student cited by Megan Scott in her AP article? What tone does he use? Why?
5. What does Schipul hope to achieve with this article? What change does he hope to influence? Explain.

It's Consumer Spending Stupid

James Livingston

Many of us feel guilty when we carry a high balance on our credit cards. Especially in today's economy, we may feel that consumerism is a luxury we cannot afford. But in this next essay, history professor James Livingston explains why consumer culture is good for the economy, *and* good for us.*

AS YOU READ

What are your consumer spending habits? Do you try to save, or do you prefer to spend money as quickly as you receive it? When you do spend, have you ever defended the purchase as "helping the economy"?

BEFORE YOU READ

Livingston refers to the characters of the ant and the grasshopper. Who are these characters? To what story do they refer? How are they applicable to his argument?

1   As an economic historian who has been studying American capitalism for 35 years, I'm going to let you in on the best-kept secret of the last century: private investment—that is, using business profits to increase productivity and output—doesn't actually drive economic growth. Consumer debt and government spending do. Private investment isn't even *necessary* to promote growth.

2   This is, to put it mildly, a controversial claim. Economists will tell you that private business investment causes growth because it pays for the new plant or equipment that creates jobs, improves labor productivity and increases workers' incomes. As a result, you'll hear politicians insisting that more incentives for private investors—lower taxes on corporate profits—will lead to faster and better-balanced growth.

3   The general public seems to agree. According to a *New York Times*/CBS News poll in May, a majority of Americans believe that increased corporate taxes "would discourage American companies from creating jobs."

4   But history shows that this is wrong. Between 1900 and 2000, real gross domestic product per capita (the output of goods and services per person) grew more than 600 percent. Meanwhile, net business investment *declined* 70 percent as a share of G.D.P. What's more, in 1900 almost all investment came from the private sector—from companies, not from government—whereas in 2000, most investment was either from government spending (out of tax revenues) or "residential investment," which means consumer spending on housing, rather than business expenditure on plants, equipment and labor.

5   In other words, over the course of the last century, net business investment atrophied while G.D.P. per capita increased spectacularly. And the source of that growth? Increased consumer spending, coupled with and amplified by government outlays.

---

*James Livingston, *New York Times*, October 25, 2011.

6   The architects of the Reagan revolution tried to reverse these trends as a cure for the stagflation of the 1970s, but couldn't. In fact, private or business investment kept declining in the '80s and after. Peter G. Peterson, a former commerce secretary, complained that real growth after 1982—after President Ronald Reagan cut corporate tax rates—coincided with "by far the weakest net investment effort in our postwar history."

7   President George W. Bush's tax cuts had similar effects between 2001 and 2007: real growth in the absence of new investment. According to the Organization for Economic Cooperation and Development, retained corporate earnings that remain uninvested are now close to 8 percent of G.D.P., a staggering sum in view of the unemployment crisis we face.

8   So corporate profits do not drive economic growth—they're just restless sums of surplus capital, ready to flood speculative markets at home and abroad. In the 1920s, they inflated the stock market bubble, and then caused the Great Crash. Since the Reagan revolution, these superfluous profits have fed corporate mergers and takeovers, driven the dot-com craze, financed the "shadow banking" system of hedge funds and securitized investment vehicles, fueled monetary meltdowns in every hemisphere and inflated the housing bubble.

9   Why, then, do so many Americans support cutting taxes on corporate profits while insisting that thrift is the cure for what ails the rest of us, as individuals and a nation? Why have the 99 percent looked to the 1 percent for leadership when it comes to our economic future?

10   A big part of the problem is that we doubt the moral worth of consumer culture. Like the abstemious ant who scolds the feckless grasshopper as winter approaches, we think that saving is the right thing to do. Even as we shop with abandon, we feel that if only we could contain our unruly desires, we'd be committing ourselves to a better future. But we're wrong.

11   Consumer spending is not only the key to economic recovery in the short term; it's also necessary for balanced growth in the long term. If our goal is to repair our damaged economy, we should bank on consumer culture—and that entails a redistribution of income away from profits toward wages, enabled by tax policy and enforced by government spending. (The increased trade deficit that might result should not deter us, since a large portion of manufactured imports come from American-owned multinational corporations that operate overseas.)

12   We don't need the traders and the C.E.O.'s and the analysts—the 1 percent—to collect and manage our savings. Instead, we consumers need to save less and spend more in the name of a better future. We don't need to silence the ant, but we'd better start listening to the grasshopper.

QUESTIONS FOR ANALYSIS AND DISCUSSION

1. Livingston states his credentials in his first sentence. Why does he do this? Does it make you take what he has to say more seriously? Is he an expert?

2. How does consumer debt drive economic growth? Does it seem strange that the more people owe, the better the economy seems to be?

3. Livingston notes that his view is controversial. What is controversial about it? Why does he feel private investment is not necessary to promote growth?
4. The author observes that "a big part of the problem is that we doubt the moral worth of consumer culture." What does he mean? What is the "moral worth" of consumer culture? What are our public attitudes toward consumerism?
5. To what famous quote does Livingston's title refer? How does his title contribute to the argument of his essay?
6. How do you think Daniel Akst (next article) would respond to Livingston's argument that in order to improve the economy, we need to save less and spend more? What is your own response? Explain.

Thrift: The Rebirth of a Forgotten Virtue
Daniel Akst

America's enduring love affair with big spending is coming up against some unromantic realities. The spending of the Baby Boomers, coupled with the instant gratification demanded by Gen-Xers and Millennials have created unheard of levels of personal debt. In this next essay, columnist and author Daniel Akst wonders what happened to the forgotten virtue of thrift. Here, Akst defines what it means to be thrifty and explains how thrift can be much sexier than the alternative—poverty.*

BEFORE YOU READ

In this next article, the author describes "spenders" and "savers." Which are you and why?

AS YOU READ

What cultural influences drive our spending habits? How does where we live and with whom contribute to our ideas of thrift? Explain.

1 Remember Jack Benny? Cheapness was his shtick; on his radio and television shows he occasionally made hilarious subterranean visits to his money, which was protected by locks, alligators, and an ancient security guard who, from the look of him, had last seen action at the Second Battle of Bull Run. "Your money or your life," to the rest of us, is Hobson's choice; to Benny, it was an existential crisis.

2 Ah, those were the days—a halcyon time when, the Depression still a fresh memory, Americans enjoyed both affluence and restraint. Willy Loman's refrigerator payments notwithstanding, consumer indebtedness at midcentury now looks like a mere flyspeck, at least from the towering mountain of debt atop which we sit.

---

*Daniel Akst, *Wilson Quarterly*, Summer 2009.

3   We have managed since Benny's heyday to get a little carried away. Alan Greenspan and the Chinese gave us too much credit, unfettered bankers chose greed over sobriety, and consumers snapped up McMansions financed by loans they could never repay. In 1980, American household debt stood at what must have seemed the enormous sum of $1.4 trillion. Last year the figure was 10 times as large, only 24 percent of us were debt free, and more than half of college students carried at least four credit cards. Is it any wonder there were more than a million consumer bankruptcy filings last year? Or that the nation's banking system came close to collapse? The result of all this excess is a people hung-over from its recent intoxication with spending and flabbergasted by the bill from the wine merchant.

4   So thrift, supposedly, is back, implying, as the dictionary tells us, "using money and other resources carefully and not wastefully." (The word's etymological connection to "thrive" may come as a shock to some big spenders, but not to the truly thrifty.) Personally, I'm not certain that the resurrection of thrift—heralded on the covers of *Time* and *Business Week,* among other places—is anything more than temporary. But as a lifelong cheapskate, I'm grateful that at least thrift no longer carries quite the musty and ungenerous connotations it once did. If we skinflints are the last ones to step out of the closet, it only means we can appreciate all the more heartily how nice it is to escape the smell of mothballs.

5   I'm talking here about real thrift, which for the most part involves *not spending money.* It's not to be confused with the smug species of faux thrift that's been in vogue for a while. You see it in shelter magazines and newspaper home sections, where rich people boast of furnishing their multimillion-dollar homes with zany castoffs and repurposed industrial *objects.* Or how about the children of one Joan Asher? The *Wall Street Journal* reports that after three had inpatient nose jobs—attended by a private nurse each time—the fourth had to suffer through an outpatient procedure after which she was nursed at home by mom.

6   Real thrift, the skeptical, calculating kind that can make a difference between being solvent and not, is not a matter of cut-rate rhinoplasty. The quotidian penny-pinching I'm talking about used to have a bad name indeed, in much the same way as "spinster" and "cardigan," as we know very well from Jack Benny. Like his preening insistence that he was always 39—or that he was an accomplished violinist—Benny's pretend niggardliness was funny but also geriatric, unsexy, and possibly even emasculating. Men do in fact make passes at women who wear glasses, but do women melt for men who hoard gelt?

7   Evolutionary biologists, who seem to know everything about everything, suggest otherwise. The males of many species, including our own, evolved to attract females by means of costly displays—for example, the tail of the peacock, which he drags around to demonstrate his vitality to peahens. Lacking such plumage, human males resort to exotic European automobiles, pricey dinners, vulgar wristwatches, and other forms of showiness. (Human females are supposed to be seeking signs in such ostentation that a mate will spend on them and their offspring. In the modern world, of course, women themselves earn and spend plenty, often supposedly in answer to their own evolutionary imperative to look young and beautiful.)

8   Spending and sex thus are inextricably connected. "Easy come, easy go" might well have been our motto on both fronts until relatively recently. During the boom, people spent freely and were implored to do so on every side by purveyors of every conceivable thing, in terms designed to penetrate directly to the unrestrained limbic brain. Sex, after all, sells, and thrift is the opposite of sexy. Kooky Scotsmen are thrifty. Flinty New England farmers are thrifty. Elderly pensioners are thrifty. Brad Pitt isn't thrifty.

9   This lack of sex appeal is one reason modern life has produced no great constituency for saving. Saving has often found itself the subject of negative stereotyping in popular culture. In *McTeague* (1899), the novelist Frank Norris tars all three with the same broad brush in a melodramatic portrait of greed and its tragic consequences. *McTeague* is a good example of how, in literature, the prudently thrifty (who are perhaps inherently too boring for drama) tend to be overshadowed by the fanatically miserly. From Shylock through Silas Marner and Ebenezer Scrooge right up to Mr. Potter (*It's a Wonderful Life*), Fred C. Dobbs (*Treasure of the Sierra Madre*) and C. Montgomery Burns (*The Simpsons*), it's clear that writers have always taken seriously St. Paul's assertion that the love of money is the root of all evil. Financial profligacy, it would seem, is nothing compared with being a greedy skinflint.

10   To the extent that thrift produces wealth, it breeds envy. The thrift, future-mindedness, and sobriety of the Jews have fueled prodigious achievements and equally prodigious anti-Semitism, and the association of thrift with a despised minority probably didn't do any good for the trait's public image. Shylock was far from the last moneygrubbing Jew to besmirch popular culture; a coarse and monied Jewish stock manipulator is at the center of Anthony Trollope's *The Way We Live Now* (1875), and lesser such figures flitted in and out of books and movies well into the 20th century. Before Harold Lloyd finds himself hanging from the hands of a clock high above the sidewalk in the silent classic *Safety Last* (1923), he encounters such a character practically salivating with greed behind the counter of a jewelry store. One wonders uneasily whether it was by sheer chance that Jack Benny—né Benjamin Kubelsky—chose a penny-pinching stage persona for himself. The man was by all accounts as generous in his private life as he was tightfisted on screen.

11   There was a time, of course, when thrift was in favor. It was practically a matter of life and death for the Puritans and a cornerstone of their work ethic, along with temperance, diligence, and piety. They excelled at deferring gratification, and it is one of the great ironies of American history that their preternatural self-discipline and industry launched us on the path to such unimaginable riches that thrift would be forgotten in the stampede to the mall. (On the other hand, if you have to be a victim of something, it might as well be your own success.)

12   Benjamin Franklin, who was hardly puritanical in any modern sense of the term, none-theless embraced thrift and famously reminded us that "a penny saved is a penny earned" even before the advent of income taxes (which have made a penny saved worth *even more* than a penny earned). A relentless self-improver, Franklin as a young man "conceived the bold and arduous project of arriving at moral perfection," and as an aid in this venture developed a kind of moral spreadsheet, writing the days of the week across the top and listing 13 virtues along the side, so he could plot his failings by date and category in a grid. Frugality ("waste nothing") was number five on the list.

13   Thrift was so important to Samuel Smiles, the great 19th-century Scottish self-help guru, that in 1875 he published an entire book devoted to it. Smiles's *Thrift* was a sequel to his earlier bestseller, *Self-Help,* which appeared in the landmark literary year of 1859 (when readers first encountered John Stuart Mill's *On Liberty* and Charles Darwin's *Origin of Species*). Smiles's oeuvre, which also included *Duty* and *Character,* made the case for the overriding Victorian virtue of self-control, a characteristic then associated not with the timid but the strong. For in those days, people understood the connection between

money and virtue. "No man can be free who is in debt," Smiles tells us in *Thrift*. "The inevitable effect of debt is not only to injure personal independence, but, in the long-run, to inflict moral degradation."

14   We have self-help gurus today, of course, and some of them (the ubiquitous Suze Orman, for example) even stress the connection between money and morals, but that's not why they are known or attended. We simply want the advantages of financial security and a higher standard of living. The reward for good financial management is a big house, a nice car—all the things that come from bad financial management, without the debt.

15   How did we get here? The transformation of thrift from a virtue into something verging on a social disorder occurred sometime between the 1880s and 1920s, when America transformed itself from a nation of want into one of, well, *wants*. Unbridled economic growth (fueled by decades of self-restraint and invested savings) undermined the Protestant ethos of self-denial and reticence, while the rising merchant class did its best to change the country's long-ingrained aversion to luxury. Consumer credit became more widely available, and religious denominations laid off the hellfire and brimstone in favor of a therapeutic approach to happiness in the present. Vast new big-city "department stores" leveled the full force of their merchandising grandeur at women, who understandably preferred to purchase items they had once laboriously made. Catalyzed by mass communications (which made possible the stimulation of mass desire through advertising) and the rise of an urbanized middle class, consumerism exploded.

16   The loud noise caught the attention of two important social theorists, one of them famous and the other largely forgotten. It's yet another irony in the saga of America's love/hate relationship with thrift that we live by the precepts of the thinker whose name hardly anyone remembers.

17   First, the one you know about. Thorstein Veblen, the peripatetic Norwegian-American economist (he died in 1929, shortly before the great crash that might have brought him grim satisfaction), is best known today for his theory of conspicuous consumption, which argued that a lot of spending is just a wasteful attempt to impress. In effect, Veblen explained consumerism in terms of status and display, bringing evolutionary ideas to bear on economics and consumer behavior to powerful effect. Reading Veblen is a little like reading Freud or Darwin, albeit on a smaller scale: Do so and you'll never look at the world in quite the same way again.

18   As you might imagine, the iconoclastic Veblen took a dim view of all the conspicuous consumption around him, regarding it as a species of giant potlatch in which competitive waste had run amok. You might call Veblen's the voice of thrift, and it is still heard today from leftist intellectuals who, from their tenured pulpits and Arts and Crafts homes, reliably denounce the spending of others. The truth is that nobody listens to these people, except to submit to their periodic floggings as a kind of penance for sins we have no intention of ceasing.

19   But there was another voice heard back when thrift was in its death throes—that of Simon Patten (1852–1922), like Veblen a maladjusted economist who had strong ideas about spending. Patten can seem naive and even crass to us today, for he used his pulpit at the University of Pennsylvania's Wharton School to advocate the very thing that Marx feared: that business and consumer spending should sweep away all the old arrangements and remake the world according to the doctrine of plenty. And he imagined a large role for economists in the running of it.

20   Unlike Veblen, Patten came on the scene not to praise thrift but to bury it. The old values that "inculcated a spirit of resignation" and "emphasized the repression of wants" must be abandoned, Patten argued, adding, "The principle of sacrifice continues to be exalted by moralists at the very time when the social structure is being changed by the slow submergence of the primeval world, and the appearance of a land of unmeasured resources with a hoard of mobilized wealth."

21   Patten was hugely influential in his time, especially in helping liberals to see that something like Adam Smith's "universal opulence" should be a goal and not a cause for shame. His genius was in recognizing capitalism's potential for realizing something like a modern Cockaigne, the mythical land of plenty that beguiled the suffering masses in the Middle Ages. Patten's thinking opened the door to such later fulfillment-oriented intellectuals as Abraham Maslow and Herbert Marcuse, who implicitly (or explicitly) disparaged the idea of deferring gratification—a notion that would come to seem as pointlessly self-sacrificial as postponing happiness until the afterlife.

22   In important ways Patten and Veblen were both right about consumerism, but of the two Patten was the true radical. Beside his starry-eyed utopianism Veblen's sour conservatism is plain to see. As things turned out, it's Patten's world we live in, even if we use the language of Veblen to understand it.

23   Patten and Veblen both died in the 1920s, a decade when affluence, technology, and changing social mores joined forces to drive a stake through the heart of pecuniary restraint. Since then, modern America has effectively banished thrift by foisting on the world those four horsemen of the financial apocalypse: the automobile, the television, the credit card, and the shopping cart. Besides costing money to buy and operate, cars opened up the landscape so that more Americans could have bigger houses on bigger lots. To fill them up, people enjoyed the dubious guidance of television, which helped them figure out what they should want. Credit cards enabled us to conjure money on the spot to pay for stuff. And the shopping cart, unthinkable in traditional department stores but indispensable in their demotic successors—Wal-Mart and Target—gave Americans a way to get all that booty out to the automobile, which they could use to drive it home.

24   After the hardships of the Great Depression and the rationing and other deprivations of World War II (during which Americans saved roughly a quarter of their income), nobody was too focused on thrift, and I can't say I blame them. Besides, spending stimulated the economy, which was something like a patriotic duty. In his 1954 study *People of Plenty: Economic Abundance and the American Character,* David M. Potter said of the contemporary American that "society expects him to consume his quota of goods—of automobiles, of whiskey, of television sets—by maintaining a certain standard of living, and it regards him as a 'good guy' for absorbing his share, while it snickers at the prudent, self-denying, abstemious thrift that an earlier generation would have respected." Or as William H. Whyte put it in *The Organization Man* (1956), "Thrift is becoming a little un-American."

25   Unfortunately, for a people who love money, we've become very good at making it disappear, a task to which we've brought characteristic ingenuity and verve. Reckless overspending was until recently a course open to practically every American, just like reckless investing. And suddenly we were all Emma Bovary, bent on financial suicide. "It is because she feels that society is fettering her imagination, her body, her dreams, her

appetites," Mario Vargas Llosa once wrote, "that Emma suffers, commits adultery, lies, steals, and in the end kills herself."

26   He might well have been describing America, circa 2007. Four-dollar coffee drinks? Fourteen-dollar cocktails? Bottled water from Fiji, priced higher than gasoline? You've got to be kidding. Now that it's safe to come clean, I will confess to having been a bit of a refusenik about all this for most of my, er, 39 years on this earth. Every stick of furniture in my house is second-hand, as are many of my family's clothes, computers, bicycles, books, pieces of art, and other items. We've mostly had used cars, and we still have the new ones we bought in a single mad burst in 2001. The funny thing is, it's amazing what a nice life you can have with a middle-class income and Jack Benny's attitude about money.

27   More people are waking up to this particular old-time religion. Since early 2008 personal saving has crept back up a few percentage points above zero (much to the consternation of stimulus-minded economists), and some long-term trends are likely to reinforce today's renewed interest in controlling spending.

28   It helps that conspicuous consumption, like tobacco, has fallen into social disrepute, a change that removes some of the pressure felt by many families to keep up with the Joneses (who may well have been foreclosed by now). Veblen was right that much spending is meant to be conspicuous, and if the display incentives surrounding consumption have changed, so will consumption.

29   Rising environmental consciousness ought to be a further spur to thrift, for what could possibly be greener—or more demonstrative of piety—than eschewing wasteful consumption? Although cutting global greenhouse emissions by building new power plants and the like can be expensive, many of the ways individuals can make a difference will actually put money in your pocket: eating less red meat, driving a fuelefficient car, and taking fewer planet-warming plane trips, to name a few. The same goes for buying less stuff; making do with what you have or going secondhand uses fewer resources and of course reduces spending as well. A rising scavenger subculture threatens to erase the stigma that was associated with "garbage picking" when I was a kid, transforming shame into virtue. Like so many other things, this "freecycling" is abetted by Craigslist.

30   You'll need to consider garbage picking now and then because in the years ahead we'll have to pay not only for our individual and collective overspending in the boom years, but also for our gigantic national outlays during the ensuing crash to bail out banks, insurers, and automakers and stimulate the economy to stave off a depression. We've been paying for all this by borrowing, so expect to pay higher taxes to retire these debts. Speaking of retirement, have I mentioned Social Security and Medicare? Maybe I shouldn't.

31   So do our straitened circumstances give Jack Benny any more sex appeal? It's hard to believe he could make it on *American Idol,* but we might learn something from him nonetheless, for as any behavioral economist can tell you, there was method in his money-storing madness. From whom, after all, was he protecting his savings if not himself? Self-protective "commitment devices" like Benny's moats and alligators are already being used here and there—deposits to your retirement account are defended by hungry tax collectors, after all—and if we're smart, we'll use them even more in the future.

32   Fortunately, thrift is far from the worst thing we can have thrust upon us. To be thrifty, after all, is to save, and to save is not only to keep but to rescue. Thrift is thus a way to redeem yourself not just from the unsexy bondage of indebtedness but also from

subjugation to people and efforts that are meaningless to you, or worse. Debt means staying in a pointless job, failing to support needy people or worthwhile causes, accepting the strings that come with dependence, and gritting your teeth when your boss asks you to do something unethical (instead of saying "drop dead"). Ultimately, thrift delivers not just freedom but salvation—which makes it a bargain even Jack Benny could love.

QUESTIONS FOR ANALYSIS AND DISCUSSION

1. What assumptions does Daniel Akst make about his readers? Would you consider yourself Akst's target audience? For example, what do you need to know in order to understand Akst's first paragraph? His historical references? Explain.
2. What is thrift? What associations does the word have for you? Is it negative, positive, or neutral? Is being thrifty "un-American"? Why has it gained a bad reputation, despite sage advice that saving is a good thing to do?
3. Akst uses many synonyms in his essay to define *thrift* and *thrifty*. Which other words does he use in its place? What words have more negative meanings, and which ones have a more positive meaning?
4. The author states that going green is equal to becoming thrifty. What are some examples he gives that prove his point? Besides the examples that Akst lists in his essay, which other ways can leaving a smaller carbon footprint actually put money in your pocket?
5. According to Akst, you can have a "nice life" with a middle-class income and Jack Benny's attitude about money. What is your definition of a "nice life"? Do you agree with the author that a nice life can be had this way?
6. Do you agree with Akst's thesis: being thrifty is more honorable and intelligent than being a spend-thrift? Is there a middle ground? Explain.

Are Student Loans Destroying the Economy?

Derek Thompson

Most students today assume some debt during their college years, mostly through student loans, but some as credit card debt, often related to school expenses. Most students must begin paying off their student loan debt six months after graduation Without the guarantee of a good job after graduation, something many new graduates once took for granted, many students are taking a hard look at their finances and making tough decisions on what to buy and when. In this next essay, business editor Derek Thompson explains what happens to the economy when large numbers of young people trade cars for college and homes for homework.*

---

*Derek Thompson, *Atlantic*, April 22, 2013.

Before you began school, did you know how you were going to pay for it? Did you save in advance? Count on loans or scholarships? A combination of these? If you do have college loans, how long do you think it will take for you to pay off your debt?

Do you own a car? A house? How do these big ticket items factor into your spending plans? Are they essential items, or luxuries? Why?

1   Recoveries are powered by two things. Houses and cars. And young people aren't buying either.

2   That's the conclusion from a new study out of the New York Fed, via Brad Plumer, that can be easily read as blaming student debt for holding back the recovery by squashing home and auto sales. The share of 30-year-olds with student debt who have taken out a mortgage has collapsed since the recession struck (ditto those without student debt).

Proportion of Borrowers with Home-secured Debt at Age 30

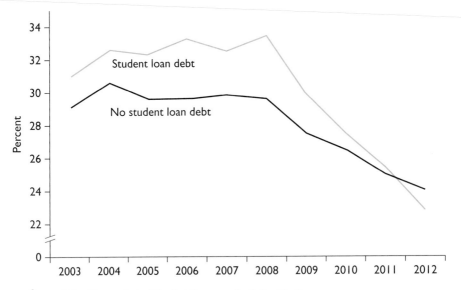

Source: Federal Reserve Bank of New York Consumer Credit Panel/Equifax.

3   And the share of 25-year-olds with student debt who also have an auto loan has fallen since the crash, as well (ditto again those without student debt).

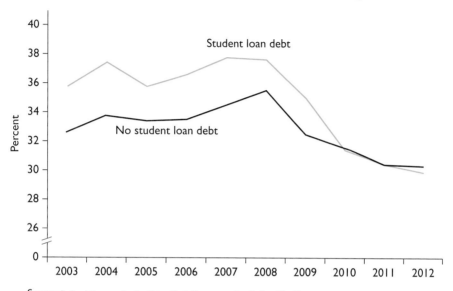

Proportion of Borrowers with Auto Debt at Age 25

Student loan debt

No student loan debt

Source: Federal Reserve Bank of New York Consumer Credit Panel/Equifax.

4   This study seems to feed into a familiarly scary story about student debt as a dangerous bubble that is piling unprecedented levels of debt on young people, and is wrecking the economy by preventing them from starting their lives.

5   There are two problems with that story. First, there are so many reasons that cars and houses are falling out of favor with young people beyond student loans (and even beyond the miserable economy) that it's impossible to pick a single culprit. For example, companies like Ford are vocally worried that smartphones are replacing cars as symbols of grown-up sociability, and young people are bunching in urban and urban-lite areas with many apartments and good public transit.

6   Second, it's a myth that college graduates have more debt than they used to. In fact, they have less. Total debt for 20-somethings has fallen since its peak in 2008, as it has for every age group in this period of deleveraging. Families that feasted on credit in the last decade have spent the last few years paying back what they owe and cutting back their excessive spending. Young people, with and without student loans, have done the very same.

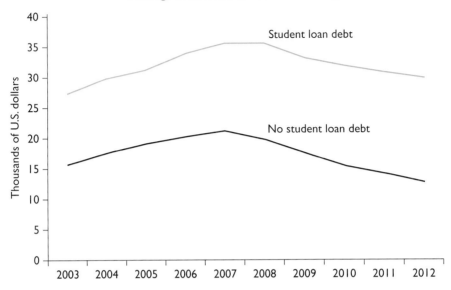

Average Total Debt of Borrowers at Age 25

Source: Federal Reserve Bank of New York Consumer Credit Panel/Equifax.

7   Average debt among twenty-somethings is at its lowest since 1995, according to a recent Pew Research Center report. More than a fifth of young households in 2010 didn't have any debt at all—the lowest in 30 years.

8   What's really changed is *what kind of debt* they have. Young people have swapped student loans for mortgage and auto loans. They've traded cars for college and homes for homework.

9   And that's okay! Compared to cars and houses, higher education is a much safer investment. For all the media criticism about college losing its luster, you could make a good argument that it's never been more important. While the returns to college have flattened recently, wage growth has been even weaker (or negative) among non-college grads. As a result, the "bonus" that young workers get from going to college, which economists call, the "college premium," has tripled in the last 30 years. Today, the share of the 18-24-year-old population enrolled in school is at an all-time high 45 percent today.

10   I tend to regard the most educated generation in American history as good news, but even good news has its downsides. The downside here is that millions of young people invested in their human capital *during a period of overall deleveraging*. Little was left over for cars and houses. And the twin engines of the consumer economy were starved for fresh fuel.

11   Meta Brown and Sydnee Caldwell, the authors of the New York Fed study, (available at http://libertystreeteconomics.newyorkfed.org/) end on a pessimistic note:

> While highly skilled young workers have traditionally provided a vital influx of new, affluent consumers to U.S. housing and auto markets, unprecedented student debt may dampen their influence in today's marketplace.

12   But here's a more optimistic read. With youth unemployment kissing 18 percent through 2010, more young American realized that the opportunity cost of leaving the labor force to go to school had never been lower. They wouldn't have bought homes, anyway. They wouldn't have bought cars, anyway. The economy was too rotten. So for many of them, the choice wasn't been a four-bedroom house and four more years of school. It was between school and underemployment. They chose wisely.

13   So, optimistically, today's debt swap could work like a reverse-stimulus, sucking energy from the economy in the short-term but empowering our labor force in the long-term when, eventually, some of these students will get married, buy a house, and put some wheels in their garage, having invested in their education before they took out their first car loan.

QUESTIONS FOR ANALYSIS AND DISCUSSION

1. Thompson notes that the study conducted by the New York Federal Reserve can be easily read as blaming student debt for holding back the recovery by squashing home and auto sales. Why does he feel this conclusion is invalid? Explain.

2. Review the graphs. Based on what you see, what conclusions can you draw on the connections between student debt and car and auto sales? What other conclusions might you draw? As a student, is there something the New York Fed and Thompson missed when drawing conclusions from the data?

3. Thompson observes that companies like Ford are worried that smartphones are replacing cars as symbols of adulthood. Do you agree? What are the symbols of adulthood? What things do you wish to own that will reflect your adult independence and social standing? Explain.

4. According to Thompson, why is it better to invest in college than in cars? Why is it important for the economy?

Reading the Visual

Scenes from the Depression

Photos from *The Boston Globe*

A sign informing readers that Fremont Pontiac GMC is permanently closed is seen on a door at the Newark, Calif. dealership, Tuesday, March 3, 2009. The dealership closed due to economic conditions earlier this year. (AP Photo/Paul Sakuma)

A RE/MAX Central bus advertises tours of foreclosed homes March 7, 2009 in Las Vegas, Nevada. The real estate group began giving tours for prospective buyers three times a week in February 2008, in an effort to clear inventory of foreclosed properties. They have seen a steady decrease in foreclosure listings since the summer of 2008 in the Las Vegas area. (Ethan Miller/Getty Images)

As new home sales and housing starts hit record lows, empty lots, partially constructed homes, and abandoned ones are seen in a subdivision on January 30, 2009 near Homestead, Florida. Prices in November of 2008 declined 8.7 percent from a year earlier, the biggest drop in records going back to 1991, the Federal Housing Finance Agency reported. (Joe Raedle/Getty Images)

QUESTIONS FOR ANALYSIS AND DISCUSSION

1. Why do you think *The Boston Globe* chose these photos, among others, to represent the recession? What exactly do these photos represent?
2. "A picture is worth a thousand words." In a single paragraph for each, summarize what story these photographs are trying to visually convey.
3. During times of economic hardship, certain areas of the country are hit harder than others. Has this recession been more equalizing than others? Why or why not? How has the economic downturn impacted the area and industries around where you live?

Why Won't Anyone Give Me a Credit Card?
Kevin O'Donnell

Many of today's graduates carry credit card debt. For many years, credit card companies were falling over themselves trying to entice college students to sign on the dotted line, much to the chagrin of credit counselors and parents alike. While carrying credit card debt is never a good idea, it turns out that college may be the best time to start building your credit profile. As recent graduate Kevin O'Donnell explains, he doesn't have bad credit, but the companies keep turning him down. Why the change of heart?*

BEFORE YOU READ

Do you have a credit card? If so, did you get it through a campus offer? Through a department store? How old were you when you got your first card, and how well have you managed your credit profile?

AS YOU READ

O'Donnell complains that no one will offer him a credit card. Why are credit card companies so eager to offer college students cards while they are still in school, but reluctant once these students graduate?

1   While picking up a new shirt at J.Crew a few months ago, I asked about opening one of those store credit cards—you know, the ones that give you a discount on the first purchase. I filled out the paperwork, and the cashier phoned the lending bank and gave them my information. "You'll hear if you've been approved by mail in a few days," he said. A few weeks later, I got a letter from World Financial Network National Bank (how dubious does that sound?) saying they would not be able to extend me a line of credit.

2   The J.Crew card was the fourth one I'd applied for over the past year, and it was my third rejection. I am a 27-year-old professional with a full-time job, no mortgage, no children, and no student loans. With the exception of one outstanding dental bill, I have absolutely no debt. I pay my bills on time; I never miss rent. I should be an ideal candidate for a credit card, right? Not so.

3   With the economy in the dumps, it's harder than ever to get a card. The amount of credit card offers mailed to U.S. households has dropped precipitously in 2009, from an estimated 1.13 billion in the first fiscal quarter of 2008 to 372.4 million in the same period this year. Why the decline in junk mail? Last month, credit card default rates reached their highest point since the recession began. Bank of America claimed its rate hit 14.54 percent, while Citigroup (which issues MasterCard) saw its default rate go from 10.03 percent to 12.14 percent. American Express, however, reported a slight decrease—from 8.9 percent to 8.4 percent—in default rates. Perhaps that decline is related to AmEx offering certain customers a $300 bribe to *close* their accounts.

---

*Kevin O'Donnell, *Slate Magazine*, September 18, 2009.

4   Well, that explains why my American Express application got rejected. But why, despite my decent financial record, am I a particularly bad candidate for a credit card? I've got no credit history. Typically, the best time to get your first credit card is in college, when banks litter campuses with offers. One study estimated that students receive 25 to 50 applications per semester. I was always wary of getting a credit card as an undergrad. I was living hand-to-mouth, and it was always easy enough to pick up a bar tab with a debit card. What I didn't realize was that I'd very soon need a credit card to live. If I'm doomed to a life without plastic, what am I going to do if I want to buy a house or lease a car? There are certain things you can't put on a debit card.

5   My quest for credit is a paradoxical one: How can I establish a credit history when banks won't let me create one in the first place? When my American Express, MasterCard, and Continental Chase Rewards applications were denied, I did what friends and relatives advised—try to take out a card with a department store, hence the J.Crew Card. It turns out they gave me bad advice—J.Crew, just like everybody else I had tried before, requires applicants to have a prior credit history. Gail Cunningham, the spokeswoman for the National Foundation for Credit Counseling, told me that, historically, gas cards and department store cards have been relatively easy to get because the companies' "risk is pretty small—how much can you charge at the filling station?" But in this time of economic decline, even those once-freewheeling retailers are cutting back on the number of applications they approve. Standard & Poor's recently reported that U.S. retail outlets that extend credit claimed losses of 12.2 percent in May, the highest since S&P started tracking such data in January 2000.

6   So what *should* I do to get a credit card? I could just keep filling out applications— and I'd probably have a better chance with smaller community banks, as they didn't suffer the financial blows that the larger institutions did. But sending in loads of applications will probably hurt me in the end. When lenders review applicants, they look at five factors: identification, account history, public records (bankruptcy filings, court records of tax liens), consumer statements (challenges to the status of an account with a lender), and inquiries. That last item is the most crucial for those of us with no credit: It shows how many times lenders have requested to review an applicant's credit history. The more times that information has been reviewed (and rejected), the more suspicious you look as an applicant. Since I have no credit history, I basically don't exist to these lenders—and since I've only started applying for credit in earnest since the start of the credit crunch, I pose more of a gamble to these banks, who aren't willing to take risks on applicants who can't prove their fiscal prudence.

7   As a last resort, I went to a branch of Chase Bank, the place that happily accepts my twice-monthly direct deposits. "You don't have credit?" the *customer* service rep asked. "Well, it's going to be very hard to get [a card]." I had heard about secured credit cards, which require you to put up cash as collateral—think of it as a credit card with training wheels. When I asked the financial adviser about that option, she laughed—laughed!— and said Chase didn't offer those. It was like that scene in *Pee-wee's Big Adventure*, when Pee-wee asks to see the basement of the Alamo and gets heckled off the grounds by the tour guide.

8   My quest for credit does have a happy ending, however. Bank of America actually does offer one of those secured credit cards, the BankAmericard Visa Secured Card. Mine

just arrived three weeks ago. First purchase? A hotel stay for a friend's wedding out of town. (My balance is almost maxed out for the month, alas.) It will take about a year before I've proven my worth and can get those ridiculous credit-card training wheels removed—my account will be evaluated periodically and, provided I'm in good standing, my credit score will increase. And you know what? If my mailbox suddenly becomes flooded with offers, I promise I won't complain.

QUESTIONS FOR ANALYSIS AND DISCUSSION

1. Some students are given credit cards by their parents "for emergencies." Do you think this is a good idea? If you have such an arrangement, have you ever used your card for something other than an emergency? What constituted an "emergency"?
2. O'Donnell is very eager to get a credit card. Why does he want one? Is it a marker of adult life? Simply a way of life? Can you survive in this world without credit cards and the debt that comes with them? Explain.
3. O'Donnell experiences difficulties in getting a credit card after he graduates. Do you have any credit cards? Do you worry that you won't be able to procure one once you graduate? Why or why not?
4. Why is credit important? How can it be useful and valuable? Explain.

Regrets of a Stay-at-Home Mom
Katy Read

There was a time not so long ago when most women didn't have a choice to stay home and raise their children. They were expected to. Today, most women (70%) are part of the paid workforce, and many remain working while their children are still young. Some women, usually ones who have another source of income from a fully employed partner, "opt out"—a term used for women who decide to forgo a career, at least for a while, to focus on raising a family. The problem is that once out of the paid workforce, it is very difficult to get back "in." In the next essay, writer Katy Read gives a warning to young women considering the "opt out" route once starting a family. Fourteen years ago, she "opted out" to focus on her family. Now, she's broke.*

BEFORE YOU READ

A poll taken by ABC News in 2012 reported that 21 percent of respondents said "more mothers of young children working outside the home" was a good thing for society; 37 percent, said it was a bad thing; and 38 percent said it doesn't make much difference. Where does your opinion fall on this question?

*Katy Read, *Salon Magazine*, Jan 6, 2011.

What does it mean for a woman socially and economically to "opt out" of paid work? Explain.

1   We had wonderful times together, my sons and I. The parks. The beaches. The swing set moments when I would realize, watching the boys swoop back and forth, that someday these afternoons would seem to have rushed past in nanoseconds, and I would pause, mid-push, to savor the experience while it lasted.

2   Now I lie awake at 3 a.m., terrified that as a result I am permanently financially screwed.

3   As of my divorce last year, I'm the single mother of two almost-men whose taste for playgrounds has been replaced by one for high-end consumer products and who will be, in a few more nanoseconds, ready for college. My income—freelance writing, child support, a couple of menial part-time jobs—doesn't cover my current expenses, let alone my retirement or the kids' tuition. It is a truth universally acknowledged that a single woman in possession of two teenagers must be in want of a steady paycheck and employer-sponsored health insurance.

4   My attempt to find work could hardly be more ill-timed, with unemployment near 10 percent, with the newspaper industry that once employed me seemingly going the way of blacksmithing. And though I have tried to scrub age-revealing details from my résumé, let's just say my work history is long enough to be a liability, making me simultaneously overqualified and underqualified.

5   But my biggest handicap may be my history of spending daylight hours in the company of my own kids. Just having them is bad enough. Research shows that mothers earn 4 to 15 percent less than non-mothers with comparable jobs and qualifications, that as job candidates, mothers are perceived as less competent and committed than non-mothers (fathers, in contrast, rate higher than men without kids). Heather Boushey, senior economist at the Center for American Progress, told me that the outlook for an at-home mother returning to work in this economy "kind of makes my stomach drop a little bit." I know the feeling.

6   When Paul Krugman warns that many of the currently jobless "will never work again," I am petrified—hello, 3 a.m.!—that he means me. I long ago lost track of how many jobs I have applied for, including some I wouldn't have looked twice at in my 20s, but I can count the resulting interviews and have fingers left to twiddle idly. Before I left full-time work in 1996, my then-husband and I, both reporters at the same newspaper, earned the exact same salary. Now my ex, still a reporter, is making $30,000 a year more than that, while I have been passed over for jobs paying $20,000 less.

7   As I wander the ghost-town job boards, e-mailing my résumé into oblivion, I tamp down panic with soothing thoughts: I have a comfortable house, for now, some money in the bank, for now, a 9-year-old Mazda that rattles alarmingly but runs, for now. Millions of people are hanging by far thinner threads, and I am genuinely grateful for what good fortune I have.

8   So this is not a plea for sympathy. More like a warning from the front lines.

9   The recession has already shifted habits and attitudes and will likely usher in long-term cultural changes about which economists, sociologists and political strategists are

churning out predictions as we speak. Here's mine: The economic crisis will erode women's interest in "opting out" to care for children, heightening awareness that giving up financial independence—quitting work altogether or even, as I did, going part-time—leaves one frighteningly vulnerable. However emotionally rewarding it may be for all involved, staying home with children exacts a serious, enduring vocational toll that largely explains the lingering pay gap between men and women as well as women's higher rate of poverty. With the recession having raised the stakes, fewer mothers may be willing to take the risk. If it's not yet the twilight of the stay-at-home mother, it could be her late afternoon. Certainly it is long past nap time.

10   Statistics suggest mothers are reaching that conclusion. Between 2008 and 2010, the number of stay-at-home mothers fell from 5.3 million to 5 million. (Stay-at-home dads held steady at around 150,000.) Who knows how many others are frantically sending out résumés? Whether they have paying jobs or not, mothers still handle most of the country's child care, but that "feels like the last gasp of a dying age," journalist Hanna Rosin wrote last year in *Atlantic Monthly*. She quotes Boushey noting that "the idealized family—he works, she stays home—hardly exists anymore." The image of a mother pushing a stroller down the street at midday may come to seem as quaint as that of a 1950s housewife pushing a vacuum in stockings and pumps.

11   Stay-at-home mothers obsolete? Those among the 5 million who are alive and well and reading this may already be clicking indignantly to the comments section to defend their choices. Go ahead and vent, stay-at-home mothers. I get it. Fourteen years ago, I struggled with my own decision amid a tangle of internal and external messages. Some still seem valid and others now less so, but the difference was hard to tell amid the hormone-saturated, sleep-deprived, advice-swamped bewilderment of new parenthood.

12   I became a mother during a moment in history when women faced unprecedented career opportunities yet were expected to maintain a level of interaction with their children that would have made my own mother's eyes roll practically out of their sockets. I was a busy reporter and naive new mom, two jobs that I was led to believe could not, for all practical purposes, be performed adequately and simultaneously. Oh, and while one was commendable, the other was morally imperative.

13   Like I needed the extra pressure. I already felt responsible for giving my sons childhoods—those fleeting years that would forever loom large in their lives—full of adventure and learning and treasured memories. If I could have enriched their experience by moving to a farm or hitting the road in an Airstream, I would have considered it. But according to the parenting manuals I dutifully consulted, what my boys required was constant engagement with a loving, omnipresent figure, sort of like if God engaged in daily floor time. The parenting experts never said exactly how children like mine, overseen by an ever-shifting cast of underpaid near-strangers in a commercial daycare center, would be damaged. But I got the impression I might as well have gone through pregnancy throwing back shots of tequila.

14   Meanwhile, my work/life balance . . . wasn't. My husband and I kept erratic hours, handing off babies like batons. At work, I lost choice assignments as I dashed out before the stroke of 6, when the daycare began charging a dollar a minute. My editors, probably well-meaning, set me on what suspiciously resembled a mommy track. While an intern handled the tragic late-breaking news of an honor student murdered by her mother's crack

dealer, I yawned through meetings where citizens complained about potholes. (Though who knew how fabulous a steady-paying pothole gig would look to my underemployed future self?)

15   And the emotional turbulence! I drove to work with spit-up-stained shirt and tear-streaked face, cried at baby-food commercials featuring mothers and infants bonding in what looked like a weekday-afternoon glow. I felt the time flying past. My firstborn wasn't yet crawling when I began gazing nostalgically at newborns in the park, with their impossibly delicate fingers and mewing cries. Over at the playground, hulking 4-year-olds hoisted themselves around with huge, capable hands, conversing in vast vocabularies. Soon my son would be one of these giants, his infancy vanished into the chaotic past.

16   My second son was born. Two weeks later, my father was diagnosed with a brain tumor. Sitting near my dad's bedside, I showed off the baby to my Aunt Millicent, mentioning my plans to return to my job. She shook her head sadly. "You won't believe how fast those years go by," my aunt said. "Try not to miss them, if you can help it."

17   My father died two months later. That fall, my husband found a new job in a different city. And I—feminist, ambitious journalist, daughter of a woman with a successful advertising career—quit a full-time job at a big-city paper and began part-time freelancing work that brought in less, some years, than I'd made as a waitress in college.

18   I wasn't worried, frankly, about the long-term economic consequences, partly because nobody else seemed to be. Most articles and books about what came to be called "opting out" focused on the budgeting challenges of dropping to one paycheck—belt-tightening measures shared by both parents—while barely touching on the longer-term sacrifices borne primarily by the parent who quits: the lost promotions, raises and retirement benefits; the atrophied skills and frayed professional networks. The difficulty of reentering the workforce after years away was underreported, the ramifications of divorce, widowhood or a partner's layoff hardly considered. It was as though at-home mothers could count on being financially supported happily ever after, as though a permanent and fully employed spouse were the new Prince Charming.

19   I myself witlessly contributed to the misinformation when I wrote an article about opting out for a now-defunct personal-finance magazine. Amid chirpy budgeting tips and tales of middle-class couples cheerfully scraping by, I quoted a financial advisor bluntly outlining the long-term risks. My editor wasn't pleased. "It's so . . . negative," she said, and over the phone I could almost hear her nose wrinkling. So I, neophyte freelancer eager to accommodate well-paying client, turned in a rewrite with a more positive spin.

20   Since then, a few writers have reported the financial downsides, notably Ann Crittenden, who calculated in *The Price of Motherhood* (2001) that having a child costs the average college-educated woman more than a million dollars in lifetime income. More recently, Linda Hirshman (*Get to Work*, 2006) and Leslie Bennetts (The Feminine *Mistake*, 2007) wrote manifestos scolding women who opt out. In 2010, Karine Moe and Dianna Shandy outlined the risks of downsizing a career on behalf of family in *Glass Ceilings & 100-Hour Couples.*

21   But I might not have realized such warnings even applied to me: After all, I was working. Downsizing my career seemed ideal—research shows 60 percent of mothers would choose part-time work if they could. While my kids spent three afternoons a week in daycare, I did what the experts advised: developed my skills, undertook new challenges,

expanded my professional contacts. I advanced creatively if not financially, published essays in respected literary journals that often paid (cue ominous music) in copies of the magazine.

22   But who had time for long-term financial planning amid the daily demands of two small boys? I took them sliding, skating, swimming and skateboarding, supervised art projects, helped with homework, conferred with teachers, drove to music lessons and dentist appointments and baseball practices. I handled all of their sick days, some involving lingering health problems that, if I'd had an office job, would have exasperated the most flexible employer. Not every moment, of course, was sunny and delightful; there was plenty of crying, screaming and slamming doors (sometimes by the kids, too, ha ha). It was harder than any paying job I've ever held.

23   Salary experts estimate the market value of a stay-at-home parent's labor (child care, housecleaning, cooking, laundry, driving, etc.) at about $118,000. This hollowly cheerful calculation has always struck me as patronizing, with the effect, if not the intention, of further diminishing our status. Moms—aren't they the greatest? They should be pocketing as much as a registered pharmacist or the mayor of Chula Vista, Calif., yet they'll happily accept payment in the form of adorable gap-toothed smiles. An implied, faintly sinister coercion—a good mom doesn't want money—fuels a system that relies on our unpaid childcare, household chores and volunteer work but offers no safety net.

24   Few of the arguments for staying home seem as persuasive now as they did 14 years ago. I long ago stopped trusting most advice from so-called parenting experts. The kids I know who attended full-time daycare seem fine, and I doubt my sons would have been damaged if I had kept my job. In at least one crucial way, they'd be far better off: I'd have more money to contribute to their college educations.

25   Still, like most mothers, I have mixed feelings about my choices, and like most mothers writing complaining first-person essays, I feel compelled to note the upside. I am deeply thankful to have witnessed as much of my sons' childhoods as I did. I'm a procrastinator, and I can imagine myself thinking of those long playground afternoons as something I would get around to eventually, not noticing the swing set's shadow stretching ever longer across the sand.

26   So if some young woman with a new baby were to ask me about opting out I would tell her, as my Aunt Millicent told me 14 years ago, how quickly a child's early years zip past, how challenging but wonderful they are, how grateful I am for every single moment I was privileged to witness.

27   And then, unlike my aunt, I would warn her not to do it.

QUESTIONS FOR ANALYSIS AND DISCUSSION

1. Why is Read scrubbing age-revealing details from her résumé? Explain.
2. As the reader, what take-away message do you have after finishing the essay? Is Read telling women to remain fully employed? Is she warning them not to have children? Explain.
3. Why would mothers be considered less competent and less committed than nonmothers. What about men? What accounts for the difference in opinion?

4. Read states that her essay is not a plea for sympathy, but a warning from the frontlines. Who is she warning? What is she warning against, and why?

5. What is Read's tone in this essay? Identify phrases that identify her tone.

6. What reasons does Read give for her own choice to "opt out"?

7. What arguments are given to women to encourage them to "opt out"? Why does Read feel that these arguments seem "as persuasive now as they did 14 years ago"?

WRITING ASSIGNMENTS

1. Research recent articles on the current financial crisis. Have things improved since the articles in this chapter were written? Based on your research and the information in this chapter, write a short essay in which you forecast what your personal economic future might look like over the next five to ten years.

2. Several writers in this chapter accuse the Baby Boomers for much of the current economic crisis. Why is this particular group scapegoated? How might Baby Boomers respond to these accusations? Identify several points raised in the articles in this section and interview at least three people between 55 and 65 about their views on the economy and the reasons why things got so bad. Do they admit any culpability?

3. Anya Kamenetz calls post-Millennial youth "generation debt." Is this an appropriate title for this generation? Explain why or why not.

4. Write about a time when you had to make a personal choice that involved incurring debt. Describe the circumstances and your feelings about the incident.

5. What, if anything, can the younger generation learn from the older generation about debt? Speak to a few people older than you about their views of debt, including student loans, credit card debt, and car loans. What is their view of debt? Does it differ from your view? Explain.

6. Several authors refer to parents or grandparents who came of age during the Great Depression with reverence and hold them as examples of a time when people lived better, more financially responsible lives. Research the social impact of the Great Depression. What are the merits of thrift? What role does it play in our social consciousness? Is it as important today as it was 50 years ago? As America once again faces the most challenging economic climate since the Great Depression, how might your generation measure up?

7. What are your expectations of the economy after graduation? Do you expect to get a good job? Did the economy influence your choice of major? Will it influence how choosy you are when seeking full-time work? Explain.

16

Our Lives Online

Before 1990, very few people had ever heard of the Internet. Only a handful had a cell phone, and those that were available were clunky and cumbersome, requiring a suitcase-sized transmitter. Social networking meant meeting your friends after work at the local bar where you might exchange a home telephone number or a business card, which was filed in a card index called a Rolodex. No one could have guessed how different things would be in 2013, or how much the Internet would change American culture, education, personal and business relationships, journalism, commerce, and medicine. Today, three-quarters of the U.S. and Canadian population is online.

Today we use the Internet to network for business, friendships, and dating. It is inextricably connected to the daily life and social experience of most Americans. Web communities have changed the way many of us think about meeting people and sharing information. Online databases and encyclopedias have transformed the way we research information and share ideas. Almost 80 percent of charitable contributions come through the Web. Social networking sites such as Facebook and Twitter have revolutionized the way we communicate with friends and share information. They have even changed the way we find out breaking news. During the Boston Marathon bombings in April of 2013, Boston Police used Twitter to provide updates to the public before news media could even broadcast on the air.

This chapter explores how technology, the Internet, and especially social networking sites influence our relationships with each other and how we relate to the world around us. Is the Internet redefining friendships and what it means to be a "friend"? Is it changing the way we think and speak? Is it rewiring our brains? And if so, should we be worried? The arguments may surprise you.

Is Google Making Us Stupid?

Nicholas Carr

Only a generation ago, researching information could take weeks or months, and consisted of countless hours of reading through mounds of printed magazines, newspapers, and academic journals. To find original sources for research papers, students waded through microfiche, card catalogues, and volumes of reference books, reading every detail, looking for just the right phrase or statistic that could prove their point or help make their case. Now researching takes only a few hours working with databases and search engines to find that perfect phrase or statistic to cut and paste into a research paper. The Internet has changed the way we work and study, and it may even be changing the way we think. Are we getting more efficient, or are our brains getting lazy? In this next essay, author Nicholas Carr discusses what the Internet is doing to our brains and how new ways of thinking will change us forever—for better or for worse.*

BEFORE YOU READ

Do you tend to skim through long pieces of writing or do you become deeply involved in longer works? Which do you prefer—longer articles or short abstracts of information and why?

AS YOU READ

How is society affected by the media? How do new technologies change our way of thinking?

1 "Dave, stop. Stop, will you? Stop, Dave. Will you stop, Dave?" So the supercomputer HAL pleads with the implacable astronaut Dave Bowman in a famous and weirdly poignant scene toward the end of Stanley Kubrick's *2001: A Space Odyssey*. Bowman, having nearly been sent to a deep-space death by the malfunctioning machine, is calmly, coldly disconnecting the memory circuits that control its artificial brain. "Dave, my mind is going," HAL says, forlornly. "I can feel it. I can feel it."

2 I can feel it, too. Over the past few years I've had an uncomfortable sense that someone, or something, has been tinkering with my brain, remapping the neural circuitry, reprogramming the memory. My mind isn't going—so far as I can tell—but it's changing. I'm not thinking the way I used to think. I can feel it most strongly when I'm reading. Immersing myself in a book or a lengthy article used to be easy. My mind would get caught up in the narrative or the turns of the argument, and I'd spend hours strolling through long stretches of prose. That's rarely the case anymore. Now my concentration often starts to drift after two or three pages. I get fidgety, lose the thread, begin looking for something else to do. I feel as if I'm always dragging my wayward brain back to the text. The deep reading that used to come naturally has become a struggle.

3 I think I know what's going on. For more than a decade now, I've been spending a lot of time online, searching and surfing and sometimes adding to the great databases of the Internet. The Web has been a godsend to me as a writer. Research that once required days in the stacks or periodical rooms of libraries can now be done in minutes. A few Google searches, some quick clicks on hyperlinks, and I've got the telltale fact or pithy quote I was after. Even when I'm not working, I'm as likely as not to be foraging in the Web's info-thickets reading and writing e-mails, scanning headlines and blog posts, watching videos and listening to podcasts, or just tripping from link to link to link. (Unlike footnotes, to which they're sometimes likened, hyperlinks don't merely point to related works; they propel you toward them.)

4 For me, as for others, the Net is becoming a universal medium, the conduit for most of the information that flows through my eyes and ears and into my mind. The advantages

*Nicholas Carr, *Atlantic*, Jul./Aug. 2008.

of having immediate access to such an incredibly rich store of information are many, and they've been widely described and duly applauded. "The perfect recall of silicon memory," *Wired*'s Clive Thompson has written, "can be an enormous boon to thinking." But that boon comes at a price. As the media theorist Marshall McLuhan pointed out in the 1960s, media are not just passive channels of information. They supply the stuff of thought, but they also shape the process of thought. And what the Net seems to be doing is chipping away my capacity for concentration and contemplation. My mind now expects to take in information the way the Net distributes it: in a swiftly moving stream of particles. Once I was a scuba diver in the sea of words. Now I zip along the surface like a guy on a Jet Ski.

5   I'm not the only one. When I mention my troubles with reading to friends and acquaintances—literary types, most of them—many say they're having similar experiences. The more they use the Web, the more they have to fight to stay focused on long pieces of writing. Some of the bloggers I follow have also begun mentioning the phenomenon. Scott Karp, who writes a blog about online media, recently confessed that he has stopped reading books altogether. "I was a lit major in college, and used to be [a] voracious book reader," he wrote. "What happened?" He speculates on the answer: "What if I do all my reading on the web not so much because the way I read has changed, i.e. I'm just seeking convenience, but because the way I THINK has changed?"

6   Bruce Friedman, who blogs regularly about the use of computers in medicine, also has described how the Internet has altered his mental habits. "I now have almost totally lost the ability to read and absorb a longish article on the Web or in print," he wrote earlier this year. A pathologist who has long been on the faculty of the University of Michigan Medical School, Friedman elaborated on his comment in a telephone conversation with me. His thinking, he said, has taken on a "staccato" quality, reflecting the way he quickly scans short passages of text from many sources online. "I can't read *War and Peace* anymore," he admitted. "I've lost the ability to do that. Even a blog post of more than three or four paragraphs is too much to absorb. I skim it."

7   Anecdotes alone don't prove much. And we still await the long-term neurological and psychological experiments that will provide a definitive picture of how Internet use affects cognition. But a recently published study of online research habits, conducted by scholars from University College London, suggests that we may well be in the midst of a sea change in the way we read and think. As part of the five-year research program, the scholars examined computer logs documenting the behavior of visitors to two popular research sites, one operated by the British Library and one by a U.K. educational consortium, that provide access to journal articles, e-books, and other sources of written information. They found that people using the sites exhibited "a form of skimming activity," hopping from one source to another and rarely returning to any source they'd already visited. They typically read no more than one or two pages of an article or book before they would "bounce" out to another site. Sometimes they'd save a long article, but there's no evidence that they ever went back and actually read it. The authors of the study report:

> It is clear that users are not reading online in the traditional sense; indeed there are signs that new forms of "reading" are emerging as users "power browse" horizontally through titles, contents pages and abstracts going for quick wins. It almost seems that they go online to avoid reading in the traditional sense.

8   Thanks to the ubiquity of text on the Internet, not to mention the popularity of text-messaging on cell phones, we may well be reading more today than we did in the 1970s or 1980s, when television was our medium of choice. But it's a different kind of reading, and behind it lies a different kind of thinking—perhaps even a new sense of the self. "We are not only *what* we read," says Maryanne Wolf, a developmental psychologist at Tufts University and the author of *Proust and the Squid: The Story and Science of the Reading Brain.* "We are *how* we read." Wolf worries that the style of reading promoted by the Net, a style that puts "efficiency" and "immediacy" above all else, may be weakening our capacity for the kind of deep reading that emerged when an earlier technology, the printing press, made long and complex works of prose commonplace. When we read online, she says, we tend to become "mere decoders of information." Our ability to interpret text, to make the rich mental connections that form when we read deeply and without distraction, remains largely disengaged.

9   Reading, explains Wolf, is not an instinctive skill for human beings. It's not etched into our genes the way speech is. We have to teach our minds how to translate the symbolic characters we see into the language we understand. And the media or other technologies we use in learning and practicing the craft of reading play an important part in shaping the neural circuits inside our brains. Experiments demonstrate that readers of ideograms, such as the Chinese, develop a mental circuitry for reading that is very different from the circuitry found in those of us whose written language employs an alphabet. The variations extend across many regions of the brain, including those that govern such essential cognitive functions as memory and the interpretation of visual and auditory stimuli. We can expect as well that the circuits woven by our use of the Net will be different from those woven by our reading of books and other printed works.

10   Sometime in 1882, Friedrich Nietzsche bought a typewriter—a Malling-Hansen Writing Ball, to be precise. His vision was failing, and keeping his eyes focused on a page had become exhausting and painful, often bringing on crushing headaches. He had been forced to curtail his writing, and he feared that he would soon have to give it up. The typewriter rescued him, at least for a time. Once he had mastered touch-typing, he was able to write with his eyes closed, using only the tips of his fingers. Words could once again flow from his mind to the page.

11   But the machine had a subtler effect on his work. One of Nietzsche's friends, a composer, noticed a change in the style of his writing. His already terse prose had become even tighter, more telegraphic. "Perhaps you will through this instrument even take to a new idiom," the friend wrote in a letter, noting that, in his own work, his "'thoughts' in music and language often depend on the quality of pen and paper."

12   "You are right," Nietzsche replied, "our writing equipment takes part in the forming of our thoughts." Under the sway of the machine, writes the German media scholar Friedrich A. Kittler, Nietzsche's prose "changed from arguments to aphorisms, from thoughts to puns, from rhetoric to telegram style."

13   The human brain is almost infinitely malleable. People used to think that our mental meshwork, the dense connections formed among the 100 billion or so neurons inside our skulls, was largely fixed by the time we reached adulthood. But brain researchers have discovered that that's not the case. James Olds, a professor of neuroscience who directs the Krasnow Institute for Advanced Study at George Mason University, says that even the

adult mind "is very plastic." Nerve cells routinely break old connections and form new ones. "The brain," according to Olds, "has the ability to reprogram itself on the fly, altering the way it functions."

14   As we use what the sociologist Daniel Bell has called our "intellectual technologies"—the tools that extend our mental rather than our physical capacities—we inevitably begin to take on the qualities of those technologies. The mechanical clock, which came into common use in the 14th century, provides a compelling example. In *Technics and Civilization*, the historian and cultural critic Lewis Mumford described how the clock "disassociated time from human events and helped create the belief in an independent world of mathematically measurable sequences." The "abstract framework of divided time" became "the point of reference for both action and thought."

15   The clock's methodical ticking helped bring into being the scientific mind and the scientific man. But it also took something away. As the late MIT computer scientist Joseph Weizenbaum observed in his 1976 book, *Computer Power and Human Reason: From Judgment to Calculation*, the conception of the world that emerged from the widespread use of timekeeping instruments "remains an impoverished version of the older one, for it rests on a rejection of those direct experiences that formed the basis for, and indeed constituted, the old reality." In deciding when to eat, to work, to sleep, to rise, we stopped listening to our senses and started obeying the clock.

16   The process of adapting to new intellectual technologies is reflected in the changing metaphors we use to explain ourselves to ourselves. When the mechanical clock arrived, people began thinking of their brains as operating "like clockwork." Today, in the age of software, we have come to think of them as operating "like computers." But the changes, neuroscience tells us, go much deeper than metaphor. Thanks to our brain's plasticity, the adaptation occurs also at a biological level.

17   The Internet promises to have particularly far-reaching effects on cognition. In a paper published in 1936, the British mathematician Alan Turing proved that a digital computer, which at the time existed only as a theoretical machine, could be programmed to perform the function of any other information-processing device. And that's what we're seeing today. The Internet, an immeasurably powerful computing system, is subsuming most of our other intellectual technologies. It's becoming our map and our clock, our printing press and our typewriter, our calculator and our telephone, and our radio and TV.

18   When the Net absorbs a medium, that medium is re-created in the Net's image. It injects the medium's content with hyperlinks, blinking ads, and other digital gewgaws, and it surrounds the content with the content of all the other media it has absorbed. A new e-mail message, for instance, may announce its arrival as we're glancing over the latest headlines at a newspaper's site. The result is to scatter our attention and diffuse our concentration.

19   The Net's influence doesn't end at the edges of a computer screen, either. As people's minds become attuned to the crazy quilt of Internet media, traditional media have to adapt to the audience's new expectations. Television programs add text crawls and pop-up ads, and magazines and newspapers shorten their articles, introduce capsule summaries, and crowd their pages with easy-to-browse info-snippets. When, in March of this year, *The New York Times* decided to devote the second and third pages of every edition to article abstracts, its design director, Tom Bodkin, explained that the "shortcuts" would give harried readers a quick "taste" of the day's news, sparing them the "less efficient" method of

actually turning the pages and reading the articles. Old media have little choice but to play by the new-media rules.

20   Never has a communications system played so many roles in our lives—or exerted such broad influence over our thoughts—as the Internet does today. Yet, for all that's been written about the Net, there's been little consideration of how, exactly, it's reprogramming us. The Net's intellectual ethic remains obscure.

21   About the same time that Nietzsche started using his typewriter, an earnest young man named Frederick Winslow Taylor carried a stopwatch into the Midvale Steel plant in Philadelphia and began a historic series of experiments aimed at improving the efficiency of the plant's machinists. With the approval of Midvale's owners, he recruited a group of factory hands, set them to work on various metalworking machines, and recorded and timed their every movement as well as the operations of the machines. By breaking down every job into a sequence of small, discrete steps and then testing different ways of performing each one, Taylor created a set of precise instructions—an "algorithm," we might say today—for how each worker should work. Midvale's employees grumbled about the strict new regime, claiming that it turned them into little more than automatons, but the factory's productivity soared.

22   More than a hundred years after the invention of the steam engine, the Industrial Revolution had at last found its philosophy and its philosopher. Taylor's tight industrial choreography—his "system," as he liked to call it—was embraced by manufacturers throughout the country and, in time, around the world. Seeking maximum speed, maximum efficiency, and maximum output, factory owners used time-and-motion studies to organize their work and configure the jobs of their workers. The goal, as Taylor defined it in his celebrated 1911 treatise, *The Principles of Scientific Management*, was to identify and adopt, for every job, the "one best method" of work and thereby to effect "the gradual substitution of science for rule of thumb throughout the mechanic arts." Once his system was applied to all acts of manual labor, Taylor assured his followers, it would bring about a restructuring not only of industry but of society, creating a utopia of perfect efficiency. "In the past the man has been first," he declared; "in the future the system must be first."

23   Taylor's system is still very much with us; it remains the ethic of industrial manufacturing. And now, thanks to the growing power that computer engineers and software coders wield over our intellectual lives, Taylor's ethic is beginning to govern the realm of the mind as well. The Internet is a machine designed for the efficient and automated collection, transmission, and manipulation of information, and its legions of programmers are intent on finding the "one best method"—the perfect algorithm—to carry out every mental movement of what we've come to describe as "knowledge work."

24   Google's headquarters, in Mountain View, California—the Googleplex—is the Internet's high church, and the religion practiced inside its walls is Taylorism. Google, says its chief executive, Eric Schmidt, is "a company that's founded around the science of measurement," and it is striving to "systematize everything" it does. Drawing on the terabytes of behavioral data it collects through its search engine and other sites, it carries out thousands of experiments a day, according to the *Harvard Business Review*, and it uses the results to refine the algorithms that increasingly control how people find information and extract meaning from it. What Taylor did for the work of the hand, Google is doing for the work of the mind.

25   The company has declared that its mission is "to organize the world's information and make it universally accessible and useful." It seeks to develop "the perfect search engine," which it defines as something that "understands exactly what you mean and gives you back exactly what you want." In Google's view, information is a kind of commodity, a utilitarian resource that can be mined and processed with industrial efficiency. The more pieces of information we can "access" and the faster we can extract their gist, the more productive we become as thinkers.

26   Where does it end? Sergey Brin and Larry Page, the gifted young men who founded Google while pursuing doctoral degrees in computer science at Stanford, speak frequently of their desire to turn their search engine into an artificial intelligence, a HAL-like machine that might be connected directly to our brains. "The ultimate search engine is something as smart as people—or smarter," Page said in a speech a few years back. "For us, working on search is a way to work on artificial intelligence." In a 2004 interview with *Newsweek*, Brin said, "Certainly if you had all the world's information directly attached to your brain, or an artificial brain that was smarter than your brain, you'd be better off." Last year, Page told a convention of scientists that Google is "really trying to build artificial intelligence and to do it on a large scale."

27   Such an ambition is a natural one, even an admirable one, for a pair of math whizzes with vast quantities of cash at their disposal and a small army of computer scientists in their employ. A fundamentally scientific enterprise, Google is motivated by a desire to use technology, in Eric Schmidt's words, "to solve problems that have never been solved before," and artificial intelligence is the hardest problem out there. Why wouldn't Brin and Page want to be the ones to crack it?

28   Still, their easy assumption that we'd all "be better off" if our brains were supplemented, or even replaced, by an artificial intelligence is unsettling. It suggests a belief that intelligence is the output of a mechanical process, a series of discrete steps that can be isolated, measured, and optimized. In Google's world, the world we enter when we go online, there's little place for the fuzziness of contemplation. Ambiguity is not an opening for insight but a bug to be fixed. The human brain is just an outdated computer that needs a faster processor and a bigger hard drive.

29   The idea that our minds should operate as high-speed data-processing machines is not only built into the workings of the Internet, it is the network's reigning business model as well. The faster we surf across the Web—the more links we click and pages we view— the more opportunities Google and other companies gain to collect information about us and to feed us advertisements. Most of the proprietors of the commercial Internet have a financial stake in collecting the crumbs of data we leave behind as we flit from link to link—the more crumbs, the better. The last thing these companies want is to encourage leisurely reading or slow, concentrated thought. It's in their economic interest to drive us to distraction.

30   Maybe I'm just a worrywart. Just as there's a tendency to glorify technological progress, there's a countertendency to expect the worst of every new tool or machine. In Plato's *Phaedrus*, Socrates bemoaned the development of writing. He feared that, as people came to rely on the written word as a substitute for the knowledge they used to carry inside their heads, they would, in the words of one of the dialogue's characters, "cease to exercise their memory and become forgetful." And because they would be able to "receive a quantity

of information without proper instruction," they would "be thought very knowledgeable when they are for the most part quite ignorant." They would be "filled with the conceit of wisdom instead of real wisdom." Socrates wasn't wrong—the new technology did often have the effects he feared—but he was shortsighted. He couldn't foresee the many ways that writing and reading would serve to spread information, spur fresh ideas, and expand human knowledge (if not wisdom).

31   The arrival of Gutenberg's printing press, in the 15th century, set off another round of teeth gnashing. The Italian humanist Hieronimo Squarciafico worried that the easy availability of books would lead to intellectual laziness, making men "less studious" and weakening their minds. Others argued that cheaply printed books and broadsheets would undermine religious authority, demean the work of scholars and scribes, and spread sedition and debauchery. As New York University professor Clay Shirky notes, "Most of the arguments made against the printing press were correct, even prescient." But, again, the doomsayers were unable to imagine the myriad blessings that the printed word would deliver.

32   So, yes, you should be skeptical of my skepticism. Perhaps those who dismiss critics of the Internet as Luddites or nostalgists will be proved correct, and from our hyperactive, data-stoked minds will spring a golden age of intellectual discovery and universal wisdom. Then again, the Net isn't the alphabet, and although it may replace the printing press, it produces something altogether different. The kind of deep reading that a sequence of printed pages promotes is valuable not just for the knowledge we acquire from the author's words but for the intellectual vibrations those words set off within our own minds. In the quiet spaces opened up by the sustained, undistracted reading of a book, or by any other act of contemplation, for that matter, we make our own associations, draw our own inferences and analogies, foster our own ideas. Deep reading, as Maryanne Wolf argues, is indistinguishable from deep thinking.

33   If we lose those quiet spaces, or fill them up with "content," we will sacrifice something important not only in our selves but in our culture. In a recent essay, the playwright Richard Foreman eloquently described what's at stake:

> I come from a tradition of Western culture, in which the ideal (my ideal) was the complex, dense and "cathedral-like" structure of the highly educated and articulate personality—a man or woman who carried inside themselves a personally constructed and unique version of the entire heritage of the West. [But now] I see within us all (myself included) the replacement of complex inner density with a new kind of self—evolving under the pressure of information overload and the technology of the "instantly available."

34   As we are drained of our "inner repertory of dense cultural inheritance," Foreman concluded, we risk turning into "'pancake people'—spread wide and thin as we connect with that vast network of information accessed by the mere touch of a button."

35   I'm haunted by that scene in *2001*. What makes it so poignant, and so weird, is the computer's emotional response to the disassembly of its mind: its despair as one circuit after another goes dark, its childlike pleading with the astronaut—"I can feel it. I can feel it. I'm afraid"—and its final reversion to what can only be called a state of innocence. HAL's outpouring of feeling contrasts with the emotionlessness that characterizes the human figures in the film, who go about their business with an almost robotic efficiency.

Their thoughts and actions feel scripted, as if they're following the steps of an algorithm. In the world of *2001*, people have become so machinelike that the most human character turns out to be a machine. That's the essence of Kubrick's dark prophecy: as we come to rely on computers to mediate our understanding of the world, it is our own intelligence that flattens into artificial intelligence.

QUESTIONS FOR ANALYSIS AND DISCUSSION

1. In this essay, Nicholas Carr uses a full-circle approach in which he links his introduction to his conclusion. What hook does Carr use in the introduction and how does he revisit it in his conclusion? Do you find the full-circle approach to be an effective writing strategy? Explain.

2. The psychologist Maryanne Wolf is quoted as saying, "We are not only *what* we read. . . . We are *how* we read." What does she mean by this statement? How might this effect the reading of literature for future generations?

3. The article illustrates several examples of how technology has given us great advancements, but in the process has taken something away from our ability to think. Find three textual examples of this phenomenon. In the author's opinion is the price we are paying worth the gain? What do you think?

4. Sergey Brin, one of the founders of Google, says, "Certainly if you had all the world's information directly attached to your brain, or an artificial brain that was smarter than your brain, you'd be better off." What is Nicholas Carr's opinion of this statement? What is your opinion of this statement?

5. According to Carr, Google seeks to develop the perfect search engine that will "understand exactly what you mean and gives you back exactly what you want." Which search engine do you commonly use? Try experimenting with at least three different search engines to see which one is most effective. What makes one search engine better than another?

6. How does Nicholas Carr show that money may be the underlining cause of the recent change in the way we are reading and thinking? Summarize this section of the article, and then state if you find this business model to be ethical. What, if anything, can individuals do to influence the trend?

I Tweet, Therefore I Am: Life in the Hall of Mirrors

Andrew Lam

Some critics argue that tweets, posts, and public cell phone calls were cries for attention and reassurance that we matter and have importance. Most people believe that social networking sites allow users to connect with people in a way they never could before. Twitter allows us to instantly capture moments in time. Facebook allows for debate, family updates, reminiscing on last night's party (complete with embarrassing photos), and sharing of favorite hobbies, interests, and causes. But what do our online postings reveal about how we connect with the world and how we view ourselves? When we post, we publicly share whom we know, where we are, what we think, what we do, and even who we wish to be. But is social networking taking a bizarre turn? In this next essay, author Andrew Lam explores the strange psychology of online posting, in which people have begun to capture their final moments, surgical traumas, and violent activities. How much has online posting changed our behavior and what we feel should be recorded?*

BEFORE YOU READ

The author of this essay wonders if social networking has become so much of who we "are" and that we "are beginning to believe that we do not fully exist without some sort of electronic imprint in the virtual world." Would you feel complete without social networking (Facebook, Twitter, etc.)? Why or why not?

AS YOU READ

In which ways does modern technology help enhance and deepen our life experiences? Can you imagine your life without a cell phone, handheld communication devices, the Internet, or social networking tools like Facebook and Twitter? How would your life be different?

1   A tragic and disturbing story involves tweeting. A young woman who was being stalked tweeted her impending doom a few days before her murder. "So scared right now," "I got me an uglyass stalker" were some of her tweets, then closer to her death, she tweeted, "This can't be happening . . ." In essence, she was broadcasting events leading to her demise.

2   In the same week, a teenager in the suburb of Baltimore posted on Facebook murder-suicide references before taking a shotgun to school and wounding one of his classmates on the first day of school.

3   Going back a month or so and there's that horrific story about a teenager who lost an arm to an alligator in Florida while swimming with his friends. He heroically fought the reptile and managed to get away minus one limb. But this incident couldn't fully be a modern story until somehow it involved the social media. According to ABC News, before going into surgery to close up his wound, he asked his friend "to snap a photo of him in the trauma unit and post it on Facebook."

4   The examples, of course, are endless. Yet they all seem to suggest man's 21st century response to dramatic events is not necessarily just to simply interact with it, but to also record it. If communication technology was created to enhance our daily lives, something has dramatically shifted along the way: More and more, we are altering our behaviors in service of the digital world.

---

*Andrew Lam, *Huffington Post*, September 5, 2012.

5   So many of us have been raised on video games, cell phones and iPods, and who spent the large bulk of their lives in chatrooms, Skypes and posting on YouTube that we become news reporters and newsmakers without much of an effort. We announce our actions and, in some cases, our impending demise online without giving it much thought. We have been so conditioned to invest our emotional life in the virtual space that it has become second nature. And many of us have learned to split our attention, with one eye on the electronic mirror, and the other on reality.

6   Indeed, more and more, we are beginning to believe that we do not fully exist without some sort of electronic imprint in the virtual world, a digital projection of ourselves, a validation of our existence.

Pipiatum ergo sum? I tweet, therefore I am?

7 Wafaa Bilal, a photography professor at NYU a couple years ago went a step further and implanted a camera in the back of his head as part of an art project. The camera broadcast a live stream of images to a museum in Qatar. On his skull, the real and the digital converge, and the real is photographed for the benefit of the digital.

8   The trend is "self-tracking," according the *Economist*, and a market for these devices is rapidly emerging. There are wireless devices that can track people's physical activity, while other devices measure brainwave activity at night to chart people's sleep patterns online.

9   "People around the world are now learning how to leverage the incredible power inherent in the URL to create what is essentially a parallel universe of digital identities," noted Robert Young, an Internet entrepreneur. But in this new industry, he observed, "the raw materials for the 'products' are the people . . . the key is to look at self-expression and social networks as a new medium and to view the audience itself as a new generation of 'cultural products.'"

10   Perhaps it's too early to tell the long-term effects of an over-saturated information age on human evolution. But according to the *New York Times*, scientists say the constant use of computers and cellular telephones is causing a significant, evolutionary shift in our brain's wiring.

11   But one of the most troubling consequences of devoting so much attention to the virtual world is the death of empathy. Clifford Nass, a communications professor at Stanford, told the *New York Times* that empathy is essential to the human condition. However, given the virtualization of the real world, and tendency for many to multitask, "we are at an inflection point," he said. "A significant fraction of people's experiences are now fragmented."

12   Which may very well explain a story that involves professor Bill Nye, popularly known as "the Science Guy" on TV a couple years ago. He collapsed on stage out of exhaustion as he prepared to give a lecture. But instead of rushing to the stage to help him, the *LA Times* and other media reported, many students in the audience took out their cell phones, snapped photos, texted and tweeted the event.

13   Or consider this now famous story that involves YouTube. On March 30, 2008, a group of teenagers in Florida lured one of their own peers to one of the girl's homes and videotaped her beating. With one girl behind the camera to record the episode, and two

boys guarding the door, the rest mercilessly beat the young woman into a concussion. It was for a dual purpose: to "punish" the victim for allegedly "trash talking" about them on MySpace, and to post the footage on YouTube. The most telling line during the beating, however, was when the young woman behind the camera yelled out: "There's only 17 seconds left. Make it good."

14   Seventeen seconds left, that is, in a 10-minute slot—the maximum time one can post a video segment on YouTube. The time frame and the incident prompted a journalist to quip, "Well, Warhol was only off by five minutes."

The 10 Minutes of Fame

15 What makes that incident unusual is not the violent acts themselves—girl fights have been well-reported, after all—but that the girls' actions were dictated not by a pure act of revenge but by a kind of exhibitionism rarely seen before. Stranger still is that increasingly the electronic world dictates exactly how an action should be carried out. The collective beating of the young woman, for instance, were directed to intensify as the video neared its 10-minute mark. (Did their beating lose steam, one wonders, when the camera stopped rolling?)

16   This modern mindset has given psychologists and anthropologists enough material to study what they call the "disinhibitive effect" on the Internet. Road rage is quickly giving into Net wrath. Like actors who are trained to lose their reservations on stage, many now take daring risks for the virtual world—nevermind that they might have repercussions in the real one. They show all, or do something enormously bizarre or violent to garner lots of hits, lots of eyeballs.

17   Andy Warhol was off by five minutes but he otherwise frighteningly prophetic. A future in which everyone can be famous for about 10 minutes has indeed arrived. We have all become actors, filmmakers, reporters. We begin to believe that we are not fully ourselves, that we are not viable in the new system, unless we make some sort of electronic imprint, some sort of projection of ourselves, in the virtual world. Diaries, once locked away and hidden, have now gone electronic in the form of blogs and vlogs. The real event to some may no longer be as important as its virtual image, which can be relived online.

18   No one doubts that communication technology has enhanced humankind in marvelous ways. But it comes with a price. Mary Shelley's *Frankenstein; or, The Modern Prometheus* was a seminal work and a warning that the discovery of electricity at the cusp of the industrial revolution could create a monster, and of the divine punishments that await those who dared to steal powers from the Gods. The Wachowski brothers' extraordinary movie *The Matrix*, made at the end of the 20th century, in which humans are enslaved and permanently trapped in a simulated reality, was in a way the same warning. Man in the 21st century has transcended geographical and even biological constrains, and found the power to translate and project himself in various media across the globe. But as a result he is seriously fragmented.

19   The new hero in this new myth necessarily needs to become a prophet. For his is the arduous task of reintegrating the various fragments of the self, hearing the symphony in the cacophony, reclaiming the human in the digital—or else suffers being trapped forever in the labyrinthine halls of mirrors.

1. What is the meaning of Lam's title, "Life in the Hall of Mirrors"? Explain.
2. Lam observes that the demands of digital technology have encouraged us "to split our attention, with one eye on the electronic mirror, and the other on reality." Drawing from your personal experience and behavior you have observed in others, respond to Lam's statement. Are we constantly monitoring two lives?
3. Lam notes that the digital world has caused many people to "create what is essentially a parallel universe of digital identities." Are there two identities—the digital one and the "real" one, or are they one *and* the same? Explain.
4. Lam feels that living our lives in the digital world has caused "the death of empathy." What does he mean? What support does he offer? Do you agree that we are less empathetic of others in our eagerness to be the first to tweet, record, or post a comment?
5. In what ways has social media made us all "actors, filmmakers, [and] reporters"?
6. When you post something online, do you think carefully about what you are about to post and how it might sound to others? Do you consider how people will think about you and react to your post? Or do you shoot from the hip, writing whatever comes to mind? Explain.

The Flight from Conversation

Sherry Turkle

Human beings are a social species. From the tribes and clans of the past to the cliques and clubs of the present, we naturally gravitate to each other and seek a sense of belonging and inclusion. Conversation allows us to connect with others, share ideas and feelings, and receive important feedback we need to live our lives productively and happily. While many people agree that social media has allowed people to "reconnect" with friends they would not otherwise have remained in touch with, it may harbor a darker side. If we are conducting most of our communication online, what happens when we meet face to face? Are we losing our ability to meaningfully converse with one another? In this next essay, psychologist and professor Sherry Turkle wonders if we are becoming "alone together."*

Do you read and send e-mail and texts while engaged in face-to-face activities such as meetings, small social gatherings, and dates? Is it okay to pull out your phone when you are at dinner with someone else? Why or why not?

*Sherry Turkle, *New York Times*, April 21, 2012.

In which ways does modern technology help enhance and deepen our life?

1   We live in a technological universe in which we are always communicating. And yet, we have sacrificed conversation for mere connection.

2   At home, families sit together, texting and reading e-mail. At work, executives text during board meetings. We text (and shop and go on Facebook) during classes and when we're on dates. My students tell me about an important new skill: it involves maintaining eye contact with someone while you text someone else; it's hard, but it can be done.

3   Over the past 15 years, I've studied technologies of mobile connection and talked to hundreds of people of all ages and circumstances about their plugged-in lives. I've learned that the little devices most of us carry around are so powerful that they change not only what we do, but also who we are.

4   We've become accustomed to a new way of being "alone together." Technology-enabled, we are able to be with one another, and also elsewhere, connected to wherever we want to be. We want to customize our lives. We want to move in and out of where we are because the thing we value most is control over where we focus our attention. We have gotten used to the idea of being in a tribe of one, loyal to our own party.

5   Our colleagues want to go to that board meeting but pay attention only to what interests them. To some this seems like a good idea, but we can end up hiding from one another, even as we are constantly connected to one another.

6   A businessman laments that he no longer has colleagues at work. He doesn't stop by to talk; he doesn't call. He says that he doesn't want to interrupt them. He says they're "too busy on their e-mail." But then he pauses and corrects himself. "I'm not telling the truth. I'm the one who doesn't want to be interrupted. I think I should. But I'd rather just do things on my BlackBerry."

7   A 16-year-old boy who relies on texting for almost everything says almost wistfully, "Someday, someday, but certainly not now, I'd like to learn how to have a conversation."

8   In today's workplace, young people who have grown up fearing conversation show up on the job wearing earphones. Walking through a college library or the campus of a high-tech start-up, one sees the same thing: we are together, but each of us is in our own bubble, furiously connected to keyboards and tiny touch screens. A senior partner at a Boston law firm describes a scene in his office. Young associates lay out their suite of technologies: laptops, iPods and multiple phones. And then they put their earphones on. "Big ones. Like pilots. They turn their desks into cockpits." With the young lawyers in their cockpits, the office is quiet, a quiet that does not ask to be broken.

9   In the silence of connection, people are comforted by being in touch with a lot of people—carefully kept at bay. We can't get enough of one another if we can use technology to keep one another at distances we can control: not too close, not too far, just right. I think of it as a Goldilocks effect.

10   Texting and e-mail and posting let us present the self we want to be. This means we can edit. And if we wish to, we can delete. Or retouch: the voice, the flesh, the face, the body. Not too much, not too little—just right.

11   Human relationships are rich; they're messy and demanding. We have learned the habit of cleaning them up with technology. And the move from conversation to connection

is part of this. But it's a process in which we shortchange ourselves. Worse, it seems that over time we stop caring, we forget that there is a difference.

12   We are tempted to think that our little "sips" of online connection add up to a big gulp of real conversation. But they don't. E-mail, Twitter, Facebook, all of these have their places—in politics, commerce, romance and friendship. But no matter how valuable, they do not substitute for conversation.

13   Connecting in sips may work for gathering discrete bits of information or for saying, "I am thinking about you." Or even for saying, "I love you." But connecting in sips doesn't work as well when it comes to understanding and knowing one another. In conversation we tend to one another. (The word itself is kinetic; it's derived from words that mean to move, together.) We can attend to tone and nuance. In conversation, we are called upon to see things from another's point of view.

14   Face to face conversation unfolds slowly. It teaches patience. When we communicate on our digital devices, we learn different habits. As we ramp up the volume and velocity of online connections, we start to expect faster answers. To get these, we ask one another simpler questions; we dumb down our communications, even on the most important matters. It is as though we have all put ourselves on cable news. Shakespeare might have said, "We are consum'd with that which we were nourish'd by."

15   And we use conversation with others to learn to converse with ourselves. So our flight from conversation can mean diminished chances to learn skills of self-reflection. These days, social media continually asks us what's "on our mind," but we have little motivation to say something truly self-reflective. Self-reflection in conversation requires trust. It's hard to do anything with 3,000 Facebook friends except connect.

16   As we get used to being shortchanged on conversation and to getting by with less, we seem almost willing to dispense with people altogether. Serious people muse about the future of computer programs as psychiatrists. A high school sophomore confides to me that he wishes he could talk to an artificial intelligence program instead of his dad about dating; he says the A.I. would have so much more in its database. Indeed, many people tell me they hope that as Siri, the digital assistant on Apple's iPhone, becomes more advanced, "she" will be more and more like a best friend—one who will listen when others won't.

17   During the years I have spent researching people and their relationships with technology, I have often heard the sentiment "No one is listening to me." I believe this feeling helps explain why it is so appealing to have a Facebook page or a Twitter feed—each provides so many automatic listeners. And it helps explain why—against all reason—so many of us are willing to talk to machines that seem to care about us. Researchers around the world are busy inventing sociable robots, designed to be companions to the elderly, to children, to all of us.

18   One of the most haunting experiences during my research came when I brought one of these robots, designed in the shape of a baby seal, to an elder-care facility, and an older woman began to talk to it about the loss of her child. The robot seemed to be looking into her eyes. It seemed to be following the conversation. The woman was comforted.

19   And so many people found this amazing. Like the sophomore who wants advice about dating from artificial intelligence and those who look forward to computer psychiatry, this enthusiasm speaks to how much we have confused conversation with connection and collectively seem to have embraced a new kind of delusion that accepts the simulation of

compassion as sufficient unto the day. And why would we want to talk about love and loss with a machine that has no experience of the arc of human life? Have we so lost confidence that we will be there for one another?

20   We expect more from technology and less from one another and seem increasingly drawn to technologies that provide the illusion of companionship without the demands of relationship. Always-on/always-on-you devices provide three powerful fantasies: that we will always be heard; that we can put our attention wherever we want it to be; and that we never have to be alone. Indeed our new devices have turned being alone into a problem that can be solved.

21   When people are alone, even for a few moments, they fidget and reach for a device. Here connection works like a symptom, not a cure, and our constant, reflexive impulse to connect shapes a new way of being.

22   Think of it as "I share, therefore I am." We use technology to define ourselves by sharing our thoughts and feelings as we're having them. We used to think, "I have a feeling; I want to make a call." Now our impulse is, "I want to have a feeling; I need to send a text."

23   So, in order to feel more, and to feel more like ourselves, we connect. But in our rush to connect, we flee from solitude, our ability to be separate and gather ourselves. Lacking the capacity for solitude, we turn to other people but don't experience them as they are. It is as though we use them, need them as spare parts to support our increasingly fragile selves.

24   We think constant connection will make us feel less lonely. The opposite is true. If we are unable to be alone, we are far more likely to be lonely. If we don't teach our children to be alone, they will know only how to be lonely.

25   I am a partisan for conversation. To make room for it, I see some first, deliberate steps. At home, we can create sacred spaces: the kitchen, the dining room. We can make our cars "device-free zones." We can demonstrate the value of conversation to our children. And we can do the same thing at work. There we are so busy communicating that we often don't have time to talk to one another about what really matters. Employees asked for casual Fridays; perhaps managers should introduce conversational Thursdays. Most of all, we need to remember—in between texts and e-mails and Facebook posts—to listen to one another, even to the boring bits, because it is often in unedited moments, moments in which we hesitate and stutter and go silent, that we reveal ourselves to one another.

26   I spend the summers at a cottage on Cape Cod, and for decades I walked the same dunes that Thoreau once walked. Not too long ago, people walked with their heads up, looking at the water, the sky, the sand and at one another, talking. Now they often walk with their heads down, typing. Even when they are with friends, partners, children, everyone is on their own devices.

27   So I say, look up, look at one another, and let's start the conversation.

QUESTIONS FOR ANALYSIS AND DISCUSSION

1. What does Turkle mean when she says the technical universe has caused us to sacrifice conversation for connection? What is the difference and why does it matter?

2. Turkle says that phones "are so powerful that they change not only what we do, but also who we are." How can a phone change who we are? Explain.

3. Turkle observes that "texting and e-mail and posting let us present the self we want to be." Deconstruct one of your latest tweets or online postings. What did you say? How long did it take to write, and what thought did you put into it, and why? What were you trying to share with your friends, and what did you hope they would think of your message? In what ways is what you posted a presentation of the "self [you] want to be"?

4. Turkle states that while e-mail, Twitter, Facebook all have their places, they do not substitute for conversation. What is conversation? What is the difference between conversation and engaging in posts online? What is missing in an online post or text message?

5. Why, in this digital age in which you can have hundreds of friends on Facebook, is it ironic when people say "no one is listening to me"? What is the essence of listening? How do you know when you are listened to, and how do others know you are listening? Is this clear on social media?

6. What is Turkle's objective in this essay? Who is her audience? What action is she hoping her audience will take after reading her essay?

My Facebook, My Self

Jessica Helfand

Many people feel that there is no better way of keeping in contact with high school friends, old neighbors, and new acquaintances than on Facebook. Facebook allows us to keep in touch with as many people as we wish, and in different ways. We see posts about everything from our friends' most recent travels, their comments on world news, to what they had for dinner. Social networking has allowed us to not only view others, but also present ourselves to the world. More than simply connecting us with each other, social networking sites allow us to present a persona to the world—publicly sharing who we know, what we think, what we do, and even what we own. However, in the next essay, writer Jessica Helfand warns us that we need to think carefully about what we put on Facebook, how we create our "profile," and how privacy on Facebook may just be an oxymoron.*

BEFORE YOU READ

Have you ever thought about what your Facebook profile says about you? What image do you project? What do you hope people will learn about you from what you share?

*Jessica Helfand, *Observatory*, March 11, 2009.

AS YOU READ

Have you ever put anything on a social networking page or blog that could potentially embarrass you in five, ten, even twenty years? Consider the information you have personally shared online (include e-mails) and the ramifications of having a record of your online activity possibly accessible in the future.

1   In a recent interview on the *Today Show*, Mark Zuckerberg—the young founder of Facebook—observed that the single most distinctive feature of his revolutionary social networking site was its capacity to let users control various degrees of privacy.

2   I would have listened to more of the interview were it not for my laptop notifying me that I was being invited to chat by someone I went to high school with. For anyone unfamiliar with this practice, Facebook also has a questionable feature displaying everyone who you've "friended" who happens to be online while you're online, which in turn allows them to spontaneously engage you in an online chat. (Even if you're sitting in your pajamas, watching the *Today Show*.) Mind you, the sheer fascination of this surprise encounter—this particular guy never uttered a single word to me when I was a teenager—struck me then, as it does now, as remarkably un-private.

3   Turns out, the very perception of what is public versus what is private is a fundamentally generational conceit. It is also, as it happens, a visual one.

4   I am often asked whether people made scrapbooks, a century ago, intending to share them with others. There's no explicit visual cue that tells us people wanted their stories projected to the world, nor is it clear that any single scrapbook maker believed this to be a clear-cut, black-and-white issue. (Couldn't it be both?)

5   What it does point to is perhaps the more profound question of the projected self: who, after all, doesn't want to look a certain way to others? Scrapbooks and photo albums represent a genre unto themselves because they are unique autobiographical efforts—unvalidated by external approvals, often asynchronous and even wrong in their depiction of real-world events, and stunningly prone to the occasional willfully-constructed fiction. Among other things, this explains why so many scrapbooks celebrate a kind of curious "episodic" time—leapfrogging from happy event to happy event and ignoring the arguably more revealing, if banal, moments in between. Reconstructing biographical narratives within the context of so much idiosyncrasy is ridiculously hard. (And devilishly fun.) There's also something deeply engaging in the ebbs and flows of personal stories in which actual truth is gloriously trumped by an individual's own flawed, if heartfelt rendition of life as he or she deems fit. The resulting palimpsest-like volumes offer extraordinary reflections of authors no longer here to speak for themselves, in which visual cues become biographical cues: pictures speak at least as loud as the words that accompany them. Often, they speak louder.

6   Where Facebook is concerned, the line between public and private exists in a sort of parallel (though oddly torqued) universe: like scrapbooks, Facebook is comprised of pages with amalgamations of diverse content, all held together by an individual's own process of selection. Generally speaking, there is a pronounced appreciation for nostalgia, alternately endearing (how adorable you were at 15!) and excruciating (how appalling you look at 50!). Just like scrapbooks, there is a fair amount of posturing and proselytizing,

bad grammar and bizarre juxtapositions. There's a scarcity of snark. And an almost evan-gelical devotion to stuff: where scrapbook-makers once pasted in pictures of their favorite film stars, Facebook encourages the construction of fan pages, as well as groups to join, causes to support, and so forth.

7   But when it comes to posting actual images, the similarity ends somewhat abruptly: first, because the emphasis on networked sharing is Facebook's *lingua franca*, whereas scrapbooks inhabit a more diary-driven personal landscape; and second, because online, the degree to which pictures are deployed takes the projected self and splinters it into mil-lions of tiny satellite identities leading who knows where.

8   And it begins with the no-holds-barred domain of the Facebook portrait, or portraits *plural*, since that is more the rule than the exception for most users. Why have one self-portrait when you can have twenty or thirty or more? I predict—within the next ten years or so—a magnificent exhibition in some great museum that examines the aesthetic permu-tations of the iterative self-portrait: retouched and re-engineered, Googled and canoodled and oh-so-public. But the social consequences of such wanton picture-posting are not without concern: paradoxically, while this endless and myopic self-branding may breed a generation of really thoughtful image-makers, what are they jeopardizing, even sacrific-ing, in the process?

9   For anyone under the age of, say thirty or so, the whole notion of open-source think-ing is a native habitat that can be applied to everything from group-table seating in res-taurants to sharing playlists to data clouds (I tag, you tag, we all tag)—in short, there's nothing proprietary because people in this particular demographic group don't perceive space as anything you can own. They see it as infinite real estate, to be grazed but not com-mandeered, shared but not colonized. The beauty of this thinking, besides the fact that it is inherently democratic and gracious, is that it lends itself to a kind of progressive evolution in which everyone wins. It's commendable, really, and speaks well for us all.

10   On the other hand (and I'm not the first, nor will I be the last to mention it) there are implicit pitfalls in this rapidly growing virtual arena, particularly for those for whom social skills have not caught up with, say, their computational skills. On Facebook, this leads to huge numbers of pictures by kids of kids at parties acting stupid—yes, stupid—with ciga-rettes and sunglasses and cans of beer and face paint. It's kind of sweet and sort of sad and probably meaningless (or so way too many parents of teenagers tell me) and lighten up, I'm told, because they're just posturing, showing the world just how radical they can be. It's safe, because after all, they're not drinking and driving. They're just on screen.

11   Or are they? Even if you are super-careful—ell, even if you don't have a Facebook account yourself—say you find yourself at some random party where there's someone brandishing a mobile phone. And that someone (or, for that matter, someone else) snaps your picture. Soon thereafter, somebody *with* a Facebook account "tags" you and there you are—*whammo*—your questionable behavior rendered spectacularly public. Sure, the same thing can happen on Flickr (and does) but there's something about those intercon-nected six-degrees-of-separation orbits on Facebook that make a seemingly innocent act like "posting" a random image seem both insidious and scary. (Scarier still, many of the more provocative pictures being posted are actually seen as badges of honor by the people posting them.)

12   Naturally, people in their thirties and forties (and fifties and sixties) are just as likely to parade themselves through their Facebook albums, and do. But the control mechanism is more conscious, and the editorial process itself is typically a bit more cogent. Sure, there are people my age posting images of themselves with big hair back in the 1980s, but this seems more silly (and sentimental) than self-destructive. (After all, those of us who remember a world before Starbucks are old enough to know better.) No—self-destructive is a thirteen-year old girl posting images of herself in a bikini, and all the boys in her class, and her school, and her neighborhood, and even her friends' friends commenting on it, all of it screamingly public. Self-destructive is a seventeen-year old high school senior posting images of himself with a bong, or downing shots of whiskey, or lap-dancing with that thirteen-year old in the bikini. Self-destructive is the as-yet unknown ramifications of so much self-publishing, when what we're publishing is our selves.

13   Who is to say what's right or wrong, what's appropriate or not, what's shared, what's seen, what's hidden? Plenty of what's taking place on Facebook is inherently innocuous, and most of us are willing to take responsibility for what we post and where we post it. A lot of Facebook is seamless and fast, streamlined and effective and fun. But as projections of ourselves, a Facebook identity, made manifest through a person's posted photo albums, inhabits a public trajectory that goes way beyond who and what we are. And it all starts with what—and more critically, who—we actually show.

QUESTIONS FOR ANALYSIS AND DISCUSSION

1. The founder of Facebook, Mark Zuckerberg, contends that Facebook lets "users control various degrees of privacy." On the other hand, the author of this essay shows how Facebook allows for very little privacy. In your opinion, which is the stronger argument? Have the new privacy features recently added by Facebook addressed the issue, or made it more complicated?

2. The author states that one of her Facebook friends "never uttered a single word to me when I was a teenager." Why would someone want to "friend" someone with whom they have little connection? Is Facebook redefining the definition of a "friend"? Explain.

3. Helfand compares and contrasts traditional scrapbooks to Facebook. How are they similar and different? Add your own observations.

4. Helfand predicts that one day a great museum will exhibit the iterative self-portrait, such as seen on Facebook. What predictions do you make about how Facebook will evolve in the future? Will it perhaps lend itself to great art or will it eventually become obsolete? Explain.

5. Jessica Helfand belongs to the older generation, which she views as "cogent"; she views the younger generation as in part "democratic and gracious" and in part "self-destructive." Is Helfand fair in her assessment?

6. Evaluate your own Internet relationships and friendships. Are you a different person online than you are in "real" life?

Strictly Private

QUESTIONS FOR ANALYSIS AND DISCUSSION

1. When you enter information about yourself online, do you think about who else may see it? Explain.
2. What do you need to know in order to understand the point of this cartoon? Explain.
3. Would this cartoon have made any sense ten years ago? Why or why not?
4. Respond to the character's comment, that she expects "all of this to remain strictly private." If you use social media, explain why you use it. How much information do you willingly give away? What do expect others to do with the information? Do you ever worry about what you say online? Why or why not?
5. What message is this cartoon conveying? Explain.

Facebook, the Mean Girls and Me

Taffy Brodesser-Akner

There are many popular movies that highlight the phenomenon of teen aggression in high school. There are popular "queen bees" who bully and control the popular crowd, and everyone else takes the abuse or risks getting singled out for ridicule. For the underdogs in Hollywood films, the unpopular usually prevail and the "mean girls" or "jock-heads" get their due. What about in real life? Our experiences in middle school and high school can influence our self-image even into adulthood. In this next essay, Taffy Brodesser-Akner explains her own experience as a not-so-popular girl who now finds that at 34 years old, she finally feels "like a popular seventh-grader," thanks to networking on Facebook.*

BEFORE YOU READ

When you were in high school, was there a particularly popular group of kids? Did you belong to this popular crowd? Did you know any "mean girl" type of kids and did they affect you?

AS YOU READ

What can *Facebook* tell you about your friends? Is it a superficial way to stay in touch or do you get to know people on a deeper level? When someone asks to be your Facebook friend, how much thought do you put into the decision to say "yes"?

1   I sit at my computer and wait for Barbara, who once poured yogurt on my head in front of the entire field hockey team, to tell me the details of her breakup with her current boyfriend. While I wait, I chat with Alison, who, years ago, stole my pants during gym and cut a hole in the crotch area, and who needs advice on how to sleep-train her baby. Still, while all this is going on, I play online Scrabble with Rachel, who, when I was 12, told everyone I had faked getting my period for attention.

2   I am someone with a life. I have a career, a son, a husband, an active volunteer life, and many current and real-life friendships that need maintenance. I have a work deadline in three hours, plus dinner isn't ready. The laundry remains unlaundered. Why, then, am I sitting at my computer, concerned to distraction over the activities of the people who were cruelest to me during my formative years?

3   They weren't always horrible to me. I loved fifth and sixth grades. I had a clique of friends, complete with secret nicknames, passed notes, knowing looks, friendship bracelets, friendship pens, friendship songs. We moved through the school as a group and took turns slumber-partying at each other's houses.

4   We traded the title "best friend" regularly among different pairings in our group. Nancy and Barbara had spent two weeks together in Nantucket over the summer, and

*Taffy Brodesser-Akner, *Salon,* November 20, 2009.

though Nancy and I had been best friends prior to that, apparently they had decided that their time had come to be best friends. They made this announcement to me via conference call the week before school started. I took it OK; after all, I'd been meaning to get to know Amy better.

5 Late in sixth grade, something changed, and I wasn't a part of it. One day, all my friends came in with matching training bras. "I didn't know we were getting bras," I said. They looked at each other, a shared glance I used to be on the comfy side of, and my heart sank with the unspoken answer: *We* weren't. *They* were.

6 Seventh grade began, and I found out we had grown out of things like changing best friends. I met a girl named Emily who had transferred to our school. After a good day of getting to know her, I asked if she wanted to be best friends. "You're such a loser," she spat. I looked around one day, and my group of friends had wandered away. Adults like to generalize and say things like, "Aren't kids cruel?" But we kids, the ones who are left out in the cold, have a role in what happens to us. Not necessarily a fair one, but the facts of our unpopularity are not mysterious. We get fat, we say the wrong thing, we wear outdated clothing. Me, I was too needy. Long after my friends stopped needing superlative titles to know how much they meant to each other, I still did.

7 I did not go quietly into that lonely and unpopular night. Each morning, I tried to assume a casual air of friendship. Big mistake. My efforts backfired, and my former friends' apathy toward me turned to hatred. Soon, I was not just ignored at school. I was tripped as I came out of the shower. People made flatulent noises when I sat down in class. My locker was magic-markered with the word "loser." We are tempted to remember this behavior and make light of it. Oh, it couldn't have been that bad, we said. But I remember it well. It was that bad.

8 Now, all these years later, there's Facebook, allowing us to put the past to rest, to erase the mystery that used to be inherent in the subject of wondering whatever happened to those people you once knew.

9 After accumulating college friends and ex-boyfriends, as we all do when we join Facebook, I took a chance and looked up Barbara. With the nervousness that accompanied me on every bus trip to school following my fall from grace, I pressed the button that would send her a friend request. Immediately, I received confirmation: She had agreed, finally, to be my friend. Brave now, I found Alison, then Amy, then Nancy. I was euphoric. Here I am, back in the inner sanctum. I sort through their pictures, their posts, their lives. I cheer their triumphs, their babies' birthdays, photos from their ski trips. I cobble together the story of how life has been since we knew each other, deliberately, forcefully forgetting how it was we parted.

10 I check their updates and their statuses with eagerness each day. Like an addict, I am euphoric when I am practicing my addiction, remorseful and self-hating when I'm not. I am shocked at how easily I have forgiven these people. I am filled with the warm light of acceptance; I am wrapped in the cozy blanket of belonging.

11 In my imagination, my old clique's renewed friendship tells me that they know they were wrong, that they were just being cruel. They're sorry, they say with every LOL or emoticon. We were wrong, they say when they press the "like" button on my status update. If I'm honest, I bet they don't think about it. I bet they regard me as a name that is familiar— a new person in their lives, more than an old one.

12   There is no way to go back in time and undo things—not the insults, not the humili-
ations. We can pretend some events never happened, though we are always still a little
plagued. But, sometimes, we can also find a way to make what happened in the past right.
I'm not saying you can do that with everything that haunts your past. But some things, you
can. Maybe the way women in the '90s took back the word "bitch," calling themselves and
each other by the ugly slur so that it wouldn't hold power when men said it, maybe that's
what I'm doing with my former friends.

13   Why do you need to be loved by people who rejected you a hundred years ago, asks
my husband, though I have explained it. He believes I have Stockholm syndrome, that I
have fallen in love with my torturers. I tell him that these are just old friends, that I'm over
it, that it's nice to be in touch with a piece of my past. But I'm not exactly over it, am I?
What I am, though, is someone who has finally found a way to put my life's ugliest social
chapter to rest. Maybe I didn't come by it the honest way—through a true reckoning with
my past, a fearless inventory of what happened that year and why I can't get over it. But
who is to say that we shouldn't try to find peace any way we can? Who says it always has
to be so hard?

14   Whatever my intention was when I contacted my former friends, it's different now.
I no longer want validation; I no longer am testing the waters to see if they now find me
worth their time. These women are not who I thought they'd be. They're people having
a hard time in the economy, people who are struggling through their days, their relationships. I don't have enough in common with them to think that, had we not fallen out, our
friendships would have survived. But here, now, I am someone who also struggles with
these things. I have stretched across a social divide that was narrower than I thought, and
I found community where I least expected it. Am I pathetic? Maybe. But what I also am,
finally, is a popular seventh-grader. I think of my younger self, eating her lunch alone,
wondering when this agony will be over. I wish I could tell her I haven't forgotten about
her. I wish I could tell her I've made it OK.

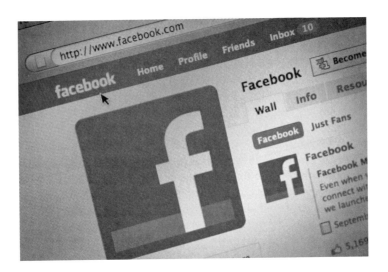

1. Brodesser-Akner comments in her essay that she no longer wants or needs validation. Describe what she means by this statement. Do you believe her? Draw from textual evidence to support your point.
2. The author states that she is finally "a popular seventh-grader" due to Facebook. What does it mean to be "popular"? Can you be truly popular on Facebook? Can Facebook or other social networking sites help people right the wrongs in their past?
3. Most narrative essays use chronological order to tell their stories. Show how Brodesser-Akner progresses through her own essay. Do you find the author's style to be effective?
4. What was the author's purpose for writing this essay? Explain. Use textual evidence in your explanation.
5. Look up the definition of "Stockholm syndrome." Why does the author's husband use this term to describe her relationship with her "friends" on Facebook?
6. Brodesser-Akner asserts that in the 1990s, women "took back the word, 'bitch,' calling themselves and each other by the ugly slur so that it wouldn't hold power when men said it." She then claims that this is what she's doing with her former friends. Explain what she means by this analogy.

You Gotta Have (150) Friends
Robin Dunbar

Can social networking sites fulfill the need to connect with others in the same way face-to-face relationships do? Can they really be as meaningful as our in-person interactions with others? In this next essay, anthropologist Robin Dunbar, professor of evolutionary biology, explains that they can, to a certain extent. Social networking sites allow us to broadcast to (and thereby connect with) a large group of people. But the number of people we can truly handle, offline and on, is capped—at about 150. Dunbar is best known for formulating "Dunbar's number," a measurement of the "cognitive limit to the number of individuals with whom any one person can maintain stable relationships." Which of course begs the question, what's the point of having more than 150 "friends" on Facebook?*

How many friends do you have on Facebook? Are they all people you know? How many of them do you follow or interact with on a regular basis? Do you try to connect with the friends you have, or is it more a place where you can just talk about yourself?

---

*Robin Dunbar, *New York Times*, December 25, 2010.

AS YOU READ

Dunbar states that we can only maintain around 150 meaningful relationships, online and off. What does it mean to "maintain" a real friendship? Do you agree that it is impossible to "maintain" more than 150 friends?

1   More than anything since the invention of the postal service, Facebook has revolutionized how we relate to one another. But the revolution hasn't come in quite the way that the people behind it and other social networking sites assume.

2   These sites may have allowed us to amass thousands of "friends," but they have not yet devised a way to cut through the clunky, old-fashioned nature of relationships themselves. Our circle of actual friends remains stubbornly small, limited not by technology but by human nature. What Facebook has done, though, is provide us a way to maintain those circles in a fractured, dynamic world.

3   Social networking and other digital media have long promised to open up wonderful new vistas, all from the comfort of our own homes. The limitations of face-to-face interaction that have, until now, bound us to our small individual worlds—the handful of people we meet in our everyday lives—would be overcome.

4   The critical component in social networking is the removal of time as a constraint. In the real world, according to research by myself and others, we devote 40 percent of our limited social time each week to the five most important people we know, who represent just 3 percent of our social world and a trivially small proportion of all the people alive today. Since the time invested in a relationship determines its quality, having more than five best friends is impossible when we interact face to face, one person at a time.

5   Instant messaging and social networking claim to solve that problem by allowing us to talk to as many people as we like, all at the same time. Like the proverbial lighthouse blinking on the horizon, our messages fan out into the dark night to every passing ship within reach of an Internet connection. We can broadcast, literally, to the world.

6   I use the word "broadcast" because, despite Facebook's promise, that is the fundamental flaw in the logic of the social-networking revolution. The developers at Facebook overlooked one of the crucial components in the complicated business of how we create relationships: our minds.

7   Put simply, our minds are not designed to allow us to have more than a very limited number of people in our social world. The emotional and psychological investments that a close relationship requires are considerable, and the emotional capital we have available is limited.

8   Indeed, no matter what Facebook allows us to do, I have found that most of us can maintain only around 150 meaningful relationships, online and off—what has become known as Dunbar's number. Yes, you can "friend" 500, 1,000, even 5,000 people with your Facebook page, but all save the core 150 are mere voyeurs looking into your daily life—a fact incorporated into the new social networking site Path, which limits the number of friends you can have to 50.

9   What's more, contrary to all the hype and hope, the people in our electronic social worlds are, for most of us, the same people in our offline social worlds. In fact, the average number of friends on Facebook is 120 to 130, just short enough of Dunbar's number to allow room for grandparents and babies, people too old or too young to have acquired the digital habit.

10   This isn't to say that Facebook and its imitators aren't performing an important, even revolutionary, task—namely, to keep us in touch with our existing friends.

11   Until relatively recently, almost everyone on earth lived in small, rural, densely interconnected communities, where our 150 friends all knew one another, and everyone's 150 friends list was everyone else's.

12   But the social and economic mobility of the past century has worn away at that interconnectedness. As we move around the country and across continents, we collect disparate pockets of friends, so that our list of 150 consists of a half-dozen subsets of people who barely know of one another's existence, let alone interact.

13   Our ancestors knew the same people their entire lives; as we move around, though, we can lose touch with even our closest friends. Emotional closeness declines by around 15 percent a year in the absence of face-to-face contact, so that in five years someone can go from being an intimate acquaintance to the most distant outer layer of your 150 friends.

14   Facebook and other social networking sites allow us to keep up with friendships that would otherwise rapidly wither away. And they do something else that's probably more important, if much less obvious: they allow us to reintegrate our networks so that, rather than having several disconnected subsets of friends, we can rebuild, albeit virtually, the kind of old rural communities where everyone knew everyone else. Welcome to the electronic village.

QUESTIONS FOR ANALYSIS AND DISCUSSION

1. The author's research indicates that we devote 40 percent of our social time each week to the five most important people we know. First, think about how many people you would define as the "most important people" in your life and then determine how much time per week you actually spend with those people. Does it seem to be about 40 percent of your social time? Does the author's research reflect your lifestyle and experiences? Explain.

2. What is "Dunbar's number"? How many friends do you have on Facebook (or another social networking site)? Does it fit with "Dunbar's number"?

3. Consider the author's words: "The emotional and psychological investments that a close relationship requires are considerable, and the emotional capital we have available is limited." Explain what you think the author means here. Have any of your own friendships required emotional and psychological investment? Explain.

4. What point is Dunbar making in the final sentence of his article?

5. If the number of friends—online and offline—we can handle is about 150, is there any point to having more than that on a social networking site? Why or why not?

6. Do you have any personal examples of long-distance friendships? Dunbar asserts, "Emotional closeness declines by around 15 percent a year in the absence of face-to-face contact." Do you find this assertion to be true according to your own examples of long-distance friendship?

7. According to a blog post by Path's founder Dave Morin, "Path allows you to capture your life's most personal moments and share them with the 50 close friends and family in your life who matter most. Because your personal network is limited to your closest friends and family, you can always trust that you can post any moment, no matter how personal. Path is a place where you can be yourself." Analyze Morin's comments and argue which site is better for college students, Path or Facebook, and state whether you think Path will take over Facebook in the future.

Streams of Content: Limited Attention

danah boyd

For much of history, information was something that was given to us—controlled by governments, companies, and other groups in power who decided what we needed to know, and when we would know it. Until recently, most consumers of information received news at the same time, filtered by the outlets conveying the information itself. Today, however, information can hit us from multiple avenues, both official and unofficial, complimented by video and as-it-happens updates. In this next essay, danah boyd, a professor of media, culture, and communications, explains how the Internet is changing the way we consume information and how we interact with content and with each other.*

BEFORE YOU READ

Many students use multiple network media at the same time. Does it feel natural for you to receive a text message at the top of your screen, while you are tweeting about something else, all while taking notes in class? Or do you find yourself getting distracted with so much information demanding a bit of your attention?

AS YOU READ

In what ways is our use of Internet media an act of consumption? Explain.

1 In his seminal pop-book, Mihaly Csikszentmihalyi argued that people are happiest when they can reach a state of "flow." He talks about performers and athletes who are in the height of their profession, the experience they feel as time passes by and everything just clicks. People reach a state where attention appears focused and, simultaneously, not in need of focus at the same time. The world is aligned and everything just feels right.

2 Consider what it means to be "in flow" in an information landscape defined by networked media, and you will see where Web 2.0 is taking us. The goal is not to be a passive

---

*danah boyd, *UX Magazine*, February 5, 2010.

consumer of information or to simply tune in when the time is right, but rather to live in a world where information is everywhere. To be peripherally aware of information as it flows by, grabbing it at the right moment when it is most relevant, valuable, entertaining, or insightful. Living with, in, and around information. Most of that information is social information, but some of it is entertainment information or news information or productive information. Being in flow with information is different than Csikszentmihalyi's sense, as it's not about perfect attention, but it is about a sense of alignment, of being aligned with information.

3   As of late, we've been talking a lot about content streams, streams of information. This metaphor is powerful. The idea is that you're living inside the stream: adding to it, consuming it, redirecting it. The stream metaphor is about reaching flow. It's also about restructuring the ways in which information flows in modern society.

4   Those who are most enamored with services like Twitter talk passionately about feeling as though they are living and breathing with the world around them, peripherally aware and in-tune, adding content to the stream and grabbing it when appropriate. This state is delicate, plagued by information overload and weighed down by frustrating tools.

5   For the longest time, we have focused on sites of information as a destination, of accessing information as a process, of producing information as a task. What happens when all of this changes? While things are certainly clunky at best, this is the promise land of the technologies we're creating. This is all happening because of how our information society is changing. But before we talk more about flow, we need to step back and talk about shifts in the media landscape.

From Broadcast to Networked

6 For the last few centuries, we have been living in an era of broadcast media, but we have been switching to an era of networked media. This fundamentally alters the structure by which information flows.

7   Those who believe in broadcast structures recognize the efficiency of a single, centralized source. There's some nostalgia here. The image is clear: 1950s nightly news, everyone tuning in to receive the same message at the same time. There are the newspapers, the radio stations, magazines—all telling the same newsy story. Centralized sources of information are powerful because they control the means of distribution. There is also the town gossip, the church, and the pub. These too were centralized channels for disseminating information.

8   Broadcast media structures take one critical thing for granted: attention. There is an assumption that everyone will tune in and give their attention to the broadcast entity, even though that was never true in the first place. As TV channels and publishing brands proliferated, we've seen that attention can easily be fragmented. Over the last few decades, increasing numbers of entities have been fighting for a smaller and smaller portion of the pie. Even gossip rags started competing for attention.

9   The opportunities for media creation have been rising for decades, but the Internet provided new mechanisms through which people could make their own content available. From blogging to social network sites to media sharing sites to sites that provide social streams, we are seeing countless ways in which a motivated individual can make their

personal content available. There were always folks willing to share their story but the Internet gave them a pulpit on which to stand.

10   Internet technologies are fundamentally dismantling and reworking the structures of distribution. Distribution is a process by which content creators find channels through which they can disseminate their creation. In effect, they're pushing out the content. Sure, people have to be there to receive it, but the idea is that there are limited channels for distribution and thus getting access to this limited resource is hard. That is no longer the case.

11   As networked technologies proliferate around the world, we can assume that there is a channel of distribution available to everyone and between everyone. In theory, anyone could get content to anyone else. With the barriers to distribution collapsing, what matters is not the act of distribution, but the act of consumption. Thus, the power is no longer in the hands of those who control the channels of distribution, but those who control the limited resource of attention. This is precisely why YOU were *Time* magazine's the Person of the Year in 2006. Your attention is precious and valuable. It's no longer about push; it's about pull. And the "Law of Two Feet" is now culturally pervasive.

12   While we're dismantling traditional structures of distribution, we're also building out new forms of information dissemination. Content is no longer being hocked, but links are. People throughout the network are using the attention they receive to traffic in pointers to other content, serving as content mediators. Numerous people have become experts as information networkers.

13   To many people, this seems like old news. Isn't that the whole point of Web 2.0? Isn't that what we've been living? Sure, of course. But now that we're seeing Web 2.0 go mainstream, we're seeing all sorts of folks get into the game. What they're doing often looks different than what early adopters were doing. And the business folks are all trying to turn the Internet into a new broadcast channel (don't worry, they're failing). But we need to talk about these shifts so we can talk about what innovation needs to happen.

14   If folks are going to try to get in-flow with information, we need to understand how information flows differently today. Let me highlight four challenges, points where technological hope and reality collide.

Four Core Issues

1. Democratization

15 Switching from a model of distribution to a model of attention is disruptive, but it is not inherently democratizing. This is a mistake we often make when talking about this shift. We may be democratizing certain types of access, but we're not democratizing attention. Just because we're moving towards a state where anyone has the ability to get information into the stream does not mean that attention will be divided equally. Opening up access to the structures of distribution is not democratizing when distribution is no longer the organizing function.

16   Some people might immediately think, "Ah, but it's a meritocracy. People will give their attention to what is best!" This too is mistaken logic. What people give their attention to depends on a whole set of factors that have nothing to do with what's best. At the most basic level, consider the role of language. People will pay attention to content that is in

their language, even if they can get access to content in any language. This means Chinese language content will soon get more attention than English content, let alone Dutch or Hebrew content.

2. Stimulation

17 People consume content that stimulates their mind and senses. That which angers, excites, energizes, entertains, or otherwise creates an emotional response. This is not always the "best" or most informative content, but that which triggers a reaction.

18 This isn't inherently a good thing. Consider the food equivalent. Our bodies are programmed to consume fat and sugars because they're rare in nature. Thus, when they come around, we should grab them. In the same way, we're biologically programmed to be attentive to things that stimulate: content that is gross, violent, or sexual and that gossip which is humiliating, embarrassing, or offensive. If we're not careful, we're going to develop the psychological equivalent of obesity. We'll find ourselves consuming content that is least beneficial for ourselves or society as a whole.

19 We are addicted to gossip for a reason. We want to know what's happening because such information brings us closer to people. When we know something about someone, there's a sense of connection. But the information ecology we live in today has twisted this whole thing upside down. Just because I can follow the details of Angelina Jolie's life doesn't mean she knows I exist. This is what scholars talk about as parasocial relations. With Facebook, you can turn your closest friends into celebrities, characters you gawk at and obsess over without actually gaining the benefits of social intimacy and bonding.

20 Stimulation creates cognitive connections. But it is possible for there to be too much stimulation. We don't want a disconnected, numb society, nor a society of unequal social connections. So driving towards greater and more intense stimulation may not be what we want.

21 Of course, there's money here and people will try to manipulate this dynamic for their own purposes. There are folks who put out highly stimulating content or spread gossip to get attention. And often they succeed, creating a pretty unhealthy cycle. So we have to start asking ourselves what balance looks like and how we can move towards an environment where there are incentives for consuming healthy content that benefit individuals and society as a whole. Or, at the very least, how not to feed the trolls.

3. Homophily

22 In a networked world, people connect to people like themselves. What flows across the network flows through edges of similarity. The ability to connect to others like us allows us to flow information across space and time in impressively new ways, but there's also a downside.

23 Prejudice, intolerance, bigotry, and power are all baked into our networks. In a world of networked media, it's easy to not get access to views from people who think from a different perspective. Information can and does flow in ways that create and reinforce social divides. Democratic philosophy depends on shared informational structures, but the combination of self-segmentation and networked information flow means that we lose the common rhetorical ground through which we can converse.

24   Throughout my studies of social media, I have been astonished by the people who think that XYZ site is for people like them. I interviewed gay men who thought Friendster was a gay dating site because all they saw were other gay men. I interviewed teens who believed that everyone on MySpace was Christian because all of the profiles they saw contained biblical quotes. We all live in our own worlds with people who share our values and, with networked media, it's often hard to see beyond that.

25   Ironically, the one place where I'm finding people are being forced to think outside their box is the Trending Topics on Twitter. Consider a topic that trended a while ago: #thingsdarkiessay. Started in South Africa, this topic is fundamentally about language and cultural diversity but, when read in a U.S.-context, it reads as fundamentally racist. Boy did this blow up, forcing a lot of folks to think about language and cultural differences. Why? Because Trending Topics brings a topic that gained traction in a segment of the network to broader awareness, often out of context. Unfortunately, it's hard to get meaningful dialogue going once a Trending Topic triggers reactions.

26   In an era of networked media, we need to recognize that networks are homophilous and operate accordingly. Technology does not inherently disintegrate social divisions. In fact, more often *than* not, *it* reinforces them. Only a small percentage of people are inclined to seek out opinions and ideas from cultures other than their own. These people are and should be highly valued in society, but just because people can be what Ethan Zuckerman calls "xenophiles" doesn't mean they will be.

4. Power

27 When we think about centralized sources of information distribution, it's easy to understand that power is at stake. But networked structures of consumption are also configured by power and we cannot forget that or assume that access alone is power. Power is about being able to command attention, influence others' attention, and otherwise traffic in information. We give power to people when we give them our attention and people gain power when they bridge between different worlds and determine what information can and will flow across the network.

28   In a networked culture, there is also power in being the person spreading the content. When my colleagues and I were examining retweets in Twitter, we saw something fascinating: a tension between citationality and attribution. In short, should you give credit to the author of the content or acknowledge the person through whom you learned of the information? Instinctually, many might believe that the author is the most important person to credit. But, few ideas are truly the product of just one individual. So why not credit the messenger who is helping the content flow? We found that reasonable people disagreed about what was best.

29   In a broadcast model, those who control the distribution channels often profit more than the creators. Think: Clear Channel, record labels, TV producers, etc. Unfortunately, there's an assumption that if we get rid of limitations to the means of distribution, the power will revert to the creators. This is not what's happening. Distribution today is making people aware that they can come and get something, but those who get access to people's attention are still a small, privileged few.

30   Instead, what we're seeing [is] a new type of information broker emerge. These folks get credit for their structural position. While the monetary benefits are indirect, countless

consulting gigs have arisen for folks based on their power as information brokers. The old controllers of information are losing their stature (and are not happy about it). What's emerging is not inherently the power of the creators, but the power of the modern-day information brokers.

Making It Work

31 As our information ecosystem evolves, we will see some radical changes take place. First, I believe that information spaces will get more niche. We will see evidence of this in the ways people direct their attention, and also in what new enterprises are succeeding. Successful businesses will not be everything to everyone; that's the broadcast mentality. Instead, they will play a meaningful role to a cohort of committed consumers who give their attention to them because of their relevance.

32 To be relevant today requires understanding context, popularity, and reputation. In the broadcast era, we assumed the disseminator organized information because they were a destination. In a networked era, there will be no destination, but rather a network of content and people. We cannot assume that content will be organized around topics or that people will want to consume content organized as such. We're already seeing this in streams-based media consumption. When consuming information through social media tools, people consume social gossip alongside productive content, news alongside status updates. Right now, it's one big mess. But the key is not going to be to create distinct destinations organized around topics, but to find ways in which content can be surfaced in context, regardless of where it resides.

33 Making content work in a networked era is going to be about living in the streams, consuming and producing alongside "customers." Consuming to understand, producing to be relevant. Content creators are not going to get to dictate the cultural norms just because they can make their content available; they are still accountable to those who are trafficking content.

34 We need technological innovations. For example, tools that allow people to more easily contextualize relevant content regardless of where they are and what they are doing and tools that allow people to slice and dice content so as to not reach information overload. This is not simply about aggregating or curating content to create personalized destination sites. Frankly, I don't think this will work. Instead, the tools that consumers need are those that allow them to get into flow, that allow them to live inside information structures wherever they are, whatever they're doing. The tools that allow them to easily grab what they need and stay peripherally aware without feeling overwhelmed.

35 Finally, we need to rethink our business plans. I doubt this cultural shift will be paid for by better advertising models. Advertising is based on capturing attention, typically by interrupting the broadcast message or by being inserted into the content itself. Trying to reach information flow is not about being interrupted. Advertising does work when it's part of the flow itself. Ads are great when they provide a desirable answer to a search query or when they appear at the moment of purchase. But when the information being shared is social in nature, advertising is fundamentally a disruption.

36 Figuring out how to monetize sociality is a problem, and not one that's new to the Internet. Think about how we monetize sociality in physical spaces. Typically, it involves

second-order consumption of calories. Venues provide a space for social interaction to occur and we are expected to consume to pay rent. Restaurants, bars, cafes . . . they all survive on this model. But we have yet to find the digital equivalent of alcohol.

37   As we continue to move from a broadcast model of information to a networked one, we will continue to see reworking of the information landscape. Some of what is unfolding is exciting, some is terrifying. The key is not [to] be all utopian or dystopian about it, but to recognize what changes and what stays the same. The future of Web 2.0 is about information flow and if you want to help people, help them reach that state.

QUESTIONS FOR ANALYSIS AND DISCUSSION

1. What is "flow"? What happens when true flow occurs? How does the concept of flow connect to the Internet and how we use information?
2. What does boyd mean when she states that with the Internet, we are "living inside the stream"?
3. What is the difference between broadcast media and networked media? What are the primary attributes of each?
4. How does the advancement of networked media over broadcast media represent a significant power shift for both producers of content and consumers of content? Explain.
5. Summarize boyd's primary points. What is her argument?
6. Boyd warns that if we are not careful, we are going to "develop the psychological equivalent of obesity." What does she mean? Explain.
7. In what ways does advertising impede flow? Why does boyd feel that in order to advance the effective and useful consumption of information, advertising cannot be part of the solution?

WRITING ASSIGNMENTS

1. Track all of your online correspondence—received and sent—for a period of one week. This should include e-mail, blogging, text messaging, and posting on social networking sites such as Facebook and Twitter. Develop categories for the communication (social, family, work, school, junk, etc.) and chart how many of each you receive and send in each category. Keep track of how much time you spend online. In a short essay, discuss how the Internet both enhances and complicates life, and whether it is indeed changing your personal relationships for better or for worse.

2. Several of the writers in this chapter are critical of social networking sites, noting that they promote self-centeredness, reduce our ability to cope with emotions, and cheapen what it means to be "a friend." Interview at least ten people of different age groups about how they use online communication and their views of social networking sites. Create simple questions, but make them broad enough to allow for the expression of detailed viewpoints and options. Write a short essay evaluating the role of social networking in the lives of people today. Include any differences or similarities you

noticed between age groups, professions, and/or social backgrounds. Based on your surveys, can you predict the role social networking will have in our lives in the next decade?

3. Is there a connection between how we communicate and relate to others online and how we develop our own sense of identity? How others perceive us? Print the profiles of at least ten people you know (you may need to ask for permission if you are not part of a social network) and compare the profiles they present to the people you know in "real life." Alternatively, you could ask an acquaintance to share five profiles of people you don't know for analysis.

4. A popular television commercial for an Internet employment agency features a man writing an insulting letter to his boss only to have a toy fall off his monitor and hit the "enter" key, sending his message. Have you ever had a mishap with online communication, or found yourself sending a message that you shouldn't have simply because you hit the "enter" key in the heat of the moment? Describe your experience. Did it influence your future use of online communication?

5. Evaluate your own online communication style. Are you brief and to the point, or do you compose in more detail? What do you think your style says about you? What does it communicate to others? Do you have different styles for different situations? Explain.

6. Write about a relationship, romantic or merely friendly, in which online networking was an essential component of the connection you had with the other person. Cite examples of how social networking contributed to your relationship, and how it enriched the quality of your relationship.

7. Research how the Internet is influencing how we think and how it may be even changing our brains. Will the Internet be the next influence on our physical evolution? Explain.

8. Watch the film *The Social Network* and do research on the beginnings of Facebook. Then write an essay arguing whether Robin Dunbar is correct in stating: "Facebook has revolutionized how we relate to one another. But the revolution hasn't come in quite the way that the people behind it and other social networking sites assume."

9. Check and see how many "friends" you have on Facebook or equivalent social site, followers on Twitter or Pinterest, or blog readers if you maintain a blog. What does the number of friends or followers mean to you? Why do you have the friends you do? Do you know all of your friends or followers personally? Does it matter whether you do or not? Write an essay in which you explore the meaning of followers and friends in social media.

Family Values

The American family has always been in a state of transition, influenced by the social and economic landscape. How we envision the concept of family is based in part on our personal history, peer group, and the values we share. Many of our ideas regarding "traditional family" and "family values" are based on models generations old, touted by politicians, and perpetuated by media archetypes, especially television.

However, the role the American family plays as a social, economic, and moral barometer continues to influence our expectations and behaviors. Stepfamilies, same-sex relationships, single-parent households, and extended families with several generations living in one home all force us to redefine, or at least reexamine, our definitions of *family*.

Divorce, for example, is a widely accepted reality of life that is no longer viewed as a deviation from the norm. Single motherhood is no longer ascribed the social stigma it had 30 or 40 years ago, with almost half of children born to mothers under 30 now born out of wedlock. In 2012, the Annie E. Casey Foundation's Kids Count reported that 35 percent of children under the age of 18 live with only one parent. Marriage has also come under scrutiny. Cohabitation is growing more popular in some communities than marriage. Almost 7 percent of children today are born into two-parent households to parents who are unmarried. Over a dozen states have legalized same-sex marriage, and many more have ballot measures and bills supporting same-sex marriage drafted.

From traditional models of a married nuclear family—with a husband, wife, and children—to cohabiting multigenerational stepfamilies and same-sex unions, this chapter takes a look at how our concept of family has changed over the last several decades. What are American family values today?

Family: Idea, Institution, and Controversy
Betty G. Farrell

Although the family has always been in a state of transition, many politicians expound that the family is not just in a state of change, it is in a state of decline—to the detriment of society. And whether this is true or not, it seems that many people agree that most of society's ills are directly connected to the decline of the family. The truth is the American family is more than an icon in our culture. It is an American institution, subject to intense scrutiny and criticism. In this essay,

Professor Betty G. Farrell explores the importance of the institution of family in American culture and how this importance is inextricably linked to our social and political consciousness.*

BEFORE YOU READ ————————————————

Social scientists and family historians often comment that the American family is in a "state of transition." What do they mean? What is *transition*? Is it a positive or negative thing?

AS YOU READ ————————————————

How do we construct our concept of family? What cultural myths and social forces contribute to our construction of this institution? How does nostalgia influence our view? Explain.

1 Q: What did Eve say to Adam on being expelled from the Garden of Eden?
2   A: "I think we're in a time of transition."
3   The irony of this joke is not lost as we begin a new century, and anxieties about social change seem rife. The implication of this message, covering the first of many subsequent periods of transition, is that change is normal; there is, in fact, no era or society in which change is not a permanent feature of the social landscape. Yet, on the eve of the twenty-first century, the pace of change in the United States feels particularly intense, and a state of "permanent transition" hardly seems a contradiction in terms at all. To many, it is an apt description of the economic fluctuations, political uncertainties, social and cultural upheaval, and fluidity of personal relationships that characterize the times. For a large segment of the population, however, these transitions are tinged with an acute sense of loss and nostalgia. Moral values, communities, even the American way of life seem in decline. And at the core of that decline is the family.

4   In a nationwide poll conducted by the *Los Angeles Times* [. . .], 78 percent of respondents said they were dissatisfied with today's moral values, and nearly half of that group identified divorce, working parents, and undisciplined children as the key problems. Only 11 percent of the respondents believed that their own behavior had contributed to the moral problems in the United States, and a resounding 96 percent believed that they were personally doing an excellent or good job of teaching moral values to their children. Conversely, 93 percent thought that other parents were to blame for the inadequate moral upbringing of their children. The sense of loss and decline many Americans feel today is filled with such contradictions. Americans want their families to offer unconditional love yet also to enforce and uphold strict moral values. They want flexibility, mobility, and autonomy in their personal lives but yearn for traditional communities and permanently stable families. When the substance of the debate over families is this ambiguous and contradictory, it is important to look more closely at the underlying issues in this time of transition.

———————————————

*Betty G. Farrell, *Family: The Making of an Idea, an Institution, and a Controversy in American Culture*

5   For most people in most eras, change seems anything but normal. Periods of social change can evoke much social anxiety, because the unknown is inherently unsettling and because many people are stakeholders in the status quo. Those who seek change generally want to effect a shift in the relations of power, either for themselves or for others. But such shifts are always unpredictable, and they can seem treacherous to those who hold the reins of power, as well as to those who feel their social, economic, or political power eroding. The groups with eroding power are the ones most likely to resist, through active strategies and passive resistance, the ideas, values, symbols, and behaviors associated with change. This describes such groups in the contemporary United States as militias who see minorities, foreigners, and new cultural values as a threat to the American way of life; whites who see blacks, Latinos, and Asians as challenging their privileges and claim on limited resources in a zero-sum game; pro-life advocates who see pro-choice supporters as threatening traditionally defined family roles; and antigay proponents who see gays and lesbians as subverting the gendered social order. Although social structural forces are ultimately responsible for the realignment of prestige and power among social groups in any society, these forces are always complex, abstract, intangible, and invisible. So those who symbolize or represent the forces of the new—women, minorities, immigrants, the poor, and other marginalized groups—tend to be singled out and blamed for the disruptions and upheaval associated with change. Social psychologists identify this process as scapegoating, the act of displacing generalized anxiety onto a conveniently visible and available target. Scapegoats have been identified in every era; but in periods in which the pace of change is particularly fast and a sense of unsettling disruption is acute, those social newcomers who challenge established values and behavior can all too readily become the targets of the rage, fear, and ambivalence of people feeling the earthquake tremors of social change.

Popular Perspectives on the Family

6 The family values debate has been generated against just such a backdrop in the late-twentieth-century United States. Fundamental changes in the expectations, meanings, and practices defining American family life have characterized much of the twentieth century, but especially the final 30 years. Consequently, concern about the family moved to the center of the political arena. Threats to the family on the one hand and salvation through the family on the other are the two most prominent themes in the recent family politics discourse. That the American family is broken and in need of repair is a common assumption of many social observers. Its complement is that families are worth fixing, because making them strong (again) is the key to solving most of society's ills. Neither of these assumptions has been subject to much critical scrutiny, nor has the historical image of the strong, vital, central family institution of the past on which they rest. Longing for order is one of the impulses behind the current turn to family politics in the United States; and feminists, gays and lesbians, single-parent mothers, absent fathers, pregnant teenagers, and gang-oriented youth, among others, have all at one time or another been made the scapegoats for family decline in the United States.

7   Longing for a more orderly, mythic past is most commonly associated with the conservative position on the family politics spectrum, and it would be easy to caricature the nostalgia for a family modeled on the classic 1950s television sitcom as the sum total of

this side of the family values debate. But if we assume that concerns about The Family, writ large, are only those of conservative politicians attempting to manipulate public sentiment, we would overlook the vast reservoir of social anxiety about contemporary family life that is also being tapped by many others from a variety of political and social perspectives: working mothers who are consumed with worry about child care; adolescents seeking the emotional attachment of family ties among peers and in gangs when it is found lacking in their own homes; committed gay and lesbian couples fighting for inclusion in the legal definition of family even as they retain a skeptical stance toward this fundamentally heterosexual institution. Why such concern about the family? One reason is that the metaphor evoked by family is a powerful one. A family is defined not so much by a particular set of people as by the quality of relationships that bind them together. What seems to many to be the constant feature of family life is not a specific form or structure but the meanings and the set of personal, intimate relationships families provide against the backdrop of the impersonal, bureaucratized world of modern society.

8   The core sentiments of family life that define the nature and meaning of this social institution for most Americans are unconditional love, attachment, nurturance, and dependability. The hope that these qualities are common to family relationships accounts for the shock with which we react to reports of violence, abuse, and neglect occurring inside the sanctuary of the private home. In popular culture, as in real life, stories of families beset by jealousy, envy, lust, and hatred rather than by the ideals of love, loyalty, and commitment provide an endless source of titillation and fascination. Family stories are not only the stuff of life we construct through our daily experience but the narrative form used to entice us as consumers into a marketplace adept at presenting all sorts of products as invested with emotional qualities and social relationships.

9   The widely promoted "Reach Out and Touch Someone" advertising campaign developed by AT&T in 1978 was a prototype of this genre. In this set of ads, a powerful multinational company hoped to pull at the heartstrings and the pocketbooks of the consuming public by promoting itself as the crucial communication link between family members separated by great global distances. The copy in the print advertisements told heartwarming personal tales of mothers and sons, uncles and nephews, and grandmothers and grandchildren reunited by AT&T's implied commitment to family values, albeit at long distance phone rates. The family metaphor works as an advertising ploy because there is widespread sentimentality in American society about family life. What makes families so compelling for those of us who actively choose to live in them, as well as for those of us who just as actively reject them as oppressively confining, is that families reside at the intersection of our most personal experience and our social lives. They are institutions we make, yet they are in no small part also constructed by cultural myths and social forces beyond any individual's control.

10   A desire for the kind of care and connection provided by the ideal family cuts across class, race, and ethnic lines in the United States. A commitment to family seems to be so widely shared across groups of all kinds in the hybrid mix that makes up American culture as to be nearly universal. It therefore comes as some surprise that the qualities many accept as natural components of family ties today—unconditional love, warmth, enduring attachment—were not the same expectations most American families had until 150 years ago. The historical variations in family life challenge the claim that the family, even within

the same culture, has had the same meaning or has offered the same timeless experiences to its members.

11   Assumptions about American family life in the past are widely shared. These include the beliefs that families were large and extended, with most people living in multigenerational households; that marriages occurred at an early age and were based on permanent, unwavering commitment between spouses; that the ties between kin were stronger and closer than those experienced today; and that family life in the past was more stable and predictable than it is currently. These assumptions about the family of the past have collectively produced an image that one sociologist has called "the Classical Family of Western Nostalgia." It is the image upon which politicians and advertisers, among others, routinely draw as they explain contemporary social problems by reference to family breakdown or as they tap consumer desires by associating a product with positive family values and warm family feeling. The family is a potent symbol in contemporary American society, because it touches our emotional needs for both intimate personal attachments and a sense of embeddedness in a larger community.

12   Is there truth to the fears that family values are weaker today than in the past—that children are more vulnerable, adolescents more intractable, adults less dependable, and the elderly more needy? In both popular culture and political discourse, sentimentality and nostalgia about the family have often prevailed, and a social and historical context for framing the issues has largely been missing. It is important to challenge the popular understanding of the family as an institution that is biologically based, immutable, and predictable with a more culturally variable and historically grounded view. Because families are central to the way we talk about ourselves and about our social and political lives, they deserve to be studied in their fullest scope, attached to a real past as well as a present and future.

Academic Perspectives on the Family

13 Assumptions about the nature of the family abound not only in popular culture but in social science as well. The disciplines of anthropology, sociology, history, and psychology all have particular orientations to the institution of the family that define their theoretical positions and research agendas. Among sociologists and anthropologists, for example, a starting premise about the family has been that it is one of the central organizing institutions of society. Its centrality comes from having the capacity to organize social life quite effectively by regulating sexuality, controlling reproduction, and ensuring the socialization of children who are born within the family unit. Many social science disciplines start with the question "How is society possible?" and they recognize that the organization of individuals into family units is a very effective means of providing social regulation and continuity. Through the institution of the family, individuals are joined together and given the social and legal sanction to perpetuate their name and traditions through their offspring. Whole societies are replenished with future generations of leaders and workers.

14   In the early twentieth century, the anthropologist Bronislaw Malinowski made the argument that the most universal characteristic of family life in all cultures and all time periods was the "principle of legitimacy." He had noted that the rules for sexual behavior varied widely across cultures but that control over reproduction was a common feature of

every social order. Every society made the distinction between those children (legitimate) born to parents who had been culturally and legally sanctioned to reproduce and those children (illegitimate) whose parents were not accorded this sanction. The function of the principle of legitimacy, according to Malinowski, was to ensure that a child born into a society had both an identifiable mother and father. The father might, in fact, not be biologically related to the child, but his recognized sociological status as father was the affiliation that gave the child a set of kin and a social placement in that social order.

15   In addition to being the only sanctioned setting for reproduction, families are important sources of social continuity, because they are most often the setting in which children are cared for and raised. The power of social forces is such that parents normally can be counted on to provide long-term care for their dependent children, because the emotional closeness of family bonds makes them want to do so. Families are therefore particularly effective institutions, because they press people into service for their kin by the dual imperatives of love and obligation. Although it is possible that food, shelter, physical care, and emotional nurturance could be provided through alternative means by the state or other centrally administered bureaucratic agencies, it would require considerable societal resources and effort to ensure that these needs were effectively met for a majority of individuals in a society. What families seem to provide naturally, societies would otherwise have to coordinate and regulate at great cost.

16   To argue that families are effective or efficient as social institutions is not, however, to claim that they are necessary or inevitable. One common fallacy that some sociologists have promoted in studying the family at the societal level is the equation of its prevalence with the idea that it is functionally necessary. The assumption that societies "need" families in order to continue, based on the observation that some form of family exists in all known societies, ignores the range of variation in or the exceptions to this institution. Individuals and subgroups within all societies have constructed alternative arrangements to the traditional family of parents and their children. But the very fact that they are considered alternatives or experimental social organizations suggests how powerful the dominant family norm continues to be.

17   Another assumption that is shared across several social science disciplines is that family harmony and stability constitute the basis for order and control in the larger society. From this perspective, the family is a microcosm of the larger society, and social regulation in the domestic sphere helps promote order and control at all social levels. Individual social analysts might alternatively celebrate or lament the kind of control, regulation, and social order that was understood to begin in the family and radiate outward to the larger society; but the assumption that society was built on the foundation of the family was rarely challenged.

18   As a microcosm or a miniature society of the rulers and the ruled who are bound together by reciprocal rights and obligations, the family helps maintain social order first by its capacity to place people in the social system. It does so by providing them with identifiable kin and establishing the lines of legitimate succession and inheritance that mark their economic, political, and social position in society. Because individuals are located in an established social hierarchy by their birth or adoption into a particular family group, the nature of power and access to resources in a society remain largely intact from one generation to the next. Thus, one meaning of the family as a central institution of the

social order is that it reinforces the political and economic status quo. Families ensure that the distribution of resources both to the advantaged and disadvantaged will remain relatively stable, since the transmission of wealth, property, status, and opportunity is channeled along the lines of kinship.

19   In another important way, families help to regulate the social order. Family life, according to both law and custom, prescribes roles for men, women, and children. Although these roles are really the products of social and cultural forces, rather than biological imperatives, and are therefore highly fluid in times of change, they appear to most people to be prescribed by stable and immutable rules governing everyday life. The meaning of "traditional" family life is that people are conscripted into established roles. Everyone knows his or her place and tends to keep to it by the pressures of community norms and social sanctions. But such traditional family roles exact a toll as well. What promotes social harmony and order to the advantage of some produces severe constraints on others. Women and children, whose roles in the family have traditionally been subordinate to those of men, have sometimes resisted such prescriptive expectations and have led the charge for social change in both overt and covert ways. It is not surprising that in times of rapid social change the family has been identified as an inherently conservative institution, one that not only helps to perpetuate the status quo but is perceived as being oppressively restrictive to many of its own members.

20   Although many changes have characterized American family life over time, we should be mindful of important continuities as well. The most striking continuity is the importance that the family holds for so many people. The reasons that the family is important have varied historically, but there is no doubt that it has been a central institution, one on which people have pinned all manner of beliefs, values, and prejudices, as well as fears about and hopes for the future. Families reside at the intersection of private and public experience. We are all experts, since most of us have lived within one or more families at some point in our lives. Families can house both our highest hopes and our greatest disappointments, and their fragility or resilience therefore carries great personal meaning, in addition to social significance. The novelist Amos Oz has called the family "the most mysterious, most secret institution in the world." Its mysteries and secrets are not fully revealed in the social and historical record, but in reconstructing some of the patterns of family life, we can begin to understand why it has continued to play such a central role in American culture, as an organizing social institution, a lived experience, and a powerful metaphor.

QUESTIONS FOR ANALYSIS AND DISCUSSION

1. Farrell notes that in a poll on moral values, 78 percent of respondents said that they were dissatisfied with today's moral values, but that only 11 percent believed that their own behavior had contributed to this moral decline. What is your own opinion about today's moral values, and how does your own behavior fit in with these values?

2. Evaluate Farrell's opening joke about Adam and Eve. How does it connect to her material? Is it an effective means of drawing in readers and orienting them to her topic?

3. Farrell notes that Americans want their families to "offer unconditional love yet also to enforce and uphold strict moral values. They want flexibility, mobility, and autonomy . . . but yearn for traditional communities and permanently stable families" (paragraph 4). What, according to the author, is problematic with this yearning? Do you agree? Explain.

4. In her fifth paragraph, Farrell discusses our social fear of change. How does our fear of change connect to the practice of scapegoating? Identify some social scapegoats of the last century. For what were they blamed and why? Who represents "the forces of the new" today?

5. Farrell comments that our social concern for "The Family" is rooted in the "metaphor evoked by family" (paragraph 7). What does she mean? How does she define *family* in this paragraph, and how does this definition connect to our social concerns about the decay of the family in general? Explain.

6. According to Farrell, what assumptions about family span many academic disciplines, such as anthropology, sociology, history, and psychology? How do these assumptions form the basis for the theoretical approaches of these disciplines? Explain.

7. How do families "help to regulate the social order" (paragraph 19)? How can this regulation "exact a toll" on certain members of society? Do you agree or disagree with Farrell's assessment? Explain.

8. At the end of her essay, Farrell quotes novelist Amos Oz, who calls the family "the most mysterious, most secret institution in the world." How is the family "secret"? If almost everyone has a family and understands what the term implies, how can it be "mysterious"?

Five Myths About Marriage
Stephanie Coontz

Marriage is considered by many to be a sacred institution. This is clear by the number of people fighting for the right to marry, as well as the number of people arguing against same-sex marriage. People have strong opinions about marriage and what it means. But many of our beliefs about marriage—entering into it, preserving it, and ending it—are based on cultural assumptions and social constructs. In this next article, author and family studies professor Stephanie Coontz debunks five "myths" about marriage.*

BEFORE YOU READ

If you decided to live with your significant other, do you think you would feel social pressure to marry after a period of living together? Would your family approve? What are your personal expectations of living together? Are you in favor or against it? Explain.

---

*Stephanie Coontz, *Washington Post*, May 25, 2012.

AS YOU READ

Coontz notes that, contrary to popular belief, divorce is not necessarily harmful for women and children. What is your personal viewpoint on divorce? Does it make it too easy to leave when the going gets rough? Or is it important to be able to leave a relationship when it no longer is working for you?

1. People don't value marriage the way they used to.

1 Modern Americans do put less emphasis on marriage as an institution that should organize everyone's life, but they put much more value on it as a relationship based on fairness, intimacy and fidelity. That is, paradoxically, one reason they have become more tolerant of divorce. For example, a May 2010 Gallup poll found that while only 23 percent of Americans believe divorce to be morally wrong, 92 percent believe it is immoral for a married man or woman to have an affair—the highest disapproval of any topic in the survey.

2 The value placed on fidelity—especially male fidelity—has arguably never been higher. In the late 19th century in the United States, an epidemic of venereal disease plagued respectable middle-class wives because so many of their husbands frequented prostitutes. In the 1920s, Somerset Maugham's play *The Constant Wife* raised eyebrows because its heroine rejects the urging of friends and family to follow convention and ignore her husband's affair. And as late as the 1950s and early 1960s, marriage counselors routinely responded to a woman's complaints about her husband's infidelity by asking whether she had provoked it by not keeping herself "well groomed."

2. Married women who work put in a "second shift" at home.

3 Employed wives with young children do, on average, spend 2⅓ hours more per week on housework and paid work than their husbands do. But that comes out to an extra 20 minutes a day, hardly a full second shift. And once the early months of child-rearing are over, the average total workload of most husbands and wives (time spent in paid and unpaid work combined) is now virtually identical, according to the Bureau of Labor Statistics. Wives spend more time on unpaid household work than their husbands, but husbands spend more time on paid work.

4 The real gender inequality in marriage stems from the tendency to regard women as the default parent, the one who, in the absence of family-friendly work policies, is expected to adjust her paid work to shoulder the brunt of domestic responsibilities. Women who quit their jobs or cut their hours suffer a wage penalty that widens over the years, even if they return to the job market and work continuously for two more decades. Over a lifetime, even a temporary absence from the workforce can cost a woman hundreds of thousands of dollars, making her more economically vulnerable in case of divorce or the death of her spouse.

3. Divorce is harmful for women and children.

5 Divorce rates have been falling for 30 years, but the freedom to leave a dysfunctional marriage can be a lifesaver for women, who initiate two-thirds of divorces. Economists Betsey Stevenson and Justin Wolfers found that every state that adopted no-fault divorce,

beginning with California in 1970, experienced an 8 to 13 percent decline in wives' suicide rates and a 30 percent decline in domestic violence in the next five years.

6   On average, children of divorce exhibit more behavioral problems and do more poorly in school than children of intact marriages. But in many cases, the problems blamed on divorce can be seen in children many years before their parents split up and are actually a result of the dysfunctional family relations that eventually led to divorce.

7   One large survey found that experiencing their parents' divorce lowered the well-being of 55 to 60 percent of children but improved the well-being of 40 to 45 percent. And when demographer Allen Li controlled for problematic characteristics in children that preexisted their parents' separation, he found no average negative impact of divorce itself.

8   Children of divorced parents are themselves more likely to divorce. But a recent study using data from the National Survey of Families and Households found that people who grew up in houses where their parents fought frequently were more likely to divorce if their parents remained together.

4. Married parents spend less time with their kids than they used to.

9 In 1965, according to data from the federal study of how people use their time, mothers spent 10 hours each week, on average, focused on their children. Since that time, all moms have increased the time they spend with their kids, even as they have also increased their work hours. But college-educated mothers, the people most likely to have careers and to return to work in the first year after childbirth, increased time with their kids at more than twice the rate of less-educated mothers. By 2007, according to economists Garey Ramey and Valerie Ramey, college-educated women were, on average, spending 21.2 hours a week focused on their kids, while moms with less education were doing 15.9 hours a week.

10   In 1965, fathers averaged barely three hours a week doing primary child care. By 2007, economists Betsey Stevenson and Dan Sacks report, that had risen to almost 7 hours a week for less-educated dads, and almost 10 hours for those with a college degree.

5. Married couples are the building blocks of community life.

11 All that time couples invest in their children comes at the expense of being involved in the world beyond the family's front door. Sociologists Naomi Gerstel and Natalia Sarkisian report that married women and men are less likely to visit and give practical assistance to their extended families than are the unmarried. Men without wives are much more likely to call their parents than their married peers.

12   Economically as well as emotionally, modern marriage has become like an affluent gated community. It has become harder for low-income Americans to enter and sustain. But for the educated, two-income families whose divorce rates have been falling and who spend more time with their children than they used to, marriage brings more relative advantages than in the past.

13   The notion that marriage is an impediment to commitments to the larger community is a long-standing one -- and one reason early Christians did not place the institution at the top of their moral hierarchy, complaining that married couples cared more about pleasing each other than doing the Lord's work. It wasn't until 1215 that marriage became a sacrament.

1. In what ways have our values of marriage changed? In you view, are these current values better than ones held 50 or 100 years ago? Explain.
2. Evaluate the support Coontz gives for why she feels these myths are untrue? State whether you agree or disagree with her arguments on each of the five issues she identifies as "myths."
3. In marriages with children, where does gender inequality arise?
4. Did any of the myths Coontz debunks surprise you? Change your perspective? If so, which one(s) and why?
5. According to Cootnz, what is the price married families pay when it comes to community involvement? Explain.
6. Coontz states that "modern marriage has become like an affluent gated community." Do you agree or disagree with her assessment? Explain.

Reading the Visual

Burgers Done?

QUESTIONS FOR ANALYSIS AND DISCUSSION

1. What message is the cartoonist conveying? What is he saying about marriage and relationships?
2. What is the comedic element in this cartoon?
3. What visual clichés are present in this cartoon? How do these elements convey a sense of time, place, gender, and situation?

In Defense of Single Motherhood

Katie Roiphe

Although some people may lament the decline of "traditional family" structures of married father, mother, and children living in harmony under one roof, many others have come to accept and even embrace a variety of new family configurations. Most prominent among these is single motherhood. In 2012, Child Trends, a Washington research group that analyzes government data, reported that more than half of births to American women under 30 occur outside marriage. Yet, many people still believe that single motherhood is bad for kids and bad for society. In this next essay, author Katie Roiphe defends single motherhood.*

BEFORE YOU READ

Does society tend to blame single mothers for its ills? What reputation do single mothers face? Is our opinion different for single fathers? If so, what accounts for the difference?

AS YOU READ

How does Roiphe's references to her own children contribute to her essay and her points? Why do you think Roiphe chose to include her son in her essay?

1   In a season of ardent partisan clashing, Americans seem united in at least one shared idea: Single mothers are bad. A Pew Research Center poll on family structures reports that nearly 7 in 10 Americans think single mothers are a "bad thing for society." Conservatives obsess over moral decline, and liberals worry extravagantly—and one could argue condescendingly—about children, but all exhibit a fundamental lack of imagination about what family can be—and perhaps more pressingly—what family is: we now live in a country in which 53 percent of the babies born to women under 30 are born to unmarried mothers.

2   I happen to have two children with two different fathers, neither of whom I live with, and both of whom we are close to. I am lucky enough to be living in financially stable, relatively privileged circumstances, and to have had the education that allows me to do so. I am not the "typical" single mother, but then there is no typical single mother any more than there is a typical mother. It is, in fact, our fantasies and crude stereotypes of this "typical single mother" that get in the way of a more rational, open-minded understanding of the variety and richness of different kinds of families.

3   The structure of my household is messy, bohemian, warm. If there is anything that currently oppresses the children, it is the idea of the way families are "supposed to be," an idea pushed—in picture books and classrooms and in adults' casual conversation—on American children at a very early age and with surprising aggressiveness.

4   At 2, my son, Leo, started to call his sister's father, Harry, "my Harry." When he glimpsed Harry's chocolate-brown 1980s car coming down our block he would say, "My

---

*Kate Roiphe, *New York Times*, August 11, 2012.

Harry's car!" To me this unorthodox use of "my" gets at the spirit of what we're doing: inventing a family from scratch. There are no words for what Harry is to him, but he is definitely his Harry.

5   The other day Leo brushed his mop of blond hair in front of the mirror and announced, "Now I look like Harry." People are quick to tell me that this is not the real thing. But is it necessarily worse than "the real thing"? Is the physical presence of a man in the home truly as transfiguring, magical and unadulteratedly essential as people seem to think? One could argue that a well-loved child is a well-loved child.

6   To support the basic notion that single mothers are irresponsible and dangerous to the general order of things, people often refer vaguely to "studies." I am not a huge believer in studies because they tend to collapse the complexities and nuance of actual lived experience and because people lie to themselves and others. (One of these studies, for instance, in order to measure emotional distress asks teenagers to record how many times in a week "you felt lonely." Is there a teenager on earth who is a reliable narrator of her inner life? Can anyone of any age quantify how many times in a week they have felt lonely?) But since these studies provide fodder for those who want to blast single mothers, it's worth addressing what they actually say.

7   Studies like those done by the Princeton sociologist Sara S. McLanahan, who is one of the foremost authorities on single motherhood and its impact on children, show that conditions like poverty and instability, which frequently accompany single-mother households, increase the chances that the children involved will experience alcoholism, mental illness, academic failure and other troubles. But there is no conclusive evidence that, absent those conditions, the pure, pared-down state of single motherhood is itself dangerous to children.

8   Professor McLanahan's studies over the years, and many others like them, show that the primary risks associated with single motherhood arise from financial insecurity. They also offer evidence that, to a lesser extent, particular romantic patterns of the mother— namely introducing lots of boyfriends into children's lives—contribute to the risk. What the studies don't show is that longing for a married father at the breakfast table injures children. And Professor McLanahan's findings suggest that a two-parent, financially stable home with stress and conflict would be more destructive to children than a one-parent, financially stable home without stress and conflict.

9   There is no doubt, however, that single motherhood can be more difficult than other kinds of motherhood. In France, the response to the added difficulty is to give single mothers preferential access to excellent day care. Here the response is moralism disguised as concern and, at other times, simply moralism.

10   The idea of "single mothers" may itself be the convenient fiction of a fundamentally conservative society. In fact women move in and out of singleness, married parents break apart, men and women live together without marrying, spouses or partners die, romantic attachments form and dissolve. Those who brandish research like Professor McLanahan's ongoing Fragile Families study and Paul R. Amato's 2005 paper on changing family structures to critique "single mothers" conveniently ignore the fact that such investigations rely on shifting, differing and extremely complex definitions of the households involved.

11   What gets lost in the moralizing conversation is that there is a huge, immeasurable variety in households, and there are great ones and terrible ones, arduous ones and

inventive ones, drab ones and exuberant ones, among families of all structures and economic strata.

12   It's useful and humbling to remember that no family structure guarantees happiness or ensures misery: real life is wilier and more fraught with accident and luck than that. If you think that being married ensures a good life for your children you need only enter a bookstore and open any novel, or go to the theater and watch practically any play, or have dinner with nearly anyone you know. Suffering is everywhere, and married parents, even happily married parents, raise screwed-up or alcoholic or lost children, just as single parents raise strong, healthy ones. What matters most, it should go without saying, is the kind of parent you are, not whom you sleep with, and even that matters only up to a point.

13   With the steep rise of children born to unmarried parents, America's prevailing fantasies of family life no longer match the facts on the ground. But as the children born to unmarried women under 30 come of age in the majority, these faded archetypes will have to evolve. Our narrow, constricting, airless sense of the isolated nuclear family has not always, if we are honest, served us well, and it may now be replaced by something more vivid and dynamic, and closer to the way we are actually living.

14   All of the liberal concern about single motherhood might more usefully be channeled into protecting single mothers, rather than the elaborate clucking and exquisite condescension that get us nowhere. Attention should be paid to the serious underlying economic inequities, without the colorful surface distraction of concerned or judgmental prurience. Let's abandon the fundamentally frothy question of who is wearing a ring. Young men need jobs so they can pay child support and contribute more meaningfully to the households they are living in. The real menace to America's children is not single mothers, or unmarried or gay parents, but an economy that stokes an unconscionable divide between the rich and the not rich.

QUESTIONS FOR ANALYSIS AND DISCUSSION

1. Roiphe admits that she has two children with two different fathers, neither of whom she lives with. How does this orient the reader to her point of view? Does it stregthen her position? Explain.

2. Who is the "typical single mother" that Roiphe refers to in her second paragraph? Explain.

3. Why is Roiphe "not a huge believer in studies"? Explain.

4. Roiphe observes that anyone who thinks being married ensures a good life for their children need only open a book or see a movie and learn otherwise. Evaluate this point. Does it provide good support for her argument? Why or why not?

5. Roiphe predicts that as the children born to single mothers come of age themselves, public opinion of single motherhood will likewise evolve. What is your current view of single motherhood? Do you agree that the last vestiges of stigma will be erased in the next 20 years? Why or why not?

6. What, according to Roiphe, is the "real menace to American's children"? Respond to her statement with your own viewpoint.

Why Gay Marriage Is Good for Straight America
Andrew Sullivan

Much of the debate about same-sex marriage hinges on how we define marriage itself—is it a partnership between two loving, consenting adults or a sanctified or legal union between a man and a woman? Many arguments supporting gay marriage focus on the issue of love: if two people love each other, goes the argument, they should be allowed to marry. Opponents to this view contend that marriage is more than about love: It has traditionally been a legal and social bond between a man and a woman, foremost to support the upbringing of children. To redefine this definition of marriage would be to undermine the institution itself and threaten the family. Should same-sex couples be afforded the legal right to marry? As state after state legally sanctions the practice, it would seem as if the country is leaning toward "yes." A longtime advocate for gay marriage, journalist Andrew Sullivan reflects on his own life, love, and pursuit of happiness—and why gay marriage is good for everyone.*

BEFORE YOU READ

According to Sullivan, why do homosexual couples want to marry? What motivates them? Do heterosexual couples marry for the same reasons as gay couples?

AS YOU READ

In your opinion, should same-sex couples be permitted to legally marry? Are you likely to be swayed by hearing different points of view on the subject? Why or why not?

1   As a child, when I thought of the future, all I could see was black. I wasn't miserable or depressed. I was a cheerful boy, as happy playing with my posse of male friends in elementary school as I was when I would occasionally take a day by myself in the woodlands that surrounded the small town I grew up in. But when I thought of the distant future, of what I would do and be as a grown-up, there was a blank. I simply didn't know how I would live, where I would live, who I could live with. I knew one thing only: I couldn't be like my dad. For some reason, I knew somewhere deep down that I couldn't have a marriage like my parents.

2   It's hard to convey what that feeling does to a child. In retrospect, it was a sharp, displacing wound to the psyche. At the very moment you become aware of sex and emotion, you simultaneously know that for you, there is no future coupling, no future family, no future home. In the future, I would be suddenly exiled from what I knew: my family, my

---

*Andrew Sullivan, *Daily Beast*, July 18, 2011.

friends, every household on television, every end to every romantic movie I'd ever seen. My grandmother crystallized it in classic and slightly cruel English fashion: "You're not the marrying kind," she said. It was one of those things that struck a chord of such pain, my pride forced me to embrace it. "No, I'm not," I replied. "I like my freedom."

3   This wasn't a lie. But it was a dodge, and I knew it. And when puberty struck and I realized I might be "one of them," I turned inward. It was a strange feeling—both the exhilaration of sexual desire and the simultaneous, soul-splintering panic that I was going to have to live alone my whole life, lying or euphemizing, concocting some public veneer to hide a private shame. It was like getting into an elevator you were expecting to go up, the doors closing, and then suddenly realizing you were headed down a few stories. And this was when the future went black for me, when suicide very occasionally entered my mind, when my only legitimate passion was getting A grades, because at that point it was all I knew how to do. I stayed away from parties; I didn't learn to drive; I lost contact with those friends whose interest suddenly became girls; and somewhere in me, something began to die.

4   They call it the happiest day of your life for a reason. Getting married is often the hinge on which every family generation swings open. In my small-town life, it was far more important than money or a career or fame. And I could see my grandmother's point: the very lack of any dating or interest in it, the absence of any intimate relationships, or of any normal teenage behavior, did indeed make me seem just a classic loner. But I wasn't. Because nobody is. "In everyone there sleeps/A sense of life lived according to love," as the poet Philip Larkin put it, as well as the fear of never being loved. That, as Larkin added, nothing cures. And I felt, for a time, incurable.

5   You can have as many debates about gay marriage as you want, and over the last 22 years of campaigning for it, I've had my share. You can debate theology, and the divide between church and state, the issue of procreation, the red herring of polygamy, and on and on. But what it all really comes down to is the primary institution of love. The small percentage of people who are gay or lesbian were born, as all humans are, with the capacity to love and the need to be loved. These things, above everything, are what make life worth living. And unlike every other minority, almost all of us grew up among and part of the majority, in families where the highest form of that love was between our parents in marriage. To feel you will never know that, never feel that, is to experience a deep psychic wound that takes years to recover from. It is to become psychologically homeless. Which is why, I think, the concept of "coming out" is not quite right. It should really be called "coming home."

6   In the end, I had to abandon my home in order to find it again and know the place for the first time. I left England just after my 21st birthday for America and its simple foundational promise: the pursuit of happiness. And I gave myself permission to pursue it. I will never forget the moment I first kissed another man; it was as if a black-and-white movie suddenly turned into color. I will never forget the first time I slept next to another man—or rather tried to sleep. Never for a moment did I actually feel or truly believe any of this was wrong, let alone an "intrinsic evil," as my strict Catholicism told me that it was. It was so natural, so spontaneous, so joyous, it could no more be wrong than breathing. And as I experienced intimacy and love for the first time as an adult, all that brittleness of the gay adolescent, all that white-knuckled embarrassment, all those ruses and excuses and dark, deep depressions lifted. Yes, this was happiness. And America for me will always represent it.

7   And that is why marriage equality is, to my mind, the distillation of America. If you're a heterosexual reading this, have you ever considered for a millisecond that your right to pursue happiness did not include your right to marry the person you love? And that is why, over the centuries, the U.S. Supreme Court has upheld the right to marry for everyone, citizen or even traveler, as a core, inalienable right, bestowed by the Declaration of Independence itself. The court has ruled that the right to marry precedes the Bill of Rights; it has decided that prisoners on death row have a right to marry, even if they can never consummate it. It has ruled that no limitations may be put on it for anyone—deadbeat dads, multiple divorcées, felons, noncitizens. Hannah Arendt wrote in 1959 that "the right to marry whoever one wishes is an elementary human right . . . Even political rights, like the right to vote, and nearly all other rights enumerated in the Constitution, are secondary to the inalienable human rights to 'life, liberty and the pursuit of happiness' proclaimed in the Declaration of Independence; and to this category the right to home and marriage unquestionably belongs." And, of course, after a long struggle, interracial marriage was finally declared a constitutional right, in perhaps the most sweeping ruling ever, with the court declaring that civil marriage was one of the "basic civil rights of man, fundamental to our very existence and survival." Barack Obama is a historic American figure not because he is black, but because he is the son of a black father and a white mother. He is the living embodiment of the pursuit of happiness that marriage represented.

8   I still didn't think it would ever happen to me. I thought I was too emotionally damaged, my emotions and sexuality severed by all those years of loneliness and arrested emotional development. I thought my heart had too much scar tissue, and I could live my life well enough with just friendship and occasional sexual encounters or dates. But when I first set eyes on my husband, I knew I had lucked out. Some things you simply know. And when we finally got married, a few years later, and our mothers walked us down the makeshift garden aisle, and my sister gave the reading through tears, and one of our beagles howled through the vows, and my father put his arms around me and hugged, I did not hear civilization crumble. I felt a wound being healed. It is a rare privilege to spend your adult life fighting for a right that was first dismissed as a joke, only finally to achieve it in six states and Washington, D.C. But how much rarer to actually stumble upon someone who could make it a reality. And to have it happen to me in my own lifetime! This joy is compounded, deepened, solidified by the knowledge that somewhere, someone just like I was as a kid will be able to look to the future now and not see darkness—but the possibility of love and home. That, I realized, was really what I had been fighting for for two decades: to heal the child I had once been—and the countless children in the present and future whose future deserved, needed, begged for a model of commitment and responsibility and love.

9   And that is why it has been such a tragedy that conservatives decided this was a battle they were determined to fight against, an advance they were dedicated to reversing. It made no sense to me. Here was a minority asking for responsibility and commitment and integration. And conservatives were determined to keep them in isolation, stigmatized and kept on an embarrassing, unmentionable margin, where gays could be used to buttress the primacy of heterosexuality. We were for them merely a drop shadow for heterosexuality. What they could not see was that the conservative tradition of reform and inclusion, of social change through existing institutions, of the family and personal responsibility, all led inexorably toward civil marriage for gays.

10   Yes, the main stumbling block was religion. But we were not talking of religious marriage and were more than eager to insist, as in New York state, on the inviolable religious freedom of churches, mosques, and synagogues to retain their bans on gay marriage. We were talking about civil marriage—and in that respect, religious tradition had long since ceased to apply. Civil divorce changed marriage far more drastically for far more people than allowing the small percentage who were excluded to be included. And no one doubted an atheist's right to marry, outside of any church or any religion, just as no one doubted the marriages of childless couples, or infertile ones. In fact, every single argument against marriage equality for gays collapsed upon inspection. And when the data showed that in the era of gay marriage, straight marriage had actually strengthened somewhat, divorce rates had declined, and marriages lasted longer, even those who worried about unintended consequences conceded that the argument was essentially over. And that is why it remains so appropriate that George W. Bush's solicitor general, Ted Olson, would lead the legal fight against Proposition 8 in California; that a Reagan-appointed judge, Anthony Kennedy, would be the foremost Supreme Court justice affirming gay and lesbian equality; and that in Albany, in the end, the winning votes came from Republicans who voted their conscience.

11   Of course this is new and not so new. For a long time, gays and lesbians braver than I was were effectively married and lived together, risking violence and opprobrium and isolation. For decades these bonds existed, and we knew of them even if we never spoke of them. I saw them up close as a young man in the darkest years of the AIDS plague. I saw spouses holding their dying husbands, cradling them at the hour of their death, inserting catheters, cleaning broken bodies, tending to terrified souls. This proved beyond any doubt for me that gay couples were as capable of as much love and tenacity and tenderness and fidelity as heterosexual couples. And when I heard their bonds denigrated or demonized, dismissed or belittled, the sadness became a kind of spur. For so long, so much pain. For so many, so much grief compounded by stigma. But we did not just survive the plague. We used it to forge a new future. And in the years of struggle, as more and more heterosexuals joined us, we all began finally to see that this was not really about being gay. It was about being human.

12   Just like being gay is no longer necessarily about being an outsider. It is about being an American.

QUESTIONS FOR ANALYSIS AND DISCUSSION

1. Identify the primary points of argument Sullivan uses to support his case that gay marriage makes marriage overall a stronger institution.
2. What does Sullivan mean when he refers to the "red herring of polygamy"? What arguments have been made against same-sex marriage and how are they dismantled?
3. Will legalizing gay marriage increase or decrease the problems gay men and women now encounter in America in gaining social acceptance? What benefits might all gay people receive, whether or not they choose to marry? Do you think that a legal change in marriage will help to change the beliefs of people who now disapprove of homosexuality? Why or why not? Explain.

4. Sullivan laments that marriage conservatives often cite religious reasons for being against same-sex marriage. Why does he feel such arguments against same-sex marriage are invalid on religious grounds? Explain.

5. What emotional and psychological toll is taken on by gay men and women when they are denied the right to marriage? Explain.

6. Much of Sullivan's argument is based on his own perspective, feelings, and experiences. In your opinion, does this recounting of his personal history support or detract from his argument? Explain.

Tie the Knot

W. Bradford Wilcox

Judging from the tabloids, it seems like America just loves a wedding. Yet, half of children born to parents under 30 are born into unwed families. This sharp decline in marriage may have deep economic consequences. Many socialists feel that there is a correlation between the decline in marriage rates and the increase in children living at or below the poverty line. Research indicates that stable families enable children to thrive, shore up communities, and help all members of the family unit to succeed during good times and to weather the bad times. Why is marriage in decline? In this next essay, sociology professor W. Bradford Wilcox explains that social policy can help staunch the trend. The result, he argues, would be a stronger economy, happier and healthier children, and a stronger country overall.*

BEFORE YOU READ

Why should people consider remarrying if they have children? What are the pros and cons?

AS YOU READ

Would a national campaign that provided incentives to marry sway you more toward marriage rather than living together? Would incentives influence your decision as to when to have children—before or after marriage? Why or why not?

1   The picture of the twentysomething years painted by the pop culture—think *Girls* or *The Mindy Project*—suggests that young adults use their 20s as a kind of "odyssey years" to bridge adolescence and adulthood. Judging by Hannah, Adam, and Mindy, the 20s are about getting educated and established at work, enjoying drinks and coffee with friends, trying your hand at relationships, all before the press of adult responsibilities sets in.

2   This picture is largely accurate for college-educated young adults as we show in our new report, "Knot Yet: The Benefits and Costs of Delayed Marriage in America," and it's

---

*W. Bradford Wilcox, *Slate*, March 25, 2013.

a picture that ends up relatively rosy, even if the 20s have difficult moments. These highly educated adults have embraced a "capstone" model of marriage that typically leads them to put off marriage until they have had a chance to establish themselves professionally, personally, and relationship-wise. This capstone model is paying big dividends to the college-educated: Their divorce rate is low, and their income is high. We find, for instance, that college-educated women who postpone marriage to their 30s earn about $10,000 more than their college-educated sisters who marry in their mid-20s.

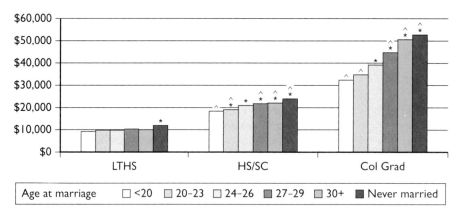

SOURCE: *American Community Survey, 2008–2010*

NOTE: Figure depicts mean income. An asterisk (*) above the bar indicates a statistically-significant difference (p <0.05) between the age group and that of individuals who married when they were less than 20 years old, controlling for race/ethnicity, urbanicity, and census region derived from an *OLS regression model* (not shown). A caret (^) above the bar indicates a statistically-significant difference (p <0.05) between the age group and that of individuals who married when they were 24–26 years old, controlling for the same factors derived from an *OLS regression model* (not shown).

Courtesy of Brandon Wooten/The "Knot Yet" report

3   But one major and more dystopian feature of actual contemporary twentysomething life is conspicuously absent from small-screen depictions: parenthood. Hard as it might be for Hannah and Mindy—and their viewers—to imagine, most American women without college degrees have their first child in their 20s. These young women and their partners— who make up about two-thirds of twentysomething adults in the United States—are logging more time at the diaper aisle of the local supermarket than at the local bar.

4   This would not be such a big deal except for the fact that many of these twentysomethings are drifting into parenthood, becoming moms and dads with partners they don't think are fit to marry or at least ready to marry. For instance, almost 1 in 2 babies—47 percent, to be precise—born to twentysomething women are now born to unmarried parents. In fact, twentysomething women now have the majority of children outside of marriage, which—given that 30 is the new 20—makes them the new teen moms.

5   The reality is that children born to unmarried twentysomething parents are three times more likely to grow up with a disorienting carousel of adults coming and going in the home, compared to children born to married parents. This kind of carousel, as sociologist

Andrew Cherlin notes in his book *The Marriage-Go-Round*, is associated with higher rates of teen pregnancy, behavioral problems in school, and substance abuse. By contrast, "stable, low-conflict families with two biological or adoptive parents provide better environments for children, on average, than do other living arrangements."

6   How did twentysomethings become the new teen moms? Progressives stress economics as a cause, conservatives stress culture, but both are a factor. Among college-educated couples who have access to stable, high-paying, and meaningful work, only 12 percent have their first child before marriage. By and large, college-educated women and men don't want to derail their professional and economic prospects by having a baby before they have established a strong economic foundation for themselves and their future family.

7   But 58 percent of women who have a high-school degree or some college—women we call "middle Americans" and who make up a majority of young adult women—are now having their first child outside of marriage—a rapid and quite recent development. (Among women without a high-school degree, 83 percent do.) The biggest economic issue is that men without college degrees are less likely to hold the kind of stable, decent-paying jobs that will secure their financial future. Chris, 22, a welder in Ohio interviewed for the *Love and Marriage in Middle America* project at the Institute for American Values, said his recent stint of unemployment "drove the final nail in the coffin" of his relationship with a young woman he was hoping to marry. "[I] was depressed; I was bored out of my mind—no income, not able to do anything. It basically was just like hell," he said.

8   Two cultural factors are also in play here. The rise of the "capstone" model of marriage is one such factor, as Cherlin has noted. All Americans, not just the college educated—watch the same TV shows and movies and pick up the idea that adults have to have all their ducks in a row—a middle-class lifestyle, a soul mate relationship—before they settle down. This model sets a high bar for marriage and minimizes marriage's classic connection to parenthood. So large numbers of less-educated twentysomethings who view the capstone model as unattainable end up having the child before the marriage.

9   Second, as Kathryn Edin and Maria Kefalas point out in *Promises I Can Keep: Why Poor Women Put Motherhood Before Marriage*, many young adults have been scarred by the divorce revolution—which hit poor and middle American communities harder than upper- and middle-class communities—and have become gun-shy about marriage. They have seen too many friends and family divorce to have the trust required to move forward with a wedding. So, living amid a climate characterized by a trust deficit, they often choose, or drift "unintentionally" into, parenthood with partners who are not marriageable *or* who seem good but to whom they are not yet ready to marry.

10   Melissa, a 31-year-old single mother, had this to say about why she has never married any of her boyfriends: "I just never felt that anyone's as loyal to me as I am to them," she said. "Even when I feel like I'm in a good relationship, there'll be little things that they'll do that will make me start wondering, 'Do they really have my back?'" What's striking about Melissa's comment—which is all too representative—is that it's not just the bad guys who give her pause about marriage; it's also the good guys. She just seems to harbor a general suspicion about the possibility of lifelong love and the whole institution of marriage.

11   So what can be done to bring women like Melissa and the "good guys" back together? Progressives are right to point to the importance of shoring up the economic foundations

of family life in middle America. New infrastructure projects, better vocational training, and the elimination of the marriage penalties built into many of the nation's public policies serving lower-income Americans are all steps that could help to boost the fragile foundations of middle American families. President Obama was right to call in his State of the Unions address for measures "to strengthen families by removing the financial deterrents to marriage for low-income couples."

12   But conservatives are also right in calling for a new ethic of parental responsibility that is equally binding on all Americans and all parents, regardless of their income, education, or gender. We need a national campaign—like we have had around teen pregnancy—encompassing public, civic, and pop-cultural efforts (yes, Lena Dunham should get in on the action) to encourage twentysomethings to wait until they have a plan and a partner who will enable them to give their children the life and family they deserve. Isabel Sawhill, a fellow at the Brookings Institution, says young adults need to treat parenthood, not marriage, as the capstone.

13   This is because becoming a parent, for both mothers *and* fathers, is a big deal, arguably a bigger deal than getting married. Young adults owe it to their children to try to bring them into a home with two loving parents who are ready to support them and one another in the exhausting, exhilarating, and quotidian adventure that is parenthood. And, at least in the United States, that's most likely to happen within marriage.

14   The bottom line is this: Today's twentysomethings need to approach parenthood with the same seriousness that they approach marriage. For some, this will mean postponing parenthood into the later 20s or 30s, after their ducks are all in row. But for others, this will mean marrying earlier to someone with whom they are in a "good relationship." But either way, contemporary young adults need to be more intentional about sequencing the baby carriage after marriage, just as the country needs to be more intentional about stabilizing the fragile foundations of family life in poor and middle American communities across the United States.

QUESTIONS FOR ANALYSIS AND DISCUSSION

1. How are college-educated adults doing marriage "better"? Why does it work for them? What attracts them to marriage?
2. What might be wrong with the "capstone" model of marriage? Explain.
3. Wilcox notes that many twentysomethings, especially those without college degrees, are "drifting into parenthood." What does he mean? What does he think is problematic with this phenomenon?
4. How did twentysomethings become the new teen moms? What factors have contributed to this shift in parenthood? Explain.
5. Wilcox notes that young adults approach parenthood with a more relaxed attitude than they do marriage. According to Wilcox, what is faulty with this reasoning? Explain.
6. Wilcox gives several reasons why children are better off being raised within a marriage than outside of one. Evaluate each of his reasons.

Who Are You Calling a "Mama's Boy"?
Kate Stone Lombardi

For generations, popular psychology warned mothers to avoid getting to close to their sons, out of fear that "mama's boys" would fail to grow up to be strong independent men. While it is quite all right for girls to be close to their fathers—so called daddy's girls—mama's boys" suffer from a negative stereotype. Moms are warned not to coddle their boys, out of fear of emasculating them. Recent research, however, indicate that the popular theory simply isn't true. In fact, explains author and journalist Kate Stone Lombardi, boys who grow up close to their mothers are more likely to "man up" later in life.*

BEFORE YOU READ

How close are you to each of your parents? Are you closer to your mother or your father? Do you think popular cultural beliefs about raising boys and girls influenced how your parents treated you and nurtured your relationships with them? Explain.

AS YOU READ

What cultural influences do boys and girls face when growing up? What role do parents play in navigating these influences? How can parental bias impact child development?

1   My daughter Jeanie and I use Google chat throughout the day to discuss work, what we had for lunch, how we're avoiding the gym, and emotional issues big and small. We may also catch up by phone in the evening. I can open up to Jeanie about certain things that I wouldn't share with another soul, and I believe she would say the same about me. We are very close, which you probably won't find particularly surprising or alarming.

2   Many mothers are anxious when it comes to raising boys. If her teenage son is crying, should she comfort him, or will this embarrass and shame him? Now switch genders. Suppose I told you that I am very close to my son, Paul. That I love hanging out with him and that we have dozens of inside jokes and shared traditions. Even though we speak frequently, I get a little thrill each time I hear his signature ringtone on my cellphone. Next, I confess that Paul is so sensitive and intuitive that he "gets me" in a very special way.

3   Are you starting to speculate that something is a little off? Are you getting uncomfortable about the kind of guy my son is growing up to be?

4   For generations mothers have gotten one message: that keeping their sons close is wrong, possibly even dangerous. A mother who fosters a deep emotional bond with her son, we've been told, is setting him up to be weak and effeminate—an archetypal mama's boy. He'll never be independent or able to form healthy adult relationships. As

---

*Kate Stone Lombardi, *Wall Street Journal*, February 25, 2012.

the therapist and child-rearing guru Michael Gurian wrote in his 1994 book about mothers and sons, "a mother's job . . . is very much to hold back the coming of manhood." A well-adjusted, loving mother is one who gradually but surely pushes her son away, both emotionally and physically, in order to allow him to become a healthy man. This was standard operating procedure for our mothers, our grandmothers and even our great-grandmothers. Amazingly, we're still encouraged to buy this parenting advice today.

5   Somehow, when so many of our other beliefs about the roles of men and women have been revolutionized, our view of the mother-son relationship has remained frozen in time. We've dramatically changed the way we raise our daughters, encouraging them to be assertive, play competitive sports and aim high in their educational and professional ambitions. We don't fret about "masculinizing" our girls.

6   As for daughters and their fathers, while a "mama's boy" may be a reviled creature, people tend to look tolerantly on a "daddy's girl." A loving and supportive father is considered essential to a girl's self-esteem. Fathers are encouraged to be involved in their daughters' lives, whether it's coaching their soccer teams or escorting their teenage girls to father-daughter dances. A father who flouts gender stereotypes and teaches his daughter a traditionally masculine task— say, rebuilding a car engine—is considered to be pretty cool. But a mother who does something comparable—like teaching her son to knit or even encouraging him to talk more openly about his feelings—is looked at with contempt. What is she trying to do to that boy?

7   Many mothers are confused and anxious when it comes to raising boys. Should they defer to their husband when he insists that she stop kissing their first-grade son at school drop-off? If she cuddles her 10-year-old boy when he is hurt, will she turn him into a wimp? If she keeps him too close, will she make him gay? If her teenage boy is crying in his room, should she go in and comfort him, or will this embarrass and shame him? Anthony E. Wolf, a child psychologist and best-selling author, warns us that "strong emotional contact with his mother is especially upsetting to any teenage boy."

8   None of these fears, however, is based on any actual science. In fact, research shows that boys suffer when they separate prematurely from their mothers and benefit from closeness in myriad ways throughout their lives. A study published in Child Development involving almost 6,000 children, age 12 and younger, found that boys who were insecurely attached to their mothers acted more aggressive and hostile later in childhood—kicking and hitting others, yelling, disobeying adults and being generally destructive.

9   A study of more than 400 middle school boys revealed that sons who were close to their mothers were less likely to define masculinity as being physically tough, stoic and self-reliant. They not only remained more emotionally open, forming stronger friendships, but they also were less depressed and anxious than their more macho classmates. And they were getting better grades.

10   There is evidence that a strong mother-son bond prevents delinquency in adolescence. And though it has been long established that teenagers who have good communication with their parents are more likely to resist negative peer pressure, new research shows that it is a boy's mother who is the most influential when it comes to risky behavior, not only with alcohol and drugs but also in preventing both early and unprotected sex.

11   Finally, there are no reputable scientific studies suggesting that a boy's sexual orientation can be altered by his mother, no matter how much she loves him.

12   With all of the concern—some even call it a "crisis"—about boys falling behind girls academically, getting lower grades, exhibiting more behavior problems and going to

college in falling numbers, you would think that this research about the benefits of mother-son closeness would warrant some consideration. If staying close to mothers helps boys to perform better in school, act less aggressively and avoid behaviors that will derail their lives, why is it still so discouraged?

13   Boys need and want a close connection with their mothers. But the pressure for mothers and sons to disengage begins at a shockingly tender age (one mother I know who was comforting her weeping 3-year-old was told that he should "man up"), and the pressure escalates at every stage, until a mom actually begins to believe that the best kind of parenting that she can offer is to leave her depressed, silent teenage son alone to work out his own problems. Heaven forbid that she threatens his masculinity by giving him a hug and trying to get him to talk about what's bothering him!

14   I am not the only mother who has rejected this kind of thinking. A great many mothers keep their sons close; it is our little secret. And for the record, Paul, a young man now, is more than six feet tall, plays ice hockey, has lots of male friends and had a steady girlfriend in college. He's self-assured and independent. The fact that I feel the need to reassure you—and myself—that our deep emotional bond has not compromised my son's masculinity is telling. But, yes, we have a tight connection and my son is still OK, even "a guy's guy."

15   I'm tired of making excuses for our closeness, and I'm not alone.

QUESTIONS FOR ANALYSIS AND DISCUSSION

1. Evaluate Lombardi's examples of her relationship between her daughter Jeanie and her son Paul. How does her introduction set up her argument?
2. Lombardi states that for many years, popular culture dictated that "A well-adjusted, loving mother is one who gradually but surely pushes her son away, both emotionally and physically, in order to allow him to become a healthy man." Where does this belief come from? How is it a cultural construct?
3. Why is our treatment of boys somewhat hypocritical when you consider social opinions of raising girls? Explain.
4. How do socially constructed expectations of men and women dictate how we relate to our children?
5. In what ways could strong mother–son bonds be helpful for boys? Explain.

Being a Dad Is Fun, but Nothing Like a Mom
Richard Fabrizio

Roughly 85 percent of all adults will have a child at some point in their lives. Today, most parents share child-rearing responsibilities, but not always evenly. In this next editorial, journalist Richard Fabrizio takes a funny look at parenting differences in this tribute he wrote for his wife, Maureen, on Mother's Day.*

------

*Richard Fabrizio, *SeaCoast Online*, May 9, 2010.

BEFORE YOU READ

When you were growing up, who shouldered most of the child-rearing respon-sibilities in your family? If you have children, who does the bulk of the work? Is it 50/50?

AS YOU READ

What is Fabrizio's tone in this article? How does his tone help him connect to the reader? Does his writing convey a sense of who he is? Evaluate his tone and style.

1   This past Wednesday, after feeding my two children, I immediately gave in to their requests for "treats" despite it being 7:30 in the morning. A Hershey's Kiss for my 5-year-old daughter and Dum Dum lollipop for my 2½-year-old son. They'd eaten their breakfasts.

2   It will certainly be my fault if the kids join the ballooning epidemic of childhood obesity in America and yet one more thing for my supermom wife to take on at the fam-ily level. You see, I'm what some might refer to as a push-over dad. I know, it's somewhat redundant. I have turned spoiling into an art. The smiles, the laughs; I love it.

3   The boy jumps and flops on the furniture and I tell him to stop when his mom is watching and wink at him when she's not. There's not much better than getting crazy with the kids when I walk in at 7 p.m. after work. You'd be amazed where an imaginative 2½-year-old can stuff himself in a game of hide and seek. Though the downside of all this fatherly fun is their mom trying to *corral* them back into the evening routine to get them to bed at a reasonable hour.

4   She's actually able to bathe both of them—at the same time—when I would fear one of them drowning if pressed into the same situation, and I used to guard Water Country's Wave Pool back in the day. "Have some fun . . ."

5   I'm slowly but surely imparting my sense of humor upon my daughter, which as a dad is kind of Jerry Seinfeld meets Jerry Lewis. Imagining her with my sense of humor as a teenager even makes me cringe. The "big personality" thing has on occasion led to my daughter racing right past her mom into my arms when we sometimes pick the kids up together from day care. That can't be easy.

6   And while the boy greatly prefers his mom, he didn't sleep through the night but a handful of times—seriously—until he was more than 2 years old. I was never acceptable to him at 1 a.m., 2 a.m. or any other darkened a.m. hour. Two years without a good night's sleep? Yup, supermom.

7   Then, of course, there's the boy's use of words inappropriate for an average 2½-year-old, which is not funny at all (and my fault). It's one more thing for his mom to rein in. Not that I leave this to my wife, but it's just another of the many, many reasons why today is the most important day of the year: Mother's Day.

8   I was talking to one of my reporters this past week who was interviewing a group of Seacoast moms for a Mother's Day story. I suggested she ask where the line is drawn between woman and wife, and mother, and how hard it is to maintain some separate iden-tities. It must be hard to be a great mom while making sure to not become just a mom.

As much as I would like to think I know how hard that is for my wife, I honestly don't; not in a spiritual sense that comes with being a mom. I do know disasters would loom if I attempted to do all that she does.

9   Being a dad is different. It just is. I'm the fun guy. I put the fun in funky, if you recall. Sure, I worry when one of the kids is sick, but my wife becomes nurse and doctor. She knows exactly what medicine to buy when they need it. Have you seen those drug store aisles for fever medicines? Infant, children's, different flavors, dosing forms, brand names, generics. Different flavors?! I get dizzy trying to find what she has clearly explained I need to pick up on the way home from work.

10   I get the kids off to day care three days a week when my wife works, but she lays out their outfits the evening before. I cannot imagine what I would dress them in if it were left up to me. I'd only buy Garanimals with the matching tag system, or they'd embody the Einstein one suit theory. Lots of sweatpants. However, my daughter more than qualifies as a fashionista, so that's out. I honestly struggle to know in which drawer the particular clothes are stored.

11   I hate sounding like a dad from the 1950s (c'mon, 1960s, 1970s and early 1980s, too), no offense to them, because I'm not. I do some cooking and a little cleaning. I know how to make the bed. I mow the lawn. But, I can admit in true admiration of my wife and mother of children that I would be lost without her both as husband, and especially as a father.

12   So on the most important day of the year, Happy Mother's Day Maureen!

QUESTIONS FOR ANALYSIS AND DISCUSSION

1. How does Fabrizio refer to his son and daughter in this editorial? Are his references parallel? Explain.
2. Research the history of Mother's Day and Father's Day. What are their origins? How do they connect back to the values of family, parents, and children?
3. According to Fabrizio, how is being a dad different from being a mom? Is it easier or harder? Why?
4. What is Fabrizio saying about fatherhood? Do you think other fathers would agree with his perspective? Object to it? What about mothers? Explain.
5. Would your reception of this editorial be different if Fabrizio's wife, Maureen, wrote it from her perspective? What might she say on Father's Day?
6. Who is Fabrizio's audience? Select a few sentences from the article and explain how Fabrizio uses words to effectively connect with his audience.

WRITING ASSIGNMENTS

1. In your own words, define what *marriage* is. Then, define *family*. How does marriage connect to your definition of *family*? Are the two related? Why or why not?

2. Select one or two of the articles in this chapter and write an essay in which you argue for or against its premises. As you formulate your response, pay attention to the

author's personal bias, his or her tone, and how the arguments involved were supported by evidence or opinion.

3. What images of gay life has television presented to viewers? How do the images correspond to claims that many gay men and women just want what marriage affords: social stability, anchors in relationships, and family and financial security? What influence, if any, does the media have in swaying public opinion in the gay-marriage debate?

4. Write a personal narrative in which you describe the structure of your family during your childhood, focusing specifically on the role of marriage in your family. Were your parents married? Divorced? If you could have changed anything about your parents' marital relationship, what would it have been?

5. Is marriage about love? Is it about family? Children? If a couple has children, but find that they no longer feel the marriage is a loving one, should they stay together anyway? Write an essay in which you describe what you think marriage is and on what grounds individuals have to terminate it.

6. Draft a letter to a pair of married friends with children who are filing for divorce to reconsider their decision, or to support it, considering the impact the new arrangement is likely to have on their children. Assume that both parents are working and they are considering an amicable divorce in which they intend to continue a close relationship with their children.

7. Do you feel that marriage is an important consideration for the rearing of children? Do you think cohabitation will confer the same stability for children as a marriage would? What factors influence your decision to marry or not to marry? Explore your perspective in a well-considered essay.

8. Interview several people who have children under the age of 18. Describe the family units of the people you interviewed. Are they married with children, or are they living in a different family arrangement? What circumstances led to their family situations? Finally, how satisfied are they with their family arrangements, and what are their hopes for the future? After completing your interviews, write a short article reporting your results.

9. Will legalizing gay marriage increase or decrease the problems gay men and women now encounter in America in gaining social acceptance? What benefits might all gay people receive, whether or not they choose to marry? Do you think that a legal change in marriage will help to change the beliefs of people who now disapprove of homosexuality? Why or why not? Explain.

Credits

Image Credits

Page: 215 Art Resource, © 2009 Estate of Pablo Picasso/Artists Rights Society (ARS), New York. Page: 218 Norman Rockwell Museum Collections/IMG Worldwide Inc; Page: 223 FRESH STEP is a registered trademark of The Clorox Company and is used with permission ©2014 The Clorox Company, Inc. Reprinted with permission; Page: 226 ForestEthics; Page: 228 Creators Syndicate, Inc.; Page: 230 Courtesy of Pat Bagley; Page: 231 Daryl Cagle/Cagle Cartoons, Inc.; Page: 232 Spencer Platt/ Getty Images; Page: 235 Boston Globe/Getty Images; Page: 320 Courtesy of adbusters.org; Page: 329 Image Courtesy of The Advertising Archives; Page: 331 Image Courtesy of The Advertising Archives; Page: 332 Image Courtesy of The Advertising Archives; Page: 333 Image Courtesy of The Advertising Archives; Page: 334 Image Courtesy of The Advertising Archives; Page: 335 Maximillian Pinegger/ Justin Salice-Stephan; Page: 338 The Advertising Council; Page: 353 Reprinted with permission from National Eating Disorders Association; Page: 354 Image Courtesy of The Advertising Archives; Page: 373 Courtesy of Adam Zyglis; Page: 409 Jessmine /Shutterstock; Page: 412 Mike Sullivan, www.savingdowns.com; Page: 456 Courtesy of Brice Hall; Page: 474 Associated Press; Page: 503 David Fitzsimmons/Cagle Cartoons, Inc.; Page: 520 Associated Press; Page: 521 Ethan Miller/Getty Images; Page: 522 Joe Raedle/Getty Images; Page: 551 Mike Keefe/Cagle Cartoons, Inc.; Page: 554 PSL Images/ Alamy; Page: 577 James and Ellen Hrkach/Full Quiver Publishing.

Text Credits

Daniel Akst. "Thrift: The Rebirth of a Forgotten Virtue." *Wilson Quarterly,* Summer 2009. Reprinted by permission of the author.

Arthur Allen. "Prayer in Prison: Religion as Rehabilitation" by Arthur Allen. Reprinted by permission of the author.

Arthur Allen. Excerpt from "Prayer in Prison: Religion as Rehabilitation." Reprinted by permission of the author.

Jennifer Baumgartner. Excerpt from *You Are What You Wear: What Your Clothes Reveal About You.* Copyright © 2012 by Jennifer Baumgartner. Reprinted by permission of Da Capo Press, a member of the Perseus Book Group, as conveyed by Copyright Clearance Center.

danah boyd. "Streams of Content: Limited Attention." *UX Magazine,* February, 5, 2010, © 2010. Reprinted by permission of the author.

Taffy Brodesser-Akner. "Facebook, the Mean Girls and Me." This article first appeared in Salon.com, at http://www.Salon.com. An online version remains in the Salon archives, © Nov. 20, 2009. Reprinted with permission.

Sara Inés Calderón. "Why Latinas Aren't Allowed to be Angry, and other Stereotypes," as appeared in *News Taco,* February 8, 2012. Permission by the author.

Daniel Callahan and Sherwin B. Nuland. "The Quagmire," from *The New Republic,* May 19, 2011. Reprinted courtesy of Drs. Daniel Callahan and Sherwin Nuland.

Nicholas Carr. "Is Google Making Us Stupid?" *Atlantic,* Jul./Aug. 2008.

James C. Carter. "Letter to the Editor," S.J, from *The Times-Picayune.*

Danise Cavallaro. "Smoking: Offended by the Numbers." Reprinted by permission of the author.

Philip N. Cohen. "Still a Man's World," from *Boston Review,* January/February 2010. Reprinted courtesy of Philip N. Cohen.

Index

Page numbers followed by an *f* refer to figures.

APPENDIX A
THE ANNOTATED
BIBLIOGRAPHY

THE ANNOTATED BIBLIOGRAPHY

In ENG 102, all students are required to develop an annotated bibliography as part of Writing Project #3. The annotated bibliography is an important tool when writing a research paper. The primary goal for developing an annotated bibliography is more than simply locating sources. As you conduct your search, evaluating each source for its relevance and usefulness in supporting your thesis is equally important. You are required to include at least three scholarly sources in your annotated bibliography. Other sources may be substantive news sources, government sources or additional scholarly sources. You should consider the annotated bibliography a search record for academic sources that you will consider using to support your discussion in the final research paper. Creating an annotated bibliography helps the writer

- Discover information about a topic
- Find out which writers are the authorities on a topic
- Find information to help support an argument
- Discover the voice of opposition

You will have the opportunity to learn how to find scholarly sources during the Library Class that is provided for all ENG 102 students. Because the annotated bibliography should be considered a search record, every source that you identify does not have to be used in your final paper. Some sources may provide background information, other source will help support your discussion or provide the opposing argument, while you may discover that some sources you have identified will not be useful.

EVALUATING SOURCES

Once you have identified sources, it is important to evaluate each source to make sure it is an appropriate source for an academic paper. You will learn that while certain sources are appropriate for preliminary research, *Wikipedia* and *CQ Researcher* (which you will learn about during a classroom visit from one of the librarians), these sources should not be used in your final paper.

When you construct your annotated bibliography, sources should be listed alphabetically and include the following elements in each annotation:

1. THE CITATION

MLA Format

Brookhart, Susan M. "The Public Understanding of Assessment in Educational Reform in the United States." *Oxford Review of Education*, vol. 39, no.1, 2013, pp. 52-71.

APA Format

Brookhart, S. M. (2013). The public understanding of assessment in educational reform in the United States. *Oxford Review of Education*, *39*(1), 52-71. doi:10.1080/03054985.2013. 764751

2. **AUTHOR'S CREDENTIAL**

   - Who the author is or what organization created your source

   - What education, background and experience makes the author and expert on your research topic. This information can be found at beginning or end of an article. If you do not find it in either of there, Google the author to find out the credentials they had at the time the article was written.)

   - What other research the author has produced that is related to your topic

3. **SUMMARY**

   - What is the source about

   - What is the author's claim/or does the source provide information only

   - Is there a specific claim and how does the author come to that conclusion

4. **RELEVANCE**

   - How does the source relate to your topic

   - Does the source provide background information

   - Does the source support your thesis or provide a counter claim

The length of the annotation depends on the length of the source but, in general, each annotation should be approximately 100-200 words long. Below is a sample of one annotation using MLA Format:

DeBoer, George E. "The Scientific Literacy: Another Look at Its Historical and Contemporary Meanings and Its Relationship to Science Education Reform." *Journal of Research in Science Teaching,* 37.6 (2000): 582-601. **(CITATION)** In an attempt to define scientific literacy, George E. DeBoer, Emeritus Professor, Colgate, focuses on science in education. As one whose primary interest has been on scientific literacy and, the history of secondary school science teaching in the U.S. **(AUTHOR'S CREDENTIALS)** DeBoer contextualizes the inclusion of science in education by providing an historical background that offers readers the shifts in approaches to making science part of the general curriculum. In his efforts to provide an extensive overview of the history of science in education, DeBoer's includes a discussion about the 1957 launching of Sputnik that became of the impetus for the first wave of revising the importance of and approach to teaching science. The goals of science teaching are summarized and the implications of scientific literacy and education reform are discussed. **(SUMMARY)** This article provides background information on the events that have led to the focus on STEM disciplines in the K-12 experience in the twenty-first century. **(RELEVANCE)**

INTRODUCTION TO ANNOTATED BIBLIOGRAPHY

As part of Writing Project #3 (the annotated bibliography), you are required to develop an introduction. When done correctly, the introduction helps writers discover what they know about their topic, what sources will help them produce the final paper, and what additional work needs to be done. This element of Writing Project #3 can also help writers determine what kind of argument will best serve their purpose. The introduction should include all from the following checklist:

- ☐ Provide research question
- ☐ Indicate the kind of paper you intend to write (e.g. position paper, proposal, refutation argument)
- ☐ Provide thesis/claim/position
- ☐ Discuss background information readers will need and which sources you will use to supply this information
- ☐ Identify which sources will be used to support the planned claim
- ☐ Identify other point(s) of view that you plan to address and which source(s) will be used for this purpose
- ☐ Discuss strategies in your effort to locate sources (e.g. where you looked, keywords used and the success you had)
- ☐ Discuss what additional material may be needed
- ☐ Discuss any problems with the sources listed in the annotated bibliography
- ☐ Discuss any concerns or difficulties anticipated in writing the essay

STUDENT SAMPLE

Name

Instructor's Name

Course and Section

Date

Introduction: The Role of a Global Economy on Americans and Their Education

Americans in the twenty-first century are required to compete in a global market. This reality affects more than the economy – it affects the education system as well. In order to remain competitors in the job market, Americans must not only have a high school diploma, but pursue a higher education as well. My main concern in researching this topic was how the American education system is preparing its students for one day obtaining a job and/ or career in a highly competitive global job market. I've found that high dropout rates, a lack of college preparation programs, and student performance in science, technology, engineering, and math (STEM) subjects are hurting American job prospects. In terms of education reform, it is imperative the focus is centered on ensuring that all students, of any background, are provided with an education allowing them to compete in the global market. I began with the research questions – How does education affect America's ability to compete in a global economy? My thesis evolved into the following statement: With an ever changing economy, the job market in America no longer holds a place for those without at least a basic education; therefore, if Americans hope to have a chance at competing in this new global economy, education must be made a priority.

In researching this topic, I drew from academic articles and scholarly journals dealing with various topics related to American dropout rates, dropout job prospects, the global market, and international STEM education success. "Rising Powers in the Global Economy: Issues and Questions" by Edward Mansfield discusses contrasting elements between the United States and European economies versus Brazil, Russia, India, and China (BRIC) and provides good background information on the global economy. This source is used as material to discuss the opposition. "Barriers to Employment among Out-of-School Youth" by Cynthia Miller and Kristen E. Porter highlights key elements of my argument regarding the struggle for gaining employment for those who have dropped out of school. I use this source as support for my claim of education reform. "Revisiting the Global Market for Higher Education" by Tim Mazzarol and Geoffrey N. Soutar and "Higher Education in the Global Market: Opportunities and Threats" by Navin Singh reinforce my claim that a global economy requires job seekers to have higher education and are also used as evidence to support my thesis. Finally, "U.S. students improving – slowly – in math and science, but still lagging internationally" by Drew Desilver illustrates American shortcomings in math and science education and is used to further supports my point that education reform is needed to improve these areas. The Center on Education and the Workforce and the National Center for Education Statistics both provide reports that analyze national trends in education and labor. I will be using each of the reports as support for my argument using the data discussed. "U.S. Falls in Global Ranking of Young Adults Who Finish College" by Daniel Vise provides background information on U.S. goals to improve higher education attendance and reports evidence of not only a lack of progress, but actual regress. I will use this source as support for my claim that competing countries in the global market are gaining populations that are more highly educated than Americans.

Name

Instructor's Name

Course and Section

Date

Annotated Bibliography: The Role of a Global Economy on Americans and Their Education

Aspen Institute College Excellence Program. The Aspen Institute, http://www.aspeninstitute.org/topics/
college-excellence-program. Accessed 12 October 2015. The Aspen Institute is an educational
and policy studies organization based in Washington, DC. The Aspen Institute's College
Excellence Program specifically pursues the goal to advance higher education practices, policies,
and leadership and bring improvement to U.S. college completion rates, employment rates after
graduation, and education reform ensuring the success of students in higher education settings. In
this report, the Aspen Institute notes various findings on higher education and employment after
college graduation. This report provides support for higher education specifically addressing low
wages and unemployment rates.

"Education and Workforce Trends through 2025" Center on Education and the Workforce. Georgetown
University, cew.georgetown.edu/wp-content/uploads/Iowa_Wrkfrce2025.pdf. Accessed 12
October 2015. The Center on Education and the Workforce, an independent, non-partisan
research institute affiliated with Georgetown University in Washington, DC, focuses on research
aimed to improve education and training for the purpose of gaining a better workforce and
decreasing unemployment rates. The research suggests that by the year 2025, over sixty percent
of jobs, including those in industry, will require higher education, eight percent of which will
actually require a graduate degree. This report provides clear statistics and analysis supporting the
claim that the demand for a workforce with higher education is mounting in the twenty-first
century – even in positions and industries that traditionally, Americans do not generally
think will require a higher education.

DeSilver, Drew. "U.S. Students Improving – Slowly – in Math and Science, but Still Lagging

Internationally." Pew Research Center, 2 February 2015. http://www.pewresearch.org/fact-

tank/2015/02/02/u-s-students-improving-slowly-in-math-and-science-but-still-lagging-

internationally/. Accessed 12 October 2015. Drew DeSilver, senior writer at the Pew Research

Center, a nonpartisan American think-tank based in Washington, D.C., provides information on

the U.S. science and math education rankings compared to global counterparts. DeSilver

discusses U.S. improvement in two of the four STEM subjects in regards to student education, but

goes on to explain that as a nation, America is still falling far behind the other countries across

the globe. This report provides statistics showing U.S. STEM education shortcomings and further

analyzes the negative trends between American students and their global competitors.

Mansfield, Edward D. "Rising Powers in the Global Economy: Issues and Questions." *International

Studies Review*, Vol. 16, 2014. pp. 437-466. Edward D. Mansfield, Director of the Christopher H.

Browne Center for International Politics at the University of Pennsylvania, focuses on the

international political economy in his journal article specifically addressing mounting interest in

the growing economies of Brazil, Russia, India, and China (BRIC). He discusses the global

market and analyzes the U.S. and European economies compared to those of BRIC. In his

discussion of the BRIC economies, Mansfield provides an argument claiming the BRIC countries

do not pose a threat to Americans as they are not nearly as strong. This article addresses the

opposition of the claim that the global economy is creating a more competitive job market for

Americans.

Mazzarol, Tim and Geoffrey N. Soutar. "Revisiting the Global Market for Higher Education." *Asia

Pacific Journal of Marketing and Logistics*, Vol. 5, 2012, pp. 717-737. Tim Mazzarol,

professor at the University of Western Australia and an affiliate professor with the Burgundy

School of Business, France, and Geoffrey Soutar, professor at the University of Western

Australia and member of the Australian and New Zealand Academy of Management, analyze

the global market and the effects of on the higher education around the world in their journal article. Mazzarol and Soutar contextualize international industrial reliance and commercialization and further explain how these elements affect educational requirements and costs across the globe. This journal article provides strong evidence to support the idea that a) there is a global economy, b) jobs are now requiring high education to accommodate for international reliance of industry, and finally c) the effects of a and b on education systems around the world.

Miller, Cynthia and Kristin E. Porter. "Barriers to Employment among Out-of-School Youth." *Children and Youth Services Review*, Vol. 29, 2007, pp. 572-587. Cynthia Miller, economist whose work focuses on policies and programs to increase the employment and earnings of low-wage workers and disadvantaged young adults, and Kristin Porter, statistician with a PhD in biostatistics from the University of California, Berkeley discuss the statistics surrounding youth that dropout of school and further analyze their obstacles to employment thereafter. Miller and Porter found that youth without at least a GED or high school diploma face extreme unemployment rates and often very low wages. Furthermore, those with children had the longest unemployment spells and often faced the most instability. This journal article supports education reform to improve dropout rates and favors the claim that pursuing higher education will improve the status of Americans in the job market.

"Projections of Education Statistics to 2021" National Center for Education Statistics. U.S. Department of Education, http://nces.ed.gov/programs/projections/projections2021/. Accessed 12 October 2015. The National Center for Education Statistics, the primary federal institution for collecting and analyzing data related to education, reports various educational statistics from 1996 to 2013 and further projects data through 2021. This report gives specific statistics for current college attendance rates and anticipated enrollment for the next six years. This source provides great background and support for the claim that other nations have been more highly educated in 2015, and America is falling behind in terms of students pursuing college degrees.

Vise, Daniel. "U.S. Falls in Global Ranking of Young Adults Who Finish College." *The Washington Post*, 13 September 2011. www.washingtonpost.com/local/education/us-falls-in-global-ranking-of-young-adults-who-finish-college/2011/08/22/gIQAAsU3OK_story.html. Accessed 12 October 2015. Daniel Vise, higher education reporter at the Washington Post and author of College Inc., discusses the United States' dropping ranking among other countries across the globe regarding college attendance and graduation rates. Vise contextualizes the educational goals of the U.S. government, specifically Barack Obama, and further analyzes the shortcomings of such goals. This article provides support for the claim that other nations in the world better prepare their students for college and are now benefiting from a highly educated populations, whereas, the U.S. is falling behind further every year.

APPENDIX B: OVERVIEW OF ENGLISH 102 PROGRAM AND WRITING PROJECTS

COURSE SYLLABI: OVERVIEW

English Composition instructors create and distribute a course syllabus to their students within the first week of the semester. Each course syllabus is a record of the course terms between the faculty member and the student. In accord with the University's policy for all courses, the syllabi for composition courses include the following important information:

- Instructor contact information
- Specific course location and meeting times
- Required and/or recommended books and materials
- Course description
- Course requirements
- Learning outcomes for the course
- Assignment descriptions
- Grading standards
- Policy statements regarding attendance, missed or late work, and disability resources.

An organized, detailed syllabus and specific detailed assignment sheets for each major writing assignment protect both faculty and students from ambiguous interpretations of work and grade expectations. Students should read through the syllabus carefully. A student who ignores or neglects any of the requirements or policies stated in the syllabus will not be successful in a composition course. Be sure to ask your instructor about anything in the syllabus that is not clear.

Many instructors include the following statement in their syllabus: "A syllabus is a contract. Your continued attendance in my class means that you have read and understood the rules, policies, and guidelines that the syllabus details." All students should expect both instructors and students to adhere to the terms of the syllabus "contract."

The Composition Program adopts approved texts for English 102. All composition instructors are required to use the approved texts. All students should plan on purchasing the approved texts for their composition courses during the first week of class.

Composition students should expect to devote 2-3 hours to composition work outside of class for every hour spent in the composition class. Students read 20-60 pages of text each week for their composition class. The reading assignments may include chapter content, sample essays, resources or samples posted on the Web Campus site for the class or reserved in the library, or classmates' drafts. They can expect to submit a writing assignment for every class meeting and write in class during every class meeting. These writing assignments may be journal entries, answers to reading comprehension questions, directed freewriting or other prewriting strategies in preparation for a longer writing assignment, quizzes, notes on in-class discussions, collaborative exercises, written responses to classmates' writing, or reflection on their own writing. Students will receive an assignment sheet for major writing assignments, which details the requirements of the assignment and the evaluation standards. Students should expect to share their writing with their instructor and their classmates. Successful students arrive on time, attend class daily, and complete the reading and writing assignments required for each class according to the instructor's directions.

The writing projects in ENG 102 are designed for you to practice the skills required to complete the research paper. As you work through each project, you will learn how to effectively summarize material, use your own ideas to support a thesis, evaluate sources, and integrate source material into your paper to support your thesis. The following provides you with the criteria for each assignment you will have to complete in ENG 102.

ENG. 102 WRITING PROJECT ONE ASSIGNMENT – SUMMARY/RESPONSE

Part I – Summary

This assignment will require you to write an objective summary of an article assigned by your instructor.

Your summary should be **no less than one page and no more than one and a half pages** long. The purpose of this assignment is for you to learn how to fairly and accurately write a condensed version of an original source. You should pay careful attention to providing the most relevant information in the one-page summary as well as identifying the writer's thesis/position on the issue.

"Summary" Defined: A summary presents only a text's major points and eliminates supporting details. Writers often incorporate summaries of other writers' views into their own arguments. You will make use of summaries in your argument analysis essay, your critical annotated bibliography, and your researched argument essay. For Part I of Writing Project, you should not use any direct quotes.

Part II – Synthesis and Response

In the synthesis and response, you will read a second essay on the same topic and write an essay of no less than two full pages that connects the ideas of the first article you read to a second article.

The Synthesis and Response paper: Your task is to write an essay of **no less than two pages** that goes beyond simply summarizing the second text. Your response should be thesis-driven, which means that you will have to provide your own claim or position on the topic and write a short essay in which you discuss the ideas about the topic that you found in the two pieces. The thesis in academic essays can sometimes be two or three sentences in length rather than a single sentence. In a synthesis/response essay, the thesis expresses your reaction to the sources; it may express your level of agreement or disagreement or indicate the ways in which you will extend or build on the sources. When developing the two-page essay, your position should be supported by examples from the text. This support can be presented in the form of quotes and paraphrased material. The purpose of this portion of the assignment is for you to learn how to expand on the ideas provided in a text by offering original ideas that either complement or run counter to the text and to learn how to use direct quotes and paraphrase information to effectively support your work.

Project Learning Objectives:

- to learn and practice the skills of Reading critically
- Identifying claims and reasons
- Quoting, paraphrasing, and summarizing
- Citing sources

Related Readings: Summarizing, Paraphrasing and Direct Quotes, pp. 266-268

ENG. 102 WRITING PROJECT TWO ASSIGNMENT – THE POSITION PAPER

This assignment will require you to write a paper stating your tentative position on some facet of a broader topic. You must clearly state your position and develop a thesis on some element of a topic that you would like to explore as you work towards the 8-10 page research paper for Writing Project #4.

For this assignment you will use readily-available sources to gather background information on your topic, i.e., magazines, newspapers, appropriate websites, or the texts you have explored in class. Examine the issues and positions around your topic and use the information you find to help formulate your position on some facet of a controversial topic. While you will be required to find scholarly/academic sources for Writing Projects #3 and #4, for this assignment you do not have to use them. The sources you rely on should be used to provide you with information and the prevailing discussions about the topic.

When you choose your topic and construct a tentative thesis, you should avoid engaging in any pro/con arguments but rather enter the discussion to explore the prevailing points of view about the topic and decide how you feel about the issue. As you develop your paper, you should construct a tentative thesis that can be supported with academic sources in Writing Project #4 and provide sufficient arguments to support your thesis/claim. . This paper should be considered the foundation for the final paper so that you should maintain an objective, formal, academic tone. You can change your position/claim/thesis after you have done more formal research, but once you have made a choice, you should be prepared to continue focusing on the same topic. The paper should be 3-5 pages long and double spaced. Please use MLA format and adhere to the guidelines of academic writing.

Audience: UNLV students who are neutral and <u>uninformed</u> about your topic.

Project Learning Objectives

- topic development
- developing an effective introduction
- developing a tentative thesis/position
- performing background research
- working towards a research paper

Related Readings – Chapter 3 (Finding Arguments)

ENG. 102 WRITING PROJECT THREE ASSIGNMENT – CRITICAL ANNOTATED BIBLIOGRAPHY & INTRODUCTION

For this assignment, you will write a critical annotated bibliography consisting of eight academic-level sources and corresponding annotations. You will also write a two-page introduction in which you explain your search strategy and your plan for using your sources to write your researched argument essay.

Annotated Bibliography Defined: An annotated bibliography is a list of source citations, each followed by a brief annotation – a paragraph or two summarizing the content of the source. In addition, a <u>critical</u> annotation includes an assessment of the credibility of the material.

Project Learning Objectives:
- Choosing and narrowing a research topic
- Designing search strategies
- Conducting academic research
- Evaluating sources
- Writing citations
- Planning a research-based argument essay

Related Reading Assignments – Chapter 9 and Appendix A

Your Purpose: To conduct necessary research and planning in preparation for writing a research-based argument essay.

Your Research Question/Thesis: The annotated bibliography is centered on a research question based on the topic you have chosen. The answer to this research question will evolve into your claim and will be the foundation of your researched argument essay.

The Introduction to Your Bibliography: The annotated bibliography requires a two-page introduction. Your introduction will describe the specific topic of your research and the research question that you wanted to answer. It will include your planned working thesis (your claim and primary reasons) and discuss how the sources you have listed will assist you in writing the researched argument paper (background information, evidence to support your claim, discussion of counter arguments, etc.)

Your Sources: The number of sources required for this assignment is eight. At least three of your sources must be scholarly. Other sources may be substantive news sources, government sources or additional scholarly sources. See "Evaluating Sources" in Chapter 9 (260-265). Sources from popular magazines/web sites are not acceptable.

Your Audience: A university group whose members are neutral and uninformed about the topic.

Your Title: The title of this project should be: Annotated Bibliography: Your Topic

Required Length: Two-page introduction, eight sources, and their annotations. The length of each annotation will vary depending on the source itself, but each should consist of at least one substantial paragraph (about 100-200 words).

ENG. 102 WRITING PROJECT FOUR ASSIGNMENT – Researched Argument Essay

This is where you will bring it all together and show what you have learned this semester. You will demonstrate your skill in articulating complex ideas, examining claims and evidence found in your research materials, supporting your ideas with relevant reasons and examples, sustaining a coherent discussion, and using standard written English.

Assignment: Using the sources that you listed on your Annotated Bibliography, as well as any additional sources, write a research-based argument essay of eight to ten pages.

Topic: Same as that for your Annotated Bibliography. *No topic changes allowed!*

Project Learning Objectives:
- Synthesizing research materials
- Establishing a claim
- Organizing a research-based argument
- Developing your own argument using evidence consisting of expert opinion, facts and statistics, your own experience and observations (if appropriate to the topic), and your analysis and evaluation of the ideas found in your research
- Integrating and documenting research sources
- Integrating your own ideas with those of others
- Using visual tools such as tables, charts, graphs, and illustrations

Related Reading in the Text:
- Chapter 5: "Shaping Arguments: Thinking Like an Architect"
- Ancillary Graphics: Tables, Charts and Graphs pp. 235-242

Purpose: To convince your readers to agree with your stand on the issue *or* at least to believe in the soundness and reasonableness of your position

Focus: You must address your topic on a "local" level. The way in which you do this will depend on your specific topic. You might relate it to Nevada, to Las Vegas, to UNLV specifically, or to university students in general. This is part of audience analysis: you are appealing to the interests and concerns of your readers. (For example, if you are writing about factory farms, your reader will be interested in knowing about factory farms here in Nevada; if you are writing about recycling, we will want to know about recycling here at UNLV.)

Audience: UNLV students who are neutral and <u>uninformed</u> about your topic – so to meet the needs of your readers, you will need to provide sufficient background information for them to understand your argument.

Sources: At least five academic-level secondary sources. Newspaper articles, magazine articles, non-academic websites, etc., may be cited in addition to, but may not replace, the five academic sources. You may also make use of interviews and surveys. Note that you are not required to use all of the sources on your annotated bibliography, and you may use sources that were not included on your bibliography.

Including graphics in your research paper:

A graphic such as a table, chart, graph, or diagram:
- You may include one or more pages of graphics in your paper, BUT they CANNOT substitute for text in the length requirement
- Font used in graphics must not exceed 12-point font
- Tables, charts, and graphs are used most commonly to show numerical data or statistics
  - If you conducted a survey, you can use a graphic to show your results.
  - If you found a research source that supplies statistical data about your topic, you can put the data into a graphic; don't forget to cite the source of the data.
  - If you found a graphic in one of your research sources that you want to use, you can design a copy of the graphic or, if it is an electronic source, you can download it or you can copy and paste it into your document. <u>Don't forget to cite the source.</u>
- You may compose a graphic(s) yourself, or you may use one(s) that you found in your research materials.

An IMAGE such as artwork, an advertisement, a cartoon, or a news photo that communicates information or an idea about your topic:
- Images may account for up to one page of the length requirement.
- You may include more than one page of images, BUT the amount in excess of one page CANNOT substitute for text in the length requirement.
- Visuals are used to relay opinion, inspire reaction, or influence emotion.
- Tip: Use Google's Image Search feature to find images related to your topic. On the Google home page, click on *Images.*

Required Length: 8-10 pages, <u>PLUS</u> a "Works Cited" page

Format: MLA Style

APPENDIX C:

UNLV ENGLISH COMPOSITION

POLICIES AND PROCEDURES

COURSE-WIDE POLICIES

The English Composition Program adopted a number of policies as well as University policies to enhance the learning experience and ensure consistent and fair treatment of composition students.

Attendance: The following attendance policy is standard for all composition classes to ensure that students benefit from the critical reading and discussion and writing practice that occur in class daily. Uniform application of the policy ensures that students who are in class and students who miss class are treated fairly.

> **Regular attendance and participation in class,** specifically at least 80% of class meetings is required. Missing more than 20% of class meetings will result in a failing grade for the course (*7 or more absences during ENG 102*). See below especially as they apply to religious holidays and official extra-curricular events. Other exceptions must be approved by your instructor. Coming to class late or leaving early may be counted as partial absences.

> **Class Attendance Policy:** Registration in a class obligates the student to be regular and punctual in class attendance. Students who without previous arrangement with the instructor or department fail to attend the first two class meetings of a course that meets multiple times per week or the first meeting of a class that meets one time per week may be dropped from the course. Nonattendance for a web-based course shall be defined as failure to log onto WebCampus or other instructor-designed website within one week of the course start date without previous arrangements with the instructor or department. Nonattendance does not release the student from the responsibility to officially drop any course for which they have enrolled and choose not to complete, nor from financial obligation to pay for the course.

> **Class Absences:** There are no official absences from any university class. It is the student's responsibility to consult with the teaching faculty regarding absences from their class. Students may be dropped from classes for nonattendance during the first week of instruction.

> It is the policy of the Nevada System of Higher Education to be sensitive to the religious obligations of its students. Any student missing class quizzes, examinations, or any other class or lab work because of observance of religious holidays shall be given an opportunity during that semester to make up missed work. The makeup will apply to the religious-holiday absence only. It shall be the responsibility of the student to notify the instructor within the first 14 calendar days of the semester, of his or her intention to participate in religious holidays that do not fall on state holidays or periods of class recess. This policy shall not apply in the event that administering the test or examination at an alternate time would impose an undue hardship on the instructor or the university that could not reasonably have been avoided.

Religious Holidays Policy – Any student missing class quizzes, examinations, or any other class or lab work because of observance of religious holidays shall be given an opportunity during that semester to make up missed work. The make-up will apply to the religious holiday absence only. It shall be the responsibility of the student to notify the instructor no later than the end of the first two weeks of classes of his or her intention to participate in religious holidays which do not fall on state holidays or periods of class recess.

Any student who is denied a make-up option after appropriately notifying the teaching faculty, shall have the right to appeal that decision through the normal appeal mechanism in place.

Policy for Missed Work: Students who represent the University of Nevada, Las Vegas, at any official extracurricular activity shall have the opportunity to make up any assignments or examinations missed as a result of this event. It is the responsibility of the student to provide official written notification to the instructor of the course(s) at the earliest time possible of his or her intention to participate in a university-sponsored event but no less than one week prior to the date of the missed class(es). This policy shall not apply in the event that completing the assignment or administering the examination at an alternate time would impose an undue hardship on the instructor or the university that could reasonably have been avoided. There should be good-faith effort by both faculty and student to come to a reasonable resolution. When disagreements regarding this policy arise, they can be appealed to the department chair, dean of the college, and the Faculty Senate Academic Standards Committee. For purposes of definition, extracurricular activities may include, but are not limited to, intercollegiate athletics, band, drama, forensics, recruitment, or any other activity sanctioned by the dean and/or the Executive Vice President and Provost.

Office Hours: Composition instructors reserve a minimum of three hours per week to be available to their students for questions and additional help. Meeting with an instructor to discuss questions about reading or writing assignments, or to engage in a one-to-one review of a student draft is one of the most beneficial steps a student can take toward success in a composition class.

Office hours take place on campus in a location provided by the English Department or one designated by the instructor. The instructor will be available by phone and email, as well. Students should look for the specific location, days and times for contact hours on the course syllabus distributed by the instructor.

Class Schedule Change or Cancellation: To further students' educational experience while still meeting course goals, instructors may on rare occasions change the scheduled meeting time or location for a class. For instance, students may be instructed to meet in Lied Library for a lesson on research resources. These schedule changes will be announced in class in advance and shared with the Composition Program administrators. Students with questions should contact their instructors or the Composition Program Office.

In the rare event that an instructor must cancel a class meeting, a representative of the Composition Program will post a "class cancelled" sign on the classroom door. Since instructors also alert students to cancellations by posting an announcement in WebCampus and/or contacting students via email, students should check both WebCampus and Rebelmail regularly. Students should always check the syllabus, including updates in WebCampus, for weekly reading and writing assignments due for each class meeting. Instructors cancelling class are expected to give their students an out-of-class assignment, which is typically posted to the WebCampus site for the class.

Students with questions about a cancelled class should contact the Composition Program Office for information or instructions (702-895-3165).

Submitting or Retrieving Papers Outside of Class: Students should consult their syllabus for their instructor's policy concerning late papers. Although some instructors require paper submissions from their students, most instructors allow or require electronic submissions, typically through WebCampus. Therefore, even if a student is absent, he or she usually can submit his/her essay by the deadline.

Students do not have access to instructor mailboxes for dropping off or retrieving work and English Department staff are not responsible for forwarding papers to instructors.

Academic Dishonesty/Plagiarism: A composition course gives students the opportunity to practice writing in an environment created to help students succeed. Students cannot benefit from writing instruction, practice, and evaluation if they do not compose and complete their own writing assignments.

Plagiarism is "using the words or ideas of another, from the Internet or any source, without proper citation of the sources. Submitting the same paper in two different classes, without prior instructor approval, is also considered a form of academic dishonesty. More information about this can be found in the *Student Academic Misconduct Policy* (approved December 9, 2005) located at http://studentconduct.unlv.edu/misconduct/policy.html. Instructions on incorporating and documenting sources are available through the Writing Center. Students should always check with their instructors when they have questions about the appropriate use of sources or the ways to incorporate sources into their essays.

If a student in a particular course is suspected by the instructor to be guilty of academic dishonesty, the faculty member may initiate disciplinary review under procedures described in the *Student Academic Misconduct Policy* (http://www.unlv.edu/studentconduct/misconduct/policy).

Conferences: A one-on-one review of an essay is often the best way to address concerns the reader and/or writer might have about a text. The Composition Program therefore encourages all of its instructors to meet individually with each student at least once during the semester for this type of review.

Conferences may take place in the instructor's office or at a designated location on campus. If instructors cancel class meetings in order to meet with each student individually, attending the conference is equivalent to attending class meetings. Students failing to attend their scheduled conference will suffer the same penalties they would incur for missing the classes.

When a conference is scheduled, a student should plan on spending 15-20 minutes reviewing one or more papers assigned in the composition class. It's important to bring copies of all papers to the conference, as well as a list of questions for the instructor about writing, specific assignments, or class progress.

The University requires that all students be informed of their grade at midterm, in advance of the final withdrawal date of each semester. Conferences are often scheduled around mid-semester so that instructors can inform students of their midterm grades, in addition to discussing specific writing assignments.

Final Exam: UNLV requires that all classes meet for a final exam at the end of each semester. The University prepares a final-exam schedule for each semester's classes and posts it on the University website under "Calendars and Schedules" at http://www.unlv.edu/registrar/calendars. Composition instructors are required to offer a final exam on the day and at the time determined by the University. Students should check this schedule to avoid making plans to leave campus for the semester before exams have been completed.

Final exams in ENG 102 always require students to write an argumentative essay. Class time will be devoted to learning strategies for writing timed essays. Students can apply these strategies to other timed writing they'll be asked to complete in their university courses.

Right to Privacy: Students at UNLV benefit from the protections of the Family Educational Right to Privacy Act (FERPA). To protect students' privacy, instructors may not post grades outside their office or leave student work to be retrieved in hallways outside of offices. (Instructors may choose to enter grades into the WebCampus Grade Center, which enables each student to see his/her grades throughout the semester. All students may see their mid-semester and final grades through MyUNLV.)

Instructors also may not speak to anyone other than the student about the student's progress or grades in a composition course, including parents or friends. If a student wishes a friend or a parent to speak on his/her behalf or retrieve information for him/her, then the student must give the composition instructor written permission to share this information.

Instructors may not use a student's work as part of a lesson or sample in subsequent semesters without gaining a release for that use from the student. Instructors may ask students to complete a consent form for this purpose, but students are not required to give their consent.

COURSE-WIDE PROCEDURES

The Composition Program recognizes that students may encounter problems during the semester with their schedule, their classes, or their instructors. We have established procedures for addressing these problems so that all students are treated uniformly and fairly.

Dropping a Class: When a student's schedule changes, making it impossible to attend class on time or on a regular basis, the best course of action may be to drop the class. Composition courses are structured around regular, punctual attendance, and an attendance policy is enforced. Tardiness and irregular attendance will affect the student's grade. Unfortunately, students often quit coming to class due to a schedule conflict or other reason and assume that the instructor will drop them from the course. Composition instructors cannot drop students from a course for non-attendance, nor can they assign an Incomplete (I) to such students. Instead, the students will fail the class due to accumulated absences and missed work. Students wishing to avoid an F in their composition class must remember to drop the class by the final date for withdrawing from a class. This can be found in the calendar for the semester in "Calendars and Schedules" on the UNLV website at http://www.unlv.edu/registrar/calendars.

Incompletes: Since students in composition courses are usually just beginning their studies at UNLV and often must complete the composition sequence before enrolling in essential classes in their majors, we rarely award Incompletes. When assigned, the grade must meet the following UNLV mandates:

> The grade of I – Incomplete – can be granted when a student has satisfactorily completed three-fourths of course work for that semester/session but for reason(s) beyond the student's control, and acceptable to the instructor, cannot complete the last part of the course, and the instructor believes that the student can finish the course without repeating it. The incomplete work must be made up before the end of the following regular semester. If course requirements are not completed within the time indicated, a grade of F will be recorded and the GPA will be adjusted accordingly. Students who are fulfilling an Incomplete do not register for the course but make individual arrangements with the instructor who assigned the I grade.

Grade Disputes: If a student disagrees with an instructor's evaluation of an assignment and the grade that has been assigned to it, the student should attempt to meet with the instructor to discuss the problem and request reevaluation of the assessment. Prior to this meeting, the student should

- Take the time to reread the paper and carefully consider the instructor's comments on it
- Define the specific reasons the student feels the essay deserves a different grade.

Grievances: Although a discussion with the instructor is always the first and most beneficial step in resolving a dispute, students with complaints about their teacher or the course may bring those complaints to the Composition Office. We ask students to complete a grievance form and then talk with the student and the instructor to resolve the issue. To investigate the problem, we may ask for samples of graded work, copies of emails, or other records. Both the student and the instructor will be informed of the Composition Office's decision. Students who are not satisfied with our response to their complaint may consult the Chair of the English Department and then the Dean of the College of Liberal Arts.

Semester Evaluations: The end-of-semester course evaluation is the primary venue students have for sharing information about the class with us. In it students may evaluate the class curriculum and materials as well as the instructor and level of instruction. To encourage an honest evaluation, students submit these forms anonymously.

The evaluation form is a standard one used by the department. Students may simply mark the appropriate responses to each question and be finished in a few minutes. There is a place for additional comments for each prompt and at the end of the form. Most instructors appreciate comments on what students found most valuable and/or problematic in the class.

Student course evaluations are usually distributed during the last of week of class. Before the students complete the forms, instructors must leave the room. The students then have approximately fifteen minutes to finish the evaluation. A student or other volunteer collects all of the completed forms and places them in their original envelope. After class, the student or volunteer delivers the evaluations to the English Department.

Students are encouraged to be completely honest in this process. Since instructors may not read the evaluations until after they have submitted their grades and records, the evaluations cannot affect students' grades. For that reason, it will not hurt students to say something negative, and it will not help them to say something positive.

Remember, the evaluations are anonymous and confidential.

UNIVERSITY RESOURCES

A number of resources are available to students at UNLV. A few are described below. Students can find a complete listing on the University website and in the Undergraduate Catalog.

Web Campus: Every course offered at UNLV has its own website through Web Campus. When students register for classes, they are automatically authorized access to the Web Campus site for each of their courses. Class syllabus and assignment calendars are posted on the course website. Many instructors also use these sites to post and distribute course material, lecture notes, and handouts. Some instructors administer timed quizzes and monitor class discussions through the website. Web Campus also offers an easy format for instructors to communicate with individual students and with the entire class through e-mail and/or announcements. Instructors may post information on the Web Campus site daily or use it infrequently. For instructions on how to log in to Web Campus, go to https://wchelp.unlv.edu/students/home.

E-mail: The University requires faculty and staff to communicate with students through Rebelmail, UNLV's official e-mail system for students. All students enrolled in courses at UNLV are given a Rebelmail account. The suffix is always @unlv.nevada.edu. For instructions on how to establish a UNLV e-mail account go to https://rebelmail.unlv.edu/. Instructors may also ask their students to use the email tools of *WebCampus*.

E-mail is often the most efficient and direct way to contact instructors. This is particularly true for composition instructors, who share an office and phone with a number of other instructors.

Writing Center:
Staffed primarily by English Department graduate students, the Writing Center offers all UNLV students assistance with any writing project. Consultants are available to discuss any stage of the writing process, from generating ideas to developing and polishing drafts, and can help with a wide variety of projects, such as reports, newsletters, essays in any discipline, and graduate school applications. However, the Writing Center is *not* a proofreading or editing service. Instead, consultants teach writers to identify and correct problems in their own writing.

One-on-one or small group assistance with writing is available at the Writing Center, located in CDC-3- 301. Although walk-in consultations are sometimes available, students with appointments will receive priority assistance. Appointments may be made in person or by calling

702-895-3908. Students with appointments should bring their Rebel ID card, a copy of the assignment and two copies of any writing to be reviewed.

The Writing Center also offers workshops each semester on topics that writing students often have problems with. Composition instructors may announce these workshops in class and encourage students to attend. A list and descriptions of classes offered each semester is available on the Writing Center's website.

Computer Facilities: Computer Labs open to UNLV students can be found at ten locations on campus. Many locations have both PC's and Mac's. Students should expect to show their student identification (RebelCard) when using campus computers. For more information on computer lab locations see https://www.unlv.edu/maps/computer-labs. Guidelines for using the computer labs are available at http://oit.unlv.edu/labs-classrooms/lab-rules.

Special Accommodations: Students with a documented disability that may require accommodations will need to register with the Disability Resource Center (DRC) for the coordination of services. This is an online process. For instructions and the online form, go to http://drc.unlv.edu/students/register.html. The DRC is located in the Student Services Complex. (SSC-A 143) and can be reached at 702-895-0866/Voice; 702-895-0651/Fax; or drc@unlv.edu. For additional information please visit http://drc.unlv.edu/.

UNIVERSITY UNDERGRADUATE LEARNING OUTCOMES

The five University Undergraduate Learning Outcomes (UULOs) define what all UNLV students should know and be able to do when they graduate. Because students engage with the UULOs in both their general education and academic majors, the UULOs help make the undergraduate experience intentional and coherent.

The UULOs create a purposeful sequence of learning from the first year, to the middle years, to the senior year. Student learning develops through both curricular and co-curricular experiences which expose students to the UULOs in diverse contexts.

UNLV defines specific student outcomes for each UULO. Jump to each UULO's section to read its description and specific outcomes.

INTELLECTUAL BREADTH AND LIFELONG LEARNING

Graduates are able to understand and integrate basic principles of the natural sciences, social sciences, humanities, fine arts, and health sciences, and develop skills and a desire for lifelong learning. Specific outcomes for all students include:

1. Demonstrate in-depth knowledge and skills in at least one major area.
2. Identify the fundamental principles of the natural and health sciences, social sciences, humanities, and fine arts.
3. Apply the research methods and theoretical models of the natural and health sciences, social sciences, humanities, and fine arts to define, solve, and evaluate problems.
4. Transfer knowledge and skills gained from general and specialized studies to new settings and complex problems.
5. Demonstrate lifelong learning skills, including the ability to place problems in personally meaningful contexts; reflect on one's own understanding; demonstrate awareness of what needs to be learned; articulate a learning plan; and act independently on the plan, using appropriate resources.
6. Achieve success in one's chosen field or discipline, including applying persistence, motivation, interpersonal communications, leadership, goal setting, and career skills.

INQUIRY AND CRITICAL THINKING

Graduates are able to identify problems, articulate questions, and use various forms of research and reasoning to guide the collection, analysis, and use of information related to those problems. Specific outcomes for all students include:

1. Identify problems, articulate questions or hypotheses, and determine the need for information.
2. Access and collect the needed information from appropriate primary and secondary sources.
3. Use quantitative and qualitative methods, including the ability to recognize assumptions, draw inferences, make deductions, and interpret information to analyze problems in context, and then draw conclusions.
4. Recognize the complexity of problems, and identify different perspectives from which problems and questions can be viewed.
5. Evaluate and report on conclusions, including discussing the basis for and strength of findings, and identify areas where further inquiry is needed.
6. Identify, analyze, and evaluate reasoning, and construct and defend reasonable arguments and explanations.

COMMUNICATION

Graduates are able to write and speak effectively to both general and specialized audiences, create effective visuals that support written or spoken communication, and use electronic media common to one's field or profession. Specific outcomes for all students include:

1. Demonstrate general academic literacy, including how to respond to the needs of audiences and to different kinds of rhetorical situations, analyze and evaluate reasons and evidence, and construct research-based arguments using Standard Written English.
2. Effectively use the common genres and conventions for writing within a particular discipline or profession.
3. Prepare and deliver effective oral presentations.
4. Collaborate effectively with others to share information, solve problems, or complete tasks.
5. Produce effective visuals using different media.
6. Apply the up-to-date technologies commonly used to research and communicate within one's field.

GLOBAL/MULTICULTURAL KNOWLEDGE AND AWARENESS

Graduates will have developed knowledge of global and multicultural societies, and an awareness of their place in and effect on them. Specific outcomes for all students include:

1. Demonstrate knowledge of the history, philosophy, arts, and geography of world cultures.
2. Respond to diverse perspectives linked to identity, including age, ability, religion, politics, race, gender, ethnicity, and sexuality; both in American and international contexts.
3. Apply the concept of social justice.
4. Demonstrate familiarity with a non-native language, or experience living in a different culture.
5. Function effectively in diverse groups.
6. Demonstrate awareness of one's own place in and effect on the world.

CITIZENSHIP AND ETHICS

Graduates are able to participate knowledgeably and actively in the public life of our communities and make informed, responsible, and ethical decisions in their personal and professional lives. Specific outcomes for all students include:

1. Acquire knowledge of political, economic, and social institutions.
2. Identify the various rights and obligations that citizens have in their communities.
3. Apply various forms of citizenship skills such as media analysis, letter writing, community service, and lobbying.
4. Explain the concept of sustainability as it impacts economic, environmental, and social concerns.
5. Examine various concepts and theories of ethics, and how to deliberate and assess claims about ethical issues.
6. Apply ethical concepts and theories to specific ethical dilemmas students will experience in their personal and professional lives.